WAUGH'S WORLD

IAIN GALE

To my parents

Waugh's World

A GUIDE TO THE NOVELS OF EVELYN WAUGH

IAIN GALE

SIDGWICK & JACKSON
LONDON

First published in 1990 by
Sidgwick & Jackson Limited

Photosetting by Florencetype Ltd, Kewstoke, Avon BS22 9YR
Printed by

for Sidgwick & Jackson Limited
1 Tavistock Chambers, Bloomsbury Way
London WC1A 2SG

ISBN 0 283 99835 0

ACKNOWLEDGEMENTS

I should like to thank Auberon Waugh for his kind permission to include quotations from the works of Evelyn Waugh and for his Introduction to the book.

Thanks are also due to all those who have encouraged me with this work over the years: in particular, to Alison Greenshields for the peace of the Sussex Downs; to the staff of the London Library for their help in locating essential reference material, otherwise unobtainable; to Jane Shaw for endless cups of tea; to Brian Robson and Harry Quinn for first stimulating my interest in the work of Evelyn Waugh; and, of course, to Anne.

AUTHOR'S NOTE

Evelyn Arthur St John Waugh was born on October 1903 into the small Hampstead household of Arthur and Catherine Waugh. He was the second son of the family, his elder brother being Alec Waugh, the popular novelist. Arthur Waugh was a respected publisher and literary critic, and such a background clearly had an early influence on the young Evelyn, who wrote his first story, 'The Curse of the Horse Race', at the age of seven.

Evelyn was educated at Lancing College on the Sussex Downs, which features in two of his works, and at Hertford College Oxford, the setting for the early chapters of his most celebrated novel, *Brideshead Revisited.*

At Oxford Waugh formed the friendships and the opinions which were to shape his life and art. It was here that he met such aristocratic aesthetes as Harold Acton, Patrick Balfour and Hugh Lygon, who served to lift him from the middle-class, minor public school drudgery of which he was terrified, into the 'enchanted garden' which he was to attempt to re-enter throughout his life.

In 1924, coming down from Oxford with what he himself called 'a bad third', Waugh was found employment as a junior master at a preparatory school in Wales which later served as the model for Llanabba Castle in his first novel.

Thankfully for us, schoolmastering did not prove to be Waugh's vocation and, after brief flirtations with carpentery and journalism, in 1927 he published his first book, a biography of Dante Gabriel Rossetti, the Pre-Raphaelite artist. This was followed in 1928 by *Decline and Fall*, the satirical tale of Paul Pennyfeather and his brief excursion into the whirlwind of inter-war upper-class society. In this first novel Waugh clearly owes a debt, which he was later to admit, to Ronald Firbank, and in many ways also to his idol, Max Beerbohm.

Decline and Fall was followed in 1930 by the even more deeply satirical *Vile Bodies*, which, being taken up by the very society which it sought to vilify, made of Waugh an overnight success.

Following the break-up of his first marriage in 1930, Waugh was converted to the Roman Catholic faith. The influence of both of these events can be traced in all of his subsequent work, and forms the heart of what he considered his masterpiece, *Brideshead Revisited.*

With nothing to keep him in England, and a hundred painful memories to escape, Waugh embarked on the first of a series of expeditions to Africa and South America. His experiences in Africa are recorded in several volumes of travel writing, and provide the backdrop for his two hilarious novels of colonial life: *Black Mischief* (1932) and *Scoop* (1938).

Back in England between travels, Waugh continued to write novels dealing with the fragile fabric of the British upper-class world of which he was so avid and meticulous an observer. For many, *A Handful of Dust* (1934) is Waugh's most accomplished novel, chronicling with close and savage detail the breakdown of an apparently idyllic marriage, and the eventual ruin of Tony Last – a symbol of all the enduring virtues of English landed society – by his capricious and selfish young wife, Brenda, the Nina Blount of *Vile Bodies* transformed from harmless Bright Young Thing into ruthless herald of the modern age.

The relentless onset of the 'modern world' and the idiocy with which it is filled was to be Waugh's subject in his next five novels. In 1939, with the outbreak of war, he immediately joined the army and began a military career which, together with his divorce, his Catholicism and his time at Oxford, can be seen as a fourth profound influence on his work. On his own admission, Waugh was not a born soldier and despite his reckless heroism during the battle of Crete and in the Balkans, where he served in British liaison with Randolph Churchill, his chief monuments to the war are the novels which it prompted him to write.

Put Out More Flags, published in 1942, continues the story of Basil Seal – and those other characters first encountered in *Black Mischief* – into the first days of the war. It is written very much in the vein of Waugh's early social satires and is of an entirely different nature to his next book.

There is no need to summarize the events or characters of *Brideshead Revisited*, so firmly have they become imprinted upon the British literary mind. Suffice it to say, in the words of Christopher Sykes, that: 'The reception of the book on the issue of the first edition was so enthusiastic that one can almost use the word ecstatic. . . .'

After the war Waugh settled down to living the life of a country squire at his house in Somerset and, after a brief, caustic excursion into the world of the American funeral parlour (*The Loved One*, 1948), he set about writing a trilogy in which he would be able to convey his feelings about the war and its effect upon the world.

Sword of Honour, published in three volumes between 1952 and 1961, follows the career of one of Waugh's most memorable characters, Guy Crouchback, younger son of a dispossessed Catholic family. In these three books Waugh progresses even further down the road which he had taken with *Brideshead*, and writes with an ever-increasing sense of nostalgia and regret about the vanished England of the Flytes and the Crouchbacks.

Although published before the final volume of the trilogy, *The Ordeal of Gilbert Pinfold* fits most coherently into the Waugh canon, alongside the short story, 'Basil Seal Rides Again' (1963), as Waugh's final work: a self-consciously autobiographical account of the temporary madness of an elderly English man of letters with an unhealthy prediliction for drink and drugs.

Evelyn Waugh died on Easter Sunday, 1966, in a setting worthy of one of his own books: the cloakroom of the country house where he had lived with his second wife, Laura Herbert, since 1956. He left five children and a body of work which forms an unequalled chronicle of life among the British upper classes between 1920 and 1960.

The aim of *Waugh's World* is to provide a comprehensive guide to the fiction of Evelyn Waugh. As such it covers all of his novels apart from one: *Helena*, the tale of the mother of the Emperor Constantine, which cannot be viewed alongside Waugh's other novels, being, as it is, an essentially historical novel set in the fourth century.

As well as being a guide, this is a bedside book, intended to be read and enjoyed in itself. Primarily, however, this is an easy-to-use reference to Waugh and his work.

Included within the text is an entry on every character and location, actual or fictional, as well as any major subject which might help to illuminate Waugh's own personality.

The characters from one book frequently reappear in another – often with completely different central figures – thus creating the illusion of a completely self-contained world within the books, forever functioning behind the scenes against which Waugh's complex dramas are played.

The emphasis placed upon each entry depends entirely upon its own importance within the books. While they may also have a separate entry of their own, many subjects of a similar nature are grouped under generic headings such as Dress, Drink, Food, Battles, Games, Cars, Churches, Clubs, Expressions, Schools, Hotels and Newspapers.

The book is organised alphabetically and within each entry, a brief description and analysis of the subject is followed by an explanation of how it is related to each of the novels in which it occurs.

At the foot of most entries there is an appropriate abbreviated page reference to the original novels. Any further entries on related topics are indicated within the text either by the designation 'q.v.' or '*See also*'.

Should there be no entry on the subject on which you are interested, nor any cross-reference, it is always advisable to think of another heading under which it might be found.

In the case of there being more than one character or location of the same name, each one is given a specific entry in order of either literary or social importance. In the case of families, entries are in alphabetical order.

ABBREVIATIONS USED IN THE GUIDE

DF *Decline and Fall* (1928)
VB *Vile Bodies* (1930)
BM *Black Mischief* (1932)
HD *A Handful of Dust* (1934)
Sc *Scoop* (1938)
PF *Put Out More Flags* (1942)
BR *Brideshead Revisited* (1945)
LO *The Loved One* (1948)
MA *Men at Arms* (1952)
OG *Officers and Gentlemen* (1955)
US *Unconditional Surrender* (1961)
WS Work Suspended and other stories (1967) Also includes 'Mr Loveday's Little Outing' (1934), 'Cruise' (1932), 'Period Piece' (1936), 'On Guard' (1934), 'An Englishman's Home' (1939), 'Excursion, in Reality' (1936), 'Bella Fleace Gave a Party' (1932), 'Winner Takes All' (1935), 'Scott-King's Modern Europe' (1946), 'Basil Seal Rides Again' (1963) and 'Charles Ryder's Schooldays' (1945).
GP *The Ordeal of Gilbert Pinfold* (1957). Also includes *Tactical Exercise* (1962) and *Love Among the Ruins* (1953)

All page numbers refer to current editions, published in England by Penguin Books. As this format might be subject to change, readers might find some discrepancies in the pagination. We shall attempt to correct these with suitable revisions as and when such changes occur.

IAIN GALE, SUMMER 1990

INTRODUCTION

In January 1946 the magazine *Life* wrote to Evelyn Waugh proposing an illustrated *Companion* to his novels. He got it into his head that the magazine wished to print pictures of the real people from whom his fictitious characters were drawn, and answered threatening them all with legal action. Mrs Reeve of *Life* had written that the magazine planned 'a photographic feature dramatizing characters and scenes from your novels . . . we face a monumental job'.

Waugh replied, 'the only "monumental" work Mr Scherman is likely to perform is breaking stones at Dartmoor (our Sing Sing)". Later, the correspondence was taken up by Mr Osborne, and Waugh to some extent relented.

To *Life* Magazine, 7 February 1946

Dear Mr Osborne,

I don't know how I have given you and Mrs Reeve and Mr Scherman the impression that I seek popularity for my books among those who cannot read. I have tried to give the literate all the information they need about my characters. If I have failed, I don't believe you can help me.

I am sure it is not your fault and you are being bothered by some boss in the United States. Take heart; he has forgotten all about it already. . . .

But if this preposterous subject has become a fixed idea with the man and you would like to see me, by all means come. . . . Have you a bicycle? I am always here and can give you a glass of port on arrival and plenty of dry bread.

Please do not telephone.

Yours sincerely

Evelyn Waugh

On 24 February Waugh wrote in his diary:

'The American journal *Life*, with whom I have been in acrimonious correspondence for some time, today sent a feeble-minded young man named Osborne to see me. . . . To bed early but unable to sleep; took sleeping draught at 1.15. . . .

Next day he wrote to A.D. Peters, his agent:

Piers Court, 25 February [1946]

Dear Pete,

I have been bothered for some weeks by some yanks named Life & Lime. . . .

No amount of rudeness has shaken off these pests and yesterday a feeble-minded young man named Osborne arrived on my doorstep. . . . I told the balmy [sic] fellow to apply to you for terms. Make them stiff. . . .

Mr Osborne has an impediment in his speech, perhaps due to drink.

Yours
Evelyn

That is more or less the last we hear of the first attempt to publish a *Companion* to Evelyn Waugh's novels. Iain Gale has been less ambitious. There is practically no attempt to identify the fictional characters with real people, and no attempt at all to demonstrate photographically what they might have looked like for the benefit of those who cannot read. This is surely a good idea, since fictional characters come to life in the reader's imagination or not at all. Even the better, later television versions of P.G. Wodehouse will have upset many admirers of the Master through interpretations which do not coincide with their own fantasy. No doubt many uses will be found for this book. I would like to think it will occupy much the same place in readers' affections as Cruden's *Concordance* to the Bible.

Auberon Waugh
Combe Florey
Summer 1990

A

ABDUL AKBAR, JENNY
'Charming girl' first encountered by Brenda Last at the block of flats in London, where she too has an apartment. The ex-wife of a Moulay of Morocco, who treated her appallingly ('I remember the scars'). When she enters a room she is always preceded by the heavy odour of musk. Her hair is deep black and curled, and John Last thinks her: 'the most beautiful lady I've ever seen'. Flirts with Tony Last whom she insists upon calling 'Teddy', and whom she tells: 'If you're nice to me I'll purr'.
HD 82, 84–85, 87

ABDUL KRIM ***(1884–1963)***
Leader of Berber rebels in Morocco in the 1920s. Trained with the Spanish Army. In July 1926 he led his rebels against Mellila and wiped out the Spanish garrison. Krim eventually surrendered to a combined Franco–Spanish force.
• In 1926 the British Consul at Fez tells Charles Ryder that a party of young Englishmen on bicycles have come to join his army.
BR 201

ABEL, MRS
Cook to Charles Ryder's father, she possesses ten menus given to her by Charles' Aunt Philippa, from which she never deviates.
BR 65

ABER, MRS
The dentist's wife who gave Mr Prendergast (q.v.) his copy of the Encylopaedia Britannica while at his first living in Worthing.
DF 33

ABERCROMBIE, SIR AMBROSE
Eminence Grise of the British acting community in Hollywood. Ex-Eton and the Coldstream Guards. In summer he dresses in a regimental blazer and sports an I Zingari ribbon on his boater.. On other days he wears a deer stalker and an Inverness cape. In his late fifties in 1948, he is particularly keen to be known as a 'Grand Old Boy'. Is instrumental in sending Dennis Barlow back to England.
LO 30

ABERCROMBIES, THE
Servants, man and wife, at Broome. Employed by Arthur Box-Bender. In 1940 they emigrate to Jamaica.
MA 22

ABERDEEN
Apparent origin of the stone from which the Lovers' Seat at Whispering Glades (q.v.) was hewn.
LO 98

ABINGDON
Town in Buckinghamshire close to where Lucy Simmonds has relatives with whom she stays before her confinement.
WS 173

ABORTION
An infrequent topic in the novels. Virginia Crouchback attempts unsuccessfully to find a doctor who will abort her pregnancy in wartime London.
• Clara has an abortion to get rid of Miles Plastic's child.
US 76–84; GP 212

A BRAND FROM THE BURNING
Film based on the life of John Wesley made by the Wonderfilm Company of Great Britain. Starring Effie La Touche

as Selina, Countess of Huntingdon, and filmed on location at Doubting Hall (q.v.).
VS 209

'ABROAD'
Mr Prendergast thinks that if they had not been told that it existed, no one would want to go abroad.
• In Mrs Leonard's 'film-clouded' imagination 'abroad' is one great rose-coloured adventure that mixes Honolulu, Algiers and Quetta.
DF 103; MA 217

ABUSIVE LETTERS
The clergy receive many letters of abuse.
DF 41
(*See also* PRENDERGAST)

ABYSSINIANS
The senior officers' club in Bari is, in fact, a disused seminary for Uniate Abyssinians.
US 156

ABYSSINIAN CRISIS
The conflict (December 1934–May 1938) between the Ethiopian Empire of Haile Selassie and the Italians, who were in search of an empire, under Mussolini.
• For Mr Hornbeam (q.v.), the horror of the crisis could be dispelled by meditating with a Japanese mystical practice.
• Its effect in Santa Dulcina had been to cut off the flow of tourists, thus destroying Guy Crouchback's tourist agency.
• Hitchcock reports the Abyssinian crisis for the *Daily Beast* from Asmara with 'some of the most colourful eye-witness stuff we ever printed'. (Asmara is some miles from the front line.)
MA 85; WS 53; Sc 32

ACCENTS
The waiter at the Château de Madrid restaurant in Glasgow, in November 1940, has such an appalling French accent that Trimmer is tempted to ask him whether he acquired it in the Mile End Road or the Gorbals.
OG 73

ACCESSORIES
Listed alongside their owners (all of whom, q.v.):

False beard – Father Rothschild; Simon Balcairn (*VB 9*)
Cigarette case with 'Tony' engraved on it – Tony Last (*HD 164*)
Little red leather-covered address book – Barbara Sothill (*PF 88*)
A human skull engraved, '*Et in arcadia ego*' – Charles Ryder (*BR 43*)
Pigskin satchel – Mr Samgrass (*BR 145*)
Emerald ring – Julia Flyte (*BR 264*)
Japanned tin medicine chest – Apthorpe (*MA 60*)
'Thunder Box' – Apthorpe (*MA 00*)
Tobacco jar with the arms of New College – Mr Crouchback (*US 71*)
Ivory Crucifix – Mr Crouchback (*US 71*)
Elliptical violet sunglasses – Miss Thanatogenos (*LO 70*)
Foolscap paper and English ink – Gilbert Pinfold (*GP 28*)
Blackthorn stick and a malacca cane – Gilbert Pinfold (*GP 30*)
Cigarette lighter, 'a most uncertain apparatus' – Miles Plastic (*GP 223*)
Gold cigarette case – Mr Loveday (*WS 14*)
Silver watch – Mr Loveday (*WS 14*)
Cleft stick – William Boot (*Sc 42*)
Gold fountain pen embossed with eagles (stolen) – The ex-King of Ruritania (*VB 41*)
(*See also* LAST, TONY and APTHORPE.)

ACCIDENTS
Sebastian Flyte alarms Charles Ryder with a telegram announcing: 'Gravely injured, come at once', putting into Charles' mind visions of all sorts of horrendous accidents – 'a loaded gun held carelessly at a stile, a horse rearing and rolling over, a shaded pool with a submerged stake, an elm bough falling suddenly on a still morning, a car at a blind corner, . . .'. In fact, Sebastian has only cracked a bone in his ankle 'so small that it hasn't a name'.
• A driver overturns his slag lorry in the back drive at Boot Magna.
• John Plant's father is knocked down

and killed by a motor-car driven by Arthur Atwater (q.v.)

• Tony and Brenda Last's son John Andrew (q.v.) is killed in a hunting accident when a motorcycle backfires.

• Guy Crouchback twists his knee while playing rugby in the Halberdiers' mess. He twists the same knee again during parachute training and has to go to an RAF hospital.

• Basil Seal blows off the toes of one foot while demonstrating to his commandos at the start of WWII a device for blowing up bridges.

HD; Sc 203; BR 72–73; MA 78; US 103; WS 108, 256

(*See also* STITCH, JULIA)

ACHILLES

Mythical son of Peleus and Thetis. A renowned warrior during the Trojan War and the greatest of heroes – Slayer of Hector, he was himself killed by Ajax.

• Major Graves is compared to Achilles by Guy Crouchback for his approach to training the commandos on Mugg.

OG 89

ACHON ***(d. 1934)***

Son of Amurath, popularly supposed to have been eaten by a lioness in the Ngumo mountains of Azania. In fact he was taken as a boy to the monastery of St Mark the Evangelist and locked up by order of his sister and the Patriarch Gorgias. He is next seen naked and old with a long white beard both blind and crippled. Having been kept in a cave near the monastery he is 'liberated' by the Earl of Ngumo and created Emperor in opposition to Seth. However, at his coronation the great gold tiara of Amurath proves too heavy for his weak old head and it kills him.

BM 164, 177, 205

ACRE

City in Phoenicia successfully besieged by the crusaders in 1191. In Charles Ryder's thoughts as he leaves Brideshead for the last time, dwelling on: 'the flame which the old knights saw from their tombs which they saw put out; that flame burns again for other soldiers, far from home. . . .'

BR 331

ACTORS

(*See* THORNE, PABLO, PLAYS, THEATRE, GARBO, JOKES)

ACTS OF GOD

What Captain Grimes (q.v.) considers his meeting with 'Bill', who manages a 'place of entertainment. A sort of night club . . .' in the Argentine, and who offers him a job.

DF 140

ADA

Fifteen-year-old housemaid of Colonel Blount (q.v.) at Doubting Hall. When she suggests hanging mistletoe over Captain and Mrs Littlejohn's bed, Mrs Florin tells her that she is too young to be thinking such things.

VB 201–202

ADDERFORD, ***GLOUCESTERSHIRE***

Family home at the old Rectory of the Grace family (q.v.). The Connollys stay there for two days in 1940.

PF 116

ADDIS

Sign on a door in the War Office, where Colonel Plum is in charge. Its meaning is 'Assistant Deputy Director Internal Security'. In 1940 Basil Seal is keen to work there.

PF 146

ADEN

From where transport planes are sent to rescue the British Legation in Azania in 1932.

• Destination, according to Gilbert Pinfold, of Mr Angel and his BBC team to make recordings of Arab dance music. Pinfold also relates that there was at one time in Aden a stuffed mermaid in a box in one of the hotels. It is at this hotel that William Boot and Corker stay, noticing the mermaid, while awaiting the ship to take them to Ishmaelia in 1938. During this time they also buy some Japanese shawls, Benares trays, cigarette boxes, an amber necklace and a model of Tutankhamen's sarcophagus.

Guy Crouchback is offered a security job here in 1942.

BM 213; Sc 71; US 18; GP 136

ADMIRALS

Beryl Muspratt was married to an Admiral.

• A Rear Admiral snatches the last leg of chicken at the United Services Club in 1941.

BR 270; OG 22

ADOLESCENCE

'What,' wonders Everard Spruce, 'is adolescence without trash.' He is referring to Iris Storm.

• In the opinion of the station psychologist at Mountjoy (q.v.), arson is inseparable from adolescence.

US 200; GP 184

ADRIATIC SEA

Setting of one of Ruth Mountdragon's novels.

PF 219

ADVERTISING

'Every Molassine dog cake wags a tale', seen by Mr Outrage from the window of the train from Dover.

• Charles Ryder's fellow art students in Paris in 1926 want to earn a living 'doing advertisements for Vogue'.

VB 28; BR 147

(*See also* BEAVER, JOHN)

AEGEAN

From where Mrs Stitch gleans bronzes in the 1930s.

Sc 221

AESTHETIC MOVEMENT

English artistic movement flourishing in the 1890s in the wake of the Pre-Raphaelites, and spearheaded in literature by Oscar Wilde, in painting by J.A.M. Whistler, and in illustration by Aubrey Beardsley, (*all* q.v.).

For John Plant's father the Aesthetic Movement curtailed the development of English painting from the proper channels in which it had been moving in the spirit of Millais and Winterhalter.

WS 128

(*See also* SILK, Ambrose)

AESTHETICS

At Oxford, Charles Ryder has 'the fallacy of modern aesthetics' exposed to him by Collins, thus: 'the whole argument from Significant Form stands or falls by VOLUME. If you allow Cezanne to represent a third dimension on his two-dimensional canvas, then you must allow Landseer his gleam of loyalty in the spaniel's eye.' However, Sebastian Flyte becomes Charles' real tutor in aesthetics when he reads aloud to him from Clive Bell's 'Art': '"Does anyone feel the same kind of emotion for a butterfly or a flower that he feels for a cathedral or a picture?" "Yes, I do".'

BR 30

AFGHAN FRONTIER

Area of Northern India in which Colonel McAdder (q.v.) had been 'a veteran of numberless unrecorded campaigns'.

DF 166

AFGHANISTAN

Topic on which Sanders (q.v.) had written to Lord Monomark.

BM 73

AFRICA

Charles Ryder paints equatorial Africa as an antidote to his pictures of country houses.

• The Superior of the monastery in Morocco where Sebastian Flyte ends his days is a Dutchman who has spent fifty years in Central Africa.

• In WWI Africa was the destination for officers who had blotted their copy-books.

• In 1940, Guy Crouchback is involved in a debacle on the African Coast, off Dakar, when he leads a raiding party.

• Apthorpe and 'Chatty' Corner are old inhabitants of Bechuanaland.

• Sanders (q.v.) has a brother in Kasanga, 1200 miles from Makarikari. According to Apthorpe, Kasanga is 'a perfectly awful hole', the real Africa being anywhere between Chad and Mozambique.
• Ritchie-Hook (q.v.) once shot a killer rhino on the Somaliland/Ogaden border.
• Before his divorce Guy Crouchback had a farm in Kenya (q.v.).
• In the experience of Sir Ambrose Abercrombie, if a white man disgraces himself in Africa he is sent home. He laments that he is unable to do the same for Dennis Barlow (*both* q.v.).
• Arthur Atwater (q.v.) has a pal who emigrated to Rhodesia (he thinks).
• In Africa, Hitchcock (q.v.) always sends his dispatches in a cleft stick.
• Frau Dressler (q.v.) has spent her entire life in Africa, drifting from Tanganyika to Ishmaelia.
BR 254, 290; OG 11, 58; MA 55, 58, 69, 74; LO 31; WS 137; Sc 42
(*See also* KENYA)

AGADIR
Town on the west coast of Morocco.
• According to Dr Messinger (q.v.) it is 'an interesting little place', so he informs Tony Last.
• The home of Zingermaun (q.v.).
HD 158

AGAMEMNON
King of Mycenae, commander-in-chief of the Greek force against Troy. Plotted against on his return and murdered by his wife, Clytemnestra. His memory is invoked by Aimee Thanatogenos (q.v.) to summon the Greece she has never seen.
LO 116

AGE OF THE IVORY TOWER
A mythical name for the Late Edwardian era of aesthetics and leisured gentlemen used by Ambrose Silk (q.v.) to describe his own attitude to life.
PF 35

AGRARIAN LEAGUE
Revolutionary group in Neutralia, infamous for burying alive ten priests.
WS 207

AGRICULTURAL SHOWS
During Charles Ryder's early days at Brideshead, an agricultural show is held which he and Sebastian watch through a telescope from the roof, while sunbathing. It is 'a modest two-day show serving the neighbouring parishes, and surviving more as a fair and social gathering than as a centre of serious competition'. The show is judged by Lord Brideshead.
BR 85

AIR RAIDS
Just the place, thinks Basil Seal, for a surrealist: 'limbs and things lying about'.
• 'In an air raid it is the duty of every officer and man not on duty to take the nearest and safest cover . . .', says Air Marshal Beech from beneath the billiard table at Bellamy's.
• In 1939 Air Raid Wardens roam the countryside persecuting any yokels walking home from the pub at night with their pipes aglow.
OG 13; PF 31, 49

AIRCASTLE CORRESPONDENCE SCHOOL
School of journalism at which, for fifteen shillings a month, Bateson becomes a graduate. It is a qualification which leads to his being employed by the *Daily Beast* (q.v.): 'They guarantee a job to all their star pupils. They've a big advertising account with us, so we sometimes take one of their chaps "on space" for a bit' (Lord Copper).
Sc 187

AIRSHIPS
A party is held in a 'dirigible' moored in a London suburb, in 1930. No one really enjoys it.
VB 122

AKONANGA, DOCTOR
Black doctor practising at 14 Blight Street, London, who describes himself as a 'nature-therapeutist and deep psychologist'.

Virginia Crouchback visits him, on the recommendation of Mrs Bristow (q.v.), in a vain attempt to rid herself of Trimmer's baby. She finds that he has moved to Brook Street, where he is employed by H.O.O.H.Q. to practise witchcraft against the Nazis.

He is small and neatly dressed with grey in his 'sparse little tangle of beard; he was wrinkled and simian and what should have been the whites of his eyes were the colour of Trimmer's cigarette-stained fingers . . . his smile revealed many gold-capped teeth'.
US 81–83

ALABAMA
American home of Mr Samuel Smiles Jackson, 'a pious old darky' and first president of Ishmaelia.
• Also the home of the Adventist University of Alabama, attended by the Negro who attempts to persuade William Boot to part with his parcel of geological specimens, and who proclaims himself to be the welter-weight champion of his year.
Sc 75, 153

ALAPOV, NADA
Friend of Anthony Blanche (q.v.) who, with Jean Luxmore, uses the same drug dealer.
BR 196

ALBANIA
Eastern European country on whose hills the sunset changes 'with the crude brilliance of a German picture-postcard, from green to violet', as Paul Pennyfeather observes while gazing across the water from Margot Metroland's villa in Corfu.
DF 205

ALBERT I
King of the Belgians who succeeded Leopold II in 1909. Greatly admired for his pride and steadfastness when his country was occupied by the Germans between 1914 and 1918.

In February 1940, it seems to Guy Crouchback that Mannerheim holds that place in English hearts held by King Albert in 1914.
MA 141–142

ALCAZAR
Fortified palace in Madrid laid seige to by the Republicans in September 1936 during the first months of the Spanish Civil War. One of the places where Miss Bombaum (q.v.) had 'popped up' as a young reporter.
WS 203

ALCIBIADES ***(c.450–404 BC)***
Athenian statesman.
• Angela Lyne wonders why he cut off his hair.
PF 28

ALCOHOLICS
According to Lady Marchmain (q.v.) dipsomania is 'simply a great misfortune'. However, her son, Sebastian Flyte (q.v.), is an incurable alcoholic.
BR 158
(See also LYNE, ANGELA)

ALDERSHOT
Town in Surrey dominated by the Army, where 'Julia' lives with her father, a major.

One of the Emperor Seth's claims to a knowledge of the modern age is having seen 'the great tattoo of Aldershot'.
BM 17; WS 162

ALEPPO
Coastal town in Turkey and one of the stops on the tour of the Near East undertaken by Mr Samgrass and Sebastian Flyte (*both* q.v.).
BR 145

ALEXANDER THE GREAT ***(356–323 BC)***
King of Macedonia, trained by Aristotle, victorious over the Persians, and conqueror of Asia Minor, Egypt, Babylon and part of India.
• Guy Crouchback compares Apthorpe's feud with Dunn (q.v.) to Alexander's visit to Siwa.
• Julia Stitch points out Alexander's tomb in Alexandria to Guy Crouchback in 1941.

• Scott-King compares his own self-confidence to that of Alexander, when invited to Neutralia.
MA 183; OG 127; WS 199

ALEXANDRIA
Clara's smile is compared to that of a fifth-century deacon in Alexandria.
• Guy Crouchback recovers in a hospital in Alexandria, where he is subsequently entertained by Julia Stitch (q.v.), who drives him about.
• Mr Metcalfe of Much Malcock (q.v.) used to work in Alexandria. In his Alexandria office there hung a calendar proclaiming, 'God gave all men all earth to love'. His wife misses the silent Bereber servants.
OG 126–128; GP 200; WS 47–48

ALFRED
Husband of one of the women in Adam Fenwick-Symes' carriage on the train to Aylesbury.
VB 138

ALGECIRAS, SPAIN
Port – in Gilbert Pinfold's mind – into which the *SS Caliban* puts for an examination of her cargo and passengers.
GP 87

ALGIERS
Whence Sebastian Flyte takes a motor bus to a monastery near Carthage, wanting to join as a lay-brother.

According to the young lady on board the *SS Glory of Greece*, Algiers is 'not very Eastern, in fact full of frogs'.

Location for a film of St John's Gospel in which Miss Grits is responsible for the continuity.
BR 289; WS 21, 76

ALI
Loyal Indian secretary of Seth, Emperor of Azania (q.v.). Bribes Major Joab to kill Mr Youkoumian.
BM 7

ALLAN
Character from one of Lottie Crump's parties who is best remembered for having been 'beaten up by some chaps'.
BM 75

ALLBRIGHT, CHARLES *(b 1938)*
Supposed son of Clarence Allbright (q.v.), and boyfriend of Barbara Seal. Borrows one of Peter Pastmaster's shirts. Plays the guitar and is aged twenty-one when he first meets Basil Seal.

Has 'a mop of dishevelled black hair and a meagre black fringe of beard and whiskers; formidable, contemptuous blue eyes above grey pouches, a proud rather childish mouth'.

One of his uncles is a Duke. He is a friend of Robin Trumpington and is, in fact, the son of Basil Seal and Betty Stayle. Basil uses this fact to ensure that he does not marry Barbara.
WS 51, 254, 258, 260, 273–275, 279

ALLBRIGHT, CLARENCE *(d 1943)*
'Awful chap' with no money; killed in action in 1943. Married to Betty Stayle. One supposed son, Charles (q.v.).
WS 254, 258, 275, 279

ALLGOOD, BILLY
Fellow officer in Cedric Lyne's company in WWII who is unable to accompany the troops in the attack, having broken his collarbone while on leave.
PF 178

ALOYSIUS
Teddy bear belonging to Sebastian Flyte whom Charles Ryder first encounters at Germer's, the Oxford barbers: 'What do you suppose Lord Sebastian wanted? A hair brush for his teddy bear . . . to threaten him with a spanking when he was sulky.' From Sebastian we later learn that although Aloysius is an excellent artist, he is rather more modern in his style than Ingres (q.v.).

He is discarded by Sebastian during his second, disastrous, year at Oxford.
BR 30, 53, 100, 102

ALPHONSE
The maître d'hôtel at Chez Espinosa (q.v.).

Always keeps a typewritten list of the diners, expressly for gossip columnists.
• Name used by Corker (q.v.) to attract the attention of a French steward on board the *Francmaçon*
VB 84; Sc 62

ALPS
Where Peter Postmaster's 'very secret corps' trains in 1939.
• Charles Ryder's father, reminiscing about 'reading parties', wonders why Alpine scenery should ever have been thought conducive to study.
PF 77; BR 62

AMBROSE
One of the boys taught by Scott-King at Granchester.
• Butler to the Prime Minister, Sir James Brown (q.v.), in 1930.
• Butler to Tony Last at Hetton.
WS 200; VB 58

AMELIA, LADY
Subject of *Period Piece* (1936). Has novels read to her by her companion Miss Mayers. Particularly fond of that type of story known by the local library as 'strong meat'. Friend of Etty Cornphillip (q.v.). Has a pekinese called Manchu. In her sitting room there is an heraldic fire-screen.
WS 23, etc.

AMERICA
American soil is 'peaceful and fecund'. Perfect, in fact, for Pimpernell's (q.v.) art.
• In America, where they have 'heroes of their own', Trimmer (q.v.) is a huge flop.
PF 39; US 186

AMERICAN PARCELS
Parcels of food sent from the USA to beleagured Britain during the early days of the Second World War. One such, sent to Mr Crouchback by his grandchildren, contains six tins of Pullitzer's soup, a packet of prunes, and such unfathomable items as a tin of Brisko, a tin of Yum-crunch and a bottle of Cocktail Onions: 'Could it be that this remote and resourceful people . . . have contrived an alcoholic onion?'
OG 25

AMERICANS
Paul Pennyfeather believes, in 1922, that the next war will be against the Americans.
• John Boot, the novelist, has an American girlfriend from whom he is desperate to get away, 'or else go crazy'.
• At Cannes, Angela Lyne finds that it is only the Americans who are aware of the war which faces Europe in 1939.
• Charles Ryder's father insists on treating his friend Jorkins as an American, from 'across the herring pond', much to Charles' embarrassment.
• Cara (q.v.) has some American friends living on the Brenta canal. Also in Venice, an American woman tries to sit bare-shouldered at Florian's, but is driven away by a persecuting crowd.
• Charles Ryder, at one time, becomes 'concerned' with two 'emancipated' American girls who have a garconière in Auteuil.
• To Mr Crouchback, the Americans are a 'remote and resourceful people . . . whose chief concern seemed to be the frustration of the processes of nature . . .'.
• After the allied invasion, Italy is full of Americans 'clamouring for dough-nuts and *Coca-Cola*'.
• Brigadier Cape says, sarcastically, that the Americans are bound to perfer an amphibious landing on the Côte d'Azur.
• Dennis Barlow notices that all American young ladies are: 'exquisite, amiable, efficient', although they do all look alike. American mothers must be able to tell their daughters apart: 'A man could leave such a girl in a delicatessen shop in New York, fly three thousand miles and find her again in the cigar stall at San Francisco'.
• According to Aimee Thanatogenos (q.v.), any American man would hate himself if he were to live off his wife.
• In Venice, Ralph Bland runs off with an American woman whom he far prefers to Etty Cornphillip.

• Apart from everything else being new, the Americans also invent new types of parties, one of which is the 'happening' (q.v.), which Barbara Seal tries to explain to her father.
DF 68; Sc 10; PF 24; BR 68, 95, 96, 194; US 95, 166; LO 36, 45, 88; WS 30, 155, 260
(*See also*, individual entries)

AMPLEFORTH
Catholic public school in Yorkshire, attended by Beryl Muspratt's (q.v.) three sons.
• Father Phipps travels here to witness the induction of the Abbot.
BR 82, 270

AMURATH
Emperor of Azania and grandfather of Seth (q.v.), he is: 'a slave's son, sturdy, bow-legged, three-quarters Negro'. He is educated by Nestorian monks, then enters the service of the Sultan at Matodi. He is promoted to commander-in-chief of the Sultan's army and finally assumes the title Emperor Amurath the Great. Defeats the Wanda and creates the Azanian Empire and the new capital of Debra Dowa.
BM 9, 10

ANABAPTISTS
Sixteenth-century religious sect practising the re-baptism of adults; to whose doctrines Dennis Barlow is inclined in the matter of his becoming a priest.
LO 100

ANARCHISTS
According to Lady Marchmain, Venice is full of Anarchists.

That they must also be very active in Spain is made clear later when, while dining onboard ship, Charles Ryder overhears a bishop declare it to be his aim to reconcile the Anarchists and Communists in Barcelona in 1936.
BR 96, 234

ANCHORAGE, LADY
Society hostess and friend of Brenda Last and her mother, to whom she always lends her chalet on Lake Geneva in August. described by Julia Flyte as 'stuffy'.
• Has her London house painted by Charles Ryder in 1936, before it is demolished to make shops and flats.
• Discovered by Viola Chasm (q.v.) to be paying her maid five pounds a week to send on to her all of Ralph Bland's letters.
• Friend of Mrs Kent-Cumberland (q.v.).
HD 172, 200; BR 192, 221; WS 26, 100

ANCHORAGE HOUSE
London residence of Lord and Lady Anchorage (q.v.).
HD 171; BR 221
(*See* London)

ANCIEN RÉGIME
Pre-revolutionary hierarchy of France, generally supposed to be reactionary and traditionalist.
• Lady Circumference's criticism of Mrs Melrose Ape (q.v.) sounds 'the hunting cry of the ancien régime'.
VE 101

ANCIENT GREECE
Thoughts of this civilization are invoked by Aimee Thanatogenos before her suicide.
LO 116

ANCIENTS, THE
Believed that you can bring upon yourself your own doom or nemesis, as is realised by Corporal-Major Ludovic (q.v.) in the summer of 1941.
US 87

ANDERSEN, HANS CHRISTIAN *(1805–1875)*
Danish author and storyteller. Chiefly renowned for his collection of fairy tales including the 'Tale of the Ugly Duckling', 'The Little Mermaid', and 'The Tinderbox'.
• Guy Crouchback is barely able to distinguish the stories of the Old Testament from those of Hans Andersen.
US 226

ANDERSON
Butler to Lady Seal (q.v.).
PF 18

ANDERSONS, THE
Couple immortalized in Robert Burns' poem 'John Anderson, My Jo'.
LO 98
(*See* POETRY)

ANDREW
Friend of Celia Ryder who, with his wife Cynthia, takes the Ryders' flat in London on a lease while Charles is away.
BR 251

ANGEL OF THE LORD
The vision which brought to Egdon Heath the psychopath who is later to decapitate Mr Prendergast:

> 'An angel clothed in flame, with a crown of flame on his head, crying "kill and spare not, the Kingdom is at hand"'.

DF 177

ANGEL, MR
Leader of a team of BBC reporters who interview Gilbert Pinfold (q.v.) at Lychpole. Has a thick beard and wears spectacles, corduroys and a tweed coat. His voice has no accent and is 'ridiculously plebian'.

Later Pinfold becomes convinced that Angel is one of those persecuting him on board the *SS Caliban*.
GP 19, 127

ANGELA
Friend of Brenda Last. Tony Last is not keen to stay with her and her family over New Year.
HD 17

ANGELIC SALUTATION
Murmured to Gilbert Pinfold by the nurse on the *SS Caliban*, after she gives him a sedative injection.
GP 49

ANGELS, THE (1)
Real family travelling on the *SS Caliban*, who lend foundation to Gilbert Pinfold's belief that he is being persecuted by Mr Angel (q.v.).
GF 124

ANGELS, THE (2)
Faith, Charity, Fortitude, Chastity, Humility, Prudence, Divine Discontent, Mercy, Justice and Creative Endeavour: the young female assistants of Mrs Melrose Ape, the evangelist (q.v.). Each of them carries a pair of costume wings in a black box like a violin case.

• Charity eventually ends up as a prostitute, first being sent by Margot Metroland to Buenos Aires, then being shunted around the Army and then off to the East, before finally ending up with a General, and Adam Fenwick-Symes (q.v.) in a staff car on the western front in WWII.
VB 9, etc.; VB 223–224

ANGMERING, BILLY
Said by London society in 1931 to be having 'a terrific walk out with a girl called Sheila Shrub' – so John Beaver tells Brenda Last.
HD 17

ANNABEL
Priscilla Boot's dog. Quite old and does not like to be moved. Consequently Mr Salter (q.v.) is compelled to spend the night in her company.
Sc 203

ANNAMESE STUDENTS
Paul Pennyfeather is informed by his scout at Oxford that an Annamese student at Scone has attempted to buy one of the Senior Tutor's daughters.
DF 210

ANSTRUTHER, GEORGE
Family doctor to the Marchmain family. Visits Lady Marchmain in the autumn of 1926.
BR 168

ANSTRUTHER, JEAN
Jean Anstruther of Glenaldy married Kerr of Gellioch, the uncle of Angus Anstruther-Kerr (q.v.), with whom Colonel Campbell (q.v.) confuses Guy Crouchback.
OG 61

ANSTRUTHER-KERR, ANGUS
One of the commandos with Guy Crouchback on the assault course on Mugg, led by Chatty Corner. Notable for sustaining a bad fall and being shipped back to the mainland.
OG 49

ANSTRUTHERS, THE
British couple, inhabitants of Azania and friends of the Courteneys. They have a daughter, Betty, who takes a fall from her pony. They are the epitome of English colonial ex-patriots, making every country in which they live into a sort of cosy suburbia.
BM 54

ANTHEA
Girl at school with 'Julia', who has a crush on Gilbert Warwick (q.v.), the writer. He writes her the same three-page letter twice, and she becomes very cynical.
WS 159

ANTHONY, SAINT, OF PADUA *(1195–1231)*
Preacher, born at Lisbon, who worked with the Franciscan missionaries among the Moslems in Morocco. Fell ill and returned to Europe, where he became a preacher in Italy. Buried at Padua. Known as the 'hammer of the heretics'.
• After he loses Aloysius (q.v.) Sebastian Flyte prays like mad (ironically) to St Anthony of Padua. The bear is immediately returned to him by Mr Nichols, a cab driver.
BR 84

ANTIBES
Resort in the South of France, near Nice, where Mr Baldwin (q.v.) has a villa and where he longs to be whenever he is in England on a frosty winter's morning, out hunting with the Fernie.

To where Rex Mottram is moved by Brenda Champion after having flirted with Julia Flyte at Cap Ferrat.
Sc 56; BR 178

ANTIC HAY
BR 48
(*See* BOOKS)

ANTIGONE
In Greek myth she is the daughter of Oedipus and Jocasta, doomed to destruction. Wandered with her father until his death and then returned to Thebes where Creon condemned her to death. Subject of two tragedies by Sophocles.
• 'Proud Antigone' is one of Aimee Thanatogenos' (q.v.) figures of ancient Greece.
LO 116

ANTIGUA
Island in the Antilles and home of the Baptist College of Antigua, of which the consul general of Ishmaelia is a graduate.
Sc 50

ANTOINETTE
Girl at school with Jenny Abdul Akbar (q.v.) who once came to Mass wearing lipstick: 'She was an ugly girl, always eating chocolates'.
HD 163

ANTONIC, DOCTOR BOGDON
International Secretary of the Committee for the Bellorius Tercentenary at Simona University, Neutralia. He is 'a middle-aged, gentle man whose face was lined with settled distress and weariness'.

He is a Croat and his wife is a Czech. He unsuccessfully attempts to emigrate from Neutralia to England with the help of Scott-King (q.v.).
WS 199, 217

ANTROBUS, MRS VAN
London society hostess of the 1930s; said to be 'seriously thinking' of Peter Pastmaster (q.v.) marrying one of her daughters.
PF 143

APE, MRS MELROSE

American evangelist preacher. Creator of the Angels, with whom she travels to England from France on the ferry in 1927. Is full of axioms, one of which is 'if you feel queer, sing'. Her favourite axiom is 'Salvation doesn't do them the same good if they think it's free'. Drinks rum. Leads community singing on the ferry; tells people that she has Hope, and Hope is what England wants.

Margot Metroland gives a party for her on 11 November 1927. She does not invite Simon Balcairn who turns up nevertheless and publishes a story in the *Daily Excess* about various society figures testifying to Mrs Ape and giving her their jewels.

Once, in Kansas City, she had got no further than her opening words: 'brothers and sisters, look at yourselves' before a huge tumult of emotion in which all of the seats in the hall had been broken up. It looks very much as though she has managed to instil some remorse among the rich, until Lady Circumference's voice breaks through with: 'What a damned impudent woman', and the moment is saved.

VB 9, 10, 19–20, 22, 84, 95, 99, 101

APHRODITE

Greek goddess of love and beauty (Venus).

• Poppet Green (q.v.) is working on a painting of the head of the Aphrodite of Melos. Basil Seal embellishes the picture with a ginger moustache and it is subsequently admired by Ambrose Silk (q.v.) who declares that Poppet has crossed one of the 'artistic rubicons'.

PF 31–34

(See SCULPTURE)

APPENDROTS, THE

London-based friends of Roger and Lucy Simmonds (q.v.).

WS 152

APPLEBY

Regular at the Wimpole Club (q.v.); friend of Arthur Atwater (q.v.). 'A good scout' who knows of a cave in Bolivia which contains a cache of Jesuit treasure. He has the idea of organizing an expedition to recover the treasure.

WS 182

APTHORPE *(c.1903–1940)*

The only one of Guy Crouchback's company to look like a soldier. He is well-built, moustachioed, has a tan and talks in military shorthand. We never learn his Christian name. Apthorpe's chief concerns are his boots (q.v.) and his 'thunder-box' (q.v.).

Prior to joining the Halberdiers he had been living in Africa. Plays golf and is 'above' sex: 'you have to be in the bush, or it gets a grip on you'.

Suffers from 'Bechuana tummy' which he treats with the contents of bottles kept in a japanned medicine chest, and copious amounts of whisky.

Has one old friend 'Chatty' Corner (q.v.), the famous 'gorilla man', whom he invites to a mess dinner at which the latter becomes so drunk that he has to leave.

To Guy Crouchback there seems about Apthorpe 'a sort of fundamental implausibility'. This is supported when Apthorpe admits that his second aunt at Peterborough is an invention, and by the later revelations of Chatty Corner.

In his huge kit bag he carries a collapsible bed, chair, bath, washstand and coat-rack.

Conducts a one-man war with Dunn of the Royal Corps of Signals (q.v.), whose men, he believes, come under his command.

In his conceit he reminds Guy of Mr Toad in *Wind in the Willows* (q.v.).

It is eventually revealed that Apthorpe was almost an alcoholic. This only becomes clear following his death, after Guy has smuggled a bottle of whisky into him when he is in hospital with 'Bechuana tummy'. It is generally concluded that it is the whisky which kills him.

The Adjutant reveals that he always thought Apthorpe 'a bit mad'.

According to Chatty Corner he was very well informed and read anything that he picked up, also being the soul of hospitality.

MA 44, 58, 59, 60, 97, 98, 107, 111, 162, 175, 181, 237, 242; OG 19, 57, 58

APTHORPE
House Captain in Charles Ryder's house at Lancing in 1919.
WS 287

APULEIUS, LUCIUS *(b. AD 125)*
Latin satirist, born in Numidia. Famous as the author of *The Golden Ass*, a satire on religious mysteries and their inherent vice, to which Ambrose Silk alludes as a parallel to his own self-mimicry.
PF 61

APULIA
Area in the south-east of Italy, between Foggia and Bari.

Guy Crouchback finds himself here at Bari, towards the end of the war. He is keen to buy the local merchandise, but is told that there is nothing to be had.
US 157

ARABS
The Arabs at Matodi live in a ghetto behind the bazaar. They consider the marriage of the daughter of Amurath into the house of the Sultan a disgrace.
• In Gilbert Pinfold's hallucinations, Mr Angel is leading a team from the BBC to Aden to make recordings of Arab dance music.
BM 14; GP 136

ARCADY
Mythical land of pastoral innocence where Paul Pennyfeather supposes Captain Grimes (q.v.) follows the Bacchic Train (q.v.).
DF 199

ARCHBISHOP OF CANTERBURY
Jakes, the reporter (q.v.), concocts a story that the Archbishop of Canterbury is behind Imperial Chemicals.
• According to 'Mr Chatterbox' the Archbishop is apparently so overcome at the public appearance of Mrs Melrose Ape (q.v.), that he confesses to doing 'something' at Eton in the 1880s with Sir James Brown (q.v.).
VB 106; Sc 102

ARCHIMANDRITE ANTONIOS
Greek priest expelled in 1939 from Sofia by the Bulgars; supposedly for 'fornications', but in reality as a political move. Turns up at the Ministry of Information, desperate to be an 'ally'.
PF 67

ARCHITECTURE
Margot Metroland (q.v.) employs Otto Silenus to demolish King's Thursday and rebuild it as 'something clean and square'. Nothing can be done to save it, for Jack Spire, the conservationist is too busy at the time saving St Sepulchre's Egg Street. In Silenus' opinion the problem of architecture is that the only perfect building can be the factory. To him it is impossible for domestic architecture to be beautiful.

He decorates the interior of the new King's Thursday with a glass floor, rubber furniture, a porcelain ceiling and leather-clad walls. A lift leads to the top of a great pyramidal tower from which one can survey the glass and aluminium roofs.

King's Thursday is again rebuilt once Margot's enthusiasm for modernism wears off.
• Charles Ryder prefers buildings which have grown eclectically over the centuries to the work of the great architects: 'In such buildings England abounded'.

He recognizes, sadly, that the English have only come to realize their wealth of architectural heritage of this sort at the very moment of its destruction.
• Guy Crouchback finds a piece of undateable architecture in a church at Begoy (q.v.).
• The apotheosis of modernism is Satellite City (q.v.) and in particular the Dome of Security, whose dome itself is hidden by the various ancillary wings which support it. It is made entirely of glass and concrete and the huge sheets of glass designed to 'trap' the sun are eventually camouflaged with coats of tar during a period of national panic.

• Mr Metcalfe (q.v.) describes modern architecture as: 'functional monstrosities in steel and glass and concrete'.
• Two architectural historians appear in the books: Archie Banks and Jack Spire (*both* q.v.).
• John Plant considers 'a decent home' that of his father – built in 1840 in stucco and weather-boarding. He admits to a preference for 'domestic architecture': 'It was one of the peculiarities of my generation . . . When the poetic mood was on us we turned to buildings and gave them the place which our fathers accorded to Nature – to almost any buildings, but particularly those in the classical tradition, and, more particularly, in its decay'.
• Neutralian buildings are in a different tradition altogether (as Scott-King discovers). The Ministry is in the 'severe one-party style' with a portico of straight, unadorned columns and a huge plain doorway. The Hotel 22nd March is in 1890s Rococo. The National Memorial is 'like all modern state-architecture' – a huge, plain stone pyramid.
DF 119–120; BR 215; Sc 109, 228, 303; OG 9; US 198; GP 191; WS 59, 80, 118, 143, 144, 207, 208, 209
(*See also individual buildings*, LONDON and LYNE, Cedric)

ARDINGLY
Soldier–servant shared by Ludovic (q.v.) and Captain Fremantle, to whom he reveals that Ludovic is 'going on funny . . . acting soft'.
US 114

ARGENTINA
Home of Anthony Blanche (q.v.) who, at the age of fifteen, is taken, disguised as a girl, to the Jockey Club at Buenos Aires.
• Where, in Buenos Aires, Margot Metroland (q.v.) has a brothel, managed by 'Bill'.
BR 47

ARGENTINES
The Argentine representative at the Bellorius Conference was simply a student who happened to be in Neutralia at the time.
• The Argentine chargé d'affaires gives Paul Pennyfeather the works of Longfellow as a wedding present.
WS 226; DF 156

ARISTOCRACY
The young of the 'real' aristocracy do not bother to wear fancy dress for Miss Mouse's party, but stand aloof: 'amused, but not amusing'.
VB 53
(*See also* individual families)

ARKWRIGHT
A don at Oxford, recommended to Charles Ryder by his cousin Jasper for his lectures on Demosthenes.
BR 28

ARLEN, MICHAEL *(1895–1956)*
Novelist, born in Bulgaria and educated at Malvern College. His major novel was *The Green Hat* (1924), (*see* BOOKS), which sold tremendously well. It concerns high society and, to Paul Pennyfeather in 1928, 'All Mayfair seemed to throb with the heart of Mr Arlen'.
• He is one of the authors considered by Seth (q.v.), along with Shaw and Priestley. to represent modern literature.
• For a time he was so famous that in 1943, Everard Spruce supposes that Frankie and Coney (all q.v.) will think he is the author of a passage he quotes from Aldous Huxley.
DF 147; BM 17; US 200

ARMENIANS
The most memorable of Waugh's Armenians is Mr Youkoumain (q.v.), proprietor of the Grand Hotel et Bar Amurath at Matodi.
• There is an Armenian merchant in Main Street, Jacksonburg, who unwisely lays in huge quantities of white cotton shirts only to discover that the White Shirt Movement (q.v.) is not as successful as might have been hoped.
• On their ill-fated expedition to the Near-East, Mr Samgrass and Sebastian

Flyte take with them an Armenian cook, Begedbian.
BM 97; SC 78; BR 145

ARMISTICE DAY
As Adam Symes boards the train for Aylesbury he sees people selling artificial poppies in the streets.
VB 65

ARMSTRONG
Fellow member of the Royal Academy whom Mr Plant (q.v.) describes as living 'like a hottentot'.
• Tony Last's agent at Hetton.
WS 109; HD

ARMY OF AZANIA
The ten-thousand-strong, Prussian-officered army built up by Amurath (q.v.). By the time of Emperor Seth (q.v.) the Imperial Guard are in tattered, field-grey uniforms; the infantry in bare feet and armed with every kind of weapon. The army is commanded by General Connolly (q.v.)
BM 13, 35–36

ARMY TRAINING MEMORANDUM NO. 31 WAR
Memorandum issued to all officers and officer cadets in April 1940, of which General Ironside said: 'I direct all commanding officers to ensure that every junior officer is thoroughly examined in the questions set in Part 1 of this memorandum . . .' thus provoking a state of great studiousness in the Halberdiers' mess. (There were one hundred and forty-three questions.)
MA 170

ARP
Air Raid Police of 1939–45, whose distinctive letters were written in white on a black helmet, as seen by Guy Crouchback and Ian Kilbannock outside Bellamy's in St James's.
OG 10
(*See also* AIR RAIDS)

ART
According to Professor Silenus (q.v.) the problem of all art is: 'the elimination of the human element from the consideration of form'.
• Art also serves to bring Basil Seal to the studio of Poppet Green (q.v.).
• Mr Bentley is an advocate of 'art for art's sake'.
• Lord Brideshead wants to know whether the chapel at Brideshead is 'Good Art' and asks Charles Ryder his opinion.
• Mr Ryder divides painters into two categories – serious and amateur (oils and watercolour).
• According to Charles Ryder, art students in Paris never go near the Louvre.
• Cordelia Flyte thinks that Modern Art is 'all bosh', and Charles Ryder agrees.
• Just such modern art is published in *Survival* (q.v.), as a supplement chosen by Coney and Frankie. To Guy Crouchback these reproductions look like 'squiggles'.
• 'Bertie' thinks Egyptian art 'inartistic'.
• According to Simon Lent 'vital art implies a corresponding set of social relationships'.
• It is Mr Plant's opinion that if you want to write books on art you should study the masters; but to paint, you should watch him.
DF 120; PF 43, 111; BR 89, 142; US 124; WS 20, 72, 114, 128
(*See also* AESTHETICS *and individual artists*)

ART CRITICS
According to Celia Ryder it is better for Charles' exhibition to open on Friday in order to give the critics the weekend to turn out their reviews.
BR 252

ART DEALERS
After Adam Symes invents Provna (q.v.) a steady output of his work travels from Warsaw to California via Bond Street.
• 'Dealers in abstract painting from the Danubian Basin' are part of the anti-fascist force quartered in Penkirk castle, near Edinburgh, in the spring of 1940 when they are reinforced by the Halberdiers.

• Goodchild and Godley of Duke Street handle Mr Plant's work – in particular copies of Lely and other English portraitists which are sent off to the US.
• The Mansard Gallery was a London gallery which specialized in 'vague assemblages of picnic litter' in the 1920s.
• The Grosvenor Gallery in Bond Street was the seat of the Aesthetic movement in the 1890s.
VB 112; MA 161; WS 115, 117

ART HISTORIANS
WS 80
(*See* BANKS, Archie)

ARTHUR
Legendary King of England who restored it to an age of chivalry, but was ultimately overcome by his barbarous enemies.

Sir James Macrae, after having proposed the idea of introducing King Arthur into the film of *Macbeth*, which is being written by Simon Lent, eventually concedes to abandoning his proposal.

• Fellow traveller of Bertie and Mabel on-board the *SS Glory of Greece*. At first thought to be 'a pansy' but then engaged to the young lady correspondent.

• Friend of Mrs Pinfold who works at the BBC.

• Artist employed by Mrs Stitch (q.v.) to paint murals on the ceiling of her bedroom. Criticized by her for putting 'too much ivy on the turret'. Just why she has commissioned him to do so is uncertain, for she admits: 'I think all Arthur's work is banal'.

• The porter at Basil Seal's club.
WS 75; WS 20; GP 152; Sc 7, 8; BM 69

ARTISTS
While in the 1850s Poppet Green would have painted knights in armour and ladies in distress, in the 1880s 'nocturnes', and in 1920 pierrots, in 1939 she paints bodiless heads.

• Anthony Blanche first spots that Charles Ryder is an artist – 'that very rare thing'. However, he tells him that: 'artists are not exquisite. I am . . . but the artist is an eternal type, solid, purposeful, observant – and, beneath it all, p-passionate'.
• Drawing on the Bellini family, Cara observes to Charles that during the Renaissance, painting was a family business.
• Lord Marchmain supposes that Charles Ryder will become a war artist and is surprised that he is applying for a commission. He implies that to be a war artist is to avoid danger.
• Dennis Barlow considers himself a sort of artist – versatile, precise, only unhappy when overtaken by monotony and chaos.
• Aimee Thanatogenos wonders if many artists are inspired in the evenings.
• According to Mr Hornbeam (q.v.), 'There is no place for the Artist in the Modern World'.
• This is, no doubt, a view with which Mr Plant would agree. He lives in the house of an unfashionable 1880s artist and considers English art to have ended with the Aesthetes.
• For Simon Lent, the artist should be the mirror of his age and, 'must share the weekly wage envelope of the proletarian'.
• The young Charles Ryder, perhaps in anticipation of his future career, declares that if he were an artist: 'I shouldn't do things I'd be dissatisfied with'.
PF 30; BR 52, 53, 96; LO 22, 72; WS 53, 72, 127, 128, 309

ART NOUVEAU
The chapel at Brideshead is described by Sebastian Flyte as

> 'a monument of art nouveau': 'The whole interior had been gutted, elaborately refurnished and re-decorated in the arts-and-crafts style of the last decade of the nineteenth century. Angels in printed cotton smocks, rambler roses, flower-spangled meadows, frisking lambs, texts in Celtic script, saints in armour, covered the walls in an intricate pattern of clear,

bright colours . . . The sanctuary lamp and all the metal furniture were of bronze, hand-beaten to the patina of a pock-marked skin; the altar steps had a carpet of grass-green, strewn with white and gold daisies. "Golly," I said'.

BR 39–40

ARUNDEL
Final destination of the indecisive Nina Blount and Adam Fenwick-Symes when attempting to decide where to dine. They have a dreary dinner in a hotel where Adam then takes her to bed.
VB 79

ARUNDELLS
Family of recusant Catholics connected to the Crouchbacks.
US 60

ARYANS
The fascist legation from Ishmaelia in London informs William that the Ishmaelians are pure Aryans – 'in the course of the years the tropical sun has given to some of us a healthy, in some cases almost a swarthy tan'.
Sc 51

ASCOT
Small town in Surrey, notable for Royal Ascot week in June.
• A determination to keep one's tickets for the Royal enclosure at Ascot is, Cedric Lyne surmises, one of the factors which makes society people shy of divorce.
PF 170

ASHANTI WARS
Series of wars (1824–1831, 1873–1874, 1893–1894, 1895–1896) precipitated by British colonial expansion on the Gold Coast.
• In 1939 the entrance to the war office is guarded by veterans of the Ashanti War.
• The Corps of Halberdiers played a distinguished part in the First Ashanti War and have a drum captured during that campaign in their mess.
PF 144; MA 49

ASHFORD, DAISY
Authoress of *The Young Visiters* (*See* Books), written when she was a small child.
HD 16

ASMARA
Town in Abyssinia from where Hitchcock reported the Abyssinian crisis.
Sc 32

ASQUITH, HERBERT HENRY, 1ST EARL OF OXFORD AND ASQUITH *(1852–1928)*
British Liberal Statesman and MP for East Fife, 1886–1918. Home Secretary, 1892–1895. Chancellor of the Exchequer, 1905–1908. Prime Minister, 1908–1916.
• Sir Joseph Mainwaring (q.v.) reflects on how easy it is to oust a Prime Minister in time of war, just as Asquith was replaced by Lloyd George in 1916.
• Ruby's husband was in Asquith's cabinet – a fact that would probably make her appreciate the figure of Gladstone bought by Lieutenant Padfield for Guy Crouchback.
PF 117; US 123

ATATURK, MUSTAFA KEMAL *(1881–1938)*
Turkish leader of the Nationalists from 1909. Elected President in 1923 and died in office.
• Mr Samgrass and Sebastian Flyte encounter a band of brigands – stragglers from his army, at the top of a pass in Turkey in 1925.
BR 145

ATHEISM
Ambrose Silk (q.v.) is Atheistic representative in the religious department of the Ministry of Information.
PF 110

ATHOL, MRS (NÉE JACKSON)
Holder of one of the chief posts of state in Ishmaelia, by virtue of being the aunt of Rathbone Jackson, the President.
Sc 75

ATLANTIC, THE

The Atlantic Ocean is used symbolically in several of the novels.

• It is described as 'Ponderous waves rising over murky, opaque depths'.

• A storm in the Atlantic provides the backdrop for Charles Ryder's first affair with Julia Flyte.

• John Plant sees the Atlantic as taking him from Spring into Winter.

• Mr Pelecci is drowned here in 1940.

HD 161; BR 193; WS 125; OG 40

ATROCITIES

Unspeakable atrocities are committed by the bimetalists on the wife of Senator Mendoza of Neutralia.

WS 207

ATWATER, ARTHUR

A 'bad character', Arthur Atwater is the mysterious assailant of John Plant's father, who kills him with his motor car. He introduces himself to John at the latter's club under the name of Thurston and appears to have a high opinion of himself: 'I wasn't brought up and educated to sell stockings'. (Atwater works as a commercial traveller.)

He later telephones John under the alias of Long and persuades him to send him ten shillings. He pops up again some months later at the Zoo and tells John that he is descended from Henry VII. They subsequently go to his club, the Wimpole (q.v.), and get very drunk. Atwater goes off to sleep rough on the Embankment.

Plant meets Atwater again during the war on several occasions and we learn that he advances in rank until, by 1944, he 'holds sway over a large area of Germany'.

WS 136, 137, 179, 180, 189, 191

AUCHINLECK, SIR CLAUDE JOHN EYRE *(1884–1981)*

British General. Served in Egypt and Mesopotamia from 1914–1919. In WWII served in Norway and India. Took over from Wavell in Middle East in July 1941 and advanced into Cyrenaica before being driven back by Rommel. Made a scapegoat and replaced by Alexander in August 1942. Created Field-Marshal in 1946.

• De Souza (q.v.) tells Guy Crouchback that he might as well agitate Auchinleck about Scottish Nationalism as isolate the Jewish faction from the rest of the anti-fascists in Yugoslavia in 1944.

US 204

AUCTIONEERS

Charles Ryder often arrives to paint a picture of a country house, only a few paces ahead of the auctioneer who is to sell it.

• Gilbert Pinfold's local doctor is the brother-in-law of the local auctioneer.

BR 216; GP 17

AUCTIONS

When the contents of Broome (q.v.) are sold at auction, Guy Crouchback's father attends and marvels at the prices paid as he sits on the edge of the rostrum eating pheasant sandwiches and drinking port.

• Kerstie Kilbannock frequents sale rooms.

• Gervase Kent-Cumberland sells two Romneys and a Hoppner 'at a poor price', in order to modernize Tomb (q.v.).

MA 35; US 149; WS 99

(*See also* CHRISTIE'S)

AUGUSTAN AGE

Originally the age of Ovid and Virgil. Later adopted to describe that of Pope and Swift. Geoffrey Bentley looks back to the Augustan Age.

PF 175

AUGUSTUS

One of Virginia Crouchback's many suitors. She never marries him and describes him as 'fat as butter'.

MA 85

AUNTS

Deceased Anglican aunts are a feature of the lives of both Gilbert Pinfold and Apthorpe (q.v.).

GP 71; MA

AUSTRALIA
Destination of Charles Ryder's cousin Melchior after he 'got into queer street'.
• When drunk, Boy Mulcaster compares himself and Charles to 'the poor dead Australians' of the Great War, when they become special constables during the General Strike (q.v.).
• Supposed destination of the Kanyis (q.v.) before they are abandoned by the Zionists.
• Tom Kent-Cumberland is sent away to a sheep farm in South Australia, where he meets the McDougalls (q.v.). He eventually settles in one of Mr McDougall's more remote estates with Gladys Cruttwell (q.v.).
BR 63, 198; US 235; WS 99

AUSTRALIANS
Two Australian soldiers are found dead in a side street in Alexandria, used as a short cut by Mrs Stitch.
• In Australia, because he is gentle, dignified and cultured, Tom Kent-Cumberland is completely different to everyone else.
OG 128; WS 103

AUSTRIANS
One of the peoples whom Mr Goodall believes, in 1941, will join together in a glorious crusade to redeem the modern age.
• In 1914, one of John Plant's schoolmates – who had betrayed the fact that John's father was an artist – had an aunt who was married to an Austrian nobleman and was thus hounded by the schoolboys as a 'German spy'.
OG 40; WS 168

AUTEUIL
Town in France, where, in 1926, Charles Ryder becomes 'concerned' with two American girls.
BR 194

AVIGNON
Town in Provence, France, where the restaurant car leaves Angela Lyne's train as she journeys back to England from the Riviera in the autumn of 1939.
PF 24

AVON, RIVER
River in Wiltshire into which the river Bride flows, near Brideshead (q.v.).
BR 21

AYLESBURY
Town in Buckinghamshire, and the nearest town to Doubting Hall (q.v.); seat of the Blounts, 'You go to Aylesbury by train and then take a taxi'.
VB 64

AYRSHIRE
Scottish county West of Glasgow. Ian Kilbannock's grandfather, the first baron, built a castellated house on the Ayrshire coast.
US 88

AZANIA
Small fictitious island in the Indian Ocean, off the coast of Italian Somaliland and below the gulf of Aden. The capital city is Debra Dowa (q.v.), and the chief port is Matodi.

Originally a Portuguese colony, successfully besieged in the 1630s by the Omani Arabs. The Arabs controlled the island from Matodi until the coming of Amurath (q.v.) from Basra.

Amurath established the Azanian Empire and founded the new capital. The indigenous population is divided into two tribes – the Wanda and the Sakuyu (q.v.).

In the sixteenth year of Amurath's reign, the French built the Chemin de Fer Impérial. Also under Amurath came the abolition of slavery (never properly enforced) and the Christian religion (likewise).

A cosmopolitan trading population gradually grew up, made up of Greeks and Jews, Indians and Armenians. Amurath was succeeded by his daughter, and she by his grandson, Seth (q.v.). After a revolution in 1932 Azania was mandated by the League of Nations as Joint Protectorate between the French and the British.

• Basil Seal (q.v.) is involved in this later episode of Azanian history, having financed the trip by the theft of his mother's emeralds.
BM 7, 10, 233; PF 16, 49

AZTECS
Ancient Mexican civilization with a highly developed, stylized artistic style and a predilection for human sacrifice.
• Julia Stitch's (q.v.) face, encased in a mud-pack, is thought by John Boot to be 'as beautifully menacing as an Aztec mask'.
• Anthony Blanche compares Lord Brideshead's face to an Aztec carving.
Sc 6; BR

B

BABALI INN
Position in the British lines on Crete held by the Halberdiers in May 1941.
OG 198

BABBIT
Official at the Foreign Office in London with whom 'Percy' is playing a game of chess by cable from Azania.
BM 57

BABY
Friend of Dan (q.v.) whom she accompanies to Brighton, where she thinks that the hotel 'stinks of yids'. Gets drunk at a party and quarrels with Dan.
HD 138–140

BACCHIC TRAIN
The huge and exuberant group of followers of the Greek god Bacchus, god of wine, and representative of its benign influence on civilization. He is always seen surrounded by these Bacchantes, all of them singing and dancing with joy.
• It is as part of this company that Paul Pennyfeather sees Captain Grimes (q.v.).
• Miss Mouse has a burning desire to tear off her dress and dance like a Bacchante at the savage party.
DF 99; VB 53

BACHELORS
Fashionable bachelors tend to occupy upper rooms in Shepherd's Market and North Audley Street and 'lurk' there on evenings at home.
• In Victorian times bachelors were apparently hardy and did not object to the barrack-like guest room, known as 'the bachelors' wing' at Malfrey (q.v.).
• Simon Lent is a depressed, half-in-love bachelor, living in a mews on £800 a year.
DF 149; PF 75; WS 63
(*See also individual entries*)

BAD CHEQUES
Colonel Blount gives Adam Fenwick-Symes a cheque for £1000 signed 'Charlie Chaplin'.
• Adam Fenwick-Symes writes a bad cheque to Lottie Crump, to pay his bill at Shepheard's.
• Basil Seal cashes a bad cheque at his club.
• Simon Lent is on the verge of writing cheques which will not be honoured.
• Sebastian Flyte gives a bad cheque to Anthony Blanche's drug dealer, 'a s-s-stumer, my dear'.
• Philbrick moves about the country leaving bad cheques for dinners at hotels.
BM 67; VB 82, 195; BR 196; WS 64; DF 112

BADGERS
Subject of one of William Boot's columns – 'Lush Places'. Unfortunately the word badger is substituted by his sister Priscilla with 'crested grebe', giving rise to a torrent of letters of which two are notable. One from a Major in Wales challenges William to produce one case of a young rabbit being attacked by a grebe; and another, from a lady, asks him why he condones baiting a rare bird.
Sc 20

BAGSHOT HEATH
Small heath between Bagshot and Camberley in Surrey. Requisitioned by the army as a training area in WWII.
PF 127

BAGNOLD, COLONEL AND MRS
Neighbours of the Pinfolds at Lychpole.
GP 11

BAKIC
'Interpreter' assigned to Guy Crouchback in Begoy. He is in fact a Yugoslavian partisan spy. He pronounces 'th' as 'd', e.g.: 'I tell dese people dey better talk Slav'. A thoroughly ruthless, bullying Communist.
US 173, 175, 176

BALCAIRN, SIMON, EIGHTH EARL OF (VISCOUNT ERDINGE, BARON CAIRN OF BALCAIRN, RED KNIGHT OF LANCASTER, COUNT OF THE HOLY ROMAN EMPIRE AND CHENONCEAUX HERALD TO THE DUCHY OF AQUITAINE) *(c.1903–1930)*
Gossip columnist on the *Daily Excess* (q.v.). Takes Adam Fenwick-Symes for lunch at Chez Espinosa to ask him why he has not received an invitation to Margot Metroland's (q.v.) party. (He has in fact snubbed her by writing 'things' in the paper.)

His cousins are all in lunatic asylums 'or else they live in the country and do indelicate things with wild animals except my mamma . . . and that's worse'.

Lives in Bourdon Street, London, where his flat is furnished with oilcloth and Lalique glass.

Is ejected by Lord Metroland from his party, his disguise of a beard undone, and is eventually left so short of copy that he has to invent a completely fictitious story about 'society' being convulsed by paroxysms of religious ecstasy at Mrs Ape's preaching. He telephones this story into his paper and then puts his head in the gas oven and commits suicide.
VB 50, 84–86, 104–106

BALDWIN, MR
Baldwin is an alias and we never learn his real name.

First encountered by William Boot as an extra passenger on the private aeroplane from Croydon to Paris, 'a small man in a hurry'.

William thinks that he may be Turkish. His accent is impossible to pin down. He takes pills for his health, enjoys the Côte d'Azur and has a pack of hounds in the Midlands, next to the Fernie, a house in Antibes, and a vineyard in Bordeaux, opposite Mouton Rothschild.

He also has a pied-à-terre in Jacksonburg, where M. Giraud is an employee of his.

Friend of Lord Copper. Is able to compose succinct journalistic memos.

• He is next encountered by William as a parachutist on the roof of the Pension Dressler (q.v.).

• He is an excellent ping-pong player and is able to speak Swedish to the Swede, arranging for him to kill Dr Benito (q.v.) and thus for the counter-revolution to prevail.
Sc 53–58, 166, 167, 168, 170

BALDWIN, STANLEY
British statesman, educated Harrow and Cambridge. MP in 1906 and Prime Minister in 1923. His policy of non-intervention in Spain in 1936 was seen to be a betrayal of the League of Nations. He was reluctant to rearm and resigned in 1937.

In a conversation at Charles Ryder's table on his trip across the Atlantic in 1936, Baldwin's name is mentioned in connection with Spain.
BR 262

BALKAN TERRORISTS
On liaison with whom Sir Ralph Brompton (q.v.) delivers an informal talk in London, just before Christmas 1943.
US 141

BALLET
The head of ballet in Miles Plastic's new Britain insists upon all of his girls being sterilized because, once you have had a baby, you can never dance well again.

• Roger Simmonds describes his play *Internal Combustion* (q.v.) as 'an old-fashioned ballet'.
GP 199; WS 133

BALLINGAR
Market town in Ireland, four and a half hours' train journey from Dublin and fifteen miles from Fleacetown. It has a late Regency Gothic church, an unfinished cathedral and a number of general stores – Mulligan's, Flannigan's and Riley's.

The barracks are now an empty memorial to liberty. It is 'A typical Irish town'.
WS 77

BALLIOL, DEAN OF
(*See* URQUART, Sligger)

BALLON, MONSIEUR
French Minister and diplomatic representative in Debra Dowa. A freemason (his apron is purloined by the Legation butler), he keeps his last cartridge for his wife during the Azanian crisis.

Plays a political game against Sir Samson Courteney and Seth (q.v.). Wears a false nose at the victory ball; arranges the removal of Achon (q.v.) from the monastery, and fails in his attempt at a coup.
BM 47, 53, 56

BALLON, MADAME
Wife of M. Ballon (q.v.) who makes assignation with the Duke of Ukaka (General Connolly). Is never seen to be drunk and refuses to tell anyone where General Connolly is.
BM 10, 111, 123, 219

BALLS
After a provincial Conservative ball, one of Basil Seal's friends is arrested.
• The Victory ball at the Perroquet, Debra Dowa, (q.v.) is a success beyond all expectations. The dance floor is 'awash' with turbans and 'women of all complexions in recently fashionable gowns, immense imitation jewels and lumpy ornaments of solid gold'. Both the British envoy and M. Ballon wear false noses.
• The Duchess of Stayle holds a ball to which John Boot is invited. It is full of elderly princesses but dancing is not an important feature. Mrs Stitch is there eating *foie gras* with an ivory shoe-horn in a bedroom.
• Charles Ryder's college at Oxford (Hertford), holds a ball during Eights Week in 1922.
• Vittoria Corombona asks Lord Marchmain and Cara to her ball at the Corombona Palace in Venice, but they do not attend. Charles and Sebastian do attend.
• The ball given for Julia Flyte in 1922 is the last of its type to be seen at Marchmain House (q.v.).
• At the ball onboard the *SS Glory of Greece*, Bertie dresses as an Apache and gets plastered.
• Roger and Lucy Simmonds first meet at a ball in Pont Street given by one of his relatives.
• Alastair Trumpington sees Peter Pastmaster in full dress uniform at a Court ball and feels sorry for him because he cannot come on to a club afterwards.
BM 81, 106; Sc 72; BR 78, 173; WS 19, 147; PF 44

BALZAC, HONORÉ DE *(1799–1850)*
French novelist and author of *Comédie Humaine*, in which he attempts to give a complete picture of modern civilization. Wrote eighty-five novels in twenty years.
• Angela Lyne (q.v.) has a paperback volume of Balzac which, she thinks, tells something about her personality.
• Gilbert Pinfold believes that to have written as many books as Balzac smacks of 'professional trickery'.
PR 25; GP 10

BAMFSHIRE, SONIA
Ailing friend of Rex Mottram who is put 'back on her feet' by a doctor in Vienna.
BR 168

BANKES
Schoolmate of Charles Ryder at Lancing who is sent out of Greek Testament class for saying 'who will rid me of this turbulent priest'.
WS 302

BANKS, ARCHIE
Distant cousin of Bella Fleace (q.v.) who wears horn-rimmed spectacles and has a 'BBC voice'.

Works at the Victoria & Albert Museum in South Kensignton, where he also lives. Later draws on his experiences at Fleecetown to write a short story for the *Spectator*. Photographs the door-cases and chimney-pieces and discovers six rare first editions in the library which Bella subsequently sells for £1000.

Later writes an essay on Fleacetown for the *Architectual Review*.
WS 80, 81

BANKS, OLIVE
One of the people Cordelia Flyte prays for – a hard case.
BR 91

BANNISTER, JACK
Prep-school friend of William Boot (q.v.), nicknamed 'Moke'. Has ginger hair. In 1938 is the vice-consul in Ishmaelia. Has a pet cheetah and a collection of skins and eggs.
Sc 95, 96, 98, 99

BANQUO
Character in Shakespeare's *Macbeth*.

Guy Crouchback, offering Ludovic dinner, seems to him to have turned from Banquo's ghost to host.
US 53

BARBADOS
Caribbean island where the trans-Atlantic liner puts in on the way to South America, allowing Tony Last and Thérèse de Vitre to bathe and tour the island's churches by car.

They eat flying fish at dinner in a hotel out of town and buy a stuffed fish which Thérèse then leaves behind.
HD 166–167

BARBERS
The barber at Jacksonburg who cuts Katchen's hair also shaves the Minister of the Interior.
• Charles Ryder first sees Sebastian Flyte at Germer's, the Oxford barbers (q.v.).
• A barber comes from Trumper's to Rex Mottram's London house to shave Charles Ryder, Sebastian Flyte and Boy Mulcaster on the morning after their arrest.
• The barber onboard the ship carrying the Ryders back from New York in 1936 manages to shave Charles 'with extraordinary dexterity'.
• In one of Gilbert Pinfold's hallucinations, 'Margaret' tells him that he should visit the barber's shop. She asks him what barbers do apart from cutting one's hair: 'They try and sell one hairwash . . . They make conversation. They massage the scalp. They iron moustaches. They sometimes, I believe, cut people's corns –.' 'Oh Gilbert, something much simpler. Think darling. Sh . . . Sh . . .' 'Shave?' 'Got it.'
Sc 141; BR 30, 115, 239; GP 111

BARBIZON
Village in the Forest of Fontainebleau, France, and centre for a school of painters in the 1850s, including Millet, Diaz and Theodore Rousseau, who, influenced by Corot, themselves had an influence on Impressionism.

In the Summer, according to Mr Crouchback, all art students go to Barbizon to paint in the open air.
BR 63

BARCELONA
Where Doctor Beamish (q.v.) first 'raised his fist' during the Spanish Civil War.
• Where Basil Seal says he will join Lord Monomark's yacht, but does not.
• A bishop, a fellow passenger of Charles Ryder on his journey across the Atlantic, is on a goodwill mission to Barcelona to reconcile the Anarchists with the Communists (1936).
• The fall of Barcelona (January 1939) is covered by Scab, Bum and Joe (q.v.).
BM 73; BR 234; OG 214; GP 195

BAREBONES-ABRAHAM, TOM
Supposed ring-leader of a group of enemy agents in London in 1940. In fact he is a fictitious contributor to Ambrose Silk's magazine *Ivory Tower* (q.v.), concocted by Mr Bentley to appease the police.
PF 199–200

BARI
Adriatic coastal town near Taranto, Italy. Does not see many foreign visitors from the Crusades until 1943. Has many fine Norman buildings and is also the resting place of the bones of St Nicholas. Is the only place in WWII to be gassed when a ship carrying mustard gas explodes in the harbour.
• Guy Crouchback is first based here early in 1944 and returns in 1945.
US 167–169, 233

BARINESE
The people of Bari, whose every aim in 1944 is to be employed by the occupying forces.
US 160

BARKER
Oxford student who was to share digs with Collins and Tyngate, but who, as he is standing for presidency of the Union, feels that he should be nearer the centre of town.
BR 140

BARLOW, DENNIS ***(b. c.1903)***
A 'young man of sensibility rather than sentiment'. Assistant at the Happier Hunting Ground (q.v.).

During the war deals with air priorities in Air Transport Command at an Italian port. Before the war he had been a poet and had received some praise. After the war goes to Hollywood to help write a film on the life of Shelley, but finds Megalopolitan Studios no different from service life.

Leaves the world of letters to work for the Happier Hunting Ground animals' cemetery.

Takes up with Aimee Thanatogenos, a trainee embalmer at Whispering Glades (q.v.) and impresses her with poems which he deftly takes from the major English poets.

When it is clear that advancement will be slow in his new career he decides to become a 'non-sectarian clergyman'. Is engaged to marry Aimee; however, when it is revealed to her by Mr Joyboy (q.v.) that Dennis has been deceitful, she breaks it off.

Is eventually sent back to England courtesy of a subscription fund raised by the English cricket club at Hollywood.
LO 22–23, 31–33, 123

BARNET, MRS
'Silent woman' in the village of Broome (q.v.) to whom Guy Crouchback was taken as a child by his mother with provisions and comforting words. She sat silent under a patchwork quilt surrounded by plaster statues of saints.
OG 226–227

BARNEY, MRS
At whose house, near Brideshead, Cordelia Flyte has one of her two teas after the hunt.
BR 160

BAROQUE
Style of Italian art and architecture beginning in 1630 in Rome with Bernini and Poussin. Used in France for political buildings by Lebrun and others, and carried over into England by Wren, Hawksmoor and Vanbrugh.
• Charles Ryder is converted to the Baroque by Brideshead Castle (q.v.), where he rejoices in 'all its clustered feats of daring and invention'.
• Cedric Lyne has a love of Baroque art.
BR 79; PF 168

BARRIE, SIR J.M. ***(1860–1937)***
Scottish-born novelist and the author of *Peter Pan*.
• Ruby (q.v.) invites an American General to met him at dinner in 1943, at which time he has been dead for six years.
US 122

BARS
Bar Basque – in either Jibouti, St Jean de Luz or Prague – where Colonel Plum once got drunk with Basil Seal.
• Harry's Bar, Venice – where Sebastian Flyte and Charles Ryder eat hot cheese sandwiches and drink champagne cocktails.

• Mooney's Saloon, Hollywood – haunt of the editorial staff of the local newspapers.
• The Regina Bar – haunt of the drug-pusher friend of Anthony Blanche.
PF 148; BR 98, 196; LO 113

BARTOLOZZI, FRANCESCO
(1727–1815)
Italian engraver who settled in London in 1764. One of the original members of the Royal Academy. Renowned for his sepia line engravings of classical and pastoral subjects.
• Roger and Lucy Simmonds, on moving into their house in Victoria Square, take down the Bartolozzi prints provided by the landlord and hang their own pictures.
WS 145

BARTON, MISS
Assistant at the store where William Boot buys the equipment for his expedition to Ishmaelia.
Sc 44

BAT, OLD
One of the estate workers at Brideshead met on his bicycle by Charles and Sebastian.
BR 40.

BATES, FRANK
Son of a bishop. Popular young master at Lancing, in 1919, and idol of the young Charles Ryder. He is lame from a football injury which precludes his service in the Great War. Has 'innocent blue eyes'.
WS 304, 305

BATESON
Young journalist on the *Daily Beast* (q.v.). Graduate from the Aircastle Correspondence School (q.v.).

Is sent to collect William Boot from Victoria Station on his return from Ishmaelia. 'Loses' him and is subsequently fired.
Sc 187–189

BATH
Town in Somerset, a mile or two outside which stands 'A composed Hermitage in the Chinese Taste', built in 1767, which Roger Simmonds proposes as a house for John Plant (q.v.).
WS 144

BATHS
The baths at King's Thursday are sunken and made of malachite.
• The Grand Azanian hotel in Debra Dowa (q.v.) has only one bath.
• Lady Seal always has a touch of ammonia in her bath.
• Ambrose Silk's bathroom has only a gas-burning apparatus to heat it which explodes in 'a cloud of poisonous vapours'.
• Prudence Courteney and William Bland play with an inflatable rubber sea-serpent in the bathroom at the legation, as does Sir Samson Courteney who day-dreams about the pleistocene era.
• Angela Lyne drinks a large cocktail in her bath, suffused with 'an aura of naughtiness'.
• Charles Ryder's bathroom at Brideshead is a converted dressing-room with a mahogany-framed copper bath, filled by pulling a heavy brass lever. There is always a coal fire in Winter. Watercolours decorate the walls and there is a chintz armchair. It is in stark contrast, Charles tells us, to the 'uniform, clinical little chambers, glittering with chromium-plate and looking-glass which pass for luxury in the modern world.'
DF 135; PF 119, 194; BM 38, 62–63, 76; BR 148–149.

BATTLES
• Agincourt (1415): Decisive battle between the victorious English under Henry V and the French; after which the first Baron Marchmain was created.
• Balaclava (1858): Scene of the Charge of the Light Brigade. Called to mind by Charles Ryder.
• Bannockburn (1314): Scottish victory over the English. Called to mind by Charles Ryder.
• The Battle in the West (*c.* 537): The great battle in which King Arthur was killed. Called to mind by Charles Ryder.

• Crécy (1346): Famous victory of the English over the French. Its name rings in Lady Sea's ears.
• Culloden (1745): Final defeat of the Scottish Jacobites. Mr Plant compares its aftermath with the disappearance of the artistic class of the Edwardian era.
• Gallipoli (1915): Disastrous but heroic Allied landing against the Turks. Called to mind by Charles Ryder.
• Inkerman (1854): Where the British thin red line held off the Russians. Where Colonel Prentice's grandfather served.
• Lepanto (1571): A great Christian victory over the Turkish fleet. Called to mind by Charles Ryder.
• Marathon (490 BC): Massive Greek victory over the Persians. Called to mind by Charles Ryder.
• Quebec (1759): The English under Wolfe stormed the Heights and defeated Montcalm. Called to mind by Charles Ryder.
• Roncesvalles (778): The gallant last stand of Charlemagne's Paladins under Roland. Called to mind by Charles Ryder.
• Thermopylae (480 BC): Leonidas and his three hundred Spartans were massacred by the Persians. In Charles Ryder's mind.

BATULLE, BARONESS
One of the guests at the banquet for Mildred Porch. Her ballgown exposes her tattoed and cicatrized back.
BM 168

BATUM
Visited by Mr Samgrass on his trip to the Near East with Sebastian Flyte.
BR 145

BAUHAUS, THE
German art and craft school founded at Weimar in 1906 under Van de Velde. In 1919 he was succeeded by Gropius who re-organized the school along modernist lines of industrial design. Moved to Dessau in 1926. It became a byword for utilitarian design.
• Otto Silenus studied here.
DF 122

BAUMBEIM, OTTO
Assistant director of Megalopolitan Studios (q.v.) who, according to Mr Medici, is 'screwy'.
LO 27

BAVARIANS
Thought by Mr Goodall (q.v.) to be among the peoples of Europe who will take part in the great Pilgrimage of Grace (q.v.).
OG 40

BAVERSTOCK, PETER
Friend of Lucy Simmonds (she only has two) who lives in the Malay states. He had wanted to marry Lucy since she was seven, and until she is married he proposes to her every eighteen months. Lucy writes him a letter every fortnight.
WS 166

BBC
In the 1930s Basil Seal gives the first of what is meant to be a series of talks for the BBC.
• Spotty BBC announcers live in basement flats and give cocktail parties, or so it is reported by Adam Fenwick-Symes, the gossip columnist of the *Daily Excess* in 1930.
• The BBC invite Gilbert Pinfold to record an interview and send down to Lychpole a team of three young men, led by a Mr Angel (q.v.). Later, on the Third Programme, Pinfold hears himself attacked by Clutton-Cornforth (q.v.) in a broadcast entitled 'Aspects of Orthodoxy in Contemporary Letters'.

Another writer featured by the BBC is James Lance, who also attacks Pinfold on the radio.

Arthur, a friend of the Pinfolds', works at the BBC.
• Some of Scott-King's classical ex-colleagues are recruited by the BBC.
PF 48; VB 111; GP 18, 19, 62, 82, 152; WS 195

BEACH, SYLVIA
Important American ex-patriot figure in Parisian literary society from the 1920s

to the 1950s. Founder of the American bookshop, Shakespeare and Co., she was also a friend of all the major writers of the period including Hemingway, Joyce, Pound, Eliot and Gide. She published the first edition of Joyce's *Ulysses* in 1922.

Publications by her are one of Lieutenant Padfield's thank-you presents to his hosts and hostesses in London in 1943.
US 25

BEACHES
'Rather jovial' room of the Royal Victorian Institute, Brompton, which, during its time as command centre of HOOHQ (q.v.), houses a Victorian locomotive engine, six sailors and a number of naval charts.
US 28

BEACON HILL
Hill near Brideshead on which the fire was lit to celebrate Nelson's victory at Trafalgar in 1805.
BR 316

BEAMISH, DOCTOR
Director in charge of euthanasia at Satellite City (q.v.). His patients are kept waiting so long that they often die of natural causes. He grew up during the 'nervous' thirties, fought in the Spanish Civil War (q.v.), painted abstract pictures for *Horizon* magazine (q.v.), aligned himself with Stephen Spender (q.v.) and wrote 'publicity' for the last Viceroy (q.v.). His is the most envied position in Satellite City.
GP 195

BEANO
Nickname of a major-general friend of Jumbo Trotter; encountered by him and Guy Crouchback on the Duke of York's steps in 1941.

Is narrowly missed by a bomb during the blitz.
OG 43–44

BEAR ISLAND
Island in the Irish Sea.
• Basil Seal, once sailed a yawl around Bear Island, or so he tells Ambrose Silk.
PF 175

BEARD, THE REVEREND SEPTIMUS
Author of *Prayers on Various Occasions of Illness, Uncertainty and Loss* (1863) – one of the books which Paul Pennyfeather finds in his cell at Egdon Heath.
DF 168

BEARDS
Clara (q.v.) has a long beard the colour of golden corn which is eventually removed, having been a side effect of Klugmann's Operation.
GP 198

BEARS
A bear was once kept in one of the outhouses at Doubting Hall (q.v.).
• There is a stuffed bear in the foyer at Boot Magna Hall.
• In Hollywood a dead she-bear was once kept in the ice-box by its owner for over a week before she decided to call the taxidermist.
VB 67; Sc 00; LO 23

BEASLEY, ROBIN
Gentleman with whom Brenda Last's sister Marjorie St Cloud has an affair, which she later plays down.
HD 57

BEAUTY
In comprehending a woman's beauty, thinks John Plant, one automatically imagines how her face might look when she is in love.
WS 161
(*See also* AESTHETICS)

BEAVER, MRS
Widow, interior decorator and mother of John Beaver (q.v.). Has a house in Sussex Gardens and a little shop nearby where she always arrives at 9.00am precisely. She drives a two-seater motor car and her clients include Mrs de Trommet and Brenda Last.

Persuades Brenda Last to lease a flat and then to have it decorated. Her taste is modernist, 'white chromium plating and natural sheepskin carpet'.

(Mrs Beaver is probably based, as a designer, upon Syrie Maugham.)
HD 8, 35; Sc 7

BEAVER, JOHN ***(b. 1909)***
Son of Mrs Beaver (q.v.), with whom he lives in Sussex Gardens. Constantly impecunious. Twenty-five years old in 1934.

His income is £6 a week and he passes his life in idleness and being invited at the last minute by hostesses who are one man short.

Unpopular member of Bratt's club (q.v.). Is invited to Hetton by Tony Last (q.v.) where he is put into the least comfortable room. John Last thinks him 'a very silly man'.

He has been engaged, but lack of money put an end to it; has never had 'a proper affair'.

Following his being taken up by Brenda Last, he is looked at by women in a new way and welcomed by the members of Bratt's. Having helped in the destruction of the Lasts' marriage, he abandons Brenda when she runs out of money, and goes to New York.
HD 7, 8, 28, 35, 51, 58, 176, 200

BEAVERS
John Plant (q.v.) compares himself and his friends to beavers who, 'inhabiting a concrete pool, will if given timber, fatuously go through all the motions of damming an ancestral steam'.
WS 191

BEDDOES, THOMAS LOVELL ***(1803–1849)***
English poet, educated at Charterhouse and Oxford. Author of *The Bride's Tragedy* (1822) and *Death's Jest Book* (1825). Committed suicide in 1949.
• His death is alluded to by Ambrose Silk when ruminating on his own career.
PF 42.

BEECH, AIR MARSHAL
Air Marshall in WWII whose wife plays bridge with Kerstie Kilbannock (q.v.). Kerstie's husband, Ian, thinks him 'the most awful shit'.

First meets Guy Crouchback at the Kilbannocks' party where he recites, to everyone's embarrassment, a rhyme about Elinor Glyn (q.v.) of whose identity he is unaware.

He is 'a stout man, just too short to pass for a Metropolitan policeman with a cheerful manner and shifty little eyes'.

Guy is forced by Ian Killbannock into seconding his proposal to Bellamy's, to which he is duly elected. The air marshall is not, however, impressed by the sense of humour of Bellamy's members and is apt to question whether becoming a member was a wise move.

Later writes his reminiscences of the war (1951), which Elderberry is seen to be reading at Bellamy's.
MA 26, 125–126; OG 13, 99; US 238

BEECHAM'S PILLS
Patent indigestion tablets advertised by 'a face of flawless Florentine quattrocento beauty', to which Anthony Blanche compares Julia Flyte.
BR 54

BEERBOHM, SIR (HENRY) MAXIMILLIAM ***(1872–1956)***
English novelist, wit and caricaturist. Author of *Zuleika Dobson* (1912).
• There exists a caricature of John Plant's father by Max Beerbohm in a defiant pose, saying 'I am a Dodo'.
WS 111

BEETHOVEN, LUDWIG VAN ***(1770–1827)***
Pre-eminent German composer of the nineteeneth century.
• According to 'Soapy' (q.v.) 'no late Beethoven comes off'.
• The string quartet at Mountjoy (q.v.) play the 'Grosse Fugue as the last movement of the B Flat'.
GF 181

BEFORE NEED ARRANGEMENT
Euphemism for booking a plot in Whispering Glades (q.v.).
LO 36

BEGEDBIAN
Armenian cook to Mr Samgrass and Sebastian Flyte on their trip to the Near East.
BR 145

BEGOY
Town in Northern Croatia to which Guy Crouchback is posted in 1944. It is mostly abandoned but still has about it the vestiges of the Habsburg Empire – thermal springs and ornamental gardens.
• Guy asks the local priest to say a Mass for Virginia.
US 172, 198

BELGIANS
Charles Ryder meets a Belgian Futurist calling himself Jean de Brissac de la Motte during the General Strike (q.v.).
• Guy Crouchback thinks of King Albert of the Belgians (q.v.).
BR 193; MA

BELGIUM
Where Mr Hardcastle, chairman of the St John's Wood Residential Amenities Company (q.v.), has a daughter in 1938.
WS 141

BELGRADE
Capital of Yugoslavia, close to the area where Guy Crouchback spends the last few weeks of the war.
• Its bombing on Palm Sunday 1941 is not of any great concern to Major-General Whale.
OG 115

BELISARIUS ***(AD 505–565)***
Byzantine general under the Emperor Justinian. Defeated the Persians in 530; recovered the African provinces in 533; captured Ravenna in 540 and repelled the Huns in 559.
• A book (1938) based upon his life by Robert Graves (q.v.), recounts the legend that he ended as a blind beggar. Miss Bombaum confuses him with Bellorius (q.v.).
WS 203, 230

BELL, CLIVE ***(1881–1962)***
Art critic. Author of *Art* (1924), *Since Cezanne* (1922), *Civilization* (1928) and *French Painting* (1931).

Friend of Roger Fry and founder with him of the Bloomsbury group. Developed theory of Significant Form outlined in *Art*, which postulates that form subornes content. Champion of the Post-Impressionists.
• Sebastian Flyte quotes from *Art* (*see* AESTHETICS) and opens Charles Ryder's eyes.
• According to Mr Plant (q.v.), Sir Lionel Sterne, though an important patron of painting, has no time to read Clive Bell.
BR 30; WS 115

BELL, MONSIGNOR
Catholic priest at the Old Palace, Oxford, in 1923. Asks Sebastian Flyte to lunch, at the request of Lady Marchmain. Gives Sebastian a fourth talking-to in October 1922.

Lady Marchmain wants Sebastian to lodge with him; Sebastian refuses.
BR 59, 101, 136

BELLACITA
Capital city of Neutralia (q.v.).
WS 207

BELLINI
Surname of a family of Venetian painters of the Renaissance.
• Jacopo (*1400–1470*), by whom there are four known pictures. Father of Gentile and Giovanni.
• Gentile (*1429–1507*). Works in the Doges Palace, Venice and St Marco, Milan.
• Giovanni (*1430–1516*). Best known of the three. Influenced by Mantegna and Antonello; had an influence on Titian. Renowned as a painter of Madonnas.
(*See his* PORTRAIT OF THE DOGE; ST JEROME *and* FEAST OF THE GODS)
• Charles Ryder, when asked by Lord Marchmain which Venetian painter he likes best, answers wildly 'Bellini', unaware that there are three.
BR 95–96

BELLORIUS *(1646)*
Fictitious Neutralian poet whose life's work was a poem of 1500 lines of Latin hexametres, reprinted in the mid-nineteenth century in Germany where it is discovered by Scott-King (q.v.). The subject is a visit to an imaginary utopia.
• Scott-King translates the work into Spenserian stanzas but it is rejected by the OUP.
WS 190, 197

BENFLEET, SAM
Junior director of Adam Fenwick-Symes' publishers in Henrietta Street – 'A competent young man with a restrained elegance of appearance'.
VB 30

BENGERS
Field on the Brideshead estate over which the hunt rides.
BR 160

BENITO, DOCTOR GABRIEL
Minister of Foreign Affairs and Propaganda, and director of the Press Bureau of Ishmaelia. Holder of the Star of Ishmaelia, 4th Class.

A short, brisk man 'soot-black in face, with piercing boot-button eyes'. Dresses in a black suit and while linen shirt. According to Pigge (q.v.), he is 'creepy'.

Denies Russian involvement in Ishmaelia and is responsible, with the Russians, for locking up the President.

Attempts to buy Katchen's stones from William Boot. Is forced to leap to his death from the balcony of the presidential residence, by 'the Swede'.
Sc 95, 98, 119, 145, 152, 176

BENNETT, ARNOLD *(1867–1931)*
English novelist, and author of the Clayhanger series and numerous other works – many set in the centre of the pottery industry.
• Paul Pennyfeather (q.v.), on encountering Philbrick during his second sojourn in Oxford, replies 'Arnold Bennett', when asked his identity.
DR 212

BENSON, MRS
One of Gilbert Pinfold's fellow travellers aboard the *SS Caliban*.
GP 36

BENSON
Chauffeur to Sir James Macrae (q.v.).
• Butler to Barbara Sothill. Basil Seal borrows twelve pounds ten from him and tells him that he will pay it back. Does not admit that Barbara has already given him a fiver in part payment.
WS 66; PF 12, 87

BENTHAM, MRS
Evening secretary to Sir James Macrae (q.v.).
WS 65–76

BENTLEY, GEOFFREY
Publisher of the work of Ambrose Silk (q.v.); declares that he has never liked authors, but thinks books 'a good thing'.

Distantly related to King George III. During the war becomes head of a department at the Ministry of Information.

In 1963 organizes a public banquet to celebrate Ambrose Silk's sixtieth birthday and his investiture with the Order of Merit.
PF 61–66, 183; WS 253

BENWELL, MR
John Plant's (q.v.) publisher.
WS 130

BERBERS
The natives of North Africa who provide the servants in Alexandria that Mrs Metcalfe (q.v.) misses so much.
WS 48

BERGSON, AMELIA
American writer who buys a 'before needs reservation' at Whispering Glades (q.v.).
LO 38

BERKSHIRE DOWNS
Berkshire hills below which John Plant

and Lucy Simmonds (q.v.) go to look at a house which John might want to buy.
WS 173

BERLIN
One of the places to which Basil Seal thinks he might go in 1932.
BM 232

BERMUDA
Atlantic island where Canon Chatterbox was chaplain.
• Where Angela Lyne has a beach and a bungalow, acquired in the 1950s.
• Basil Seal takes his family here in 1962.
VB 150; WS 256, 281

BERT
Gardener to the Flytes at Brideshead.
BR 37

BERTIE
Adjutant of X Commando, Isle of Mugg. Captain in the Grenadier Guards. Friend of Eddie (q.v.). According to him, the kick of an ostrich can kill three horses. Visits the zoo in Cape Town with Eddie and Ivor Claire in February 1941.

Tommy Blackhouse meets him at Bellamy's dancing with joy.
• Passenger on *SS Glory of Greece*.
OG 50, 108, 114; WS 17

BERTRAND, MONSIEUR
Editor of the *Courier d'Azanie* – does not look of any importance, and neither is he. Three-quarters of his time is taken up with printing stationery. Twice a year he and his wife dine at the French Legation, by virtue of his position. He is thus unwilling to sell the newspaper to Basil Seal (q.v.).
BM 124

BEST-BINGHAM, EDDIE
Sir Joseph Mainwaring has an interesting talk with him at the Beefsteak Club about the RDF (q.v.).
PF 22

BETTY
'Homely' nurse who accompanies Brigadier Cape at Bari (q.v.).
US 170

BETTY, AUNT
Owner of Buckborne House and relative of the Flytes, who gives Julia as a wedding present a pair of Chinese vases which used to stand on the stairs at Buckborne.
BR 188

BEVAN, ANEURIN *(1897–1960)*
British Labour politician. Member for Ebbw Vale in 1929; brilliant orator; Minister of Health in 1945; introduced National Nealth Service in 1948 and was Minister of Labour in 1951.
• In the New Britain of Miles Plastic, an improbable coalition between Bevan and Anthony Eden (q.v.) has introduced euthanasia to the Health Service.
GP 194

BEVIS
(*See* BOOKS)

BIARRITZ
Fashionable French seaside resort on the Bay of Biscay.
• Where Engineer Garcia (q.v.) claims to have seen the Duke of Westminster.
• Where Jock Grant-Menzies first meets Mrs Rattery (q.v.) in the Summer of 1933.
HD 97; WS 213

BICESTERS
London society family in the 1930s. 'The Bicesters' Dance' is used as an excuse to the parents of many young ladies attending Johnnie Hoop's savage party (q.v.).
VB 54

BICYCLES
Whitemaid conjectures that Miss Svenningen (q.v.) might ride a bicycle in shorts.
WS 216
(*See also* TRANSPORT)

BILL
Passenger on *SS Glory of Greece* who has a row with Bertie.

• Acquaintance of Captain Grimes (q.v.). An 'awful stout fellow' who had served with Grimes in Ireland and gone to Argentina, where he manages the brothel run by Margot Metroland. Takes on Grimes as an assistant.
WS 17; DF 140

BILLY
Member of the crew of the *SS Caliban* who, in Gilbert Pinfold's mind, is berated by the clergyman for being impure, apparently having 'filthy pictures' of girls stuck up by his bunk.
GF 39

BIMETALISTS
Radical political faction in Neutralia responsible for commiting 'unspeakable atrocities' on the wife of Senator Mendoza.
WS 207

BIRMINGHAM
Final wartime destination of the Prentices' evacuees.
• Fifty families from Birmingham are sent as evacuees to Malfrey. Barbara Sothill takes in five and thus provokes her housemaids to leave. The others feel unwanted in Malfrey, where the mothers in the party are keen to drink at the two inns.
• The inhabitants of Debra Dowa (q.v.) have, among their treasured possessions, 'trinkets' from Birmingham.
MA 29; PF 11; BM 27

BIRTH CONTROL
Topic discussed by Paul Pennyfeather and Arthur Potts at Queens Restaurant.
• Seth (q.v.) reads about birth control in the newspapers and is very keen to have it in Azania. He seeks to achieve this through an advertising campaign showing on the one hand an impoverished man with many children, one of whom is mad, and on the other a rich man with a few healthy children.

The message is, however, misunderstood by the natives who take it that the poor man is blessed with many children, one of whom is 'holy', and that the Emperor's 'juju' must therefore be a good thing as it gives you many children.
DF 121; BM 129, 147

BISLEY
Town in Surrey which plays host to an annual international small-arms shooting competition.
• Major Hound (q.v.) won many prizes here before the war.
OG 119

BITHYNIA, BISHOP OF
A bishop of Bithynia in the second century denied the divinity of Christ, the immortality of the soul, the existence of good, the legality of marriage and the validity of the sacrament of Extreme Unction. He was, of course, condemned as a heretic.
DF 212

BLACKALL
Porter at Scone College, Oxford, in 1927.
DF 14

BLACKBIRDS, THE
Members of a production – *Dover Street to Dixie* – presented by Charles B. Cochran at the London Pavilion in 1923. The lead was Florence Mills. The show took London by storm and the first party given to welcome them was thrown by Oliver Messel at the Abbey Road Studios of John Wells, the portraitist.
• In *Brideshead Revisited*, the Blackbirds are a coloured orchestra from the United States who arrive in England in the Spring of 1926. A party is held in their honour at a private house in Regent's Park, at which they appear happier to gamble on dice than play music. One of them hits Mrs Arnold Frickheimer on the head with a bottle of milk.
BR 195

BLACK BITCH
Duchess of Ukaka and wife of General Connolly (q.v.). Frequently thumped and locked in a cupboard when excited. Very keen on etiquette. Enjoys the Victory Ball (q.v.). Cannot bear another woman to touch her husband's clothes.
BM 43, 135

BLACKHOUSE, MAJOR-GENERAL TOMMY
A Captain in the Coldstream Guards in the 1920s. Member of Bellamy's and friend of Guy and Virginia Crouchback. Falls in love with Virginia while Guy is in Kenya (q.v.) and subsequently marries her. Guy identifies him for the divorce proceedings from a solicitor's window at Lincoln's Inn. After the divorce he leaves the Guards but refuses to abandon the Army and transfers to a line regiment. Parts from Virginia before the war but has a brief affair with her in 1939.

Next seen by Guy on 31 December 1939 at Bellamy's, by which time he has managed to rejoin the Coldstream as a Major.

Guy meets him again in November 1940 on the Isle of Mugg where, now a Colonel, he is organizing X Commando, which he fills with old friends. Guy detects a difference in him here. He is 'Tommy, the perfect soldier'.

Finally returns to England in May 1951. Retires from the Army with a pretty new wife at the rank of Major-General; organizes X Commando reunion in 1951.
MA 18, 19, 80; OG 45, 47, 51, 61, 69, 118; US 237

BLACK MAGIC
Practised by the witch doctor, Dr Akonanga (q.v.), who is employed by HOOHQ to give Herr Ribbentrop nightmares. His equipment includes a decapitated cockerel, human bones, a skull, a bowl of ashes, a statue of the Sacred Heart and scorpions (q.v.).
• Anthony Blanche (q.v.) admits to having dabbled in black magic in Cefalu (q.v.).
US 83, 84; BR 47

BLACKMAIL
According to Peter Pastmaster (q.v.), his mother, Margot Metroland, is blackmailed by Sir Humphrey Maltravers into marriage in return for Paul Pennyfeather's release from prison.
• It costs Mr Harkness thirty pounds to get rid of the Connollys (q.v.) and Basil Seal uses this fact to extract some sherry from the cellars of the girl at Grantley Green.
DF 161; PF 125

BLACKPOOL
Venue for the 'slow valse' competition, for which Halberdier Shanks' request for leave is denied by Guy Crouchback.
MA 205

BLACK SEA
Inland Sea between Russia and Turkey.
• Gilbert Pinfold, looking over the rail of the *SS Caliban* thinks of 'the iceflows of the Black Sea that raced past Constantinople and Troy'.
GP 89

BLACKSTONE GAOL
Where Paul Pennyfeather passes the first period of his prison sentence. The Governor is Sir Wilfred Lucas-Dockery.
DP 161

BLACKWATER, KITTY
Sister of Lady Throbbing (q.v.) and the subject of a portrait by Sir J.E. Millais (q.v.) which achieves a rock-bottom price at Christie's.

Fellow passenger of Adam Fenwick-Symes across the Channel. Frequently mentioned in the social columns; so much so that a piece about her has to be cut from one such by the social editor of the *Daily Excess*.

Leads the 'old brigade' in an 'orgy of litigation' against Simon Balcairn's last, posthumously published, story in that newspaper (q.v.).
VB 11, 12, 87, 109

BLADE, MILLICENT
Fair-haired girlfriend of Hector (q.v.); particularly notable for her nose which 'pierced the thin surface crust of the English heart to its warm and pulpy core'. She is given a poodle called Hector, by Hector, to ensure that she will not forget him while he is away in Africa establishing their farm.

When Millicent makes it clear that she

intends to flirt with a great many men, in particular Major Sir Alexander Dreadnought (q.v.), Hector (the dog) bites her nose so savagely that she has to have it remodelled by a plastic surgeon. Bereft of her beauty, she finishes a spinster.
WS 31–43

BLAKE, CORPORAL
Member of X Commando's establishment; wounded in manouvres on the Isle of Mugg (q.v.).
OG 52

BLAKE, TUBBY, LIEUTENANT
'Stoutish schoolmaster' in the Halberdiers with Guy Crouchback. Member of the Mess Committee at Kut al Imara.
MA 99

BLAKE-BLAKISTON, LT. COMMANDER
Captain of *HMS Plangent* in May 1941.
OG 168
(*See* SHIPS)

BLANCHE, ANTHONY
(b. circa 1903)
Friend of Sebastian Flyte (q.v.) and a flamboyant homosexual of indeterminate nationality. When Charles Ryder first meets him he takes him for 'part Gallic, part Yankee, perhaps part Jew'.

Educated: Eton, 1914–1916 (expelled after two years); Argentina, 1916–1918: Europe 1918–1920; Christ Church, Oxford 1921–1922 (sent down).

At the age of fifteen he was taken, dressed as a girl, to the casino of the Jockey Club in Buenos Aires.

He is tall and slim with 'large saucery eyes'. He claims to be an acquaintance of Proust, Gide, Cocteau, Diaghilev and Firbank (all q.v.).

While in Europe after the Great War, he started three feuds on Capri and practised black magic in Cefalu. He was cured of his Oedipus complex in Vienna and, in 1920, of drug addiction in California.

Dresses in a loud brown suit and yellow leather gloves at Oxford in 1922. He has a bad stammer and he seems to Charles Ryder 'the aesthete *par excellence*, a byword of iniquity'. He reminds Charles of a Neapolitan urchin, with a streak of cruelty.

In the Summer of 1922 he attends a luncheon party at Sebastian Flyte's rooms in Christ Church, where he first meets Charles and after which he addresses a party of rowers from the balcony with passages from *The Wasteland* (q.v.). Is very taken by Charles and threatens to come to his 'burrow and ch-chivvy you out like an old st-t-toat'.

He takes Charles to dinner at the Spread Eagle at Thames (q.v.). Beforehand he drinks four Brandy Alexanders at the George bar. Attempts to poison Charles' mind against the Flytes. Tells him that he is an artist, but that he himself is 'exquisite'.

Reads *Antic Hay* (*see* BOOKS). Attends houseparty at Garsington.

Paints his toe nails and drinks green Chartreuse.

Goes down from Oxford in 1922, having had an affair with a policeman in Munich, where he takes a flat and, it seems to Charles, taking with him all the abandon of that first year. Meets Sebastian at Constantinople.

Moves to Marseilles where, in 1925, he is joined by Sebastian Flyte who pawns his suits to get drunk. Takes Sebastian to his drug dealer; travels with Sebastian to Tangier and returns to England when Sebastian takes up with Kurt.

Charles' final meeting with him is at his own exhibition of South American paintings in 1936. He is completely unchanged and calls the pictures 'an imposture'.
BR 34, 43, 47, 50, 51, 59, 102, 104, 145, 148, 158, 195–197

BLAND, RALPH
Closest relative of Billy Cornphillip. Came to a bad end.

Viola Chasm is in love with him. Writes letters to Viola Chasm which are intercepted by Lady Anchorage's maid. He is married with two children. Spends his wife's money. Does not get on with Billy. Borrows money from Billy and loses it

in the City. Spends Christmas with the Cornphillips. Stands as a radical against Billy and is elected. Accused of corrupt practises (he gave £3 to a gardener discharged by Billy). Becomes slightly mad. Gets drunk often. Threatens Billy. Is taken to court to keep the peace. Takes Etty off to Venice. Leaves her for an American. He is Etty's son's father.
WS 26–30

BLAND, THE HONOURABLE WILLIAM

Honorary Attaché at the British Legation, Azania, where he lives with the Courteneys. Boyfriend of Prudence Courteney (q.v.). Smokes cigars. Enjoys the gramophone. Gambles. Is essentially lazy and has a mutual antipathy to Basil Seal.

Leaves Debra Dowa by bomber to return to England.
BM 44–46, 50, 58–59, 61, 126, 215

BLANK, PRUDENCE

'The Mary Selena Wilmark of Britain'. One of the guests of Silas Shock at the Savoy Grill on 11 December 1936.
Sc 80

BLENKINSOP, MAJOR

Doctor in the RAMC, who treats Guy Crouchback's knee in March 1943.
US 125

BLENKINSOP

London butler to Lady Metroland (q.v.).
• Tobacco grower from Latakia. Alias adopted by Basil Seal on his journey to Smyrna for the British Government in September 1939.
VB 98; PF 51

BLITZ

Guy Crouchback and Ian Kilbannock converse on the steps of Bellamy's (q.v.) during an air raid in the Blitz: 'The sky over London was glorious, ochre and madder'. Guy compares it to Turner and Ian to John Martin.

Virginia Crouchback, however, is less enthusiastic and moves out of Claridges and then out of London altogether.

Once, when staying in London during the Blitz, Gilbert Pinfold occupied an hotel bedroom just vacated by an Allied statesman.
OG 9, 14, 48; EP 48

BLOCK, SERGEANT

Sergeant in Charles Ryder's company of the Halberdiers.
BR 329

BLOGGS, NANNY

Richest member of the Boot household at Boot Magna Hall (q.v.). Bedridden for thirty years. Keeps her savings in a red flannel bag under her bolster. Promises William Boot (q.v.) a flight in an aeroplane if she should win the Irish Sweepstake. Decides, however, after having failed to win, that it is just a Popish trick.

William plays dominoes with her every evening from six to seven o'clock, after which he owes her thirty-three shillings.
Sc 18, 46, 205

BLOUNT, COLONEL

Father of Nina Blount (q.v.) and owner of Doubting Hall (q.v.). Absent-minded, he believes Adam Fenwick-Symes has come to mend the vacuum cleaner. Gives Adam a cheque for £1000 signed Charlie Chaplin.

Eats copious amounts of food (q.v.). In need of extra funds and passionately keen on motion pictures, he lets his house to the Megalopolitan Film Company as location for *A Brand From the Burning* (q.v.) in which he himself is given a walk-on part.
VB 69, 142–143, 150

BLOUNT, NINA

One of the Bright Young People. Pretty daughter of Colonel Blount (q.v.) and engaged to Adam Fenwick-Symes (q.v.). Always has 'a pain'.

Loses her virginity to Adam in a hotel at Arundel. According to Adam, naked she looks 'like a fashion drawing without the clothes'. Seems cold but admits to Adam that one could grow quite fond of love after a time – like smoking a pipe – but doubts whether it is worth it.

Attends party on the airship. Becomes engaged to Ginger Littlejohn (q.v.), according to whom she is 'a girl who likes nice clothes and things'.

Adam sells her to Ginger for £78 16s 2d and she marries Ginger. Has affair with Adam; becomes pregnant – but is the child Ginger's or Adam's?

VB 33, 118, 122, 183–184

BLOUSE, MISS

Cook to Margot Metroland at Pastmaster House (q.v.).

VB 93

BOAR'S HILL

House near Oxford (q.v.).

• Charles Ryder is advised by his cousin Jasper to keep clear of it.

• Sebastian Flyte thinks it a place where conventional undergraduates go to tea.

BR 28, 101

BOAZ, VISCOUNT

Azanian Minister of the Interior. Responsible for the death of Seth. Killed in turn by Joab.

BM 106, 223–226

BOB

Son of one of the two women with whom Adam Fenwick-Symes shares a carriage on the train to Aylesbury. Very keen to go into the motor business and has friends at the local hockey club.

VB 138

BOEOTIA

Aimee Thanatogenos pines for the Boeotian waterfront before committing suicide.

LO 116

BOERS

South African inhabitants of Dutch origin who fought two bloody wars against the British for control of the colony.

• If one looks at the medals worn by the commissionaires at Espinoza's restaurant (q.v.), one can see in one's minds eye: 'Boer farms sink to ashes'.

WS 63

BOGGETT

Mr Metcalfe's gardener at Much Malcock.

WS 43

BOGOLOV, MRS

Widow who is keen to have a wreath placed on her husband's grave at Whispering Glades (q.v.). She is informed that they just 'do not do' that sort of thing.

LO 36

BOHEMIANISM

It is not easy to appear Bohemian when wearing evening dress; however, Scott-King's neighbour at dinner in Neutralia is able to do so.

WS 219

(*See also* Ambrose SILK, Anthony BLANCHE, MR PLANT)

BOLIVIA

South American country between Brazil and Peru, where at one time Basil Seal (q.v.) worked for the secret police.

• Appleby (q.v.) knows of a cave in Bolivia where the Jesuits stored their treasure. He has an aerial photograph of the area and is particularly keen to take an expedition there.

PF 49; WS 182

BOLSHEVISM

Early name for Communism, based on the principal that the community as a whole should own all property.

• According to Colonel Hodge, the local parson at Much Malcock preaches Bolshevism 'Sunday after Sunday'.

WS 52

BOMBAUM, MISS MARTHA

Middle-aged reporter who had, before the war, always been at the centre of 'unpleasantness' from Danzig to Wal-Wal (q.v.). Does not look respectable to Scott-King. Wears a hat that is too feminine and has a 'lavish' hairstyle. Believes that the Bellorius convention is Neutralian propaganda and confuses Bellorius with Count Belisarius (q.v.). Smokes cigars.

Eventually proves her usefulness by arranging to get Scott-King out of Neutralia by the underground network.
WS 203, 217, 230, 240

BOMBAY
Town on the west coast of India, where in a huge teetotal hotel, Gilbert Pinfold spends one night on his return to England from his cruise.
• Some of the inhabitants of Debra Dowa (q.v.) possess 'shoddy trinkets' from Bombay.
GP 144; BM 27

BOMBS
In 1939, a small man carrying a suitcase filled with bombs wanders the corridors of the Ministry of Information and the War Office, trying to find out what to do with them.
PF 68, 144

BONE SETTING
Form of massage practised in London by Dr Cruttwell and much enjoyed by Brenda Last and her sister (q.v.).
HD 38

BONI DE CASTELLANE
Friend of 'Ruby' (q.v.).
US 80

BOOBY-TRAPS
Particular favourite amusement of Colonel Ritchie-Hook (q.v.), for whom war is a series of practical jokes: 'the wet sponge on the door . . . he saw war itself as a prodigious booby-trap'.

This is later borne out when he contrives to blow up Apthorpe (q.v.) on his Thunder Box (q.v.).
MA 72

BOOKMAKERS
Sebastian Flyte teases Charles Ryder that he spends his money 'like a bookie' on 'ducks and drakes'. (In fact, it is mostly spent on Sebastian.)
BR 61

BOOKS
• *ABC*: Universal British railway timetable. Tony Last has a copy in his bedroom at Hetton.
• *A La Recherche du Temps Perdu*, Marcel Proust (1913–1922). Read by Mr Samgrass at Brideshead.

A set of Proust is bought by Paul Pennyfeather while staying at the Ritz.
• *Alexandria*, E.M. Forster. Julia Stitch gives a copy to Guy Crouchback in 1941.
• *Algerian Grammar*. Read by Pappenhacker (q.v.).
• *Alice in Wonderland*, Lewis Carrol (1865). The croquet match in it is likened to Dawkins' selfless act of rescuing the general's valise from the burning aircraft.
• *Antic Hay*, Aldous Huxley (1923). To Anthony Blanche it is forbidding, but nevertheless he reads it, until he is thrown into the fountain.

Everard Spruce reads it aloud to Frankie (q.v.) in 1944.
• *Art*, Clive Bell (1914). Read and discussed by Charles Ryder in his first term at Oxford.
• *Barchester Towers*, Anthony Trollope (1857). Bishop Goodchild realizes that one 'cannot expect the calm of Barchester Towers in Azania'.
• *Bases of Design*, Walter Crane (1898). Charles Ryder reads it at Lancing in 1919.
• *Bessie Cotter*. Enjoyed by Lady Amelia.
• *Bevis, The Story of a Boy*, R. Jeffries (1882). Tony Last has a copy in his bedroom at Hetton.
• *Bible, The*. Guy Crouchback compares his position with the parable of the labourers in the market place waiting to be hired. He also recalls the tale of Uriah the Hittite. Guy is not well versed in the Old Testament.

According to Lady Marchmain, the gospel is 'simply a catalogue of unexpected things'.

St John's Gospel is made into a film by Sir James Macrae.

Nannie Bloggs reads only the Bible and *The Turf Guide*.

• *Bleak House*, Charles Dickens (1853). First novel read to Mr Todd by Tony Last.

• *Book of Sonnets about Venice and Florence*, Etty Cornphillip.

• *Byzantine Art*, Collins. Dedicated to Charles Ryder.

• *Can You Forgive Her?*, Anthony Trollope (1864). Read aloud to Virginia Crouchback by Peregrine.

• *Carmina, The*, Horace (23 BC), translation by Pyne. Left by Virginia Crouchback as a present for Ian Kilbannock in 1944.

• *Charterhouse of Parma, The*, Stendhal (1839). One of the books read by the commandos on Mugg.

• *Conjuring for All*. Tony Last has a copy in his bedroom at Hetton.

• *Cyropedia, The*, Xenophon (*c.* 400 BC). Mr Crouchback brushes up on his Xenophon.

• *Death in the Dukeries*, John Plant (1935). The professor of poetry at Oxford thinks it a work of art.

• *Death Wish, The*, Ludovic. Twice the length of *Ulysses* and has a heroine who is exquisite and doomed. Frankie thinks it a pure novelette. Sells nearly a million copies in the US and made into a film in 1951.

• *Decameron, The*, Boccaccio (1351). Building proposals in Much Malcock are compared to the mark of the plague in the court of the Decameron.

• *Diary of a Nobody*, George and Weedon Grossmith (1892). Read by Lady Marchmain aloud on the evening before the hunt at Brideshead in 1924.

• *Divine Comedy, The*, Dante Aligheri (1321). Provokes particular disgust when found in Adam Symes' luggage by customs officers at Dover.

• *Dombey and Son*, Charles Dickens (1848). Second novel read to Mr Todd by Tony Last.

• *Don't*. One of the books available to the commandos on Mugg.

• *Eminent Victorians*, Lytton Strachey (1918). Charles Ryder has a copy during his first term at Oxford.

• *Farewell to Arms, A*, Ernest Hemingway (1929). Tony Last has a copy in his bedroom at Hetton.

• *Forsyte Saga, The*, John Galsworthy (1922). Read by Paul Pennyfeather at Scone in 1922.

• *Fortitude*, Hugh Walpole (1913). In 1919 Charles Ryder thinks it 'strong meat and rather unnecessary in places'.

• *Free Man Greets the Dawn, A*, Sir Francis Hinsley (*c.* 1920). One of a number of 'charming books' by the author. A book of Belles Lettres – half autobiography, a quarter politics and a quarter mystical. It went 'straight to the heart of every Boots subscriber' in the early 1920s, and earned the author a knighthood.

• *Frightened Footman, The*, John Plant. Set in Frasham.

• *Georgian Poetry*, Ed. Edward Marsh; (5 volumes (1912–1922). Frank Bates has a set at Lancing in 1919.

• *Greek Anthology, The*, Cephalas (10th century AD). Symonds keeps a leather-bound copy in the chapel at Lancing.

• *Heart of the Matter, The*, Graham Greene (1948). Guy Crouchback reflects that at the time of 'Operation Truslove', Scobie would have been very near at hand.

• *Lady Almina's Secret*. Read by the religious maniac at Blackstone Gaol.

• *Lady into Fox*, David Garnett (1922). Read by Charles Ryder in Sebastian Flyte's rooms at Oxford.

• *Law of Landlord and Tenant, The*. Tony Last has a copy in his bedroom at Hetton.

• *Little Dorrit*, Charles Dickens (1857). Fifth novel read to Mr Todd by Tony Last, and read again after *Oliver Twist*, Mr Todd's particular favourite.

• *Lost Chord, The*, Adelaide Procter (1858). Borrowed from the library of the *SS Caliban* by a traveller in 1953.

• *Martin Chuzzlewit*, Charles Dickens (1844). Third novel read to Mr Todd by Tony Last.

• *Modern English Usage*, Henry Watson Fowler (1926). Frequently consulted by Ludovic (q.v.).

• *Mr Disraeli*. One of the books available to the commandos on Mugg.

• *Murder at Mountrichard Castle*, John Plant (1939).

• *No Orchids for Miss Blandish*, James Hadley Chase. One of the books available to the officers on Mugg. Guy Crouchback finds it unreadable and Ivor Claire enjoys it.

• *North and Hilliard's Latin Prose*. Used by Mr Crouchback to teach Latin.

• *Nicholas Nickleby*, Charles Dickens (1839). Fourth novel read to Mr Todd by Tony Last.

• *Oliver Twist*, Charles Dickens (1838). Sixth novel read to Mr Todd by Tony Last.

• *Oxford Book of English Verse*, Ed. Sir Arthur Quiller Couch (1900). Scoured by Dennis Barlow in search of poems for Aimee Thanatogenos (q.v.).

• *Panorama of Life, The*, Prudence Courteney (unpublished). A view of the world (mainly sex).

• *Pensées*, Ludovic (1944). Book of poems based on his time in Crete.

• *Plays Pleasant and Plays Unpleasant*, George Bernard Shaw (1898). Taken by a party of Indians from Balliol to a picnic by the river in 1923.

• *Prayers on Various Occasions of Illness, Uncertainty and Loss*, The Reverend Septimus Beard (1863). One of the books in Paul Pennyfeather's cell at Egdon Heath.

• *Pre-Raphaelitism*, John Ruskin (1851). Charles Ryder reads Julia Flyte Ruskin's description of Hunt's 'The Awakened Conscience'. There is a copy in the library at Brideshead.

• *Reminiscences*, Air Marshal Beech (1951). Read by Eldeberry at Bellamy's.

• *Roget's Thesaurus*. Consulted by Ludovic.

• *Sanctuary*, William Faulkner (1931). Enjoyed by Lady Amelia and known in the local library as 'strong meat'.

• *Self Help*, Samuel Smiles (1859). Copy given by the chaplain at Egdon Heath to Captain Grimes.

• *Shropshire Lad, A*, A.E. Housmann (1896); Medici edition. Charles Ryder has a copy in his first term at Oxford.

• *South Wind*, Norman Douglas (1917). One of Charles Ryder's books in his first term at Oxford.

• *Sinister Street*, Compton MacKenzie (1914). Charles Ryder has a copy in his first term at Oxford.

• *Sun Also Rises, The*, Ernest Hemingway (1926). Everard Spruce compares Brett Ashley to Virginia Crouchback.

• *Spiritual Combat, The*, St Francis de Sales. Tony Box-Bender asks for a copy to be sent to his P.O.W. camp.
Christ, the Ideal of the Monk, Abot Marmion; *Spiritual Letters*, Don John Chapman; *The Practice of the Presence of God*, Laurence – these are all asked for by Tony Box-Bender.

• *The Turf Guide*, Guide to the British racing season. Nannie Bloggs reads only this and the Bible.

• *Ulysses*, James Joyce (1922). Half the length of *The Death Wish*.

• *Under the Ermine*, Wenlock Jakes (1938). A survey of 'the undercurrents of English political and social life'. Jakes receives an advance of £20,000.

• *Vengeance at the Vatican*, John Plant (1927). The first of his crime novels.

• *Vice Versa*, F. Anstey (1882). Guy Crouchback reads it in the winter garden of the Grand Hotel, Southsand, in November 1940.

• *Vision and Design*, Roger Fry (1920). Charles Ryder has a copy during his first term at Oxford.

• *Warning Shadows*. Anthony Blanche compares the footman in this book to Kurt (q.v.).

• *Waste of Time*, John Boot (1937). Travel book on time spent with the Patagonian Indians, some of whose names are remembered by everyone in London society.

• *Westward Ho!*, Charles Kingsley (1855). Borrowed by Gilbert Pinfold from the library of the *SS Caliban* in 1953. He reads it aloud to confuse his voices.

• *Wind in the Willows, The*, Kenneth Grahame (1908). Guy Crouchback likens Apthorpe's conceitedly clever giggle to that of Mr Toad.

• *The Wisdom of Father Brown*, G.K. Chesterton (1900). Lady Marchmain reads aloud having discovered Sebastian's drunkenness at Brideshead.

• *Woodwork at Home*. Tony Last has a copy in his bedroom at Hetton.

• *Word to the Unwise, A*; *Prolegomenon to Destruction*; *Berlin or Cheltenham: The Choice for the General Staff*; *Policy or Generalship*; *Policy or Professionalism*; *The Gentle Art of Victory*; *The Lost Art of Victory*; *How to Win the War in Six Months: A Simple Lesson Book for Ambitious Soldiers* – all potential titles for Basil Seal's unpublished work on strategy.

• *Yellow Book, The*, H. Harland (1894–1897). Poppet Green and her friends look on Ambrose Silk as a survival from the age of.

• *Young Visiters, The*, Daisy Ashford (1919). Tony Last has a copy in his bedroom at Hetton.

BOOT, ANNE (LADY TRILBY)
Widowed great-aunt of William Boot (q.v.); resident at Boot Magna Hall (q.v.). Owner of a motor car adapted to suit her tastes, with a horn workable from the rear seat, which she uses noisily on her weekly trip to church.
Sc 18

BOOT, BERNARD
Uncle of William Boot (q.v.) and resident of Boot Magna Hall. Devotes his life to scholarship for which he has little recognition. Traces the Boot family back to Ethelred the Unready and the Barons de Butte. Has rheumatism for which he drinks cider.
Sc 18, 29

BOOT, JOHN COURTENEY *(b. 1903)*
Novelist and member of a cadet branch of the Boots of Boot Magna (q.v.). His novels sell 15,000 copies in their first year, and are popular in society. Also writes on history and travel. His works include a life of *Rimbaud* (1921), written when he was eighteen, and *Waste of Time* (1938), an account of his travels among the Patagonian Indians. (*See* BOOKS).

Friend of Julia Stitch (q.v.) who persuades Lord Copper (q.v.) to send him to Ishmaelia. However, he is confused with William Boot, the countryside columnist, who is sent in his place (q.v.).

By further mistakes, he is created KCB in William's place. Is sent off to the Antarctic by the *Daily Beast* (to escape his American girlfriend).
Sc 5, 12, 19, 72, 183, 213

BOOT, MRS
Widowed mother of William Boot (q.v.). Owner of the contents of Boot Magna Hall (q.v.), where she resides.
Sc 18

BOOT, OLD MRS
Widowed grandmother of William Boot (q.v.) and resident of Boot Magna Hall (q.v.). Owns the family money and keeps a scrapbook.
Sc 18

BOOT, PRISCILLA
Sister of William Boot (q.v.) and resident of Boot Magna Hall. claims to own the horses. While in a 'playful mood', substitutes the word 'grebe' for that of 'badger' (q.v.) in one of William's 'Lush Places' columns; thus engendering a stream of outraged correspondence. At dinner she is preoccupied with killing wasps in the honey on her plate. Hunts.

Wakes Mr Salter (q.v.) by ransacking her wardrobe for a lost tie.
Sc 18, 20, 195, 213

BOOT, RODERICK
Least eccentric uncle of William Boot (q.v.) and resident of Boot Magna Hall, where he is estate manager.
Sc 18

BOOT, THEODORE
Monocled, oldest and jolliest uncle of William Boot (q.v.) and resident of Boot Magna Hall. Has a 'purplish, patrician face . . . ruddy, Hanoverian'.

Makes occasional, ill-fated journeys to London. Attempts to steal Nanny Bloggs' savings. Is in the habit of singing one line of a hymn repeatedly, such as: 'Change and decay in all around I see' or 'In thy courts no more are needed, sun by day nor moon by night'.

Tries to get into William's car to London, saying that he has some business with a man in Jermyn Street. Is compared to 'a surfeited knight of the age of Heliohabilus'.

The author of numerous dirty stories about London of the 1890s, which he wants Lord Copper to publish. Is persuaded to take William's place at the Boot Banquet. Salter persuades Lord Copper that he is the Boot; Theodore is responsible for Salter's transfer to 'Home Knitting'.

Is installed at the *Daily Beast* on £2000 a year, with a future he can hardly believe.
Sc 18, 19, 23, 201, 212, 215, 216

BOOT, WILLIAM

Owner of Boot Magna Hall (q.v.) where he lives with eight relatives and numerous retainers. Journalist on the *Daily Beast* (q.v.) for which paper he writes the 'Lush Places' countryside column – a position passed on to him by the late rector of Boot Magna, on whose style he has modelled his own.

Is called to the offices of the *Daily Beast* to be, he thinks, berated for the episode of the grebe and the badger (q.v.) but, in fact, through a misunderstanding, he is to be sent as a war correspondent to Ishmaelia (q.v.).

Travels to Paris and Marseilles and thence to Ishmaelia; meets Mr Baldwin (q.v.) on the Blue Train and meets Corker (q.v.). Arrives in Ishmaelia and books into the Hotel Liberty and then the Pension Dressler where he meets Katchen, with whom he falls in love.

Is the only journalist left in Jacksonburg. Attends tea party at British consulate; refuses to sell Katchen's rocks to Dr Benito (q.v.). After the imprisonment of Katchen, decides to attack Dr Benito and sends news to the *Beast*.

Decides to marry Katchen, who then goes back to her husband, leaving him heartbroken.

Returns to England where on his arrival is responsible for the dismissal of Bateson, after the latter has lost him. Is hailed as a maker of journalistic history but refuses to attend the banquet in his honour and returns to Somerset to resume his column.
Sc 16, 19, 23, 24, 126, 185, 191, 207

BOOT MAGNA HALL

Country house, near the Vale of Taunton Deane, Somerset. Station – Boot Magna Halt (One hour from Taunton). Ancestral home of the Boot family (q.v.).

Encircled by enormous trees, drives, rides and a lake prone to becoming marshy. On the south terrace there is an ornamental dolphin waterspout (which no one can remember how to work).

A large house, it is home to the entire Boot family, also Nannie Price, Nannie Bloggs, Sister Watts, Sister Sampson, Miss Scope, Bentinck the butler, James the footman, Nurse Grainger and ten servants, who spend most of the day at one of their five obligatory meals.

It has stucco pillars on the entrance porch and ivy-covered windows on the first floor. In the lobby there are sporting implements, including a couple of bicycles, and a stuffed bear. Beyond this, glass doors lead into the hall, which has a double staircase, a black-and-white-chequered marble floor, and potted palms. By the glass door is an armchair in which no one ever sits.

Mrs Boot's bedroom is sunny. Priscilla Boot's bedroom, in which Mr Salter stays, has an oil lamp on the dressing table. It is homely and girlish with twenty or thirty china animals on the shelves, along with deer slots, foxes' brushes, otter pads and a horse's hoor. The door does not close properly. On the washstand is a flowered basin and ewer.

The gentlemen use the lavatory in the library. The house contains long corridors lit with oil lamps, and doors covered in faded baize. The carpet is threadbare and the stairboards creak.
Sc 17 etc.

BOOTS

A subject of particular interest to Apthorpe (q.v.), who is extremely proud of his 'porpoises', made from the skin of the white whale. Cow, he says, is a great mistake.

He later takes an army boot to pieces before a party of signalmen to show them its appalling construction; an event which antagonizes his relations with Dunn (q.v.).
• According to General Connolly, the Azanian soldiers will not wear boots. Basil Seal will not have this and orders a thousand pairs from England. The boots duly arrive and are a great success. Basil, feeling vindicated, questions General Connolly about then:

'No cases of lameness yet I hope?'

'No cases of lameness. One or two of bellyache though.'

The shoes, all one-thousand pairs, have been eaten.
MA 44–45; BM 137–138

BORDEAUX, FRANCE
Where Mr Baldwin (q.v.) has a small vineyard on the opposite slope to Château Mouton-Rothschild.
Sc 55

BORDIGHERA
Town in Italy.
• Charles Ryder's Aunt Philippa takes refuge here from his father.
• Here, on a tennis lawn, Peregrine Crouchback once strained his knee.
BR 70; US 125

BORETHIUS, DOCTOR
Doctor in Zurich who is apparently able to cure the most hardened of alcoholics – Even Charlie Kilcartney (q.v.).
• Rex Mottram takes Sebastian Flyte to see him, but loses him in Paris.
BR 159, 160

BOSANQUET, CAPTAIN
Adjutant of the Halberdiers in 1940. Instructs Guy Crouchback and Apthorpe to wear greatcoats (q.v.).
MA 47

BOSCH, JEROME (HIERONYMOUS) *(1450–1516)*
Born and died at Hertogenbosch, the Netherlands. Painter of fantastic allegorical visions. See his 'Ship of Fools' (Louvre) and 'Earthly Paradise' (Prado).
• Guy Crouchback compares soldiers in gas masks to figures from his paintings.
OG 16

BOSNIA
Area of Yugoslavia, East of Belgrade, between Croatia and Hercegovina, in whose uplands Charles Ryder's mother is killed by a German shell, while on nursing service at the front towards the end of the Great War.
WS 301

BOSTON, MASSACHUSETTS
Where Lieutenant Padfield had lived and worked before the war, as the junior member of a firm of eminent lawyers.
US 25

BOSWELL, MIKE
Friend of Millicent Blade, mistaken for a suitor by her poodle, Hector, who bites him hard on the hand, thus engendering a three-month love affair between the two young people.
WS 36

BOTANY BAY, AUSTRALIA
Renowned for its nineteenth-century convict settlement.
• In Cedric Lynes' mind, one of the features of the Regency age.
PF 171

BOTLEY
Small town to the west of Oxford; by the road to which Sebastian Flyte and Charles Ryder leave the city on their way to Brideshead in 1922.
BR 25

BOUCHER, FRANÇOIS *(1703–1770)*
Painter of the Rococo age specializing in erotic nudes of mythological title. There are many fine examples in the Wallace Collection.
• Angela Box-Bender laments their absence from Kemble (q.v.) after the evacuation of works of art from London in 1939, at which time the house becomes a repository for art treasures.
• The girl at Grantley Green (q.v.) looks

to Basil Seal like the sort of girl Boucher would have painted, 'half-clothed in a flutter of blue and pink draperies, a butterfly hovering over a breast of white and rose'.

• Thinking of 'Margaret', Gilbert Pinfold conjures up 'a nymph by Boucher'.
MA 27; PF 122; GP 116

BOUCHER'S
Boarding house at Lancing (q.v.).
WS 302

BOUGHTON
Home village of Charles Ryder (q.v.).
• The name of the house of Charles' cousin Jasper, which is approached through an avenue of Wellingtonias, and has a pitch-pine minstrels' gallery.
BR 264; WS 305

BOULLE, ANDRÉ CHARLES
(1642–1732)
Seventeenth-century Parisian cabinet-maker whose synonymous work (inlaid with precious metals and pearls) epitomizes the late Baroque of Louis XIV.
• In 1939 Angela Box-Bender is surprised not to receive any Boulle furniture from the Wallace Collection (q.v.), when her house becomes a repository for national art treasures.
MA 27

BOX, THE
Device for diagnosing maladies; looks like a wireless set. A hair or a drop of the invalid's blood is brought to the box and the operator then 'tunes in' to the life waves of the patient to find the cause of the illness.
• The box cures Lady Fawdle-Upton's nettle rash. However, when Fanny Graves tries it on her spaniel for worms, the life force is misdirected and they become as 'big as serpents'.
• Gilbert Pinfold says that it counts as sorcery and that his wife should confess it, but really he considers it to be harmless. Pinfold, however, later imagines that the box was first developed as a means of interrogation by the Nazis and that the Communists now have it.
GP 12, 13, 136

BOX-BENDER, THE RIGHT HONOURABLE, ARTHUR, MP
(b. 1883)
Brother-in-law of Guy Crouchback (q.v.) and twenty years his senior. Serves in the Rifle Regiment 1914–1918. Marries Angela Crouchback in 1914.
• One son – Tony – and three daughters. Bought Kemble (q.v.) in Gloucestershire when elected to Parliament. Is not from an 'old', nor a Catholic family. He is described as being 'Protestant and plebian'. For some years he expects Guy to go insane.
MA 17–19, 21, 25, 29; US 201, 238

BOX-BENDER, THE MISSES
The three daughters of Arthur and Angela Box-Bender who are evacuated to Connecticut during the war. They send Mr Crouchback an american parcel (q.v.).

In 1951 their father throws a party for one of them.
OG 25–26

BOX-BENDER, TONY
Son of Arthur and Angela Box-Bender. Serves in the Rifle Brigade in WWII, when he declares that he wants 'an MC and a nice neat wound'.

Thinks that his Uncle Peregrine (q.v.) is going mad and is unable to tell one sherry from another.

His regiment is at Calais during the fall of France. Captured 2 June 1940. In 1940 sends home requesting food and Trumper's Eucris, but by 1943 these have changed to pleas for religious works by St Francis de Sales and others. Arthur Box-Bender construes this as religious mania.

By 1951 he has entered a monastery.
MA 26, 29, 30, 201, 202; OG 247; US 240

BOXING
Philbrick's purported father 'Chick Philbrick' is a 'very useful little boxer' at Lambeth Stadium before the Great War.

• In the 1920s Rex Mottram takes Julia Flyte to prize fights at which he is able to get ringside seats; after the matches he introduces her to the boxers.
DF 52; BR 179

BOY SCOUTS
Organization formed in 1908 by Lord Baden-Powell, with the aim of training boys to be good citizens and self-sufficient.
• Colonel Hodge is involved in the running of the local Boy Scouts at Much Malcock.
• Apthorpe's aunt is interested in a group of high church Boy Scouts at Tunbridge Wells, to whom Apthorpe worries she might give his 'kit' if he should die.
• Paul Pennyfeather feels a 'flush about his knees' as Boy Scout Honour tells him to own up.
• A troop of Boy Scouts scores the laps at the motor-racing circuit visited by the Bright Young People.
• Charles Ryder sees a troop of Boy Scouts 'church bound' and looking unmilitary, one Sunday at Oxford.
• A naughty scoutmaster is exposed in the *News of the World* read by Sebastian Flyte after church at Brideshead.
WS 46; MA 238; DF 187; VB 165; BR 59, 84

BRACE, MRS
Editor of the social pages of the *Daily Excess* (q.v.) and immediate boss of Lord Balcairn (q.v.). Looks business-like and wears her hair in an Eton crop.
VB 87, 104

BRACE, SAM
Acquaintance of the station-master at Hetton, who has to go up to London in order to retrieve his wife.
HD 54

BRADSHAWE
Butler to Lady Seal (q.v.).
BM 85

BRADSHAWES, THE
Friends of Guy Crouchback, who, on a day before the Second World War take General Cutter to visit him at Santa Dulcina (q.v.).
MA 23

BRAKEMORE'S
Aeroplane factory near Malfrey where Barbara Seal's housemaids – Edith and Olive – are keen to go and work in 1940.
PF 11

BRAKENHURST, LORD
Owner of a large estate at Much Malcock, of which one pasture borders on Mr Metcalfe's paddock.
WS 45

BRANCUSI, CONSTANTIN
(1876–1957)
Romanian abstract sculptor, influenced by Rodin but who turned to abstractism in 1907 and had an influence on Modigliani. His major work is a ninety-foot-high column at Tirgu Jin in Rumania, and his studio in Paris is preserved.
• Ambrose Silk owns a sculpture by Brancusi: 'an object like an ostrich egg', in 1940.
• Anthony Blanche has two sculptures by Brancusi in his rooms at Oxford in 1921.
PF 194; BR 50

BRAY
Town in Berkshire where, according to the chauffeur of Adam Fenwick-Symes' hired car, there is a very nice hotel.
VB 79

BRAZIL
Where Tony Last goes with Dr Messinger to find the City, and where he ends his days with Mr Todd (all q.v.).
• South American country of which one of Mr Loveday's fellow inmates of the mental institution expects hourly to be announced Emperor.
HD 159; WS 12

BRAZZAVILLE
Town in the Congo, on the Congo river, where Ritchie-Hook and the brigade

major board an aeroplane which subsequently disappears.
OG 113

BREMEN, GERMANY
Where, in 1939, cruelty to animals provokes an oratory from the Church of England.
PF 113

BRENDA
Friend of Kerstie Kilbannock who she takes in as a paying guest in 1941.
OG 133

BRENT, LIEUTENANT
'Dull young regular' officer and Guy Crouchback's second in command of D Company in June 1940. Successfully attacks a German mortar position in the battle for Crete, May 1941.
• Last heard of in a trench in Crete with Sergeant-Major Rawkes (q.v.).
MA 207; OG 209

BRENT'S
Boarding house at Lancing.
WS 302

BRENTA CANAL
Canal in Venice (q.v.) where Cara has some American friends.
BR 95

BRETHERTON, MR
Sanitary inspector in the British Legation in Azania. Not on dining terms with the Lepperidges (q.v.).
BM 234–235

'BRETT' (LADY BRETT ASHLEY)
One of the major characters in Ernest Hemingway's *The Sun Also Rises* (1900), which deals with her wanderings around Europe with American reporter Jake Barnes.
• Recalled by Everard Spruce when comparing her to Virginia Crouchback as one of 'the last of twenty years' succession of heroines'.
US 200

BRIDE, THE
Stream on the Brideshead estate; a tributary of the River Avon.
BR 21

BRIDESHEAD CASTLE
Stately home in Wiltshire, near Chippenham (reached by the A420 from Oxford to Swindon). Ancestral home of the Earls of Marchmain (q.v.). Stands in a man-made landscape, enclosed by the winding valley of a stream, the Bride, a tributary of the Avon which rises two miles away at the farm of Bridesprings.

The Park: The River Avon is dammed here to form two lakes, one very small and shallow; both surrounded by beech trees. The woods are of oak and beech. Fallow deer graze in the park where there is a Doric temple by the lake and an ivy-covered arch over one of the weirs.

The park was planned circa 1790 and the house itself is surrounded by lime trees. There is a fountain of rocks and carved animals before the steps of the house.

The Drive: The house, which stands at the head of the valley, is approached through wrought-iron gates with twin neo-classical lodges set on a small green; then another set of gates. At the gates there is a small grey church. On the front side there are steps of water.

The House: Baroque in style, it was built circa 1670, from the stones of the old castle which stood a mile away, down by the village church at Brideshead in the field called Castle Hill. The New House was one hundred years old when Lord Marchmain's Aunt Julia was born (q.v.). It was designed by a follower of Inigo Jones, although the dome is of a later period. Known as the 'New House' before Lord Marchmain's day.

The dome is false, like those of Chambord. Its drum contains additional rows of nurseries, and Nanny Hawkins' rooms.

The hall (1671), is hung with tapestries and furnished with a marble table and pilasters, and small heraldic chairs. There is an open fireplace with caryatid supporters on either side. It is used as a conference room by the army in 1942.

The library is on one side of the house, overlooking the lakes and is Soanesque in design.

The Chinese drawing room has gilt pagodas, mandarins, painted paper and Chippendale chairs. In 1942 it is used by the army as the officers' mess. Lord Marchmain dies here in 1938 in the Queen's Bed, a huge velvet-hung four-poster ('like the baldachino at St Peter's'), of twisted gilt and velvet columns for posts, and plumes of feathers in gold-mounted ostrich eggs.

The Cardinal's dressing-room contains a silver basin and ewer.

The office is a small room off the colonnade. Designed as a study and decorated with painted panels in the Rococo style, and a groined ceiling, it is this room that is decorated by Charles Ryder in 1922 (q.v.). It is destroyed by the army in 1942.

Lady Marchmain's room has a creeper outside the window. It is decorated with *bondieuserie*, has a low ceiling, chintz, views of Florence, bowls of hyacinths and pot pourri and petit-point.

Charles Ryder's room is next to Sebastian's and has a shared bathroom which was once a dressing room. It is hung with watercolours and has a chintz armchair. The bath is deep and of copper with a mahogany surround and a brass lever.

In the night nursery there is a crucifix over the bed.

The painted parlour is octagonal and of a later style than the rest of the house. The walls are painted with wreathed medallions and on the dome, Pompeiian scenes. The furniture here is of satin-wood and ormolu. There is a hanging bronze candelabra.

The side entrance to the house is through the stone-vaulted passages of the servants' quarters, with stone flagstones. The back stairs are of scrubbed elm and uncarpeted and the passages here are of bare wood with a drugget carpet or linoleum. The walls are lined with red and gold fire buckets.

Through green-baize servants' doors, one walks into plaster-decorated corridors with gilded cornices. Doors are of mahogany and the windows have shutters.

One room has twin fireplaces in marble. On its coved ceiling are painted classical gods and heroes. It has gilded mirrors and scagiola pilasters.

The chapel (*circa* 1883), decorated by Lord Marchmain as a wedding present for his wife, is one of the two pavilions which flank the house and which, with the colonnade are later additions. It has two doors – one public, one private – to the house. It is decorated in the late arts-and-crafts style with angels, roses, fields of flowers and lambs, Celtic texts and armoured Saints. On the altarpiece is a triptych of softly carved pale oak. All of the metal is 'hand-beaten bronze'. There is a green carpet with white daisies on the altar steps.

The cellars have, in 1922, huge empty bays. Only one area is by then used for wine.

The Fountain: Designed in the seventeenth century; Neapolitan. It consists of an oval basin with rocks and carved vegitation in the centre, around which there are carved camels, leopards and a lion – all waterspouts. In the centre of the rocks is a massive obelisk of sandstone as high as the house's pediment.

The terrace: Built on massive stone ramparts overlooking the lakes the terrace is flanked on either side by the colonnade. Beyond each pavilion at the end, there are lime groves. The terrace is partly paved, and partly given over to flowerbeds and dwarf-box hedges. In the centre is the fountain.

The nearest village is Flyte St Mary with one pub; the nearest big towns are Melstead Carbury and Marchmain (ten miles away).

- Lord Marchmain leaves the Castle to his daughter Julia. In 1942 it is requisitioned by the army. To the commanding officer of 2 Company in 1942, Brideshead is 'a big private house with two or three lakes'.
- To Hooper (q.v.), it is a 'great barrack

of a place with a sort of RC church attached'.
BR 20, 21, 22, 36, 39, 40, 75–79, 80, 83, 120, 133, 146, 148–149, 274, 300–303, 316–318, 325–327, 330

BRIDESHEAD
Village near Chippenham, Wiltshire. In the old church are buried the earls of Marchmain, including Sir Roger Flyte.
BR

BRIDESHEAD, LORD *(b. 1900)*
Eldest son of Lord Marchmain (q.v.). Known as 'Bridey'. Everyone has their own opinion of him:
• According to Charles Ryder's barber at Oxford he is 'a very quiet gentleman, quite an old man';
• According to Anthony Blanche he 'has the face as though an Aztec sculptor had attempted a portrait of Sebastian; a learned bigot, a ceremonious barbarian, a snow-bound llama';
• According to Sebastian he is 'much the craziest of all of us . . . He's all twisted inside. He wanted to be a priest you know'.
• Educated at Stonyhurst, he attempted to become a Jesuit priest, but was persuaded to go to Oxford to think it over. Toys with the idea of going into the Guards or being an MP.

Rarely smiles, but when he does it is lovely. Finds it difficult to get drunk; dislikes drink.

In his own opinion he does not think that he would be a good priest. Rex Mottram calls him a 'half-baked monk'.

Reveals that Rex has been married before and thus destroys his and Julia's plans for a grand wedding (Bridey Bombshell).

Refuses to do public service in the General Strike because he is not convinced that the owners are right.
• According to Charles Ryder, 'He had a kind of mad chivalry about everything which made his decisions swift and easy'. Commissions Charles to paint pictures of Marchmain House (q.v.) before it is demolished (although he considers it 'rather ugly').

Wants to close Brideshead after the death of Lady Marchmain. Lives in two rooms up in the dome.

Julia thinks him 'like a character from Chekhov'. For Charles and Julia he is always mysterious, 'a hard-snouted, burrowing, hibernating animal'.

His hobby is a collection of match boxes which he keeps at his small house in Westminster.

Joint-master of the Marchmain Hunt – has few friends; visits his aunts; attends Catholic dinners; member of a dining club at which he is known as 'Brother Grandee' and to which he invites Charles.

Marries Beryl Muspratt (q.v.); is insensitive and a virgin. Serves (from 1940–1943) with the Wiltshire Yeomanry in Palestine.

BRIDESPRINGS
Farm on the Brideshead estate where the Bride Stream rises; to where Charles and Sebastian would sometimes walk to tea.
BR 21

'BRIDEY'S BOMBSHELL'
Julia Flyte's nickname for Lord Brideshead's revelation that she cannot be married to Rex Mottram because he has already been married and divorced to Miss Sarah Evangeline Cutler of Montréal in 1915.
BR 188

BRIGADE MAJOR, THE
Unnamed major of the Halberdiers who recommends that Guy Crouchback take Apthorpe the bottle of whisky which kills him. Afterwards he is somewhat embarrassed and apologetic to Guy, without admitting his own culpability.
MA 235, 243

BRIGGS
Pupil in Paul Pennyfeather's form at Llanabba (q.v.). Known as Brolly 'because of the shop, you know'. Wins the long jump at the sports day because of his spiked shoes.
DF 26, 47

BRIGHTON
Where Tony Last and Milly (both q.v.) go to contrive his 'infidelity'.
• Where Simon Lent is summoned to a conference with Sir James Macrae (*both* q.v.).
HD 134; WS 73

BRIGHTON COLLEGE
Where the son of Mr and Mrs Bundle (q.v.) is educated.
DP 32

BRIGHT YOUNG PEOPLE, THE
Generic term coined by the press for the smart society set in the late 1920s. Favourite pastimes are parties (q.v.), treasure hunts and practical jokes. In reality they included Babe Jungman, the Guinness sisters, Lady Eleanor Smith, Brian Howard, Patrick Balfour, David Tennant, Tom Driberg and Loelia Ponsonby.
• In Waugh's fiction they are characterized by Miles Malpractice, Agatha Runcible, Archie Schwert, Mary Mouse, Simon Balcairn, Lord Vanbrugh, Johnnie Hoop and Pamela Popham.
• Mr Outrage does not understand them. As far as he is concerned they have neglected the chance they had to remake a civilization by playing the fool. Father Rothschild is more philosophical about them, and thinks that it is all in some way historical. They all to him seem to have 'a fatal hunger for permanence'. Their motto is 'if a thing's not worth doing well, it's not worth doing at all'.
VB 14, 21, 29, 131, 132 etc.

BRINDISI
Coastal town on the Gulf of Taranto, Italy, where, in mid-February 1945, Guy Crouchback is set ashore, having come from Dubrovnik.
US 233

BRINK, COLONEL
Inhabitant of Little Bayton with whom Tony Last has some business.
HD 78

BRINK, MR
'Cheery' fellow-traveller of Tony Last on the journey to South America.
HD 162

BRINKMAN
Fellow pupil of Apthorpe at Staplehurst prep school. Goalie for the first XI.
MA 110

BRISBANE
Town in Queensland, Australia.
• The hopeful destination of M. *et* Mme Kanyi (q.v.), which they never reach.
US 177

BRISTOL CHANNEL
It is rumoured that Ginger (q.v.) buys a small island in the Bristol Channel to turn into a country club.
VB 120

BRISTOW, MRS
Kerstie Kilbannock's charwoman who 'knows everything'.
US 80

BRITAIN
According to Mr Baldwin (q.v.), while other nations use force, the British alone use 'might'.
Sc 172

BRITISH COUNCIL, THE
Organization responsible for cultural operations in the Commonwealth.
• Some of Scott-King's classical colleagues fall away from teaching classics to work for the British Council.
WS 195

BRITISH LEGION
Association of British ex-servicemen and -women.
• Colonel Hodge of The Manor, Much Malcock, is keenly involved in the affairs of the local branch of the British Legion.
WS 46

BRITTANY, FRANCE
Location of the German submarine pens which are the objective of 'Operation

Hoopla' (q.v.) in the Autumn of 1943.
US 27

BRITTLING

Maid to Mrs Algernon Stitch who reads the crossword clues aloud.
Sc 7

BRITISH ARMY

The men of Peter Pastmaster's regiment in 1939 are 'all either weather-beaten old commissionaires or fifteen stone valets'.
• Crosse and Blackwell's regiment is a sobriquet for the general-service list.
• For Charles Ryder the army is like a love affair which by 1943 has gone sour. All that is left are 'the chill bonds of law and duty and custom'.
• According to Charles' Sergeant-Major, 'If you get on the wrong side of senior officers they take it out of you in other ways'.
• Charles Ryder enters the army on a commission in the special reserve.
• According to the Cuthberts (q.v.) you cannot trust the army in business.
• Hooper is of a similar opinion.
• The classic pattern of army life is 'the vacuum, the spasm, the precipitation'.
• Guy Crouchback is in favour of a drug for soldiers so that they can sleep when they are not needed.
• In a really modern army, Ivor Claire supposes, the men would respect their officers if they had the cleverness to desert.
• Tony Box-Bender is not keen on being 'chased round' in barracks.
• Mr Crouchback tells Guy that the army is full of temptations.
• Mess traditions reign supreme: Junior officers may not drink in the ante-room before luncheon.
• The war office is too busy with the private soldiers and has no time for the officers (according to Leonard).
• Before WWII, soldiers were simply trained by standing to attention and stamping their feet.
• The typical army attitude is exempified for the porter at Southsand station in the abandonment of Guy and Leonard by the rest of their company.
• De Souza thinks all army courses are like prep school.
• Sergeants, according to Gilbert Pinfold, are 'absurd to many but to some rather formidable'.
• Fosker reminds him of the sort of subaltern who was so disliked by his regiment that they would post him to SOE.
• Officers should be fair to their men and not let them dwell on 'imaginary grudges'.
• One of an officer's main abilities must be to 'appreciate the situation'.
• John Verney is a company commander during the war and hates 'all the annoyances of army life': 'Defaulters, subalterns playing the wireless in the mess, the staff-sergeant mislaying a file, the driver of his car missing a turning.'
• John Plant finds 'plain regimental soldiering . . . an orderly and not disagreeable way of life' in WWII.
• Guy Crouchback notices how the army is able to put itself in order with remarkable ease, rather like a colony of ants.
• According to the army, an officer's job is quite simply to sign things, take the blame and walk in front of his men and get shot.
• If, in the army, you make one mistake, it will follow you throughout your career, opines Guy's CO.
• Regiments include:

The Bombadier Guards – Basil Seal offends the Colonel at an interview in 1939.

The Coldstream Guards – Tommy Blackhouse.

The Blues and Royals – Ivor Claire; Ludovic.

The Halberdiers – 'every bit as good as the Foot Guards'. Guy Crouchback Colonel Tickeridge, Colonel Green, Ritchie-Hook, Apthorpe and others. Raised by the Earl of Essex under Queen Elizabeth for service in the low-countries. Properly 'The Earl of Essex's Honourable Company of Free Halberdiers'. Nicknames are 'The

Copper Heels' and 'The Applejacks' (after a fight in an orchard at Malplaquet). Battle Honours include Malplaquet and the First Ashanti war.

The Commandos (q.v.) – Guy Crouchback, Tommy Blackhouse, Trimmer, Basil Seal, Alastair Trumpington, Peter Pastmaster.

The Lancers – Colonel Blount was in the Lancers.

(*See also* individual officers)

BROMPTON, SIR RALPH

Homosexual diplomatic adviser to HOOHQ (q.v.), he is a character out of light comedy: 'a tall grey civilian dandy'. Wears a monocle; smokes Turkish cigarettes; is an ex-ambassador.

Before the war he accosts Ludovic (q.v.) at a society wedding reception in St James's Square (1931). Ludovic becomes his 'valet' and 'secretary'.

Lives in Hanover Terrace and has a 'retreat' at Ebury Street which is known only to fifty men.

He is also a 'friend' of Lieutenant Padfield (q.v.). At one time he was first secretary at the same embassy as Peregrine Crouchback, who he tried, unsuccessfully, to make the 'chancery butt'.

Having previously shyed away from the secret service in peacetime, he enjoys his involvement with it in time of war.

US 29, 33, 35, 124, 141

BROOK PARK

Where the Brigade of Halberdiers goes 'under canvas' in September 1940, before moving to Liverpool.

MA 213

BROOKE, RUPERT *(d.1915)*

English poet who died of disease on his way to fight at Gallipoli (q.v.). A handsome romantic, he was a favourite poet among the young between the wars.

• In 1940, he is seen by Ian Kilbannock as emblematic of the outdated romanticism of the Great War.

• Barbara Sothill sees Basil Seal as Rupert Brooke.

• Dennis Barlow's poetry is successful in wartime Britain, partly because people are looking for a new Rupert Brooke.

PF 17, 29; OG 101; LO 22

BROOKWOOD

Town between Woking and Pirbright in Surrey, at which Guy Crouchback's company de-trains before marching to its quarters in Aldershot in April 1940.

• Close to where Alastair Trumpington (q.v.) is posted in 1940 – in a 'horrible villa on a golf course'.

PF 127; MA 193

(*See* NECROPOLIS)

BROOME HALL, SOMERSET

Family home of the Crouchbacks, situated between the Blackdown Hills and the Quantocks, in the vale of Taunton Deane.

Built in the late seventeenth century around an earlier medieval shell. Improved in the eighteenth century, and added to in the 1900s.

Reached from London (Paddington) by the train to Taunton which takes three hours, and then another train to the town of Broome.

Outside the gates is 'the Lesser House' whose stucco façade masks an earlier structure. This is owned by the Crouchbacks and their factor lives there in 1943. The street before it is a cul-de-sac and the back looks onto the park, in which there are yew trees.

Broome Hall has iron gates and the drive is a continuation of the village street which had been the main road to Exeter until the eighteenth century.

There is a forecourt between the house and the main road. The forecourt is guarded by a tower, where the Blessed Gervase was taken. Behind the tower are two medieval quadrangles built in the Caroline style. There is also a massive gothic wing added by Gervase and Hermione in the 1900s and designed by the same architect as the church.

The house has long, panelled galleries. The Great Hall, which is Caroline, was given a plaster ceiling in the eighteenth century, which was removed by Gervase and Hermione to reveal the timbers. When Guy was a child the walls above the wainscott were hung with weapons in radiating circles. These were sold with the furniture at the auction of the contents.

Let by Mr Crouchback to a Catholic girls' school. At the time of the school's occupation the walls are hung with German nineteenth-century religious paintings. Above the dais, where family portraits used to hang, is a cinema screen.
MA 9; OG 22; US 17, 25, 60, 61, 63, 68, 69, 240

BROOME VILLAGE
Most of Broome village is Catholic. The Catholic church is visible from the station yard. It is Puginesque, dates from the 1860s and was erected by Guy Crouchback's great-grandfather. There is also a medieval Anglican church whose burial grounds are still Catholic and belong to the Crouchbacks.

In the Catholic church the sable and argent cross of the family hangs in Ivo's funeral diamond.

The town pavements are cobbled.

Mr Crouchback's funeral takes place in the Catholic church. It smells of beeswax and chrysanthemums and incense.

Opposite the church the lesser house has a stucco façade and a porch. The street in front is a cul-de-sac and at the back is a park. It is here that Guy Crouchback eventually takes up residence after the war.
(Refs as above)

BROTHELS
Captain Grime's friend Bill is in charge of a brothel – 'a place of entertainment' – in the Argentine, owned by Margot Metroland (q.v.).

• On his visit to Marseilles, Paul Pennyfeather finds himself surrounded by brothels: 'a bare leg in a lighted doorway'. He eventually finds one called 'Chez Alice', where Margot has been sending her girls.

• When abroad, Gilbert Pinfold, in his younger days, was wont to patronize brothels 'with the curiosity of a traveller who sought to taste all flavours of the exotic'.
DF 140, 152, 153; GP 115
(*See also* JOHN PLANT)

BROWN, BESSY *(b. 1906)*
Under the alias Pompilia de la Conradine, tries unsuccessfully to get a position with Margot Metroland. Has worked at Mrs Rosenbaum's for two years.
DF 145

BROWN, SIR JAMES
Conservative Prime Minister in 1930; comes from Gloucestershire.

Is surprised in his study by Agatha Runcible (q.v.) dressed as a Hottentot.

Is discredited in a newspaper article by Vanburgh (q.v.) detailing his daughter's midnight party at 10 Downing Street, and forced to resign.
VB 48, 76

BROWN, MISS JANE
Youngest daughter of Sir James Brown (q.v.). Friend of Mary Mouse and Agatha Runcible (q.v.). Invites the Bright Young People (q.v.) back to 10 Downing Street after Johnnie Hoop's savage party and ingratiates herself with them by making omelettes and giving them her father's whisky.

Is ultimately responsible for bringing down the government.
VB 52, 56, 57

BROWN, CAPTAIN
Successor to Captain Mayfield in command of Cedric Lynes' company in WWII. Worries about his men's position. Pores over the map. Gets a rocket from the CO.
PF 130

BROWNIES, THE
Junior Girl-Guide association founded by Lady Baden-Powell.

• Dame Midred Porch (q.v.) remembers the Brownies crying during a hail-storm at an August rally in England.
BM 185

BROWNING, ROBERT *(1812–1889)*
English poet and husband of Elizabeth Barrett Browning. Travelled to Russia and Italy; eloped in 1846. His works include *The Ring and the Book* and *Childe Roland to the Dark Tower Came.*
• Guy Crouchback has the latter in his mind when standing before the old castle, Mugg.
• Charles Ryder feels himself a man 'of Browning's renaissance' after he has first begun to paint Marchmain House (q.v.).
BR 213; OG 55

BRUCE, INSPECTOR
Police inspector from Scotland Yard who arrests Paul Pennyfeather at the Ritz.
DF 157

BRUNNER, MRS HACKING
Resident of Venice who Cara asks to come to lunch with Sebastian and Charles on account of her beautiful daughter.
BR 97

BUCHAREST, RUMANIA
Where one of the Jewish refugees who besieges Guy Crouchback with questions, has a sister.
US 180; Sc 180

BUCKINGHAMSHIRE
Location of Doubting Hall (q.v.).
VB 141

BUDAPEST, HUNGARY
One of the places where Dr Antonic studied as a young man.
• Birthplace of Katchen.
• Jean de Brissac la Motte tells Charles Ryder that he should have been there 'when Horthy marched in' (q.v.).
• Jepson of the *Daily Beast* writes a long story about a pogrom in Budapest.
WS 218; Sc 134; BR 195; Sc

BUDE, CORNWALL
Home of the correspondent of the *Daily Excess* who enjoys the Titled Eccentrics feature.
VB 111

BUDWEIS, CZECHOSLOVAKIA
Where Madam Antonic's father had a factory.
WS 240

BUENOS AIRES
Capital of Argentina where Margo Metroland (q.v.) has a brothel managed by 'Bill' and later by Grimes.

Where Fanny Throbbing's daughter works until 1930, and where the 'Angel' Chastity is sent (q.v.).
• In 1918, at the Jockey Club in Buenos Aires, Anthony Blanche, aged fifteen, is disguised as a girl and taken to play roulette.
VB 27; BR 47

BUFFS, PRIVATE OF THE
Is recollected by Gilbert Pinfold when he realizes that Captain Steerforth alone represents British justice.
• Scott-King also stands 'like the immortal private of the Buffs' in Elgin's place, when accused by Miss Bombaum of being drunk.
GP 88; WS 223

BULGAR PEOPLES
In 1939 they are dealt with by Mr Pauling of the Ministry of Information, who is told by the Archimandrite Antonios (q.v.) that they have ejected him from Sofia for 'fornications'.
• According to Guy Crouchback, the Yugoslavians 'hate their guts'.
• Bulgarian terrorists are among the refugees with whom Scott-King uses the Underground system to escape from Neutralia (q.v.).
PF 67; US 225; WS 244

BULLDOG DRUMMOND
Fictitious character invented by 'Sapper' (H.C. McNeile, 1888–1937). He is a charming ex-army officer turned amateur sleuth and features in books published between 1920 and 1937.
• In 1939 Basil Seal is seen by the younger generation as 'a kind of dilapidated Bulldog Drummond'.
PF 34

BULL-FIGHTS
In August 1934 Marjorie and Allan join Lord Monomark on his yacht coming down the coast of Spain attending bull-fights.
HD 200

BUNDLE, MR AND MRS
Acquaintances of Mr Prendergast's mother in Woking. He is a retired insurance salesman. The Prendergasts have supper with the Bundles after Sunday evensong.

They have a son, a spotty boy at Brighton College, and Mr Bundles' mother, Mrs Crump, also lives with them.
DF 32

BUNYAN, LADY
Mother of one of the boys at Llanabba; taken ill at a previous sports day.
DF 61

BURGES, WILLIAM *(1827–1881)*
English architect and designer; the embodiment of the High-Victorian preoccupation with medieval romanticism.
• Gilbert Pinfold is given a remarkable washstand by James Lance (q.v.). It is 'by an English architect of the 1860s, a man not universally honoured but of magisterial status to Mr Pinfold and his friends'.

The architect is indisputably Burges. Waugh was given an identical washstand by Sir John Betjeman which became known as the 'Betjeman Benefaction', with panels painted by 'a rather preposterous artist who later became President of the Royal Academy'.
GP 24

BURGOS
Town in Old Castile, Spain, where Cordelia Flyte is based during the Spanish Civil War (q.v.). A journalist here tells her that Sebastian is dying in a monastery near Carthage.
BR 289

BURIAL
Gilbert Pinfold once assisted in a burial at sea on a troop ship.
GP 65
(*See also* WHISPERING GLADES)

BURMA
Place of origin of the gilt idol in the Halberdiers' mess.
• Offered as a posting to Ian Kilbannock in 1943. (He refuses.)
OG 18; US 186

BURMESE
The young Burmese on board the *SS Caliban* remind Gilbert Pinfold of officers by the way they pace about in pairs in their blazers and fawn trousers.
GP 53

BURNS, HALBERDIER
Aged soldier-servant of Colonel Jumbo Trotter (q.v.).
OG 32

BURNS, ROBERT
Scottish poet and author of, among other poems, 'John Anderson, My Jo' (q.v.) and 'My Love is like a Red Red Rose', which is inscribed on the lovers' seat in Whispering Glades Memorial Park (q.v.).
• Fortunately, Dennis Barlow is not tempted to steal any of Burns' poetry.
• Aimee Thanatogenos thinks Burns' poetry coarse.
LO 98

BURTON, LADY ISABEL *(1831–1896)*
Designer of the extraordinary mausoleum in the Roman Catholic cemetery near the church of St Mary Magdalen, Mortlake. It takes the form of a tent made of stone and contains the tomb of her husband, Sir R.F. Burton (1829–1890), the explorer and writer of books on Africa.
• Virginia and Peregrine Crouchback are buried in the Catholic cemetery 'in sight of Burton's stucco tent'.
US 199

BUSH, MAJOR
Officer of Cedric Lyne's battalion in WWII.
PF 133

BUSINESS
John Plant lies to a prostitute in Fez, telling her that his business is the exporting of dates.
• According to Lieutenant Hooper (q.v.) you could never get away in business with the waste of man hours he experiences in the army.
BR 15; WS 122

BUTTE
Ancient family name of the Boots of Boot Magna Hall (q.v.).
Sc 18

BUTTER
Tony Last is embarrassed by a drop of melted butter on Jenny Abdul Akbar's chin.
• Basil Seal rejoices in noticing a dribble of melted butter on a woman's chin, making her look ridiculous while she does not realize it.
HD 85; PF 31

BYRON, GEORGE GORDON, LORD *(1788–1824)*
English poet who, in 1809, embarked on a grand tour of Spain, Malta, Albania, Greece and the Aegean. Lover of Lady Caroline Lamb. In 1810 went to Europe again. Spent two years in Venice where Countess Teresa Guiccioli became his mistress. Went to Greece in 1823 and died at Missolonghi.
• Lord Marchmain has a 'Byronic aura' about him.
• Charles Ryder imagines the Corombona Ball (q.v.) as being such a Venetian night as those which Byron might have known, and spends another 'Byronic night fishing for scampi in the shallows of Chioggia'.
BR 94, 98

BYZANTINE ART
The Byzantine Empire flourished from the fifth to the eleventh century, taking over that of Rome after its fall in 476. Mosaics were used frequently in church decoration and excellent examples exist in Rome, Ravenna, Venice, Sicily and Greece. The main features are the lily, the cross and the head of Christ Pantocrator.
• In 1927, Paul Pennyfeather discusses Byzantine mosaics with Arthur Potts at Queen's restaurant in Sloane Square.
• Collins (q.v.) writes an unfinished work on Byzantine Art which he dedicates to Charles Ryder 'with the aid of whose all-seeing eyes I first saw the Mausoleum of Galla Placidia and San Vitale'.
DF 121; BR 45–46

C

CACHET FAIVRE

Lady Seal always has her *Cachet Faivre* and clear China tea brought to her at 7:30, on the evening of one of her dinner parties.
PF 17–19

CAESAR, (CAIUS) JULIUS

(100–44 BC)
Roman emperor.
• Introduced by Simon Lent into his screenplay of *Macbeth* for Sir James Macrae.
• Observed by Theodore Boot not to have enjoyed the devotion he deserved.
WS 75; Sc 218

CAFE ROYAL, THE, PICCADILLY, SW1

London restaurant frequented in the 1890s by the aesthetic set under Oscar Wilde and Aubrey Beardsley; later by Augustus John and his associates.
• Because of these associations Ambrose Silk feels at home here.
• Basil Seal comes here in the Spring of 1940 to keep a watch on Poppet Green.
• Frank de Souza tries to persuade Guy Crouchback to join him and Pat there on 30 December 1939.
PF 173, 174; MA 80
(*See also* RESTAURANTS *and* LONDON)

CAINE, (SIR THOMAS HENRY) HALL *(1853–1931)*

English novelist and friend of Rossetti. See his *Public Recollection of D.B. Rossetti* (1882), many novels, and *Sonnets of Three Centuries* (1882).
• To Everard Spruce he is one of the 'masters of trash'
US 203

CAIRO

Mr Youkounian desperately cables Cairo for fresh supplies of prophylactics for the Azanians.
• Where Ben Hacket once saw a woman who looked like a fish.
• While in Cairo for a few hours in 1932, Corker (q.v.) buys cigarette boxes, an amber necklace and a model of Tutankhamen's sacrophagus.
• According to Major Cattermole, 'those people' in Cairo send arms to Mihijlovic to be used against the British.
• Gilbert Pinfold's voices talk about a scandal in Cairo involving him during WWII when his Brigade Major shot himself. They also say that they have a letter written by Pinfold from the Mecca House Hotel in Cairo in 1929.
• Location of HQ of Allied Command in Egypt.
• In February 1941, bankers dine at the Mohamed Ali Club. Where Major Hound is based in 1941.
HD 44; BM 147; Sc 71; US 163; GP 104, 130; OG 119

CALAIS

One of the possible destinations of the Halberdiers in May 1940.
MA 197

CALDICOTE, LADY

Neighbour of the Boots of Boot Magna Hall, Somerset. Priscilla Boot stays with her when Mr Salter comes to stay.
Sc 196

CALDICOTE, MISS

Daughter of Lady Caldicote. She is the young lady to whom, it is believed at Boot Magna, William Boot is romantically attached; it is not so.
Sc 126

CALEDONIAN BALL
Scottish Ball held in London once a year.
• To Guy Crouchback, the group of Bonnie Prince Charlie and his followers in a film on the 1745 rising look like a party dressed for the Caledonian Ball.
MA 160

CALIFORNIA
Mrs Beaver takes John Beaver there in July 1934 to stay with Mrs Arnold Fischbaum.
• Where Anthony Blanche is cured of drug-taking.
• The grass in Southern California is not suitable for cricket.
• Dennis Barker lives in Los Angeles (q.v.).
• Simon Lent has an admirer in Fresno, California, from whom he receives a box of preserved figs as a present.
• In 1947, Basil Seal and Angela Lyne visit California.
• Home, according to Gilbert Pinfold, of gurus with whom he feels an affinity when parachuting from an aeroplane in WWII.
HD 182; BR 47; LO 29; WS 64, 266; GP 142

CALLIGRAPHY
In 1919 Charles Ryder, as a schoolboy, is keen on calligraphy and has evolved his own method. He illuminates a poem by Ralph Hodgson in this way, but makes a mess of the letter 'I'.
WS 308

CALVINISM
Most nannies are Calvinists. One of the interests of Mr Sweat and Soapy (q.v.) at Mountjoy.
GP 38, 180

CAMBRIDGE
Where, in 'New Britain', some girls are 'put down', having been the unsuccessful results of an experimental operation.
• Source of a group of undergraduates who come down to London in May 1926 to run messages for Transport House during the General Strike.
GP 199; BR 194

CAMPBELL OF MUGG, COLONEL HECTOR
The Laird of Mugg; known as Mugg; he is a little deaf, and mistakes Guy Crouchback for Angus Anstruther Kerr (q.v.).

His chief concern is the demolition of the hotel. Obsessed with explosives. Served under Kitchener (whom he disliked) at Spion Kop.

Gives dinner to Guy Crouchback and Tommy Blackhouse in 1940.
OG 59–60

CAMPBELL, MRS
Wife of Sir Hector Campbell of Mugg (q.v.).
OG 61

CAMPBELL, KATIE *(b. circa 1913)*
Mentally unstable; great-niece of Colonel Campbell (q.v.). From Edinburgh, she stays with Mugg from 1937.

Encountered by Guy Crouchback at dinner in Mugg. Has a freckled face, short black curly hair with a tartan ribbon, regular features and mad eyes.

Her mother was a Meiklejohn and grandmother a Dundas. She is passionately fascist and tells Guy she is a 'Political Prisner' [sic].
OG 61, 63, 65, 66

CANEA
Town in North-west Crete which forms the base for X Commando's raiding parties in 1941.
OG 172

CANNES, FRANCE
Where Margot Metroland has a villa in 1928. Her caretaker wins at the Casino and gives her notice.
• Where Angela Lyne holidays every Summer until 1939.
• Where Anthony Blanche has an affair with Stephanie, Duchess of Vancouver, in 1920.
DF 135; PF 24; BR 60

CANNIBALISM
In 1939 Basil Seal claims to have once eaten a girl in Africa. He is, in fact, quite

truthfully referring to the rumours of his eating Prudence Courteney in a stew in the interior of Azania in 1932.

• In the 1870s every European missionary, ambassador, tradesman, prospector, or scientist venturing into Ishmaelia, was eaten – either raw or in a stew. The Christian cannibals will not eat uncooked human flesh without Diocesan permission.

• When a weakened alcoholic in North Africa, Sebastian Flyte has a desire to become a lay brother and go into the African bush to preach to the cannibals.

Sc 74; BR 290

CANADA

In 1927, Lord Edward Throbbing, according to the gossip columns, is living in a log shack in Canada. He is, in fact, staying at Government House in Ottawa.

• A Canadian woman has the walls of her London Apartment covered with chromium plating by Mrs Beaver.

• Rex Mottram (q.v.) is Canadian; he has Canadian courtesey. According to him, the Canadians 'don't take much mind' of Catholics.

• Mr Pelecci is drowned in a ship bound for Canada, to where he is being deported.

• Jasper Cumberland (q.v.) emigrated to Canada after the Peninsular War.

HD 56; BR 108, 109, 170; OG 40; WS 95; VB 51

CANVEY ISLAND

Island in Essex, at the mouth of the River Thames.

• House of a doctor who Mrs Bristow thinks might be able to 'help' Virginia Crouchback; Kerstie Kilbannock does not think it a promising suggestion.

US 90

CAP FERRAT, FRANCE

Where Lady Rosscommon (q.v.) has a villa. Julia Flyte stays there in the summer of 1922. Rex Mottram and Brenda Champion stay at the same time in the next villa, rented by a newspaper owner. Politicians are frequent visitors. It is here that Rex begins to court Julia.

• Angela Lyne also has a villa at Cap Ferrat.

BR 176, 177; WS 256

CAPE, BRIGADIER

Officer commanding the HQ of the British Mission to the Anti-Fascist forces of National Liberation (Adriatic) in 1943. He is wounded at Salerno and he goes to a conference at Caserta.

US 153

CAPE TOWN

Stopping-off place for Hookforce on their way to Crete in February 1941.

In 1941 it is a 'ville lumière'. Ivor Claire thinks the inhabitants very civil. Eddie and Bertie went to the zoo, and Guy Crouchback to the art gallery, to see the Patons. To Guy Crouchback it is an Ali Baba's lamp – with something for everyone.

OG 107, 108, 110

CAPRI, ITALY

Island off the Salerno peninsula, Italy, where Anthony Blanche claims to have started three feuds.

• Julia Flyte follows Charles Ryder there in 1936.

BR 47, 265

'CAPTAIN'S SALUTATION', THE MATTER OF THE

De Souza's name for Apthorpe's obsession with being saluted – and his subsequent raging.

MA 179

CARA

Italian wife of a Mr Hicks and mistress of Lord Marchmain. She is middle-aged, well dressed and pretty. Charles Ryder is surprised that she is not more disreputable looking.

She appoints herself as guide to Charles and Sebastian in Venice; she embarrasses Charles with intimate questions.

Prophesies Sebastian's drunkenness and comes to Brideshead with Lord Marchmain in 1938.

BR 97–100, 302

CARDENAS, GENERAL
Neutralian general shot by the anarchists.
WS 207

CARDIFF
Jane Grimes is sent to Margot Metroland's 'agency' by a 'gentleman' at Cardiff.
• One of the stops on the Sword of Stalingrad's tour of Britain.
DF; US 22

CARDS
Sir Humphrey Maltravers (Metroland) is keen to play 'a hand of cards' while staying at King's Thursday.
• Miles Malpractice thinks cards are 'divine', especially the Kings: 'Such naughty old faces!'
DF 132

CARICATURISTS
Humphrey Maltravers bears 'a preternatural resemblance to his caricatures in the evening papers'.
• According to society, Julia Stitch is desperate for Lord Copper's caricaturists to 'lay off Algy', her husband.
• Mr Outrage is 'a source of low income to caricaturists'.
• There is a caricature of Mr Plant by Spy.
• Lottie Crump has Spy drawings in her hall.
DF 129; Sc 12; WS; VB 38
(*See also* OLD BILL)

CARMICHAEL, MR A.A.
Master at Lancing in 1919; known as 'A.A.'; a dandy and wit. Renowned in the Oxford Union and writes reviews of clerical works for the *New Statesman*. Charles Ryder has never spoken to him, yet worships him from afar.
WS 304

CARPACCIO, VITTORE
(1460–1526)
Venetian painter. Pupil of Gentile Bellini (q.v.) and assistant of Giovanni. Best known work is *The Legend of St Ursula* (Venice).
• Lady Seal has a small work by Carpaccio, her most valuable possession, which she sends in 1939 to Malfry for safe-keeping.
PF 17

CARPENTIER
French boxing star of the 1920s.
• In 1923 Rex Mottram is on easy terms with him.
BR 107.

CARS
• Margot Metroland (Beste-Chetwynde) has two Hispano Suizas.
• Lady Circumference has 'a little motor car' (a 1912 Daimler).
• The Minister of Transportation has a Daimler.
• Mr Reppington has a two-seater.
• A Riley is mentioned by one of the 'Speed Kings' at the Imperial hotel.
• Adam Symes hires a Daimler to take Nina to Arundel.
• Mrs Mouse has a Rolls Royce.
• The general reader has an Austin Seven.
• Motor cars we are told 'offer a very happy illumination of the metaphysical distinction between "being" and "becoming". Some are purely for travel and have "being". *Real* cars (racing cars) are in a perpetual state of flux. Their owners are part of them'.
• Captain Marino drives an Italian red Omega and completes the race circuit in twelve minutes, one second at 78.3 mph.
• The General's car is a Daimler.
• The C.O. of Alastair Trumpington's unit in 1939 has a Humber Snipe.
• Algernon Stitch has a 'sombre and rather antiquated Daimler'.
• Julia Stitch always has the latest model of mass-produced baby car; brand new twice a year, . . . always black 'tiny and glossy as a midget's funeral hearse', which she drives on the pavement.
• The commercial salesman who visits Doubting Hall drives a Morris.
• Hardcastle has a two-seater Morris-Cowley with a removable soft top, driven open by Sebastian Flyte to Brideshead and then to London for the Ball and then

almost crashed by him in Shaftesbury Avenue. Hardcastle is subsequently not allowed to use it for a term.
• The Flytes have a Rolls Royce.
• Rex Mottram has a Hispano Suiza.
• Charles' Uncle at Boughton has a Humber.
• Gervase Kent-Cumberland is given a model motor car in pillar-box red, intended for his brother, Tom. He later has an old two-seater.
• Roger Simmonds writes a play – Internal Combustion – in which all the characters are parts of a motor car.
• Arthur Atwater has a two-seater with which he kills Mr Plant. He *says* that he has a Rolls Royce.
• Agatha Runcible crashes a Plunket-Bowse.
• The New Zealand Brigadier on Crete has 'a small shabby sports car'.
DF; VB; PF; Sc; BR; WS; OF

CARTHAGE, TUNISIA
Ancient town in North Africa near Tunis.
• Sebastian Flyte is taken in by the father of a monastery near Carthage.
BR 289

CARTIER
Renowned French jeweller.
• Professor Silenus has a Cartier watch – a platinum disc.
• Julia Flyte expects Rex Mottram to buy her a ring from Cartier's rather than Hatton Garden.
DF 127; BR 183

CARTOONS
(*See* OLD BILL and CARICATURISTS)

CARVER, MRS
Caretaker to Ambrose Silk. A 'motherly old Cockney', she continually teases him for not being married.
PF 196

CASABLANCA, MOROCCO
To where Charles Ryder flies to see Sebastian Flyte in 1926.
• Kurt wants to live in a nice flat in Casablanca with Sebastian.
BR 210, 205

CASATI, MARCHESA
Friend of Ruby (q.v.).
US 80

CASERTA, ITALY
Town in Campania, twenty miles north of Naples.
• In January 1944, Brigadier Cape and Joe Cattermole attend a conference here.
• Location of Allied HQ in 1944; Tito is a guest here in August of the same year.
• Dennis Barlow is based here during the war.
US 155, 203; LO 22

CASTELLO CROUCHBACK, SANTA DULCINA, ITALY
Castle in Italy and home of Guy Crouchback (q.v.). Originally home of a Genoese lawyer. Gervase Crouchback buys it in 1889 and builds a new house in the ramparts.

Originally called Villa Hermione but locals always refer to it as Castello Crouchback. For fifty years it was 'a place of joy and love' (1889–1939).

Sold in 1951 to Ludovic (q.v.) who lives there with Padfield (q.v.).
MA 11; US 239

CASTLE HILL, BRIDESHEAD, WILTSHIRE
Site of the old Brideshead Castle.
BR 316

CASTLES
A castle built *c.* 1890 on the coast of Ayrshire is the family seat of the Kilbannocks (q.v.) and the home of the dowager Lady Kilbannock.
• The Castle, Mugg is the billet of Chatty Corner in 1940.
• The New Castle, Mugg is the home of Colonel Campbell.
OG

CAT O'NINE TAILS
A whip with nine knotted lashes.
• The threat that the law allows punishment with the cat for prostitution and white-slaving, galvanizes Paul Pennyfeather into a defence at his trial.

• One of the punishments on offer at Blackstone Gaol (q.v.).
DF 159

CATS

As a boy Ginger Littlejohn is very cruel to cats.
• The cat at the Old Hundredth is called Blackberry.
VB 214; HD 73

CATHCART, MAJOR JACK

Officer billeted with Barbara Sothill at Malfrey in 1940.
PF 136, 141

CATHERINE THE GREAT *(1729–1796)*

'Enlightened despot' – Empress of Russia from 1762 to 1796.
• Guy Crouchback compares himself to the Russian sentry posted every day on the spot where Catherine the Great had once wanted to preserve a wild flower.
OG 40

CATHOLICS

Philbrick tells Prendergast that he is a Catholic.
• According to Jasper Ryder, all Anglo-Catholics are 'sodomites with unpleasant accents'.
• The most prominent Catholic families in Waugh's fiction are the Flytes and the Crouchbacks (q.v.).
• Sebastian Flyte attends Mass at Oxford and at Brideshead. His faith is initially an enigma to Charles Ryder. Sebastian himself admits that being a Catholic is 'very difficult'. He is in love with the 'loveliness' of his faith. Brideshead and Cordelia are fervent in their Catholicism. According to Sebastian, Catholics are not just a clique 'as a matter of fact, they're at least four cliques all blackguarding each other half the time'. They look at life differently from other people, although they try to hide this fact.
• Lady Marchmain is keen to turn Charles Ryder into a Catholic and talks to him often on the subject. He eventually becomes a convert.
• Sebastian never mixes with other Catholics at Oxford.
• In Canada, according to Rex Mottram, no great notice is taken of Catholics. He notices, however, that in Europe there are some very posh Catholics.
• In the 1930s there are a dozen rich and noble Catholic families none of which have an heir suitable for Julia Flyte.
• A Catholic husband might demand yearly pregnancies.
• Rex Mottram is of the opinion that, if capable of nothing else, at least the Catholic church can 'put on a good show'. He is misinformed by Cordelia, during his conversion, that Catholics have to sleep with their feet pointing East, so they can walk to heaven (among other things).
• When Lord Marchmain was converted to Catholism he told his wife that she had brought his family back to the faith of their ancestors.
• Beryl Muspratt is a member of the Catholic Players' Guild.
• Julia Flyte is cynical of Catholicism; 'You can get anything there for a penny, in black and white'.
• Most of the village of Broome is Catholic, of the type found in parts of Lancashire and the Hebrides.
• Peregrine and Mr Crouchback are both devout Catholics. Virginia Crouchback eventually converts to Catholicism, having heard that the Catholic Church is 'the church of sinners'.
• Gilbert Pinfold is a Catholic convert, although his wife is one by birth.
• At one time Mr Plant used to hold Catholics in esteem: 'their religious opinions are preposterous . . . but so were those of the ancient Greeks . . . grant them their first absurdity and you will find Roman Catholics a reasonable people – and they have civilized habits'.
DF; BR; MA; OG; US; GP; WS

CATTERMOLE, MAJOR JOE *(b. 1903)*

Third in command at Bari in 1943; a 'sort of professor' in civilian life. Educated at Balliol, Oxford, 1921–24; not in Sligger Urquhart's set; spoke at the Union.

The only man able to stand Gilpin (q.v.). He is 'emaciated, totally unsoldierly, a Zurbaran ascetic with a joyous smile'.

Serves 1943 Yugoslavia, Sixth Offensive. Wounded. Speaks of the enemy with impersonal hostility. Speaks of his comrades with a mystical love.
US 155, 162, 165

CAVAFY, CONSTANTINE P. *(1863–1933)*
Pen name of C.P. Kavafis. A Greek tragic poet, he lived in Alexandria. Many of his poems are concerned with erotic homosexuality. Others with the Hellenistic world.
• At Julia Stitch's lunch party in Alexandria, an English cabinet minister expounds on Cavafy to Guy Crouchback – who is told by an Egyptian lady that he is not much in favour in the 1940s.
OG 130

CAVANAGH, BINKIE
'Poor Binkie' is a member of Bellamy's. Quite mad, he was known to hide under the billiard table.
OG 12

CAVOUR, COUNT CAMILLO BENSO DI *(1810–61)*
Architect of Italian nationalism. In 1847 he set up the *Risorgimento* newspaper. Gained power in 1848 and helped Garibaldi in Southern Italy.
• To Guy Crouchback Cavour was a hooligan 'from out of town, causing a disturbance'.
US 15

CEFALU, AFRICA
Where Anthony Blanche (q.v.) admits to having practised black magic.
BR 47

CELIBACY
According to Joe Cattermole, 'patriotic passion has entirely extruded sex' among the Yugoslavian partisans.
US 165

CERVANTES, MIGUEL DE SAAVEDRA *(1547–1616)*
Spanish novelist and author of *Don Quixote* (1615).
• Poppet Green and Ambrose Silk both know the analogy of Cervantes in the galleys at Lepanto – one of many writers and artists to have served their country.
PF 40

CETNICS
Serbian quislings fighting on the side of the Germans in Yugoslavia in 1944.
US 163

CEYLON
Ginger Littlejohn serves five years in the army in Ceylon.
• Destination of the *SS Caliban* and Gilbert Pinfold. His first visit took place in 1953. According to him there is little to do here – it is full of elephants and orange-robed monks.

Pinfold visits the Buddha's tooth at Kandy, and goes to mass in Colombo.
VB 118; GP 27, 144–46, 148

CÉZANNE, PAUL *(1839–1906)*
French Impressionist painter and father of many of the ideas behind Cubism. Formalized impressionist techniques into basic forms. See his 'Bathers' and 'Mont St Victoire'.
• Ambrose Silk and Poppet Green are well aware that Cezanne deserted from the French Army in 1870.
• According to Collins (q.v.), 'if you allow Cezanne to represent a third dimension on his two-dimensional canvas, then you must allow Landseer his gleam of loyalty in the spaniel's eye'.
• Cezanne is abhorred by Mr Plant (q.v.), who calls him 'a poor booby – a kind of village idiot who had been given a box of paints to keep him quiet. He very properly left his canvases behind him in the hedges'.
• According to Mr Plant, the Jews 'hired a lot of mercenary lunatics to write him up'.
PF 40; BR 30; WS 112, 113

CHALLONER, RICHARD *(1691–1781)*
Catholic convert, writer, missionary and Bishop of Debra (1741).
• According to Mr Crouchback, he misread a transcript from the St Omers' records attributing the betrayal of the blessed Gervase Crouchback to his steward.
OG 21

CHAMBERLAIN, (ARTHUR) NEVILLE *(1869–1940)*
British statesman: Chancellor of the Exchequer 1924–34; Minister for Health 1924–9; Prime Minister 1937. Tried 'appeasement' with Germany and Italy but was forced into war in 1939. Gave up premiership in June 1940, shortly before his death.
• On September 1939 Barbara and Freddy Sothill (q.v.) listen to Chamberlain's declaration of war on the wireless. Lady Seal also hears this and thinks that he speaks rather well. She had never liked him or his brother (Sir Austen); they were 'uncomfortable, drab fellows'. She intends, however, to invite him to lunch.
• According to one of Rex Mottram's friends, Chamberlain is the only thing stopping Hitler from scuppering himself in 1938. Delirious crowds greet his return from Munich on 29 September 1938.
• For Mr Crouchback he is lumped together with Lloyd George and the rest of mankind, on the opposite side to the Crouchbacks and Allied Anglo-Catholic families.
PR 9, 18; BR 280, 284; MA 34

CHAMBERS
Cook to Mrs Beaver (q.v.).
HD 9

CHAMPION, BRENDA
English society figure ('the innermost of a number of concentric ivory spheres . . .'), with whom Rex Mottram has an affair.
She has cold eyes, wears sun-glasses and lives in Charles Street.
Rex and Brenda stay at the same villa on Cap Ferrat and at the same house party at Sunningdale. While courting Julia Flyte, Rex has a brief affair with Brenda.
Charles Ryder meets her at the party before his arrest in 1923.
BR 109, 170, 177, 178, 179, 181, 245

CHANDLER, MRS
Cook at Brideshead Castle.
BR 37

CHANEL
Firm of couturiers established in Paris in 1912 by Gabrielle (Coco) Chanel (1883–1971). Her 1920s secret was freedom from the corsets of the *belle epoque* in a combination of simplicity and elegance. She also introduced a vogue for costume jewellery.
• Chanel diamonds are, according to Simon Balcairn, just one example of the jewellery thrown to Mrs Ape by her adoring London society audience.
VB 106

CHAPLAIN GENERAL, THE
Is the victim of an assassination attempt in 1940, in which the bomb blows off his eyebrows. The culprits are presumed to be the Russians.
PF 150

CHAPLIN, CHARLIE SIR CHARLES SPENCER *(1889–1977)*
London-born English comedian and star of silent-film comedies.
• Colonel Blount (q.v.), signs his cheque to Adam Symes: 'Charlie Chaplin'.
VB 82

CHARLES I *(1600–49)*
King of England; revered by many with that reverence which Ambrose Silk reserves for George IV.
PF 40

CHARLIE
Unfortunate soldier in the rear-guard on Crete; killed by mortar-fire.
OG 195

CHARLUS, BARON PALAMEDE (MEME) DE
Character in Proust's *À La Recherche du*

Temps Perdu (1922). A secret homosexual, he professes to be a ladykiller.

• While staying at Brideshead, Mr Samgrass spends 'a cosy afternoon before the fire with the incomparable Charlus'.
BR 120

CHASM, LORD ARCHIE
Member of the Carlton Club. Interviewed there regarding the conduct of his daughter, Agatha Runcible, in 1927.

Stays away from Julia Flyte's wedding in 1923. Described as 'stuffy' by Cordelia Flyte.

Stays with his wife at Claridges in 1934. Knows the Macdougals (q.v.).
VB 35; BR 192; WS 101

CHASM, LADY VIOLA (VIOLA RUNCIBLE)
Wife of Lord Chasm and mother of Agatha Runcible.

Friend of Kitty Blackwater, Fanny Throbbing, Mrs Beaver, Mrs Stitch, Julia Flyte, Rex Mottram, Lady Amelia and Ralph Bland.

Runs a 'Distressed Area'; falls in love with Ralph Bland. Does not feed her guests well at a weekend house party and is described by Lady Amelia as being 'chic and plump'.
VB 26; HD 9; Sc 7; BK 107; WS 129

CHASTITY BELTS
In the Middle Ages chastity belts performed the same function as 'Hector' in 1933.
WS 33

CHATTERBOX, CANON *(b. 1860)*
University friend of Colonel Blount (q.v.) at New College. Has a living at Worcester, having been chaplain in Bermuda. Confused by the Colonel with Mr Chatterbox of the *Daily Excess*.
VB 150

CHATTERBOX, MR
Society gossip columnist of the *Daily Excess*, first embodied by Simon Balcairn (q.v.) and after his death by Adam Fenwick-Symes (q.v.). His pay is £10 a week plus expenses.
VB 108

CHEKHOV, ANTON *(1860–1904)*
Russian playwright and author of *The Seagull* (1896), *Uncle Vanya* (1900) and *The Cherry Orchard* (1904).

• Julia Flyte thinks her brother, Lord Brideshead, like a character from Chekhov – a recluse, met unexpectedly upon the stairs.
BR 246

CHELTENHAM SPA
Among whose society the same principle prevails as that with which Colonel MacAdder runs Egdon Heath – 'If you make a prison bad enough people'll take jolly good care to keep out of it'.
DF 167

CHEMICAL WARFARE
Tony Box-Bender thinks chemical warfare 'the end' and managed to escape a chemical warfare course in 1940.
MA 30
(*See also* Arsenical Smoke)

CHERBOURG, FRANCE
Town in Normandy, close to where Trimmer and Ian Kilbannock find themselves in operation Popgun, when they blow up a train.
OG 147

CHERTSEY, BISHOP OF
The Bishop's younger sister's engagement is one of Adam Fenwick-Syme's 'stories' as Mr Chatterbox of the *Daily Excess*.
VB 111

CHESTER
At which racecourse Ben Hackett (q.v.) once won 'five Jimmy-o-goblins' on a horse called Zero.
HD 19

CHESTER-MARTIN, MR AND MRS
Couple in front of whom Lord Moping attempts to hang himself.
WS 11

CHESTERTON, G.K. ***(1874–1936)***
Catholic convert, English novelist and author of the *Father Brown* stories. Read aloud by Lady Marchmain in times of trouble.
BR 128, 212

CHIANG, KAI-SHEK ***(1887–1975)***
Chinese statesman and soldier. In command of the Army of Chinese Unification in 1926. Opposed the Communists. President of the Republic 1928–31; CIC against the Japanese 1935–45.
• According to Sir Ralph Brompton, Chiang is a collaborator.
US 29

CHINDITS
Unit of elite jungle troops, originally the Seventy-Seventh Brigade, founded by Orde Wingate in Burma in February 1943.
• Joined by Ivor Claire in 1943.
US 127

CHINESE, THE
According to Philbrick they are 'nasty inhuman things'. One of his friends is murdered by one.
• According to Ambrose Silk, the military hero is a laughable figure in China.
• Basil Seal knows a Chinaman in Valparaiso.
• Nanny Price (q.v.) gives her wages to Chinese missions.
• The Chinese, so Dennis Barlow has heard, can distinguish one of their race from another.
• It is said that Chinese gentlemen and philosophers are able to converse on complex topics while their minds wander through beautiful subconscious dreams.
• According to Gilbert Pinfold, you can always get a Chinaman, outside Europe, to make you a suit in an afternoon.
• The Chinese delegate to the Bellorius Conference is killed by partisans.
DF 78; PF 170, 176, 177; Sc 19; LO 45; WS 169, 232; GP 28

CHIOGGIA, ITALY
Coastal town near Venice where Charles Ryder and Sebastian Flyte spend a 'Byronic' night fishing for scampi in the shallows.
BR 98

CHIPPENDALE, THOMAS ***(1718–1779)***
English neo-classical-style cabinet-maker; worked predominately in mahogany.
• The Chinese drawing room at Brideshead is described by Charles Ryder as 'a splendid, uninhabitable museum of Chippendale . . .'.
BR 301

CHIPPENHAM, WILTSHIRE
Mr Bentley's maternal grandfather was three times mayor of Chippenham.
PF 65

CHOBHAM COMMON, SURREY
Area of land between Chobham and Sunninghill. One of the training areas for the army in 1940.
PF 127

CHOIRS
To Gilbert Pinfold it seems as though 'Margaret' is attended by a choir of bridesmaids, chanting an epithalamium.
GR 115

'CHOKEY' (SEBASTIAN CHOLMONDELEY)
Black boyfriend of Margot Metroland in 1922. Impeccably dressed; once shot a man at a party: 'He gets gay at times'.

Very keen on church architecture and English culture. He is a jazz musician, but says he will give all the jazz in the world for one stone from an English cathedral.
DF 75, 77, 79, 80–82

CHRISTIES
(*See* AUCTIONS and LONDON)

CHRISTMAS

Adam Symes and Nina Blount hang up stockings on Christmas Eve at Doubting Hall and view the decorations in the servants' hall.

• Peregrine Crouchback's Christmases are consistently dismal. He spends them with cousins named Scrope-Weld in Staffordshire.

• In the 1920s it was customary to have a 'poor' relation in most English homes at Christmas.

• Christmas is the worst time for Gilbert Pinfold – when he needs his drink and drugs most.

• In the New Britain Christmas is called Santa-Claus-Tide and children sing songs of goodwill. The nativity becomes an obscure old folk play shown on television.

• Christmas at Hetton means a big Christmas tree in the hall, a little one in the nursery, the choir singing carols in the gallery, Mr Tendrill's improbable sermon, and charades.

• Ralph Bland stays with the Cornphillips for a Christmas party.

• Bella Fleace gives a Christmas Party. There are several parties near Ballingar at Christmas.

• Sebastian Flyte spends Christmas 1925 drinking himself insensible in the Near East.

VB 213; HD 60; US 143; GP 25, 209, 210; WS 27, 79, 81; BR 154

CHUMS

Periodical for boys; popular in the Edwardian era.

• Read by Alastair Trumpington.

PF 217

CHURCH, THE

Mr Prendergast, being a failed priest, is very interested in church matters.

• In Hollywood, liturgy is the concern of the stage rather than the church.

• Paul Pennyfeather is reading for the church at Scone.

DF 11, 72; LO 51

CHURCH AND GARGOYLE

Scholastic agents who find Paul Pennyfeather a position at Llanabba school. The proprietor is Mr Levy. Their fee is five per cent of a year's salary.

DF 16–19

CHURCHES

Llanabba Parish Church: where Grimes marries Flossie Fagan in 1922.

• St Magnus, Little Bechley: where Arthur Potts (q.v.) makes brass rubbings.

• St Barnabas, St Columba, St Aloyious, St Mary's, Pusey House and Blackfriars: the churches of Oxford.

• Parish church of the Halberdiers' HQ: high-tower and earlier apse.

• St Augustin's, Southand: where Guy Crouchback meets Ambrose Goodall.

• St Margaret's, Westminster: where Ludovic forms part of the guard of honour for a society wedding in 1931. Sonia and Alastair Trumpington are married there.

• Broome Catholic Church: Puginesque in style, built in early 1860s.

• Broome Anglican Church: medieval.

• Westminster Cathedral: where Virginia Crouchback makes her first confession, then prays at a side altar.

• University Church, Whispering Glades: small, stone, square tower and gloss walls.

• Wee Kirk o' Auld Lang Syne, Whispering Glades: low building with a tartan carpet.

• Four Square Gospel Temple: frequented by Aimee Thanatogenos's father.

• St Michael and the Angels, Colombo: visited by Gilbert Pinfold.

• Ballingar Church: Protestant, 1820s Gothic in style.

• Ballingar Cathedral: unfinished Catholic structure.

• The Norman Church, Tomb: admired by Bessie MacDougal.

• Lancing Chapel: bare and unfinished, but huge. Admired by Charles Ryder.

• St Botolph's: near Lancing.

• Farm Street, Mayfair: (*see* LONDON).

• Brompton Oratory: Guy and Virginia Crouchback are married here.

• The Savoy Chapel: Rex Mottram and Julia Flyte are married here.
• The Church, Santa Dulcima: contains the tomb of Roger de Waybrooke.
• St Sepulchre's Egg Street: (*See* LONDON).
• St Peter in Chains, Rome: where Moses lays down the law, in Guy Crouchback's mind.
WS 77, 102, 278, 303, 312; MA 126, 129; DF 43; BR 58; MA 62, 108; US 32, 60, 171; LO 39, 63, 97, 116; GP 148

CHURCHILL, SIR WINSTON SPENCER *(1874–1965)*

British statesman and Prime Minister from 1940–45 and 1951–55. Lord Haw-Haw blames Churchill for the attempt on the life of the Chaplain-General (q.v.).
• According to Guy Crouchback, Churchill developed late in life.
• On the day that Churchill becomes Prime Minister (10 May 1940), Apthorpe is made a Captain.
• To Guy Crouchback, Churchill is 'a master of sham–Augustan prose, a Zionist, an advocate of the Popular Front in Europe, an associate of the press-lords and of Lloyd-George'.

He describes him to the younger officers as being like Hore-Belisha 'except that for some reason his hats are thought to be funny'. Guy finds Churchill's wireless broadcasts pompous.
• Is said to read Everard Spruce's newspaper.
• Mme Kanyi believes that Churchill is a friend of the Jews.
• According to de Souza, Tito could run rings round Churchill as a politician.
PF 151; MA 112, 175; US 49, 177, 204

CIGARETTES

Fat Turkish cigarettes are smoked at parties at Oxford by the Bright Young People and by Charles Ryder and Sebastian Flyte at their picnic on the way to Brideshead.
• *Players* are smoked by Trimmer (q.v.).
• Ludovic (q.v.) smokes Greek cigarettes in Crete.
• Cigarettes made from the sweepings of canteen floors are smoked by Londoners in 1943.
• Turkish cigarettes are smoked by Sir Ralph Brompton in 1943.
• Macedonian cigarettes are smoked by the Yugoslavian partisans.
• Cigarettes prepared by doctors are smoked by Mr Slump (q.v.).
VB 123; BR 26; OG 134, 223; US 23, 142, 182; LO 93

CIGARS

Lord Rending's cigars are destroyed by the Bollinger club (he smokes them in the college garden after breakfast).
• Paul Pennyfeather's guardian smokes cigars.
• Grimes gives cheap cigars to Clutterbuck (q.v.) which he smokes in the boiler room.
• Reggie St Cloud smokes a cigar after luncheon.
• Térèse de Vitre's father smokes cheroots.
• Basil Seal smokes Burma cheroots.
• Corker smokes large cheroots.
• Adam Fenwick-Symes gives Colonel Blount a box of cigars for Christmas in 1927.
• Charles Ryder smokes Partagas.
• Rex Mottram smokes Havanas (and gives one to the police sergeant at Bow Street).
• Lieutenant Padfield is given a box of cigars by the American minister in Algiers.
• According to Major Marchpole, 'A woman's only a woman, but a good cigar is a smoke'.
• Simon Lent smokes cigars.
• Julia buys a box of expensive cigars for Andrew Plant, which he plans to smoke in less than six weeks.
• Miss Bombaum smokes cigars.
DF 11, 16, 36; VB 213; HD 150, 167; BM 141; Sc 65; BR 43, 115; US 158; WS 64, 164, 217

CIGS

Commander in chief of the General Staff in 1941.
OG 43

CINCINNATI, COUNT
Popular young attaché at the Italian Embassy; invented by Adam Fenwick-Symes who says that he is descended from the Roman Consul Cincinnati and is the best amateur cellist in London.

Dances at the Café de la Paix; is taken up in Lord Vanbrugh's column and goes to Monte Carlo.
VB 113

CINCINNATI, OHIO, USA
Where Jack Spire proposes to re-erect the original King's Thursday.
DF 118.

CINEMA
John and Elizabeth Verney go to the cinema and see a murder story in which a bride murders her husband by pushing him off a cliff.
• Andrew Plant visits the cinema in Fez.
• Guy Crouchback sees a film about the 1745 rebellion.
• Nina Blount and Adam Fenwick-Symes go to the cinema and quarrel throughout the film.
• Colonel Blount's local cinema at Doubting Hall is the Electra Palace.
• Angela Lyne is found drunk outside a cinema in Curzon Street by Peter Pastmaster and Molly Meadowes who are on their way inside.
GP 169; WS 120; MA 160; VB 90; PF 154

CIRCUMFERENCE, LORD
Father of Lord Tangent (q.v.). Has long fair moustache and watery eyes. Talks to Paul Pennyfeather about sport. Cannot stand Americans, and calls Paul 'Mr Pennyfoot'.
DF 68

CIRCUMFERENCE, GRETA, COUNTESS OF
Aunt of Alastair Trumpington and mother of Lord Tangent (q.v.). Presents the prizes at Llanabba Sports Day in 1922. Admires Flossie Fagan's frock.

She is stout and elderly, wears tweeds and a Tyrolean hat; has a deep voice and hearty manner. Considers the only way to control her son is to beat him. Does not appreciate the Llanabba Silver Band.

Wishes that she were back in the early 1890s and disapproves of Paul's wedding to Margot Beste-Chetwynde (Metroland).
DF 47, 67, 69, 149

CIRCUSES
Ben Hacket once saw a woman who looked like a fish, in a circus in Cairo.
• During Eights Week in 1923 it seems to Sebastian Flyte, that Hertford College has become a circus.
• Philbrick claims to be the proprietor of a circus.
HD 44; BR 24; DF 60

CITADELS OF THE PLAIN
In Paul Pennyfeather's eyes, Grimes is like the Pompeiian sentry who stood while the citadels of the plain fell about him.
DF 199

CITY, THE
Fabled city of South America which Dr Messinger and Tony Last set out to discover. The legend began in the sixteenth century and its location varies between the Matto Grosso, upper Orinoco and Uraricuera.

In fact it is between the head waters of the Courantyne and the Takutu. It came about from an exodus from Peru in the early fifteenth century. Known as 'Shining', 'Glittering', 'Many Watered' and 'Bright Feathered'. Its name in *Pie Wie* also means 'Aromatic Jam'.
HD 159

CIVIL SERVANTS
The tradition of the Civil Service, according to Mr Bentley, is to lounge about talking.
• Mr Plant's father was in the Bengal Civil Service.
PF 62; WS 111

CLAIRE, IVOR
Captain in the Blues and Royals. Young show-jumper and member of X Commando (q.v.). Member of Bellamy's. Owner of a white pekinese called Freda

whose eyebrows he plucks. Before the war Guy Crouchback sees him jump on a horse called Thimble at the Concorso Ippico in Rome. Guy sees him as 'salty, withdrawn, incorrigible'; the finest of all the men in the Commandos, 'quint-essential England'. At Dunkirk (q.v.).

In Egypt he leads a party armed with mallets against Arab marauders, during which he twists his knee and goes into a nursing home in Alexandria.

Joins Chindits in Burma; stays there for six months; wins DSO; survives the war, and spends his days in Bellamy's.

OG 48–53, 68, 81, 114, 122; US 127, 237

CLARA

Beautiful, bearded love of Miles Plastic. Lives in a Nissen hut hung with eighteenth-century paintings and containing a looking glass with porcelain flowers and a gilt clock.

Ballet dancer who becomes pregnant, disappears, has an abortion and her beard removed.

GP 202, 203–4, 209, 213

CLARENCE, WILLIAM, DUKE OF *(later William IV) (1765–1837)*

His daughter Henrietta married Gervase Wilbraham of Acton, whose daughter married Mr Bentley's maternal grand-father.

PF 65

CLARENCE, DUKE OF

Attends, with his wife, the private view of Charles Ryder's exhibition in 1936. Expresses the opinion that South America must be 'pretty hot'. Celia Ryder suggests that Charles dedicate *Ryder's Latin America* to the Duchess of Clarence.

BR 254

CLARK, MRS

Stewardess to Celia Ryder on her Atlantic crossing with Charles in 1936.

BR 239

CLAUSEWITZ, KARL VON *(1780–1831)*

Prussian general and military theorist.

• The Germans attacked by Ritchie-Hook are perplexed at not being able to find a precedent for a single-handed assault on a fortified position in the works of Clausewitz.

US 222

CLEOPATRA *(69–30 BC)*

Queen of Egypt.

• Malfrey, lying defenceless and splen-did, is compared to her by Barbara Seal.

PF 9.

CLIFF PLACE, WORTHING, SUSSEX

Private sanitorium in Worthing run by Augustus Fagan MD (q.v.).

• On the seafront a few miles outside the town, a large house with a long drive and broken windows.

DF 202

CLIVE, SIR ROBERT *(1725–74)*

British soldier and politician. Instrumental in British supremacy in India. Won a famous victory over the French at Plassey (1757).

• In 1936 Rex Mottram's friends are jingoistic about the land of Clive and Nelson.

BR 262

CLOVIS *(465–511 AD)*

Merovingian King of the Salian Franks. In 493 married Clotilda, a Christian, and, having invoked God to defeat the Alemanni at Cologne, was converted to Christianity with all his soldiers.

• Julia Flyte supposes that not all of Clovis' men can have been 'exactly Catholic-minded'.

BR 186

CLUBS

Athenaeum, 107 Pall Mall

Founded 1824.

• Philbrick is a member and is ap-proached with a peerage here by the Archbishop of Canterbury.

• Charles Ryder's Warden at Hertford

talks to his father here about his future. They are both members.

- Mr Plant is a member.

Bachelors
John Plant and Jimmie Grainger are members.

Beefsteak, 9 Irving Street
Sir Joseph Mainwaring is a member and talks to another member about the Germans in 1939, and also to Eddie Beste-Bingham about RDF.

***Bellamy's, St James's* (based on White's)**
Members: Guy Crouchback, Ian Kilbannock, Air Marshal Beech, Tommy Blackhouse, Binkie Cavanagh, Arthur Box-Bender, Elderbury, Gervase Crouchback, Mr Crouchback, Ivo Crouchback, Peregrine Crouchback, Gilbert Pinfold, Roger Stillingfleet, Crambo, Nailsworth, Basil Seal, Bertie, Lieutenant Padfield, Ivor Claire.

- The Crouchbacks have been members for generations – Gervase's name is on the role of honour. Mad Ivo used to sit in the window and stare at passers-by.
- It is 'an historic place. Once fuddled gamblers attended by link men had felt their way down these steps'.
- It has two sets of glass doors (the first are painted out during the Blitz), a small vestibule and the smell of cigar smoke and whisky. During the Blitz the windows of the card room are blown in and those of the coffee room which front St James's are covered in sticking plaster.
- The night porter is Job and the barman, Parsons.
- It is a tolerant club, accepting eccentricities. Before joining the army Guy Crouchback writes from here to secure a commission.
- Peregrine Crouchback finds it 'awfully rowdy' and only goes to read the papers. The conversation is quite liberated and Guy's friends feel free to talk about Virginia's reputation. Peregrine Crouchback overhears a conversation about aphrodisiacs.
- After the war Roger Stillingfleet does not frequent the club.
- Virginia Crouchback would like to burn down Bellamy's, 'bless her'.

Bollinger Club, Oxford
Oxford undergraduate dining club. Based on the Bullingdon. It is steeped in tradition and numbers among its members reigning kings, epileptic royalty in exile, uncouth peers, smooth young men from embassies, illiterate lairds, ambitious young barristers and Conservative candidates.

- Among its activities are the stoning to death of a fox with champagne bottles and destroying anything vaguely aesthetic. Members include Alastair Trumpington, Peter Pastmaster and Lumsden of Strathdrummond. In 1922 they break Austen's piano; destroy Rending's cigars and break his china; tear up Partridge's black sheets and ruin his Matisse; break Sanders' windows and tear up his Newdigate poem; and debag Paul Pennyfeather in the quad.

***Bratt's, St James's* (based on White's)**
Established 1919. Nearest bus stop is on the corner of Bond Street.

- Members: Alastair Trumpington, Peter Pastmaster, Tony Last, John Beaver, Jock Grant-Menzies, Rex Mottram, Charles Ryder, Boy Mulcaster, Bill Meadows, Cedric Lyne, Freddie Sothill.
- Has an elegant Georgian façade and panelled rooms. When founded it was intended for young men who, by the 1930s, are all old and bald.
- In the evening it is often filled with young men in white tie who have failed to find a party. Holds an annual golf tournament at Le Touquet.
- Peter Pastmaster and his colonel discuss the formation of the commandos here in 1940.
- In 1934 Tony Last and Jock Grant-Menzies get drunk and call up Brenda.
- In May 1926 Bill Meadows forms his group of special constables here.

Brooks's, St James's
Founded 1764.

• A young man takes refuge on the steps from Julia Stitch's car.

Brown's
Tony Last is a member.

Carlton, 69 St James's Street
Conservative club founded in 1832.
Lord Chasm is interviewed about Agatha here in 1927.

Garrick, 15 Garrick Street
Founded 1831.
• Sir James MacRae invites Simon Lent to lunch here.

Greville
Tony Last is a member and stays here after Brenda's infidelity. It is here that he meets Dr Messinger.

Palm Beach, Wimpole Street
Known to John Plant in the early 1930s.
WS 185

RAC, 89 Pall Mall
Founded 1897.
• To William Boot, Copper House seems to be a less exclusive rival of the RAC.

Travellers', 106 Pall Mall
Founded 1819.
• Sir Joseph Mainwaring always takes Basil Seal here for luncheon (q.v.). The atmosphere is sombre. Basil Seal joins in later life.

Turf, 5 Carlton House Terrace
Founded 1864.
• Where, in 1939, old men talk about the evacuees scheme.

***Turtles, St James's Street* (based on Brooks's)**
Half-way down St James's. Has a direct hit during the Blitz which destroys the spirit store, spilling the contents into the gutter.
• Ian Kilbannock's father was a member, but Ian does not rate it very highly.

United Services, Duke of York's Steps, St. James
Guy Crouchback visits with Jumbo Trotter in 1941.

Wimpole, Wimpole Street
(*See* ATWATER)

CLUTTERBUCK, MR AND MRS JOHN
Parents of Percy Clutterbuck – both are stout. Also have an older son, Sam, at Cambridge and two younger children, Joan and Peter. Mr Clutterbuck has stood three times as a Liberal candidate and is in business as a brewer. He offers a job to Grimes.
• Sam discovers greyhound racing with Philbrick.
DF 72, 74, 76, 81, 84, 110

CLUTTERBUCK, PERCY
Pupil at Llanabba school. 'Delicate', according to Dr Fagan. 'Nasty', according to Mr Prendergast. Is sick after eating mutton. Grimes gives him some cheap cigars which he smokes in the boiler room and is sick. Tells Paul Pennyfeather that he is Tangent.

Goes for 'walks' with Grimes. Is given half a crown by Paul for an essay on self-indulgence. Wins the 'Three-Mile Open' by cheating and does well in the jumping.
DF 24, 26, 34, 36–38, 74

CLUTTON-CORNFORTH, ALGERNON
Obsequious editor of a literary weekly and acquaintance of Gilbert Pinfold for thirty years. In Pinfold's mind he 'speaks on Aspects of Orthodoxy in Contemporary Letters' in a 'fluting, fruity voice'. He attacks Pinfold verbally.
GR 62, 116

COCHRANE (COCHRAN), SIR CHARLES BLAKE *(1872–1951)*
British theatrical producer and agent of Mistinguett. Presented *The Miracle* (1911) and Noel Coward's *Cavalcade* (1931).
• Ambrose Silk designed stage sets for him in the 1920s.
PF 43

COCKPEN, THE LAIRD OF
A follower of Bonnie Prince Charlie represented in a film on the 1745 rebellion seen by Guy Crouchback.
MA 161

COCKPURSE, LADY POLLY
Friend of Brenda Last and John Beaver. According to Brenda's sister, she hasn't known anyone longer than five years. She is popular with women by virtue of her clothes.

She is an ardent and successful social-climber. Meets Brenda at a restaurant in Albemarle Street. Tony Last tells John that she *looks* like a monkey and the child tells the village people that she *is* a monkey.

In 1932, her party is a success – very smart and straight. Even her husband is there. People had previously treated her more flippantly.

She is also a friend of Margot Metroland, and Julia Stitch and an admirer of the works of John Boot. Visits Hetton in 1932. Stays in Lyonesse. Hosts the party for Mrs Northcotes' fortune telling.

Lunches with Julia Stitch in 1937.
HD 26, 41, 44, 48, 77, 116; Sc 12

COCKSON, MRS
Fellow passenger of Gilbert Pinfold aboard the *SS Caliban* in 1953.
GP 36

'COCO-NUT'
Colonel Ritchie-Hook's name for the severed head of a French colonial native soldier which he brings back as a trophy from the raid on the African coast, and later pickles.
MA 231

COCTEAU, JEAN ***(1889–1963)***
French poet and playwright – convert to Catholicism; opium addict; patron of Picasso and Stravinsky.
• Ambrose Silk, in the Paris of the 1920s, frequents the company of Cocteau.
• Anthony Blanche is on close terms with Cocteau, whom he professes to have told about Charles Ryder – 'he is all agog'.
PF 43; BR 47, 52

CODES
Kt to QR3 CH is in fact not a code, but a move in a chess game Percy Legge is playing with Babbit of the Foreign Office.
BM 57

COFFINS
A vast selection are available in California, of which the mid price is £2000. Dennis Barlow chooses a walnut chest with bronze trimmings and quilted satin interior for Sir Francis Hinsley's corpse.
LO 40

COISTREL
'A groom, knave, base fellow: The swarming rabble of our coistrell curates' (*Oxford English Dictionary*). Word found by Ludovic (q.v.) when trying to find new description for reports on his men in 1943.
US 85

COKE-UPON-LITTLETON
'Cant name of a mixed drink . . .' Term found by Ludovic in the *Oxford English Dictionary.*
US 86

COLAPHIZE
'To buffet and knock'. Term found by Ludovic in the *Oxford English Dictionary.*
US 86

COLENSO
A malcontent. (Name is that of a nineteenth-century Bishop of Natal who championed the Negros).
• One of the batch of Halberdiers from the Training Depot, to who to Guy Crouchback is 'their' Sarum-Smith.
MA 93

COLLEONI, BARTOLOMMEO ***(1400–1475)***
Italian condottière from Bergamo; generalissimo of Venice, 1454.

Charles Ryder and Sebastian Flyte

admire his equestrian statue by Verrochio (1495) in Venice.
BR 98

COLLINS ***(b. 1902)***
Contemporary of Charles Ryder at Oxford. A Wykehamist 'an embryo don, a man of solid reading and childlike humour . . .' Shows Charles 'the fallacy of Modern aesthetics'. Charles and Collins spend the Easter vacation in Ravenna.
• Sebastian Flyte is sure that Collins will become prematurely bald.
• Makes notes for a thesis on the Ravenna mosaics. He dedicates the first column of his unfinished work on Byzantine Art to Charles, who wonders in later life if he might not have gone the same way himself, but for Sebastian.
• Charles sells his Omega screen to Collins for £10. Charles visits Collins in Hertford College and is not asked to share his digs.
BR 29, 30, 44–45, 60, 140

COLOMBO
Capital of Ceylon.
• Has a hotel – the Galleface – to which Gilbert Pinfold intends to go. It also contains some good tailors, at one of which, Pinfold has three suits made. There is not much to see or do. Pinfold goes to mass at the Church of St Michael and all Angels.
• Ginger Littlejohn spent five years there.
GP 137, 140, 144–148; VB 118

COLONELS
Térèse de Vitre, having thought that Tony Last was Colonel Strapper, wonders whether all colonels are old.
HD 162.
(*See also* PLUM, TICKERIDGE, GREEN, BLACKHOUSE)

COLONIAL DAMES
Association of right-wing American ladies of the deep South.
• Ambrose Silk recounts a tale of a cellist who was burned to death by communists when playing a concert for the Colonial Dames.
PF 112

COLONY BOG
Heathland in Surrey used as an army training area in WWII.
PF 127

COMMANDOS
Specialist raiding forces raised in 1940; battalion-size. Name taken from that of similar units used by the Boers. Made up of men from various regiments.
• One such unit is X Commando raised in 1941 on the Isle of Mugg by Tommy Blackhouse (q.v.).
• 'They have special knives and tommy-guns and knuckle dusters; they wear rope-soled shoes.'
• To Alastair Trumpington they sound like something from 'Chums' (q.v.).
PF 29; OG 45, 47, 109

COMMISSIONAIRES
The commissionaire at Esponoza's can summon only the most decrepit taxis in London. He is a veteran of the Boer War and the north-west frontier.
• In the Black-Out Londoners learn to find their destination by feeling commissionaires' buttons.
PF 49; WS 63

COMMUNISTS
Lord Copper explains Communism to Salter over dinner.
• Most of the staff of the *Daily Twopence* are Communists, 'they're University men, you see'.
• In Ishmaelia the Bolshevists like to be known as 'blacks'. Their vice-consul wears a violet shirt and calls Karl Marx a negro.
• The Communists take over in Ishmaelia and devise a new calendar for the Soviet State.
• Rex Mottram flirts with Communists and Fascists alike in his speeches.
• A bishop encountered by Charles Ryder in mid-Atlantic is travelling to Barcelona to reconcile the Anarchists and Communists.

• It is the opinion of Rex Mottram's friends that the Communists will tear Hitler limb from limb.
• In 1939 the Communists, as well as the Nazis wanted war.
• De Souza would not call Communism a sect. He is, in spirit, a Communist.
• During the 1920s many well-educated Englishmen were turning to Communism, while Gilbert Pinfold became a Catholic.
Sc 14, 32, 165; BR 224, 234, 280; US 206, 232; GP 13
(*See also* PAPPENHACKER, DE SOUZA, SIR Ralph BROMPTON)

COMPLEXIONS
There are three complexion types at Whispering Glades – 'Rural', 'Athletic' and 'Scholarly' (red, brown or white).
LA 47

COMPTON LAST
Village near Hetton, to the South.
HD 101

CONCENTRATION CAMPS
(*See* HANS AND KURT)

CONCERT PARTIES
A concert party entertains the Halberdiers. It is made up of three elderly women, a cadaverous old man and a 'neuter beast' at the piano, dressed as pierrots and pierrettes.

Later, the Halberdiers themselves put on a concert – 'a strange piece of mummery traditional in the Halberdiers' in which the characters are 'Silly Bean, Black Bean, and Awful Bean'.
MA 55, 206

CONEY
Secretary to Everard Spruce. She has long black hair and wears espadrilles.
US 50

CONGREVE
One of the characters in the story of *Captain Truslove*, remembered by Guy Crouchback. Congreve is a flashy polo player who resigns from the regiment when it is posted overseas. His fiancée returns the ring. However, he reappears in the penultimate chapter and rescues Truslove.

Guy compares him to Leonard (q.v.).
MA 217

CONNAUGHT, DUKE OF
Sponsor for Betty Stayle.
WS 279

CONNECTICUT, USA
State on the American East coast to which Arthur Box-Bender evacuates his three daughters to a business associate in 1940.
MA 20

CONNELLYS
Manufacturer of the 'Thunder-box'.
MA 144

CONNOLLY, GENERAL (DUKE OF UKAKA)
A stocky Irishman, middle-aged, ex-Black and Tans, South African police force, and Kenya Game Reserves. CIC of Emperor Seth's forces. Calls the tank a tin can. Has a red beard, smokes a pipe.

Opposes issue of boots to Azanian army. Argues with Basil Seal. Married to Black Bitch. Accepted into the French set and leaves the country.
BM 30, 35, 121

CONNOLLYS, THE
Family of three refuges taken in by the inhabitants of Malfrey and a source of constant trouble.

No one knows how they got there; they simply appeared. Nothing is known of their parents.

Doris is a pubescent girl of between ten and eighteen, with dark, bobbed hair and pig's eyes. Micky is her younger brother and Marlene is a year younger than Micky.

They go first to the Mudges, where they kill six ducks and a cat and are incontinent.

The longest they stay in one place is ten days. Micky bites a roadman's wife; Marlene has a seizure; they are sent to an institution and then sent back.

At Malfrey House Micky tears up a

folio and Marlene eats the dog's dinner.

Basil Seal finds them a billet with the Harknesses whose lives they destroy, driving out their two maids. Basil makes £30 retrieving them. Basil next gives them to the Graces and makes £20. Then he gives them to the girl at Grantly Green, and gets some sherry and much else. Finally he takes them to Mr Todhunter who is the billeting officer and sells them as a going concern.
PF 79, 86, 141

CONRADINE, POMPILIA DE LA
One of Margot Beste-Chetwnyde's 'girls' in the Latin American Entertainment Co.
DF 144

CONSCIENTIOUS OBJECTORS
Sir Wilfred Lucas-Dockery's appendix to a report on Conscientious Objectors gets him his position of governor of Blackstone.
• The attendant of Guy Crouchback's ward in the RAF hospital is a CO whose objections are founded on the dimensions of the Great Pyramid.
DF 166; YS 115

CONSERVATIVE PARTY
The local Conservative women of Wiltshire come to Brideshead for tea.
• In the mid 1930s, with Rex Mottram in possession, 'young Conservatives' in their early forties are among those who gather at Brideshead. However, the orthodox Conservatives look down on Rex's dealings.
• In Azania the Conservative Party is headed by the Earl of Ngumo.
BR 37, 261, 283; BN 143

CONSTANTINOPLE
One of the stops on Sebastian Flyte's trip to the Near East with Mr Samgrass. They stay with the Ambassador.

Sebastian also wins money at cards here, gives Samgrass the slip and meets Anthony Blanche at the bar of the Takatlian. Sebastian then runs away before returning here.
BR 145, 152, 153

CONVERTS
Rex Mottram is the most difficult convert to Catholicism Father Mowbray has ever had. 'He doesn't correspond to any degree of paganism known to the missionaries.'

In Julia Flyte's mind Rex is only one of a number of strange converts in the history of the church such as Clovis (q.v.).
• When Lord Marchmain converts he tells his wife that she has brought him back to the faith of his ancestors. According to Cordelia such pomposity is only one way in which conversion takes people.
• Charles Ryder becomes a Catholic in the late-1930s, as does Gilbert Pinfold, in the mid-1920s.
BR 185, 186, 212, 331; GP 13

COOK, COLOUR SERGEANT
Given charge of the training of the Halberdiers' new intake of officers in 1940.
MD 45

COOK'S
British travel agency used by Sebastian Flyte, Mr Samgrass and Tony Last.
BR 184–6; HD

COPPER, LORD
Owner of the Megalopolitan Newspaper Corporation. Stands for 'self-sufficiency at home, self-assertion abroad'. Has a massive head.

Usually lunches at one with Julia Stitch. Believes civil war in Ishmaelia inevitable. Lives in 'a frightful mansion' in East Finchley. Decides on 'Boot' for Ishmaelia; meets Boot and gives him advice; draws picture of a cow.

Prepares to send Boot to the South Pole; procures Knighthood for John Boot.

Often gives banquets in which he exults. Throws banquet for Boot's return.

Sees himself as deserted leader. Makes speech lasting thirty-eight minutes.
• According to Sprat he has always had it in for the regular army.
Sc 1–15, 179, 215; OG 154.

(LE) CORBUSIER, CHARLES EDOUARD JEANNERET
(1887–1965)
Swiss architect and father of Modernism.

Inventor of the 'machine à habiter'.
• Otto Silenus has, according to Arthur Potts, 'got right away from Corbusier'.
• To Paul Pennyfeather, Corbusier is in fact not modern at all but 'a pure nineteenth-century, Manchester school utilitarian'.
DF 122

CORFU
Where Margot Metroland has a villa with a great bed, carved with pineapples, that once belonged to Napoleon III.
• Paul Pennyfeather and Otto Silenus stay there in 1923.
DF 150

CORKER
Corker of *Universal News*. British journalist who calls waiters 'Alphonse' or 'you black bum'. Drinks pints of bitter and wears striped flannel suits.

Meets William Boot. Seats himself at the Captain's table. Tells William stories of Fleet Street and Wenlock Jakes. Finds a peer's widow trapped in a lift. Develops nettle-rash. Buys souvenirs in Aden.

Friend of Pigge (q.v.). Married to 'Madge'. Takes William under his wing. Tries to leave for Laku; is instructed to remain; compelled to travel to Laku and left stranded in a lorry with Pigge, twelve miles out of Jacksonburg.
Sc 61–68, 85, 92, 147

CORNER, MRS *(d. 1944)*
Housekeeper to Peregrine Crouchback, killed by the same flying bomb as Virginia and Peregrine.
US 126, 195

CORNER, CHATTY (JAMES PENDENNIS)
Friend of Apthorpe (q.v.) according to whom, he is known everywhere between Chad and Mozambique. Son of a Bishop; educated at Eton and Oxford; plays violin and is an expert on gorillas and Bechuanaland.

Invited by Apthorpe to Mess dinner at the Halberdiers' barracks, where he becomes drunk and has to leave. He is tanned and has wiry hair and shaggy eyebrows. He is bequeathed Apthorpe's kit. Does not respond to Guy's message in *The Times*. Encountered by Guy on Mugg where he is training the Commandos.

Known as 'Kong'. Lives in the Old Castle. Used to get drunk with Apthorpe in Africa. In charge of a Jungle Warfare school before Dunkirk.
MA 74, 75, 77; OG 21, 39, 51, 54–58

CORNPHILLIP, LORD BILLY
Lives in Wiltshire. Husband of Etty Cornphillip. A very dull man. In Lady Amelia's husband's regiment.

Friend of Lady Instow. Conservative. Relative of Ralph Bland. Forbids Etty to talk to Ralph. Has the magistrate make Ralph keep the peace. Has a son (whose real father is Ralph).
WS 25–50

CORNWALL
Location of Brook Park (q.v.).
• John and Elizabeth Verney take a holiday there at Good Hope Fort.
• On 12 June 1940 Guy Crouchback and his company are quartered in a seaside hotel in Cornwall.
MA 203; US 14; GP 170

COROMBONA, VITTORIA
Venetian aristocrat who throws a ball at her palace in 1923 attended by Charles Ryder and Sebastian Flyte.
• Virginia Crouchback fell down the stairs at the Palazzo Corombona.
BR 97; US 56

CORONATIONS
During Coronation Week, 1936, Charles Ryder runs away from London.
• Achon dies during his own coronation, killed by the enormous weight of the great gold crown of Azania.
BR 265; BM 205

CORPSES
'Bodies', 'cadavers', 'the meat' – have it as you will.
LO 54

CORRESPONDENCE COURSES
To Guy Crouchback, Army Training Memorandum No. 31 War, April 1940 appears like a correspondence course in Business Efficiency.
Sc 187

CORYBANTES
Young men who, dancing and playing musical instruments, celebrate the orgiastic rites of Cybele, a Roman and Greek goddess (Rhea).
• Gilbert Pinfold compares himself with them when free-falling from an aeroplane.
GP 142.

COSTA RICANS
Mr Baldwin (q.v.) carries a Costa Rican passport, and passes, with William Boot, through customs at Aden.
Sc 71

CÔTE D'AZUR
Where the Americans would have preferred to land in the South Front in WWII.
• Mr Baldwin has a villa there, to which he tries to get every year.
YS 166; Sc 56

COTSWOLDS
Location of Much Malcock, Little Chipping Manor, and other houses (q.v.).
WS 45

COTTESMORE COUNTRY
Area of land around the village of Cottesmore, Lincolnshire, hunted by the Cottesmore Hunt.
• Home of Major Rattery (q.v.).
HD 97

COUNTRY HOUSES
A castle in Ayrshire: Lady Kilbannock
A house in Hampshire: Cedric Lyne
Boot Magna Hall, Somerset: The Boots
Boughton: Jasper Ryder
Brideshead Castle, Wiltshire: The Flytes.
Broome Hall, Somerset: The Crouchbacks
Buckbourne: 'Aunty Betty' Flyte
Doubting Hall, Bucks: Colonel Blount
Fleacetown, Ireland: Bella Fleace
Garesby: The Wrottmans
Hetton, the West Country: Tony Last
Inverauchty, Scotland: Angus Stuart-Kerr
King's Thursday, Hants: Margot Metroland
Lower Chipping Manor, Glos: The Box-Benders
Lychpole, the West Country: Gilbert Pinfold
*Malfrey, Glos:*Freddy and Barbara Sothill
Mountrichard Castle: Lady Mountrichard
Much Malcock House, Glos: Lady Peabury
The Old Mill House, North Grappling: The Harknesses
Tomb, Norfolk: The Kent-Cumberlands

COUNTRY LIFE MAGAZINE
Julia Stitch tells Arthur to telephone *Country Life* for a back issue in which there is a photograph of a lion's head over the gate of Twisbury Manor.
• Celia Ryder's barn conversion at the Ryder's rectory is the subject of an article in *Country Life.*
Sc 7; BR 220–221
(*See* MAGAZINES)

COUNTRY, THE
In Mr Salter's mind, country conversation is chiefly on the topic of Mangel Wurzels and Zider. There, is something, he thinks 'un-English and not quite right about the country'.
• In Mr Metcalfe's mind the true countryman wears a dark suit on Sundays, loves a bargain (by private treaty), is fascinated by gadgets, is 'genial *but* inhospitable', and has three hundred other such characteristics.
Sc 27; WS 43

COURT
The most notable appearances are those of Paul Pennyfeather and Sebastian Flyte, Charles Ryder and Boy Malcaster (all q.v.).
BR 116; DF 159

COURTENEY, PRUDENCE
Daughter of Sir Samson Courteney (q.v.). Lover of William Bland. Nymphomaniac – thinks men 'hard to keep amused'.

Knows lot of stories. Author of *The Panorama of Life* (q.v.).

Wants to be in love. Seduced by Basil Seal. Eaten by Basil and cannibals in a stew.
BM 44–6, 55, 61, 139, 141, 230

COURTENEY, SIR SAMSON
His Britannic Majesty's Minister in Azania. A charming man although not successful in diplomacy.

A promising young man, he had passed through the Foreign Office. Third secretary at Peking, transferred to Washington, where he took up cycling and would vanish for days. Moved to Copenhagen.

Married to the daughter of a liberal cabinet minister. Moved to Stockholm as Chargé d'Affaires. In Sweden his career was doomed.

Speaks bad French. At age fifty is created Knight of St Michael and St George, and sent to Azania.

Known henceforth as the Envoy Extraordinary.
BM 47–48; WS 235

COWARD, SIR NOEL ***(1899–1973)***
English author, playwright and composer; author of *The Vortex* (1924), *Private Lives* (1930) and *Cavalcade* (1931).
• Ian Kilbannock does a good impression of Noel Coward and often quotes from his play *Private Lives* (notably on Operation Popgun).
OG 145–46

COWES, ISLE OF WIGHT
Location of the HQ of the Royal Yacht Squadron and Cowes Week, every July.
• On those lawns in Lady Seal's mind the member of the Royal Yacht Squadron are forever portrayed.
• Lt Padfield is a 'fellow who used to come to Cowes'.
PF 29; VS 25

COWS
Lord Copper draws a picture of a cow on his blotter, and finds a problem with the horns and the ears – which is the higher?
Sc 179

CRAIG, EDWARD GORDON ***(1872–1966)***
English actor and stage designer. Friend of Isadora Duncan. Had a strong influence on set design.
• To Guy Crouchback, the Old Castle on Mugg seems like a set designed by Craig for a play by Maeterlinck.
OG 55

CRAMP
Injured soldier in Ivor Claire's company of X Commando.
OG 52

CRANE, WALTER ***(1845–1915)***
English painter, designer, and illustrator of children's books. Principal of the RCA. Wrote textbooks on illustration. Associated with the Arts and Crafts Movement (q.v.).
• In 1919 the young Charles Ryder is reading Crane's *Bases of Design*.
WS 302

CRESSIDA
Lover of Troilus in Homeric myth, Chaucer and Shakespeare.
• Charles Ryder compares the park at Brideshead to the land 'where Cressida lay that night'.
BR 280

CRICKET
It is difficult to play cricket in California because of the lack of turf.
• Granchester school plays an annual cricket match at Lord's.
• To Nanny Hawkins, Sebastian must spend all his days at Oxford playing cricket, like Lord Brideshead.
LO 29; WS 195; BR 37

CRICKET CLUB
Strongly English, non-playing club of Los Angeles. The members club together to

send Dennis Barlow back to England.
LO 123

CRICKLEWOOD
Where, at the Stadium, in 1937, a cycling championship takes place, covered in depth by the *Beast*.
• Where in 1931 Ivo Crouchback is found starving to death in a lodging.
Sc 21; MA 18

CRIMINALS
According to Mr Prendergast, criminals are as bad as schoolboys, inventing horrors to shock him at confession and singing the wrong words to hymns.
• The criminal class in Morocco generally have Maltese papers.
• Mr Sweat tells Miles Plastic that 'there's no understanding of crime these days like what there was'.
DF 165; WS 123) GP 181
(*See also* PRISONS)

CROATS
Dr Antonic is a Croat, born under the Habsburgs. As a Croat he has no hope.
WS 218, 239

CROCK
Duty servant to the Halberdiers' officers at Kut-al-Imara in 1940.
MA 143

CROSSE & BLACKWELL'S REGIMENT
Synonym for the general service list.
PF 150

CROSSWORDS
Julia Stitch does the morning crossword in bed. Brittling reads her the clues: 'Terracotta is too long, madam, and there is no r'. 'Try hottentot. It's that kind of word.'
• During the channel storm the Captain and Chief Officer of the ferry are on the bridge doing a crossword puzzle: 'Word of six letters beginning with ZB', said the Chief Officer ... 'Z, can't be right, said the Captain after a few minutes' thought'.
• Gilbert Pinfold has dreams about doing *The Times* crosswood puzzle.
VB 21; Sc 8; GP 16

CROUCHBACK
Family name of Guy Crouchback of Broome (q.v.) Arms are a cross of sable and argent. Traditional family Christian name is Gervase.

One Martyr, Gervase. Old Catholic family.

Two medieval excommunications and an apostacy in the seventeenth century. Their decline is completed by the 1930s. In 1914 they had seemed assured.
MA 18, 36; US 63

CROUCHBACK, THE BLESSED GERVASE
Catholic martyr and priest. Ancestor of Guy Crouchback and brother of Guy's direct ancestor.

Betrayed by a spy when himself at Broome (q.v.). Examined by the Council and tortured.
OG 21, 22; US 69

CROUCHBACK, GERVASE AND HERMIONE *(m. 1889)*
Grandparents of Guy Crouchback. Leading Catholics. Of Broome House. Gervase has side-whiskers and set views on Ireland and India. Hermione paints Roman ruins and speaks three languages.

They play cards together in the schoolroom at Broom. Visit Italy on their honeymoon in 1889. Have an audience with Pope Pius.

Cruise from Naples up the coast to Santa Dulcina. Gervase buys castle in 1889. Removes the eighteenth century plaster ceiling at Broome and replaces it with beams.
MA 9–11

CROUCHBACK, GERVASE *(1865–1943)*
Father of Guy Crouchback (q.v.) and son of Gervase and Hermione. Lives at the Marine Hotel, Matchet with his dog, Felix, a golden retriever. Taller than Guy, with a kinder expression.

Joyful in the face of his life's misfortunes. Widowed early. Sees the world as being Crouchbacks and the Catholics on one side and everyone else on the other.

His memory only retains good things. Goes to Mass every day. Punctual; intensely religious; gives Guy Gervase's holy medal. Smokes a pipe; abstains from wine and tobacco during Lent, but drinks port.

Teaches Greek as a temporary schoolmaster at a prep school in 1940. In his rooms are a brass bedstead, oak presser and book rack, circular shaving glass and mahogany priedieu from Broome.

Keeps his own wine in the hotel cellar. Sits on county council in the 1900s; makes benevolent visits and dislikes the wireless.

Is puzzled by the contents of an American food parcel from his grand daughter. Does not know what Trumper's Eucris is. Acnowledges no monarch since James II.

Friend of Miss Vavasour and the Tickeridges (q.v.). Has blood clots. Gives up the school in October 1943. Dies in winter 1943. Buried at Broome.

To Guy he is a 'just' man ('in the sense of the psalmist'), and the only good man he had ever known.

MA 17, 33–35, 158, 203; OG 28; US 48, 59, 64, 65, 72

CROUCHBACK, MRS

Mother of Guy. Gives a set of vestments for St Dulcina's bones.

Guy's memory of her is of walks beside the lake at Broome, under a sunshade, and of her helping him on winter afternoons with a scrapbook. She dies during his childhood.

MA 16; US 72

CROUCHBACK, GUY
(b. October 1903)

Youngest son of Gervase Crouchback and grandson of Gervase and Hermione. Educated at Downside. His home is Castello Crouchback, Santa Dulcina delle Rocce, Italy, and he is a farmer by profession.

He is 'slight and trim' and belongs to Bellamy's. He speaks good Italian; feels kinship with Roger de Waybrooke (q.v.) and is solitary in his religion.

Marries, *c* 1926, a fashionable society beauty, Virginia Troy. Honeymoons at Castello Crouchback. Settles in Kenya and farms. Wife returns to England and her affair with Tommy Blackhouse (q.v.). Leaves Kenya. Returns to Italy and tries to grow vines at Santa Dulcina – unsuccessfully.

Attempts to capitalize on tourist trade in Italy – unsuccessfully.

Divorced 1931 and has a few 'sad little love affairs'. Leaves Santa Dulcina July 1939 intent on taking part in the struggle against the Modern Age. Thinks of Virginia frequently – when he awakes. Intrigues for a commission; is unsuccessful. Tries to get into the Irish Guards. Visits Kemble and Matchet.

Makes up mind to join Foreign Office. Meets Major Tickeridge through whose influence he enters the Halberdiers as a Lieutenant in November 1939.

Befriends Apthorpe (q.v.). Hates PT and finds army life difficult. Is called 'uncle'. Meets Virginia at Claridges on 1 January 1940 and 'lays a ghost'. Posted to Southend.

Grows a moustache; acquires a monocle; visits the Garibaldi restaurant. Finds Apthorpe implausible. Attempts to seduce Virginia on 14 February 1940 at Claridges. Returns to Scotland 15 February 1940. Is filled with military pride by Ritchie-Hook's speech. Is good at cross-country warfare training. Is put on Most Secret Index.

Given a company in X Battalion in May 1940. Posted to Brook Park. Visits Matchet for a day. Embarks at Liverpool. Sails to Africa. Leads raiding party on African coast. On beach is promoted to Captain but loses it immediately. Visits Apthorpe in hospital on the African coast. Takes a bottle of whisky which eventually kills Apthorpe.

Caught in the Blitz with Ian Kilbannock in late 1940. Places advert in *The Times* on 2 November 1940 for Chatty Corner. Leaves barracks on 14 October 1940. Posted to Southsand. Posted to X Commando Isle of Mugg. Finds Chatty Corner on 7 November 1940. Dines with Colonel Campbell. Unable to read *No Orchids for Miss Blandish*. Thinks there should be a drug for soldiers to keep them asleep until they are needed. Drawn closer to Ivor Claire by night manoevre.

November 1940–May 1941: meets Dr Glendining Rees, sees Julia Stitch's yacht (he knows her of old when she came to Santa Dulcina). Sails to Cape Town. Views the Patrons. Arrives at Sidi Bishr, near Cairo, Egypt in April 1941. Visits Alexandria and dines with Mrs Stitch.

Reads *Country Life* in the library of the club at Alexandria. Posted to Crete in mid-May 1941. Lands at Suda on 26 May 1941; fights in withdrawal from Crete. Finds a dead English soldier. According to Ludovic he has 'the gravity of lead within a vacuum'. 31 May 1941 – on the beach at Sphakia. Refuses to surrender.

Swims out to boat and escapes with Ludovic. Has hallucinations. Carried ashore by Ludovic. Awakes in Alexandria in hospital. Rescued by Mrs Stitch. Stays at the Stitch's villa. Boards ship to England at end of June 1941. Returns to London in September 1941. Posted to Halberdier HQ.

Continues with the Halberdiers for two years from September 1941 to September 1943.

In August 1943 is told he is too old to fight. Thinks the Lateran Treaty a mistake. Disinterested in victory. Promoted to Captain. Posted to No. 6 Transit Camp, London. Posted to Special Service Forces Liaison Office; meets Ralph Brompton. Learns of his father's illness; encounters Ludovic; is selected by EPS and father dies.

September 1943: Attends father's funeral who was the only good man he has ever known. Remembers his childhood at Broome. Sees himself as one of the biblical labourers in the market place (q.v.). Does not expect to be a hero. Gives his father's tobacco jar to Miss Vavasour.

Visited by Virginia on 7 December 1943 in hospital, where he is convalescing after spraining his knee. They spend Christmas together. She tells him she is carrying Trimmer's child. They decide to marry.

Posted to HQ of British mission in the Adriatic at Bari. Attempts to help the Jews.

Receives news of Trimmer's son's birth (4 June) and of Virginia's death. Is not greatly affected. Pays for a Mass for Virginia. Is suspected of spying. Flies out to observe an attack. Crashes in aeroplane. Sets out again. Sees death of Ritchie-Hook.

Tries to help get the Jews out of Begoy. Ends his Crusade. Leaves Begoy. Goes to Split. At Bari again. Visits the Jews near Lecce. Tries to find the Kanyis. Realizes he has been instrumental in their death. In 1951 attends X Commando reunion at Bellamy's. Marries Domenica Plessington. Moves into the Lesser House and puts on weight.

MA 129, 167, 176, 241; MA 9, 12, 14, 17, 19, 82, 84, 105; OG 57, 104, 162, 164, 206, 240; US 9, 23, 66, 70, 103, 239, 196

CROUCHBACK, PEREGRINE
Privy Chamberlain, the Knight of Devotion and Grace of the Sovereign Order of St John of Jerusalem (*d. 1944*).

Bachelor uncle of Guy Crouchback. Member of Bellamy's.

Address: Carlisle Place, Belgravia, London, SW1. Served Dardanelles in 1915 and Colonies from 1915–18. Student of heraldry and of Roger de Waybrooke (q.v.). 'A bore of international repute,' his presence can empty any room. He is liked by the Italians.

In 1940 he collects binoculars and sends them to the War Office. Collector of bibelots. Papal Knight. In him, Guy sees his own 'indefinable numbness' and the 'saturnine strain' of Ivo Crouchback.

Contracts dysentry in the Dardanelles and is made ADC to a colonial governor. Honorary attaché in diplomatic service in 1920s. Is made the chancery butt (without success) by Sir Ralph Brompton (q.v.). He is 'impervious to ridicule'. His housekeeper is Mrs Corner. From 1929–44 he lives in London in his old-fashioned flat near Westminster Cathedral.

Enjoys the war as a fulfilment of his own

predictions. Sends food parcels to occupied countries and collects first editions.

Dislikes Christmas and as a young man spends it abroad. Later goes to the Scrope-Welds (q.v.). Strains his knee playing tennis at Bordighera. Does not drink gin or gamble. Has made love twice, once aged twenty and once forty-five, both times with the same woman.

Sees Virginia Crouchback as a scarlet woman but takes her to dinner at Overtons in 1943. Perceives, mistakenly that she is keen on him.

Is killed by the same flying bomb as Virginia and Mrs Corner at Carlisle Place. Buried at Mortlake (q.v.).
MA 13, 15, 31; US 9, 124, 131, 136, 138, 143, 195

CROUCHBACK, IVO *(1902–1931)*
Brother of Guy (q.v.). Always rather odd. Sits at the window of Bellamy's alarming passers-by with his mad stare. In 1928, he disappears aged twenty-six. He is found, barricaded into a lodging in Cricklewood, where he starves himself to death.

Dies raving mad.
MA 17, 21

CROUCHBACK, GERVASE *(1897–1916)*
Brother of Guy (q.v.). Educated at Downside. Goes into the Irish Guards 1916. Has a medal of our Lady of Lourdes bought in France in 1914 on holiday. Gets drunk in London while in training and compares medals with a prostitute. Killed on his first day in France by a sniper.

In June 1940 he seems very distant from Guy.
MA 17, 37; OG 41

CROUCHBACK, GERVASE *(b. 4 June 1944)*
Son of Virginia Crouchback and Trimmer (q.v.). Initially Virginia cannot bear the sight of him. Midwife is Sister Jenkins.

When Virginia is killed by a flying bomb, Gervase is with Angela Box-Bender and thus saved. (Virginia has sent him there not because she is worried for his safety but because she cannot bear to see him.)

Adopted in July 1944 by Eloise Plessington (q.v.). Subsequently brought up by Guy as his own son, with his wife Domenica (q.v.).
US 184, 189, 191, 202

CROUCHBACK, VIRGINIA
(*See* TROY)

CROWN JEWELS, AZANIAN
A huge gold crown and an ivory sceptre are given to Emperor Amurath by the French President.
BM 28

CROYDON, SURREY
Location of the airport used by Basil Seal, William Boot, Paul Pennyfeather and Arthur Potts to fly to France.
BM 88; Sc 46; DF 151–5

CRUMP, LOTTIE
Notorious proprietress of Shepheard's Hotel, Dover Street, on the corner of Hay Hill, Mayfair. A character from the Edwardian era, oblivious to changes in the social order. Has two cairn terriers.

In 1914 relegates her signed photograph of the Kaiser to the servants' lavatory. A reassuring figure in a time of uncertainty.

Insults her servants. Has entertained at one time most male members of all European royal families. She is not keen on artists or intellectuals, only on money and aristocracy. Forgets everyone's names. Adjusts the bills so that the rich pay more.

Verbally attacks Mr Outrage on the telephone. Expert at avoiding publicity.

Basil Seal frequents her establishment.

(Based on Rosa Lewis, proprietress of the Cavendish Hotel).
VB 31, 36–47; BM 75

CRUMP, MRS
One of Mr Prendergast's friends from Worthing: 'rather deaf, but a very good churchwoman'.
DF 32

CRUSADES
Eight medieval military expeditions to free the Holy Land from Saracen rule.

Roger de Waybrooke (q.v.) was a Crusader, to whom Guy Crouchback sees himself as successor in the war against the Nazis.
MA 13
(*See also* GOODALL, PILGRIMAGE OF GRACE)

CRUTTWELL, GENERAL, FRGS
Eminent explorer encountered by William Boot in the department store. Advises him on what to take to Ishmaelia.

In Ishmaelia with Sprat Larkin in 1897. Paid £600 a year by the shop. Has a false tan. Many places are names after him – Crutwell Glacier, Spitzbergen; Cruttwell Falls, Venezuela; Mount Cruttwell, the Pamirs; Cruttwell's Leap, Cumberland; Cruttwell's Folly, Salonika.
Sc 43–44

CRUTTWELL, GLADYS
First love of Tom Kent-Cumberland. Employed in his firm as a clerk. She is, 'a virtuous, affectionate, self-reliant, even-tempered, unintelligent, high-spirited girl . . . .'

Two years Tom's elder, she has fluffy yellow hair. After Mrs Kent-Cumberland separates them, Gladys is twice engaged. Mrs Kent-Cumberland then orchestrates their marriage and they emigrate to Australia.
WS 97, 105

CRUTTWELL, TOBY
Criminal and friend of Philbrick. Brain behind the Amalgamated Steel Trust robbery of 1910, the Isle of Wight burglaries of 1914, and the Buller Diamond robbery of 1912. He also arranged for a Dr Peterfield to do something unspeakable to Alf Larrigan.

Won a VC for his feats at Gallipoli. Worked with Philbrick for five years. After the war he became Major Cruttwell and went into Parliament as Conservative member for a South-Coast town. As Captain Cruttwell, he is a last-minute dinner guest of Lady Seal's.
DF 53–54; BM 83–84

CRUTTWELL, MR
London bone-setter to Brenda Last and her sister Marjorie.
HD 40

CRUTTWELL
Scoutmaster at Much Malcock.
WS 50

CUMBERLAND
Location of Cruttwell's Leap.
Sc 43

CUMBERLAND, COLONEL JASPER *(b. 1800)*
Ancestor of the Kent-Cumberlands (q.v.) and author of a diary of the Peninsular War, later published under the title *The Journal of an English Cavalry Officer During the Peninsular War.*
WS 94

CUMBERLEIGH, JUNE
BBC interviewer in Gilbert Pinfold's mind. Interviews Jimmy Lance (q.v.). Known to Pinfold. Clever girl and friend of Lance.
GP 82, 83

CURRENCY
At the bazaar in Matodi, money changers traditionally exchanged Austrian, Spanish and Portuguese guineas.
• The normal currency of the capital and railway of Azania is Indian Rupees. However, East African shillings, French and Belgian colonial francs and Maria Theresa (Austrian) thalers are also in use. In the interior, rock salt and cartridges are used.
• In the South American jungle a bush pig's leg is worth a handful of shot or twenty gun caps; a game-bird or a necklace.
BM 9; 153; HD 187

CURTISS-DUNNE, SIR SAMSON
Conservative Member of Parliament for Lancing. Has a mansion at Steyning.
WS 302, 312

CURTISS-DUNNE ***(b. 1903)***
Contemporary of Charles Ryder at Lancing in 1919. Calls himself a Socialist. Fails Dartmouth Naval College. Keen to start a political group. In Brent's house, they all think he's 'balmy'. Wears soft black shoes.
WS 302, 310

CURZON, LORD GEORGE ***(1859–1925)***
English statesman. Travelled extensively in the East. In 1898 he was Viceroy of India and Foreign Secretary from 1919–24.
• Friend of 'Ruby' who tells Lieutenant Padfield all about him.
US 78

CUSTOMS OFFICERS
The walls of the customs shed at Dover are lined with confiscated pornography and 'strange instruments'. They confiscate Adam Fenwick-Syme's manuscript and strip-search Miss Runcible.
• At Le Bourget, the French customs officers search William Boot's kit. For them it is alleviation of their normally humdrum lives, only equalled by the time an Egyptian lady tried to smuggle in a doll stuffed with hashish.
VB 24; Sc 54

CUTHBERT
'Soldierly' valet to Mr Baldwin (q.v.). Brave and true, he was Baldwin's batman in the Great War. Carries a gun.
Sc 57

CUTHBERT, MR AND MRS
Old servants of the Crouchbacks at Broome and later proprietors of the Marine Hotel, Matchet. During the war they become avaricious, and are unable to understand Mr Crouchback's generosity.
OG 37, 38

CUTLER, MISS SARAH EVANGELINE ***(m. 1915)***
Canadian first wife of Rex Mottram whom he married in Montreal in 1915. Instrumental in disrupting Rex's wedding plans with Julia Flyte. Divorced in 1919.
BR 188

CUTTER, GENERAL
Acquaintance of Guy Crouchback who had spent a day with the Bradshawes at Santa Dulcina. Guy writes to him asking for a commission.
MA 23

CUTTINGS, THE
American aristocratic family. One of the families whose hair Trimmer has cut.
OG 217

CYMPRYDDYG
Nearest large town to Llanabba Castle School (q.v.). Home of the Metropole Hotel.
DF 98

CYRENAICA
Town in the Libyan desert to which every available unit is sent after the fall of Greece, leaving Hookforce alone in Alexandria.
OG 156

CYRIL
Page-boy at the Megalopolitan Building in Fleet Street.
• One of Anthony Blanche's boyfriends at the Blue Grotto club where he is the barman. Calls him Toni.
Sc 25, BR 260

CZECHS
Rex Mottram's friends believe that in 1938 the Czechs are bound to rise against Hitler.
• According to Lord Marchmain the only job that the Czechs are good at is being coachmen.
• Dr Antonio's wife is a Czech and they are, as a race, more optimistic than Croats.
BR 280, 316; WS 218, 239

D

DAGOS
According to Grimes' friend, Bill, the 'Dagos' are not good at running his 'place of entertainment' in Buenos Aires on account of their inability to be dispassionate towards women.
DF 140

DAIMLER HIRE COMPANY
Adam Fenwick-Symes orders a chauffeur-driven Daimler from the DHC while staying at Shepheard's in which he takes Nina Blount to Arundel for the night.
VB 78

DAISY
Proprietor of a restaurant in Albemarle Street, opened in 1933. Friend of Brenda Last and her sister Marjorie. Attends Mrs Northcote's party at Polly Cockpurse's. Opens a club in 1934 to which Brenda and John Beaver go for breakfast after a party.
HD 40

DAKAR
Port in French Senegal close to which Guy Crouchback leads a raiding party in 1940.
• The Halberdiers are given lectures on Dakar while off the African coast.
MA 217

DALI, SALVADOR *(1904–1989)*
Spanish artist and principal member of the Surrealist movement. Particularly interested in the symbolism of dreams. See his *The Persistence of Memory* (New York).
• Poppet Green is influenced by Dali in her paintings of 1939 – particularly in her rendition of the Aphrodite of Melos. She arranges surreal objects in the same 'conventional' manner.
PF 30

DALMATIA
Coastal area of Yugoslavia stretching from Croatia to Montenegro. Main town is Split (q.v.).
• Frank de Souza once spent a month here and found it agreeable. In 1944 it is occupied by the Germans.
US 95, 211

DAN
Friend of Milly (q.v.). Meets her by chance while she and Tony Last are staying in Brighton. Dresses in fur coat, plus fours, patterned shirt, beret and correspondent shoes. He is accompanied by a girl called 'Baby' whom he takes to a party. His dinner jacket is midnight blue. Thinks Milly a 'nice kid'. Takes her to Dieppe for the weekend.
HD 138–141

DANCING
The Bright Young People, staying at King's Thursday in 1922 go to a dance and whist drive in the village hall.

Charles Ryder's college (Hertford) gives a ball during Eights Week in 1922, a quite unprecedented thing. His servant, Lunt, puts it all down to the effect of the War. According to Lunt some students even go dancing at the Masonic Halls with the rest of Oxford.
• Miles Malpractice dances with David Lennox at King's Thursday in 1922.
• In 1940 one of Guy Crouchback's company puts in a request for leave in order to compete in the slow valse competition in Blackpool.
• Basil Seal, in the interior of Azania, sleeps through the frenzied dancing of the natives around their campfire. The tribesmen slash themselves with knives or they dance in one chain, and the women in another.

• Clara (q.v.) is a dancer and tells Miles Plastic that one can never dance really well after one has had a baby.
DF 129, 128; BR 24; MA 205; BM 229, 230; GP 199
(See also BALLS)

DANDRUFF
According to Corker, dandruff is caused by acidity. He suffers from it badly.
SC 91

DANTE ALIGHIERI *(1265–1321)*
Florentine poet and author of *Vita Nuova* and *The Divine Comedy* (*c.* 1314), a copy of which, owned by Adam Symes, disgusts a customs officer at Dover in 1927. He confiscates *Il Purgatorio.*
• Mr Antonic admits that the Neutralian Ministry has not even heard of Dante.
VB 24; WS 226

DANZIG, POLAND
Baltic Port to which American warships are sent on 16 August 1920 as the Bolsheviks advance on Warsaw.
• Miss Bombaum reports on this incident.
• In July 1930 the Germans smuggle arms and military advisers into the Free City and the Poles there are attacked.
WS 203

DARDANELLES
Straits off the Hellespont and scene of the battle of Gallipoli in December 1915.
• Where Peregrine Crouchback caught dysentery in 1915.
• Dennis Barlow, on reading Sir Francis Hinsley's poetry, presumes that he was killed in the Dardanelles.
US 124; LO 53

DAR ES SALAAM, TANGANYIKA
One of the destinations for dhows from Matodi.
In 1918 Edward Seal (q.v.) is a brigadier here.
BM 9; DF 18

DARTMOOR, DEVON
Where Angela Lyne's son's school is moved during WWII.
PF 118

DARTMOUTH
Town in Devon and location of the Royal Naval College which Apthorpe's aunt wants him to attend.
• Curtiss-Dunne is expelled from the same establishment.
MA 111; WS 302

DARWIN, AUSTRALIA
Out-of-the-way Australian town to which Charles Ryder's cousin Melchior is driven by debt.
BR 70

DAUMIER, HONORÉ *(1808–1879)*
French painter and caricaturist, well-known for his drawings of lawyers, government figures and literary characters.
• Sebastian Flyte has two drawings by Daumier hanging in his rooms at Oxford.
• Some of the robes worn by the visiting academics to the conference on Bellorius in Neutralia recall Daumier's lawyers.
• To the young Charles Ryder, Mr A.A. Carmichael looks like the prosecuting counsel in a cartoon by Daumier.
BR 33; WS 211, 304

DAVID
Friend of Ambrose Silk in the 1920s who commits suicide by throwing himself under a train.
PF 43

DAVIDSON
Commander of X Battalion, the Halberdiers. Tells Guy Crouchback to fall in, in the station yard at Brookwood.
MA 193

DAWKINS
Soldier-servant of General Ritchie-Hook; with him from 1940–1944. His legs set alight during the aeroplane crash in Yugoslavia. Asks permission to remove flaming trousers. Legs swell with enormous blisters. Does not complain about tetanus

injections. Does not display sadness when informed by Guy about Ritchie-Hook's death. Is thankful that he was not with the General.
US 209, 212, 215, 223

DAWKINS, MISS
One of the staff stenographers with Sir James Macrae assigned to Simon Lent.
WS 71

DEANE, MRS JIMMY
London society hostess who is upset at not being asked to have John Beaver to dinner.
HD 45

DEATH
'A solemn thought', the warden of Egdon Heath tells Paul Pennyfeather.
• To Angela Lyne, death summons up images of dead Greeks by Flaxman; riddled corpses in no-man's land; sixteenth-century woodcuts and frock-coated undertakers.
• Dennis Barlow is afraid of Death but is told by the girl at Whispering Glades that it is best to talk openly about it.
DF 201; PF 29; LO 44

DEATH-WISH, THE
Ludovic finds Major Hound lacking in The Death-Wish.
• Almeric Griffiths tells Guy Crouchback that he has The Death-Wish.
OG 159; US 170
(See also BOOKS)

DEBATES
Sarum-Smith organizes a debate for the Halberdiers on the theme of 'Any man who marries under thirty is a fool', which develops into a 'series of testimonies'.
MA 206

DEBRA DOWA
Capital City of Azania. Two hundred miles inland of Matodi at the foot of the Ngumo Mountains. Has a cosmopolitan population and legations from Britain, France and the USA.
• Basil Seal arrives. Seth has plans to rebuild the city. Renames site of Anglican Cathedral 'Place Marie Stopes'. Has irregularly shaped houses and one main street which splits to the barracks one way and to the Christian quarter the other. There are ten places of worship and many side alleys. Set on fire by the army. The palace is enclosed by an irregular stockade and consists of a 'large stucco villa of French design'. There are various sheds around it serving as servants' quarters, stables and kitchens, a wooden guard house and a thatched barn used for state banquets. There is also a domed, courtyard chapel and the Princesses' residence. The courtyard is filled with kitchen refuse, derelict wagons, cannon and donkey carcasses. In the time of Amurath eucalyptus trees are planted.
BM 10, 14, 46, etc.

DEBRETT
Debrett's Peerage and Baronetage: comprehensive list of the noble families of the British Isles, first compiled by John Debrett (1752–1822).
• Sebastian, bored with Charles Ryder's enquiries about his family, tells him to look it up in Debrett's.
• Does not contain any information on Mrs Muspratt.
BR 41, 287

DEBUSSY, CLAUDE ***(1862–1918)***
French composer and exponent of 'Musical Impressionism'.
• According to Soapy (q.v.), the Debussy pizzicato played at Mountjoy has no feeling in it.
GP 181

DEBUTANTES
Not always as pure as they might seem, as Alastair Trumptington finds out to his relish, becoming absorbed in seeing how far he can go with 'various lewd debutantes'.
PF 35

DELACROIX, EUGENE ***(1798–1863)***
French Romantic painter renowned for using vivid colours and loose form in dramatic and violent historical subjects.

• The art teachers in Paris in the 1920s are still trying to make their students paint like Delacroix – so Charles Ryder tells Cordelia Flyte.
BR 147

DELHI, INDIA
Where one of Mrs Komstock's sons lives.
LO 74

DELUGE, THE
The great flood of the Old Testament.
• In Paul Pennyfeather's eyes, Captain Grimes has, 'like some Channel-swimmer', swum through the Deluge.
DF 199

DEMERARA
River which marks the start of Tony Last and Dr Messigners' expedition into Brazil in 1934. They stay there at a hotel.
HD 153, 168

DEMONIC POSSESION
Gilbert Pinfold wonders sometimes whether he is not posessed by the Devil.
GP 146

DEMOSTHENES ***(383–322 BC)***
Greatest Greek orator and Athenian politician. Led Athens against the Macedonians.
• At Oxford Jasper Ryder advised his cousin Charles to attend Arkwright's lectures on Demosthenes.
BR 28

DENTISTS
Nina Blount thinks that she would rather go to her dentist for pleasure any day, than have sex.
VB 90

DESERT, ANDREW
Sociable friend of Andrew Plant, invited by him to lunch with the Simmondses in 1938.
WS 154

DE SOUZA, FRANK ***(b. 1917)***
'A cynic' and Jewish. One of Guy Crouchback's intake into the Halberdiers in 1940: 'a dark, reserved, drily humourous, efficient man'. Has a 'sallow face'. Has a girl called Pat who lives in London.

In 'mufti' wears a brown suit, green shirt and orange tie. Goes straight from Cambridge into the Halberdiers. Meets Guy at the Café Royal. Inclined to classical allusions. Devises cruel techniques for baiting Apthorpe by saluting. Is one of Guy's Subalterns. Comes under heavy enemy fire on Crete. Is wounded in the head: 'lost a bit of my ear'.

Wins the MC. Thinks all army courses are like prep schools. Is confided in by Captain Fremantle (q.v.).

Admits to being changed by four years of war. Wonders whether Guy Crouchback and Ludovic are lovers. Wherever he goes he leaves people feeling anxious. Telephones 'Jumbo' and tells him of Guy's plight.

Promoted to Major. Lives in a cave in Bosnia.

Guy decides he has never really liked De Souza.
MA 44, 79–80, 178–179; OG 209, 211; US 9, 94–96, 111, 113, 193, 204–206, 225

DETECTIVES
Two detectives, Mr James and Mr Blenkinsop, accompany Tony Last and Molly to Brighton to witness his 'infidelity'.
HD 135

DEUS EX MACHINA
Basil Seal, appealing to the Great Crested Grebe to release him from his exile in Ishmaelia, remembers that even in antiquity there was 'a god from the machine'.
SC 166

DEVONSHIRE, DUKE OF
Is cut from the social pages of the *Daily Excess* in 1930.
VB 87

DIAGHILEV, SERGEI ***(1872–1929)***
Russian impressario and head of the eponymous ballet company founded in 1911, which acted as a catalyst for leading

composers, dancers and painters in the 1920s.
• For Ambrose Silk the 1910s are 'the days of Diaghilev'.
• Anthony Blanche is on close terms with Diaghilev in the 1920s and 1930s.
PF 43; BR 47

DIAMOND JUBILEE
The Diamond Jubilee of Queen Victoria takes place in 1898, at the time of the crisis between Billy Cornphillip and Ralph Bland.
WS 79

DIARIES
Guy Crouchback keeps a war diary which follows him, intact though battered, out of Crete. Disillusioned, he burns it, in Alexandria.
• Charles Ryder keeps a diary as a schoolboy at Lancing.
OG 238; WS 290

DICKENS, CHARLES ***(1812–1870)***
Pre-eminent British author of the Victorian era.
• Tony Last is compelled to pass his days reading Dickens to Mr Todd. According to Mr Todd, Dickens believed in God – 'it is apparent in all his books'.
• To Gilbert Pinfold, Dickens' ability to write so many words is professional trickery.
• The spirit of Dickens suffuses the painting of John Plant's father.
HD 209, 213; GP 10; WS 128

DIEPPE, FRANCE
Dan tells Tony Last he has tried to take Milly to Dieppe for a weekend.
• General Whale is partly responsible for the disasterous raid on Dieppe on 19 August 1942, in which the Canadians suffer heavy casualties.
HD 140; US 187

DIETS
Lord Monomark insists on two raw onions and a plate of oatmeal porridge for luncheon: 'I feel two hundred per cent better'.
• In 1933 Tony and Brenda Last are on a diet in which they cannot mix protein and starch. They have a printed catalogue.
VB 108, HD 24

DIGBY-SMITH
In charge of propaganda and subversive activity behind enemy lines, at the Ministry of Information.
PF67

DIGBY-VANE TRUMPINGTON, SIR ALASTAIR ***(Alastair [or Alistair] Trumpington) (1903–c.1941)***
At Scone with Paul Pennyfeather in 1922. Member of Bollinger Club. Hosts party; feels ill and is helped to bed and thus not directly involved in de-bagging Paul. Sends Paul £20 for damages.

Nephew of Lady Circumference. Attends Eton. Reads *Chums*. Lord Parakeet attends his twenty-first birthday party in London. Falls out of Parakeet's car. Chosen by Paul Pennyfeather as his best man. Borrows money from Paul for a new top hat. Helps arrange Paul's release from prison. Compared in this enterprise to Sir Bedivere. Becomes Margot Metroland's 'young-man' for one year when he is twenty-one.

Friend of Peter Pastmaster, with whom he attends a *Palais de Danse* in Reading. Carries out experiments into how far lewd debs will go.

Drinks port at Mickleham. In General Strike of May 1926, drives around East End breaking up meetings. Has schoolboy honour and habits in general. Enjoys winter sports, sailing, squash and golf. Member of Bratt's. Wears a bowler hat in London until week after Goodwood. Marries Sonia.

Is notoriously fashionable in 1929. Has a five-day party after a Conservative ball with Basil Seal and Peter Pastmaster in 1932.

Married by 1932 and lives in Montagu Square. Has two dogs – a bull terrier and a chow. Never pays his rent. Basil Seal dines with him and Sonia and plays Happy Families.

Moves house and is suddenly very poor;

with no servants. Goes to a cocktail clubs. Moves house once a year and in 1939 lives in Chester Street. Is unfaithful to Sonia for one week every year while taking part in Bratt's golf tournament at Le Touquet.

Uses an electric razor in 1939. Is shocked by advent of war in 1939. Joins army and becomes a fitter. Refuses commission; hates PT; wears tweeds when off-duty.

Sonia conceives his child in February 1940. Becomes mortar-man in Mr Smallwood's platoon. Posted to a seaside town in summer 1940. Volunteers for Commandos and accepts commission with Peter Pastmaster and Basil Seal.

Killed in the war.

DF 10–11, 42–43, 69, 129, 148, 203, 215; BM 77–70, 231; PF 35–8, 44–46, 105–109, 132–133, 213, 217; WS 251, 254, 278

DIGBY-VANE TRUMPINGTON, SONIA

Wife of Alastair Digby-Vane Trumpington (q.v.). Meets him at Peter Pastmaster's twenty-first birthday party. Married at St Margaret's, Westminster. At centre of fashionable society in 1929 but forgotten by 1939. Lives in Chester Street in 1939 and Montagu Street in 1932. Moves house once a year to avoid paying bills. Her bedroom is always the centre of the household. Has a dog – a chow – and photograph albums. Holds three to four levées every day.

As a deb she admits mixed company to her bathroom and bath. Drinks Black Velvet. Her bed is always surrounded by a confusion of letters, newspapers, bottles, parcels, flowers and dogs. She embroiders on silk. Visited by Basil Seal and Peter Pastmaster in 1940.

Friend of Margot Metroland. Does not re-marry after Alastair's death. Has no servants in 1962. Becomes involved in two charitable organizations. Visited by Basil Seal in 1962. One son – Robin – born in 1941.

PF 36–37; BM 78, 231; WS 265, 277

DIGBY VANE-TRUMPINGTON, ROBIN *(b.1941)*

Son of Alastair and Sonia. Basil Seal thinks his daughter is engaged to him. Is in love in 1962. Lives with his mother. Friend of Charles Allbright.

WS 273, 277

DINING CLUBS

Lord Brideshead is a member of a dining club which meets once a month. He is known as 'Brother Grandée' and wears a special jewel, and they all have club buttons. Charles Ryder is invited as Bridey's guest.

• The Bollinger Club (q.v.) at Oxford is responsible for Paul Pennyfeather's being sent down.

BR 268; DF

DIPLOMATS

Julia Flyte sees her prospective husband as being an English diplomat with ambitions for the Paris Embassy.

• Charles Ryder dines with the British Consul in Fez, 'a kind, serious man'.

• Sir Samson Courteney is the British Minister in Azania – 'A not altogether successful diplomat' (q.v.).

• M. Ballon is French minister in Azania (q.v.).

BR 176, 201; BM

(See ALGERNON STITCH AND TONY SEAL)

DISC JOCKEYS

An early version of a 'disc jockey' broadcasts music to the troops at Bari in 1944.

US 168

DISGUISE

Grimes disguises himself with a long red beard after his faked suicide.

• Paul Pennyfeather wears a heavy cavalry moustache during his second sojourn at Scone.

• Sebastian Flyte dines at the George in Oxford in false whiskers.

• Ambrose Silk escapes to Ireland disguised as an Irish priest.

• Simon Balcairn attends Margot's party wearing a false beard and medals, and is discovered.

DF 139, 210; BR 30 PF 195; VB 97

DIVORCE

There are six notable divorces in the novels:

1. Brenda divorces Tony Last on grounds of adultery to enable her to marry John Beaver;
2. Virginia Crouchback is divorced by Guy, enabling her to marry Tommy Blackhouse;
3. Rex Mottram, it is revealed, has been divorced from Sarah Cutler, and therefore cannot be married to Julia Flyte in the Catholic church;
4. Mrs Simpson is a divorcee, and thus cannot marry Edward VIII if he remains on the throne;
5. Charles Ryder divorces Celia so that he can be with Julia Flyte;
6. Julia Flyte divorces Rex Mottram.

• Brenda Last's brother Reggie attempts to negotiate a divorce settlement with Tony who refuses point-blank.

• Rex Mottram does not realize the importance of being divorced in the Catholic faith.

• Julia's Italian cousin Francesca has had an annulment.

• According to friends of Rex Mottram, nobody cares about divorce now (1938) 'except a few old maids who aren't married . . .'.

• To Boy Mulcaster, his sister Celia's divorce from Charles Ryder is by far the happiest he has ever seen. The details, he has always noticed, make enemies of the parties.

• Rex Mottram says to Charles that he has never known a divorce do anyone any good.

• Tommy Blackhouse, marrying a divorced woman (Virginia), is forced to resign from the Guards.

BR 188–9, 262, 281, 282–4; MA 80, 22; HD 128, 145–152

DOCTORS

A tipsy surgeon signs Paul Pennyfeather's death certificate in 1922.

• An English doctor in Corfu is a bore and pesters Margot Metroland.

• Virginia Crouchback has never had a doctor of her own – only a man in Newport who gives her sleeping pills and a man in Venice who patched her up after a fall.

• There is apparently a doctor in Monte Carlo who will give you a miracle cure.

• Kerstie Kilbannock has 'a man in Sloane Street'.

• Gilbert Pinfold's doctor is Dr Drake.

• Dr Mackenzie is a first-class doctor in the Cornish village visited by John Verney.

• Dr Beamish operates on Clara.

• Bella Fleace is badly treated by 'a tipsy sporting doctor'.

DF 192, 203; US 56; GP 173, 198; WS 80

DODO

Extinct species of bird.

• Mr Plant considers himself to be a Dodo and calls John 'a petrified egg'. He is portrayed by Max Beerbohm saying this.

WS 111

DOGE

Head waiter at Shepheard's Hotel (q.v.). Partially deaf and blind. Suffers from gout. One-time butler to the Rothschilds. Dandled the young Father Rothschild on his knee.

VB 37

DOGS

Lottie Crump has two Cairn terriers.

• Colonel Blount has an overweight liver-and-white spaniel.

• The matron at Agatha Runcible's nursing home has a 'very nasty' fox terrier called Spot.

• Sonia Trumpington has a chow.

• Alastair Trumpington has a bull terrier.

• Marjorie (Rex) and Allan have a colourless pekinese named Djinn: 'a very unrepaying dog'. He is always dragged along by his lead; he snaps at a child; gets lost and, to Marjorie, he does not have 'a spark of human feeling'.

• The wife of the Captain of the *Franc-maçon* has 'a tiny, hairless dog'.

• Priscilla Boot has a 'dirty old dog' named Annabel. Mr Salter has to have her to sleep in his room.

• Julia Flyte has a small pekinese which

she carries, almost buried, in her fur coat in 1923.

- Mr Crouchback has a smelly golden retriever named Felix.
- Ivor Claire has a white pekinese named Freda.
- The Gestapo have bloodhounds.
- Colonel Campbell has six dogs, including two deerhounds, a hairless pomeranian – Hercules – and Jason.
- Ludovic has a pekinese called Fido.
- Reginald Graves-Upton has a Cairn terrier.
- Fanny Graves has a spaniel (with worms).
- The 'golfer' in the next cabin to Gilbert Pinfold has 'an imaginary dog'.
- There is a plaster cast of a dead dog in Naples.
- Lady Amelia has a pekinese named Manchu.
- Millicent Blade has a poodle named Hector who causes her downfall.
- Frau Dressler has a three-legged dog.
- Lady Peabury has 'many Cairn terriers'.

WS 17, 23, 33, 34, 46; OG 23, 48, 145; US 107, 119, 121; GP 11, 12, 38; MA 33, 40; VB 36, 73, 185; BM 78; HD 38, 39; Sc 60, 203, 287; BR 117, 129

DOLBEAR AND GOODALL

Oxford chemists.

- Sebastian Flyte puts himself 'unreservedly in the hands of Dolbear and Goodall'.

BR 33

DOMOBRANS

Local home guard of Begoy.
US 206

DOTHEBOYS HALL

Fictitious school in *Nicholas Nickleby* by Charles Dickens.

- Trimmer compares it to Kut-al-Imara.
- De Souza compares it to No. 4 Special Training Centre.

MA 88; US 94

DOUBTING HALL, BUCKINGHAMSHIRE

Home of Colonel Blount (q.v.). Nearest station is Aylesbury. It could do with 'a lick of paint', according to the taxi driver. The taxi from the station costs fifteen bob.

In the local village every house seems to be a garage or a filling station.

You leave the main road and drive between twin octagonal lodges and heraldic gateposts with wrought-iron gates. A mile up the drive is a stone wall, then a rough track with sheep either side, stables, potting sheds, a huge kennel – where a bear was one kept – and finally the house.

It has a palladian façade and in front is an equestrian statue pointing down the drive.

Inside, a long corridor lined with marble busts on yellow marble pedestals leads to a room with a rococo fireplace furnished with a large leather-topped writing table under the window. In the library, there is a stuffed owl, some early British remains and the remains of Nina's collections – butterflies, beetles, fossils, eggs and stamps. The bookcases are filled with 'superbly unreadable books'. There is also a gun, an alpenstock and a butterfly net.

Before the fire is a heraldic firescreen. The chimney-piece is hung with the embroidered saddle cloths of Colonel Blount's regiment of lancers. There is also an engraving of the Royal Yacht squadron.

Featured in *A Brand from the Burning* (q.v.). During WWII becomes a hospital.
VB 64–70, 140–141

DOWAGERS

According to Agatha Runcible, the female customs officers at Dover who strip-search her are 'just like dowagers'.
VB 25

DOWNSIDE

Catholic public school near Midsomer Norton, in Somerset.

- Guy Crouchback is a pupil; in 1941 he is reminded of it by Turtle's being on fire.
- Gervase Crouchback goes straight from Downside into the Irish Guards.

OG 9; MA 17

DOWSON, ERNEST, CHRISTOPHER *(1876–1900)*
English poet and aesthete. Friend of Wilde and Beardsley. Originator of the saying 'if you ever come to read it, you will understand' – evoked by Dennis Barlow to explain his putative opus on Whispering Glades to Aimee Thanatogenos.
LO 111

DOYLES, THE
One of the familes merged with Bella Fleace's line on her family tree.
WS 79

DRAGE, JIMMY
Friend of Philbrick and old colleague of Toby Cruttwell.

Attempts to kidnap Lord Utteridge's son from Belgrave Square. Fails.

Has a motor bike. Has a bet with Philbrick resulting in the latter's employment at Llanabba.
DF 55–57

DRAKE, SIR FRANCIS *(1540–1596)*
English Admiral; victor over the Armada in 1588.
• In 1938 Rex Mottram's friends are proud to talk of themselves as being from 'the Land of Drake'.
BR 262

DRAKE, DR
Doctor to Gilbert Pinfold and local G.P. at Lychpole. A true countryman, he is lean and weather-beaten. His brother is the local auctioneer and his brother-in-law the local solicitor.
GP 17

DREADNOUGHT, MAJOR SIR ALEXANDER, BART, MP *(b.1890)*
Suitor of Millicent Blade and eventual cause of her disfigurement by Hector the poodle. It is impossible for Hector to upset Sir Alexander. Forty-five year old widower. Conspicuously gallant in WWI. Lives in the Midlands. Has an Aubusson carpet.

Gives Hector sugar lumps; is bitten by Hector and helps to wash him.
WS 41

DREAMS
On the trans-Atlantic crossing, Charles Ryder dreams of Julia Flyte in 'a hundred fantastic and terrible and obscene forms'.
• William Boot dreams, after his interview with Mr Salter, of Lord Copper 'in a hundred frightful forms'. He is chased by Copper down badger runs wearing the plumage of the great-crested grebe. In Ishmaelia he imagines that Bengal lancers and highlanders in kilts will come to his aid against Doctor Benito, and imagines himself throttling him.
• At school, Charles Ryder day-dreams of having his own private printing press.
BR 238; Sc 35, 155; WS 296

DRESS
• A.A. (Carmichael): Thirty ties.
• Abdul-Akbar, Jenny: A striped berber silk dressing gown; a hat with a veil.
• Albright, Charles: A pleated white silk shirt, flannels, green cummerbund, sandals (in 1963).
• Sir Ambrose Abercrombie: Summer – Dark grey flannels, Eton Rambler tie, boater with I Zingari ribbon. Winter – A deer stalker and Inverness cape.
• Art Master at the Ruskin School of Art: A dark blue shirt, lemon-yellow tie and horn-rimmed spectacles.
• Arthur Atwater: A raincoat and a soft grey hat.
• Baldwin, Mr: A three-piece suit, crêpe de chine shirt, snakeskin shoes.
• BBC Interviewers in 1953: Cord trousers, tweed jackets and horn-rimmed spectacles.
• Benito, Dr: A black suit.
• Berber Servants: White robes with red sashes.
• Peter Beste-Chetwynde: At Llanabba: a Charvet dressing gown.
• Blanche, Anthony: A chocolate-brown suit with white stripes, from Lesley and Roberts, suede shoes, a large bow tie and yellow wash-leather gloves.
• Blount, Nina: Hats from a shop in Hanover Square.
• Viscountess Boaz: A backless frock.
• The Bollinger Club: Bottle-green and white evening tails.

• Incorrect dress for an off-duty officer of the Bombardier Guards: Suede shoes.
• Boot, Theodore: To a banquet – old evening tails, black waistcoat, tall collar.
• Box-Bender, Arthur: To a funeral – black tie, subfusc suit and a bowler hat.
• Brideshead, Lord: A bottle-green velvet smoking suit. The robes of the Knights of Malta.
• Brompton, Sir Ralph: A light, herring-bone tweed suit and black brogues.
• Burmese Young Men: On a cruise – blazers and pale fawn trousers.
• Circumference, Lady: Tweeds and a Tyrolean hat.
• Clarence, Duke of: A greatcoat.
• Connolly, General: Shorts, an open shirt and a white topee.
• Copper, Lord: Coronation robes.
• Corker: Striped flannel suits fitting well at the waist and wrists, braces and double-breasted waistcoats.
• Court Ladies in Azania: Green and violet frocks trimmed with sequins and ostrich feathers.
• Crouchback, Hermione: A yachting cap and shawl.
• Crouchback, Guy: Off-duty in 1940 – flannels and a leather-patched tweed jacket. In hospital in 1943 – flannel pyjamas.
• Countrymen: A dark suit on Sundays.
• Coney: Espadrilles and long hair.
• Courteney: A pillar-box red beret.
• Curtis-Dunne: At Lancing in 1919 – soft black house shoes.
• Dan: A fur coat, beret, tartan stockings, black and white shoes, purple tweed plus fours, a patterned-silk shirt and a midnight blue dinner jacket.
• Daytrippers to the country: Flannels on Sundays.
• The daughter of a Dean: Flowered muslin.
• Drunken Major, The: A bowler hat and a Burberry overcoat.
• Everyman, Lady: A fur coat.
• Fagan, Dr: A pale-grey morning coat (at the sports). A velvet dinner-jacket (at home in the evenings).
• Fagan, Flossie: A knitted woollen frock 'the colour of indelible ink on blotting paper', with green and pink flowers.
• Fremlin, Mrs: Fur gloves and high rubber boots.
• The French Press in Africa: Breeches, open shirts, chocolate-brown riding boots and Spahi capes.
• Excelsior Movie-Sound Newsmen: Silk shirts and horsehair capes.
• Fe, Dr Arturo: A white waistcoat with onyx buttons; a gardenia.
• Fleace, Bella: A crimson satin evening gown, white gloves and satin shoes.
• Flyte, Julia: A light coat, flowered silk shirt, charm bangle, gold earrings and furs; a green hat with a diamond arrow, and a fur coat; a tight gold tunic dress and a white gown. An emerald ring; when dining alone – a gold silk Chinese robe embroidered with dragons.
• Flyte, Sebastian: A dove-grey flannel suit, white crêpe de chine shirt, Charvet tie with a pattern of postage stamps. When hunting – red coat or a tweed jacket, hat and gloves.
• The girl at Grantley Green: A tweed suit, woollen jumper, and soft, fur-lined boots.
• Grimes, Captain: A stiff celluloid evening collar and prison clothes.
• Grant-Menzies, Jack: A rat-catcher coat (hunting at Hetton).
• Graves, Mr: Lovat tweed and an old Rugbeian tie.
• Girls on a cruise ship: Trousers, duffle coats, tweed skirts and sweaters.
• Hacket, Ben: A handkerchief round his neck; later a stock with a fox-head pin; a Sunday suit.
• Harkness, Mr: In England – home-spun knickerbockers, a silk cravat with a cameo ring. In India – white ducks.
• Harkness, Mrs: Hand-woven woollen dresses.
• The Harkness's maid: An apple-green dress, muslin apron and Dutch hat.
• Homosexuals in the New Britain: Colourful clothes.
• Hornbeam, Mr: Home-spuns.
• The Ishmaelite Consul-General in London: Communists – A violet shirt. Fascist – A white silk shirt, buckskin breeches and hunting boots.

• The Ishmaelite Foreign Minister: A Derby hat and a military cape.
• Indian Students at Oxford: White flannels, blazers and white turbans.
• Jews in Yugoslavia in 1944: Military greatcoats, balaclavas, and woollen gloves.
• Journalists in Ishmaelia: Sombreros, dungarees, jodphurs, bullet-proof waistcoats, and Newmarket boots.
• Kilbannock, Kerstie, in 1944: A coat and a skirt made from her husband's evening clothes. Virginia Crouchback's cast-offs.
• Last, Brenda: Pyjamas at dinner at home with Tony.
• Last, Tony, On Sundays – A dark suit and stiff white collar. A lemon carnation buttonhole with crimson edges: a greatcoat; a dry shirt and flannel trousers (evening in the jungle); cotton gloves, hats with muslin veils (Brazil).
• Lift attendants at Copper House: Caucasian uniform.
• Loved ones: A dark suit or a fake suit in a one-piece 'dickey'.
• Macrae, Sir James: Ginger plus fours.
• Lyne, Angela: Only the highest fashion. Arrow earrings designed by herself, with an emerald shaft and a ruby point.
• Man in a train at Berkhamstead: A bright brown suit.
• Marchmain, Lord: In England in winter – a greatcoat, white muffler, cloth cap, grey wollen gloves and a leather jerkin.
• Lord Marchmain's Venetian Gondoliers: Green and white livery with a silver shield.
• Lord Marchmain's Venetian Footmen: Striped livery.
• Messinger, Doctor: Dry shirt and flannel trousers (evening in the jungle). Cotton gloves and a hat with a muslin veil.
• Metroland, Lord: A coat with an astrakhan collar.
• Metroland, Margot: A Boulanger wedding dress; lizard-skin shoes; silk stockings; chincilla coat; a tight little black hat, pinned with platinum and diamonds.
• Milly: A backless vermilion evening frock, high red shoes and a bracelet.
• Mottram, Rex: A check Ulster; a fur-lined overcoat with astrakhan lapels; a silk top hat in the evening.
• Motor Racing fans: Bright jumpers, belted trousers, old school ties, checked tweeds.
• Mouse, Miss: an 'enterprising' frock by Cheruit.
• Neutralian Aristocrats: Dark suits, stiff collars, black ties, and black, buttoning boots.
• The State Trumpeters of Neutralia: Medieval tabards.
• Ngumo, the Earl of: A lion's mane busby, fur mantle, red satin skirt, brass bangles and a lions' teeth necklace.
• Officials of Debra Dowa in time of bereavement: Blue cotton cloaks.
• Pennyfeather, Paul: Brown shoes, fancy socks, black silk sock suspenders. A morning coat and silk top hat, with a gardenia in his buttonhole. A prison suit; a dressing gown and cuff links.
• Pie Wie Indians: Red cotton loin cloths (men). Grubby calico dresses (women).
• Philbrick: A suit of mustard-coloured plus fours; a prison suit.
• Pigge: A mackintosh.
• Pinfold, Gilbert: Soft, fur-lined boots; a Brigade tie, tweed suit and matching cap; ten pairs of shoes; three pale pink buff suits made for him in Colombo.
• Plant, John: Eleven hats – tall silk, hunting topper, bowler, panama, black, brown and grey soft, a green hat from Salzburg, a sombrero, a tweed cap for onboard ships and trains. Four overcoats.
• Plant, Mr: Poncho capes, checked suits, sombrero hats, stock ties.
• Plastic, Miles: Drab serge clothes; a hat.
• Politicians of the New Britain: Open flannel shirts, blazers, baggy trousers.
• Potts, Arthur: An Ulster.
• Prendergast, Mr: A faded, striped blazer; prison clothes.
• Rattery, Mrs: Leather flying helmet, overalls (flying); tall hat and cutaway coat (hunting).
• Reppington, Mrs: Black lace evening dress
• Reppington, Mr: White mess-jackets.
• Riley: Knee breeches and black-silk stockings.

- Ritchie-Hook, General: In Yugoslavia – shorts and a bush shirt.
- Ryder, Charles: At Lancing in 1919 – heliotrope silk socks with white clocks. At Oxford – 'An unhappy compromise between the correct wear for a theatrical party at Maidenhead and a glee-singing competition in a garden-suburb'; – Silk shirts, Charvet ties (one with a design of postage stamps), and a gardenia. In later life: a greatcoat.
- Ryder, Jasper: Always a suit from a London tailor, plus fours, a Leander tie.
- Ryder, Mr: A tall hat on Sundays. When dining at home – A frogged-velvet smoking jacket. On formal occasions – A tail coat, black waistcoat, high collar and white ties. As a young man – salt and pepper knickerbockers and a panama hat.
- Runcible, Agatha: Trousers (to the motor-races).
- Salter, Mr: A bowler hat.
- Silenus, Otto: Batik ties.
- Shumble: A mackintosh.
- Stuart-Kerr: Black suede shoes and a bottle green bowler.
- Stayle, Lady Ursula: A 'puckered and puffed up' frock with old lace in improbable places.
- Seth: Spotted silk pyjamas from Charvet.
- Seal, Sir Christopher: Always a silk top hat and an orchid in his buttonhole
- Seal, Barbara: In 1963 – tight short trousers, slippers, a thin jersey; pyjamas and a fur coat; Stilettoes.
- Seal, Basil: A stiff white collar and bowler hat (to an interview). A topee (in Azania). Monogrammed underclothes ('B') (Ambrose Silk's). As an older man: A stiff evening shirt, black pearl studs and a buttonhole. A bowler hat. Suits from English tailors. Tie pins and cuff-links.
- Silk, Ambrose: In his Fascist phase – a brown shirt. A dark suit slightly too close at the waist. A plain cream silk shirt, dark-brown bow tie with white spots. A Charvet tie. Crêpe de chine pyjamas. Monogrammed underclothes ('A'). As Father Flanagan – a clerical collar, a black clerical vest with jet buttons.
- de Souza, Frank: A 'British Warm'; a brown suit, green silk shirt and orange tie.
- Spruce, Everard: Charvet shirts and pyjamas; voluminous suits; heavily striped silk shirts; bow ties; 'non commital' trousers. No jacket at home.
- Stitch, Julia: In Egypt – linen, Mexican sombrero, white leather shoes, crimson slippers with high, curled toes.
- Stitch, Algernon: Bowler hats.
- Simmonds, Lucy: A quilted bed-jacket.
- Simmonds, Roger: Dark shirts and light ties.
- Sveningen, Miss: An evening gown of chocolate-coloured silk, low black satin shoes, a tartan ribbon in her hair, a wide patent-leather belt and a handkerchief tied to her watch strap.
- Tendril, Miss: A mackintosh.
- Trimmer: A kilt.
- Trumpington, Alastair: A bowler hat in London until the week after Goodwood.
- Undergraduates at Oxford in the 1920s: Tweeds; broad trousers and high-necked jumpers.
- De Vitre, Mr: A panama hat and smart silk clothes.
- Whelper: A mackintosh.
- Wisemen of Moshu: Leopard's feet, snake skins, necklets of Lions' teeth, shrivelled bodies of toads and bats, masks of painted leather and wood.
- Young ladies at parties in the 1920s: Pyjamas.
- Young men in 1951: Hired evening clothes – soft shirts and dinner jackets.
- Yoshiwara, Baroness: A gold Paquin frock.

DRESSLER, FRAU

Proprietress of the German pension in Jacksonburg. Has lived her life in Africa and moved to Ishmaelia from Tanganyika in 1919, leaving Herr Dressler somewhere else.

Her pension is centre of the German population in Jacksonburg. Large and shabby and vociferous; William Boot meets her; calls the natives villains.
Sc 104, 110–112

DREYFUS, ALFRED *(1859–1935)*

Jewish Captain in French army, falsely accused of giving defence documents to a foreign power. Court-martialled and transported. Provoked wave of anti-semitism in France. Re-tried and pardoned in 1906.

• To Mr Plant, Dreyfus was always guilty, until in the 1930s anti-semitism became popular.

WS 113

DRINKS – *Alcoholic*

Alcoholic drinks are listed in alphabetical order, followed by their most prominent consumers.

• Absinthe: William Boot, Katchen, Erik Olafsen, Mr Baldwin.

• Absinthe *Frappé*: Margot Metroland.

• Absinthe and Vodka Cocktail: Peter Pastmaster.

• Brandy Alexander: Anthony Blanche (at the George).

• Brandy and Crème de Menthe: Gilbert Pinfold.

• Brandy and ginger ale: John Beaver.

• Home-made brandy: Mr Youkoumnian.

• Brandy and soda: Peter Pastmaster.

• Beer (pints of bitter): Corker (Bass, Worthington), Sebastian Flyte and Charles Ryder in a pub on the way to Brideshead; (in tankards): the officers in Charles Ryder's mess before dinner, the Halberdiers' officers at lunch; Ludovic at a society wedding in 1931.

• Black Velvet: Sonia and Alastair Trumpington (in a deep jug).

• Bottled Beer: Gilbert Pinfold in Colombo.

• Calvados and Vodka Cocktail: Angela Lyne (in private).

• Cassiri (fermented Cassava – thick and purplish): Dr Messinger and Tony Last with the Pie Wies in South America.

• Champagne Cocktails: Charles Ryder and Sebastian Flyte at Harry's Bar in Venice.

• Chartreuse (Green): Anthony Blanche and Charles Ryder at Thame, ('there are five distinct tastes as it trickles over the tongue. It is like swallowing a sp-spectrum...').

• Cider (*Zider*): Bernard Boot, and, in Mr Salter's mind, every countryman.

• Claret Cup: Ladies at Oxford during Eights Week.

• Mulled Claret: Sebastian Flyte and his friends at Oxford.

• Cognac: Rex Mottram and Charles Ryder, at Paillards; the guests at Lord Copper's banquet, Agatha Runcible, Tony Last and Jock Grant-Menzies at the Old Hundreth, Sebastian Flyte when ill in Morocco, Basil Seal on a health farm in 1962, John Beaver at Espinoza's.

• Cointreau: Sebastian Flyte, Charles Ryder and Anthony Blanche at Oxford.

• Crème de Menthe: Gilbert Pinfold to disguise his sleeping draught.

• Dubonnet: one of the drinks on the advertising hordings in Morocco seen by John Plant in 1938.

• Egg with port and brandy: Basil Seal, in the morning, at his club.

• Gin: Charles Ryder (regularly has three glasses before dinner in the mess in 1943), the Colonel of Charles Ryder's regiment.

• Gin and bitters (Pink Gin): Major Tickeridge, in the evening, Virginia and Guy Crouchback in 1943, Guy Crouchback and the major in Bari, Captain Bosanquet at lunch, the Halberdier officers to celebrate Apthorpe's promotion.

• Gin and vermouth: Charles Ryder on the train to Brideshead in 1923, Sebastian Flyte at the height of his drunkenness at Brideshead, Charles Ryder and Julia Flyte on the Train to Brideshead in 1936, Guy Crouchback and Apthorpe before dinner at Kut al Imara.

• Greek Absinthe: Sebastian Flyte in North Africa.

• Irish Whiskey: Adam Fenwick-Symes.

• Jim's Specials: Arthur Atwater and John Plant at the Wimpole Club (strong and agreeable).

• Kummel: the officers' mess of Cedric Lyne's regiment, Ivor Claire and the officers' mess of X Commando; one of the members of the Royal Household of Azania drinks too much of Sir Samson Courteney's Kummel.

• Lager: Simon Balcairn and Adam

Fenwick-Symes at luncheon at Espinoza's; Alastair and Sonia Trumpington and Basil Seal at a cocktail club in 1932.

• Liqueurs: Sebastian Flyte and Charles Ryder at Oxford.

• Mastik and water: Mr Youkoumian.

• Mead: the Earl of Ngumo, for breakfast.

• Peach Brandy: William Bland and the Legation (in cocktails).

• Pernod and water: Basil Seal.

• Pivari: Tony Last and Mr Todd in South America.

• 'Progress Port': New Britons, one month of the year.

• Port: Mr Sniggs and Mr Postlethwaite; Tony Last and Jock Grant-Menzies at Bratt's; 'Bill'; Sebastian Flyte and Charles Ryder at Brideshead; Guy Crouchback and his father after dinner at Matchet; Mrs Jellaby; Tamplin, aged sixteen at the Berkeley; William Boot and Jack Bannister; Mr Crouchback at the auction at Broome; Mr Salter and William Boot at a grill-room in the Strand.

• Rum: Basil Seal ('better for you than whisky'), Guy Crouchback, after a freezing cold military exercise.

• Slivovic: The Yugoslav partisans and Guy Crouchback.

• Sherry (Brown): Paul Pennyfeather at Egdon Heath.

• Sherry: Bill; The Halberdiers' women before Sunday luncheon; Reginald Graves-Upton, with the Pinfolds on Sunday morning; William Boot and Jack Bannister; Guy Crouchback and Mr Goodall.

• South African Sherry and Old Falstaffe Gin: a party at Everard Spruce's in 1943.

• South African Sherry: the Box-Benders in 1940.

• South African Brandy (called *Kommando*): Eddie and Bertie in Cape Town.

• Spirits: at Brideshead in individual decanters.

• Stout: Virginia Crouchback (with oysters at Overton's); Basil Seal (with oysters, at his London hotel).

• Toddy: Basil Seal and the chiefs in Azania.

Wine

• Barolo: Guy Crouchback and Apthorpe at the Garibaldi.

• Burgundy: Basil Seal (a bottle on his own in a restaurant); Anthony Blanche and Charles Ryder at the Spread-Eagle at Thame; Mr Crouchback (a pint at luncheon); Guy Crouchback and his father at dinner at Matchet; William Boot and Jack Bannister; Rex Mottram and Charles Ryder.

• Champagne: The Bollinger Club at Oxford; Philbrick; Paul Pennyfeather; Mr Prendergast and Grimes at the Hotel Metropole; Margot Metroland (Mumm); Peter Pastmaster; Lady Throbbing and Mrs Blackwater ('pop'); everyone at Lottie Crump's; the Lasts and John Beaver at Hetton (from a tall decanter); William Boot and Katchen; Charles Ryder in the afternoon at Oxford; Sebastian Flyte and Charles Ryder at Brideshead; Julia Flyte onboard ship; Guy Crouchback and Tommy Blackhouse at the Union Bar, Alexandria; Gilbert Pinfold, in bed, at his London hotel; Basil Seal in 1963; Charles Albright in 1913 (Veuve Cliquot Rosé); Brenda Last and John Beaver at Espinozas.

• Château Peyraguey: Sebastian Flyte and Charles Ryder, on the way to Brideshead ('heaven with strawberries').

• 'Cheap, fizzy wine': Arthur Box-Bender's guests at his daughter's dance in 1951.

• Claret: 'Bill'; Mr Baldwin, who has a small vineyard in the Bordeaux; the ladies at Boot Magna; William Boot; Barnard Boot; Sebastian Flyte and Charles Ryder at Brideshead; Guy Crouchback; the Halberdiers' officers on someone's birthday.

• Clos de Bleze, 1904 (Burgundy): Charles Ryder and Rex Mottram at dinner at Paillards in 1926; '. . . a reminder that the world was an older and better place than Rex knew'; Charles Ryder at lunch with his wine merchant in St James's Street in Autumn 1940.

• Hard, blue-red wine: William Boot on board the *Francmaçon*

• Hock: 'Bill'; Miss Sveningen; Anthony

Blanche and Charles Ryder at the Spread Eagle in Thame.
• Home-made Champagne: Mr Popotakis' clients.
• Montrachet, 1906: Charles Ryder and Rex Mottram at Paillards in 1926.
• Neutralian champagne: the Bellorius Conference.
• North African wine: De Souza and Captain Freemantle in England in 1943.
• Orvieto: Charles Ryder and Sebastian Flyte on the train to Venice.
• Veuve Cliquot Rose: Basil Seal in 1963, Charles Albright.
• Vino Scetto: Guy Crouchback and his guests at Santa Dulcina.
• Vouvray: an English boy, met by Tony Last in Tours at age eighteen.
• Whisky: Basil Seal; Angela Lyne (in secret); William Boot; Sebastian Flyte (in secret); Sir James Macrae; young people in 1963; John Verney, Mrs. Rattery, Grimes, when told to shoot himself; Gilmour, Ginger, Adam Symes, Nina Blount and Agatha Runcible.
• Whisky and Soda: Corker ('Edward VIII' made by Andre Bloc, Saigon); Guy Crouchback at sundown in hospital in Alexandria; Mr Hargood-Hood.
• Whisky and ginger ale: Tony Last.
• Whisky and water: Theodore Boot; Colonel Campbell (with water in a little china jug); Charles Ryder onboard ship (with two jugs of water – one boiling, one iced).
• Home-made whisky: Mr Popotakis' clients.

Soft
• Coca-cola: American soldiers in Italy in 1943.
• Cocoa: 'Senior' undergraduates in the evening at Oxford in the 1920s; requested by Tony Box-Bender in a POW camp; Sir James Macrae.
• Coffee: black with strychnine, Charles Ryder and other university students before exams; 'Senior' undergraduates at the Cadena Café at Oxford in the 1920s; Julia Stitch and Guy Crouchback in Alexandria in 1941. Pre-sweetened with saccharine, the mourners at Mr Crouchback's funeral in 1943.
• Lemon squash: Thérèsse de Vitre; Basil Seal on the way to Azania.
• Milk: Mr and Mrs Hornbeam.
• Orange juice: Simon Lent; Julia Stitch and Guy Crouchback in Alexandria in 1941.
• Ovaltine: Mr Salter.
• Tea: (strong) the army, all the time; (mint) John Plant and Fatima in Fez in 1938, 'a noisome beverage'; (Lapsang Suchong) Sir Ralph Brompton.
• Turnip juice: Basil Seal, at a health farm.

Waters
• Evian: Dame Mildred Porch and Miss Tin.
• Malvern: Mr Youkoumian's guests (supposedly).
• St Galmiets: Mr Youkoumian's guests (supposedly).
• Vichy: Angela Lyne; Lady Seal; Anthony Blanche.
• Vittel: M. Ballon.
• Water from a foetid well: Mr Youkoumian's guests.
DF 127, 133, 139, 192; VB 41, 42, 181; PF 24, 37, 38, 119, 120, 125, 160, 167; BM 18, 61, 64, 70, 78, 86, 88, 193; HD 11, 29, 66, 156, 164, 173, 215; Sc 28, 29, 55, 59, 62, 63, 128, 142, 173, 174, 206, 216; BR 11, 23, 25, 31, 34, 44, 46, 48, 52, 53, 57, 72, 75, 76, 81, 92, 108, 126, 127, 150, 166, 168, 171, 202, 206, 207, 226, 241, 261, 289; MA 15, 28, 39, 40, 54, 63, 103, 109, 112, 149; OG 49, 67, 97, 113, 133, 163, 221; US 33, 35, 41, 111, 132, 135, 157, 174, 228, 238; GP 12, 23, 29, 146, 207; WS 56, 66, 109, 122, 175, 185, 186, 213, 238, 260, 261, 264, 269, 271, 293; VB 16; BM 177; WS 121; HO 156

DRUGS
Margot Metroland takes Veronal to make her sleep.
• Mr Outrage and Lord Throbbing take unspecified drugs in bottles (probably Chloral).
• A general merchant in Debra Dowa ships hashish from Alexandria via Azania.

• Brenda Last, Polly Cockpurse and Mrs Beaver take Sedobral to sleep.
• Mrs Rattery has bouts of taking morphine.
• Mr Baldwin takes two types of pills – 'one round and white, the other elliptical and black', and a murky liquid. He also takes crimson cachets.
• There is a hemp plant at the Pension Dressler.
• Sebastian Flyte puts himself 'in the hands of Dolbear and Goodall' (chemists).
• Angela Lyne takes barbiturates to make her sleep.
• For Anthony Blanche there are a great many more 'delicious' ways of becoming intoxicated than drinking.
• Aimee Thanatogenos commits suicide with a brown tube of barbiturates, 'which is the staple of feminine repose'.
• Gilbert Pinfold feels at one with hashish-eaters when he makes a parachute jump during the war. He also takes a draught of chloral and bromide to enable him to sleep.

This mixture tends to make sentences run together in his head. He later takes the ingredients in crème de menthe. This makes him flushed and causes his memory to fail and eventually gives him hallucinations (q.v.).
• Morphia often has the effect of causing fornication, as in Eddie's case. Ivor Claire's aunt takes it.
• Elizabeth Verney takes '*Comprimes narcotiques, hypnotiques*', and gives them to John Verney, in the preliminary stage of his murder.
• Andrew Plant takes Dial as a sleeping draught in Fez. He supposes that having children is a habit 'like hashish'.
• Beecham's Pills for indigestion are advertised in the 1920s.
• Lord Marchmain takes pills from a little blue bottle.
• Tony Box-Bender writes home from POW camp to ask for 'Glucose D'.
DF 127; VB 12; BM 100; HD 82, 97, 161; Sc 55, 57, 99; BR 33, 54, 196, 300; LO 115: GP 17, 22, 142, 168, 173; WS 108, 189; PF 151; OG 50

DRUNKENNESS
Paul Pennyfeather reads a paper on the subject to the Thomas More Society.
• The Bollinger Club become drunk and break-up rooms in Scone College.
• Captain Grimes becomes drunk in France and fails to shoot himself when threatened with a court-martial.
• Mr Prendergast becomes drunk at the Llanabba sports day.
• Grimes is drunk at his first wedding in Ireland.
• The surgeon who signs Paul Pennyfeather's letter of release is kept drunk all day by Dr Fagan and Alastair Trumpington.
• Judge Skimp becomes very drunk at Lottie Crump's.
• According to Archie Schwert everyone is 'tight as houses' on the motor-racing course. He and Adam Fenwick-Symes become very drunk. The second stage of their drunkenness is that described in 'temperance handbooks' when feeling good becomes melancholy.
• The journalists in Azania get drunk on Popotakisis' home-made whisky, break his furniture, insult his servants, and pour champagne all over the bar.
• Basil Seal gets drunk frequently with Angela Lyne while she remains perfectly sober.
• Angela Lyne is 'stinko paralytico' and makes a scene at a cinema in Jermyn Street.

The Sakuyu warriors become drunk and re-enact their acts of valour.
• General Connolly becomes drunk and instructs Black Bitch to turn away Lady Courteney.
• Tony Last gets drunk with Jock Grant-Menzies at Bratt's in an attempt to dispel his depression: 'The best thing is to get tight'. They ring up Brenda.
• The Indians of the village near to which Dr Messinger and Tony Last pitch their camp get drunk and do not recover for a week.
• Sebastian Flyte drinks an unwise mixture and becomes so drunk that he is sick in Charles Ryder's rooms.
• According to Jasper Ryder's sources,

Charles is frequently seen drunk in the afternoon at Oxford.
• Lord Brideshead tries to get drunk when at Oxford but does not enjoy it.
• Lord Marchmain is almost a drunkard. According to Cara, it is in the Flyte blood.
• Charles Ryder, Sebastian Flyte and Boy Mulcaster get very drunk at the Old Hundredth, crash their car and are arrested.
• Julia Flyte says that she has only ever been drunk once, and then she could not move the next day.
• When drunk, Sebastian mocks Mr Samgrass in rhyme. He drinks to escape. Charles Ryder gets drunk often in an effort to 'prolong and enhance' the moment.
• Sebastian Flyte becomes hopelessly drunk at Brideshead having drunk whisky in his room during the afternoon.
• According to Lady Marchmain one of the worst things about drunkards is their deceit.
• The effect of drink on Sebastian is to cloud his eyes and thicken his voice. In the old days, according to Sebastian, the gentlemen were always too drunk to join the ladies.
• For Anthony Blanche there are 'so many much more delicious things' to do if you want to be intoxicated.
• Apthorpe becomes drunk and attempts to salute Guy Crouchback. They become drunk together at the Garibaldi (q.v.).
• An eighteen-year-old English boy met by Tony Last gets drunk for the first time on sparkling Vouvray in Tours.
• Sebastian Flyte and Charles Ryder get drunk every night on his first visit to Brideshead.
HD 66, 67, 69, 176; BR 31, 44, 82, 88, 100, 117, 124, 126, 128, 132, 138, 161, 162, 196; DF 29, 72, 101, 203; VB 42, 74, 177; PF 153–56; BM 36, 52; MA 177

DUBLIN, IRELAND
Ambrose Silk flees to Ireland, disguised as Father Flanagan of Dublin University.
• Four-and-a-half hours from Ballingar (q.v.).
• Bella Fleace sells her rare books to a bookseller from Dublin.
• On some days in a soft light, London seems like Dublin.
PF 195; WS 77, 81, 280

DUBROVNIK
Town in Yugoslavia to which Guy Crouchback is posted, in January 1945, as liaison officer with the partisans.
US 233

DUCANE, FLORENCE ***(Flossie)***
One of Lottie Crump's 'young ladies' who, having insisted on swinging from a chandelier at Shepheards, falls from it to her death. Cremated at Golder's Green.
VB 61, 76

DUELS
Ivor Claire asks Guy Crouchback what he would do if challenged to a duel. They conclude that democracy has put an end to duelling.
• Apthorpe challenges Dunn (q.v.) to a duel with heliographs.
DF 91; OG 220–21; MA 184
(See also PHILBRICK)

DUMBLETON, SIMON
Peer and friend of Mr Murdoch's business associates in Ghezira, as well as of Gilbert Pinfold.
• Goneril 'tells' Pinfold he is a snob to pretend to know him.
GP 143

DUNKIRK
Charles Ryder and Sebastian Flyte cross to Dunkirk on the way to Venice in 1923.
• At the same time as Guy and his company are billeted in Cornwall on 4 June 1940 the very ships in which they later embark are busy ferrying the BEF across from Dunkirk.
• Ivor Claire wins the MC at Dunkirk for shooting three territorials trying to swamp his boat. According to him there was 'no fuss about priorities there'.
BR 92; MA 203; OG 53, 220

DUNN
Young Signals Officer attached to the Halberdiers. Has a feud with Apthorpe. A shy man. Disliked by all.
MA 181–184, 207

'DUNS'
Colloquism for debt collectors or bailiffs. Basil Seal avoids them assidiously as do Alastair and Sonia Trumpington.
Bm 77–78

DUNZ, SCAB
Antifacist American journalist reporting on the war from London in 1941.
OG 212

DURBAN, SOUTH AFRICA
Where Dame Mildred Porch stays before visiting Azania in 1932.
BM 156

DUTCH, THE
The Superior of the monastery in Tunis, to which Sebastian Flyte goes for help, is a Dutchman from the Central African colonies.
• A battery of Dutch gunners, evacuated from Dunkirk, are still aboard the ships which the Halberdiers board for a few days at Cornwall in June 1940.
BR 290; MA 203, 207

E

EARTHQUAKES
When an earthquake hits a modern city: 'the pavements gape, the revers buckle up and the great buildings tremble and topple, men in bowler hats and natty, ready-made suitings, born of generations of literates and rationalists, will suddenly revert to the magic of the forest and cross their fingers.
PF 15

EAST FINCHLEY
Northern suburb of London and the location of Lord Copper's 'frightful mansion'.
SC 14

EASTER
There is always an Easter party at Brideshead, beginning on the Tuesday of Easter week. In 1923 it is the time of Sebastian's worst drunkenness.
BR 125

EASTER EGGS
Tony Last pictures Mrs Rattery or being a chorus girl clad 'in silk shorts and brassiere, popping out of an immense beribboned Easter egg with a cry of "Whoopee boys".'
HD 98

EASTON
Contemporary of Charles Ryder, at Lancing.
WS 290

EBONITES
A suppressed Christian sect.
• Paul Pennyfeather learns at Scone that the Ebonites used to turn towards Jerusalem when they prayed; he thinks the church quite right to have suppressed them.
DF 216

ECCENTRICS
Adam Fenwick-Symes, writing as Mr Chatterbox, runs for a week a series called *Titled Eccentrics*. Herein he includes an earl who wears Napoleonic costume; a lord who claims to have composed the Ten Commandments; and a Lady who imitates animal noises in conversation.
• When Gilbert Pinfold first joins Bellamy's (q.v.), an old Earl talks to himself all day in the hall.
VB 112; G 105

ECONOMICS
Brenda Last tells Tony that she is studying economics when she is, in fact, having an affair with John Beaver.
HD 80, 95

ECTOGENESIS
One of the sciences which fascinates Seth for a day. He is most impressed: 'Get me some of those bottles . . . and no boggling'.
BM 150

EDDIE
Officer in X Commando who tries to get Sir Angus Anstruther-Kerr's room on Mugg. Meets Guy Crouchback. Goes to the zoo in Cape Town with Bertie. Buys Kommando brandy. Gets into the ostrich cage.
OG 50, 108, 114

EDINBURGH
Katie Campbell lives in Edinburgh before coming to Mugg. According to her, Edinburgh is the heart of Scotland, although seething. Guy Crouchback thinks it 'a magnificent city'.
• Peter Ellis teaches Egyptology at the University.
OG 61, 65

EDITH
One of the maids at Malfry who decides to help with the war efforts by making aeroplanes at Brakemore's.
PF 11

EDMONTON, CANADA
Where Grimes' uncle had a brush factory.
DF 28

EDWARD – THE CONFESSOR *(1003–1066)*
Last Anglo-Saxon King, son of Ethelred the Unready. Canonized in 1161.
• By the shrine of St Edward in Westminster Abbey, the Sword of Stalingrad goes on display to the British public in October 1943.
US 23

EDWARD II, KING *(1284–1327)*
Son of Edward I. Became King 1312. Murdered infamously, in Berkeley Castle. Dr. Fagan tells Paul Pennyfeather that Edward had 'a perverse life . . . and an unseemly death'.

EDWARD, PRINCE OF WALES *(later King Edward VII) (1841–1910)*
Eldest son of Queen Victoria; became King 1902.
• Lady Circumference sighs for the 1890s and the Prince of Wales, condemning ostentatious second marriages.
• One of the suites at Hetton (Lyonesse) was fitted with satinwood in expectation that Edward VII, when Prince of Wales, would come for a shooting party.
DF 149, HD 88

EDWARD VIII, KING *(1894–1972)*
Eldest son of King George V. Ascended the throne in 1936. Abdicated that December to marry the divorced commoner Mrs Ernest Simpson. Given the title Duke of Windsor.
• Wenlock Jakes writes of the day of the King's abdication (11 December 1936) when he was dining at the Savoy Grill.
SC 80

EFFIE
One of the prostitutes at the old Hundredth. Picked up by Boy Mulcaster.
BR 109–112

EGBERTSON
Boy with whom Lady Moping hopes that Angela is not in love.
WS 13

EGDON HEATH
Penal settlement to which Paul Pennyfeather is sent. Has granite walls, is built beside quarries where the convicts undertake hard labour. Chapel has two coloured glass windows depicting St Peter and St Paul in prison. Potts gives a lecture here.
DF 185

EGDON MIRE
Mire near Egdon Heath (q.v.) in whose depths it is presumed that Captain Grimes has perished during his escape attempt.
DF 198

EGYPT
In February 1941 X Commando are told to hold Egypt to protect the Suez Canal.
• The King of Egypt has given Julia Stitch a watch.
• Gilbert Pinfold was in Egypt (Cairo) in January 1929. His voices persecute him about this.
• According to the voices people will accept traveller's cheques in Egypt.
• The *SS Glory of Greece* puts in at Cairo.
• Bertie thinks Egyptians are very inartistic.
• Egyptian merchants try to interest Mr Metcalfe (q.v.) in shady business in Alexandria.
• Peter Ellis teaches Egyptology at Edinburgh University.
OG 65, 110, 232; GP 130, 138; WS 20, 56
(See also ALEXANDRIA, CAIRO, PYRAMIDS, SPHINX and individual towns)

EIGG
Hebridian island off the west coast of Scotland from which the island of Mugg has never been seen.
OG 47

EIGHTEEN 'B'
According to his voices, Gilbert Pinfold should have been interned under this law in 1940.
GP 103

EIGHTH ARMY
British army corps of WWII famous for its endeavours in the Western Desert and Italy under Montgomery (q.v.).
• According to Colonel Grace Groundling-Marchpole (q.v.) 'the Eighth Army is not security conscious'.
US 126

EIGHTS WEEK
Week at Oxford when traditional rowing competitions take place on the river. A major social event.
• In 1923 Charles Ryder's College (Hertford) institutes dancing and cause an outcry in the servants' hall.
BR 24

ELDERBURY
M.P. 'Rather gruesome' friend of Arthur Box-Bender. Plays billiards at Bellamy's. Treads on Air Marshal Beech in 1940.
• Joins Box-Bender and Guy at the bar of the club in 1941. Is 'all for' the Russians. In 1951 sits alone in the hall of Bellamy's reading Air Marshal Beech's reminiscences. Loses his seat in the election of 1951. Spends most of his days and evenings at Bellamy's.
OG 12, 246; US 238

ELDORET
Town in Kenya near where Guy Crouchback has his farm before his divorce from Virginia.
MA 83

ELECTRICAL INSTRUMENTS
In Gilbert Pinfold's mind Angel (q.v.) possesses an electrical instrument capable of showing Pinfold's state of consciousness.
GP 133

ELECTRONIC PERSONNEL SELECTOR
'Pet' of Mr Oates (q.v.) of HOOHQ in 1943. An American invention. Takes 560 hours to install. Designed to select the perfect person for a particular wartime task.
• Comes up with Guy Crouchback's name for service in Italy in 1943.
US 31

ELENA, GRAND DUCHESS
In 1902, as a young beauty, accepts the rank of Colonel-in-Chief of the Halberdiers. In 1940 she lives in a bed-sitting room in Nice.
MA 76

ELGIN
In whose place stood 'the immortal private of the Buffs' (q.v.).
WS 223

ELIOT, T.S. ***(1888–1965)***
American born, British poet and playwright. Highly regarded in the 1920s for *The Waste Land* (1922), in the 1930s for *Ash Wednesday* (1930) and in the 1940s for *Four Quartets* (1944).
• Anthony Blanche reads passages from *The Waste Land* through a megaphone from Sebastian Flyte's balcony at Oxford to the rowers below. One is from 'The Fire Sermon' (lines 228–248).
• Everard Spruce wonders whether Ludovic's *Pensées* were inspired by *The Waste Land* in his 'drowned sailor motif'.
BR 34, US 51

ELIZABETH I ***(1533–1603)***
Queen of England.
• According to Dennis Barlow, Queen Elizabeth told her Archbishop – 'Little man, little man, "must" is not a word to be used to Princes'.
LO 121

ELLIS, HENRY HAVELOCK ***(1859–1939)***
English writer on sex. See his *Psychology of Sex* (1897). Next to *The Wind in the Willows* this is Peter Pastmaster's favourite book at the age of sixteen.
DF 128

ELLIS, PETER
Teacher of Egyptology at Edinburgh University. Friend of Guy Crouchback. Inclined to 'seethe'.
OG 65

ELPHINSTONE, MRS
Housekeeper to Sir Ralph Brompton in Ebury Street, London SW1.
US 35

EMDEN, SIR JOSEPH
Architect employed in 1935 by Celia Ryder to convert the Ryders' barn into a studio for Charles.
BR 220–221

ENDING, MAJOR
People's Warden of Mr Prendergast's (q.v.) first living at Worthing.
DF 33

ENGLAND
According to Dennis Barlow, England is 'a dying world' where the use of quotation is a national vice. 'It used to be the classics, now it's lyric verse.'
• In England servants are a major preoccupation.
• For Miss Bombaum's friend, England has few attractions: 'The women are immodest and the food upsets his stomach'.
LO 109; WS 47, 241

ENGLISH COUNTY FAMILIES
When English county families 'bay for broken glass', those who have heard them before shrink at the recollection.
DF 10

ENGLISH GENTLEMEN
In the 1940s most English gentlemen, Guy Crouchback excluded, think that they are able to endear themselves to the lower classes.
• Guy's father believes that an Englishman 'is at his best with his back to the wall'.
MA 173, 202

ENGLISH LIFE AND CHARACTER
In the last decade of English grandeur, the 1930s, Englishmen finally become curious of their heritage and Charles Ryder finds himself a popular artist.
• To Celia Ryder, Charles *is* England.
• For Anthony Blanche Charles exudes 'simple creamy English charm' . . . 'the great English blight'.
• If English life was in reality as it is in books then Basil Seal would have been sent for in time of war.
• For Guy Crouchback, England is summed up in Ivor Claire.
• In the English countryside of the 1950s one's neighbours are typically a few rich farmers; a few businessmen who come home to hunt; a majority of elderly people.
• To Bessie MacDougal all the English seem to be like Tom Kent-Cumberland
• According to Mr Plant there are only three classes in England in the 1930s – 'politicians, tradesmen and slaves'.
PF 50; BR 215, 255, 260; OG 114; GP 11; WS 103, 111

ENO'S
Blend of sparkling fruit salts popular in the 1940s.
• Sir Joseph Mainwaring feels as if he has had some Eno's after attending Church one Sunday morning in autumn 1939.
• A line in a favourite song of William Bland's in 1932 runs 'start off with cocktails and end up with Eno's'.
BM 59; PF 21

ENVOY EXTRAORDINARY
(*See* COURTENEY, SIR SAMSON)

EPHESUS
Town in Asia Minor to which Mr Samgrass travels during his trip to the Near East with Sebastian Flyte.
BR 145

EPITAPHS
Basil Seal suggests to Colonel Plum that his epitaph might read 'He drank out of chivalry'.
PF 165

EPPING, ESSEX
Where Dame Mildred Porch had led the Girl Guides among the bracken.
BM 192

EQUIPMENT
In 1940 the officers of the Halberdiers have varying amounts of equipment: Guy Crouchback has a rubber mattress, a storm lantern and a canvas wash-basin.
• Apthorpe has a collapsible bed, a mosquito net of white muslin, an incandescent oil lamp, a collapsible table, chair and wash-stand, a 'curious structure like a gallows' on which to hang his clothes, and his 'thunder-box' (q.v.).
• Tony Last takes with him to South America an automatic shot-gun, camping kit, pack saddles, a cinema camera, dynamite, disinfectants, a collapsible canoe, filters, tinned butter and, for barter – musical boxes, mechanical mice, mirrors, combs, perfume, pills, fish hooks, rockets, and artificial milk.
• William Boot takes to Ishmaelia – a tent, a collapsible canoe, a jointed flagstaff and Union Jack, a hand pump and sterilizer, an astrolabe, six linen suits, a sou'wester, a camp operating table, surgical instruments, a humidor guaranteed to keep cigars in the Red Sea, a Christmas hamper, a Santa Claus costume, a tripod mistletoe stand, a cane, a coil of rope, a sheet of tin and, of course, some cleft sticks.
MA 163; HD 155; SC 44–45

ERCHMANN
Jewish doctor who treats Poppet Green.
PF 34

ERIKSON, MR
Immediate superior to Mr Baumbeim at Megalopitan Pictures Inc. Fires Sir Francis Hinsley.
LO 28

ERITREA, ETHIOPIA
Where Mr Youkoumian (q.v.) hopes to sell the rails from the Azanian Railway.
BM 233

ERNIE
One of Tony Last's fellow passengers on the ship to Brazil.
HD 62

EROTICISM
On the *SS Caliban*, Gilbert Pinfold imagines that he hears the Captain and Goneril torturing a prisoner with 'undisguised erotic enjoyment.'
GP 59

ERSKINE, MAJOR
Commander of D Company of Colonel Tickeridge's battalion of the Halberdiers. Renowned for his intelligence. However, this is something of a fallacy, prompted by his liking for J.B. Priestley. He looks somehow dishevelled and seems to 'change shape' from time to time during the day. More like a Sapper. Does not talk much. Gets on well with Guy Crouchback. Simple and frank. Moves Hayter (q.v.) to Air Liaison. Next meets Guy in Crete. Is appalled by the retreat on Crete. Promoted to command of 2nd Battallion in 1943.
MA 167, 171, 173; OG 208; US 95

ESPERANTO
Artificial universal language of Europe, invented c. 1887 by a Pole, Dr L.L. Zamenhof.
• Suggested by Seth as a compulsory language for Azanians.
BM 148

ESSAYS
Scott-King (q.v.) writes a 4000 word essay on Bellorius entitled 'The Last Latinist'.
WS 198

ESSEX
In 1943 the location of No.4 Special Training Centre under the command of Ludovic (q.v.), in a large villa.
US 84

ESSEX, ROBERT DEVEREUX,
2nd Earl of (1566–1601)
British nobleman and General. Served at Zutphen and at Cadiz (1596). Quarrelled

with Elizabeth I. Found guilty of high treason and executed in 1601.
• Raised the Earl of Essex's Honourable Company of Free Halberdiers.
MA 48
(See BRITISH ARMY)

ESTERHAZY, SOUKI de FOUCALD
Friend of Brenda Last. Has her fortune told by Mrs Northcote.
HD 116

ETHELRED THE UNREADY (II) *(968–1016)*
Anglo-Saxon King of England, son of King Edgar and father of Edward the Confessor (q.v.).
• Bernard Boot has traced his nephew William's (q.v.) descent from Ethelred the Unready.
SC 18

ETHERIDGE
Friend of Mr Plant (q.v.) whose 37-year-old barrister son still depends on him.
WS 112

ETHERIDGE, MAJOR
Neighbour of Lady Amelia, who is informed by the vicar that Major Etheridge has put water in the petrol tank of his motorcycle and given sixpence to each choirboy to sing out of tune.
WS 28

ETON COLLEGE
Public school near Windsor, Berkshire. Founded in 1440 by Henry VI.
• The tutor of the ex-King of Ruritania was a master at Eton.
• Ginger Littlejohn sings the Eton Boating Song when drunk.
• Sebastian Flyte, Ambrose Silk, Alastair Digby-Vane Trumpington, Boy Mulcaster, Anthony Blanche, Ned Marchmain, Gervase Kent-Cumberland are all old boys.
• An old Etonian at Sebastian Flyte's luncheon party sings 'Home they brought the warrior dead'.
• Lady Marchmain's Catholic friends criticize her for not having sent Sebastian to a Catholic public school.
• In Gilbert Pinfold's hallucinations Glover says that he maintains he went to Eton. Pinfold declares every respect for the school.
• Tom Kent-Cumberland is scared by the 'magnificant' old Etonians in his brother's rooms at Christchurch.
VB 41, 119; PF 43, 45; BR 31,33, 34,47, 118,133; GP 108, 109; WS 92, 93

ETRUSCANS
Ancient non-Italian race in northern Italy in the seventh century BC.
• Charles Ryder's father talks to the warden of Hertford College about Etruscan ideas of immortality, at the Athenaeum (q.v.) and buys an Etruscan bull from Sonerscheins.
BR 26, 70

EUROPE
To the Americans of Whispering Glades, Europe is 'a treasure house of art' (to be plundered).
LO 64

'EUSTACE'
At twenty-one Julia Flyte's make-believe perfect prospective husband.

Aged thirty-two to thirty-three, handsome diplomat. Lives in a country house nearer to London than Brideshead. Tragically widowed. Needs a new young wife to secure him the Paris Embassy. Prefers to be agnostic but is in fact inclined to Catholicism. Has a private income of £12,000 per annum.
BR 176

EVERYMAN, LADY
Diner at Chez Espinoza (q.v.). Wears a fur coat. Is reported by Simon Balcairn as having confessed her sins to Mrs Ape. Talks with Lord Monomark at a party of Margot Metroland's.
VB 73, 85, 105

EXCELSIOR MOVIE – SOUND NEWS OF AMERICA
Ten Europeans form the advance party of the EMSNA in Ishmaelia. They move up to Laku in a huge armour-plated lorry.
SC 83, 124

EXETER, DEVON

Devon town on the main road to where Broome Hall stood until the eighteenth century.

• Exeter Cathedral features in a scene in *A Brand from the Burning* (q.v.) (made from pieces of canvas and match-boarding).

US 61

EXISTENTIALISM

According to Gilbert Pinfold, Angel's Box (q.v.) was first used by the Existentialists in Paris to psychoanalyse people.

GP 136, 153

EXPLETIVES

• 'Shut up you ——' says the warder at Blackstone Gaol to Paul Pennyfeather.

• 'The company' (Alistair Trumpington's) qualified every noun, verb, or adjective with the single, unvarying obscenity which punctuated all their speech like a hiccup'.

Alistair picks up the habit and shocks Sonia.

• The soldiers' vocabulary is well demonstrated in an exchange on the *SS Duchess of Cumberland*: '——y well travelling all the ——ing day. No ——ing supper. ——ed about on the ——ing quay. Now a —— won't let me have a ——ing smoke. I'm ——ing ——ed with being ——ed about by these ——ers'.

DF 164; PF 105–6, 108, 180–81

EXPLOSIVES

On 15 June 1923 Colonel Campbell blew up his stable. You could hear the bang on Muck.

• Dynamite, according to Campbell, is the safest of all explosives.

OG 91, 93

EXPRESSIONS

• A taxi driver in Marseilles: '*Gardez bien votre chapeau*'.

• Peter Beste-Chetwynde: 'Golly'.

• Nina Blount: 'Hog's Rump'.

• John Last and Ben: 'Took (cut) an arser' (fall off a horse); 'Silly old tart'; 'Cat' (vomit); 'My foot' (rubbish).

• Tony Last: 'Rotten bad'; 'be "bloody" to'.

• Brenda Last: 'Badders?' 'I'll sock you' (treat you to); 'You clod'.

• John Beaver: 'Having a walk-out with'.

• Marjorie: 'Hard cheese' (bad luck).

• Jock Grant-Menzies: 'Low joint'.

• Seth: 'Rats'; 'Stinking Curs'.

• Prudence Courtenay: 'Lovey dovey cat's eyes'; 'Cad'.

• Basil Seal: 'On a racket'; 'A jolly-up'.

• Barbara Sothill: 'Be "bloody" to'.

• Alastair Trumpington: 'Blackers' (Black Velvet).

• Ambrose Silk: 'Gawd strike me pink'; 'Lord love a duck'; (to himself) 'Cor chase my Aunt Fanny round a mulberry bush'.

• Molly Pastmaster: 'Bumbles' (Rubbish); 'Sick as cats'.

• Nigel Lyne: 'Absolutely ripping'; 'The rippingest'.

• Julia Stitch: 'Foregonners'.

• Mr Salter: 'Up to a point, Lord Copper'; 'Definitely, Lord Copper'.

• Corker: 'Alphonse'; 'Compreney pint of bitter?'; 'Black bum'; 'La belle France'; 'A cold story'; 'Bloody well no like'; 'Pansy'; 'Black booby'; 'God rot 'em'; 'A nob'.

• A photographer: 'A scab'; 'Sock me'; 'Poke in the nose'.

• Theodore Boot: 'Arrivederci'.

• Hooper: 'Rightyoh'; 'A flap'; 'Browned off'; 'Okeydoke'.

• Charles Ryder's CO: 'squared-up'.

• Soldier: 'Cheersh chum'.

• Anthony Blanche: 'Hobbledehoys'; 'Sponge'; 'Toady'; 'Poor hooligan'; 'La fatigue du Nord'; 'Sycophantic slugs'; 'Bitch'; 'Chivy you out, like an old s-s-stoat'.

• Mr Ryder: 'Stony-broke'; 'Queer Street'; 'Before the mast'; 'Come a cropper'; 'Folded up' (For Americans).

• Sebastian Flyte: 'Poppet'; 'Damn, damn, damn'; 'Being "bloody" to'; 'Sweet bulldog'.

• Charles Ryder: 'Little bit of fluff'; 'A talking to'.

• Rex Mottram: 'The worse for wear'; 'In a jam'; 'Squaring the papers'.

• Julia Flyte: 'Pickle'; 'Tight'; 'Positively

lethal'; 'Heaven'; 'Something chemical in him'.

• Major Tickeridge: 'Cheersh'; 'Pardon my glove'; 'Light shopping'; 'What's yours'; 'Lotus eaters'; 'The madam'; 'Old pussy cats'; 'In a flap'; 'Here's how'.

• Mrs Tickeridge: 'Here's how'.

• Apthorpe: 'Making a signal'; 'Bechuana tummy'.

• Miss Carmichael: 'Doing well' (eating well).

• Mrs Bristow: 'Ducks' (in 1940).

• Virginia Crouchback: 'Designs on'/ Various expletives.

• Military men: 'A general flap'.

• New Britons: 'State be with you'; 'Great State'; 'State help me'.

• Countless generations of baffled, impassioned Englishmen: 'I think I shall go for a short walk'.

• Lady Amelia: 'A very wrong thing.'

• Lucy Simmonds: 'Kulak'.

• Mr Plant's generation: 'Taking down her back hair'.

DF 151–152; VB 54;MD 20, 21, 24,25, 27, 34, 53, 57, 69, 91, 107, 125; BM 7, 44, 67, 140; PF 16, 38, 73, 124, 154, 158, 173; SC 11, 14, 62, 63, 71, 94, 106, 118, 201; BR 16, 17, 19, 49, 51, 63, 64, 68, 96, 116, 117, 125, 129, 130, 138; MA 38, 39, 60, 189; OG 64; US 90, 139; GP 190, 194, 195, 214; WS 28, 132, 167

EYRE, TROOPER

Trooper in X Commando who lands on his head during training and is delirious, although Ivor Claire thinks him 'tight'.

OG 52

F

FAGAN, DOCTOR AUGUSTUS

Headmaster of Llanabba School (q.v.). Very tall and well dressed with sunken eyes under black eyebrows, and very long white hair. Wears his hat at an angle. His voice sounds as if he may at one time have had elocution lessons. Has hairy hands and claw-like fingers. Essentially mean, he says that the reason he does not pay more is because he wants 'vision . . . not diplomas'.

Engages Paul Pennyfeather in 1922, at which date he has been running Llanabba for fifteen years (1907). Wears an orchid in his buttonhole. Pawns the Fagan cross-country running cup. Considers writing a monograph on the Welsh character. Believes that most disasters of English history can be attributed to the Welsh. Admits to a tendency for rhetoric.

Closes school late in 1922. Becomes proprietor of Cliff Place (q.v.), Worthing, having adopted the letters M.D. Like all his ideas it is on a grand scale.

Helps to secure Paul's release from prison, having had his death certificate signed by a drunken surgeon. Author of *Mother Wales* (1923), a bestseller.

DF 16–81, 35, 65–66, 202–203, 211

FAGAN, DIANA (DINGY)

Younger daughter of Dr Fagan (q.v.). Less gay than her sister. Efficient and dour. Disapproves of gaiety and fireworks. According to her sister her taste in clothes is 'all for wishy-washy greys and browns'.

DF 23, 24, 27, 48, 67

FAGAN, FLORENCE SELINA (FLOSSIE)

Elder daughter of Dr Fagan (q.v.). Middle-aged in 1922. Wears bright clothes. Talks in cockney. Calls her father 'a regular Tartar'.

Engaged to Captain Grimes, according to whom she is a bitch. Bigamously married to Grimes, who then fakes his suicide and disappears. Upset by the arrival of Jane Grimes.

Wears a bright frock made for her by Dingy.

DF 23, 24, 27, 48, 67

FALMOUTH, CORNWALL

Home of Admiral and Mrs Muspratt (q.v.). He leaves his collection of matchboxes to the town library.

BR 270

FANCY DRESS

At a fancy dress ball on the *SS Glory of Greece*, 'Bertie' comes as an apache and looks 'horribly dull'.

• The Bright Young People attend a number of such parties, dressed as savages, Victorians, Greeks, cowboys, Russians, circus acts, etc.

• Agatha Runcible has breakfast at No. 10 Downing Street still wearing her Hottentot costume from the savage party.

• Real aristocrats do not wear fancy dress.

• At the victory ball at the Perroquet in Debra Dowa the guests wear a variety of costumes – liberty bonnets, dunces' hats, jockey caps, Napoleonic helmets, pierrots' and harlequins' hats and highland bonnets.

• Between the wars Freddy Sothill's uniform is used as fancy dress.

VB 53, 58, 123; BM 111; WS 19; PF 10

FARMERS

• Basil Seal adopts the title 'farmer' after the war. This means that he 'lives in the country in ease and plenty'.

• A few rich men farm the land around Gilbert Pinfold's estate at Lychpole.

GP 11; WS 255

FASCISM
Totalitarian political system of aggressive nationalism put into practice by Mussolini and Hitler.
• Lord Copper explains fascism to Mr Salter over dinner.
• Rex Mottram is inclined in his speeches to flirt with the Fascists.
• Ambrose Silk has a brief flirtation with fascist ideas in the late 1920s.
• Gilbert Pinfold's voices say that they have evidence that he is a Fascist.
• The fascist representative of Ishmaelia in London is a negro who wears a white silk shirt, breeches and hunting boots and claims to be pure Aryan.
SC 14, 51; PF 34; BR 224; GP 103
(See also NAZIS)

FATES, THE
In Greek mythology the three daughters of Night. Controllers of men's destinies – Clotho, Lachesis and Atropos.
• Angela Lyne's affair with Basil Seal is portrayed as a terrible example of the perfect chemical reaction between man and woman 'set-up' by 'the ironic fates'.
PF 26

FATIMA
A 'chubby' little Berber prostitute favoured by John Plant at the Moulay Abdullah in Fez. She has blue and brown tattoos on her forehead and throat. She is only a prostitute to make enough money for her dowry.
WS 121

FATIM-BEY, MME FIFI
Town courtesan of Debra Dowa and protégé of Viscount Boaz (q.v.).
BM 106

FAWDLE, MR AND MRS
Neighbours of Gilbert Pinfold at Lychpole.
GP 11

FAWDLE-UPTON, LADY
Neighbour of Gilbert Pinfold at Lychpole. Suffers from nettle-rash which is cured by 'the box'.
GP 12

FE, DOCTOR ARTURO
Editor of the Neutralian *Historical Review*. Doctor of Bellacita University. Judge of the lower court. He has the appearance of an ageing film star. His hair is sparse. He has a thin moustache and short side-whiskers, three gold teeth, a monocle and dark clothes. Welcomes the Bellorius conference to Neutralia. Presents Engineer Garcia to them, who calls Fe a scholar.

Owns a third of the Neutralian Sporting Club. Leaves the ministry in disgrace with his accounts in disorder.
WS 205, 212, 214, 228, 239

FENDER, COLONEL
Land agent at Brideshead. Lunches with Lord Brideshead.
BR 85

FENWICK-SYMES, ADAM *(b.1903)*
Writer and fiancé of Nina Blount (q.v.). Has no distinguishing features. Lives in Paris for two months in 1927, writing his autobiography. Meets Father Rothschild (q.v.) at lunch with the Dean of Balliol in 1925.

Friend of Agatha Runcible and the Bright Young People. Travels to Doubting Hall to see Colonel Blount. Unable to get in. Meets Colonel Blount. Lunches with him and is given £1,000. Takes Nina to Arundel for the night in a hired Daimler.

Lunches with Simon Balcairn at Espinoza's. Visits the *Daily Excess*. Ravishes Nina on her own hearth-rug. Attends party at Margot Metroland's. Becomes Mr Chatterbox (q.v.). Invents characters – Provna, Count Cincinatti, Angus Stuart-Kerr, Imogen Quest.

Goes to the November Handicap at Doncaster. Sees Indian Runner win. Fired from the *Daily Excess* for 'bad tabulation'.

Attends motor races with Agatha Runcible and Archie Schwert. Stays at the Imperial Hotel. Remembers, as a young boy, stabbing a tailor's dummy. Watches motor races. Discovers that he has won £35,000 on Indian Runner. Buys champagne. Lends the major a fiver. Discovers that his £35,000 is invested. Telephones

Nina. Breaks off their engagement. Calls on Agatha Runcible at her nursing home. Gives her a cocktail which makes her temperature soar. Writes a bad cheque to Lottie Crump. Sells Nina to Ginger for seventy-eight pounds sixteen and twopence.

Ends up with Nina after Ginger is called to his regiment. Spends Christmas under Ginger's name at Doubting Hall. Gives Ginger a bad cheque for seventy eight pounds sixteen and twopence. Attends Agatha Runcible's funeral.

Joins the army at the outbreak of war. Meets the drunken major on a battlefield, now a general. He finally gives Adam the £35,000, which, by then, is quite worthless.

VB

FEZ, MOROCCO

In 1926 Charles Ryder takes a bus here from Casablanca to see Sebastian Flyte. He dines with the British Consul and stays for a week.

Sebastian is living here with Kurt (q.v.) in the native town in a house rented from a Frenchman. It is entered through a small courtyard with a well and an overhead vine. Inside there are a gramophone, an oil stove, rugs on the floor, silk hangings on the walls, a heavy tracery lamp on a chain, a brass tray with beer bottles and two chairs. The ceiling has carved and painted beams.

Charles visits Sebastian in the hospital.

• John Plant stays here, at a small French hotel outside the walls, for six weeks in March 1938, while writing *Murder at Mountrichard Castle*. He finds Fez the best place to write: 'a splendid, compact city' and thinks it one of the most beautiful cities in the world. On the hill is a huge hotel of 'Egyptian splendours' and in the new town 'commercial hotels'. His verandah overlooks a ravine where Senegalese infantry wash their linen.

Once a week he takes a bus to the Moulay Abdullah and dines at the consulate. He visits the local native cinema to see silent films 'in a babel of catcalls'.

On his trips to the Moulay (between the old city and the ghetto) he visits Fatima (q.v.). Fez is 'the East as adolescents would imagine it', a back lane, a water wheel, a lighted bazaar, tiled patios, one-roomed huts with women framed in the lamplight. At the brothel one evening John is caught in a police raid and decides to leave.

BR 201–204; WS 106–108, 120–124

FIFTH COLUMN

Enemy agents/traitors, working behind the lines. A term coined during the Spanish Civil War by General Mola, who at the head of four columns attacking Madrid declared that his fifth was in the city.

• Fifth columnists are the 'special concern' of the Halberdiers in Cornwall in August 1940.

• According to John Plant, grief comes to the civilized man in the form of a fifth column.

MA 208, WS 129

FIGURES OF FARCE

In 1939, Ambrose Silk thinks of himself, an aesthete born too late, as a figure of farce – along with 'mothers-in-law and kippers'.

PF 42

FILMS

• Dr Fagan (q.v.) has an offer for Llanabba from a film company whose managing director is Sir Solomon Philbrick.

• Colonel Blount is obsessed by the cinema, although he does not like Garbo, and has not seen her in *Venetian Kisses* which is playing in 1927 at the local cinema near Doubting.

• He allows the Wonderfilm company of Great Britain to film *A Brand from the Burning* at Doubting Hall. The film stars Effie La Touche as Selina, Countess of Huntingdon, and concerns the life of John Wesley. It lasts an hour and a half, speeds up at the excitingly dramatic points, and slows down during tedious conversations. It is directed by Mr Isaacs.

• *The Lion Has Wings*: Nigel Lyne is taken to see this film in the Spring of 1940 – 'The fellows say it's awfully decent'.

• Corker tells Katchen that she looks like a film star: Bergman or Garbo.
• William Boot once went to the cinema in Taunton and saw a hard-to-comprehend film about New York journalists which gives him a set impression of newspaper life.
• Guy Crouchback is influenced in the purchase of his monocle by the memory of seeing 'German Uhlans in American films'.
• He has also seen a film of the 1745 rebellion which he recalls while waiting for the Brigade to form in 1940.
• According to Elizabeth Verney, having drugs in your coffee only happens in films.
• *The Death Wish* by Ludovic is made into a film in 1951.
• Sir James Macrae engages Simon Lent to write the screenplay for his film of *Hamlet.* He wants Shakespeare in everyday language.
DF 141; VB 71, 208, 212; PF 170; SC 24, 115; MA 105, 160; GP 175; US 239; WS 68, 74
(See also BARLOW, DENNIS; HINSLEY, SIR FRANCIS)

FIRBANK, RONALD *(1886–1926)*
British novelist, Roman Catholic convert and homosexual. Best known for his *Valmouth* (1919) and *Prancing Nigger* (1924). His style is notable for its use of dialogue, fantasy and narration.
• Firbank sends copies of his novels, inscribed with endearments, to Anthony Blanche (q.v.).
BR 47

FIRST EDITIONS
• Gilbert Pinfold owns 'a few valuable books'.
• Bella Fleace's cousin, Archie Banks, discovers a number of calf-bound first editions in the library at Fleacetown, which Bella subsequently sells to a Dublin bookseller.
• John Boot's signed first editions change hands for one or two shillings more than the normal price.
GP; WS 80–81; Sc 5

FISHING
• Adam Symes is tempted to write in the *Daily Excess* that Ginger (q.v.) can only fish to the sound of the flageolet.
• While in Ishmaelia, William Boot thinks fondly of England: 'the trout lying among the cool pebbles, nose upstream, meditative, hesitant, in the waters of his home; the barbed fly, unnaturally brilliant overhead'.
• Sebastian Flyte and Charles Ryder fish for scampi in the shallows at Chioggia in 1923.
VB 141; Sc 61; BR 98

FITS
Basil Seal remembers having seen the Lieutenant-Colonel of the Bombardier Guards having a seizure in 1939.
WS 261

FITZBOURKE, KATHLEEN
'The toast of the Galway Blazers'. New name dreamt up by Sir Francis Hinsley for Juanita del Pablo (q.v.).
LO 25

FLANAGAN, FATHER, S.J.
Irish Jesuit priest and higher education correspondent of an Irish newspaper. He is keen in 1939 to visit the Maginot Line.
• Basil Seal takes his passport from the Ministry of Information and gives it to Ambrose Silk to get him out of England.
PF 189, 195

FLATS
• Anchorage House and Marchmain House in London are both demolished in the 1930s to make way for blocks of flats of the same name.
• Hill Crest Court is one of the three blocks which surround the garden of Mr Plant's house in St John's Wood. He takes delight in watching their gradual decline. Another of them is St Eustace's. Eventually, after Mr Plant's death, his son John sells the house to the Hill Crest Court Exploitation Company. It is demolished and another concrete block goes up.
BR 221, 209; WS 119, 140–143
(*See also* LAST, BRENDA)

FLAXMAN, JOHN ***(1755–1826)***
English sculptor, principally for Wedgewood, for whom he designed pottery. See his monument to Chatterton (Bristol).
• In Angela Lyne's mind the Greeks at Thermopylae are sculpted by Flaxman.
• Before Lucy Simmonds is born her mother sits in front of a Flaxman bas-relief to ensure that her child should have ideal beauty.
PF 29; WS 177

FLEACE, MISS ANNABEL ROCHFORT-DOYLE (BELLA) ***(c.1850–1932)***
Last of the Fleaces of Ballingar. Descended from the Rochforts, Fleysers and Doyles. Lives at Fleacetown (q.v.). Her mother was an O'Hara of Newhill. Her brother was killed during the Troubles. She is untidy and florid in appearance, with grey hair in a bun, a blue-veined nose, pale blue eyes and an Irish accent.

She is lame from a hunting accident and uses a stick. She is preoccupied with death. Sells first editions to a Dublin bookseller to finance a party in 1932. Prepares for the party. No one comes apart from the (uninvited) Gordons, and Mockstocks. She had forgotten to send out the invitations. She passes out and dies a day later.
WS 78–86

FLEACETOWN, IRELAND
Fifteen miles from Ballingar. Country house and home of Bella Fleace (q.v.). There is moss everywhere. All that is left of the original vast estate is the demesne land. The gates have a Georgian arch and are kept locked. The lodges are derelict. The only access to the house is through a farm gate.

The house itself has survived well, although it does not rival Gordontown. It was built in the eighteenth century and has interesting chimneypieces. It was the subject of an article in the *Architectural Review* by Archie Banks (1932).
WS 77–81

FLECKER, JAMES ELROY ***(1884–1915)***
English poet. See his *Golden Journey to Samarkand* (1913).
• Sir Francis Hinsley writes an article on Flecker's debt to William Henley (q.v.).
LO 8

FLEYSERS, THE
Irish landed family related to the Fleaces and living around Ballingar since the days of Strongbow (q.v.) (1170).
WS 79

FLINTSHIRE, LADY ETTY
Wife of Lord Flintshire. Mother of Sally and John. Thinks of marrying Sally off to Peter Pastmaster in 1939.
PF 143

FLINTSHIRE, JOHN
Son of Lord and Lady Flintshire, and brother of Sally. Friend of Basil Seal and Peter Pastmaster.
WS 254

FLINTSHIRE, SARAH (SALLY)
Daughter of Lord and Lady Flintshire. In 1939 a prospective wife for Peter Pastmaster.
• Well-proportioned. Keen on Hemingway. Has a pet dog.
• Basil Seal thinks that Charles Allbright may be her son.
PF 152; WS 254

FLORENCE, TUSCANY
Etty Cornphillip publishes a book of sonnets about Florence.
WS 29

FLORENTINE ART
Julia Flyte's face reminds Charles Ryder of 'Florentine quattrocento beauty'. The quattrocento in Italian art implies the fifteenth century and the painting of Piero della Francesca, Domenico Veneziano and Perugino.
BR 54

FLORIN, MRS
Housekeeper to Colonel Blount at Doubting Hall.
VB 72

FLOWER, MISS
Employee of the Ministry of Rest and Culture of the New Britain. Shows Miles Plastic the model of the new Mountjoy and becomes his wife.
GP 221, 222

FLOWERS
- Orchids: Dr Fagan in his buttonhole. Mr Salter suggests that William Boot send a spray of orchids to a girl. Sebastian Flyte and Charles Ryder wear orchids at Brideshead.
- Winter roses: On Paul Pennyfeather's table at Egdon Heath.
- Gillyflowers: Grow below Charles Ryder's windows at Oxford.
- The entire day's stock of a market stall: Given by Sebastian to Charles on the morning after he is sick into his rooms.
- A small red rose: Worn by Mr Ryder in his buttonhole at dinner.
- Roses: Sent by Mr Kramm to Celia Ryder and by Charles Ryder to Julia Flyte.
- Cistus and Jasmine: Among the farm buildings on Crete.
- Tuberoses: Put by Julia Stitch into Guy Crouchback's bedroom in Alexandria.
- Oleanders and Camomile: The borders in the capital of Neutralia.
- Gardenias: Charles Ryder in his buttonhole when courting girls.

DF 35, 191; Sc 33; BR 29, 32, 69, 78, 135, 238, 264; OG 185, 237; WS 206

FLYING BOMBS
Popular name for the German V1 and V2 rockets of WWII. They appear over London on 14th June 1944.
- One lands on Carlisle Place, killing Peregrine and Virginia Crouchback and Mrs Corner.
- They disturb the routine of the offices of Survival, and all seem to be heading for Cheyne Row.

US 189, 190, 195, 199

FLYING SCOTSMAN
British steam train.
- Charles Ryder expects Lord Brideshead to want to paint a picture of it.

BR 269

FLYS
Alastair Trumpington, in the army in 1939, attends a lecture about how a fly carries dysentery germs on its feet, softens its food with saliva and excretes where it has fed.
PF 105

FLYTE, CORDELIA ***(b.1912)***
Younger daughter of Lord and Lady Marchmain. Anthony Blanche is sure that she is 'abominable'. Is plain and has old-fashioned pigtails. Encounters Charles Ryder and Sebastian sunbathing on the roof of Brideshead in summer 1923. Has a pig called Francis Xavier. Admires Charles's painting in the office. Enjoys staying up late. Her school report says that she is the worst girl that the school has had 'in the memory of the oldest nun'. Her governess at Brideshead once jumped off a bridge in the park and drowned herself. Has six black Cordelias as her adopted godchildren in Africa. Makes a novena for her pig.

Plays *mah-jong*. Reveals Sebastian's drunkenness. Gives Sebastian her 'special' love.

Asks Charles to pinch her to stop her from giggling at Mr Samgrass. Is very keen on hunting. Chastises Sebastian for not dressing correctly when hunting. Writes to Charles in Paris to tell him that she was caught stealing whisky for Sebastian.

Tells Rex that Catholics have to sleep with their feet pointing East; that there is a box in the church which, if you put in it a note with someone's name on it, will ensure that they are sent to hell; and that there are sacred monkeys in the Vatican. Cannot forgive Julia for marrying in the Savoy Chapel.

Meets Charles again while he is painting Marchmain House (1926). Charles takes her to supper at the Ritz Grill. By this date she has developed the long Flyte nose and high cheekbones.

Drives an ambulance in Spain during the Spanish Civil War (1936–1938). Stays on there getting people re-settled. Visits Sebastian in Tunis. Reveals an aptitude for mimicry. Is able to imitate Father Mackay. Tells Charles that Sebastian is essentially a holy man.

Sets up home in London. In 1943 is working as a nurse with Julia in Palestine.
BR 54, 87, 88–91, 128, 133, 145, 147, 154, 160, 164, 167, 187, 190, 210, 211, 213, 246, 285–293, 296, 311, 315, 329

FLYTE, JULIA ***(b.1905)***
Elder daughter of Lord and Lady Marchmain. Sister of Sebastian Flyte (q.v.).

According to Anthony Blanche she is 'smart' and very definitely not 'greenery yallery'. Her photograph appears in the papers as regularly as advertisements for Beechams Pills. Her face has a 'flawless quattrocento beauty'.

Has her 'season' in 1923, at which she is the centre of attention. Seen as a 'bluebird'. Takes joy with her wherever she goes. Suddenly discovers that she has tremendous power as a woman. Considers marriage. Thinks of it as the beginning of adult life. Does not hope for a Royal marriage. Is hindered by the two problems of her father and her religion. Creates picture in her mind of her ideal husband. Calls him Eustace (q.v.).

Collects Charles Ryder from the station. Resembles Sebastian closely. Has dark hair, bobbed, and large eyes. Her mouth is 'less friendly' than his. Stays with her aunt, Lady Roscommon (q.v.) in Cap Ferrat. Is courted by Rex. Sebastian says that she does not care for anyone. He likes her because she is so like him. Brings Rex Mottram to Oxford. Stays with the Chasms (q.v.).

Meets Charles and Sebastian at Gunter's after their arrest. Longs to visit the Old Hundredth. Talks about Sebastian's drunkenness as 'something chemical'. Suggests that Sebastian might go to Kenya. Brings Rex Mottram to Brideshead; he gives her a tortoise inlaid with jewels. Plays *bézique.* Discover's Rex's affair with Brenda Champion. Becomes engaged secretly in summer 1924. Refuses to take Christmas Communion 1924. Is forbidden to see Rex. Lady Marchmain relents. They become engaged in May 1925. Married quietly in mid-June 1925 at the Savoy Chapel.

May 1926 telephones Charles Ryder to ask him to see the dying Lady Marchmain.

Shows a dry sense of humour. Wants a child but discovers that she will need an operation to have one. Has child, born dead.

Next meets Charles in mid-Atlantic on the way back to England (1936). Has an affair with him. Is unhappy with Rex. Has lost her quattrocento looks, but is more herself. Has a 'haunting, magical sadness'. Is feared by Rex's friends. Is painted by Charles. Goes to Capri and Naples with Charles. Wants to have Charles's child.

Secures divorce from Rex September 1938. Realizes that she cannot marry Charles.

Inherits Brideshead on the death of her father.

Gives home to a blitzed padre. Last heard of working as a nurse in Palestine with Cordelia (1943).
BR 38, 54, 73, 74, 117, 126, 156–159, 170–176, 180–193, 199, 210, 223, 227, 228, 241, 244–248, 269–265, 273–278, 286, 315, 324, 326, 329

FLYTE, JULIA ***(b.circa 1800)***
Ancestor of Lord Marchmain. Lived to be eighty-eight. Born and died at Brideshead. Never married. Saw the fire lit on Beacon Hill for Trafalgar in 1805. Called Brideshead 'The New House'.
BR 316.

FLYTE, LORD SEBASTIAN ***(b.1903)***
Younger son of the Earl of Marchmain. Educated Eton and Christ Church Oxford. Friend of Anthony Blanche and Boy Mulcaster. At Oxford 1922–1924.

Buys a hairbrush for his teddy bear, Aloysius, who he takes everywhere. Wears false whiskers in the George. Is first seen by Charles Ryder at Germer's.

Is sick into Charles's rooms. Sends Charles flowers and invites him to lunch. According to Lunt (q.v.) he is 'a most amusing gentleman'.

Is popular among London society hostesses. Takes Charles to Brideshead. Becomes short-tempered and petulant about his family. Is happiest when farthest away from Brideshead.

Drinks at the Trout.

Anthony Blanche recognizes his charm: 'He has a kind word for everyone'. According to Blanche at Eton he was 'a little bitch . . . Narcissus with one pustule'.

Breaks the smallest bone in his foot and sends for Charles: 'Gravely injured, come at once'.

He and Charles spend summer 1922 at Brideshead. Tells Charles to draw a picture of the fountain. Gets drunk every night. Always attends Mass at Brideshead. Believes in the Nativity.

Takes Charles to Venice, by way of Paris. They stay with his father. Cara tells Charles that Sebastian is in love with his own childhood and notices that he is drinking too much.

Returns to Oxford for Summer term 1923, and is more melancholy than ever. Is found by the Junior Dean of Christchurch wandering drunk at one in the morning in Tom Quad.

Mocks Mr Samgrass: 'Green arse-Samgrass'. Serenades him under his windows.

Lady Marchmain takes him away from Oxford (Summer term 1923). Travels to the Near East with Mr Samgrass (Autumn 1923). Meets Anthony Blanche in Constantinople. Is lost over Christmas 1923.

Taken in February 1924 to Zürich by Rex Mottram, who loses him in Paris. Takes Rex's money and goes to stay with Anthony Blanche in Marseilles. Gives Blanche's drug dealer a bad cheque. Pawns two of Blanche's suits. They go to Tangier where he takes up with Kurt (q.v.) in the Kasbah. Gets into trouble with the Tangier police and goes to French Morocco. Takes a house in the native quarter at Fez (q.v.) with Kurt. Becomes sick. Nursed at the Catholic infirmary. Has the grippe in one lung (May 1926).

Visited by Charles with news of his mother's death in May 1926. Is withered by drink. Has hallucinations that he is back at Oxford. Calls his mother a 'femme fatale'. Asks for brandy. Is gratified to be able to look after Kurt. Charles arranges his finances. Is found unconscious outside the monastery in Tunis, after wandering and refusing to eat and is admitted to the infirmary. Is very ill.

By 1938 he has returned to his faith. Has a beard and is very religious. Sends Christmas cards to Nanny Hawkins. Cordelia sees him in a monastery near Tunis in June 1938. Cordelia thinks that he once had a vocation and sees him ending his days in the monastery, with occasional bouts of drunkenness, until he dies.

BR

FLYTE ST MARY

Village near Brideshead. The meet of the Marchmain hounds is held here in 1923. Has a small pub, large enough to billet twenty soldiers in 1943 (out of bounds to officers).

BR 151, 325

FOGLIERE, PRINCIPESA

Venetian aristocrat who gives a ball in Venice in 1922 to which Lord Marchmain is not invited. Very proud of her English blood; 'talks of nothing else'.

BR 55, 60

FOOD

- Academy cake: Mr Plant's guests.
- Academy sandwiches: Mr Plant's guests.
- Almonds and raisins: William Boot's Christmas dinner.
- Apples: Cedric Lyne at breakfast on the ship to the war.
- Apple pie: Mrs Green's luncheon guests in 1939.
- Arab pastry: William Boot, Mr Baldwin and Cuthbert.
- Baby gazelle stuffed with truffles in its mother's milk: Mr Baldwin, William Boot and Cuthbert.

- Bacon and beans: Paul Pennyfeather in Blackstone Gaol and Egdon Heath.
- Bananas: Mr Ryder in his room.
- Bath Oliver biscuits: Charles Ryder and Sebastian Flyte while tasting wine at Brideshead in 1922.
- Beefsteak: Celia Ryder having recovered from her seasickness, John Plant and Arthur Atwater at the Wimpole club (with Worcester sauce), Miss Sveningen.
- Beetroot: The Halberdiers at Kut al Imara.
- Bird of Ishmaelia stuffed with bananas, almonds and red peppers: William Boot, Mr Baldwin and Cuthbert.
- Biscuits: From Bath and Tunbridge Wells, the Boots; Captains biscuits: Channel ferry passengers.
- Black bradenham ham: Adam Fenwick-Symes and Colonel Blount (with madeira sauce, at lunch), Charles Ryder at breakfast on board ship in 1936.
- Boiled eggs: Colonel Blount for tea, Jumbo Trotter for tea in 1940, X Commando in Alexandria, the buffet of Sir James Macrae's studios, Miss Sveningen and Whitemaid.
- Boiled goat's meat: the Earl of Ngumo for breakfast.
- Boiled turbot: Adam Fenwick-Symes and Colonel Blount at lunch.
- Bombay duck: The Boots.
- Bookbinder paste: The inmates off Blackstone Gaol.
- Bouillabaise: Paul Pennyfeather in Marseilles.
- Bread and butter: Charles Ryder in his room before breakfast at Brideshead, Cedric Lyne at breakfast on board the troop ship.
- Bread and margarine: The Halberdiers at Kut al Imara.
- Bread and milk: Julia Flyte, in bed, when upset with Rex.
- Brown bread ice: Lady Seal's dinner guests.
- Bully beef: Guy Crouchback in hospital in Alexandria.
- Cabinet pudding: Lord Copper and Mr Salter for dinner.
- Cake, large and ornamental: Guy Crouchback on his last day at Santa Dulcina.
- Cake made from dried egg, adulterated flour, nuts and preserved fruit: Mr Crouchback's funeral.
- Caneton à la presse: Charles Ryder and Rex Mottram at Paillard's.
- Carlsbad plums: Jasper Ryder's household at Christmas.
- Carrots: Basil Seal at the health farm.
- Casserole of chickens, hares, kids, pigs, peppers, cucumbers, garlic, rice, bread dumplings, grated cheese, roots, white tubers, red wine and olive oil: Deserters on Crete in 1941.
- Caviare: Paul Pennyfeather at Egdon Heath, Adam Fenwick-Symes and Simon Balcairn at Espinoza's, Celia Ryder's guests at her party in mid-Atlantic (from a large ice swan, with toast), Whitemaid in Upsala.
- *Caviare aux blinis*: Charles Ryder and Rex Mottram at Paillard's.
- Charcoal biscuits: Charles Ryder while cramming for exams.
- Cheese: The Earl of Ngumo for breakfast, Sebastian Flyte and Charles Ryder for lunch at a pub on the way to Brideshead; requested from his POW camp by Tony Box-Bender, Ludovic on Crete, Guy Crouchback in hospital after Crete, Ruben's in 1943 (French).
- Cherry cake: Adam Fenwick-Symes at Doubting Hall for tea, Jumbo Trotter for tea in 1940.
- Chicken: The Hotel Liberty, Jacksonburg.
- Chocolate: Charles Ryder's Lieutenants in 1943, requested by Tony Box-Bender from his POW camp.
- Chocolate cake: Adam Fenwick-Symes at Doubting Hall for tea.
- Chops: Mr Todhunter.
- Cocktail onions: In an American parcel sent to Mr Crouchback.
- Cod: Kerstie Kilbannock in 1943.
- Cold ham: Gilbert Pinfold on the *Caliban*.
- Condensed milk: Requested by Tony Box-Bender.
- Consommé: Lord Copper's guests.
- Cornish pasties: Supposed country food.
- Cream of chicken soup: Lord Copper's guests.

- Cream slices: The boys at the settle tea at Lancing.
- Crescent rolls: Julia Stitch and Guy Crouchback in Alexandria in 1941.
- Crumpets: The Trumpingtons for tea, the Brideshead Hunt, Mr Samgrass, the boys at the settle tea at Lancing.
- Crystallized plums: William Boot's Christmas dinner.
- Cucumber sandwiches: The British Legation in Azania for tea, Ladies during Eights Week at Oxford.
- Currant bread: Adam Fenwick-Symes at Doubting Hall for tea.
- Curry: Gilbert Pinfold on the *Caliban*.
- Dijon mustard: The Boots.
- Donkey: Major Cattermole's unit in Yugoslavia in 1942.
- Doughnuts: American soldiers in Italy in 1943.
- Dried eggs: The masters at Granchester in 1946.
- Duck: Lord Copper's guests.
- Eclairs: The settle tea at Lancing.
- Eggs: The boys at Lancing, for tea.
- Eggs and bacon: Sebastian Flyte and Charles Ryder for lunch at a pub on the way to Brideshead; Effie at the Old Hundredth.
- Fish: The Campbells of Mugg, Gilbert Pinfold on the *Caliban*.
- Fish, boiled, with sago: Guy Crouchback in hospital in Alexandria.
- Fish, fresh from the river in wine and aubergines: William Boot, Mr Baldwin and Cuthbert.
- Fish in olive oil, white truffles and garlic: An Italian restuarant near Bari in 1943.
- Flat bread and meat stew with peppers and aromatic roots: Basil Seal and Joab (the meat is Prudence Courteney).
- Fleshless fowls: Guy Crouchback's guests at Santa Dulcina.
- Flying fish: Tony Last and Thérèse de Vitre on Barbados.
- Fried eggs, sausages and bacon: The Trumpingtons in 1940 for lunch; Mr Todhunter.
- Fruit: Adam Fenwick-Symes and Colonel Blount for lunch; Anthony Blanche (supper); Gilbert Pinfold for breakfast on the *Caliban*.
- Fruit cake: Adam Fenwick-Symes at Doubting Hall for tea; Gilbert Pinfold's mother for tea.
- Fuller's walnut cake: Mary Nichols; Charles Ryder and Jasper for tea; Hector, at school.
- Galantine: Guy Crouchback at school; the Halberdiers at Kut al Imara.
- Garlic vinegar: The Boots.
- Genoese cooking: The Garibaldi.
- Gherkins: The Boots.
- Ginger biscuits: Colonel Inch.
- Golden Syrup: Requested by Tony Box-Bender.
- Goose: The Earl of Ngumo for breakfast.
- Grapefruit: Mr Prendergast (as if it were an orange).
- Green artichokes and butter: Guy Crouchback and Tommy Blackhouse at the Union Bar in Alexandria.
- Grouse: Tamplin at the Berkeley in 1919.
- Gull's eggs: Paul Pennyfeather and Peter Pastmaster before Paul's wedding; Ruben's in 1943.
- Haddock: Agatha Runcible at the Imperial Hotel.
- Hare soup: Adam Renwick-Symes and Colonel Blount at lunch.
- Haunch of roast venison: The Campbells of Mugg.
- Heather roots with oil and salt (but not bog myrtle): Dr. Glendenning-Rees.
- Honey buns: Charles Ryder and Jasper at tea.
- Hot buttered toast and gentleman's relish: Adam Fenwick-Symes at Doubting Hall for tea; Charles Ryder and his cousin Jasper for tea; The British Legation in Azania for tea.
- Hot buttered toast and honey: Jumbo Trotter for tea in 1940; Adam Fenwick-Symes at Doubting Hall for tea.
- Hot cheese sandwiches: Charles Ryder and Sebastian Flyte at Harry's bar in Venice.
- Hot muffins: Adam Fenwick-Symes at Doubting Hall for tea; a member of Basil Seal's club; Gilbert Pinfold's mother for tea; Adam Symes at tea parties.

• Hot scones: The British Legation in Azania for tea.
• Hot sheep and onions: The Imperial Banquet given by Seth.
• Human flesh: The inland natives of Ishmaelia; Basil Seal.
• Ice cream: American soldiers in Italy in 1943; Mr. Joyboy and Aimee Thanatogeno.
• Ice cream cornets: Ludovic on Crete.
• Icing sugar: The Boots.
• Italian pastries: Lord Marchmain in Venice.
• Jam: The Imperial banquet given by Seth.
• Jam sandwiches: Llanabba sports day.
• Kidneys: 'University breakfast' – the Chaplain of Scone and Paul Pennyfeather in 1923; Basil Seal and the Trumpingtons (grilled); Mr Todhunter.
• Kippers: Adam Fenwick-Symes at Lottie Crump's (they always smell better than they taste); all that is available at the St Christopher's social club.
• Lamb cutlets and mashed potato: The Ryder household.
• Lemon soufflé: Charles Ryder and Rex Mottram at Paillard's.
• Limpets: Dr Glendenning-Rees.
• Liver: Basil Seal and the Trumpingtons at a new cocktail bar in 1932.
• Lobsters: Charles Ryder at his father's house; Ruben's in 1943; Miss Sveningen.
• Lobster cream: Lady Seal's dinner guests.
• Lobster Neuberg: Sebastian Flyte's luncheon party in 1922.
• Lobster pilaff: Guy Crouchback and Tommy Blackhouse at the Union Bar in Alexandria.
• Lump sugar: Hector the poodle.
• Magyar food: One of Mr Salter's guests at a grill-room in the Strand.
• Marmalade: Scott-King.
• Mavrodaphne trifle: Anthony Blanche and Charles Ryder at the Spread Eagle.
• Mayonnaise of fresh eggs and olive oil: Ruben's in 1943.
• Melon: Julia Stitch and Guy Crouchback in Alexandria.
• Meringues: Cordelia Flyte at the Ritz Grill in 1926; Tamplin at the Berkeley in 1919; The Bright Young People at ten parties.
• Minestrone soup: The Garibaldi.
• Muscat grapes and cantaloup: Julia Flyte for breakfast on board ship.
• Mutton: Lottie Crump's (hot one day, cold the next, hot again the next); An Azanian nobleman on the train (spiced).
• Nutburgers: Aimee Thanatogenos and Dennis Barlow.
• Olives: The Earl of Ngumo for breakfast; Junior officers at Bari in 1943.
• Omelettes: Anthony Blanche for dinner.
• Onion salt: The Boots.
• Oranges: X Commando in Alexandria.
• Oseille (sorrel) soup: Charles Ryder and Rex Mottram at Paillard's.
• Oysters: Basil Seal; Adam Fenwick-Symes and Nina Blount at the Café de la Paix; Miles Malpractice at a place near Tottenham Court Road; Guy Crouchback at a restaurant beside a theatre in 1939; offered to Trimmer at the Château de Madrid in 1943; Ruben's in 1943 (from Colchester); Virginia and Peregrine Crouchback at Overton's in 1943; 'Papa' on the *SS Glory of Greece*.
• Parsley soup: Lord Copper and Mr Salter for dinner.
• Parmesan cheese: The Boots.
• Pâté de foie gras: Paul Pennyfeather in Egdon Heath; Julia Stitch, with a shoehorn in Lord Chasm's dressing-room; at the Llanabba sports day (in sandwiches).
• Peach: Charles Ryder at Brideshead while the others dine.
• Peanuts: Senior officers in Bari in 1943.
• Peanut butter: The Boots.
• Pears: The Hotel Liberty, Jacksonburg.
• Pêche melba: Lord Copper's guests.
• Pheasant sandwiches: Mr Crouchback at the auction of the contents of Broome.
• Pickled walnuts: Supposed country food; Sebastian Flyte and Charles Ryder for lunch at a pub on the way to Brideshead.
• Plovers' eggs: Sebastian Flyte's luncheon party in 1922.
• Plum pudding: William Boot's Christ-

mas dinner; the Trumpingtons, cold, in February 1940.
• Potatoes, huge and blue: The Halberdiers at Kut-al-Imara; Guy Crouchback after Crete.
• Potatoes, unpeeled: The Campbells of Mugg.
• Potted shrimps: Celia and Charles Ryder with a paper knife the night he proposed.
• Preserved figs: Simon Lent.
• Pullitzers soup: An American parcel.
• Pungent, meaty dishes: Hector the poodle.
• Quail (with muscat grapes): Guy Crouchback and Tommy Blackhouse at the Union Bar in Alexandria.
• Quail (stuffed): Bella Fleace.
• Rabbit pie: Sir James Macrae.
• Raisins and raw turnip: Mr and Mrs Hornbeam.
• Raw eggs and barley: Basil Seal at the health farm.
• Raw onions and oatmeal porridge: Lord Monomark's luncheon.
• Roast beef: The Imperial banquet given by Seth; the Hotel Liberty, Jacksonburg; Mrs Green's luncheon guests in 1939.
• Roast pheasant: Adam Fenwick-Symes and Colonel Blount (for lunch); Virginia, Guy and Peregrine Crouchback for lunch in 1943.
• Roast potatoes: the Halberdier officers for lunch.
• Roast turkey: William Boot's Christmas dinner; the Scrope-Weld's Christmas dinner.
• Roast veal: Lord Copper and Mr Salter for dinner.
• Rum omelette: Adam Fenwick-Symes and Colonel Blount (for lunch).
• Rusks: Mr Ryder, in his room.
• Saddle of mutton: Lady Seal's dinner guests; Lord Copper's guests.
• Salad (side): The Halberdier officers for lunch.
• Salad of limp lettuce with oil and garlic: Guy Crouchback's guests at Santa Dulcina.
• Salad of watercress, chicory and chives: Charles Ryder and Rex Mottram at Paillard's.
• Salad with tinned crab: Mr Joyboy and Aimee Thanatogenos.
• Salmon kedgeree: Charles Ryder at breakfast onboard ship.
• Sandwiches: Charles Ryder's lieutenants in 1943; the Halberdiers' officers at the firing range; Jumbo Trotter for tea; Gilbert Pinfold's mother for tea; Simon Lent.
• Sardines: The Hotel Liberty Jacksonburg.
• Scotch salmon: Ruben's in 1943.
• Scrambled eggs: Charles Ryder for breakfast at a tea shop at Oxford in 1922; the Marchmain Hunt; Gilbert Pinfold on the *SS Caliban*.
• Seaweed: Dr Glendenning-Rees.
• Seed cake: Adam Fenwick-Symes at Doubting Hall for tea; the British Legation in Azania for tea.
• Small roasted suckling pig: The Imperial banquet given by Seth.
• Smoked mutton: The Earl of Ngumo for breakfast.
• Smoked salmon: Offered to Trimmer at the Château de Madrid in 1943.
• Snake's flesh: Red Indians, to make them cunning.
• Snipe: William Boot and Jack Bannister for dinner.
• Sole: The Hotel Metropole (awful); the Ryder household in London (overfried) with a pink sauce; Charles Ryder and Rex Mottram at Paillard's (with a white wine sauce, simple and unobtrusive).
• Soup: The Campbells of Mugg.
• Spaghetti: Guy Crouchback on his last day at Santa Dulcina; Julia Stitch at Santa Dulcina.
• Spam cut into trefoils: Mr Crouchback's funeral.
• Spiced turkey: The Imperial banquet given by Seth.
• Stale liver pâté: Basil Seal in secret at the health farm.
• Stale sausages: New Britons, for breakfast.
• Steak and onions: The passengers on the *SS Glory of Greece* at breakfast.
• Steak and kidney pie: The Halberdier officers for lunch.
• Steak tartare: A banquet for some

Wanda notables (raw beef).
- Stewed pears in jelly sponge: The Ryder household.
- Strasburg pies: Peregrine Crouchback and the Scrope-Welds at Christmas before the war.
- Strawberries: Charles Ryder and Sebastian Flyte on a summer picnic in 1922; Philbrick at the Maison Basque in 1922 (bitter little strawberries).
- Sweetbreads: Adam Fenwick-Symes and Colonel Blount at lunch.
- Sweetcorn and pimentoes: Paul Pennyfeather and Arthur Potts at the Queen's Restaurant.
- Tinned asparagus: The British Legation in Azania.
- Tinned crab: The Bright Young People at tea parties.
- Tinned herrings: Guy Crouchback in hospital in Alexandria.
- Tinned meat and fish: Requested by Tony Box-Bender.
- Tinned noodle soup: Mr Joyboy and Aimee Thanatogenos.
- Tinned salmon: According to Lord Copper the staple diet of the agricultural classes.
- Tinned sardines: The Imperial Banquet given by Seth; X Commando in Alexandria; Ludovic on Crete; A lady in a flat in King's Road, the morning after a party (from the tin, with a shoe-horn).
- Toast and marmalade: Charles Ryder for breakfast in 1922.
- Tomato sandwiches: Adam Fenwick-Symes at Doubting Hall for tea.
- Truffles: Paul Pennyfeather at Egdon Heath.
- Toasted cheese: Adam Fenwick-Symes and Colonel Blount (for lunch); Basil Seal and the Trumpingtons (supper).
- Toffee: Requested by Tony Box-Bender.
- Turbot: Lord Copper's guests; Virginia and Pergerine Crouchback at Overton's in 1943.
- Turkish delight: Julia Stitch gives some to Ivor Claire in hospital in Alexandria.
- Whitebait: Basil Seal and the Trumpingtons, for dinner.
- White fish: Dinner aboard the *Franc-maçon*.
- White raspberries: The Flytes.
- White, tasteless soup: The Ryder household.
- Whiting: Lord Copper and Mr Salter for dinner.
- Woolton pies: The population of London in May 1941 and October 1943.
- Yoghurt: Mrs Beaver.
- Yumcrunch: Felix.
- Zabaglione: The Garibaldi.

FOOTBALL

- Anthony Blanche tells his 'P-p-preposterous tutor' that he must leave early for lunch to play 'F-f-footer'.
- Richie-Hook tells his lieutenants that they ought to follow 'footer' and remembers how, when a sergeant of his had his leg blown off, the only way to ease his dying moments was to tell him the (made-up) league results.

BR 34, MA 71

FOREIGN LEGION

French mercenary army corps, based in North Africa.
- Kurt (q.v.) has been in the Foreign Legion with a friend who is killed on exercise in the Atlas mountains. Kurt gets out by shooting himself in the foot.
- In Fez John Plant sees impoverished legionnaires at the brothel.

BR 196, WS 122

FOREIGN OFFICE

- Elizabeth Verney works in a 'clandestine branch' of the FO in 1940.
- Guy Crouchback almost joins the FO in 1939, in desperation at not being able to get a commission.

MA 41; GP 163

FORSTER, E.M. *(1879–1970)*

English writer. See his *A Room with a View*, *Howard's End*, *A Passage to India*.
- In his guide to Alexandria, of which Julia Stitch gives a copy to Guy Crouchback, he points out the gardens of the British hospital.

OG 126–127

FORT BELVEDERE
Private retreat of the Prince of Wales, later Edward VIII, in Windsor Great Park.
• From where, in 1938, one of Rex Mottram's friends has just returned.
BR 262

FORTUNE
Paul Pennyfeather's life is ruled by Fortune. He drinks a toast to 'Fortune, a much maligned lady', just before his arrest.
• The same toast is drunk by Dr Fagan (q.v.) after supper on Paul's release.
• Peter Pastmaster reminds Paul of the toast in 1923.
DF 157, 205, 215

FOSKER
One of Gilbert Pinfold's hallucinations. The juvenile lead in a play on the deck. Also a member of a jazz band.
GP 66–67

FOULENOUGH, CAPTAIN
Fictitious English comic book character.
• A small man with red hair infiltrates Celia Ryder's party onboard ship in 1936 and poses Charles the riddle that he is English, it is his first time in the Atlantic, but he is returning to England. Answer: he has been around the world.
• He is compared by Celia to Captain Foulenough and is taken off in England by two plain-clothes policeman.
BR 231, 234, 251

FOUNTAINS
• There is a fountain in the cortile of the officers' hotel at Bari with a stone triton and spiky vegetation.
• At Whispering Glades there is a fountain of Carrera statues 'allegorical, infantile and erotic'.
US 161; LO 65
(See also BRIDESHEAD CASTLE)

FOUR SQUARE GOSPEL
American evangelist cult in which Aimee Thanatogenos's father lost all his money.
LO 73

FOXES
• The Bollinger club once stoned a fox to death.
• On the beach, near Cherbourg, during Operation Popgun (q.v.) Trimmer thinks he hears a fox bark.
DF; OG 145; HD 219, 105
(See also HETTON)

FRAGONARD, JEAN HONORÉ
(1732–1806)
French painter under Louis XV and Louis XVI. Specialised in pretty *fêtes champêtres* and lightheartedly erotic works.
• Everard Spruce has a preference for Fragonard, but chooses to disguise it to promote his image.
• Gilbert Pinfold imagines 'Margaret' as nymph by Fragonard.
US 123; GP 116

FRANCE
Paul Pennyfeather travels to Marseilles.
• William Boot has never been to France before his trip to Ishmaelia.
• Charles Ryder takes up with two American girls in Auteuil.
• According to Charles Ryder the 'staples' of France are Dubonnet, Michelin and the Magasin du Louvre.
• Angela Lyne thinks that when people say they love France they mean that they love to eat.
Sc 63; BR 202, PF 28
(See also PARIS, FRENCH, and individual towns)

FRANCESCA
Italian cousin of Julia Flyte who has an annulment of her first marriage.
BR 189

FRANCIS DE SALES, ST
(1567–1622)
French Roman Catholic Bishop and writer, renowned for his *Introduction to a Devout Life*.
• Tony Box-Bender asks his father to send a copy of de Sales' 'The Spiritual Combat' to him, while a POW.
OG 246

FRANCIS XAVIER
Pig belonging to Cordelia Flyte. Receives an honourable mention at the Brideshead show in 1923.
BR 87

FRANCO, FRANCISCO ***(1892–1975)***
Military dictator of Spain. Overthrew the Socialist government between 1936 and 1939, with help from Mussolini and Hitler, in the Spanish Civil War (q.v.).
• In 1938 one of Rex Mottram's friends thinks Franco a German agent.
• Gilpin, in mocking sarcasm, tells de Souza that he hears that Franco plays a good game of golf.
• In Gilbert Pinfold's mind his 'two generals' verbally attack Franco. Pinfold admits to having had sympathy with Franco during the Civil War.
BR 262; US 96; GP 87; 109

FRANK
Footman to Lady Seal. Unable to find Basil's evening clothes.
BM 77

FRANKIE
Secretary to Everard Spruce. Wears her hair long and goes barefoot. Initiates Ludovic into Logan Pearsall Smith and Kafka. Thinks that Scott Fitzgerald wrote *Omar Khayam*.
US 40–43

FRANKS, PROFESSOR
Professor of architecture who sees King's Thursday as 'the finest piece of domestic Tudor in England'.
DF 116

FRASHAM
Fictional village in *The Frightened Footman* by John Plant.
WS 159

FRAZER, LOVAT
• At Eton Ambrose Silk collects Lovat Frazer rhyme sheets.
• Sir Francis Hinsley's books of poetry often have a scribble by Lovat Frazer on the title page.
PF 43; LO 52

FREE FRENCH
WWII Army of French liberation based in London under General de Gaulle.
• The Free French have a representative in the party sent to observe at Begoy in 1944. He is killed in the plane crash.
US 210

FREEMANTLE, CAPTAIN
Ludovic's Staff-Captain at No.4 Special Training centre in 1943. Becomes increasingly worried for Ludovic's sanity and confides in de Souza.

Before the war he had been a junior clerk in an insurance company.
US 85, 112

FREMLIN, MRS
Neighbour of Barbara Sothill at Malfrey. Middle-aged. Wears fur gloves and high rubber boots. Announces the return of the Connollys (q.v.).
PF 78

FRENCH, THE
• According to Lady Seal (q.v.) their triumphs are short-lived.
• According to Angela Lyne they are as a people 'hard boiled'. For her, French culture is like their food – messed up stuff. Stale ingredients from Spain and America and Russia and Germany, disguised in a sauce of white wine from Algeria. She thinks that the French lost their culture with their king.
• Basil Seal confuses 'Fogs' with 'Frogs': 'They're eaten hollow with communism . . . Half the thinking men in France have begun looking to Germany as their ally'.
• In Sir Joseph Mainwaring's opinion the French will have to give up a colony to bring in Italy on their side in the war.
• For Charles Ryder the French always exult at their former friend's (England's) discomfort, and see the General Strike as a revolution.
• Four French Pétainist millionaires are among Scott-King's fellow travellers on the European Underground in 1946.
PF 19, 175, 28, 54; BR 193; WS 244

FRENCH-WISE, FREDDIE
Undergraduate at Oxford at the same time as Paul Pennyfeather (1922). Friend of Alastair Trumpington.
DF 70

FREUD, SIGMUND *(1856–1939)*
Austrian founder of psychoanalysis. In *The Interpretation of Dreams* (1900) he showed that dreams and neuroses are disguised sexual urges.
• Collins (q.v.) reads Freud at Oxford in 1922 and can cover everything with one of his technical terms.
• Everard Spruce presumes that Ludovic has read a lot of Freud.
• Sir Francis Hinsley has never been able to make any sense of Freud.
BR 30; US 51; LO 8

FRICKHEIMER, MRS ARNOLD
Society hostess hit on the head with a bottle of milk in 1926, by the 'palest' member of the Blackbirds (q.v.).
BR 195

FRINTON, ESSEX
The country, for Mr Salter (q.v.) is everything that he can see from the train window between Liverpool Street and Frinton, where he and his wife sometimes take a holiday.
Sc 26

FRITH, WILLIAM POWELL *(1819–1909)*
Victorian painter. Best known for his large panoramas of social life. See his 'Ramsgate sands' (1853) (HM the Queen) and 'Derby Day' (1858) (Tate).
• Mr Plant's (q.v.) first exhibited work is 'a balloon ascent in Manchester . . . in the manner of Frith'.
WS 114

FRY, ROGER *(1866–1934)*
English painter and art historian. Organiser of the 1910 Post-Impressionist exhibition. Co-founder (1913) of the Omega Workshops (q.v.).
• Charles Ryder has a copy of Fry's book *Vision and Design* when at Oxford. Before his discovery of the Baroque, Charles's taste in art encompasses the insular puritanism of both Fry and Ruskin.
BR 29, 79

FU, MR *(d.1946)*
Scholar and expert on Bellorius on whom he has written in demotic Cantonese. Delegate at the Bellorius conference in Neutralia in 1946. Drives into the hills with the Swiss delegate and is killed by partisans.
WS 226

FULBRIGHT, JAMES WILLIAM *(b.1905)*
American politician and lawyer. Established in 1946 an exchange system between the US and other countries for students and teachers.
• Fulbright scholars are among the guests at the banquet for Ambrose Silk at the Ritz in 1962.
WS 253

FUSELI, HENRY *(1741–1825)*
Swiss-born artist who settled in England. Famous for his fantastic, nightmarish scenes. Associate of Reynolds and Blake. See his 'Nightmare' (Detroit).
• Lieutenant Padfield (q.v.) takes his hosts in wartime Britain sketches by Fuseli.
US 25

FUTURISM
Modernist artistic movement (1905–1915), founded in Paris by Marinetti and based in Italy on the work of Boccioni, Carra, Balla and Severini. It's basic aim was to capture the speed and dynamism of the machine age on canvas.
• Charles Ryder's group of Englishmen returning to London for the General Strike in May 1926 are joined by a Belgian Futurist going under the name of Jean de Brissac la Motte.
BR 193

G

GAELIC RHYMES
See STUART-KERR

GALILEO GALILEI
(1564–1642)
Italian astronomer. Author of a treatise on gravity. Perfected the refracting telescope. Advocate of the Copernican system.
• Charles Ryder, having discovered in painting Marchmain House his true vocation, feels like a Renaissance man who has seen the stars through Galileo's telescope.
BR 213

GALLA
• The Wanda of Azania are Galliac immigrants from the mainland.
BM 8

GAMAGE, SISTER
Ward sister at the health farm visited by Basil Seal.
WS 270

GAMBLING
• Sir Humphrey Maltravers is an inveterate gambler at poker.
• Rex Mottram gambles at the Travellers' Club in Paris after dinner in 1926.
• His house guests at Brideshead bet on anything they can, such as how many swans they will see on the lake.
• The Blackbirds gamble on dice at a party in Regent's Park in 1926.
• A young man at Lottie Crumps' loses a thousand pounds to Adam Symes by betting that he cannot move three half pennies around a table moving each one five times and change their position twice.
• One of the Ryders' fellow passengers on the liner across the Atlantic has a roulette wheel.
• Housey Housey is the only game which it is permissible to play for money within His Majesty's Forces.
• Ivor Claire leads X Commando in playing Baccarat for money, while the others play poker and backgammon.
• While travelling on the *SS Glory of Greece*, 'Papa' loses at the casino at Monte Carlo, and Bertie wins.
DF 132; VB 42; BR 165, 195, 243, 246; OG 68; WS 16; MA 138

GAMES
• Up Jenkins: Played by Margot Metroland, who compares it to prison visiting. Played by Gilbert Pinfold with his family.
• Chess: Percy plays a game by post with Babbit of the F.O.
• Mah-Jong: Charles Ryder plays with Cordelia Flyte at Brideshead.
• Patience: Lord Brideshead plays at Brideshead. Major Graves plays.
• Poker: Lord Metroland plays.
• Cards: Sebastian Flyte plays in Constantinople. Rex Mottram plays at the Travellers' Club in Paris.
• *Bézique*: Played by house-parties at Brideshead.
• Chemin de Fer: Rex Mottram teaches Julia Flyte at Cap Ferrat.
• Dice: The Blackbirds play at a society party in Regent's Park in 1926.
• Played at Lottie Crump's: A mysterious game which ends with someone giving a bottle of champagne to everyone in the room.
• Ping-Pong: Julia Flyte's maid plays on board ship.
• Tombola: Played on board ship.
• Bridge: Played on board ship.
• Backgammon: Played by Rex Mottram's girlfriends at Brideshead in 1936.
• Bagatelle: Played by the British Legation in Azania.
• Badminton: Played by Robin (q.v.).

• Draughts: Played by Greek traders in Tunis.
• General Post: Played by Charles Ryder who compares it to the moving of possessions following his and Julia's divorces.
• A game in which two contestants attempt to introduce a sentence into the conversation in a natural way. Played by Guy Crouchback when an undergraduate, at houseparties.
• Baccarat: Played by Ivor Claire and X Commando on Mugg.
• Peggity: Played by the Bishop and Prudence Courteney.
• A card game in which one shouts 'I claim': Played by Gervase and Hermione Crouchback, when young.
• Rugby: Played by the Halberdiers in their mess when drunk.
• Happy Families: Compared by Guy Crouchback to the questions in the ATM for April 1940.
• Housey-Housey: Played by the Halberdiers.
• Croquet: Played by the British Legation in Azania.
• Slosh: Played by Guy Crouchback at Bellamy's on the evening of his fortieth birthday.
• Piquet: Played by Virginia and Guy Crouchback during his convalescence.
• Charades: Played by Gilbert Pinfold with his family.
• Golf: Played by Glover and Apthorpe.
• Quoits: Played by the young people on board ship.
• Shuffle-Board: Played by the young people on board ship.
• A school room trick: Everyone not in the line of sight of a stranger coming into a room, puts out their tongue at a him or her. Played by bright young girls in the 1920s.
• Billiards: Played by Mr Loveday. Played in John Plant's hotel in Fez.
DF 193; BR 26, 129, 153, 165, 178, 195, 233, 236, 246, 281, 289, 296; OG 57, 68; MA 10, 77, 128; US 53, 130; GP 26,37, 45, 52, 105, 106; WS 10

GAMP, MRS
Fictitious character in *Martin Chuzzlewit* by Dickens. She is a drunken nurse who uses the imaginary character Of Mrs Harris to confirm her own opinions. In colloquial usage a 'gamp' was a lower class, alcoholic maternity nurse (or an umbrella – an implement of which she is unduly fond).
• Virginia compares Sister Jenny (q.v.) to Mrs Gamp.
US 195

GANGES
Sacred river in northern India. By ritual orthodox Hindus bathe herein on certain days of the year in order to cleanse their souls.
• Basil Seal, drinking illicit whisky at the health farm, feels transported in a mystical experience, as if he is 'on Ganges bank'.
WS 269

GARBETT, MRS
Neighbour of Gilbert Pinfold at Lychpole.
GP 11

GARBO, GRETA *(b.1905)*
• Initially Corker compares Kathleen to Garbo.
• Greta Garbo is playing in *Venetian Kisses* at the local cinema of Doubting Hall in 1927.
VB 71

GARCIA, ENGINEER
Neutralian politician and rival of Dr Fe. Talks to Scott-King. Has lived in Salford, where he worked for Green, Gorridge and Wright. Once saw the Duke of Westminster at Biarritz. Plots to take over from Dr Fe.
WS 212, 227

GARDA, LAKE, ITALY
Where Basil Seal left a party of tourists stranded in the 1930s.
PF 48

GARDENS
Lady Peabury's garden at Much Malcock contains cedars, a lawn, a box hedge, a lily pond with lead flamingoes, a rock garden with alpine plants, and flowering shrubs.
WS 59

GARESBY
• Country house which is home of the Wrottmans (q.v.). Demolished in the reign of George I, the stones being sold to a building contractor.
• Mr Goodall tells Guy Crouchback the story of the house.
MA 110

GARGE
Mr Salter's humerous name for William Boot which eases relations between them.
Sc 29

GARIBALDI, GIUSEPPE *(1807–1882)*
Italian patriot and member of the 1849 revolutionary Roman government. Fought in the Italian war of Liberation of 1859 and in 1860 to rid Sicily of the Bourbons. Helped the French Republic in 1870. Central figure of Italian independence.
• To Guy Crouchback it seems as if it would have been better had the Popes ignored the Risorgimento and treated Garibaldi as a hooligan.
US 15

GARRY, MRS
Neighbour of Guy Crouchback at Santa Dulcina who distributes Protestant tracts and opposes methods of killing octopuses. Keeps stray cats.
MA 15

GASSOWAY, JOHN
Friend of the Prime Minister's who is created a knight in 1937.
Sc 184

GASTON
Swiss manservant of Lord Marchmain in later years.
BR 298

GAUGUIN, PAUL *(1848–1903)*
French Post-Impressionist painter and friend of Pissarro. Led Pont Aven group from 1888. Associated with Van Gogh and Emile Bernard. Emigrated to Tahiti in 1895.
• London society in the 1930s talks of Charles Ryder as 'a Gauguin'.
• John Plant's father considers Gauguin's paintings to be 'disjointed negresses', although they are collected by Lionel Sterne.
BR 259; WS 115

GENERAL STRIKE
The first general strike in Britain began at midnight on 4 May 1926 and ended on the 12th, a state of emergency having been declared on Sunday 2 May. Troops were deployed, and the middle-classes, notably undergraduates, lawyers and city gents took over the trams and trains. Many others, including Charles Ryder, volunteer as special constables. The strike was vehemently opposed by Winston Churchill. On the return to work it seems to Charles 'as though a beast long fabled for its ferocity had emerged for an hour, scented danger, and slunk back to its lair'.
• Alastair Trumpington drives through London breaking up meetings, and clubs several citizens.
BR 193, 199; PF 45

GENEVA, SWITZERLAND
Where Arthur Potts is based, at the League of Nations.
• The Jews of Geneva, according to the fascist consul of Ishmaelia are responsible for the rumour that Ishmaelites are black.
DF 148; Sc 61

GENOA
Italian port in Liguria and home of an elderly lawyer who owns the Castello Crouchback before it is sold to Gervase and Hermione.
MA 11

GENTAKIAN, MR
Owner of a shop in Jacksonburg, opposite Popotakis's. Knows a great deal of news.
Sc 142

GENTLEMEN
According to Ludovic, Guy Crouchback believes that gentlemen are fighting the

war; such gentlemen as General Miltiades. Ludovic observes that all such gentlemen are now very old.

- Miles Plastic is definitely not a gentleman.

OG 186; GP 182

GENTRY, THE
It was, in Peregrine Crouchback's day, thought rather outré among the gentry for younger sons to marry.
US 135

GEOGHAN, CANON
Catholic parish priest at Southsand. Unable to 'get about' very much.
MA 109

GEOGHEGAN, FATHER
Local priest at Broome who wants to preach a panegyric at Mr Crouchback's funeral.
US 61

GEORGE I–IV
Kings of England, during whose reigns the 'greater honours' came to the Marchmain family.
BR 317

GEORGE III ***(1738–1820)***
Son of Frederick, Prince of Wales. King from 1760. He is a distant relation of Mr Bentley. His portrait hangs in Bentley's office.
PF 65

GEORGE, 'UNCLE'
Master at Lancing in Charles Ryder's day.
WS 302

GEORGIAN SOCIETY, THE
Possibly Waugh is referring to the Georgian Group, founded in April 1937 by Douglas Goldring, Lord Derwent, Robert Byron, Sir Albert Richardson, James Lees-Milne and John Summerson, with the aim of preserving the Georgian buildings and heritage of Great Britain.

- According to Celia Ryder the Georgian Society make an enormous fuss about the destruction of Anchorage House (q.v.) in 1937, but to no avail.

BR 221

GERMANY
After the Great War Lord Circumference has German prisoners on two of his farms.

- According to Kurt it is 'down the drain' in 1926.
- The Germans are behind the 'Smiles' trouble in Ishmaelia in 1937.
- Charles Ryder plans to visit at a later date.
- There are a number of Germans in business in Jacksonburg in 1937.
- Seth finds a programme of communal physical exercises in a German book in 1932.
- Lady Seal thinks war in 1939 'Very sad for the Germans'.
- According to friends of Rex Mottram, in 1938 the Germans: Have not the money, oil, wolfram, men or guts to fight. They are scared of the French, the Czechs, the Slovaks and the British. The women are barren and the men impotent. The doctors were all Jewish. They have consumption and syphilis. Germany will rise against Hitler.
- Some of Cedric Lyne's grottoes come from southern Germany.
- Angela Box-Bender believes that whereas under the Kaiser the Germans were civilised, the Nazis are brutes.
- In the 1930s Ambrose Silk lives in Germany.
- The Germans, thinks Cordelia Flyte, sometimes discover a sense of decency when in a classical country.
- A member of the Beefsteak tells Sir Joseph Mainwaring that fifty million Germans want peace in 1939.
- In 1945 Arthur Atwater is in the army and in charge of a considerable part of Germany.

DF 68; BR 204, 216, 291; MA 32; Sc 154, 110; BM 142; PF 18, 26, 43, 117
(See also Hans, Kurt, Katchen, Dressler)

GESTAPO
Nazi secret police force founded by Goering (q.v.).

• When captured and tortured by the Gestapo, foreign agents of the SOE, having been taken in the dark to their training centre in some unknown part of England, are able to tell their interrogators only that. Gilbert Pinfold's tormentors reveal that the Gestapo used the three-eight rhythm as a method of torture which would drive a man 'raving mad'.
• Gilbert Pinfold believes that the Gestapo developed a special kind of box with which to cross-examine their captives (*see* EXISTENTIALISTS).
• Half-a-dozen former Gestapo men are among those awaiting transit through Europe by way of the 'underground', with Scott-King in 1946.
US 94; GP 46, 153; WS 244

GHEZIRA
Mr Murdoch invites Gilbert Pinfold to dine with him here, together with some business associates.
GP 143

GHOSTS
Philbrick is haunted by the shade of his sister Gracie (q.v.).
DF 92–3

GI LIBERATION OF ITALY
Officer in charge of posting specially chosen agents to the Italian front in 1944. Stationed at HOOHQ Colonel in rank. Tests Guy Crouchback on his Italian.
US 57–58

GIBBONS, GRINLING *(1648–1721)*
English wood carver. Often signed with a peapod. See his work at Hampton Court Palace.
• The saloon at Malfrey is carved by Gibbons. Here the officers of the Gloucester Yeomanry set up their mess in the spring of 1940.
PF 74, 141

GIBRALTAR
British territory in southern Spain where a friend of Jumbo Trotter's is on Hamilton-Brand's staff.
• The Anglican Cathedral here was built by the Sappers.
• In Gilbert Pinfold's mind a conflict blows up about possession of Gibraltar, resulting in Spanish officials boarding the *Caliban*.
WS 87; OG 43, 64

GILBERT (W.S.) AND SULLIVAN (SIR ARTHUR)
Co-writers of the Savoy Operas. See *Patience*, *The Pirates of Penzance*, *Trial by Jury*, *The Mikado*, etc.
• Paul Pennyfeather's guardian's daughter plays records of Gilbert and Sullivan in 1922.
• The Oxford Union is, in Eights Week, suddenly afflicted with a 'facetious, wholly distressing Gilbert and Sullivan badinage'.
• The new British inhabitants of Matodi in 1932 play records of *The Mikado*.
DF 15; BR 23; BM 237–238

GILMOUR
• Friend of Ginger Littlejohn who insults Adam Fenwick-Symes in a nightclub before making friends with him and Nina and Agatha. They all go back to his flat in Ryder Street where is is sick after drinking too much.
VB 125

GILPIN
Fellow student of Guy Crouchback's at Training Centre No. 4. Rebukes de Souza for careless talk. Member of the Education Corps. School teacher before the war. 'A bit earnest'. When next encountered by Guy at Bari he is extremely unfriendly.

After the war stands for parliament against Elderberry, and wins. Although not a popular MP in the house, by 1951 he is an Under-Secretary.
US 96, 97, 153, 213, 236, 238

GIRAUD, M.
Employee of the Railway in Ishmaelia. In reality he is employed by Mr Baldwin (q.v.). Intermediate with the Russians.
Sc 86, 169

GIRL GUIDES
Girls' equivalent of the Boy Scouts,

founded in 1910 by Lady Baden Powell.

• Dame Mildred Porch is an ex Guide-Leader. She has led them through the bracken of Epping, but hurling a brandy bottle from a roof is not part of her Guide training.

BM 185, 192, 196

GLASGOW, SCOTLAND

Trimmer and Virginia Crouchback meet here in November 1940 in the restaurant of the station hotel. The city is enveloped in fog.

• A strike here is stopped in 1941 by 'Aid to Russia'.

• A Glasgow policeman receives a 'nasty poke' with one of the 'commando daggers' introduced in 1941.

• To Dennis Barlow 'Hogmanay' means 'people being sick on the pavement in Glasgow'.

• One of the places where the *Daily Beast* is printed.

• Hometown of Angela Lyne's father.

• One of the cities where the Sword of Stalingrad is exhibited.

OG 72, 79, 246; US 44; LO 100; Sc 56; PF 26

GLASS, HALBERDIER

Soldier servant to Charles Ryder in 1940. Surly, he revels in bad news, and is a 'regular'.

MA 187

GLENDENNING-REES, DOCTOR

A tall, wild looking man with a grey beard. He wears a leather suit and gold-rimmed pince-nez. Is engaged by the commandos in 1940 to teach them the means of gathering nutrition from their environment. Eats seaweed, limpets and roots.

• Served at Gallipoli in the Great War. After his initial time on Mugg, he is given a team of dieticians in Upper Norwood 'from whose experiments batches of emaciated "conscientious objectors" were from time to time removed to hospital'.

• In HOOHQ in 1944.

OG 93, 94, 95; US 26, 185

GLENOBANS, THE

London society couple, from Scotland, who throw a party in October 1943 to which Lieutenant Padfield (q.v.) is invited but Guy Crouchback is not. Guy suggests that the Lieutenant gives a Staffordshire figure of Gladstone to the Glenobans.

US 25, 123

GLOUCESTERSHIRE

Home county of the Box-Benders and Sir James Brown.

VB 41; MA 26

GLOVER, COLONEL

One of the military acquaintances to whom Guy Crouchback writes in 1939 asking for a commission. Served with Gervase Crouchback in the Irish Guards in World War One.

MA 23

GLUCK, GRAFFIN VON

Neighbour of Guy Crouchback at Santa Dulcina, where she lives in the Casa Gluck. Speaks no Italian. Lives in sin with her butler. The Italians find her 'simpatica'.

MA 12, 15

GLUCK, MR VAN

Executive at Megalopolitan Pictures.

LO 26

GLYN, ELINOR *(1864–1943)*

British novelist. Author of *Three Weeks* (1907), *Man and Maid* (1922), and *Did She?* (1934). Her books, despite being badly written were, from their sheer 'naughtiness', enormously successful.

• Air Marshal Beech recites a 'clever rhyme' about her at the Kilbannock's party:

> Would you like to sin
> With Eleanor Glyn
> On a tiger skin?
> Or would you prefer
> With her
> To err
> On some other fur?

• However, when Virginia Crouchback asks him who Elinor Glyn is he has no idea.

• Ruby tells Lieutenant Padfield all about her.
MA 125; US 78

GOA
Former Portuguese colony on India's west coast.
• In Azania Lady Courteney has a Goanese butler.
• The stewards on board Guy Crouchback's troopship in 1940 are Goanese.
• Goanese tailors abound in Jacksonburg.
Sc 94; MA 218; BM 212

GODS
Primitive people always have a God who speaks from within a cloud.
PF 175
(*See* RELIGION)

GOEBBELS, JOSEPH *(1897–1945)*
German Nazi minister and head of the Ministry of Propaganda.
• A friend of a friend of Rex Mottram is told 'something' by Goebbels in 1938.
BR 279

GOERING, HERMANN WILHELM *(1893–1946)*
Nazi leader and head of the Luftwaffe. Appointed in 1932, President of the Reichstag. Founder of the Gestapo. Committed suicide while awaiting execution.
• A friend of a friend of Rex Mottram is told 'something' by Goering in 1938.
BR 279

GOETHE, JOHANN WOLFGANG VON *(1749–1832)*
German poet dramatist, politician and philosopher. Author of *Faust* (1775–1832). Had an enormous influence on Carlyle and other Victorian writers.
• The Neutralian government have never heard of him.
WS 226

GOLD, HALBERDIER
Soldier servant to Major Tickeridge (q.v.).
• Welcomes Guy Crouchback back to the Halberdiers in 1941 on Crete.
MA 39; OG 209

GOLF
Apthorpe plays golf with one of the regular Halberdier officers.
MA 58

GOODALL, AMBROSE
Devout Catholic and member of the Southsand and Mudshore Yacht Squadron. Meets Guy Crouchback at the Catholic church at Southsand, where he carries the collection plate. Ecclesiastical historian of the Catholic church and sometime master at Staplehurst School (until 1930). He writes on heraldry for *The Tablet* (q.v.). Puts up Guy and Apthorpe as temporary members of the Squadron. Later holds the belief that a great crusade will take place 'to redeem the times'. Guy sees him as 'a gentler version of poor, mad Ivo' (Crouchback) (q.v.).
MA 108–111; OG 40–41

GOODCHILD, BISHOP
• Anglican Bishop of Debra Dowa in 1932. Brings news from the town to the Legation.
• Plays Peggity with Prudence Courteney.
BM 51, 59, 197

GOODCHILD AND GODLEY
Art dealers of Duke Street, London who pay Mr Plant a yearly retainer for 'restoration' (q.v.).
WS 115

GOODWOOD, SUSSEX
Racecourse where, every July, Goodwood week is held. Alastair Trumpington wears a bowler hat in London until the week after Goodwood.
PF 44

GORDON, GENERAL CHARLES GEORGE *(1838–1885)*
British soldier. Served in Turkey, China and the Sudan. Killed at Khartoum.
• Lady Seal tells Basil that General Gordon was a Sapper.
PF 143

GORE, SIR LIONEL
Retired Harley Street doctor. Commo-

dore of the Southsand and Mudshore Yacht Squadron (also the Secretary). Signs in Guy Crouchback and Apthorpe as temporary members.
MA 111

GORGIAS
Predecessor of the Nestorian Patriach of Azania, responsible for shutting Achon up in the monastery of St Mark the Evangelist.
BM 164

GORGON, THE
Monster of Greek legend, Medusa, whose gaze would turn any mortal to stone. She was eventually slain by Perseus.
• Basil Seal's affair with Angela Lyne seems to have been petrified by 'a Gorgon glance'.
PF 26

GOSSIP COLUMNS
• The gossip columnist of the *Daily Express* suggests sending the Sword of Stalingrad around the Kingdom.
• Everard Spruce, like many left-wingers, is a close follower of the gossip columns, which, he says allow him to know his enemy.
US 22, 199
(See also CHATTERBOX, BALCAIRN, FENWICK-SYMES, VANBRUGH)

GOVERNESSES
One of Cordelia Flyte's governesses drowns herself by jumping off a bridge at Brideshead.
BR 293

GPO
In Barbara Sothill's world these initials stand not for General Post Office but Garden Party Only. It is this list that Basil Seal uses for his exploits with the Connollys (q.v.).
PF 88

GRACE-GROUNDLING-MARCHPOLE, COLONEL
First appears as a junior officer at HOOHQ. By 1941 has been promoted to Colonel and head of the Most Secret Department of HOOHQ.
MA 160; OG 78

GRACE-GROUNDLING-MARCHPOLE, MAJOR
Major in the Halberdiers. Brother of Colonel Grace-Groundling-Marchpole (q.v.). Takes Ian Kilbannnock to dinner in Bari.
US 209

GRAFFITI
'Second Front Now' is written on a brick wall in great College Street, in October 1943.
• 'The Pope is a Traitor' is written in tar on a pillar box in Ballingar in 1932.
• 'Death to the Marshal' is written in red paint on the wall of the National Memorial of Neutralia in 1946.
US 21; WS 77, 228

GRAINGER
Maid to Angela Lyne in 1939.
PF 135

GRAINGER, JIMMIE
Friend of Arthur Atwater who knows 'almost everyone'.
WS 135, 187

GRAINGER, NURSE
One of the old nurses at Boot Magna Hall. It is thought that she will not last long. Always tells Mrs Boot that her patient is 'a little low spirited'.
Sc 19, 204

GRAMOPHONES
Paul Pennyfeather's guardian's daughter has a gramophone.
• Margot Metroland has a panotrope.
• Reggie St Cloud gives John Last a little gramophone.
• Prudence Courteney and William Bland play the gramophone at the Legation in Azania.
• Ambrose Silk owns a gramophone player.
DF 15, 128; HD 91; BM 59; PF 194

GRANCHESTER, LADY EMMA
Friend of the King (in 1939) and of Lady Seal.
• Margot Metroland tells her son Peter Pastmaster that the younger daughter, Lady Mary Meadowes (q.v.), is very pretty.
PF 27, 134, 137, 152

GRANCHESTER
Where Scott-King teaches classics. Not 'the most illustrious' of English public schools, but has a number of famous men as old boys. Holds annual cricket match at Lord's.
WS 195, 213

GRANT, DOCTOR
Doctor to Lord Marchmain who advises against administering the last rites.
BR 320

GRANTLEY GREEN, GLOUCESTERSHIRE
Village near Malfrey where Basil Seal has a brief affair with Bill's wife in 1939.
PF 121

GRASS, BARTHOLEMEW
Pseudonym adopted by Ambrose Silk for an article in *Ivory Tower* (q.v.).
• Mr Bentley tells the police that it may in fact be a woman.
PF 193, 199

GRAVES, MR *(b.1890)*
Charles Ryder's English Master at Lancing College in 1919. Charles thinks him 'a tick'. Smokes a pipe; Old Rugbeian; served in WWI. Replaces Frank's football picture with Medici prints. Owns a set of 'Georgian Poetry' and a tobacco jar with the arms of his college. Has an awkward interview with Charles, whom he calls a prig.
WS 289, 294–296

GRAVES, MR AND MRS
Neighbours of Gilbert Pinfold at Lychpole.
GP 11

GRAVES, MAJOR
Ex-Indian Cavalry officer appointed to command of the 'specialists' of X Commando on Mugg.
• He is a 'disgruntled, sandy little man whose heart was in the North-West Frontier'.*OG 89*

GRAVES-UPTON, REGINALD
Batchelor neighbour of the Pinfolds at Lychpole. Lives in a thatched cottage less than a mile from the Manor. Walks to church across the Pinfolds' fields on Sundays and has a sherry on his return. Has a Cairn terrier and keeps bees. Known by the Pinfolds as 'the Bruiser', 'Pug', 'Basher', 'Old Fisticuffs' and 'Boxer' on account of his devotion to 'the Box' (q.v.). In Pinfold's mind he becomes 'a sort of cousin' of Margaret.
US 11–12, 150

GRAYBRIDGE, LADY
Her butler lets out the North wing of her house as lodgings. She can never understand where all the fruit gets to. Falls ill and dies. Friend of Colonel Blout.
VB 204

GREAT NORTH ROAD
Route taken by Adam Symes and Archie Schwert back to London from the motor races.
VB 181

GREAT PYRAMID, CAIRO
Sir Samson Courteney receives a circular letter about the Great Pyramid. It is a 'cosmic allegory' to do with comparing the dimensions of the Great Pyramid with numbers from the Life of Christ.
• One of Guy Crouchback's fellow inmates at the RAF hospital is a conscientious objector whose argument is based on the dimensions of the Great Pyramid.
BM 104; US 115

GREECE
Professor Silenus finds the buildings of ancient Greece 'unspeakably ugly'.
• Greek traders play draughts at a small hotel, owned by a Greek, in Tunis.
• There is a Greek Hotel in Lumo (q.v.).

• Sebastian Flyte and Kurt move to Greece in 1927, where Kurt is arrested.
• To be Greek in 1941 'is to be in mourning'.
• A Greek in the carriage of the train to Debra Dowa offers Basil Seal an orange.
• Guy Crouchback tries to remember a little Greek from his schooldays to talk to an old woman on Crete.
• The Greek Royal Family attend a party thrown by Julia Stitch in Alexandria in 1941.
• In Mr Plant's opinion the religious opinions of the ancient Greeks were 'preposterous'.
DF 207; BR 289, 291; OG 131, 206, 243; WS 113; BM 12, 41, 98; Sc 93

GREEN, COLONEL GEOFFREY
Captain Commandant of the Halberdiers. Was a Brigade Major when Ritchie-Hook only had a platoon. Guy Crouchback has Sunday lunch with him. Somewhat afraid of Ritchie-Hook, and thus always smokes a pipe when in his company. Goggles in admiration at Mrs Leonard's bravery in the presence of Ritchie-Hook.
MA 61–68; OG 249

GREEN, GORRIDGE AND WRIGHT LIMITED
Salford firm who employed Engineer Garcia for seven years.
WS 212

GREEN, POPPET
Surrealist artist in 1939. Friend of Ambrose Silk. Has a brief affair with Basil Seal. Lives in South Kensington. Is terrified of air raids. Is cured before the war by Erchman. Discusses the Parsnip-Pimpernell controversy with her friends at the Café Royal. Basil Seal tells Colonel Plum that she is the head of an illegal organization smuggling young men out of the country.
PF 29–39, 166

GREENE, GRAHAM *(b.1904)*
English novelist. Author of some thirty novels including *Stamboul Train* (1932), *Brighton Rock* (1938), *The Power and the Glory* (1940), and *The Heart of the Matter* (1948).
• This last book is recalled by Guy Crouchback when years later he thinks back to his part in the raid on the coast near Dakar in 1940.
MA 232

GREENERY-YALLERY
(See GROSVENOR GALLERY).
BR 54

GREENIDGE, LADY
Confidante of John Boot.
Sc 184

GREENOCK
Scottish town at which Trimmer lands from Mugg in 1940.
OG 79

GREGSON
Solicitor to Lord Marchmain.
BR306

GRENET, ALPHONSE DE
According to Cara, Mme De Grenet had a priest waiting outside the room in which her husband lay dying.
BR 313

GRESHAM, PUSSY
Friend of Theodore Boot in the 1890s.
Sc 213

GRESWOLD
Pupil of Mr Crouchback at Matchet who diverts him on to the topic of the Blessed Gervase (q.v.). Captain of the Our Lady of Victory cricket team. Good fast bowler.
OG 21, 151

GRETNA GREEN
Village in Dumfriesshire, traditionally associated with elopement. Basil Seal threatens Charles Albright (q.v.) with 'one of those "Gretna Green" Romances'.
WS 276

GREYHOUND RACING
Philbrick discusses greyhound racing with

Sam Clutterbuck at the Llanabba sports day.
DF 76

GRIFFENBACH
Austrian dietician who exploded the onions and porridge diet in 1928.
BM 73

GRIFFITHS, SIR ALMERIC
Prominent orchestral conductor and composer. Imported to Bari by the UNRRA. Killed in the plane crash in Dalmatia. Wesleyan. Tells Guy Crouchback that he has 'the death wish'.
US 169–170, 210, 214, 224

GRIGGS
Master of Granchester School. Opposed to the teaching of classics. Talks in 'strident tones'. Is keen to go to a rally on 'Progressive Youth Leadership' held in Prague in 1946. Thinks that no decent-minded man would want to go to Ireland.
WS 200–201

GRIGSHAWE, SERGEANT
One of the best drill sergeants in the Halberdiers. Becomes a Major in the RASC. Attempts to clear room for quarters in the Marine Hotel, Matchet, but is dissuaded by Jumbo Trotter.
OG 34–37

GRIMES, CAPTAIN EDGAR
(b. circa 1892)
He is short, thick-set and has a short red moustache and a wooden leg and is slightly bald. Walks with a stick. Is always landing 'in the soup'. Is proud to be a 'public school man'. Educated at Harrow, he is expelled on his sixteenth birthday for indecency.

Goes into a brush factory owned by his uncle in Edmonton. Joins up in the Great War. Sent to Ireland in the army, connected with the postal service. Is married to Jane Grimes (q.v.) in Ireland. As far as he is concerned, 'women are an enigma'.

Lost his leg under a tram in Stoke-on-Trent when he was 'one over the eight'. Makes out that he lost it during the Great War.

Master at Llanabba School in 1922 and is engaged to Flossie Fagan. Takes Paul Pennyfeather to Mrs Roberts' pub.

Tells Paul that his trouble is 'temperament and sex'.

His homosexual conduct is uncovered at the same time as his engagement is announced. In Dr Fagan's eyes he is possessed by 'slavish poverty, abominable features, moral turpitude and an incredible vocabulary'. However, Fagan has to agree to the wedding for economic reasons. Tells Paul and Prendergast that marriage is 'rather a grim thought . . . oh why did nobody warn me? . . . I should have been told . . . They should have told me that at the end of that gay journey and flower-strewn path were the hideous lights of home and the voices of children . . . We can't escape, try how we may . . . nature always wins'. Is determined not to have any children, at least.

Marries Flossie at Llanabba Parish church and over the next few days he is seen little. Hates married life. Is offered a job by Clutterbuck's father as a beer salesman. It is too late to accept. Decides to take it nevertheless. Becomes worried about Divine Retribution. Loses his confidence and fakes his suicide.

Travels to London where, in a pub in Shaftesbury Avenue, he meets 'Bill', who offers him a job with the Latin American Entertainment Company, which he accepts. Turns up at King's Thursday, disguised with a long red beard.

Turns up at Egdon Heath where he meets Paul. Sentenced to three years for bigamy, having been discovered by his first wife. Decides to escape from prison. Rides off across the moor on the warder's horse. It is generally presumed that he is drowned in Egdon Mire where his hat is found. Paul, however, knows that he is not dead: 'Grimes, Paul at last realized was one of the immortals. He was a life force . . . Surely he had followed in the bacchic train of distant Arcady . . . had he not suffered unscathed the fearful dooms of all the offended gods . . . had he not moved unseen when the darkness covered the waters?'

DF 22, 26–30, 31, 34, 36, 39, 74, 88, 96–7, 101–103, 105, 110–111, 113, 114, 138–140, 189, 196–199

GRIMES, JANE
Wife of Captain Grimes (q.v.). Irish. Turns up at Llanabba and makes trouble after Grimes' 'suicide'. Sent to Margot Metroland by a gentleman at Cardiff. Joins Margot's girls in Marseilles and then Brazil.
DF 141, 145, 153

GRIMM, JACOB LUDWIG CARL
Author, with his brother Wilhelm, of Grimm's Fairy Tales (1812).
• In Guy Crouchback's mind the tales of Grimm are barely distinguishable from Old Testament history.
US 226

GRITS, ELFREDA
Secretary to Sir James Macrae, assigned to Simon Lent. Has 'bright eyes and a very firm mouth'. Wears a red hat at a jaunty angle. Smokes cigarettes on the film set.

Works with Simon for three weeks. He cannot think of her as anything else apart from 'Miss Grits'. Simon has 'vivid, unsentimental passages of love' with her.
WS 66, 67, 72–73

GRIZEL
Friend of Rex Mottram in 1936. 'A knowing rake', feared by his other friends, but who, in her own turn fears Julia.
BR 261

GROAT, MRS
Cook to Angela Box-Bender. Forgets to black-out the larder.
MA 31

GROGGIN, SERGEANT MAJOR
One of the senior NCOs instructing Guy Crouchback's officer intake in 1939, who shows them how to 'tell' meat.
MA 49

GROSVENOR GALLERY
London art gallery in New Bond Street which was instrumental in bringing the works of Whistler and the 'Aesthetes' of the 1890s to the public eye. Immortalised in the Gilbert and Sullivan operetta 'Patience' whose libretto includes the famous reference to 'greenery-yallery, Grosvenor Gallery' – an allusion to the paler tones used in their paintings by Whistler and his circle.
• John Plant conjectures that, confronted by a vogue for his allegorical paintings, his father may have 'retreated to the standards of the Grosvenor Gallery in the nineties'.
• According to Anthony Blanche there is 'nothing greenery-yallery' about Julia Flyte.
WS 117

GRUMPS
Previous name of Much Malcock Hall (q.v.).
WS 45

GRYLLS, THE
Ancestors of Guy Crouchback. Ambrose Goodall has a veneration for the Blessed John Gryll.
MA 109

GUATEMALA
Central American country between Mexico and Honduras, visited by Charles Ryder in 1935. Here he hears a half-caste choir sing 'Quomodo sedet sola civitas'.
BR 225

GULU
Village in the Azanian interior to which Basil Seal rides in pursuit of Seth. Here he discovers that Seth has been murdered and instructs Joab to kill Boaz.
BM 218, 221

H

HABSBURGS
In 1646 Neutralia (q.v.), was part of the Habsburg Empire. It remained such until 1919, when it was given to Serbia. In 1945 it became part of the USSR.
WS 196, 218

HACKET, BEN
Groom to Tony Last at Hetton. Renowned for swearing. Teaches John Last various oaths and expressions. Tells John about 'Thunderclap' (q.v.), also about Zero, and 'Peppermint', the company mule.
• After Tony's 'death' he stays on at Hetton and helps Teddy Last rear the silver foxes.
HD 19, 221

HAIFA
City in Israel visited by the *SS Glory of Greece*.
WS 18

HAIR
Hooper (q.v.) has his hair cut by a brother officer on the instructions of Charles Ryder's Colonel.
• Before the war, Trimmer (q.v.) was a hairdresser on Atlantic liners. General Whale considers that Trimmer's hair shows that he is proletarian.
Br 14; OE 75

HAIRSTYLING IN THE ORIENT
On which Aimee Thanatogenos writes her thesis.
LO 73

HALBERDIERS
(*See* BRITISH ARMY)

HALFPENNY, WILLIAM *(d.1755)*
English Palladian architect and author of twenty-four manuals on architecture for country gentlemen, including *Rural Architecture in the Chinese Taste* (1750).
• Architect of the composed hermitage in the Chinese taste, just outside Bath, that Roger Simmonds proposes as a house for John Plant (q.v.). Roger has a collection of his works.
WS 144

HALIFAX, EDWARD LINDLEY WOOD, FIRST EARL OF *(1818–1959)*
Conservative statesman. Viceroy of India 1926–1931; Foreign Secretary 1938–1940. Implemented Chamberlain's policy of 'appeasement'.
• One of Rex Mottram's guests at Brideshead in 1938 thinks that 'if it wasn't for Halifax . . .'.
BR 280

HALIFAX
Town in Yorkshire.
• One of the towns visited by 'Trimmer' (q.v.) on his morale raising tour in 1941, on which he is accompanied by Virginia Crouchback (q.v.).
OG 248

HALLUCINATIONS
• Agatha Runcible suffers from hallucinations in her delirium following her car crash. She imagines herself back in the car going faster and faster.
• Tony Last, fever-ridden, in the South American jungle, sees visions of Brenda, and later of the County Council, Reggie St Cloud, Lady Cockpurse and Molly.
• In the boat in which he escapes from Crete in 1941, Guy Crouchback has hallucinations. He hears whales singing, and sees the 'numberless ageless lizard-faces' of countless turtles.
• Major Cattermole (q.v.) also has hal-

lucinations during his escape from Crete.
• Gilbert Pinfold suffers from numerous, vivid hallucinations while a passenger on board the SS *Caliban*.

The first is a jazz band. This is quickly followed by a dog, a religious meeting, and a clergyman reprimanding 'Billy' (q.v.). Later he hears a band playing the 'three-eight rhythm', the crew being bullied, an oratorio, and voices accusing him of drinking.

The voices really get going however, with the torture of a Goanese steward and the appearance of Steerforth, Goneril and Margaret.

Margaret becomes the major voice in Pinfold's head. He then hears a broadcast by the third programme in which he is insulted by Clutton-Cornforth, followed by a female singer singing: 'I'm Gilbert the Filbert'. Later he hears two young men, one called Fosker, talking about him and playing him music. Margaret and another girl sing to him. A General appears and then Pinfold is accused by the boys of shirking in the war, being a foreigner, being a jewel thief, despoiling the church, being only outwardly religious, and of sodomy. They prepare to attack him, but one of them vomits and they do not carry out their threat.

He hears Margaret say that she has left presents for him in his cabin. The boys threaten him again. James Lance and June Cumberleigh insult him on the third programme. He hears the two Generals discuss a Spanish threat to take back Gibraltar and propose him as a secret agent in the affair. There is no Spanish ship or crisis, but instead of realizing that this is one of a series of hallucinations Pinfold thinks it just a hoax on the part of his imaginary tormentors.

His voices next call him a homosexual and persist in saying that he is only a Catholic because he thinks it aristocratic. They organize a petition to get Pinfold removed from the Captain's table. They accuse him of having been a Fascist, then a Communist, then a Jew. He hears Mrs Cockson and Mrs Benson insulting him in French.

The voices become increasingly nasty saying that the income tax inspectors will take every penny he has and that his wife will leave him, his children be taken away and that he will have to sell Lychpole.

Margaret tells him to have a hair cut and a shave. Margaret is 'prepared' for her 'wedding' to him. He refuses her advances and her father, the General, accuses him of being impotent. Pinfold then hears the wireless operator reading his own telegraph messages home to a party of his persecutors. He has only sent one message but imagines that he has sent a dozen.

He then decides that Mr Angel (q.v.) is behind the whole thing. He is asked why he was in Egypt in 1929, and accused of being responsible for the suicide of a staff-officer in the Middle-East.

He hears 'Operation Stock Exchange' in which the voices try to persuade him that there has been a world-wide financial slump. He is a victim of Angel's Box. They play him recordings of factory machinery, said by Swiss scientists to lull factory workers to sleep. Nightingales sing to him.

The voices follow him to Cairo, on to Colombo and to Paris. He is cured in England, when he stops taking the Bromide and Chloral which, when mixed with the grey pills prescribed by Dr Drake, had been responsible for the hallucinations.
VB 200; HD 194, 201–207; OG 238; US 162; GH 38, 51, 57, 59, 62, 68, 72, 89, 103, 134, 144, 149, 156

HALT, BERTHA VAN
Godmother of Caroline Ryder (q.v.). Gives only a fifteen shilling book-token as a christening present.
BR 219

HAMILTON-BRAND
CIC at Gibraltar on whose staff Jumbo Trotter was, along with a fellow at Area HQ.
OG 43

HAMPSHIRE
Location of King's Thursday (q.v.).
• Where the Lynes have their house.
DF 115; PF 26

HANGOVERS
Ian Kilbannock, awaking from sleep following his survival of the plane crash in Yugoslavia, feels as if he has been out on the town the previous evening.
US 215

HANNIBAL *(247–182 BC)*
Carthaginian General particularly famed for having used elephants to lead his army across the Alps in 218 BC.
PF 114

HANS
Boyfriend of Ambrose Silk (q.v.). Hitler Youth, later a Brownshirt. By 1939, however, he is in a Nazi concentration camp.
PF 42, 186–188

HAPPIER HUNTING GROUND
Animal cemetery in Los Angeles owned by Mr Schultz, where Dennis Barlow (q.v.) works. 'A dreadful place here where they bury animals'.
LO 16, 17, 50, 77

HARDCASTLE
Owner of the motor-car in which Charles Ryder and Sebastian Flyte visit Brideshead in June 1922. They leave his car out and get him into trouble with the proctors, thus forcing them to throw several dinner parties to comfort him. The parties obviously do the trick, because it is Hardcastle's car which they again borrow to travel to London for the dance after which they are arrested for drunken driving.
BR 25, 42, 108, 119

HARDCASTLE, ALFRED
'A large, neat, middle-aged, melancholy, likeable fellow. . .'. Chairman of the St. John's Wood Residential Amenities Company. Builder of the blocks of flats beside Mr Plant's (q.v.) house. Offers Mr Plant £6,000 for his freehold in 1928. Later becomes chairman of the newly named Hill Crest Court Exploitation Company.
WS 140–141

HARGOOD-HOOD, MR
Country gentleman. Lives in Gloucestershire, in 'a double quadrangle of mellow brick that was famous far beyond the county', built by his ancestors and very costly to maintain.
WS 56–61

HARKNESSES, THE
Middle-aged couple who live at Old Mill House (q.v.), North Grappling, a fifteenth century mill converted by a pupil of William Morris. He is retired. She is 'musical'. Advertise for boarders in the local newspaper at Malfrey. Basil billets the Connollys (q.v.) on them.
PF 89–98

HARLEM
Predominantly black area of New York where the cause of the Jacksons (q.v.) is taken up in 1937.
Sc 78

HAROUN AL RASHID *(785–809)*
Fifth Caliph of Arabia. Friend of Charlemagne; reigned in an enlightened way over his people, among whom he wandered in disguise. Romanticized in the *Arabian Nights*.
• Lord Monomark (q.v.) likes to appear as an 'undisguised Haroun al Rashid among his own townspeople'.
BM 72

HARPER, MISS
Secretary to Sir James Macrae.
WS 66

HARRIS, SERGEANT
'A man of excellent character, fine disciplinarian, knows his stuff backwards, the men will follow him anywhere. As such he is suggested by Captain Mayfield (q.v.) for Officer Training.

Turned down as a candidate by the company sergeant major because the company football team is unable to function without him.
PF 103

HASHISH
When leaping from an aeroplane with a

parachute, during the war, Gilbert Pinfold feels one with 'hashish eaters'.
GP 142

HASSALL
Charles Ryder writes his diary at Lancing under the cover of Hassall's *History*.
WS 287

HAT, MR
Friend of Ambrose Silk in the 1920s who with him and Malpractice (q.v.) issued a party invitation in the form of a manifesto.
PF 185

HAW-HAW, LORD
Radio name adopted by William Joyce (1906–1946), an Englishman, who broadcast morale-levering propaganda from Berlin during WWII. Angela Lyne listens to him in the Spring of 1940 blame Churchill for the bombing of the Chaplain-General.
PF 151

HAWKINS, NANNY
Nanny to the Flyte children at Brideshead (q.v.). She lives in the dome of the castle and is always the main source of gossip in the house. Charles Ryder meets her on his first trip to Brideshead in 1922. Thinks it absurd to make a nun of Julia Flyte. Believes that the upper classes spend their evenings in the ballroom. By 1938 has a small wireless set.
• Is not fond of Lord Brideshead. Considers that he has been caught by Beryl Muspratt.
• By 1943 she has aged considerably and does not at first recognise Charles. By now her dialect has reverted to 'the soft, peasant tones of its origin'.
BR 36–38, 147, 274, 286, 328

HAWKINS, SIR JOHN ***(1532–1595)***
Elizabethan Admiral who, in July 1588, with Drake, Frobisher and Howard, defeated the Spanish off Flanders.
• One of Rex Mottram's friends invokes, in 1938, the memory of Hawkins and Drake.
BR 262

HAWKSMOOR, NICHOLAS ***(1616–1736)***
English architect and exponent of the Baroque style (q.v.). Pupil of Wren and Vanburgh, with whom he worked on Castle Howard. See his Christ Church, Spitalfields; Quadrangle of All Souls, Oxford; and Doric Mausoleum at Castle Howard.
• Mrs Stitch's house is 'a suberb creation by Nicholas Hawksmoor modestly concealed in a cul-de-sac near St James's Palace'.
Sc 5

HAY, IAN (MAJOR GENERAL JOHN HAY BEITH) ***(1876–1952)***
Scottish novelist and playwright. Served WWI. Author of light novels *Pip* (1907) and *A Knight on Wheels* (1914) and war books: *The First Hundred Thousand* (1915).
• Apthorpe (q.v.) complains to Guy Crouchback that all the hospital nurses in Africa bring him are 'jigsaws and Ian Hay'.
MA 235

HAY, WILL
English star of music hall and comedy films of the 1930s. Among his characters was an eccentric schoolmaster.
• Some of the gowns worn by the scholars at the Bellorius conference in Neutralia are reminiscent of Will Hay's.
WS 211

HAYDN, FRANZ JOSEPH ***(1732–1809)***
Austrian composer. Tutor of Beethoven.
• In the opinion of Soapy (q.v.), the string quartet at Mountjoy play Mozart as if it were Haydn.
GP 181

HAYTER
Butler to Mr Ryder (q.v.).
BR 62

HAYTER
'Cocky' young regular officer in Guy Crouchback's (D) company of the Halberdiers. Guy does not respect him and believes that he himself is a better officer.

The view is shared by Major Erskine, who has him posted to Air Liaison.
MA 167, 171, 197

HEADLINES

- PRISON FOR EX-SOCIETY BRIDEGROOM. JUDGE ON HUMAN VAMPIRES.

Paul Pennyfeather is sentenced.

- WEDDING SENSATION ECHO. DEATH OF SOCIETY BRIDEGROOM CONVICT.

Paul Pennyfeather's 'death'.

- PEER'S DAUGHTER'S DOVER ORDEAL. SERIOUS ALLEGATIONS BY SOCIETY BEAUTY.

Agatha Runcible is searched by customs men.

- MIDNIGHT ORGIES AT NO. 10.

The Bright Young People have a party.

- TRAGEDY IN WEST END HOTEL.

Flossie falls from a chandelier at Lottie Crump's.

- SOCIETY BEAUTY IN PUBLIC CONVENIENCE.

Mrs Stitch drives down the gentlemens' lavatory in Sloane Street.

- MARQUIS'S SON UNUSED TO WINE. MODEL STUDENT'S CAREER AT STAKE.

On Sebastian Flyte after he is arrested.
DR 160, 206; VB 35, 59, 76; Sc 48; BR 119

HEADLONG CORNER

The best viewpoint at the racetrack where the Bright Young People go to see the motor race.
VB 158

HEARST PRESS

Newspaper empire of William Randolph Hearst (*1863–1951*)

- Pappenhacker (q.v.) is employed by them in 1939.

PF 69

HEATHER

One of John Plant's heroines in his novel *The Frightened Footman* (q.v.).
WS 159

HECTOR

Boyfriend of Millicent Blade (q.v.) who goes to Kenya to buy a farm, and before going gives Millicent 'Hector' the poodle (q.v.).
WS 31

'HECTOR'

(*See* DOGS; CHASTITY BELTS)

HEGEL, GEORG WILHELM FREDERICH *(1770–1831)*

German philosopher and author of *The Science of Logic* (1816) which contains his dialectical *Logic*.

- Mr Samgrass (q.v.) considers that one of Lady Marchmain's houseguests at Brideshead in the Christmas of 1923 has read 'too much Maritain (q.v.) and too little Hegel'.

BR 120

HELEN OF TROY

Wife of Menelaus, King of Sparta whose legendary beauty inspired her abduction by Paris, thus provoking the Trojan War and its consequences.

- Guy Crouchback's hospital in Alexandria in 1941 is stirred by 'the softly petulant north-west wind, which long ago delayed Helen and Menelaus on that strand.'

OG 226

HELM-HUBBARDS, THE

London society couple about whom Brenda Last asks John Beaver. He tells her that their marriage is not going 'too well'.
HD 27

HEMINGWAY, MRS

Friend of two women, fellow passengers of Adam Fenwick-Symes on the train to Aylesbury.
VB 138

HEMINGWAY, ERNEST *(1899–1961)*

Celebrated American novelist notable for his innovative use of the vernacular in stories whose common theme is physical determination. See his *The Sun Also Rises* (1926) and *For Whom the Bell Tolls* (1940).

- Hemingway's *A Farewell to Arms* (*see* BOOKS) is among the books in Tony Last's bedroom at Hetton.
- All the girls on whom Peter Pastmaster

(q.v.) is keen in 1939 have 'an enthusiasm for the works of Mr Ernest Hemingway'.
• Everard Spruce (q.v.) compares Virginia Crouchback (q.v.) to Bret in Hemingway's *The Sun Also Rises*.
HD 16; PF 152; US 200

HEMP
'Black sheep' of the batch of officers from the Halberdiers training depot who Guy Crouchback sees as their equivalent to Trimmer (q.v.). He is a Catholic, and 'not over scrupulous in his religious duties', from which he claims to have read that all servicemen are dispensed.
MA 93, 108

HENLEY
Town in Berkshire and home, every June, of the Henley Regatta.
• Charles Ryder supposes that Lord Brideshead's chosen subject for a picture, were he to paint one, might be the Henley Regatta.
BR 269

HENRY V ***(1387–1422)***
King of England (1413–1422). Victor of Agincourt (1415). Subject of a play by Shakespeare (q.v.).
• Hooper (q.v.) has never wept 'for Henry's speech on St Crispin's day'.
BR 15

HENRY VII ***(1457–1509)***
King of England (1485–1509). Founder of the Tudor dynasty and father of Henry VIII.
• Arthur Atwater (q.v.) claims to be descended from.
WS 180

HEPPELLS
London chemist in Mayfair to which Rex Mottram sends round for a hangover cure on the morning after Sebastian Flyte and Charles Ryder are arrested.
BR 115

HERA
In Greek mythology, the wife of Zeus and queen of the Gods.
• To Guy Crouchback, Apthorpe (q.v.), cocooned in his mosquito netting is 'soothed and wooed and gently overborne like Hera in the arms of Zeus'.
MA 164

HERESY
In the province of Mhomala on the island of Azania, a 'ridiculous heresy' springs up that the prophet Esias had wings and lived in a tree.
• The ascetic Ebionites used to turn towards Jerusalem when they prayed.
• A bishop of Bithynia (q.v.) denied the Divinity of Christ and many other things besides.
DF 212, 216; BM 144

HEROES
In 1941 heroes are 'in strong demand. Urgently required to boost civilian morale'. These heroes are found in the commandos.
• Ian Kilbannock tells Guy Crouchback that he is sure that heroes are 'delightful fellows. . .but the Wrong Period. Last-war stuff, Guy. Went out with Rupert Brooke' (q.v.). In the Second World War the heroes must, he explains, come, not from the upper classes, like X Commando (q.v.), but from the people.
OG 101

HEROINES
According to Everard Spruce (q.v.) Virginia Troy is 'the last of twenty years' succession of heroines . . . The ghosts of romance who walked between the two wars'. With her he classes Huxley's Mrs Viveash and Hemingway's Bret (both q.v.).
US 200

HESKETH-SMITHERS, SIR PHILIP
Departmental assistant director of Mr Bentley's department at the Ministry of Information. He is 'a drab, precise little man'.
PF 64

HETTON
Home of Tony Last. One reaches it

by train from Paddington. Lies midway between Hetton villlage and Compton Last.

The house was rebuilt in 1864 in the gothic style. The grounds are open to the public. The terrace has a fine view. It is not a comfortable house in modern terms.

It has battlements and a central clock tower.

Its great hall has a painted, groined ceiling in red and gold diapers, supported by polished granite pillars with vine capitals. There are lancet windows with armorial stained glass and a huge brass and wrought-iron gasolier with twenty electric bulbs. The heating is through grills in the floor by way of cast iron trefoils.

The dining hall has a hammer-beam roof and a pitch–pine minstrels' gallery.

The bedrooms all have brass bedsteads and are each named after an Arthurian character from Malory – Yseult, Elaine, Mordred, Merlin, Gawaine, Bedivere, Lancelot, Perceval, Tristram, Galahad, Morgan le Fay (Tony's) and Guinevere (Brenda's) where the bed is on a dais. In Guinevere the walls are hung with tapestry and the fireplace modelled on a thirteenth century tomb.

From the bay window you can see the spires of six churches.

The ceiling of Morgan-le-Fay is peeling. It is made of wooden slats nailed across the plaster to look like coffering, and painted with blue and gold chevrons, tudor roses and fleurs de lys. In the grounds there are a Dutch garden and an Orangery.

There is a plateroom, an estate office and collections of enamels, ivories, china, ormolu, cloisonnée and some good pictures. The library contains some interesting folios. There is also a smoking room and a billiard room.

HD 14, 26, 35–36, 99

HICKS

Former husband of Cara (q.v.) about whom little is known.

BR 303

HILL, MR

Neighbour of Gilbert Pinfold at Lychpole who grazes his cows on Pinfold's fields during the war. After the war manages to make the maximum possible profit by retreating gradually, field by field.

• According to Pinfold's voices Hill has committed suicide, forced to do so by Pinfold's greed.

GP 18, 70

HILL, CORPORAL

Member of Charles Ryder's platoon in the Halberdiers, who shoots himself at Penkirk in 1940.

MA 187

HIMALAYAS

Tibetan mountain range where, rather than in a health farm, Basil Seal feels he might be enjoying a mystical experience, when he has a drink of whisky after days of enforced abstinence.

WS 269

HINSLEY, CARDINAL ARTHUR *(1865–1943)*

English Cardinal and Rector of the English College in Rome.

• Arthur Box-Bender congratulates the local prelate at Mr Crouchback's funeral on Cardinal Hinsley's wireless broadcasts in 1943. 'You could see he was an Englishman first and a Christian second'.

US 62

HINSLEY, SIR FRANCIS

English writer at the Megalopolitan Studios in Hollywood. Vice-President of the Cricket Club. He has 'a sensitive, intelligent face, blurred somewhat by soft living and long boredom'. Describes himself as 'always the most indefatigable of hacks'. Observes that the Americans 'talk entirely for their own pleasure'. Is fired by Megalopolitan. Commits suicide by hanging himself with his braces. Body found by Dennis Barlow. Has a monocle, which he wears when embalmed. Author of *A Free Man Greets the Dawn*.

LC 7–16, 30, 47, 52, 69

HITCHCOCK, SIR JOCEYLN
English journalist: has a white moustache. Lady Cockpurse calls him 'Sir Something Hitchcock'.

Is employed by the *Daily Beast* until a dispute with Lord Copper (q.v.) about the date of the Battle of Hastings (which Copper is sure is 1066). Henceforth works for the *Daily Brute*.

Reports the Abyssinian campaign from Asmara for the *Daily Beast*. Reports from Shanghai for the *Beast* where he charges £300 for camels. Tells Lord Copper that in Africa he always sends his dispatches in a cleft stick. Is called the English 'Wenlock Jakes' (q.v.). Chronicles the Messina earthquake from his desk in London.
Sc 13, 15, 32, 33, 41–42, 66, 82, 88, 127

HITLER, ADOLF *(1889–1945)*
German dictator and originator of Nazism (q.v.).
• Barbara Sothill feels that she has transferred to herself 'all the odium which more properly belonged to Hitler'.
• Basil Seal considers 'faultless timing' to be Hitler's strong point.
• The author of 'Nazi Destiny' says that Hitler is married to a Jewess.
• The word God appears in Hitler's speeches an impressive number of times (Ambrose Silk counts them).
• Sir Joseph Mainwaring declares that if Christopher Seal (q.v.) were still alive and a German he would soon oust Hitler.
• Nigel Sothill (q.v.) asks his father whether Hitler really does have fits, and if he does, does he froth at the mouth and roll his eyes.
• In Hooper's (q.v.) opinion, Hitler would consign to the gas chambers the madmen at the asylum in whose grounds Charles Ryder's battalion is billeted in 1943.
• One of Rex Mottram's friends demands a showdown with Hitler in 1938.
• In 1943 Rex Mottram broadcasts on the wireless against Hitler. Nanny Hawkins tells Effie that if Hitler was listening, and if he can understand English, which she doubts, then he must have felt very small.
• In 1939 Arthur Box-Bender believes that the British have called Hitler's bluff and that very soon 'we shan't hear much more of Mr Hitler'.
• Hitler proclaims a taste for 'figurative' painting, prompting the Ministry of Information to announce in 1940 that it is a patriotic duty of England to defend the avant-garde.
• Gilbert Pinfold is at great pains to point out to Glover (q.v.) that he 'never had the smallest sympathy with Hitler'.
• A friend of Rex Mottram's is told that the German army keeps Hitler in power just as long as it is able to get something for nothing.
PF 12, 13, 31, 70, 110, 117, 168, 176; BR 10, 262, 280, 329; MA 20; US 123; GP 109

HITTITES
When they give their house over to the storage of artistic treasures in 1939, the Box-Benders receive not Fragonards and Boulle (q.v.) but Hittite tablets from the British Museum.
MA 27

HOARE, SIR SAMUEL (JOHN GURNEY, 1st VISCOUNT TEMPLEWOOD) *(1880–1959)*
Conservative politician. Secretary of State for Air (1922–1959); Secretary of State for India (1931–1935); Foreign Secretary (1935–1936). Resigned over the Italian invasion of Abyssinia, which he condoned in the Hoare-Laval pact with France. First Lord of the Admiralty (1936); Home Secretary (1937–1939); Ambassador to Madrid (1940–1944). In favour of the policy of appeasement.
• One of Rex Mottram's friends is of the opinion that Hitler would scupper himself in 1938 if it were not for Sir Samuel Hoare.
BR 280

HODGE, COLONEL
Owner of the Manor, Much Malcock (q.v.). Impecunious, takes an interest in the British Legion and the Boy Scouts. Is incensed by Westmacott selling his field to 'a lot of jerry-builders'. Believes that

the local parson preaches Communism. Deliberately does not register Much Matlock as a rural area because it halves the value of one's property.
WS 45–61

HODGSON, RALPH (EDWIN)
(1871–1962)
English poet whose *Poems* (1917), including his 'Song of Honour', established his reputation.
• Charles Ryder, aged sixteen at Lancing, produces an illuminated version of Hodgson's 'Twould ring the bells of heaven/The wildest peal for years,/if parson lost his senses/And people came to theirs . . .'; one of Frank's (q.v.) favourite poems.
WS 307

HOGARTH, WILLIAM *(1697–1764)*
British painter renowned for his pictures of everyday life in Georgian England in which he depicted ruined squires, debauched harlots, corrupt officials and the whole panorama of the age.
• In the days of prohibition, gin ceases to be 'Hogarthian' and becomes chic.
• To Charles Ryder, Anthony Blanche waxes in wickedness 'like a Hogarthian pageboy'.
• The Chinese Drawing Room at Brideshead, in which Lord Marchmain dies, has by evening a Hogarthian aspect.
PF 119; BR 47, 303

HOGMANAY
Dennis Barlow supposes that 'a canty day' is something like Hogmanay, which in his mind consists of 'people being sick on the pavements of Glasgow'.
LO 100

HOLINESS
'No one', Cordelia Flyte tells Charles Ryder 'is ever holy without suffering'.
BR 294

HOLLOWAY, MISS
Secretary to Julia Stitch (q.v.).
SC 6

HOLLY
Mrs Florin (q.v.) wonders whether it is not unlucky to take holly upstairs.
VB 201

HOLLYWOOD
• Paul Pennyfeather reflects that the backstreets of Marseilles in 1928 look as though they might have been created in a Hollywood film studio for a film about the Reign of Terror (q.v.).
• Dennis Barlow, Sir Francis Hinsley, Sir Ambrose Abercrombie, Aimee Thanatogenos and Mr. Joyboy (all q.v.) all work in Hollywood.
• Hollywood, according to Roger Simmonds, gives a ludicrous idea of luxury restaurants.
DR 152; LO 51; WS 155

HOLMAN-HUNT, WILLIAM
(1827–1910)
English painter and member of the Pre-Raphaelite Brotherhood. See his 'Light of the World' (1854) and 'Strayed Sheep' (1853).
• Charles Ryder compares Julia Flyte's realization of her sin to Holman-Hunt's 'Awakening Conscience'.
BR 276

HOLYWELL PRESS
Sir Humphrey Maltravers (q.v.), while impoverished at Oxford, used to proof-read for the Holywell Press.
DR 131

HOME SECRETARY
An 'ugly little man with pince-nez' who visits Lord Monomark.
VB 121

HOMER
Greek poet. Author of the *Iliad* and the *Odyssey*.
There is a statue of Homer in Whispering Glades (q.v.), below which Miss Bergson (q.v.) takes a 'before needs reservation'.
LO 38

HOMOSEXUALS

• Captain Grimes (q.v.), is a closet homosexual, who gives cigars to Clutterbuck (q.v.).

• Ambrose Silk has a love affair with a 'Brownshirt', Hans (q.v.) in Munich. Silk thinks of himself as 'a pansy. An old queen'. He wonders whether the homosexual affairs of ancient Greece, Arabia and the Renaissance had worn themselves out in the same way as his own.

• Sebastian Flyte moves in a world increasingly homosexual in nature. At Oxford he and Charles Ryder indulge in naughtiness 'high in the catalogue of grave sins'. Anthony Blanche (q.v.) is the most flamboyantly homosexual of Sebastian's friends. Sebastian himself later takes up with a German, Kurt (q.v. and see also Hans) who is imprisoned in Germany, and commits suicide. The two prostitutes at the Old Hundredth (q.v.) take Charles and Sebastian for 'fairies'.

• Sir Ralph Brompton (q.v.) carries on discreet homosexual affairs at his retreat in Ebury Street which is 'a secret known to barely fifty men'. Among his protegés are Ludovic and Lieutenant Padfield (q.v.). Ludovic points out that the badge that he wears on his tunic (that of the Intelligence Corps) is 'A pansy sitting on its laurels'.

• Virginia Crouchback asks Peregrine if he is homosexual. Although it is a subject that he rarely hears mentioned by men and never by women, he is not disconcerted by it, and points out to her that the 'o' is short as the word comes from the Greek rather than the Latin.

• His voices accuse Gilbert Pinfold of sodomy. He hears them discuss homosexuals.

• One of the passengers on the *SS Glory of Greece* is 'a lovely pansy with a camera and white suit' called Arthur, who in fact is not homosexual and becomes engaged to the writer.

DF ; PF 34, 41, 187; BR 112; US 35, 136; GP 72, 101, 182; WS 17, 20

HONEYMOONS

(*See* CROUCHBACK, GERVASE and GUY and LAST, TONY)

HONG KONG

• Lord Copper asks Salter if Great Britain still owns Hong Kong.

• The Quartermaster tells Apthorpe that he has served in Hong Kong which Apthorpe thinks 'the cushiest spot in the whole empire'.

Sc 14; MA 37

HOOHQ

The Headquarters of Hazardous Offensive Operations during WWII. A 'bizarre product of total war' which, in 1939, is housed in three flats in Marchmain House (q.v.), a block of modern flats in St. James's.

OG 44; US 185

(See also GENERAL WHALE, DR. GLENDENNING REES and DR. AKONANGA)

HOOKFORCE

Name of the force commanded by General Ritchie-Hook in Crete. All, save four men, taken prisoner by the Germans.

OG 13

HOOP, JOHNNY

London society figure among the Bright Young People in the 1920s. Publishes his autobiography, Rampoles (1930).

• His party invitations are adapted from issues of Blast (q.v.). Writes the invitations for the Savage Party (q.v.).

• Adam Fenwick-Symes writes in his Mr Chatterbox column that Johnny Hoop intends to travel to Paris to paint.

VB 31, 52, 190

HOOP, MRS

Mother of Johnny Hoop, who, as a passenger on the same ferry as Adam Fenwick-Symes, decides to abandon theosophy and 'give the Catholics the once over'. Repels sea-sickness by repeating a formula she has learned from a yogi in New York City.

VB 21

HOOPER

'A sallow youth with hair combed back, without parting, from his forehead, and a flat, Midland accent.' Newest-joined platoon commander of Charles Ryder's platoon in 1943.

• Tells Charles that the army could never get away with its customary waste of man hours 'in business'. He is a symbol for Charles of 'young England'. Charles imagines the future in terms of 'Hooper Rallies', 'Hooper Hostels' and 'the Religion of Hooper'. Is unable to come to attention smartly. Has a habit of saying 'Rightyoh' which irritates Charles. It was, ponders Charles, to make a world for those such as Hooper, that the flower of youth had died in the Great War.

• Expresses the opinion that it is strange that one family should occupy a house the size of Brideshead, 'a great barrack of a place'.

BR 10, 13–16, 134, 330

HOPE-BROWN, MR & MRS

Parents of a boy at Llanabba School in 1922.

DF 77

HORACE, (QUINTUS HORATIUS FLACCUS) *(65–8BC)*

Roman poet. Author of the *Satires*, *Epodes* and *Odes*.

• Ambrose Silk, musing on war in 1939, thinks of 'Horace singing the sweetness of dying for one's country'.

PF 40

HORE-BELISHA, LESLIE, 1ST BARON *(1893–1957)*

British politician. Chairman of the Liberal party (1931). Minister of Transport (1934). Secretary of State for War (1937–1940). Responsible for democratising the army.

• Major Tickeridge (q.v.) assures Guy Crouchback (q.v.) that the Halberdiers do not indulge in any of 'that Hore-Belisha stuff of starting in the ranks'.

• When asked by a younger fellow officer what Churchill is like, Guy Crouchback replies that he is 'Like Hore-Belisha except that for some reason his hats are thought to be funny'.

MA 41, 176; PF 46

HORNBEAMS

• Childless, middle-aged neighbours of Colonel Hodge at Much Malcock (q.v.). Mrs Hornbeam attends church and Mr Hornbeam is 'quite knowledgeable about vegetables' and at the time of the peace ballot (q.v.) canvasses every nearby cottage on his bicycle.

• Mr Hornbeam has a beard and wears homespuns. They weave their own clothes on a loom, and sing folk music to each other as they work.

WS 46, 53

HORSES

• JUMBO: Percy's horse in Azania.

• MAJESTY: Betty Anstruther's horse in Azania, which throws her.

• VIZIER: Anstruther's horse in Azania 'getting heavy in the mouth'.

• THIMBLE: Ivor Claire's clever and beautiful horse.

• THUNDERCLAP: A strawberry roan known to Ben Hacket who killed two riders and won the local point to point four years running. Stakes himself in the guts while hunting and has to be shot.

• TINKERBELL: Sebastian Flyte's mount at the Marchmain hunt in 1924.

• ZERO: Horse known to Ben Hacket on whom he once won five jimmy-o-goblins at ten to three at Chester.

• PEPPERMINT: Company mule of Ben Hacket's company during the Great War which died of drinking the company's rum ration.

• BUNNY: John Last's first pony at Hetton.

• According to Ben Hacket 'mules can't cat, neither can horses. . .'

HD 19, 34, 104; BM 56, 58, 140; BR 151; OG 48

(See also RACING)

HORTHY, (DE NAGYBANYA) NIKOLAUS *(1868–1957)*

Regent of Hungary (1920–1944). Commander in Chief of the Austro-Hungarian fleet (1918). Minister of War in the government of 1919, against Bela Kun's Communists. Aimed to restore Habsburg monarchy. Supporter of the Axis powers in WWII.

• Jean de Brissac de la Motte (q.v.) tells

Charles Ryder that he ought to have been in Budapest when Horthy marched in (February 1920): 'That was politics'.
BR 195

HOSPITAL

In the opinion of the adjutant of the Halberdiers it is not worth visiting 'a chap' in hospital unless one takes a bottle of something.
MA 235
(See APTHORPE; CROUCHBACK, GUY)

HOTELS

• THE METROPOLE, CWMPRYDDYG: The grandest hotel in North Wales, situated on a cliff overlooking Conway bay. Built before the Great War 'with a lavish expenditure on looking-glass and marble'. By 1928 it is tattered. Paul Pennyfeather, Mr Prendergast and Grimes dine there.

• THE RITZ, LONDON: Opened in 1906; named after the hotelier César Ritz. Paul Pennyfeather moves into rooms at the Ritz ten days before his wedding. He has luncheon there on the day, and it is here, in the restaurant that he is arrested. Archie Schwert (q.v.) lives at the Ritz. Agatha Runcible thinks this 'rather grand'. One can always get a drink from the night porter. Adam Fenwick-Symes telephones Nina Blount there. The Ritz restaurant is not cheap at lunchtime, and in 1933 costs eight and six. The Flytes' ball in 1923 after which Charles Ryder and Sebastian Flyte are arrested is thrown at the Ritz. Charles Ryder takes Cordelia Flyte to dinner at the Ritz Grill in 1926. John Plant invites the Simmonds to lunch with him at the Ritz in 1938.

Margot Metroland stays there in 1939. Angela Lyne dines with her.

Roger Simmonds always shows 'signs of persecution mania' in the Ritz. He calls the maitre d'Hotel 'Lorenzo' and watches him 'jostling a way through for dowdy Middle-West Americans' (who are in fact Lord and Lady Settringham). Margot Metroland lives here after the destruction of Pastmaster House, during the blitz. Basil Seal and Peter Pastmaster attend a dinner here in 1963. Basil is referred to by the cloakroom attendant as 'Florid'.

• SKINDLES, OXFORD: Philbrick is living here when Paul Pennyfeather meets him in Oxford after he has returned to the university.

• SHEPHEARD'S, DOVER STREET, LONDON: Lottie Crump's (q.v.) Hotel, 'a happy reminder' of the splendours of the Edwardian era.

The head waiter is Doge (q.v.). There are also a number of housemaids and a young Italian who is insulted by Lottie 'who once caught him powdering his nose'.

Life in Shepheard's centres around Lottie's 'parlour' which houses a collection of signed photographs which include most European Royal families and many other young men.

Adam Fenwick-Symes stays there in 1930.

A bottle of wine at Shepheards is always champagne. Mr Outrage stays there with Baroness Yoshiwara (q.v.) (in No 12, 'a suite of notable grandeur') as do Judge Skimp, the bogus major, and the Ex-King of Ruritania.

Flossie falls to her death from the chandelier.

• IMPERIAL: Hotel in the town where the racetrack is. It is in the Gothic style of 1860.

• ROYAL GEORGE: Hotel near the Imperial, by the canal. The cost of a bed is one pound a night. In Adam Fenwick-Symes' room there is 'a chest of drawers full of horrible fragments of stuff, a washstand with a highly coloured basin, an empty jug and an old toothbrush. There was also a rotund female bust . . . a thing known as a dressmaker's dummy' and a water bottle with a light green moss at the bottom. Someone else's handkerchief is under his pillow. In Agatha Runcible's room there is no looking-glass and she has to kill bed-bugs with drops of face-lotion. Everything smells. They move out to the Imperial.

• MIRAMAR, SMYRNA: Where Basil Seal, under an alias, imagines he might be told to proceed and await orders in 1939.

• GRAND AZANIAN, MATODI, AZANIA: Has 'a gloomy and unwelcoming air'.

General Connolly stays there. There is only one bath.

• GRAND CAFÉ ET HOTEL RESTAURANT DE L'EMPEREUR SETH, DEBRA DOWA: Hotel run by Mr Youkoumian (q.v.). William Bland finds rooms there for Miss Tin and Dame Mildred Porch.

• LIBERTY, JACKSONBURG, ISHMAELIA: The lounge has bare boards and the roof is made of iron and leaks. Mrs Earl Russell Jackson is the proprietor and has a rocking chair in her office. The journalists stay here in 1937. There is no bath. The menu does not vary (*See* FOOD).

• PENSION DRESSLER, JACKSONBURG, ISHMAELIA: Proprietor Frau Dressler (q.v.). It is down a side street and looks rather more like a farm than an hotel. Frau Dressler's pig roams the yard with her hens and her goat who attempts to butt the guests. Other animals present are a gander and a three- legged dog. The bathroom is a hut, full of bats. The guests are Europeans. There is a tree at Christmas. William Boot (q.v.) stays there in 1937, and meets Katchen.

• BRAGANZA HOTEL, LONDON: Where the Boot banquet is held in 1938.

• GEORGE, OXFORD: Hotel on the corner of the Cornmarket and George Street popular with undergraduates in the 1920s. (Graham Greene claimed to have fallen in love with one of the waitresses.)

Anthony Blanche takes Charles Ryder there in 1922 and drinks four Alexandra cocktails: 'One, two, three, four, down the little red lane they go. How the students stare!'.

• THE SPREAD EAGLE, THAME: Inn bought in 1922 by the idiosyncratic John Fothergill (1876–1957) and subsequently popular among London Literatii and flamboyant Oxford undergraduates. It was run entirely according to Fothergill's mercurial temperament and blatant snobbery. The habitués included John Betjeman, Tom Driberg, Terence Greenidge, Robert Byron, Harold Acton, John Sutro and Waugh.

Anthony Blanche takes Charles Ryder to dinner here in 1922. 'A delightful hotel . . . which luckily doesn't appeal to the Bullingdon' (q.v.). Over dinner he attempts to poison Charles's mind against Sebastian. They drink Hock and Burgundy and finish with Chartreuse and Mavrodaphne trifle.

• SAVOY-CARLTON HOTEL, NEW YORK: Where Charles and Celia Ryder stay before their journey back to England in 1936.

• THE HOTEL, SOUTH TWINING: Sebastian Flyte gets drunk here instead of hunting in 1924.

• MARINE HOTEL, MATCHET: Seaside hotel kept by retired servants from Broome (q.v.). Lies outside the town itself, on a cliff beside the coastguard station, overlooking Lundy. Mr Crouchback (q.v.) is a permanent resident. The original manager moves to Canada and the successors, the Cuthberts (q.v.) take on Mr Crouchback as part of the furnishings, which also include Miss Vavasour (q.v.).

• ROYAL COURT HOTEL, SOUTHSAND: Where Apthorpe's aunts had stayed when he was at Staplehurst (q.v.).

• GRAND HOTEL, SOUTHSAND: Guy Crouchback moves there from Kut al Imara in 1940. It is 'a large hotel built for summer visitors, almost empty now in war-time winter'.

• CLARIDGES, LONDON: Wheatley stays there with his father in 1919 while their London flat is being 'done up'. Tamplin's brother thinks its 'a deadly hole'. Guy Crouchback is unable to find a room there in 1940. However, Tommy Blackhouse (q.v.) is able to arrange it and Guy takes a suite 'which at all points proclaimed costliness'.

Virginia Crouchback is staying in room 650. It is on the same floor as Guy's 'not a dozen rooms away, round two corners'. Guy goes to see her there and meets Tommy coming out of her bathroom. By November 1940 Virginia has moved out of Claridges. She bumps into Leiutenant Padfield there in 1943.

• THE HOTEL, MUGG: In 1940 X Commando (q.v.) is billeted in the Hotel, Isle of Mugg, owned by Colonel Campbell (q.v.), where rooms are at a premium.

• THE STATION HOTEL, GLASGOW:

Where in November 1940 Trimmer (q.v.) meets Virginia Crouchback. Location of the Château de Madrid Restaurant (q.v.). Trimmer has been here twice before. There is a tank full of angel fish, crimson curtains with white cords and white plaster sea-horses.

• SAVOY, LONDON: Opened in 1889. César Ritz was the first manager, and Escoffier the chef. Dance music was broadcast from the ballroom in the 1920s and 30s.

Where in 1925 Rex Mottram throws the wedding reception for his wedding to Julia Flyte.

Where in 1940 Ian Kilbannock has to go to drink with American journalists who are unable to find anything 'fit to eat' there.

• MONTA ROSA BOARDING HOUSE, MATCHET: Requisitioned by the army in 1940.

• DORCHESTER HOTEL, LONDON: Opened in 1931. During WWII became the HQ of General Eisenhower. Where Virginia Crouchback meets Kerstie Kilbannock during an air raid in 1940 and confides that she is penniless and homeless. Ruby (q.v.) lives there in 1943.

• THE HOTEL, BARI: In the evenings in 1944, full of Queen Alexandra's nurses.

• THE STATION HOTEL, PENKIRK: Where the commander of the anti-fascists from the Danubian basin has billeted himself in 1940.

• A SEASIDE HOTEL IN CORNWALL: Where Guy Crouchback and his company are quartered in June 1940.

• A HOTEL ON THE SEAFRONT AT BRIGHTON: Where Tony Last goes with Milly (and Winnie) to contrive his infidelity.

• HOTEL 22ND MARCH, BELLACITA, NEUTRALIA: Named after a forgotten event in the rise of the Marshal. Previously called the Royal, the Reform, the October Revolution, the President Coolidge and the Duchess of Windsor. It is referred to by the Neutralians as 'the Ritz'.

• THE BERKELEY, LONDON: Considered by Charles Ryder, aged sixteen to be 'all right in the evening, should you want to dance'. Tamplin (q.v.) reckons it 'jolly well all right for luncheon' as well. All the men from Sandhurst go there (in 1919).

• A HOTEL IN THE NEW FOREST: Sir James Macrae stays here in 1936. For this reason alone the conference on his version of *Hamlet* is held here.

• A SMALL FRENCH HOTEL OUTSIDE THE FORTIFICATIONS OF FEZ: John Plant stays here frequently during the 1930s, to write his novels. It is cheap and chilly and the guests are all French.

• MENA HOUSE HOTEL, CAIRO, EGYPT: Where Gilbert Pinfold stays in January 1929.

• THE GALLEFACE, COLOMBO: Where Gilbert Pinfold stays in 1956.

• A HOTEL IN ADEN: Gilbert Pinfold remembers that there used to be a stuffed mermaid in a showcase in a hotel in Aden.

The same mermaid is seen by William Boot and Corker in 1937.

• THE GARDEN OF ALLAH HOTEL, LOS ANGELES: From whose roof Leo throws himself to his death.

• THE BEVERLEY-WALDORF, LOS ANGELES: Where Aimee Thanatogenos has her first job, as a hairdresser.

HOUSE OF COMMONS

• Rex Mottram's friends are 'Leathery old sharks in the. . .House of Commons'.

• At question time in Westminster Jock Grant-Menzies brings up the question of pigs.

• Basil Seal thinks it 'no great catch' being in the Commons in 1931.

HD 175; BM 75; BR 108

HOUSE OF LORDS

Where Lord Metroland enjoys from time to time making a sonorous speech.

VB 101

HOUSE PARTIES

A house party at Hetton (q.v.) is generally 'very quiet and enjoyable' without 'paper games'. The only games are Bridge, Backgammon and 'low' Poker with the neighbours. It is quite comfortable and there is always enough to drink, although a scarcity of bathrooms. No one objects if

you do not rise until the afternoon.
HD 12
(See also Country Houses)

HOUSEY-HOUSEY
(*See* Games)

HUDDERSFIELD
Town in Yorkshire on Trimmer's itinerary for his morale-boosting tour in 1940.
OG 248

HÜGEL, BARON FRIEDRICH VON *(1852–1925)*
Catholic religious writer. See his *The Mystical Element in Religion* (1909).
• Paul Pennyfeather offers to lend Stubbs (q.v.) his copy of Von Hügel while studying theology at Oxford.
DF 213

HULL
• Sebastian Flyte reads in the *News of the World* (q.v.) about 'a woman in Hull who's been using an instrument . . . "thirty-eight other cases were taken into consideration in sentencing her to six months" – golly'.
• One of the towns on Trimmer's (q.v.) itinerary for his morale-boosting tour in 1940.
BR 85; OG 248

HUMAN MIND, THE
Thinking about Hell, Ambrose Silk concludes that 'the human mind is inspired enough when it comes to inventing horrors. It is when it tries to invent Heaven that it shows itself cloddish'.
PF 60

HUNGARIANS
• Otto Silenus' design for a chewing-gum factory is reproduced in a Hungarian quarterly magazine.
• Mr Salter (q.v.) calls for 'exotic Magyar dishes' at a grill room in the Strand.
• Two 'rather forbidding Magyar cousins' of the Flytes stay with them at Christmas 1923.
• The Hungarians are among the peoples whom Mr Goodall (q.v.) believes will rise up and save Europe in 1940.
• An entire Hungarian ballet company are among the fellow travellers of Scott-King (q.v.) on his escape from Neutralia by way of the underground network.
• According to Gilbert Pinfold's voices, the Hungarians are the masters of the 'three-eight rhythm' (q.v.).
DF 119; Sc 31; OG 40; WS 244; GP 46; BR 120

HUNTING
Dr Fagan (q.v.) has noticed in women like Lady Circumference 'a tendency to regard all athletics as inferior forms of foxhunting'.
• Mr Salter asks William Boot how the hunting is: 'Well, we stop in the summer, you know'.
• Cedric Lyne detests 'the rigours of foxhunting', despite being an excellent horseman.
• Priscilla Boot goes cubbing.
• Dame Mildred Porch travels to Azania for the SPCA to investigate whether the methods used by the Wanda to hunt lions are humane.
• Mr Baldwin (q.v.) hunts with a small pack of hounds in the Midlands which marches with the Fernie Hunt. It is, he supposes the best hunting country in England.
• Hetton (q.v.) lies on the boundary of three packs.
• John Last is killed in a riding accident while out hunting.
• Mr Samgrass calls the meeting of the Marchmain hounds 'a deliciously archaic spectacle'.
• The Strickland-Venables, by 1924, have taken their grooms out of top-hats.
• Charles Ryder, like everyone else (apart from Lady Marchmain), has great faith in the merits of a day's hunting to put Sebastian right.
• Lady Marchmain hates hunting.
• Lord Brideshead is joint-master of the Marchmain, and remains so, hunting with them two days a week.
• Gilbert Pinfold hunted as a young man.
• Major Sir Alexander Dreadnought,

Bart, MP (q.v.) is joint master of a pack of hounds in the midlands.
• The Ballingar (q.v.) hounds have good hunting over the stone walls of the Fleacetown estate. Throughout her convalescence after the birth of Tom, Mrs Kent Cumberland's thoughts are all of the coming hunting season.
• Colonel Jasper Cumberland's diary (q.v.) contains 'some vigorous descriptions of fox-hunting behind the lines of Torres Vedras' (q.v.).
• Gervase Kent-Cumberland often hunts as a child and later on keeps six hunters.
• John Plant (q.v.) thinks at one time that he 'might take to' fox-hunting.
• Angela Seal once went out with the Albrighton hounds.
DF 84; HD 99; PF 168; BM 129; Sc 27, 56, 196; BR 120, 154, 157, 267; GP 16; WS 40, 77, 88, 95, 131, 262

HUSSARS
A lame Hussar brings Guy Crouchback his whisky and soda in hospital in Alexandria.
OG 227

HUXLEY, ALDOUS ***(1894–1963)***
English writer. Author of the twenties satires *Chrome Yellow* (1921) and *Antic Hay* (1923) (q.v.). His most famous novel is *Brave New World* (1932).
• Anthony Blanche reads *Antic Hay* at Oxford in 1923, being sure that it will be the topic of conversation at Garsington (q.v.). He calls it 'a rather forbidding book' and later welcomes an interruption from the 'tedium'.
• Everard Spruce compares Virginia Crouchback (q.v.) with Huxley's 'Mrs Viveash' a character in *Antic Hay* (q.v.).
BR 49; US 200

HYMNS
• 'God Rest Ye Merry Gentlemen': Played on the television in the New Britain.
• 'O God Our Help in Ages Past': Through which, with new words, Paul Pennyfeather hears of Mr Prendergast's murder (q.v.).
• 'There 'aint no Flies on the Lamb of God': Mrs Ape (q.v.).
• 'Hail Festal Day': Sung by the choir at Lancing on Sunday 28th September 1919. Wykham-Blake provides the treble cantor.
• 'Abide with me': Sung by William Boot in Ishmaelia.
• 'In Thy Courts no More are Needed Sun by Day nor Moon by Night, Abide with me': Both sung by Theodore Boot (q.v.), who takes delight in repeating the same verse over and over again. The latter is played by the Llanabba Silver Band at the Sports day.
DF 83, 183; Sc ; OG 101; WS 304; GP 214

HYPATIA ***(375–415)***
Neo-Platonist philospher and daughter of Theon, the Alexandrian mathematician. An influential teacher, she was murdered by a mob inspired by the anti-philosophical Bishop Cyril.
• A humbug, in the opinion of Ambrose Silk, 'carved up' by the desert monks.
• Julia Stitch is brought up to believe that Hypatia was murdered with oyster shells. However, EM Forster, in 'Alexandria' says that the deed was done with tiles.
PF 60; OG 128

HYSTERIA
Julia Flyte becomes hysterical while contemplating her 'sin', but recovers remarkably quickly. 'Most hysterical women', she tells Charles Ryder, 'look as if they had a bad cold.'
BR 275

I

IAGO, DOCTOR
One of Everard Spruce's guests at a party in 1943, who he is very keen to introduce to Lady Perdita.
US 42

ICELAND
Halberdier Glass reports that the Halberdiers are to be posted here in 1940.
• The rest of Trimmer's battalion is posted to Iceland in 1940. He cannot imagine that they are having much fun.
• In 1943 Sir Ralph Brompton arranges to send the bulk of the Royalist refugee volunteers to Iceland.
OG 53; US 142

ICI
Imperial Chemical Industries.
• According to Roger Simmonds (q.v.) the Imperial Defence College (q.v.) are 'up to the neck' with ICI and the oil companies.
WS 152

IDC
Imperial Defence College
• According to Roger Simmonds (q.v.) they are 'the new hush-hush crypto-fascist department' and are, in 1938, 'up to the neck' with ICI and the oil companies. They have the BBC in their pocket.
WS 152

ILLNESSES
Fever and delirium producing hallucinations: Tony Last in Brazil.
• Disease of the skin: easily contracted in the tropics.
• Nettle-rash: Corker on board ship, near Aden.
• Jaundice: Julia Flyte.
• Flu: Julia Flyte.
• 'Some long word of the heart': Lord Marchmain.
• Cancer – Kills Betty Stayle in 1956, at the age of 36.
• 'Clap' – Apthorpe suspects Sarum Smith of having it.
• An unspecified illness: Lady Marchmain.
• Bechuana tummy: Apthorpe
• Sea-sickness: Celia Crouchback and the passengers across the Atlantic; Major Hound; The Bright Young People; Fanny Thrubb; Kitty Blackwater and Father Rothschild on the cross-channel ferry.
• A complicated form of dysentery: Peregrine Crouchback on his first day in the Dardanelles.
• Arthritis: Gilbert Pinfold.
• Gout: Gilbert Pinfold.
• Rheumatism: Gilbert Pinfold
• Fibrositis: Gilbert Pinfold
• Insomnia: Gilbert Pinfold, Charles Ryder in 1923.
• Hallucinations: Gilbert Pinfold.
• Flushes and crimson blotches on the hands (an allergy): Gilbert Pinfold.
• Speechlessness, heat and strangulation, dizziness and trembling – Basil Seal in 1962.
HD 192; Sc 61, 68; BR 265, 303; OG 57, 163; MA 60; US 124; GP 12, 16, 23; WS 279; VB 12–15

IMBROS
Town on Crete to which Colonel Tickeridge moves his HQ during the retreat in 1941.
OG 180

IMMIGRANTS
Black immigrants in exile, according to John Plant, 'when their work is done, will tread out the music of Africa in a vacant lot behind the drug store'.
WS 179

IMPOSSIBILITIES
In Paul Pennyfeather's mind certain things are 'impossibilities'; things such as Margot Metroland in prison washing other prisoners' clothes.
DF 188

IN MEMORIAM
See POETRY

INCEST
Doris Connolly (q.v.) notices 'with the wisdom of the slums' that Barbara Sothill 'fancies' her brother, Basil Seal.
PF 88

INCH, COLONEL
Master of the Pigstanton hunt. Universally disliked by the hunt, he is quiet and reserved and often loses the hunt and goes off to nibble ginger biscuits. Is the director of 'various' companies and often mentions his hunting at board meetings. Offers to have the huntsmen blow 'gone to ground' at John Last's funeral.
HD 99–100, 108

INDIA
The Viceroy of India being a cousin of Ivor Claire's, finds him a post in India after he has disgraced himself during the retreat from Crete.
OG 233

INDIANS
Indian students admire the panelling from King's Thursday after its transfer to the V & A.
• Charles Ryder watches four Indian students from Balliol, 'four proud infidels' in flannels, blazers and white turbans, set off for a picnic by the river one Sunday morning in 1923.
BR 59; DF 119

INDIAN RUNNER
See RACING

INDIES, THE
Five hundred female athletes, possibly contortionists from the Indies, are promised for the gymnastic display at Simona, during the Bellorious conference (q.v.).
WS 224

INFIDELITY
Margot Metroland sells herself to Sir Humphrey Maltravers to secure Paul Pennyfeather's release from prison.
• Nina Blount throws over Adam Fenwick-Symes to marry Ginger Littlejohn. However, while Ginger is away with his regiment she has an affair with Adam.
• Brenda Last's affair with John Beaver precipitates her divorce from Tony and his subsequent downfall.
• Marjorie St Cloud once had an affair with Robin Beasley.
• Katchen seduces William Boot but then returns to her husband.
• Brenda Champion and Rex Mottram have a long-standing affair which lasts through his engagement to Julia Flyte and into their marriage.
• Julia Flyte has an affair in New York which is not a success. On the journey back to England she begins her affair with Charles Ryder that leads ultimately to both of them becoming divorced.
• Celia Ryder once had an affair which she thinks by 1936 is best forgotten.
• Virginia Crouchback is unfaithful to Guy with Tommy Blackhouse while Guy is in Kenya.
• Millicent Blade, left behind by Hector, is unfaithful to him with a number of men before her poodle destroys her good looks.
• In 1940 Basil Seal has an affair with Betty Allbright, which results in the birth of her son Charles.

INGRES, JEAN AUGUSTE DOMINIQUE *(1780–1867)*
French painter in the classical tradition and the antithesis to Delacroix. He was a superb draughtsman, saying 'a thing well drawn is well enough painted'.
• Anthony Blanche tells Sebastian Flyte that Charles Ryder draws 'like a young Ingres'. Sebastian replies that Aloysius draws well, but is more modern.
• Roger Simmonds refers to Ingres as 'a bourgeois painter'.
BR 53; WS 134

INHERITANCE
Upon his father's death in 1943, Guy Crouchback falls heir to the Lesser House and an inheritance of seven thousand pounds a year, shared with his sister, Angela Box-Bender (q.v.).
US 70

INITIATION CEREMONIES
Guy Crouchback's experience of military life before joining the Halberdiers has been limited to stories of 'gross ceremonies of initiation'.
MA 47

INKERMAN
See BATTLES

INNISFREE
Island on an artificial lake at Whispering Glades (q.v.)
LO 66

INSANITY
Edward Throbbing's butler, after the departure of the Bright Young People, has 'the horrors', sees spiders in the bath and hears musical instruments. He finally runs amok with the poker and has to be taken away in a van.
• Captain Steerforth (q.v.) once commanded a ship in which an insane stoker killed another with a sword.
VB 110, 112; GP 64
(*See also* GILBERT PINFOLD, AGATHA RUNCIBLE, MR LOVEDAY, MISS CAMPBELL, LUDOVIC, ECCENTRICS)

INSARCOPHAGUSEMENT
Invented word used at Whispering Glades (q.v.) to denote the disposal of one's 'loved one' in a sealed sarcophagus 'marble or bronze which rests permanently above ground in a niche in the mausoleum, with or without a personal stained-glass window above'.
LO 37

INSTOW, LADY
Billy Cornphillip had been 'the friend' of Lady Instow for many years until they quarrelled at Cowes in the 1910s, resulting in his marriage to Etty.
WS 26

INTELLECTUALS
Ambrose Silk wonders why real intellectuals 'always prefer the company of rakes to that of their fellows'.
• Faulty bath appliances are 'the hall mark of higher intellectuals all the world over'.
PF 59, 194

INTERIOR DECORATION
Margot Metroland has the interior of the new King's Thursday (q.v.) decorated by Otto Silenus.
• Simon Balcairn's flat is decorated with oilcloth and Lalique glass.
• Mrs Stitch (q.v.) has her ceiling painted with a mural by Arthur.
• Brenda Last is keen to have Mrs Beaver (q.v.) redecorate the morning room with chromium plating and natural sheepskin carpet.
• Angela Lyne's flat in London is decorated in 'what passes for Empire in the fashionable world'.
• The Harknesses decorate the interior of their house in a rural arts and crafts style, as do the Hornbeams (both q.v.).
• Jenny Abdul Akbar's flat in London is furnished 'with truly Eastern disregard of the right properties of things'.
• The decorations of William Boot's London hotel room have been planned by a psychologist. The colours are magenta and gamboge, 'colours which – it had been demonstrated by experiments on poultry and mice – conduce a mood of dignified gaiety'.
• Charles Ryder's rooms at Oxford (q.v.) change their appearance from being decorated with a reproduction of a Van Gogh, a Roger Fry screen, rhyme sheets from the Poetry Bookshop and a porcelain figure of Polly Peachum to containing Lalique, a human skull and a bowl of roses.
• Rex Mottram's house in Hertford Street is decorated in 1925 by 'the most expensive firm'.
• Celia Ryder has Charles's studio 'con-

verted' from a barn and destroys all its character.

• The partisans in Yugoslavia in 1944 transform the farmhouse occupied by Guy Crouchback and the observation party, with a secret store of looted furniture.

(*See also* Individual entries under COUNTRY HOUSES, RESTAURANTS, HOTELS, CHURCHES, *Countries* and *Characters*)

INTERASTRAL FILMS

Company owned by Mr Kramm with whom Celia Ryder is keen to ingratiate Charles at their shipboard party in 1936.

BR 232

INVERAUCHTY

Mythical Scottish seat of Angus Stuart-Kerr, the character invented by Adam Fenwick-Symes during his time as Mr Chatterbox.

VB 113

INVESTMENT

Rex Mottram tells Julia Flyte, 'I can make money work for me ... I expect fifteen, twenty per cent and I get it. It's pure waste tying up capital at three and a half'.

BR 183

INVITATIONS

In 1930 there are three types of invitation card:

• The normal type has a name and 'At Home', together with the date, time and address.

• The type which comes from Chelsea is such as: 'Noel and Audrey are having a little whoopee on Saturday evening; do please come and bring a bottle too, if you can'.

• The type used by the Bright Young People is that in which Johnny Hoop (q.v.) adapts a piece of artwork from Blast (q.v.) or Marinetti's 'Futurist Manifesto' (q.v.). This has two columns of print, one being a list of all the things that Johnny likes and the other being a list of the things which he hates.

• The Emperor Seth (q.v.) issues invitations for his dinner party. They are gilt edged and have silk ribbons in the Azanian colours and an embossed gold crown.

• Sebastian Flyte's luncheon invitation to Charles Ryder is written in conté crayon across an entire sheet of Charles's own Whatman HP drawing paper.

VB 52; BM 166, 167; BR 32; PF 185

IRELAND

Dr Fagan tells Paul Pennyfeather that in Ireland inter-marriage is a political necessity.

• Grimes (q.v.) tells Paul Pennyfeather that instead of being shot by the army he was sent to Ireland 'on a pretty cushy job connected with the postal service ... You can't get into the soup in Ireland, do what you like'. He is married in Ireland: 'I was tight at the time and so was everyone else'.

• Margot Metroland has a castle in Ireland which the Society for the Preservation of Ancient Buildings tries to persuade her not to demolish.

• Ambrose Silk (q.v.) flees to Ireland in 1939; to rooms in a small fishing village on the west coast.

• John Beaver and his mother (q.v.) go to Ireland for Christmas 1933, to stay with cousins. He finds it 'rather dull'.

• In Ireland, according to Ritchie-Hook the priests were 'quite openly on the side of the gunmen'.

• In 1940 there is a rumour that the German Army is in Limerick. It is the role of the Halberdiers to dislodge it.

• Sir Francis Hinsley (q.v.) attempts to transform Juanita del Pablo into an Irish maid from the Mountains of Mourne.

• The Irish (they discover at Whispering Glades) are 'just naturally poetic and won't pay that much for plantings'.

• Ballingar (q.v.) is four and a half hours from Dublin by the early train from Broadstone station, and Fleacetown (q.v.) fifteen miles from Ballingar.

• Distance is of little importance in Ireland and people will travel three hours for tea.

• One of Scott-King's colleagues reckons that he could get a decent meal in Ireland.

DF 30, 66, 101, 135, 140; PF 218; HD 59; MA 71, 204; LO 24, 25, 67; WS 77, 83, 201

IRONSIDE, GENERAL WILLIAM EDMUND, 1st BARON ***(1880–1959)***
British General. Commanded Archangel expedition 1918. Chief of the Imperial General Staff at the outbreak of WWII. Promoted Field-Marshal 1940 and given command of Home Defence Forces.
MA 169

IRPYL
The International Rally of Progressive Youth Leadership held in Prague in 1947 to which Griggs (q.v.) is keen to go, and to which he is duly sent.
WS 201

IRVING, SIR HENRY ***(1838–1905)***
English actor, the greatest of his time.
• Colonel Blount remembers his father doing a 'skit' of Henry Irving in *The Bells*.
VB 149
(*See* PLAYS)

IRWIN
Character in the newspaper remembered by the dying Lord Marchmain (q.v.).
BR 315

ISAACS, MR
Confidence trickster and producer of *A Brand From the Burning* (q.v.).

Principal of the National Academy of Cinematographic Art, in the Edgware Road. He has produced three films.
VB 144, 146, 148, 149

ISCHIA
Island off Naples, where Ambrose Silk lives after Ireland, Tangier and Tel Aviv.
WS 253

ISHMAELIA
Republic in the North East of Africa. It consists of desert, forest and swampland: all inaccessible. In the 1870s numerous Europeans went there as 'missionaries, ambassadors, tradesmen, prospectors and naturalists, and were all eaten . . . punitive expeditions were fruitless, and in the 1890s the European powers decided to abandon their claims over the territory and installed Samuel Smiles Jackson as its President with a bicameral legislature, proportional representation, religious liberty, free trade, and joint stock banking'. By the 1930s Rathbone Jackson is president (his father Pankhurst had held the post before him).

The posts of the chief ministers are held by Garnet Jackson, Mander Jackson Huxley Jackson and Mrs Athol (née Jackson).
• The capital city is Jacksonburg, which is filled with 'landless men of native and alien blood'. There is a railway to the Red Sea coast bringing in imported goods. In the outer provinces the natives are bandits, slaves and gentlemen.
• During Christmas 1937 a domestic row among the Jacksons sparks off a civil war between the Fascists and the Communists. The Fascists are led by Smiles Soum (q.v.) and the White Shirt Movement.
• Some of the beauties of the country are the forest of Popo and the waterfall at Chip. The western mountains are 'stiff' with gold ore. The Russians and the Germans find out about this and while the Russians back the Jacksons, the Germans back Dr Benito, who appears to have won until the arrival of Mr Baldwin (prompted by William Boot).
• Jacksonburg is renamed Marxville under Dr Benito.
Sc 14, 43, 44, 49, 59, 74–77, 99, 150, 154, 155, 161, 168, 172
(*See also* JACKSONS, BENITO, William BOOT.)

ISLE OF WIGHT
See CRUTTWELL, TOBY, and COWES

IT
Fanny Throbbing and Kitty Blackwater wonder whether Mr Outrage (q.v.) really has 'IT'.
VB 12

ITALY
Tony and Brenda Last spend their honeymoon in a villa borrowed from a friend on the Italian Riviera.
• The fountain at Brideshead looks as if

it belongs in a southern Italian piazza.
- Charles Ryder plans to take his 'old eyes' to Germany and Italy after he has drawn Africa and South America.
- In Italy, Lord Marchmain tells Charles Ryder in 1938, no one believes that there will be a war.
- During the retreat from Crete Guy Crouchback comes across a group of Italian prisoners who do not want to join the Germans.
- Opera, so the Halberdier Major tells Guy, is the 'most certain way to the Italian heart'.
- Dennis Barlow deals with air priorities at an Italian port during WWII.
- Mrs Komstock has a grand-daughter in Italy.

HD 156; BR 78–79, 216, 302; OG 191; US 158; LO 22, 74
(*See also* individual cities, towns and GARDA.)

ITCH
A 'ferocious young Montenegran' whose name ends in 'itch'. A 'rattling good fellow', according to Ritchie-Hook.
US 218

ITHEWAITE, MRS
One of the women sitting opposite Adam Fenwick-Symes on the train to Aylesbury (on his second visit). She agrees with Mrs Orraway-Smith (q.v.). Lives at Wendover.
VB 66

IVORY TOWER
Journal produced by Ambrose Silk for the Ministry of Information.
PF 117, 185–186
(*See also* MAGAZINES.)

IZUL
River in the North of Azania flowing down to the coast from the Monastery of St Mark, and separating Moshu from Gulu.
BM 173

J

JACKSON, MRS EARL RUSSELL
One of the Jacksons of Ishmaelia. Proprietress of the Hotel Liberty (q.v.). Smokes a pipe, and reads the bible. Is happy that the rich journalists should patronise her hotel.
Sc 79

JACKSON FAMILY, THE
Ruling dynasty of Ishmaelia. Placed in power by a combined European commission in the 1890s. They are continually feuding. Smiles Soum labels them as 'effete, tyrannical and alien'. Dr Benito proposes to bring them to trial. The word 'Jackson' to the Ishmaelites always means something exciting. They are released from prison and (under Mr Baldwin's watchful eye), returned to power.
Sc 75–77, 165, 176

JACKSONBURG
Capital city of Ishmaelia. On the main street there are many agencies for American and European companies. It is occasionally visited by foreign politicians. The main street has a single strip of tarmac down the middle, with on either side tracks for mules and camels. There is a shoddy concrete bank, a Greek general store made of wood and tin, the Café de la Bourse, the Carnegie Library, the Cinema and a number of empty sites. There are also an Armenian liquor store, a Goanese tailor, a French haberdasher. There is a statue of Samuel Smiles Jackson and an American welfare centre. The most popular venue is the Popotakis Pingpong parlour. There is also a Swedish consulate and a Press bureau.
• When it is dinner-time in Jacksonburg, it is tea-time in London.
Sc 76, 93–94, 155

JACOBITES
Guy Crouchback sees the Jacobites as a film on the rising of the '45 in which Prince Charles and his followers look like a party from the Caledonian Ball.
MA 160

JAGGER, MR
Contractor in charge of the Anglican Cathedral at Debra Dowa. Is not satisfied with being paid in Ishmaelian currency.
BM 152–153

JAKES, WENLOCK
Highest paid journalist in the United States. Scoops the world with an eyewitness account of the sinking of the Lusitania four hours before she was hit. Once covered a revolution in one of the Balkan capitals from somewhere completely different where he woke up having fallen asleep on a train. The stuff was so convincing that within a week there really was a revolution in the country. He was given the Nobel Peace prize for his description of the bloodshed.
• Stays in the Hotel Liberty in Jacksonburg, where he is at work not on the crisis, but on his book 'Under the Ermine' (q.v.), for which he has secured a $20,000 advance.
Sc 66, 67, 79, 70, 125

JAMAICA
Caribbean island to which the (fictitious) Quests (q.v.) sail on the day that Lord Monomark expresses interest in meeting Mrs Quest.
VB 115

JAMES
First footman to the Boots (q.v.).
Sc 19

JAMES, HENRY ***(1843–1916)***
American novelist, Author of *Portrait of a Lady* (1881), *The Bostonians* (1886), *The Golden Bowl* (1904) and others. His novels, with their deeply psychological character studies have had a profound influence on twentieth century literature.
• Everard Spruce reminds Frankie that Henry James, one of the 'great masters of trash' started off by writing sonnets.
• Dennis Barlow (q.v.) asks Mr Schultz (q.v.) whether he reads Henry James, who, he says, deals with 'American innocence and English experience'. Dennis has 'a Jamesian problem'.
US 203; LO 96

JANE AND CONSTANT
Friends of de Souza who meet him at the Café Royal on December 30th 1939.
MA 80

JANISSARIES
Turkish Elite troops.
• The men from the orphanages of the New Britain form the officer corps of the Forces 'a cross between Janissary and Junker'.
GP 183

JAPAN
Lord Copper believes that the capital of Japan is Yokahama.
• Two Japanese on the journey from New York to London with Charles Ryder express interest in world-brotherhood.
• Peregrine Crouchback says that he would rather see the Japanese in Europe than the Bolsheviks.
• Mr and Mrs Hornbeam (q.v.) meditate according to a Japanese mystical practice.
Sc 14; BR 250; US 126; WS 53

JAPANESE EMBASSY
Baroness Yoshiwara, at the Japanese Embassy, is the only person able to influence Mr Outrage (q.v.).
VB 12

JAPHETH, DUKE
Leader of a rebellion in Azania during which the Azanian army ran amock and terrified the sisters at the fever hospital.
BM 39

JAVA
Island south of Borneo.
• John Verney's uncle packs 'parcels for Java' three days a week in 1946.
GP 164

JAWLEYFORD COURT
Country house featured in *Mr Sponge's Sporting Tour* by Surtees (q.v.).
PF 145

JAZZ
Gilbert Pinfold abhors jazz.
GP 14
(*See also* WIRELESS, BLACK BIRDS)

JEBB, MR
Manager of the hairdressing salon where Aimee Thanatogenos used to work.
LO 74

JEHOVAH
Said to have lived on the savour of burnt offerings (so Adam Fenwick-Symes remembers when hungry and penniless).
VB 63

JELLABIES
Housekeepers to Mr Plant for over twenty years. He puts himself out on their behalf although he denies as much, saying that he pays them very little and they 'cook the books'.
• Following Mr Plant's death they leave immediately after the funeral to open a second-hand wireless shop in Portsmouth; a move they had planned some years in advance. John Plant asks them what they would like of his father's. They ask for a pair of blankets.
WS 109, 126

JELLABY, PROFESSOR
Is paid thirty guineas by the *Daily Beast* for a feature article containing not one word that anyone can understand.
Sc 15

JELLALABAD
Indian town.
• Where the Reverend Tendril (q.v.) first preached his famous sermon, 'when the Coldstream Guards were there'.
VB 33

JENKINS, NURSE
Nurse to Virginia Crouchback's baby, Gervase, in 1944. After the birth Virginia calls her 'Jenny' and compares her to Mrs Gamp (q.v.).
US 189, 195

JENKINS EAR, THE WAR OF *(1739–1743)*
War between England and Spain over the boundaries of Florida and a Spanish outrage against English sailors; notably that a Captain Jenkins claimed that his ear had been cut off by Spanish officials.
• Gilbert Pinfold thinks with pride of Jenkin's Ear when faced by the imaginary Gibraltar crisis of his hallucinations.
GP 88

JEPSON
Journalist on the *Daily Beast* who writes a story about a pogrom in Bucharest.
Sc 180

JERUSALEM
Charles Ryder, considering the flame of faith which the old knights saw put out, realizes that it now burns again for soldiers farther away in their hearts than even Jerusalem.
BR 331

JERVIS
Young officer with whom Guy Crouchback shares a tent in 1940. Requires constant supervision.
MA 173, 200

JESUITS
Appleby (q.v.) knows of some buried Jesuit treasure in Bolivia.
• Mr Plant becomes convinced of a Jesuit conspiracy to throw the world into war and writes to *The Times* on it.
WS 113, 182
(*See also* FARM STREET, PRIESTS)

JEWELLERY
Philbrick wears a huge diamond ring.
• Basil Seal steals his mother's emeralds to pay for his passage to Azania.
• Margot Metroland has a platinum and diamond hat-pin.
• Rex Mottram buys Julia Flyte's engagement ring, not from Cartier's, but from a back room in Hatton Garden.
• The Portuguese Countess has an enormous emerald ring, as big as a golf ball.
• Julia Flyte has an emerald ring.
• Lady Ursula Stayle wears long pearl drop-earrings and a pearl collar.
• In the Marchmain vaults there is a 'rather famous' ruby necklace, and a string of pearls. Also some 'hideous' diamond fenders, and a Victorian diamond collar which no one can wear.
• The Duchess of Mhomala wears a gold and garnet tiara.
• The Duchess of Stayle, according to Simon Balcairn, gives her diamond tiara to Mrs Ape.
• John Boot has a lucky pin made from bog-oak around his neck.
• Gilbert Pinfold's voices imply that he once stole a moonstone.
PF 16; BR 183, 264, 269; DF 55, 75, 91; Sc 73; GP 72; BM 168

JEWS
A Jewish nihilist from Berlin throws a bomb which does not explode during his train journey through Azania.
• A Jew in Bethnal Green, who speaks no English, has a shop discovered by Julia Stitch.
• Anthony Blanche seems to the young Charles Ryder to have the experience 'of the Wandering Jew'. He takes up with a 'Jew boy' in Constantinople.
• Guy Crouchback attempts to help a party of Jews at Begoy in 1944.
(*See* KANYI.)
• Whispering Glades is mostly patronised by 'the good-style Jews'.
• Ralph Bland has a Jewish friend in the City who runs off with his advance from Billy Cornphillip (q.v.).
• In the early thirties, when anti-Semitism

looks like becoming popular, Mr Plant starts to support the Jewish cause in letters to *The Times*.
• His voices accuse Gilbert Pinfold of being a Jew called Peinfeld.
• According to his voices most Jews are mixed up with the Communists.
• The head of Elizabeth Verney's department (q.v.) is a Jew.
• John Verney is strongly anti-Semitic.
BM 11; Sc 7; BR 47, 113; US 175, 177; LO 67; WS 27, 113; GP 70, 104, 164–165

JIBUTI
Port in French Somaliland.
• The ship carrying Basil Seal to Azania puts in at Jibuti.
• Colonel Plum (q.v.) meets Basil Seal here in 1936.
BM 89; PF 148

JIM
Barman at the Wimpole club, famous for his 'specials'.
WS 184

JOAB, MAJOR
Azanian officer of the guard on duty at Matodi. Paid by Ali (q.v.) to execute Mr Youkoumian (q.v.). Stays on in Matodi, hoping to sell the Emperor to the victorious rebel army.
BM 21–26, 225–6

JOB
Night porter at Bellamy's club (q.v.).
OG 10, 15

JOHN, AUGUSTUS, O.M. *(1878–1961)*
British painter. Essentially a portraitist, his subject matter includes gypsies and beautiful women. Reknowned for his Bohemianism, he stands as a major figure spanning twentieth century British art. See his 'Madame Suggia' (Tate, 1923) and 'Tallulah Bankhead' (1930).
• Angela Lyne (q.v.) has a portrait of herself by John painted in 1929.
• Rex Mottram is 'on easy terms' with Augustus John.
PF 155, 171; BR 107

JOHNSON, DR SAMUEL *(1709–1784)*
English lexicographer and critic. See his Dictionary (1755).
• Mr Plant states his views on art in 'Johnsonian terms'.
• The Chaplain of Scone cannot remember what Johnson said about fortitude.
WS 114; DF 14, 119

JOKES
A famous actor makes unfunny jokes at the Savage party in 1927.
VB 53

JONES, INIGO *(1573–1652)*
English neo-classical architect and stage-designer. Influenced by Palladio. See his Queen's House, Greenwich. Many buildings are attributed to him, such as the pavilions at Stoke Bruerne.
• Sebastian Flyte tells Charles Ryder that Brideshead Castle was designed by Jones, which is not neccessarily true. The dome, to Charles, looks later.
BR 78

JORKINS
School friend of Charles Ryder invited in 1923 to dinner by his father, who then proceeds to embark on 'a little fantasy for himself, that Jorkins should be an American'. Jorkins is thrown into confusion.
BR 66–68; WS 292

JORROCKS
Fictional character invented by R.S. Surtees. He is a Cockney grocer, passionately fond of field sports. See Surtees' *Jorrocks' Jaunts and Jollities* (1838) and others.
• Anthony Blanche assures Charles Ryder that when they dine at Thame they will not, whatever the case, imagine themselves 'on a j-j-jaunt with J-J-Jorrocks'.
BR 48

JOURNALISTS
The journalists in a film seen by William

Boot are all addicted to 'straight rye'.
• Corker tells William that he has a lot to learn about journalism, and relates stories of 'the heroic legends of Fleet Street'.
• According to Corker a journalist is welcome everywhere.
• William admits that not all journalists have cleft sticks.
• In 1941 it is part of Ian Kilbannock's job to drink with American journalists at the Savoy.
• The American journalists at the Savoy have limitless expense accounts.
Sc 28, 66, 80, 88, 91; OG 100, 212, 214; WS 203
(*See also* BALCAIRN, BOMBAUM, CORKER, DUNZ, FENWICK-SYMES, HITCHCOCK, JAKES, KILBANNOCK, MULLIGAN, SCHLUM, SHUMBLE, SHOCK, TITMUSS, WHELPER, PIGGE)

JOYBOY, MR

Senior Mortician at Whispering Glades (q.v.). Has 'wonderful hands'. His speciality is 'fixing' expressions at which he is 'a true artist'. Takes a Baccalaureate in embalming in the Mid West. His first appointment is as a member of the Faculty of Undertaking at 'an historic Eastern University'.
• Takes Aimee Thanatogenos home to dinner with his mother on whom she makes a great impression. Becomes engaged to Aimee. She is seduced away from him by Dennis Barlow and commits suicide. Joyboy panicks and enlists the help of Dennis to dispose of the body.
LO 47, 48, 54, 55, 59, 76, 79, 108, 111

JOYBOY, MRS

Mother of Mr Joyboy (q.v.). A difficult old woman, obsessed with listening to political commentaries on the radio. Has a parrot called Sambo.
LO 90, 91

JOYNSON-HICKS, WILLIAM, 1ST VISCOUNT BRENTFORD *(1865–1932)*

British Conservative politican. Home secretary 1924–1929. Under him many books were banned including Ambrose Silk's work on the Negroes of Montmartre.
PF 43

JUGOSLAVIANS

Brigadier Cape thinks them a 'suspicious lot of bastards'. They prefer to use their own interpreters. They like Joe Cattermole and the feeling is mutual.
• According to de Souza the Jugoslavians hate the Bulgarians' 'guts'.
US 166, 225

JULIA

Cousin of Lucy Simmonds (q.v.) who has had a crush on John Plant since being at school. Stays with the Simmonds. She is eighteen in 1938. Daughter of a Major from Aldershot. Buys John a box of cigars.
• Red-headed girlfriend of Poppet Green. Wonders why it takes both Parsnip *and* Pimpernell to write one book. Complains that Ambrose Silk's bill is always the largest.
WS 157, 162, 164; PF 58, 60

JUNGMAN

A gynaecologist from the Hague who finds himself a delegate at the Bellorious conference in Neutralia in 1946.
WS 226

JUNKERS

Prussian aristocrats, the core of the officer corps.
• Men from the orphanages of the New Britain unite the qualities of the Junkers with those of the Janissaries (q.v.).
GP 183

JUSTICE

For Captain Grimes 'Justice' stands before him with his two-edged sword.
• Justice, to Guy Crouchback, seems in 1941 to be the impetus which has brought him safe to Alexandria, while a young soldier lies unburied in a deserted village on Crete.
DF 102; OG 239

K

KAFKA, FRANZ *(1883–1924)*
Czech novelist. Author of *The Trial* (1925), *The Castle* (1926) and *America* (1927), all published posthumously. Influential on the existentialists (q.v.) and other twentieth century writers.
• Ludovic (q.v.) is uncertain who Kafka is, and is initiated into his 'occult company' by Frankie (q.v.) in 1941.
• Parsnip (q.v.) has an essay published in an issue of *Survival* in 1941 in which he compares Kafka to Klee (q.v.).
US 43, 124

KAISERS, THE
Owners of Kaisers Stoneless Peaches and one of Whispering Glades' best customers. They sponsor every day half an hour of Wagner on Los Angeles radio in the 1950s.
LO 68

KANDY
Town in the centre of Ceylon where, in 1956, Gilbert Pinfold sees the Buddha's tooth in its shrine.
GP 147

KANSAS CITY
City in Kansas, USA where Mrs Ape (q.v.) once got no further than the opening words of her oration before the hall erupted into emotion and all the seats were broken.
• Where Humility joined her Angels.
VB 100

KANYI, MR AND MRS
Two of the Jews at Begoy in 1944, survivors of an Italian concentration camp on the Isle of Rab, and before that refugees from Central Europe. In 1939, on their way to Australia, they are caught up in the war and killed by the communists.
US 176, 180, 234–236

KAPRIKI, MME
Wealthy Greek living in Alexandria in 1941.
• At her house Tommy Blackhouse meets the Flag Officer in command of the destroyers, who tells him that he is ready to take X Commando to Crete.
OG 159

KARACHI
Capital of West Pakistan.
• Gilbert Pinfold returns to England by way of Karachi.
GP 149

KASANGA, AFRICA
Twelve hundred miles from Makarikari and according to Apthorpe when drunk, 'a perfectly awful hole' where Sanders (q.v.) has a brother.
MA 58, 59

KATCHEN
'German' girl living in Jacksonburg, at the Pension Dressler. Her father is Russian, her mother is Polish and she was born in Budapest. First encountered by William Boot at the Swedish mission. She has golden hair and when first seen is wearing a mackintosh and red gum boots. Plays ping pong with William who falls in love with her.
• Is arrested on the orders of Dr Benito, an action which provokes William into action against the government, resulting in the arrival of Mr Baldwin, the death of Benito and the failure of the revolution.
Sc 104, 112–116, 126, 133, 134, 142, 152, 164, 221

KAUFFMANN, ANGELICA *(1741–1807)*
Swiss painter. Her subjects are portraits, and classical and mythological scenes,

many of which were engraved by Bartolozzi (q.v.).
• There is a ceiling painted by Angelica Kauffmann in Mr Bentley's (q.v.) room at the Ministry of Information in 1939.
PF 62

KEATINGS DURBAN
Patent insect repellent.
• Dame Mildred Porch is thankful to have remembered it when in bed at Lumo (q.v.).
BM 158

KEMP, SISTER
Nurse to Lucy Simmonds during her pregnancy in August 1939.
WS 175–176

KENT
Location of the sanitorium attended by Basil Seal (q.v.).
WS 275

KENT-CUMBERLAND, MRS
Mother of Tom and Gervase (q.v.) who sees to it that Gervase always has the best of everything. Lives at Tomb (q.v.) and has an estate in Norfolk and a house in London. Is annoyed by the advent of Tom. After the death of her husband in 1915, becomes 'more emotional and parsimonious'. Badly hit by death duties, she lets the house in London, closes a wing at Tomb, reduces the servants to four and the gardeners to two. She empties the stables of horses, will not use the car, and cuts back on hot water. Sends Tom into the motor business, and after he falls in love with Gladys Cruttwell, to Australia. Almost forgets about her younger son. Is shocked by Tom's return. Contrives to transfer Bessie MacDougal's attachment from Tom to Gervase and succeeds.
WS 87–105

KENT-CUMBERLAND, MR
Father of Gervase and Tom (q.v.). Owner of Tomb. MP. Not greatly liked by his children. Killed on active service early in 1915.
WS 91

KENT-CUMBERLAND, GERVASE PEREGRINE MOUNTJOY ST EUSTACE *(b. 1903)*
Sandy-haired eldest son of the Kent-Cumberlands (q.v.), his birth is a time of great rejoicing at Tomb (q.v.).
• More intelligent and stronger than Tom. Has a pony. Goes hunting. Goes to Eton 1915. Goes up to Christ Church, Oxford 1921. Member of the Bullingdon.
• Edits the Journal of Jasper Cumberland (q.v.) (1924). Has a Ball for his twenty-first birthday. Marries Bessie Macdougal, has two children and six racehorses.
WS 87–105

KENT-CUMBERLAND, THOMAS *(b. August 1905)*
Sandy-haired younger son of the Kent-Cumberlands (q.v.).
• Accepts his lower position with equanimity. Aged seven is keen to have a toy motor car, which he receives from his uncle Ted; but his mother, thinking that there is a mistake, gives it to Gervase.
• Remembers the air raids during the Great War as happy times at his prep school. Makes a collection of war relics including a German helmet, which is voted the best in the school. Educated at a minor public school. Gets his house colours for swimming and fives and plays for the second eleven at cricket. Platoon commander in the O.T.C. Leaves school at eighteen.
• Does not go to university. Instead he is sent to Wolverhampton to learn the Motor business.
• Compiles notes for the Journal of Jasper Cumberland published under his brother's name. Does not enjoy the ball for Gervase's birthday. Falls in love with Gladys Cruttwell. Asks her to marry him and is sent to Australia by his mother. Returns in 1926 with his fiancée, Bessie MacDougal (q.v.) and her father. Is reunited with Gladys Cruttwell who he marries and takes back to one of Mr MacDougal's farms in Australia.
WS 87–105

KENWORTHY, DOCTOR WILBUR
'The Dreamer'. Founder of Whispering Glades (q.v.).
• In 1935, while in Europe, he finds the church of St Peter in Oxford (q.v.) which he ships back to Los Angeles.
LO 34, 64

KENYA
Edward Mowbray got ill and went to Kenya or somewhere in 1926.
• Julia Flyte suggests that Sebastian should go to Kenya, 'or somewhere where it doesn't matter'.
• Basil Seal is not even the sort of man who will 'do' in Kenya, at one time though he almost goes to farm sisal.
• Guy Crouchback, in 1927, takes his share of the family fortune and settles in Kenya where he farms 'assidiously' and lives with Virginia 'in unruffled good-humour beside a mountain lake where the air was always brilliant and keen and the flamingos rose at dawn'. After Virginia returns to England and leaves him for Tommy Blackhouse (q.v.) Guy leaves Kenya.
• Apthorpe says that the 'posh ranches of Kenya' are not the 'real' Africa.
• Guy once shot a lion among the mealies, and in the army is ribbed about this fact by his firing instructor.
• Hector (q.v.) goes to Kenya in 1933 to buy a farm from Beckthorpe (q.v.) before sending for Millicent Blade to join him.
VB 29; BR 156; MA 18, 37, 74, 128, 129; US 159; WS 35; BM 81; PF 48

KERR OF GELLIOCH
Uncle of Angus Anstruther Kerr (q.v.) and friend of Colonel Campbell (q.v.).
OG 61

KEW GARDENS
A man from Kew tells Freddy Sothill that he has got the best plants in the country in his orangery.
PF 75
(*See also* LONDON)

KHARTOUM
Town in the Sudan.
• Katchen's husband was once 'in trouble' in Khartoum and thus cannot go to the Sudan.
• The wireless set at Colonel Campbell's dinner broadcasts some news about Khartoum in 1940, but Tommy Blackhouse is unable to make it out.
• After being lost in Abyssinia, Ritchie-Hook is sent to Khartoum in 1941.
Sc 159; OG 66, 241

KHAT
Chewed by the merchants in Matodi (q.v.).
BM 9

KILBANNOCK, LORD IAN
Journalist friend of Guy Crouchback who he first met in Kenya. Married to Lady Kerstie (q.v.). Before the war writes a racing column. Member of Bellamy's. During the war joins the RAF as a 'conducting officer'. Compares the Blitz to a painting by John Martin (q.v.).

Turns up on Mrs Stitch's yacht at Mugg, having been transferred to HOOHQ where he liaises with the press (drinks with American journalists at the Savoy). Tells Guy that the commandos will not make heroes because they are upper class. Sees action with Trimmer on Operation Popgun (q.v.).

Does a fair imitation of Noel Coward. His favourite play is *Private Lives*, from which he quotes while in the field.

Uses Trimmer on a morale boosting tour of Britain. Persuades Virginia Crouchback to go with him and thus sets the scene for their disastrous liaison.

Negotiates to be a special correspondent in Normandy, as a prelude for 'something more serious' than being a racing correspondent after the war.

Is posted to Bari with the observation party. He is the first journalist to be admitted to Jugoslavia. Survives the plane crash.
MA 25, 124, 126; OG 9, 99, 100, 101; US 11, 1985, 208–217

KILBANNOCK, LADY KERSTIE
Wife of Ian (q.v.). She is 'a good wife . . . personable, faithful, even-tempered

and economical'. Makes rosé wine at luncheon by mixing the previous dinner's white and red. Runs the canteen at No. 6 transit camp, London District. Attempts, with her housekeeper, Mrs Bristow, to arrange for Virginia to have an abortion (unsuccessfully). Becomes a cipher clerk (a well-paid job). Buys Virginia's furs.
OG 13, 133; US 45, 46

KILBANNOCK, THE DOWAGER LADY
Mother of Ian Kilbannock (q.v.). Lives in a castle on the Ayrshire coast. During the war the army requisition the house and gradually erode it, while Lady Kilbannock lives in the factor's house.
US 88

KILCARTNEY, CHARLIE
Friend of Rex Mottram who was an alcoholic until cured by Borethus at Zurich.
BR 159

KING OF ROME
Son of Napoleon I (q.v.). Guy Crouchback recalls that there was a 'little boy whom they called King of Rome'.
US 15

KING'S THURSDAY
Country house of Margot Metroland (q.v.), in Hampshire. It stands on a site which since the 1550s has belonged to the Earls of Pastmaster (q.v.). Between that time and the 1920s no alterations had been made, neither was any 'coal-gas or indoor sanitation' installed. The estate carpenter had inherited his post from his sixteenth century ancestor who had originally carved the panelling and the staircase. In the bedrooms there were still rushlights. In the early years of the twentieth century King's Thursday became a 'mecca' for weekend parties. According to Professor Franks it was 'the finest piece of domestic Tudor in England'.
• During his lifetime Lord Pastmaster takes a delight in showing people around the house. It is difficult to live in King's Thursday at this time with fewer than twenty servants. However, the servants of the twentieth century cannot be induced to inhabit the quarters built for their predecessors. Lord Pastmaster decides to sell the house.
• Jack Spire writes about the sale in the *London Hercules* and they establish the Save King's Thursday Fund to preserve it for the nation. The house is bought by Lord Pastmaster's rich sister-in-law, Margot. When she takes it over it has been empty for two years. She decides to rebuild. The panelling goes to the Victoria and Albert museum (q.v.). The house is remodelled by Otto Silenus who is instructed to build 'something clean and square'.
• Not long afterwards King's Thursday is again rebuilt by Margot. Paul Pennyfeather stays here with Otto Silenus, Peter Pastmaster, Humphrey Maltravers, David Lennox and Miles Malpractice in 1927. Peter Pastmaster has his twenty-first party here attended by Alastair Trumpington and Basil Seal.
DR 115, 119, 124, 126, 128, 130, 134, 139, 142, 143; WS 278

KIPLING, RUDYARD *(1865–1936)*
English writer, renowned for the *Just So Stories* (1902), *The Jungle Book* (1895) and numerous poems.
• Winston Churchill's speeches are always followed by news of some disaster as though in retribution from the God of Kipling's *Recessional*.
• A woman novelist compares Mr Plant's last painting with Kipling's *The Light that Failed*.
• Lucy Simmonds has never read any Kipling.
MA 176; WS 155

KISMAYU, AFRICA
One of the destinations of the dhows from Matodi.
BM 9

KISSING
Nina Blount tells Adam that she has invented a new type of kissing: 'you do it with your eyelashes'. William has known it for years: 'it's called a butterfly kiss'.

• Julia (q.v.) kisses John Plant's possessions in his rooms in Ebury Street.
VB 45; WS 164

KITCHENER, HORATIO HERBERT, 1st EARL KITCHENER OF KHARTOUM *(1850–1916)*
English statesman and soldier. Secretary for War 1914.
• Lady Seal tells Basil that 'even he was once a subaltern'.
• Colonel Campbell (q.v.) served under Kitchener.
PF 143; OG 66

KLEE, PAUL *(1879–1940)*
Swiss artist and founder of the Blau Reiter. Taught at the Bauhaus, and produced a great many surrealistic and abstract works. See his 'Twittering Machine' (Museum of Modern Art, New York).
• Parsnip (q.v.) writes a piece for *Survival* relating Kafka to Klee.
US 124

KLUGMANN'S OPERATION
Operation to sterilise women in the New Britain. An unfortunate side-effect is sometimes the growth of a beard.
• Dr Beamish (q.v.) has strong professional objections to it.
GP 198, 205

KNIGHTS OF MALTA
Lord Brideshead sends Charles Ryder a photograph of himself at Christmas 1937, dressed in the robes of the Knights of Malta.
• A representative of the Knights of Malta attends Mr Crouchback's funeral at Broome.
• In Neutralia the Knights of Malta rise from their places to proceed to the state banquet 'with the languor born of centuries of hereditary disillusionment'.
BR 267; US 63; WS 212

KNIGHTS OF ST MICHAEL AND ST GEORGE
Sir Samson Courteney was created a KMG in the same year that his daughter Prudence became thirteen.
BM 48

KOMSTOCK, MRS
Woman who every Saturday attends the hair dressing salon where Aimee Thanatogenos works, for a blue rinse and set. Has a son in Washington, one in Delhi, a grand-daughter in Italy and a nephew in 'indoctrination'. When she dies her son asks Aimee to do her hair as it was in real life, and thus precipitates her into her new career.
LO 74

KRAFFT EBING, RICHARD FREIHERR VON *(1840–1902)*
German specialist in nervous diseases.
• Basil Seal predicts that if Seth ever discovers psychoanalysis he will call a street after him.
BM 142

KRAK DES CHEVALIERS
Castle in the Holy Land, the stronghold of the Knights Templar.
• Mr Samgrass has himself photographed here during his trip to the East with Sebastian Flyte.
BR 145

KRAMM, MR
Owner of International Films with whom Celia Ryder tries to ingratiate Charles at her party in Mid-Atlantic.
BR 232, 250

KRONONIN, PRINCE FYODOR
Manager of the Perroquet in Debra Dowa (q.v.).
BM 106

KRUMP, SOPHIE DALMEYER
American poet, now lying in Poets' Corner, Whispering Glades (q.v.).
LO 71

KURT
Boyfriend of Sebastian Flyte in Morocco. Has long fair hair combed back without a parting, and a 'wolfish' look. Speaks with a lisp. Studies history at university in Germany. Joins the Foreign Legion. Shoots himself in the foot. Is found starving and working as a pimp in the kasbah in Tangier

by Sebastian. Meets Charles Ryder. Anthony Blanche (q.v.) describes him as 'the footman in *Warning Shadows* a great clod of a German'.

• The Germans get hold of him and take him back. Becomes a stormtrooper in a provincial town. Will not have anything to do with Sebastian who has followed him, but relents and runs away. Is caught and put in a concentration camp. Hangs himself in his hut after a week.

BR 196–197, 202, 203, 204, 206, 291–292

(*See also* HANS)

KUT AL IMARA HOUSE

Preparatory school at Southsand (q.v.). Named after the battle in 1915. The Halberdiers are billeted here in 1940. Each room contains six bedsteads and a pile of blankets and palliasses. The officers sleeping quarters are the boys' dormitories. Each is named after a battle of the Great War.

MA 87–91

L

LA PAZ
Town in Bolivia.
• At one time Basil Seal lives here in a 'gin palace'.
PF 16

LA TOUCHE, EFFIE
Actress and star of *A Brand from the Burning* in which she plays Selina, Countess of Huntingdon. Almost runs over Adam Fenwick-Symes in her 'large and ramshackle car'.
VB 142–143

LABOUR PARTY
In 1927 Miss Mouse wants to know whose party it is, and why she has not been asked.
• In 1941 'those Labour fellows in the house of commons' need to be shown by the army that once it finds good men it knows how to use them. To this end Trimmer (q.v.) is propelled into his career in propaganda.
VB 53; OG 155

LADY ALMINA'S SECRET
See Books

LADY CRIPPS' FUND
Ludovic (q.v.) says that calling his dog by a Chinese name would remind him of Lady Cripps' fund.
US 120

LAKU
Supposed city in the centre of Ishmaelia fifty miles north of Jacksonburg. It is in fact a complete fabrication resulting from the first map of the country made in 1898 being copied time and again. Each time the map was copied the word Laku (Ishmaelite for 'I don't know') was included at the site of a resting place of the original map-making team, whose leader had asked one of their boys to tell them where they were so that they could mark it on the map.
• During the Ishmaelian crisis all the foreign journalists (except William Boot), head off to Laku, where they have been informed (by Dr Benito) the action is.
Sc 99

LALIQUE
Type of Art Nouveau glassware given its name by René Lalique (1860–1945), a French jeweller.
• Simon Balcairn's London flat in 1930 is furnished with Lalique glass.
• Charles Ryder at Oxford in the 1920s has a Lalique decanter and glasses.
VB 104; BR 43

LAMENESS
Apthorpe hurts his knee at the same time that Guy Crouchback wrenches his.
MA 97

LANCASHIRE
In many parts of Lancashire one finds isolated Catholic communities.
US 60

LANCE, JAMES
Friend of Gilbert Pinfold, who shares his taste in furniture and gives him the Burges washhand stand (q.v.) In his hallucinations, Pinfold hears a broadcast by Lance and June Cumberleigh (q.v.).
GP 24, 82–83

LANDOR, WALTER SAVAGE
(1775–1864)
English writer. Influenced by Milton. See his *Grebir*, and *Imaginary Conversations*. Ambrose Silk quotes from his *I Strove with None*.
PF 43

LANDSEER, SIR EDWIN HENRY *(1802–1873)*
English painter of animal subjects. His pictures were tremendously popular during the Victorian age by virtue of their anthropomorphic sentimentality. Favourite subjects were dogs and deer. See his 'Monarch of the Glen' (18).
• Collins (q.v.) tells Charles Ryder that 'If you allow Cézanne to represent a third dimension on his two dimensional canvas, then you must allow Landseer his gleam of loyalty in the spaniel's eye'.
BR 30

LANE-FOSCOTE, SIR RODERICK MP
Member of Parliament for the constituency in which Lady Moping lives. She shows him 'extreme good will' and he writes to the Home Office to secure the release of Mr Loveday (q.v.).
WS 13

LANGLEY, BATTY *(1696–1751)*
English architect and writer of some twenty books on the subject. See his 'Gothic Architecture Restored and Improved' (1741).
• Cedric Lyne, giving way to his wife, spans the stream at their estate with a bridge in the Chinese taste taken straight from Batty Langley.
• Roger Simmonds has a collection of Langley's works.
PF 170; WS 144

LANGUAGE
Adam Fenwick-Symes calls Nina Blount 'hog's rump' in a Cockney accent in 1930.
• Agatha Runcible addresses the family of Sir James Brown, the Prime Minister, at breakfast, with a cheerful 'Good morning all', in a cockney accent, in 1930.
• Alistair Trumpington has to learn new languages when he joins the army. There is 'the simple tongue, the unchanging reiteration of obscenity, spoken by his fellow soldiers'. There is also the language in which his officers address him which includes such phrases as 'are you in the picture?'.
• Wapishiana is the local dialect of the Macushi in Brazil.
• Mr Salter, keen to address William Boot in a language which he will understand, asks him about mangel-wurzels: 'How are your boots root?'.
• Mr Baldwin's accent is 'not exactly American or Levantine or Eurasian or Latin or Teuton, but a blend of them all'.
• The Ishmaelite for 'I don't know' is Laku (q.v.).
• The language spoken by Dennis Barlow is 'a patois' derived from Whispering Glades (q.v.).
VB 54, 58; PF 128; HD 173; Sc 27, 55, 99; LO 33

LANGUISHING OF LEONARD, THE
Term, coined by de Souza (q.v.) for the episode during the equipping of the Halberdiers with tropical kit, when Leonard's wife gets into a state which results in his transfer to the Training Depot.
MA 214

LAPAD
Dr Antonic remembers sitting on the terrace at his 'little house at Lapad', and 'laughing so loudly that the passing fishermen called up to us from their decks asking to share the joke'.
WS 219

LARES ET PENATES
The household gods of Ancient Rome.
• Basil Seal makes mention of them in his speech to the more cultured of the likely candidates for 'the Connollys'.
PR 139

LARKIN, 'SPRAT'
General Cruttwell (q.v.) remembers being in Ishmaelia with 'poor "Sprat" Larkin' in 1897.
Sc 44

LARRIGAN, ALF
Unfortunate acquaintance of Philbrick (q.v.) who, when he 'tried to put it over' on one of Toby Cruttwell's girls was taken by

Toby to Dr Peterfield 'and . . . he hadn't no use for girls after that.'
DF 53

LARUE'S
According to Anthony Blanche, one of the places where Lord Marchmain sits 'with a snowy shirt front . . . in most conventional Edwardian style'.
BR 56

LASCARS
East Indian sailors.
• The crew and the stewards of the *SS Caliban* are Lascars.
GP 34

LAST, AGNES ***(b. 1922)***
Daughter of Richard Last. Lives at Hetton after Tony and Brenda. 'A neat, circumspect child of twelve, with large grave eyes behind her goggles'. She is always the last to get dressed in the morning.
HD 218–221

LAST, LADY BRENDA ***(b. 1908)***
Wife of Tony Last (q.v.). Née Rex. Daughter of Lord St Cloud (q.v.). Mrs Beaver describes her as 'lovely'. Has a 'very fair, underwater look'. Entertains John Beaver (q.v.) at Hetton. Goes to London for 'bone setting' with her sister, Marjorie (q.v.). Decides to rent a flat in Belgravia. Eats chocolates and buns on the train. Dines with Beaver who she seduces.

They go to Polly Cockpurse's party. Thinks Beaver 'second-rate and a snob'. Wears pyjamas at dinner. Spends all of her time in London. Is keen for Mrs Beaver to redecorate the Morning Room. Pretends to take a 'course in economics'. Meets Jenny Abdul Akbur (q.v.). Learns of 'John's' death and thinks it is Beaver. Says 'thank God'. Is filled with remorse.

Leaves Tony on the grounds that she is in love with Beaver. Tells him by means of a note on the breakfast tray. Compels Tony to give up Hetton. Marries Jock Grant-Menzies (q.v.) when Tony is declared dead. Is unable to get down to Hetton for the dedication of Tony's obelisk.
HD 9, 18, 24, 38, 39, 127, 200

LAST, FRANCES
Aunt of Tony Last (q.v.). Has a severe upbringing. Comes to Hetton for Christmas 1933 and attends the dedication of Tony's obelisk.
HD 14, 60, 220

LAST, JOHN ANDREW ***(1926–1933)***
Son of Tony and Brenda Last (q.v.). Has a pony called Thunderclap. Is taught to ride (and to swear) by Ben Hacket (q.v.). Thinks that John Beaver is silly. Is excited at going out with the hunt. Is killed when, after being knocked from his pony, he is kicked into a ditch by Miss Ripon's horse.
HD 19, 23, 28, 44, 53, 87, 100–105

LAST, MOLLY
Daughter of Richard Last. Lives at Hetton after Tony and Brenda. Rides a two-stroke motor-cycle.
HD 218

LAST, PETER ***(b. 1913)***
Son of Richard Last. At Oxford in 1934.
HD 218

LAST, RICHARD
Impoverished cousin of Tony Last who visits Hetton for Christmas. After Tony is declared dead he inherits Hetton. Hunts with the Pigstanton. Is instrumental in erecting Tony's obelisk.
HD 218

LAST, TEDDY ***(b. 1912)***
Eldest son of Richard Last (q.v.). Concerns himself with the rearing of silver foxes with Ben Hacket. Is badly bitten. By means of the foxes he hopes to restore Hetton to its former glory.
HD 218–221

LAST, LORD ANTHONY (TONY) ***(b. 1902)***
Educated Oxford (Balliol).

Owner of Hetton (q.v.). Marries Brenda Rex (q.v.) 1926. Jock Grant-Menzies says that he is 'one of the happiest men I know. He's got just enough money, loves the place, one son he's crazy about, devoted wife, not a worry in the world'. As a boy travels to Tours. Honeymoons on the Riviera in a borrowed villa. Has a habit of being pompous. Reads the lesson at the local church on Christmas Day and Harvest Thanksgiving. Goes to church every Sunday, returning by way of the hothouses where he picks a buttonhole before returning to the house, where he drinks sherry in the library. Invites John Beaver to Hetton.

Misses Brenda when she goes to London. Is deserted by Brenda. Tries to understand. No longer dines at Bratt's for fear of meeting Beaver, but goes to Brown's where he is also a member. Avoids Brenda. Departs for Brazil with Dr Messinger. Goes deep into the jungle in search of the City. Develops fever. Is rescued by Mr Todd. Spends the rest of his life condemned to read Dickens to Mr Todd. In England he is presumed dead after an expedition returns with his watch.
HD 9–11, 16, 30, 35, 64, 75, 77, 85, 94, 111–113, 124, 152, 156, 166, 170–217

LAST TRUMP, THE
Lady Circumference (q.v.) compares the 'fine phalanx' approaching Lady Anchorage to shake her by the hand at her ball with the elect going to meet their maker at the Last Trump.
• The horn of Lady Trilby's (q.v.) motor car resounds through Boot Magna 'like the coming of the Lord'.
• Guy Crouchback likes to think that the advertisement he places in *The Times* for Chatty Corner is 'as unambiguous as the Last Trump'.
VB 127; Sc 18; OG 39

LAST VICEROY, THE
Louis, 1st Earl Mountbatten of Burma (1900–1979) was last Viceroy of India.
• Dr Beamish (q.v.) had written 'publicity' for the last Viceroy.
GP 195

LATAKIA
Coastal town in Syria.
• Basil Seal (q.v.), in his imaginary wartime adventure in which he is called up by the Secret Service takes the alias of a tobacco-grower from Latakia.
PF 51

LATERAN TREATY, THE
Treaty, signed in 1929, between Mussolini and the Pope, setting up the Vatican State.
• When in 1943 the Italians surrender and the King flees, Guy Crouchback tells his father that it was a great mistake, but the latter reminds him that 'many souls may have been reconciled and died at peace because of it'.
US 15, 17

LATIN
• Peter Pastmaster recalls Paul Pennyfeather teaching him 'Quominus and Quin' at Llanabba.
• Guy Crouchback finds Latin an easier language in which to ask the priest at Begoy to pray for his wife.
DF 215; US 197

LATIN AMERICAN ENTERTAINMENT COMPANY LTD, THE
Organization run by Margot Metroland which ships girls from Britain to Marseilles and Buenos Aires and leads them into a life of prostitution. The cover is as an employment bureau for cabarets.

The girls include Jane Grimes (q.v.). The less experience they have the better. Employees include 'Bill', Captain Grimes and, briefly and to his cost, Paul Pennyfeather.
DF 144–146

LAUDER, SIR HARRY ***(1870–1950)***
Scottish comic singer and music hall star. Notable for his 'Roamin' in the Gloamin''. Knighted in 1919 for his morale-boosting work with the troops in the Great War.
• The Wee Kirk o' Auld Lang Syne at Whispering Glades (q.v.) is dedicated to Robert Burns and Harry Lauder, 'souvenirs of whom are exhibited in an annex'.
LO 98

LAURENCIN, MARIE ***(1885–1957)***
French artist. Reknowned for her pastel-coloured female portraits. Imogen Quest (q.v.) has 'large Laurencin eyes'.
VB 114

LAVATORIES
Julia Stitch drives down the gentlemen's lavatory in Sloane Street.
Sc 40

LAWRENCE, GERTRUDE ***(1897–1952)***
Female singer and actress. Star of numerous West End shows including those of Noel Coward (q.v.).
• Rex Mottram is on good terms with 'Gertie' Lawrence.
BR 107

LAWRENCE, T.E. (LAWRENCE OF ARABIA) ***(1888–1935)***
British soldier. Led the Arab revolt against the Turks during the Great War. After the war retired to obscurity under the alias of Aircraftsman Shaw in the RAF. See his *Seven Pillars of Wisdom* (1926).
• To Ambrose Silk in 1939, Ireland is the country of T.E. Lawrence. Barbara Sothill sees Basil Seal as T.E. Lawrence in 1939.

LE BOURGET
French airport.
• One of the stops on Basil Seal's journey from Croydon to Azania.
PF 88

LE TOUQUET
Coastal town in Artois, France.
• Every year Bratt's club hold a golfing tournament here.
• Tony and Brenda Last once went to Le Touquet with Bratt's golf team.
• Alastair Trumpington has been unfaithful to Sonia for one week of every year since they have been married, during Bratt's golf tournament.
• Boy Mulcaster joins Anthony Blanche at Le Touquet over Easter 1922 and having lost 'some infinitesimal sum' at cards, expects Anthony to pay for everything.
HD 156; PF 45; BR 49

LEAGUE OF DUMB CHUMS
William Bland's name for the SPCA (q.v.).
BM 178

LEAGUE OF NATIONS
Council of world nations inaugurated in 1920, with the express aim of preventing war. Instituted a permanent court of justice in The Hague.
• It is while returning from a meeting of the League of Nations Union at Oxford in 1927 that Paul Pennyfeather is debagged.
• Arthur Potts (q.v.) is employed by the League to investigate Margot Metroland's prostitution racket.
• Paul does not have a very high opinion of it, thinking that it makes it more difficult to move around.
• Sebastian Flyte supposes that conventional students at Oxford join the League of Nations Union.
• Azania (q.v.) is mandated as a League of Nations protectorate in the 1930s.
DF 12, 147, 154; BR 101; BM 233

LECCE
Town on the 'heel' of Italy.
• In 1944 the Jewish refugees befriended by Guy Crouchback are interned in a camp in a stony valley near Lecce.
US 233

LECTURES
While 'in the hulks' the Halberdiers entertain themselves by delivering lectures. Apthorpe lectures on 'The Jurisdiction of Lyon King of Arms compared with that of Garter King of Arms'. Guy Crouchback lectures on 'wine making'. The 'cipher officer' lectures on 'Court life in St Petersburg'.
MA 206–207

LEEDS, YORKSHIRE
Where Father Graves takes Father Phipps to see 'a first-class' cricket match after

they have been to the induction of the abbot at Ampleforth.
Br 82

LEFT BOOK CLUB, THE
Book club founded by Victor Gollancz, John Strachey and Harold Laski in 1936 with the express aim of resisting Fascism by means of circulating 'knowledge'. Had 50,000 members to which it circulated such titles as Orwell's *Road to Wigan Pier*. Ceased to exist 1948.
• Parsnip and Pimpernell are members and their works are circulated by the Club.
• The Vicar of Much Malcock attempts to interest his parishoners in the LBC.
GP 217; WS 47

LEFT WING INTELLECTUALS
Ambrose Silk, Parsnip and Pimpernell are all at the top of the government blacklist of Left Wing Intellectuals in 1939.
PF 71

LEFTISTS
Everard Spruce 'like many men of the left . . . had been an assidious student of society gossip columns'.
US 199
(*See also* COMMUNISTS and BOLSHEVISM)

LÉGER, FERNAND ***(1881–1955)***
French painter, instrumental in the formation of the Cubist movement. Later drew away and developed his 'aesthetic of the machine' in which he applied his distinctive curvilinear cubism to machine shapes and monumental figures. See his works in the Tate Gallery.
• At the time when he is fawning to the Marxists Everard Spruce (q.v.) disguises his own personal preference for Fragonard over Léger.
• In the New Britain of Miles Plastic the halls of learning are hung with reproductions of pictures by Picasso and Léger.
• The same reproductions are hung in Miles' hostel in later life.
US 123; GP 183, 196

LEGGE, PERCY AND MRS
British residents in Azania.
BM 54–56

LEGGE, MRS
Landlady to Roger and Lucy Simmonds (q.v.).
WS 163

LELY, SIR PETER ***(1618–1680)***
English portraitist, born in Westphalia. Painted for both Charles I and II and also for Cromwell. See his 'Beauties' of Charles II's court (Hampton Court).
• Mr Plant (q.v.) 'excels at copies and pastiches of Lely, which he sells through Goodchild and Godley.'
WS 115

LENNOX, DAVID
Photographer and interior decorator. Friend of Miles Malpractice and Margot Metroland (q.v.). Decorates the sports room at Margot's London residence, Pastmaster House (q.v.), in 1927. Also known affectionately as 'little Davy Lennox'. For three years has never given anyone a 'complimentary sitting'. Breaks this rule to take three photographs of Margot before her wedding to Paul Pennyfeather. Two are of the back of her head and one of the reflection of her hands in a bowl of ink.
• In 1930 Simon Balcairn has in his flat 'some enterprising photographs by David Lennox'. Angela Lyne has her London flat 'done up with Regency grisailles by David Lennox in 1938. The first issue of *Ivory Tower* in spring 1940 contains an article attacking David Lennox 'and the decorative school of fashionable artists' under the title 'The Bakelite Tower'.
DF 128, 144, 149–150; VB 104; PF 155, 186

LENT, SIMON
Young, single writer who, in 1936, lives in a six-guinea-a-week flat over a garage in a mews. Lives on £800 a year. Is 'half in love' with Sylvia and unable to pay his bills: to his tailor, his hosier, his club, his bookseller, optician, cigar merchant, barber and a number of other shops.
• Is described in the Press as a 'meteorically successful . . . enviable young novelist.
• Is invited to lunch by Margot Metro-

land. Is asked to write a screenplay for *Hamlet* by Sir James Macrae. Declares that the written word is dead and decides to give up novels and stick to screenplays. Suddenly Sir James decides to scrap the entire project. Simon slips back into his old ways.
WS 63–76

LEO
Friend of Sir Francis Hinsley who is also employed by Megapolitan Studios (q.v.) who, on being fired, commits suicide by throwing himself off the roof of the Garden of Allah Hotel.
LO 29

LEONARD, DAISY
Wife of Jim (q.v.). Pregnant (in 1940). They lodge in the town. She is sour and inclined to smutty conversation. Says that Jim is 'playing soldiers'.
MA 62–69, 215–216, 232, 238

LEONARD, JIM ***(d. 1940)***
Member of Guy Crouchback's officer intake into the Halberdiers (q.v.). Before the war he works in insurance and plays scrum half for the local rugby club. After Daisy forces him to apply for a transfer to the Training Depot becomes upset. de Souza calls it 'The languishing of Leonard'. Before he is transferred he goes on leave to South London during the Blitz, and is killed by a bomb.
MA 62–69, 215–216, 232, 238

LEPERS
Sebastian asks the Superior of the monastery near Carthage if he can send him to be a missionary among the lepers: 'lepers would do best of anything'.
BR 290

LEPPERIDGES, THE
British residents of Matodi (q.v.). He is O.C. of the native levy ... 'a very considerable man in Matodi'. Calls Bretherton (q.v.) 'the latrine wallah'.
BM 235

LESLEY AND ROBERTS
Tailors in Savile Row, London. Tailors to Anthony Blanche. Sebastian Flyte (q.v.) pawns two suits of Anthony's newly arrived from Lesley and Roberts to get drinking money in Marseilles.
BR 196

LETTERS
Seth (q.v.) writes to the King of England: 'Greeting. May this reach you. Peace be on your house'.
• Prudence Courteney writes to William Bland: 'Sweet William. You looked so lovely at breakfast you know all half awake and I wanted to pinch you only didn't . . .'
• Sir Samson Courteney receives a chain letter about the Great Pyramid: 'Good luck. Copy this letter out nine times ... 153 being the number symbolic of the Elect in Our Lord's mystical enactment of the draught of 153 great fishes'.
• Sebastian Flyte writes to Charles Ryder on black coroneted and bordered Victorian mourning paper: 'Dearest Charles, . . . I am in mourning for my lost innocence. It never looked like living. The doctors despaired of it from the start.'
• The regular soldiers in Guy Crouchback's platoon all write S.W.A.L.K. on the envelopes of their letters home.
• Letters for the East, according to Lucy Simmonds should always be written on very thin, lined paper.
• Aimee Thanatogenos writes a great many letters to the Guru Brahmin (q.v.), starting in May 1947, but does not receive a satisfactory reply and commits suicide.
BM 62, 16, 103; BR 71; MA 244; WS 166; LO 81

LEVANTINES
The proprietress of the brothel in Fez where Fatima works is 'a forbidding Levantine from Tetuan'.
WS 121

LEY, DR
Basil Seal, reading the revised edition of 'Monument to a Spartan' surmises that

it might have been written by Dr Ley himself.
PF 192

LIBERALS
Sir Humphrey Maltravers (later Lord Metroland) tells Paul Pennyfeather about the Liberal campaign of 1906.
• According to Rex Mottram's friends in 1938, the Liberals will hang Hitler.
• John Verney had stood twice for the liberal party before the war in two hopeless by-elections.
DF 131; BR 280; GP 162

LIBERIA
Basil Seal tells a colonel that they ought to do something about Liberia.
• The passions in Liberia are aroused by the Fascist attempt on the Jacksons' regime in Ishmaelia.
PF 52, 66; Sc 78

LIFE
Otto Silenus tells Paul Pennyfeather that life is like the big wheel at Luna Park (q.v.).
• In the words of Gilbert Pinfold's imaginary general, life is 'never quite what you expect when it comes to action'.
DF 208; GP 117

LIKA, THE
Desolate area of Dalmatia in which, in 1944, every village is 'ravaged and roofless'.
US 232

LILY
Daughter of one of the women who travel with Adam Fenwick-Symes on the train to Aylesbury. She is keen to be a manicurist.
VB 139

LIMBO
Limbo, thinks Ambrose Silk 'is the place. In Limbo one has natural happiness without the beatific vision; no harps; no communal order; but wine and conversation and imperfect, various humanity'.
PF 60

LIMERICK
Town in Ireland.
• In 1940 there is a rumour that the Germans have landed in Limerick.
MA 204

LIMOGES ENAMELS
Decorative enamel work produced in the town of Limoges, France.
• Limoges enamels are among the possessions of Lady Seal sent to her bank for safe-keeping at the start of WWII.
PF 17

LITTLE BAYTON
Village near Hetton where the hounds of the Pigstanton Hunt are kennelled.
• After his argument with John, Tony Last offers to take him to the kennels but, unforgiving, he declines.
HD 78

LITTLEJOHN, EDDY (GINGER)
Childhood friend of Nina Blount (q.v.). Cruel to cats as a child. In the Army in Ceylon where he does 'something military' for five years. Marries Nina Blount. During WWII gets a desk job in Whitehall and 'wears a very grand sort of uniform'.
VB 220

LITTLEJOHNS, THE
Parents of Ginger (q.v.). Residents of Oakshott. Very wealthy shipowners.
VB 203

LIVERPOOL
One of the ports to which the Halberdiers are ordered in 1940 and from where they sail to Dakar (q.v.).
• According to Gilbert Pinfold's voices one of the passengers on the *SS Caliban* has an uncle in Liverpool.
MA 218; GP 56

LIVERY COMPANIES
To the livery companies of the City of London fishmongering and cordwaining play as small a part in their interests as does cricket in those of the members of the Hollywood Cricket Club.
LO 29

LIVY (TITUS LIVIUS) ***(59 BC–AD 17)***
Roman historian and republican. See his *History of Rome.*
• Mr Crouchback teaches selections from Livy at our Lady of Victory's Preparatory School at Matchet.
OG 21

LLANABBA CASTLE SCHOOL, WALES
Minor public school in North Wales near Bangor. Proprietor Dr Fagan (q.v.). It is surrounded by a macchiolated wall and gates with towers, decorated with heraldic beasts.

It presents a 'formidably feudal' aspect . . . 'a model of medieval impregnability'. From the back it looks like any country house 'with a great many windows and a terrace, and a chain of glass houses and the roofs of innumerable nondescript kitchen buildings, disappearing into the trees'. Owned in the 1860s by a Lancashire mill owner who, during the cotton famine, employed his men on refacing the house, in the medieval style, in return for alms.

Inside are unlit passages. The common room has sixteen pipes in a rack. It also contains a set of golf clubs, a walking stick, an umbrella, and two miniature rifles. Over the chimney piece is a green baize noticeboard with school lists. On the table is a typewriter. In a bookcase are a number of old textbooks and new exercise books. There is a bicycle pump, two armchairs and half a bottle of medicinal port, a boxing glove and a bowler hat. There is a school hall, large and paneled. The drive is often waterlogged. Paul Pennyfeather is a master there, as are Grimes and Prendergast.
DF 20–21, 25, 61, 143

LLANABBA SILVER BAND
Ten men of 'revolting appearance . . . low of brow, crafty of eye, and crooked of limb . . .' Their leader is the station-master. They play at the school sports day.
DF 64

LLANDUDNO, WALES
Nearest large town to Llanabba. Grimes and Dingy Fagan go shopping there in 1922.
DF 58

LLOYD GEORGE, DAVID, 1st BARON ***(1863–1945)***
British Liberal statesman. President of the Board of Trade 1905–1908. Chancellor of the Exchequer 1908–1915. Minister of Munitions 1915. Prime Minister 1916–1922. According to Hitler he was 'the man who won the war' (WWI).
• It was 'a bitter thing' for Christopher Seal and his friends to accept Lloyd George as Prime Minister.
• One of the people for whom Cordelia Flyte prays.
• Sebastian Flyte's uncle Ned is locked up for taking a bear into one of Lloyd George's meetings.
• One of the men who in Mr Crouchback's mind stands on the other side to the Crouchbacks.
• Lloyd George's ascent to power is the last contemporary event to impress Mr Plant.
PF 18; BR 91, 118; MA 34; WS 111

LOCHIEL, DONALD CAMERON OF ***(1695–1748)***
Highland chief and supporter of Bonnie Prince Charlie (q.v.). Died in exile in France.
• Among the highlanders in Guy Crouchback's vision of the gathering of the clans (q.v.).
MA 161

LOCKJAWS, THE
Family with whom Lady Amelia stays at Christmas during the crisis at the Cornphillips, whose house is nearby.
WS 27

LOCKWOOD
Ex-pupil of Scott-King (q.v.) encountered by him at No 64 Jewish Illicit Immigrants' Camp, Palestine. At Granchester he had been a sitter for the Balliol Scholarship. Leaves to go into the army in 1939.
WS 246

LONDON

London, says Ambrose Silk, 'was meant to be seen in a fog'.

• *ACTON:* Home of Gervase Wilbraham (q.v.). Where Gilbert Pinfold starts to hear his voices again after his arrival in England.

• *ALBERMARLE STREET:* Where Brenda Last and her sister have lunch at a new restaurant in 1933.

• *ALBERT HALL:* Gilbert Pinfold declares that he is proud not to have worn a black shirt to a fascist rally at the Albert Hall.

• *ANCHORAGE HOUSE:* London residence of Lord and Lady Anchorage (q.v.). Last survivor of the noble town houses of London, 'lurking in a ravine between concrete skyscrapers'. Brenda Last dances here with Jock Grant-Menzies after Tony's disappearance. Drawn by Charles Ryder on his return from South America before being pulled down to make way for shops and two-roomed flats.

• *ARLINGTON STREET:* Location of Marchmain House. Arthur Box-Bender moves to his flat here during WWII.

• *ASPREYS, BOND STREET:* Where Archie Schwert has an account.

• *ATHENAEUM CLUB:* Gentlemen's club. Mr Plant is a member, as are Philbrick, Charles Ryder's warden at Hertford, and Mr Ryder.

• *BARTON STREET:* Location of the London house of Lord Brideshead (q.v.). Blown up during the Blitz.

• *BATT'S CLUB, DOVER STREET:* Gentlemen's club of which Philbrick is a member.

• *BAYSWATER ROAD:* The traffic noise from the Bayswater Road reaches Mr Ryder's house.

• *BEDFORD SQUARE:* Home of the 'little worker's daughter' who sends three unused penny stamps to the President of Ishmaelia. Where the offices of Geoffrey Bentley (q.v.) are to be found.

• *BEEFSTEAK CLUB, 9 IRVING STREET, WC2:* Sir Joseph Mainwaring is a member, as is Eddie Beste-Bingham.

• *BELGRAVE PLACE:* Location of the house of Harriet (q.v.).

• *BELGRAVE SQUARE:* Where Ruby lives before the war. Home, at Utteridge House, of Lord Utteridge (q.v.). Where, at the garage behind the house, his son is kidnapped by Jimmy Drage in 1920.

• *BELGRAVIA:* Where, off Belgrave Square, Brenda Last has a flat. Where in 1938, John Verney has a flat.

• *BELLAMY'S CLUB, ST JAMES'S STREET, SW1:* Gentlemen's club. Members include Guy Crouchback, Ian Kilbannock, Air Marshal Beech, Tommy Blackhouse, Binkie Cavanagh, Arthur Box-Bender, Elderbury, Gervase Crouchback, Mr Crouchback, Ivo Crouchback, Peregrine Crouchback, Gilbert Pinfold, Roger Stillingfleet, Crambo, Nailsworth, Basil Seal, Bertie, Lieutenant Padfield, Ivor Claire. (Modelled on White's).

• *BERKELEY SQUARE:* Paul Pennyfeather and Margot Metroland walk across the square in the sunshine. Where, after their court appearance, Sebastian Flyte and Charles Ryder meet Julia at Gunter's (q.v.).

• *BETHNAL GREEN:* Where Mrs Stitch finds a carpet shop kept by a man who speaks no English.

• *BLIGHT STREET, W2:* No 14 is Dr Akonanga's surgery (q.v.). During the Blitz no bombs fall here.

• *BLOOMSBURY:* Where Otto Silenus lives in a bed-sitting room. According to Mr Chatterbox (q.v.) it is an area of temperance hotels and tea dances. In whose 'sombre streets', in the top floor of a large mansion, Ambrose Silk has his flat (near the Ministry of Information).

• *BOURDON STREET:* Where Simon Balcairn lives (and dies).

• *BOW STREET:* Location of the magistrate's court in which Charles Ryder and Sebastian Flyte appear.

• *BRATT'S CLUB:* Gentlemen's club. Members include: Alastair Trumpington, Peter Pastmaster, Tony Last, John Beaver, Jock Grant-Menzies, Bill Meadows, Boy Mulcaster, Charles Ryder, and Rex Mottram.

• *BRITISH MUSEUM:* Place of employment of Miss Orme-Herrick's hard-hearted fiancé.

• *BRIXTON GAOL:* Wherein Mr Rampole (q.v.) is imprisoned.
• *BROMPTON:* Location of the Royal Victorian Institute; a Venetian-Gothic brick edifice and in 1943 the HQ of HOO.
• *BROOKS'S CLUB, ST JAMES'S:* John Boot (q.v.) is a member. Mrs Stitch almost runs over a young man outside.
• *BROOK STREET, W1:* Where there is apparently a doctor who will carry out an abortion for Virginia Crouchback. However, his house has been destroyed by a bomb. Where, in a once private large house (requisitioned by HOOHQ) Dr Akonanga works (q.v.). Where Lily (q.v.) is a manicurist.
• *BROWN'S CLUB:* Gentlemen's club. Tony Last is a member (q.v.).
• *CAFE DE LA PAIX:* Restaurant where Adam Fenwick-Symes reports seeing Count Cincinati in 1930.
• *CAFE ROYAL, 68 REGENT STREET, W1:* Restaurant, much frequented by the Bohemian set in the late nineteenth and early twentieth centuries. One of Ambrose Silk's haunts. Charles Ryder dines here during the General Strike in 1926. Where de Souza, Pat, Jane and Constant eat on 30th December 1939. Where Lucy and Roger Simmonds go to eat after the theatre.
• *CAMBERWELL GREEN:* Where Philbrick (q.v.) has a large house and where, in 1913, he buys the Lamb and Flag which he runs until 1919.
• *CAMDEN TOWN:* Where an elderly widow drops a pot of ferns on the head of Jean de Brissac de la Motte during the General Strike.
• *CAMPDEN HILL:* In the 1880s there were, from here to Hampstead, twenty or more parties on 'varnishing day'.
• *CANNING TOWN:* Where Lady Ursula Stayle helps to run a girls' club in the 1930s.
• *CARLISLE PLACE:* Where Peregrine Crouchback has a flat, in Bourne Mansions. Charles Ryder convalesces there in 1944 and effects a reconciliation with Virginia. Destroyed by a flying bomb in June 1944 which kills Virginia, Peregrine, and his housekeeper, Mrs Corner.
• *CARLTON CLUB, 69 ST JAMES'S STREET, SW1:* Gentlemen's club. Lord Chasm is a member.
• *CARLTON HOUSE TERRACE:* Where Philbrick has a large house.
• *CARTIER'S:* Bond Street jeweller's where Julia Flyte expects to be bought an engagement ring by Rex Mottram.
• *CHARING CROSS STATION:* From where Charles Ryder and Sebastian Flyte leave for Venice.
• *CHARLES STREET:* Where Brenda Champion has a house.
• *CHARLOTTE STREET:* Where, in a restaurant, Basil Seal tells Poppet Green's friends his views on the Nazis. Where Ambrose Silk, Julia Stitch and 'Tom' have lunch.
• *CHESTER STREET:* One of the Trumpington's many temporary addresses.
• *CHEYNE ROW:* All the flying bombs launched against London appear to be directed towards here.
• *CHEYNE WALK:* Where Philbrick has a large house. Where Everard Spruce lives in a fine house, cared for by four secretaries.
• *CHRISTIE'S, 4 KING STREET:* In whose auction rooms a portrait of Lady Throbbing and Mrs Blackwater as young sisters, by Millais (q.v.) made a record in rock-bottom prices in 1929.
• *CITY OF LONDON:* Where Rex Mottram has friends who are 'leathery old sharks'. Where Ralph Bland has a Jewish friend who runs off with a large sum of Billy Cornphillip's money.
• *CLAPHAM:* Where, in numerous mansions, part of HOOHQ is based in 1943.
• *CLARIDGES:* Hotel where Wheatley and his parents stay in 1919. Where the MacDougals stay, with the Chasms, in 1933. In 1940 Virginia Crouchback stays here as does, for two days, Guy. Where Basil and Angela Seal stay in 1963.
• *COVENT GARDEN:* Where, at the Royal Opera House, Adam Fenwick-Symes claims to have seen Count Cincinati.
• *DAVIES STREET:* Location of Claridges (q.v.).

- *DORCHESTER HOTEL:* Where Ruby lives during the war.
- *DOVER STREET:* Location of the Maison Basque restaurant. Location of Shepheard's hotel. Location of Bratt's Club.
- *DOWNING STREET, NO 10:* Home during 1930 of Sir James Brown and his family until the Bright Young People have a party here.
- *DUKE STREET, ST JAMES'S:* Location of Goodchild and Godley, the fine art dealers (q.v.).
- *DUKE OF YORK'S STEPS:* Where Jumbo Trotter meets Beano outside their club in 1943.
- *EARLS COURT:* Where Frank de Souza's (q.v.) girl has a flat.
- *EAST SHEEN:* Home of the widow of a trick cyclist mistakenly visited by Corker (q.v.).
- *EATON TERRACE:* Where Ian and Kerstie Kilbannock have their house.
- *EBURY STREET:* Where Sir Ralph Brompton has rooms over a shop with 'something of the air of expensive undergraduate digs'. John Plant's lodgings are in Ebury Street, with his housekeeper, Mrs Legge.
- *EDGEWARE ROAD:* Where a friend of Philbrick had his throat cut on a Saturday night. Off which road Dr Akonanga casts spells on the Nazis in 1943. Home (in one room) of the National Academy of Cinematographic Art (q.v.).
- *EMBANKMENT:* Where, according to Arthur Atwater, the police will allow you to sleep only if you have money.
- *EUSTON STATION, NW1:* Where Agatha Runcible is found staring at a model of an engine in the central hall, after her crash.
- *FARM STREET, W1:* Home of the Jesuit Church of the Immaculate Conception and monastery. Julia Flyte goes here to seek advice. Rex Mottram comes here for instruction to Father Mowbray. Guy Crouchback attends a mass here on St Valentine's day 1940.
- *FINCHLEY:* Where Winnie lives 'with a lady'.
- *FINSBURY INTERNATIONAL THEATRE:* A production is mounted here of Roger Simmonds' play *Internal Combustion*. They also mount one of the *Tractor* Trilogy.
- *FLEET STREET, EC4:* Home of the *Daily Excess* and at nos. 700–853, the *Daily Beast* (Copper House).
- *GARDEN CLUB:* Mrs Brace is a member.
- *GARRICK CLUB, 15 GARRICK STREET, WC2:* Gentlemen's Club. Sir James Macrae is a member (q.v.).
- *GLOUCESTER TERRACE:* Where tea dances take place.
- *GOLDEN SQUARE, SOHO, W1:* You generally pass through Golden Square on your way to the Old Hundredth (q.v.).
- *GOLDERS GREEN:* Where Flossie is cremated.
- *GOLDSMITHS' HALL, FOSTER LANE, EC2:* Where the Sword of Stalingrad (q.v.) is first put on view.
- *GOODE, THOMAS, SOUTH AUDLEY ST, MAYFAIR:* Purveyors of fine porcelain. Where the Pendle-Garthwaites buy a tea set as Julia Flyte's wedding present.
- *GOWER STREET, WC1:* Where Ambrose Silk sees 'the vast bulk of London University insulting the autumnal sky'. Home of the Ministry of Information.
- *GREAT PORTLAND STREET, W1:* Home of the motor-business.
- *GREAT COLLEGE STREET, SW1:* The queue to see the Sword of Stalingrad, on show in Westminster Abbey, continues up here.
- *GREEN PARK, SW1:* The windows of the long drawing room of Marchmain House look on to Green Park.
- *GREEN PARK STATION, SW1:* Underground station at which one alights for Bellamy's. Guy Crouchback notices refugees making up their beds here in 1943.
- *GREVILLE CLUB:* Gentlemen's Club. Tony Last is a member as is Dr Messinger.
- *GROSVENOR GALLERY:* Art gallery in New Bond Street (q.v.).
- *GROSVENOR HOUSE, PARK LANE, W1:* Where the mythical Polish sculptor Provna lives in a studio.

• *GROSVENOR SQUARE:* Where Angela Lyne takes a service flat in a brand new block in 1940.
• *HAMPSTEAD:* Where Mr Rampole lives, in a small but substantial house near the underground station. Home of Elizabeth Verney's parents who have a substantial Georgian villa overlooking the heath. Later in 1945 John and Elizabeth live there. Where Sir James Macrae (q.v.) has his 'low Georgian house'.
• *HANOVER SQUARE:* At a shop here Nina Blount buys her hats.
• *HANOVER TERRACE:* Where Sir Ralph Brompton has a house until the war.
• *HARLEY STREET:* Where Dr Peterfield practises.
• *HATTON GARDEN:* Where, in a back room, Rex Mottram buys Julia Flyte her engagement ring.
• *HAY HILL:* A member of Bellamy's is sandbagged here and robbed of all his poker winnings.
• *HENDON:* Where in a mansion part of HOOHQ is based until 1943.
• *HENRIETTA STREET:* Where Adam Fenwick-Symes' publishers are based.
• *HERTFORD STREET, W1:* Location of Rex Mottram's house in 1923. Where Edward Throbbing (q.v.) has his 'perfectly sheepish house' which is taken over by the Bright Young People in 1930.
• *HILL CREST COURT, ST JOHN'S WOOD:* Post-war block of flats which overshadow Mr Plant's house.
• *HILL STREET:* Location of the house of Mrs Tipping. Location of Pastmaster House (q.v.). Location of Basil and Angela Seal's house in 1963.
• *HOLBORN:* At the Holborn Grill you can, says the young Jorkins, get the best meal in London.
• *HOLBORN POST OFFICE:* Forwarding address of Arthur Atwater.
• *HOUSE OF COMMONS:* (q.v.).
• *HYDE PARK:* Where, at the foot of the Achilles statue, Philbrick kills the Portuguese count in a duel. Where William Boot watches a black man at Speakers' Corner spouting about Ishmaelia. Where Millicent Blade walks 'Hector'.
• *JERMYN STREET:* Where Mrs Rosenbaum has a brothel. Where Theodore Boot wants to go to see a chap about some business. Angela Lyne attends a matinee in a cinema here in 1939. Where Charles Ryder buys, in September 1919, a pair of heliotrope socks with white clocks. Street where one can find gentlemen who offer advances 'on note of hand only'. Charles Ryder is told by his father that they will not give him a sovereign. Where, at a new restaurant, Peter Pastmaster takes a girl out to dine (Lady Molly Meadowes), and to go to the cinema next door.
• *KENSINGTON GARDENS:* Where a baboon escaped from London Zoo goes into hiding up a tree. Where lesser nurses take their charges.
• *KENSINGTON PALACE GARDENS:* Where Sir Lionel Sterne has his house.
• *KEW:* Where Mr Pinfold's widowed mother lives, in a pretty little house.
• *KING'S ROAD, CHELSEA:* Where Basil Seal wakes up in a flat while 'on a racket'. With which in 1958 the newspapers associate the long hairstyles worn by Coney and Frankie in 1943.
• *LAMBETH STADIUM:* Where Chick Philbrick used to box, before the 1920s.
• *LEICESTER SQUARE:* Where, according to Agatha Runcible, there is a divine club, the St Christopher's Social Club.
• *LINCOLNS INN:* Brenda Last's solicitors are in Lincoln's Inn. To obtain his divorce, Guy Crouchback has to identify Tommy Blackhouse with his wife from the window of his solicitor in Lincoln's Inn.
• *LOCK'S, ST JAMES'S STREET:* Hatters, who in an interview claim that they have never seen a bottle-green bowler hat.
• *LONDON LIBRARY, ST JAMES'S SQUARE:* Private lending library. John Plant meets Basil Seal here in 1939. Gilbert Pinfold and Algernon Clutton Cornforth are members.
• *LONDON ZOO:* Mr Ryder often spends his days there. John Plant takes Lucy Simmonds there every day at noon.
• *LOWNDES SQUARE:* Location of the

town houses of Lady Seal and Arthur Box-Bender. Guy Crouchback stays here before the war whenever in London.

• *MADAME TUSSAUD'S:* Where uncles take their nephews.

• *MAIDA VALE:* Location of the Ishmaelite Legation. Where, at an obscure address, Basil Seal thinks the British Secret Service operate.

• *MARBLE ARCH;* Where John Beaver and Brenda Last are caught in a taxi in a traffic jam on their first evening out together.

• *MARCHMAIN HOUSE, ARLINGTON STREET:* London home of the Earls of Marchmain. Demolished 1927.

• *MARCHMAIN HOUSE, ARLINGTON STREET:* No 211 is the HQ of HOO in 1940. *See individual entry.*

• *MARYLEBONE STATION:* Departure point for the train to Doubting Hall (q.v.).

• *MAYFAIR:* 'Buzzes with the heart of Mr Arlen'. Bachelors lurk here in unconverted mews.

• *MILLBANK HOSPITAL:* Military hospital where Ritchie-Hook convalesces after being wounded in the raid on the African Coast near Dakar.

• *MONTAGUE SQUARE:* Where the Trumpingtons have one of their temporary residences.

• *MORTLAKE:* Where Peregrine and Virginia are buried (*See* BURTON).

• *NEW BOND STREET:* Where the Grosvenor Gallery is situated (q.v.).

• *NORTH AUDLEY STREET:* Where bachelors lurk.

• *NORTH WEST LONDON:* In whose slums Ivo Crouchback dies of starvation.

• *OLD BAILEY, THE:* Where Paul Pennyfeather is tried and sentenced.

• *OMEGA WORKSHOPS, 33 FITZROY SQUARE:* Charles Ryder buys a screen at their closing down sale in 1919.

• *ONSLOW SQUARE:* Location of the house of Paul Pennyfeather's guardian.

• *ORATORY, THE LONDON, BROMPTON ROAD:* Guy and Virginia Crouchback are married here. Rex Mottram wants to be married to Julia here.

• *PADDINGTON:* Where Virginia Crouchback thinks that one would find an abortionist.

• *PADDINGTON STATION:* Point of departure for Brideshead, Boot Magna, and Lychpole.

• *PASTMASTER HOUSE, HILL STREET:* London home of Margot Metroland. The most beautiful building between Bond Street and Park Lane. Built in the reign of William and Mary. Has a magnificent ballroom. In 1941 blown up by a bomb.

• *PICCADILLY:* Location of the bookseller supplying Paul Pennyfeather at Egdon Heath (q.v.).

• *PONT STREET:* In whose ballrooms Elizabeth Verney languishes in 1931. At a ball in Pont Street thrown by some relations of his, Roger Simmonds meets Lucy. Julia Flyte and her friends use the term 'Pont Street' as a source of amusement.

• *PORTMAN SQUARE:* Close to where Allan and Marjorie live.

• *PRAED STREET:* A grocer here supplies Mr Plant with 'Academy Cake'.

• *RAC CLUB, 89 PALL MALL, SW1:* To William Boot, Copper House seems to be a less exclusive version of the RAC.

• *REGENT'S PARK:* At a house here a party is given in 1926 for the Blackbirds (q.v.) at which Charles Ryder meets Boy Mulcaster and Anthony Blanche.

• *REGENT'S STREET: See* CAFE ROYAL

• *RITZ, PICCADILLY: See* HOTELS

• *RYDER STREET:* Where Gilmour lives, in a bed-sitting room.

• *ROYAL VICTORIAN INSTITUTE: See* BROMPTON

• *SAINT JAMES'S PALACE:* Close to which, in a cul de sac, lies the house (designed by Nicholas Hawksmoor (q.v.)) of Algernon and Julia Stitch.

• *SAINT JAMES'S SQUARE:* Where, in 1931, there was held a society wedding reception attended by Sir Ralph Brompton and Ludovic. Demolished by a bomb during the Blitz.

See also LONDON LIBRARY

• *SAINT JAMES STREET:* 'From Piccadilly to the Palace the whole jumble of incongruous facades'. Where Lock's is located. Paul Pennyfeather buys a hat here before his wedding.

See CLUBS

• *SLOANE STREET:* Where Julia Stitch drives down a Gentlemen's lavatory. Where Dr Puttock has his practice.
• *SOHO:* In 1919 Charles Ryder eats here at the d'Italie, which is full of literary people and artists. Where Virginia Crouchback supposes you could find a doctor to carry out an abortion.
• *SOUTH BANK:* In 1951 'monstrous constructions' appear here and the foundation stone for a National Theatre.
• *SOUTHGATE:* Where Gracie Philbrick is a cook.
• *SOUTH KENSINGTON:* Where Archie Banks lives and works at the Victoria and Albert Museum. Where Mary Nichols lives. Where Poppet Green has her studio.
• *STRAND, THE:* At a grill room here the staff of the *Daily Beast* always entertain on expenses. In 1943 Ian Kilbannock and Trimmer cannot find a taxi here. Adam Fenwick-Symes and Simon Balcairn are caught in a traffic jam here.
• *SUSSEX GARDENS:* Where Mrs Beaver has a house, which she shares with her son John.
• *SUSSEX SQUARE:* Where Jorkins lives in 1923.
• *TOTTENHAM COURT ROAD:* Close to where Miles Malpractice discovers a place where you can get oysters for three and sixpence a dozen.
• *TRAVELLERS' CLUB, 106 PALL MALL, SW1:* Gentlemen's Club. Where Sir Joseph Mainwaring always has his little talks with Basil Seal.
• *TRUMPERS, CURZON STREET:* Barbers by Royal Appointment, from whose establishment a barber is sent to shave Sebastian Flyte, Charles Ryder and Boy Mulcaster after they have been arrested.
• *TURF CLUB, 5 CARLTON HOUSE TERRACE, SW1:* Gentlemen's Club.
• *TURTLES CLUB, SAINT JAMES'S STREET:* Gentlemen's Club, halfway down St James's Street. A direct hit from a bomb during the Blitz in 1940 demolishes the spirit store whose contents pour into the gutters. Ian Kilbannock's father was a member. Based on Brook's.
• *UNITED SERVICES CLUB, DUKE OF YORK'S STEPS*: Jumbo Trotter is a member.
• *UXBRIDGE:* Where there is an aerodrome.
• *VICTORIA AND ALBERT MUSEUM:* Where Archie Banks works. Where the Sword of Stalingrad first goes on view.
• *VICTORIA SQUARE:* Where Roger and Lucy Simmonds take a three year lease of a furnished house.
• *VICTORIA STATION:* Bombed during the blitz. Opposite which Virginia and Peregrine Crouchback dine at Overton's in 1944.
• *WANDSWORTH:* Where a girl is found strangled with a piece of barbed wire, an event which illumines the fantasy Charles Ryder and Julia Flyte create around Lord Brideshead.
• *WAR OFFICE:* Visited by Basil Seal in 1940.
• *WESTMINSTER:* Where Lord Brideshead has a small house.
• *WESTMINSTER ABBEY:* Where the Sword of Stalingrad goes on public view.
• *WESTMINSTER CATHEDRAL:* Where Virginia Crouchback makes her first confession in 1944.
• *WHITEHALL:* Miles Plastic sees a very old man raise his hat to the cenotaph.
• *WIGMORE STREET:* Adam Fenwick-Symes buys flowers on the corner of.
• *WIMPOLE STREET:* Location of the nursing home to which Agatha Runcible is taken after her crash. Location of the Wimpole Club (q.v.). Where Sam Benfleet lives.
• *WYNDHAM'S THEATRE, CHARING CROSS ROAD, WC2:* Where, in 1919, Charles Ryder is taken to see *The Choice*.
DF52–55, 78, 81, 90, 91, 118, 122, 139, 145–149, 190, 191; VB 11, 29, 31, 55, 78, 86, 104, 110, 111, 115, 116, 118, 123–126, 128, 133–134, 148, 151, 181, 182, 185; PF 30, 36, 42, 46, 50, 51, 59, 61, 63, 65, 71, 116, 118, 124, 134–135, 152, 174, 194, 197–198, 202; BM 67, 69, 76, 78, 140; HD 7, 13, 38, 40, 42, 46, 50, 55, 70, 171, 198; Sc 5, 7, 10, 23, 24, 31, 38, 39, 48, 64, 78; BR 56, 63, 64, 67, 100, 108, 110, 113, 115, 117, 171, 172, 173, 177, 179, 181, 183, 188, 191, 194, 195,

198, 199, 210, 211, 221, 267, 275; MA 19, 22, 28, 79, 80; OG 9, 31, 41, 42, 43, 44, 218; US 21, 22, 26, 27, 32, 33, 35, 40, 43, 47, 56, 77, 78, 81, 82, 124, 132, 134, 171, 184, 199, 237; GP 30, 63, 109, 151, 154, 162, 163; WS 39, 65, 80, 101, 110, 115, 116, 117, 119, 133, 139, 145, 147, 150, 151, 154, 163, 176, 177, 178, 185, 188, 258, 259, 274, 275, 278, 279, 284, 289, 290, 292

LONDON DISTRICT
London District of HOOHQ is full of stockbrokers and wine merchants from the Foot Guards.
US 19

LONG, MR
Alias adopted by Arthur Atwater (q.v.).
WS 139

LONGFELLOW, HENRY WADSWORTH ***(1807–1882)***
American poet. Author of *Hiawatha* (1855).
• The Argentine Chargé d'Affaires gives Paul Pennyfeather a collection of the works of Longfellow bound in green leather as a wedding present.
• Colonel Blount gives Adam Fenwick-Symes a calendar for Christmas which contains a thought from Longfellow for every day of the year.
DF 156; VB 214

LORD MAYOR OF BELLACITA
'Young, lean and plainly ill at ease, he was much scarred by his revolutionary exploits, wore a patch on one eye and supported himself on a crutch stick.' Does not speak English.
WS 212

LOS ANGELES
Location of Hollywood, Whispering Glades, and the Happier Hunting Ground.
• Dennis Barlow commits the ashes of a tabby cat to the slip stream over Sunset Boulevard.
LO 23, 127
(See also Dennis BARLOW, Aimee THANATOGENOS, Sir Francis HINSLEY *and* MR JOYBOY)

LOST CHORD, THE
See BOOKS

LOVE
Paul Pennyfeather is smitten with Margot Beste-Chetwynde.
• Prudence Courteney, when in love with Basil Seal, cannot believe that she was ever in love with William Bland.
• Basil Seal's heart is pierced by a 'dart of pleasure' in the classical image of love when he sees Susie (q.v.).
• When William Boot falls in love with Katchen, he feels as if he is out at sea: 'submerged among deep waters, below wind and tide'.
• Charles Ryder in his love for Sebastian Flyte, realizes that 'to know and love one other human being is the root of all wisdom'.
• Cara tells him that his love for Sebastian is something experienced only by the English and the Germans.
• Charles calls Sebastian the forerunner for Julia and wonders whether 'all our loves are merely hints and symbols'.
• Captain Fremantle wonders whether Ludovic is guilty of 'amourous jealousy'.
• Virginia Crouchback tells Peregrine that she loves him.
• Guy Crouchback says that all American songs are about love.
• The Guru Brahmin tells Aimee Thanatogenos that she is not in love with Mr Joyboy.
• In the 1920s Gilbert Pinfold was in love with one of 'a house full of bright, cruel girls who spoke their own thieves' slang and played their own games'.
• Margaret makes a 'galloping declaration of love' for Gilbert Pinfold.
• Gilbert Pinfold has been the object of adolescent infatuation. (*See* JOHN PLANT)
• Courtship is 'free and easy' in the New Britain. However, love is 'a word seldom used except by politicians'.
• Simon Lent is a bachelor, half in love.
• How, wonders John Plant, can one write of oneself being loved with propriety? Or, indeed, at all? In his works he admits 'I have written it up as something prolonged and passionate and tragic . . . I have spoken

of it continually as a game of profit and loss'.

LOVEDAY
Lunatic, confined at the County Home for Mental Defectives for thirty-five years for murdering a young woman on a bicycle. Acts as secretary for Lord Moping (q.v.). Lady Moping arranges for him to be released. He immediately strangles a young lady on a bicycle.
WS 9–15

LOVERS' SEAT
See WHISPERING GLADES

LOWER CHIPPING MANOR
House of the Box-Benders in Gloucestershire. Bought by Arthur Box-bender when he became an MP. Nearest station is Kemble. During the war Arthur volunteers it as a store for national art treasures.
MA 25–27

LOWER GRUMPS
The field at Much Malcock over which the crisis arises (q.v.).
WS 53

LUCAS-DOCKERY, SIR WILFRED
Governor of Blackstone Gaol (q.v.). Appointed after the Home Secretary read his appendix on penology to the report on the treatment of conscientious objectors. His previous position is as Professor of Sociology at a university in the Midlands.
DF 166, 171

LUCERNE, SWITZERLAND
Destination of Sir Jocelyn Hitchcock, to cover an economic non-intervention congress after reporting on the crisis in Ishmaelia.
Sc 127

LUDOVIC *(b. 1906)*
Ivor Claire's Company Sergeant Major. Guy Crouchback thinks that he may be a Communist in 1940. Reports to Knightsbridge barracks at the start of WWII and claims the rank of Corporal of Horse as a reservist. Claire takes him to Mugg. Claire promotes him to HQ.

Has 'the manservant's gift for tongues'. Deserts. Finds Major Hound (q.v.). Only he knows of the end of Major Hound. Escapes from Crete with Guy in a boat. Carries Guy ashore at Sidi Barani. Is in hospital for two days. Tommy Blackhouse puts him in for a commission. Encounters Guy when made CO of Special Training Centre. Believes that Guy is aware of his part in the fate of Major Hound. Is posted to Britain and trained as an officer. Becomes a recluse and an addict of the English language. In 1943 he is a Major in the Intelligence corps. Is awarded the Military Medal. After the war buys the Castello Crouchback (q.v.) and employs Padfield as his 'factotum'.
OG 82, 112, 120, 12, 1, 126, 156, 161, 164, 182, 207, 235; US 10, 32, 34–39, 52, 84–87, 90–94, 98, 105, 106, 114, 160, 187, 239

LUMO
Town in Azania where a Greek hotel owner contrives to hold up the Grand Chemin De Fer for one night.
BM 12

LUMSDEN OF STRATHDRUMMOND
See CLUBS (BOLLINGER)

LUNA PARK
Where there is a big wheel, compared by Otto Silenus to life.
DF 208

LUNDY
Island off the coast of Devon.
• Visible from the Marine Hotel, Matchet.
MA 36

LUNCHEONS
Basil Seal's luncheon parties at Oxford go on late into the evening.
PF 51; BM 121
(*See also* FLYTE, SEBASTIAN)

LUNT
Charles Ryder's scout at Oxford.
BR 24

LUSH PLACES
William Boot's column in the *Daily Beast* (q.v.).
Sc 16, 21, 222

LUTIT, WILBUR, K
Late director of Megalopolitan Pictures. The Wilbur K. Lutit memorial Block of their offices is built during his lifetime.
LO 28

LUXMORE, JEAN
Uses the same drug dealer as Anthony Blanche.
BR 197

LUXMORE, COLONEL TONY
Officer in the Coldstream Guards, later promoted to command of X Commando. A 'grave, cold young man consistently unlucky at cards'. Captured on Crete. Escapes.
OG 185, 245; US 237

LYCHPOLE
Home of Gilbert Pinfold (q.v.), 'a secluded village some hundred miles from London'. His house there, of the same name, is let during the war to a convent. Reached by train from Paddington.
GP 10, 18, 22

LYNE, ANGELA, *(b. 1907)*
Wife of Cedric Lyne, and mother of Nigel. Married in 1930. Has a son by Cedric. In 1932 pays Basil Seal's expenses to allow him to stand as a parliamentary candidate. She is Scottish, the only child of a Glasgow millionaire and despite her wealth, is known among her friends as 'poor Angela Lyne'. Her dress and makeup are her hobby, and have been since 1932, since when she has been in love with Basil Seal.

Has a service flat in Grosvenor Square, decorated by David Lennox. Her husband is preoccupied with grottoes. Portrait of her by Augustus John.

Basil Seal considers marrying her after Cedric's death in 1940, and does so. Has a daughter, Barbara, by Basil (1945). Her wealth is so great as to still be intact. Gives her country house to Nigel on his twenty-first birthday (1952).

Visits a health farm with Basil in 1963. Later, they stay at Claridges.
PF 24–26, 118–120, 135, 151, 153–155; BM 70; WS 251, 254, 256

LYNE, CEDRIC *(1904–1940)*
Husband of Angela (q.v.) and father of Nigel. Dilettante architect. Collects grottoes. Lives in Hampshire in a house bought by he and Angela in 1929. In the park is a little temple bought by the Lynes on their honeymoon in Naples and a stream with a bridge in the Chinese taste, from Batty Langley.

When Angela meets him in the late twenties he is in the army, 'poor and very very soft-boiled and tall and willowy and very unhappy in a boring smart regiment because he only cared about Russian ballet and Baroque architecture'. His friends think he has had 'a raw deal'. Very romantic when first married.

Angela once bought him an octopus in a case with dolphins and silver leaf. He is accomplished at riding but hates hunting, and is a good shot.

Does not appreciate French Impressionist painting. By 1939 has been estranged from his wife for three years. Joins up again in 1939 and is worried about being killed. Is made battalion intelligence officer.

Says farewell to his wife and child. Killed in action by a bullet in France in the summer of 1940.
PF 26, 27, 43, 163, 167–172, 208, 211; WS 254, 255

LYNE, NIGEL *(b. 1931)*
Son of Cedric and Angela (q.v.). He is 'robust and unattractive' and has the misfortune to resemble Angela's father. Thinks David Lennox's painting 'awfully feeble' and does not think the portrait of his mother by John looks finished. For his twenty-first birthday his mother gives him her country house in Hampshire.
PF 26, 167–172

LYONNESSE
Mythical land.
• Charles Ryder's Oxford of the 1920s is, he says in 1944, as irrecoverable as Lyonnesse.
BR 23

M

MACKAY, FATHER

Local priest at Brideshead. Lord Brideshead asks him to see his father on his death bed. He is 'a stocky, middle-aged Glasgow-Irishman'. Is at first turned away by Lord Marchmain but eventually gives him the last rites.
BR 309, 311, 320–322

MADAGASCAR

Island off the east coast of Africa.
• Katchen and her husband head for Madagascar after they have left Ishmaelia. Her husband used to have a friend there 'and says it is more comfortable than to come to Europe'.
Sc 221

MADRAS

City on the east coast of India.
• There is a dock strike in Madras during Gilbert Pinfold's cruise in 1957.
GP 150

MADRID

Rex Mottram once attended a royal wedding here.
BR 184
(*See also* ALCAZAR)

MAETERLINCK, COUNT MAURICE *(1862–1949)*

Belgian playwright. Influenced by the Symbolists. See his *Pélleas et Mélisande* (1892).
• Anthony Blanche compares Lady Marchmain to a heroine from Maeterlinck.
• The interior of Colonel Campbell's castle on Mugg might, thinks Guy Crouchback, have been 'a set by Gordon Craig for a play on Maeterlinck's'.
BR 55; OG 55

MAGAZINES

• *APOLLO:* Dennis Barlow finds an old stained copy in Sir Francis Hinsley's handkerchief drawer.
• *ARCHITECTURAL REVIEW:* In which Archie Banks writes a piece about Fleacetown.
• *ATHEIST ADVERTIZER:* Ambrose Silk sends them a copy of the report of Nazis at a mass in Salzburg.
• *BLAST*: Vorticist magazine set up by Percy Wyndham-Lewis. One of the sources for Johnny Hoop's invitations.
• *BYSTANDER:* Read by Apthorpe at Lancing.
• *THE CASKET:* Organ of the undertaking profession in America. Mr Joyboy is a regular contributor. On the occasion of his engagement they include photographs of him with Aimee Thanatogenos.
• *COMICS:* Two tattered pictorial journals are in the Squadron Leader's office at No 4 Training Centre.
• *COUNTRY LIFE:* Guy Crouchback reads bound copies in the club in Alexandria.
• *FREE THOUGHT:* Ambrose Silk sends them a copy of the report of Nazis at a Mass in Salzburg.
• *GODLESS SUNDAY AT HOME:* Ambrose Silk sends them a copy of the report of Nazis at a Mass in Salzburg.
• *HISTORICAL REVIEW:* Dr Fe edits the Neutralian edition.
• *HORIZON:* In which during his youth Dr Beamish painted abstract pictures.
• *HORSE AND HOUND:* Sent to the British Legation in Azania.
• *IVORY TOWER:* Magazine created by Ambrose Silk for the Ministry of Information in 1939. In its first edition he 'has a blow for every possible windmill'. All of the articles apart from the last bear pen names, although all are the work of

Ambrose. Basil Seal does not think it shocking enough.
• *JOURNAL OF ORIENTAL STUDIES:* Sent to the British Legation in Azania.
• *LA VIE PARISIENNE:* Adam Fenwick-Symes tells Nina Blount that, in bed at Arundel, she looks 'exactly like la Vie Parisienne'.
• *MORTICIANS JOURNAL:* In which the engagement of Mr Joyboy and Aimee Thanatogenos is announced in a column and a half.
• *NEW DESTINY:* Publishes translations of the poetry of Scott-King's neighbour at dinner in Neutralia.
• *NEW NATION:* Carries an article on the Lucas-Dockery experiments in 1922.
• *NEW STATESMAN:* Read by Guy Crouchback. In which Mr A.A. Charmichael reviews works of Classical scholarship and Sam Benfleet suggests starting a correspondence about Adam Symes' confiscated book.
• *NEW YORKER:* Sent to the British Legion in Azania. Read by John Beaver at Bratt's.
• *PUNCH:* Adam Fenwick-Symes reads morocco-bound volumes of Punch when at Doubting Hall in 1927. Mr Salter gleans all of the jokes for Clean Fun from bound volumes of Punch. The British Legation in Azania receives eleven *Punches* at once.
• *ST JAMES'S GAZETTE:* Sent to the British Legation in Azania.
• *SPECTATOR:* Read by Guy Crouchback. Archie Banks translates his experiences at Fleacetown into a short story for.
• *SURVIVAL:* Everard Spruce's magazine. Churchill reads it.
• *TABLET:* Read by Guy Crouchback.
• *TATLER:* In which the Mottrams are often seen in the 1930s.
• *TIME:* Mr Joyboy's picture has appeared on the cover.
• *TIME AND TIDE:* Everard Spruce looks down his nose at literary competitions in *Time and Tide*. In 1943 the Sword of Stalingrad is the subject of a literary competition which Ludovic enters.
• *VOGUE:* Half of Charles Ryder's fellow students in Paris want to earn a living doing advertisements for Vogue. Sent to the British Legation in Azania.
• *WHISPERS FROM THE GLADES:* House magazine of Whispering Glades (q.v.). Devotes almost an entire issue to Mr Joyboy's romance.
VB 52, 82; PR 117, 185–186, 190; BR 147; MA 58; OG 157; US 35, 36, 49, 50, 118, 123; LO 53, 55, 89, 106; GP 195; WS 80, 81, 214, 220, 289, 304
(*See also* BLAST)

MAGNASCO
Gilbert Pinfold's voices accuse him of never having heard of Magnasco.
GP 147

MAGYARS
See HUNGARIANS

MAHARAJAS
A Maharaja in the uniform of the Red Cross, at lunch with Mrs Stitch at Alexandria in 1941, talks about racing.
OG 130–131

MAHMOUD PASHA
'Urbane pasha' who lunches with Julia Stitch in Alexandria in 1943 and declines to explain Cavafy (q.v.) to the company. He is 'a sad exile from Monte Carlo and Biarritz'.
OG 130

MAHMUD EL KHALI BIN SAI-UD
Descended from the oldest family in Matodi, he is an old man in 1932. Broods over his lapful of khat in the Arab Club.
BM 94

MAIDEN, CAROLINE
Friend of the Box-Benders at Malfrey stopped by a policeman in Stroud because she is not carrying her gas mask.
MA 30

MAIDENHEAD, BERKSHIRE
Town suggested as a suitable place

to spend the night by the chauffeur of Adam Fenwick-Symes' and Nina Blunt's Daimler.
VB 79

MAIDSTONE, KENT
Close to Maidstone Mr Outrage regains consciousness after arriving in England.
VB 28

MAINWARING, SIR JOSEPH
Old friend of Lady Seal and self-appointed guardian of Basil. Is confided in by Lady Seal about Basil. Talks to Basil, at frequent intervals (every crisis in his life). Member of the Travellers' Club. In summer 1940 he is promoted in the government.
BM 80–81; PF 20, 23, 51, 53; WS 213, 221, 256, 266

MAISKY, MRS
Unveils a picture of Stalin during Tanks for Russia Week in 1941.
OG 246

MAKARIKARI, BECHUANALAND, AFRICA
Salt pan in Bechuanaland, near Francistown.
• Apthorpe presumes that Guy Crouchback will think it is close to Kasanga. However, it is twelve hundred miles away. It is, however infinitely preferable to Kasanga.
MA 58

MAKEPIECE, MR
One of the new masters at Llanabba after Paul Pennyfeather leaves.
DF 155

MALAYA
Rample publishes 'so and so's' reminiscences of the Malay States.
• Sir Ralph Brompton believes in 1943 that Britain is 'backing the wrong horse' in Malaya.
• Where Peter Baverstock (q.v.) lives.
PF 184; US 29; WS 166

MALFREY, GLOUCESTERSHIRE
Country house of Freddy and Barbara Sothill (q.v.).

There is something 'female and voluptuous' about Malfrey.

Built in the 1720s, it is 'a Cleopatra among houses', 'sumptuously at ease, splendid'. It is approached through elaborate wrought iron gates, along a half mile of lanes from the village of Malfrey. Has a park with a lake. The saloon, around which there are drawing rooms and galleries, is carved by Grinling Gibbons. A small octagonal parlour opens onto the parterre. The orangery is one of the best in the country.

After Freddy's death during the war is made over to the National Trust and Barbara moves into the flat over the stables. Relations of Freddy's move into the bachelors' wing. In 1963 Basil Seal considers sending his daughter here to get here away from London.
PF 9, 19, 13, 22, 74–75, 87; WS 262, 272

MALINDI, KENYA
One of the destinations of the dhows from Matodi.

Mr Youkoumian plans to escape to Malindi at the start of the crisis in Azania.
BM 20

MALORY, SIR THOMAS *(d. 1471)*
English writer. Author of *Morte d'Arthur* which deals with the legend of King Arthur and the Knights of the Round Table.

All the rooms at Hetton (q.v.) are named from Malory.
HD 15

MALPRACTICE, THE HON MILES
Friend of Margot Metroland and David Lennox (q.v.). Homosexual. Attends houseparty at King's Thursday in 1927. One of the Bright Young People of 1929 who cross on the same ship as Adam Fenwick-Symes. Son of Lord and Lady Throbbing. Never visits his mother. Becomes Mr Chatterbox in succession to Adam.
DF 128, 132; VB 11, 27, 51, 152, 153, 206

MALTON, LORD
Owner of a yacht and friend of Lord Marchmain who turns up aboard it on his way to his palace, but is sent off to Trieste, Lady Marchmain being in Venice at the time (September 1922). Consequently Lord Malton is in disgrace with the smart set in Venice, no one from his yacht being asked to the Principesa Fogliere's ball.
BR 55

MALTRAVERS, SIR HUMPHREY
See LORD METROLAND

MAMMON
Ambrose Silk is proud to be one 'who made no concessions to Mammon'.
PF 35

MANCHESTER
One of the places where the *Daily Beast* is published.
• Where, in 1928, the official timekeeper pawns the trophy for the motor race.
• Mr Plant's first exhibited work is of a balloon ascent in Manchester.
• One of the places where the Sword of Stalingrad is exhibited.
Sc 156; VB 163; WS 114; US 22

MANGANESE
One of the things (with bauxite) that will, according to Sir Joseph Mainwaring, win the war for Britain.
PF 53

MANGEL WURZELS
The 'roots' to which Mr Salter is referring when he asks William Boot how they are doing.
Sc 27

MANNERHEIM, CARL GUSTAV *(1867–1951)*
Finnish statesman. Commander-in-Chief in the campaign against the Russians of 1939–1940.
• Guy Crouchback thinks that in 1940 Mannerheim holds the place in English hearts occupied in 1914 by King Albert of the Belgians.
MA 141

MARAT, JEAN PAUL *(1743–1793)*
French revolutionary politician. Murdered in his bath by Charlotte Corday.
• Looking at the embalmed corpse of Sir Francis Hinsley, Dennis Barlow thinks of the waxwork of Marat in his bath.
LO 61

MARCHMAIN, ALEXANDER FLYTE, MARQUIS OF *(1865–July 1938)*
Owner of Brideshead Castle and father of Sebastian, Julia and Cordelia Flyte and Lord Brideshead. He has a noble face 'slightly weary, slightly sardonic, slightly voluptuous'. Married 1899. Takes up religion on his marriage. Decorates the chapel at Brideshead as a present for Lady Marchmain.

Serves with the yeomanry 1914–1918. From 1915 serves dismounted in the line under Walter Venables.

After the Great War lives apart from his wife. He never returned from France, having become involved with a very talented dancer (Cara). Is excommunicated.

According to Anthony Blanche he is 'a little fleshy perhaps, but very handsome, a magnifico, a voluptuary, Byronic, bored, infectiously slothful'. However, he dare not show his 'great purple face' anywhere. 'He is the last, historic case of someone being hounded out of society'. A social leper. Lord Brideshead refuses to see him. Julia and Cordelia are forbidden to see him.

Lives in Venice with his mistress, Cara, who he does not love. She shields him from Lady Marchmain, who he hates.

Charles Ryder visits him with Sebastian. Says that he 'abominates' the English countryside. Prefers Austrian to Italian pastries. Lady Marchmain tells Charles that he used to drink in the same way as Sebastian.

Rex Mottram reckons that Marchmain will 'always be good for an odd thirty thousand a year'. Consents to Julia's marriage to Rex. Meets Charles and Julia at Monte Carlo in summer 1937. With 'a taste for the dramatically inopportune' returns to England during the divorce

proceedings between Charles and Celia and Julia and Rex, wanting to die at home. Moves into Brideshead. Occupies the Chinese Drawing Room in which he has the Queen's bed installed. Refuses the last rites. Eventually accepts the sacrament and makes the sign of the cross before he dies. Leaves Brideshead to his daughter Julia.
BR 25, 30, 42, 54, 5, 86, 94–96, 99, 132, 156, 169, 183, 212, 296, 299, 302, 303, 309, 312, 316–322

MARCHMAIN, LADY TERESA
(d. May 1926)

Wife of Lord Marchmain (q.v.). Roman Catholic. The eldest of six children. Her three brothers are all killed in the Great War. As a girl she is relatively poor but on her marriage she becomes enormously rich. Very beautiful. Marries in 1899. Four children: Brideshead (1900), Sebastian (1903), Julia (1905), Cordelia (1912).

Is abandoned by Marchmain in 1918. Lives at Brideshead Castle (q.v.). By 1923 her hair is just beginning to turn grey. Her voice is 'as quiet as a prayer, and as powerful'. Refuses to divorce her husband who hates her. Stays in Venice with Sir Adrian Porson in September 1922.

Visits Oxford in Michelmas term 1923. Tries to make friends with Charles and in so doing strikes 'at the roots' of his friendship with Sebastian. Visits Mr Samgrass who is working on her brother Ned's poems. Rex Mottram calls her 'Ma'. In 1926 is overdrawn a hundred thousand in London.

She is very ill. Abhors Rex Mottram. Is shattered by the combination of her illness, the desertion of her husband, Sebastian's alcoholism and degeneracy and Julia's loss of faith. Charles visits her on her death-bed in May 1926. Sebastian calls her 'a femme fatale. She killed at a touch'. Her obituary in *The Times* takes the form of a poem by Sir Adrian Porson.
BR 42, 54, 99, 105, 121, 122, 128, 132, 134, 157, 163, 168, 175, 182, 199, 206, 213

MARCHMAIN, WILTSHIRE

Village near Brideshead (q.v.). Ten miles from the castle 'and damn all when you get there'.
BR 325

MARCHMAIN HOUSE, ARLINGTON STREET, LONDON

London house of the Flytes. Known as 'Marchers'. It backs directly into Green Park. One of the last half dozen historic houses left in London in 1922. A ball is held there for Julia Flyte in 1923.

In 1925 Julia and Rex's wedding presents are laid out in the library. In 1926, after the death of Lady Marchmain, Lord Marchmain sells the house. At his father's instigation, and on Julia's recommendation, Lord Brideshead asks Charles Ryder to paint it. Charles thinks it 'one of the most beautiful houses I know'. Brideshead thinks it's ugly.

Charles and Cordelia walk through the garden door and into the park on their way to the Ritz Grill.

Pulled down 1926. A block of flats is erected in its place, but retains the name Marchmain House. It is here in 1940 that Guy Crouchback has to report to HOOHQ.
BR 56, 100, 172, 188, 200, 209, 210, 223; OG 44

MARGARET

Most persistent of Gilbert Pinfold's voices (q.v.).

MARINES

A squad of buglers from the US Marines sounds Taps at the burial of a canary at the Happier Hunting Ground.
LO 23

MARINETTI, EMILIO FILIPPO
(1876–1944)

Italian writer. Originator of the Futurist Manifesto (q.v.) in 1909.

• Johnnie Hoop adapts the Futurist manifesto to party invitations.
VB 52

MARINO
Italian 'ace' driver at the motor races attended by Adam Fenwick-Symes and the Bright Young People. A spanner thrown from his car hits Miles' friend on the shoulder and puts him out of the race. Crashes into Agatha Runcible and withdraws from the race on a stretcher.
VB 168, 174, 178

MARIOUT
Where Colonel Tickeridge is encamped in 1941.
OG 239

MARITAIN, JACQUES ***(1882–1973)***
French Catholic philosopher. Abandoned Bergsonism for Roman Catholicism. See his *Distinguer pour unir, ou les degres du savoir* (1932).
• Mr Samgrass thinks that the Dominican staying with the Flytes over Christmas 1922 has read too much Maritain.
BR 120

MARLBOROUGH
English public school.
• Attended by Glover (q.v.).
GP 108

MARONITES
Mr Samgrass tells the candlesticks (for want of any human audience) in the chapel at Brideshead about the Maronites.
BR 150

MARRIAGE
'Look at it how you will, marriage is rather a grim thought.'

Grimes tells Paul Pennyfeather that his first marriage 'didn't make much odds either way'. His second, however, looks like being 'a pretty solemn solemnization'. He wishes that someone would have told him about marriage. That 'at the end of that gay journey and flower-strewn path were the hideous lights of home and the voices of children . . . we can't escape, try how we may'.

Paul's marriage inspires the public to being romantic.

Mr Prendergast admits that it has always been a mystery to him as to why people should marry. He thinks that if people had not been told about marriage they would not get married.
• There is apparently an atrophy endemic to all fruitful marriages, so Barbara Sothill thinks.
• To Mr Ryder it is a mystery why any man should want to throw over one wife and take up with another immediately.
DF 101, 102, 103, 148; PF 10; BR 282

MARSEILLES
Coastal port in the South of France.
• Paul Pennyfeather travels there on business for Margot Metroland in 1927. Some of her girls are stuck there on their way to Brazil.

Paul Dines at Basso's, on the covered balcony, and watches the lights of the town reflected in the water. The next day he finds Chez Alice and Margot's girls.
• In 1932 Basil Seal flies to Marseilles on his way to Azania. He dines at the restaurant de Verdun.
• In 1937 William Boot catches the blue train to Marseilles on his way to Ishmaelia.
• Anthony Blanche, looking out on to Peckwater Quad at Oxford, is reminded as the light falls on the stone, of 'those leprous façades in the *vieux port* at Marseilles'.
• Sebastian Flyte lives with Anthony Blanche in Marseilles in February 1925, pawns two of his suits and gives a bad cheque to his drug dealer.
DF 150–153; BM 35, 88; Sc 45; BR 49, 195

MARTIN, JOHN ***(1789–1854)***
English painter. Best known for his fantastic visions of Heaven, Hell and Biblical catastrophe. See his 'The Deluge' (1826, Tate).
• Ian Kilbannock (q.v.) compares the sky over London during the blitz, 'ochre and madder, as though a dozen tropic suns were simultaneously setting round the horizon', to a painting by John Martin, but Guy Crouchback thinks it more like Turner.
OG 9

MARX, MR
One of the Emperor Seth's staff at Matodi; 'the distinguished mechanic who made the tank'. Evacuates the town in the emperor's motor boat at the start of the Azanian crisis, having been given petrol by Youkoumian.
BM 7, 19, 30

MARX, KARL ***(1818–1883)***
German philosopher and founder of Communism. See his *Das Kapital* (1867), and *Communist Manifesto* (1848) in which he condemns religion and culture as means used by the state to control the masses.
• The Communist consul of Ishmaelia tells William Boot that Karl Marx was a Negro.
• Mr Plant (q.v.) never hears much about Marxism.
• Roger Simmonds (q.v.) talks happily for hours about his Marxist ethics.
• For Lucy Simmonds her conversion to Marxist philosophy is brought about by falling in love with Roger. They read Marx together. She has 'a Marxist faith in the superior beauties of concrete and steel'.
Sc 50; WS 112, 133, 170, 172
(*See also* Communism, Socialism)

MARXVILLE
See Jacksonburg

MASEFIELD, JOHN ***(1878–1967)***
English poet. Poet Laureate 1930. See his *Reynard the Fox*, and *Nan*.
• In 1937 he writes an ode to the seasonal fluctuation of the net sales of the *Daily Beast*.
Sc 13

MASSAWA
Coastal town in Ethiopia.
• Basil Seal tells one of the officials at the Ministry of Information (q.v.) that the Germans, if they annex Liberia, will be able to cut the allies' West Africa Coast trade route by shutting the Suez Canal from Massawa.
PF 66

MATCHET, DEVON
Location of the Marine Hotel, home of Mr Crouchback. It is close to Broome (q.v.). Guy picnics there as a boy. The hotel is outside the town, on a cliff by the coast-guard station. It is approached from the harbour by a red rock track, from which Lundy Island is visible.
MA 18, 35, 36

MATODI
Coastal town in Azania. In 1632 a Portuguese garrison is beseiged here in the old fort for eight months by the Omani Arabs. Matodi becomes prosperous. It has Arab merchants' houses with latticed windows, brass studded doors, and courtyards with mango trees. The streets smell of cloves and pineapples and are only wide enough for one mule. There is a bazaar and coffee houses. Matodi is a trade centre from where dhows sail to Tanga, Dar es Salaam, Malindi and Kismayu. Then in the 1830s, trade comes to a standstill and the houses fall into ruin. After the coming of Amurath (q.v.) the old houses are turned into tenements, hotels and offices and an Arab quarter grows up behind the bazaar.
BM7, 8, 10, 14

MATTO GROSSO, BRAZIL
Close to where Dr Messinger and Tony Last explore in 1933.
• Where Ritchie-Hook spent some of the inter-war years.
HD 159; MA 66

MAVROCORDATDO, MISS
Secretary to Sir Francis Hinsley at Megalopolitan Studios who, after his dismissal, is transferred to the catering department.
LO 25

MAUREEN, AUNT
Aunt of Lucy Simmonds who tells her that when her mother was pregnant she would sit before a Flaxman bas-relief to make her baby beautiful.
WS 177

MAYFIELD, CAPTAIN
Alastair Trumpington's company commander in 1939. Offers to put Alastair in for a commission. Thinks it 'very rum' that he should decline.
PF 103–105

MAYFIELD, MA
Proprietress of the Old Hundredth, 100 Sink Street (q.v.). Boy Mulcaster claims to know her but does not recognise her. She is 'a stout woman, in evening dress'.
BR 109

MAYNOOTH
The Catholic chaplain of the Halberdiers is a recent graduate of Maynooth.
MA 61

MEADOWES, LADY MARY
Second daughter of Lord Granchester. Known as Molly. One of the girls whom Peter Pastmaster considers marrying in 1939. Is taken to dinner in Jermyn Street by Peter, and afterwards to the cinema next door where they find Angela Lyne drunk and take her back to her flat. Becomes engaged to Peter. Is married in spring 1940. In 1963 Basil Seal cannot remember whether she married Clarence Allbright or Peter Pastmaster.
PF 152–158; 162; WS 254, 259

MEADOWS, BILL
Chap in charge of a 'show' during the General Strike. Boy Mulcaster persuades Charles Ryder to join.
BR 198

MEDALS
In disguise, Simon Balcairn wears the order of St Michael and St George.
• Gervase Crouchback (d. 1915) wears a medal of Our Lady of Lourdes, which Mr Crouchback gives to Guy when he joins up in 1939.
• Seth (q.v.) designs the victory medal for General Connolly's army in Azania. It is struck by Mappin and Webb (q.v.).
• De Souza is awarded the M.C. for his part in the campaign on Crete.
• Ludovic (q.v.) is awarded the M.M. for 'running away from the enemy'.
VB 97; MA 36; BM 17–18; US 96, 105

MEDICI, LORENZO
Employee of Megalopolitan Studios who takes over Sir Francis Hinsley's office on his dismissal. He is 'a very fine young man with a very, very fine and wonderful record'. Likes his name pronounced 'Medissy'.
LO 26

MEDICI SOCIETY
London Company of fine art printers.
• Mr Graves (q.v.) hangs some Medici prints in place of the football groups in his room at Lancing.
WS 295

MEGALOPOLITAN NEWSPAPERS
See NEWSPAPERS

MEGALOPOLITAN PICTURES
Hollywood motion picture company. Employers of Sir Francis Hinsley, Mr Medici, Juanita del Pablo, Dennis Barlow, Miss Mavrocordato, Mr Van Gluck, Otto Baumbeim, Mr Erikson, and Leo (all q.v.). The eminence grise (now deceased) was Wilbur K. Lutit.
LO 24–28

MEIKLEJOHN, MISS MURIEL
Friend of Lucy Simmonds. She is pale and possessive. Shares a lodging with Lucy in Vienna where they were sent to learn to sing.
WS 166–168

MELSTEAD CARBURY, WILTSHIRE
Town near Brideshead at which one alights from the train for the castle. Charles Ryder is collected from the station here by Julia Flyte in 1923.
BR 73, 89, 308

MEMBLING, FATHER
Catholic priest taken in at Brideshead by Julia Flyte after having been 'blown up'. Is able to conclude from Cordelia's letter to

Nanny Hawkins that she and Julia are in Palestine.
BR 328, 329

MEMORY
In Lord Monomark's opinion the secret of memory is 'tabulation'.
• Charles Ryder's theme is memory 'that winged host that soared about me one grey morning of war-time'.
VB 121; BR 215

MEN OF LETTERS
One of the categories at the Ministry of Information. Mr Bentley admits that in England not much more is thought of 'men of letters' than journalists.
PF 69

MENDELSSOHN-BARTHOLDY, FELIX *(1809–1847)*
German composer. See his 'Scotch Symphony' and 'Wedding March'.
• Margot Metroland is determined that her wedding to Paul Pennyfeather is going to include 'all the barbaric concomitants of bridesmaids, Mendelssohn and Mumm'.
DF 143

MENDOZA, SENATOR
Neutralian senator upon whose wife the bimetallists commit 'unspeakable atrocities'.
WS 207

MERCER
One of the boys at school with Charles Ryder in 1919. Gives Charles a 'sloppy' poem to read.
WS 302

MERCURY
See OXFORD

MERMAIDS
There is a stuffed mermaid in a hotel in Aden. William Boot and Corker see it on their way to Ishmaelia in 1937.
• Gilbert Pinfold remembers seeing it.
Sc 71; GP 145

MESOPOTAMIA
See OXFORD

MESSINGER, DOCTOR
Explorer. Member of the Greville Club (q.v.). Meets Tony Last in the Greville Club and persuades him to accompany him to Brazil in search of the City. Knows Zingermaun (q.v.). Stays in his cabin during the journey to Brazil. Takes large doses of chloral. Nurses Tony through fever. Goes downstream to find a village. Is caught by the current and drowned.
HD 157, 158, 159, 161, 169, 170, 174, 176, 189, 192, 197

METCALFE, MR BEVERLEY
Inhabitant of Much Malcock. His house, known as Grumps until rechristened by him, is Much Malcock Hall. Has only recently moved to the country from abroad. Had been a businessman in Alexandria. President of the British Chamber of Commerce for fifteen years. Was respected by all. Looks to Boggett (q.v.) for guidance. Smokes a pipe. Reads the local paper before *The Times*. Does the crossword.

Under the Hodge Plan pays £500 for the Metcalfe-Peabury hall (q.v.). Has the local brewery change the name of the pub to the Metcalfe Arms.
WS 43–48, 56, 61

METROLAND, SIR HUMPHREY MALTRAVERS, 1st LORD *(b. circa 1881)*
Minister of Transport 1927. Home Secretary 1927. Has big red hands and a big red face. Smokes huge cigars and wears a soft hat. From a family of nine, living in two rooms. His father drinks and his mother has fits. His sister becomes a prostitute and his brother is sent to prison. Another brother is a deaf-mute.

Wins a scholarship to school and has a university career 'of brilliant successes and unexampled privations'. While at Oxford he proof-reads for the Holywell Press and takes down University sermons in shorthand for the local paper.

Becomes a lawyer. Elected to parliament in the Liberal campaign of 1906.

Guest of Margot Beste-Chetwynde at King's Thursday in 1927. Is keen to marry

Margot. Publishes his memoirs in a Sunday newspaper. Expects to become leader of the party. Wants to become a peer and keep a racehorse or two. Offers to have Paul Pennyfeather released from prison if Margot will marry him. She agrees.

Created Viscount Metroland 1928. In 1928 attends Mrs Ape's service at his own house. Accepts Margot's affair with Alastair Trumpington. Dies sometime between 1929 and 1939.

DF 129–132, 160, 207, 214; VB 101, 131–134

METROLAND, MARGOT BESTE-CHETWYNDE LADY *(b. 1891)*

South American by birth. She seems like 'the first breath of spring in the Champs Elysées'. Owns two houses in England, one in London and one in Hampshire: Pastmaster House (q.v.) and King's Thursday (q.v.). Has a villa at Cannes and a house on Corfu. Wooed by her first husband at King's Thursday 'in the odour of honeysuckle'. Has one son, Peter (b. 1906). By 1922 she is a widow, the Honourable Mrs Beste-Chetwynde, sister in law of Lord Pastmaster and a very wealthy woman. It is said that she poisoned her first husband, the brother of Lord Pastmaster (powdered glass in his coffee).

Wears an 'almost unprocurable scent'. Runs the Latin American Entertainment Company. Buys King's Thursday from her brother in law. Has an affair with Lord Monomark.

She employs Otto Silenus, her discovery, to rebuild King's Thursday.

Arrives at the Llanabba sports day in an enormous grey limousine, with Chokey (q.v.), her lover. Grimes (q.v.) reckons that she is 'the goods'. Paul Pennyfeather falls in love with her. Gives Paul a job. Agrees to marry Paul. Spends the night with Paul 'just to make sure'. Gives Grimes a job. Has two Hispano Suizas. Regarded as the most beautiful woman in society. Arranges for Paul's release from prison by marrying Sir Humphrey Maltravers (1923). Becomes Lady Metroland.

• Has her bathroom ceiling decorated by Mrs Beaver.

• In 1928 takes Alastair Trumpington (q.v.) as her lover.

• Most of the people who lunch with her read John Boot's books. At a luncheon of hers in 1936 Lady Amelia's son Simon tells Etty Cornphillip's son that Ralph Bland is his father. Simon Lent is invited to luncheon by her in 1936. In 1936 gives a party in honour of Charles Ryder. Attends Mr Plant's Academy parties. Widowed sometime between 1929 and 1939.

• In 1939 closes up Pastmaster House and moves to the Ritz (which she prefers). Pastmaster House is blown up in the winter of 1940. In 1963 she is addicted to television. She is seventy-two years old and still living at the Ritz.

DF 50, 75, 87, 88, 115, 117, 118, 134, 140, 156; VB 96, 99; HD 10; Sc 5, 11; PF 116; BR 254; WS 30, 64, 116, 251, 258, 278

MEXICO

One of the countries visited by Charles Ryder on his journey through South America in 1934.

BR 217

MHOMALA, DUCHESS OF

Guest at the banquet in honour of Mildred Porch (q.v.). Wears a gold and garnet tiara.

BM 168

MICHAEL

Writer, of whose book Sam Benfleet writes a review.

VB 99

MICKEY MOUSE

Cartoon character created by Walt Disney in 1929.

• One of the graves at Whispering Glades depicts a child clutching 'to its stony bosom a marble Mickey Mouse'.

LO 65

MICKLEHAM, SURREY

Town, south of Leatherhead.

• Where, in 1926, Alastair Trumpington tipples his port while listening to Ambrose

Silk's tales of unrequited love for a rowing blue.
PF 35

MIDLANDS, THE
Where Major Sir Alexander Dreadnought is joint master of a pack of hounds.
WS 39

MIDNIGHT ORGIES
What, according to the press, the Bright Young People indulge in at No 10 Downing Street.
VB 59

MIHAILOVIC, DRAGOLJUB, ***(1893–1946)***
Serbian soldier. Leader of the Serbian resistance from 1941. After the emergence of the Communist Tito and his own partisans, Mihailovic sided with the Germans against the Communist threat. Executed by order of Tito.
• Sir Ralph Brompton tells Guy Crouchback that Tito is their ally in 1943, not Mihailovic.
US 29

MILAN
Where Charles Ryder and Sebastian Flyte change trains on their journey to Venice in 1923.
BR 92

MILES
One of Celia Ryder's friends on the journey across the Atlantic in 1936.
BR 249

MILLAIS, SIR JOHN EVERETT ***(1829–1896)***
English painter. Leading member of the Pre-Raphaelite Brotherhood (q.v.). See his 'Isabella' (1849), and 'Ophelia' (1852) (both Tate Gallery). Married Effie Ruskin in 1855. After this time he began to turn towards portraiture, and adopted the popular, mawkishly sentimental style best seen in his 'Bubbles'.
• The portrait by Millais of Lady Throbbing and Mrs Blackwater, as young sisters, is auctioned at Christies in 1927 for a record in rock-bottom prices.
• When he hears Sebastian Flyte talk Anthony Blanche is reminded of 'that in some ways nauseating picture of "Bubbles"'.
• John Plant sees his father as 'fulfilling the promise of the young Millais'.
VB 11; BR 56; WS 128

MILLS, FLORENCE
Black American jazz singer.
• In May 1926, at the time of the General Strike, she is among the guests at a party in Regent's Park also attended by Charles Ryder, Boy Mulcaster and Anthony Blanche. Their hostess wonders whether she can be persuaded to sing. She does and everyone goes to hear her.
BR 197

MILLY ***(b. 1907)***
Prostitute. Works at the Old Hundredth (q.v.) with her friend Babs. Attaches herself to Tony Last. Jock Grant-Menzies persuades her to accompany Tony to Brighton to contrive his infidelity. At Brighton shares her bed not with Tony but with Winnie, her daughter. Her best frock is backless and vermillion. Wears red shoes and sham pearls. Is a friend of Dan (q.v.). Offers Tony a 'tongue sandwich'. Objects to Tony's conversation at dinner; it is not etiquette in her circle to express an interest in other women.
HD 71, 130–144

MILTIADES, GENERAL ***(b. circa 1870)***
Greek General (named after the Ancient Greek victor of Marathon). Before the war goes with the King of Greece to spend a week-end with the Luxmores at Wrackham, where he shoots and eats Irish stew. In his youth fights against the Turks and is wounded often. Sent into exile in middle age.
• On Crete in 1941. He is small and dignified, very tanned and has a huge white moustache. He wears three lines of decorations. Hitches a lift with Guy Crouchback.
OG 186

MILTON, JOHN *(1608–1674)*
English poet. See his *Allegro*, *Il Penseroso* and *Paradise Lost*. Worked passionately on behalf of the Commonwealth, and drove himself blind.
• Ambrose Silk, thinking of literary heroes who have served their country, includes Milton in his pantheon.
• Wykham-Blake, a fellow pupil of Charles Ryder at Lancing in 1919, chooses for his prep for Mr Graves, to learn 'Milton-on-his-blindness', which he selects because he has learned it once before.
PF 40; WS 289

MIMI
Pet name for Margaret, one of Gilbert Pinfold's voices.
GP 46

MINISTRY OF IMPERIAL DEFENCE
Where, in Whitehall, Algernon Stitch works in 1937.
Sc 6

MINISTRY OF INFORMATION
During WWII the propaganda centre of the British Government, housed in the senate building of the University of London.
• In 1939 Geoffrey Bentley heads a new department here. It is extremely difficult to gain admission to the building. His work consists of sending people who want to see him on to see someone they do not want to see. The ceiling of his office is by Angelica Kauffmann and Bentley has chosen the best pieces of furniture.
• Everyone is very keen to find a job here. Basil Seal has managed to do so. Sir Philip Hesketh-Smithers is a departmental assistant director. Mr Pauling is also employed here, as is Digby-Smith, who deals with 'propaganda and subversive activities in enemy territory'.
• The Archimandrite Antonios is another colourful figure to be encountered here.
• Basil Seal meets Ambrose Silk as they leave the building. Ambrose is given a job here, as Aetheist representative in the religious department.
• Many purges are carried out. Hesketh-Smithers is sent to the Folk-Dancing department and Pauling to 'woodcuts and weaving'. Digby-Smith is responsible for the Arctic Circle. Bentley directs a film about postmen, files press-cuttings from Istanbul and supervises staff catering, before returning to 'men of letters'.
• Ambrose Silk is commissioned to start a new magazine *Ivory Tower* (q.v.).
• In 1941 the Ministry of Information is agitating to have X Commando taken off the secret list.
• In the early days of *Survival* (q.v.) the Ministry of Information point out that as Hitler has proclaimed his love of 'figurative' painting, the avant garde should be defended as a patriotic duty.
PF 61–77, 109–110; OG 101; US 123

MINISTRY OF MODERNIZATION
Azanian organ of government instituted by royal proclamation in 1931. Its function is 'to promote the adoption of modern organization and habits of life throughout the Azanian Empire'. The chief employees are Basil Seal and Mr Youkoumian (both q.v.).

Everything is sent to them stamped REFER TO BUREAU OF MODERNIZATION.
BM 120

MINISTRY OF REST AND CULTURE
Neutralian cultural ministry in 1946, responsible for the Bellorius Conference.
WS 208

MINNEAPOLIS, MINNESOTA, USA
Parsnip (q.v.) is, by 1963, Professor of Dramatic Poetry at Minneapolis University.
WS 253

MINOTAUR
The monster, half man, half bull, of Greek legend. Offspring of Pasiphae and a bull. Inhabits a labyrinth on Crete where it is fed every ninth year until killed by Theseus.

• The Attic voices which propel Aimee Thanatogenos to her death are those which in another age had sung of the minotaur.
LO 116

MISSIONARIES
In the 1870s numerous European missionaries are eaten by the natives of Ishmaelia.
• Sebastian Flyte is desperate to be a missionary in Africa, but his request is refused (q.v.).
• Ritchie-Hook tells Guy Crouchback that you get 'a very decent type of missionary' in Africa; 'they don't stand any nonsense from the natives'.
Sc 74; BR 290; MA 71

MOABITE
One of a semitic tribe descended from Lot, living in Moab (*see* GENESIS 19:37).
• Paul Pennyfeather's insane cellmate at Blackstone Gaol calls one of the warders a Moabite, 'an abomination of Moab, a wash-pot, an unclean thing, an uncircumcised Moabite, an idolater, and a whore of Babylon'.
DF 180

MOCKSTOCK, LADY
Wife of Lord Mockstock and owner of Castle Mockstock. One of those neighbours of Bella Fleace, who are not invited to her party. The daughter of a draper.
WS 78, 86

MODERN AGE, THE
Seth declares that he is the New Age.
• Lady Marchmain's brothers died to make the Modern Age, the world of 'the travelling salesman with his polygonal pince-nez, his fat wet handshake, his grinning dentures'.
• Rex Mottram is 'something absolutely modern and up-to-date that only this ghastly age could produce'.
• Mr Hornbeam (q.v.), believes that there is no place for the artist in the Modern World.
• One of the women in Adam Fenwick-Symes' compartment of the Aylesbury train is proud to admit that she is a 'modern': 'We're not living in the Victorian Age'.
• The twentieth century is 'the century of the common man' and Elizabeth Verney is, to her husband John, its high priestess.
• Miles Plastic is the Modern Man: 'no complete man of the renaissance; no gentil knight nor dutiful pagan nor, even, noble savage'.
• Charles Allbright is 'an attempt to extract something from the rum modern world'.
• To Guy Crouchback, keen for a commission in 1939, the enemy is not only the Nazi threat, but 'the Modern Age in arms . . . whatever the outcome there was a place for him in that battle'.
• The guardian of the European underground network in 1946 has the face of 'a tricoteuse of the Terror' and bids seven Ursiline nuns: 'Welcome to Modern Europe'.
BM 17, 49; VB 139; MA 12; BR 134, 193, 331; GP 166, 182; WS 53, 244, 251
(*See also* NEW BRITAIN)

MOGADISHU, ITALIAN SOMALILAND
Post opposite Matodi (q.v.).
BM 116

MOGADOR
Town on the west coast of Morocco.
• Where, by 1933, Zingermaun (q.v.) is running a restaurant.
HD 158

MOLASSINE
Brand name of a dog food.
• Mr Outrage, waking from his drug-induced slumbers, notices an advertisement for it from his train window.
VB 28

MOLLY
Sonia Trumpington's pet kangaroo.
PF 44

MOLOTOV PACT
Russian non-aggression pact with Nazi Germany (May 1939).

• One of the main topics of conversation at Julia Stitch's luncheon party on the day of the German invasion of Russia in 1941.
OG 239

MOMBASA, KENYA
Coastal town.
• Hector arrives here in 1934.
WS 35

MONASTERIES
Achon (q.v.) is incarcerated in the monastery of St Mark the Evangelist on Azania. Within the monastery there are several holy relics. It consists of a few mud huts around a larger hut of stone.
• Sebastian Flyte ends his days in a monastery in Tunis.
• Cordelia tells Charles Ryder that there are usually a few hangers-on in monasteries.
BM 172; BR 290

MONEY
Paul Pennyfeather is sent twenty pounds, by means of compensation, by Alastair Trumpington.
• Young men are not as a rule given a thousand pounds twice on successive evenings by complete strangers, as happens to Adam Fenwick-Symes.
• For Lucy Simmonds money is of great importance. She has been brought up 'among people poorer than herself to regard herself as somebody quite singular'.
DF 43; VB 75; WS 169

MONKEYS
Cordelia Flyte tells Rex Mottram that there are holy monkeys in the Vatican.
• John Last thinks that Polly Cockpurse is a monkey.
• In August 1939 John Plant takes Lucy Simmonds to London Zoo, where they watch Humboldt's Gibbon for half an hour at a time.
HD 44; BR 187; WS 177–179

MONKS
Ambrose Silk, pondering the acceptable, destructive face of religion, thinks of the 'desert monks who carved up Hypatia', and the Inquisition 'roasting' monks in Spain.
• Amurath is educated by Nestorian monks near Basra.
• At the Monastery of St Mark the Evangelist the monks are armed with muskets.
• One of the characters painted on the ceiling of Julia Stitch's bedroom is a headless abbot.
• Sebastian Flyte is nursed by monks in North Africa; first at a Franciscan hospital in Fez, and later at a monastery near Carthage.
• Charles Ryder thinks one of the monks who takes him to Sebastian a 'poor simple monk . . . poor booby'.
• Tony Box-Bender becomes a monk after the war.
BM 9, 74; Sc 8; PR 60; BR 205, 290; US 238

MONOCLES
See CROUCHBACK, GUY.

MONMOUTH, (JAMES, DUKE OF) ***(1649-1685)***
Bastard son of Charles II. In 1685 launched an ill-fated attempt on the throne and was routed at Sedgemoor.
• Like Basil Seal he 'never condescended to the artifice of the toilet'.
PF 52

MONOMARK, LORD REX
Press baron. Owns 'those amusing papers' including the *Daily Excess*. Has a daughter. Has an affair with Margot Metroland before 1923.
• Thinks of taking up Basil Seal. Invites him for a cruise on his yacht in the Mediterranean. Discusses diet at one of Margot's parties. For lunch insists on 'two raw onions and a plate of oatmeal porridge'. Is teased by Basil Seal about his diet.
• In August 1933 Marjorie and Allan (q.v.) go for a cruise down the coast of Spain on Lord Monomark's yacht.
VB 99, 107, 108, 120, 121; BM 72–74; PF 48; HD 200

MONROVIA, LIBERIA
Coastal town of north Africa.
• If Monrovia fell into German hands, thinks Basil Seal, they could base submarines there and cut British trade routes.
PF 66

MONSTROUS REGIMENT OF GENTLEMEN, THE
Territorial searchlight battery in London in 1939, manned by fashionable aesthetes.
MA 23

MONTAGU, CAPTAIN
English naval officer present at the Battle of Ushant during the French revolutionary wars.
• Subject of a statue by Flaxman in Westminster Abbey. It is 'larger than life and portly for his years'.
US 21

MONTE CARLO
Where Adam Fenwick-Symes sends his creation, Count Cincinnati, for a holiday.
• In 1923 Rex Mottram takes Julia Flyte to Monte Carlo in his car.
• In 1925 Lord Marchmain spends the spring in Monte Carlo. Rex Mottram meets him there to ask for Julia's hand.
• Charles Ryder and Julia Flyte meet Lord Marchmain in Monte Carlo in the summer of 1937.
• Mahmoud Pasha (q.v.) is a 'sad exile from Monte Carlo'.
• Virginia Crouchback knows a magician of a doctor in Monte Carlo who will give you a 'cachet' which will cure anything.
• The cruise of the *SS Glory of Greece* (q.v.) starts at Monte Carlo.
VB 113; BR 171, 178, 299; OG 130; US 56; WS 16

MONTENEGRO
Province of Yugoslavia.
• Three Montenegran war widows look after the military mission and the airmen at Begoy (q.v.) in 1944.
• Montenegrans are among the officials of the Praesidium (q.v.) in 1944.
US 172, 203

MONTESQUIEU, MISS
Confidante of John Boot (who tells everything).
Sc 184

MONTESSORI METHOD
Method of teaching devised by Maria Montessori in 1909 for children between the ages of three and six, based on free learning.
• Seth (q.v.) proposes that the new education system in Azania be based on Montessori methods.
BM 43

MONTMORENCY WINE COMPANY
'Wine merchants' who supply the 'champagne' for the Old Hundredth.
HD 71

'MONTY', FIELD MARSHAL BERNARD LAW MONTGOMERY, 1st VISCOUNT ALAMEIN, *(1887–1976)*
British Field Marshal. Served WWI. Commander 8th Army in North Africa 1941. Victor of El Alamein (1942). Commander Ground Forces in Normandy 1944.
• In 1944 Ritchie-Hook (q.v.) has 'a bloody row' with 'Monty', and loses his command.
US 186

MONUMENTS
The National Monument of Neutralia commemorates the massacre of fifty leaders of the National Party in 1936. Built on the hillock where they fell, it is 'a loveless, unadorned object saved from insignificance only by its bulk; a great truncated pyramid of stone'.
• Tony Last's monument at Hetton is 'a plain monolith of local stone' inscribed 'ANTHONY LAST OF HETTON, EXPLORER, born at Hetton, 1902, Died in Brazil, 1934'.
• Mrs Beaver at first proposed redecorating the chapel as a chantry, but

Richard Last thinks that Tony would have preferred the monolith.
HD 220–221; WS 230
(*See also* STATUES)

MONUMENT TO A SPARTAN
See BOOKS

MOORE, GENERAL SIR JOHN *(1761–1809)*
British General. Fought in Corsica, West Indies and Holland before being sent to Egypt in 1801. 1808 sent to Spain as Commander in Chief. Forced to institute a forced march to Corunna, where on 16 January 1809 he defeated the French against far superior odds. During the battle he was mortally wounded. See Wolfe's poem and numerous paintings.
• Sarum Smith compares Apthorpe's funeral, without irony, to the burial of Sir John Moore.
MA 245

MOPING, LORD
Lunatic. Inmate since 1924 of the County Home for Mental Defectives. Mr Loveday is his secretary.
WS 7–14

MOPING, LADY
Long-suffering wife of Lord Moping (q.v.). Gives an annual garden party, at one of which her husband attempts suicide and is then taken away to the lunatic asylum. Pays seasonal calls to her husband. Sends cuttings to the asylum for the wealthier inmates' flower beds. Thinks Mr Loveday 'a very decent sort of man'. Arranges for Mr Loveday's release.
WS 7–13

MOPING, ANGELA
Daughter of Lord and Lady Moping (q.v.). Wonders whether her father has to wear a uniform at the asylum. Thinks Mr Loveday a nice man. Calls the inmates 'cuckoo' and the asylum a 'bin'. Is instrumental in having Loveday released.
WS 7–13

MOROCCO
Sebastian Flyte and Kurt live there for a while in 1926. To Charles Ryder it is 'a new and strange land'. It is 'the walled city whose streets were gentle, dusty stairways, and whose walls rose windowless on either side, closed overhead, then opened again to the stars; where the dust lay thick among the smooth paving stones and figures passed silently, robed in white, on soft slippers or hard, bare soles; where the air was scented with cloves and incense and wood smoke – now I knew what had drawn Sebastian here . . .'.
• One of Rex Mottram's friends thinks in 1938 that Franco will soon be 'skipping back to Morocco'.
• Sebastian returns to Morocco to die there.
• At the time of his father's death, John Plant is in Morocco.
• The criminal class of Morocco mostly have Maltese papers.
BR 202, 262, 292; WS 106

MORRIS, WILLIAM *(1834–1896)*
English designer and poet. Associate of the Pre-Raphaelite Brotherhood (q.v.). Exponent of the virtues of Gothic architecture. Founder of the Arts and Crafts Movement, based on socialist principles.
• The spirit of William Morris speaks to Paul Pennyfeather in Margot Metroland's motor car 'about seed time and harvest, the superb succession of the seasons, the harmonious interdependence of rich and poor, of dignity, innocence, and tradition'.
• A disciple of William Morris had turned the Harknesses' mill (q.v.) into a dwelling house.
• Charles Ryder would *like* to think that he had decorated his room at Oxford with 'Morris stuffs'.
• In 'the studio' in the Royal Victorian institute, the tone is 'derived from the disciples of William Morris'.
• Mr Plant's house has Morris wallpaper and chair-covers of 'indestructible Morris tapestry'.
DF 124; PF 93; BR 29; US 28; WS 127, 141

MORTGAGES
Abolished by Seth under his new series of reforms in 1931.
BM 148

MORVIN, CAPTAIN
Cordelia compares Sebastian's clothing for the hunt to 'something from Captain Morvin's Riding Academy'.
BR 161

MOSCOW
One of the places in which the population rallies to the aid of the Jacksons.
• The sections of X commando, re-appearing after exercise on Mugg, look like stragglers on the road from Moscow in 1812.
Sc 78; OG 86

MOSES
Ian Kilbannock compares his relationship with Air Marshal Beech with that of Pharoah and Moses.
OG 99

MOSHU
Interior town of Azania. Where Seth is cremated and Basil Seal eats Prudence.
BM 226

MOSLEY, SIR OSWALD *(1896–1980)*
English politician. Founder of the British Union of Fascists.
• An obnoxious young man at Brixton Gaol says 'heil Mosley' to Mr Rampole.
• Gilbert Pinfold denies ever having been connected with Mosley.
PF 202; GP 109

MOST SECRET INDEX
On whose files Guy Crouchback's name is to be found, along with that of Box-Bender.
MA 160

MOSTAR
Town in the east of Jugoslavia.
• A grocer from Mostar is among the Jews in Begoy.
US 175

MOTOR-CYCLES
Father Rothschild rides a motor-cycle.
• Erik Olafsen has a motor-cycle in Ishmaelia. It arrives sounding like a flight of heavy aeroplanes. He rides it into the bar of the Popotakis' Ping Pong Parlour.
• Ritchie-Hook has a 'motor-bike' in 1940.
• The vicar of Lady Amelia's parish tells her that Major Etheridge has put water in the petrol tank of his motor-cycle.
VB 133; Sc 88, 172–173; MA 72; WS 28

MOTOR RACING
The Bright Young People attend a motor race. They are made stewards. Agatha Runcible takes over from the driver of No. 13, in which she crashes.
• Agatha Runcible thinks that all Motor Men are heartless.
VB 153–175

MOTOR TRADE
See TOM KENT-CUMBERLAND and GRACIE PHILBRICK

MOTTE, JEAN BRISSAC DE LA
Belgian Futurist. Joins Charles Ryder during the General Strike. Was in Budapest 'when Horthy marched in'.
BR 193, 195, 198

MOTTRAM, REX, MP *(b. 1892)*
Canadian born, British politician. He is handsome, has dark hair which grows low on his forehead, and heavy black eyebrows. Serves 1914–1918 with the Canadians, being promoted as ADC to 'a popular General'. Wins a good MC. Married 1915 to Sarah Cutler in Montreal. Divorced 1919. By the 1920s he is in England, wealthy, and plays golf with the Prince of Wales. Is a good friend of Max Beerbohm (q.v.). Member of Bratt's Club. Member of Parliament for North Gridley. Drives a Hispano Suiza. Lives in Hertford Street, within walking distance of Marchmain House.
• Meets Julia Flyte at Cap Ferrat in 1922, where he is staying with Brenda Champion, with whom he has a long-standing affair. Decides it is time for

him to marry. Drives Julia to Monte Carlo and Nice.

• Sits on a number of charitable committees to ingratiate himself with Lady Marchmain. Offers to help Brideshead become an MP. In 1923 meets Charles Ryder at Oxford where he is taken for lunch by Julia. Invites Charles, Sebastian and Boy Mulcaster to dinner for Julia's party. According to Sebastian his friends are all 'leathery old sharks in the City and the House of Commons'.

• Liberates the three boys from the cells and takes them back to his own house. Sends to Heppell's for a hangover cure. Has a man from Trumper's shave them. Advises the boys on their court appearance.

• Spends Christmas 1923 at Brideshead. Gives Julia a diamond-encrusted tortoise for Christmas. Meets Charles Ryder in Paris, where he has lost Sebastian, and takes him to dine at Paillard's. Is worried about the Marchmain fortune. Is not liked by 'Ma Marchmain'. Does not take much account of Catholics, but does 'like a girl to have religion'. Wants to marry Julia. Wants a big wedding. Goes to Monte Carlo to ask Lord Marchmain for Julia's hand. His engagement is announced at the beginning of May 1925. Buys Julia a ring in Hatton Garden. Is forced to take out life insurance to equal Julia's dowry. Agrees to become a Catholic. Takes instruction at Farm Street. Because of his divorce they cannot be married in the Catholic church and have a 'squalid' Protestant wedding at the Savoy Chapel in mid June 1925. Gives a party the day after at the Savoy.

• To Julia he is not 'a complete human being'.

• During the General Strike organizes the gas works. Takes over Brideshead in 1927. His marriage to Julia becomes unhappy. They are often photographed in the *Tatler*. Discovers that Julia is not quite what he expected. He no longer speaks in a Canadian accent but in 'the hoarse, loud tone that was common to all his friends'.

• Charles visits Brideshead in 1938 and finds him there. Is divorced by Julia. Makes a 'rabid speech to the Commons'. Moves to London. During the war becomes 'Minister of whatever-it-is'. Makes a radio broadcast in 1943 about Hitler. Nanny Hawkins sees Mr Mottram and his friends as 'angels' during the war.

BR 107, 108, 109, 159, 160, 164–193, 201, 211, 224, 246, 261, 263, 282–283, 284, 326, 329

MOULAY, THE

Eastern potentate and former husband of Jenny Abdul Akbar (q.v.).

He is 'a beautiful and a very bad man', who sits on his throne under a crimson canopy. He mistreats her horribly.

HD 86

MOUNTDRAGON, RUTH

Pseudonym of Mrs Parker (q.v.).

PF 219

MOUNTJOY

Country house, converted into a prison of the New Britain. Planned many years before Miles Plastic is an inmate.

Before its conversion it had been the ancestral seat of a maimed VC of WWII, who now inhabits a home for the handicapped.

Burned to the ground by Miles Plastic in 1953.

GP 179, 180, 185, 214

MOUNTRICHARD, LADY

Villainous character in *Murder at Mountrichard Castle* by John Plant.

WS 120

MOUSE, MARY

One of the Bright Young People. Sends 'great hampers of caviare and things' to the perpetual party at Edward Throbbing's house. Finances most of their parties.

Falls in love with the Maharajah of Pukkapore and makes love to him in the captive dirigible.

Her mother is the owner of Indian Runner (q.v.).

VB 29, 45, 52, 122

MOUSTACHES
Paul Pennyfeather grows a heavy moustache to enable him to return to Scone in 1923.
• Guy Crouchback grows a moustache on joining the army in 1940. A barber curls it for him. It helps to 'set him up' with the younger officers. He shaves it off after Virginia declares that she thinks it horrible. He realizes that he had seen such moustaches on the faces of 'clandestine homosexuals, on touts with accents to hide, on Americans trying to look European, on business-men disguised as sportsmen'.
DF 207; MA 105–106, 123–124

MOUTON-ROTHSCHILD
Vineyard in Bordeaux, opposite which Mr Baldwin has his own vineyard on more delicate soil.
Sc 55

MOWBRAY, FATHER
Jesuit priest at Farm Street who attempts to convert Rex Mottram (q.v.). He is well known for his triumphs with the most difficult converts. Has tea with Lady Marchmain and tells her that he despairs of Rex. Lady Marchmain tells him to treat Rex 'like an idiot child'.

He is 'a gentle old Jesuit' but his unrelenting attitude on matters of faith provokes Julia into abandoning hers.
BR 182, 185

MOZART, WOLFGANG AMADEUS *(1756–1791)*
Pre-eminent Austrian composer of the eighteenth century.

The string quartet at Mountjoy play Mozart as if it were Haydn.
GP 181

MUCH MALCOCK, GLOUCESTERSHIRE
One of the most unspoilt villages in the Cotswolds. It has a memorial hall and a club, a well-kept church, a scout troop, a district nurse, and a socialist vicar. The pub is the Brakenhurst Arms. Home of Mr Metcalfe, Colonel Hodge, Lady Peabury, the Hornbeams, Boggett, Mr Westmacott and Mr Cruttwell.
WS 43, 47, 54

MUDGES, THE
A tough farming family who live in a small homestead at Upper Lamstock, near Malfrey. The first family to reject the Connollys (q.v.), who tear the head off their cat and kill six of their ducks, while Doris molests Willie Mudge.
PF 81–82

MUDIE'S
Booksellers. Source of the novels which are sent to the British Legation in Azania.
BM 104

MUDSHORE
Rifle range ten miles from Southsand (q.v.).
MA 100

MUGG
Island in the Scottish Hebrides among the other 'monosyllabic protuberances' of Muck, Rum and Eigg.

Has a laird (see Campbell), a fishing fleet, and a hotel (q.v.).

Has never been seen from Eigg. From Rum it looks like two cones.

Training ground for X Commandos in 1940.
OG 46–7

MULCASTER, VISCOUNT 'BOY' *(b. 1903)*
Educated Eton (1915–1921) and Oxford (1922–1925). Friend of Sebastian Flyte and Anthony Blanche. Brother of Celia Ryder (q.v.). He is, according to Anthony Blanche: 'everything we dagos expect of an English Lord . . . all the young ladies in London are after him . . . He's very hoity-toity with them . . . My dear, he's scared stiff. A great oaf – that's Mulcaster – and what's more, my dear, a cad'.

Joins Anthony in Le Touquet at Easter 1922. Picks up a tart and loses his virginity, which costs him three hundred francs. Expects Blanche to pay for everything.

At Oxford puts Blanche in the fountain of Mercury.

Member of the Bullingdon. Member of Bratt's.

Accompanies Sebastian and Charles to Julia's party and Rex's dinner. His high-handed tone with the policeman after their near crash in the motor car results in their being locked up.

Charles next meets him during the General Strike in May 1926, at a party in Regent's Park. Takes Charles to a number of night clubs. Joins Bill Meadows' unit of special constables with Charles. Becomes engaged in 1935 but it is called off and his parents have to give the girl money.

Lets it be known that Julia Flyte was once a girl friend of his. In 1938 negotiates Celia's divorce with Charles who he thinks has treated her 'a bit rough'.
BR 49, 108, 113, 195, 197, 198, 221, 229, 281

MULCASTER, LADY CELIA (b.1905)
Sister of Boy Mulcaster (q.v.). Friend of Julia Flyte. She is very soft, very English and very reticent. She has small perfect teeth and neat painted fingernals. She wears modern jewellery. She is pretty in a 'curiously hygienic' way. Talks of 'putting her face to bed'. Her lovemaking is also 'neat and hygienic'. Julia thinks she has 'the most delicious look of any girl in my year'. According to Mr Samgrass her conversation is 'bird-like . . . pecking away at the subject'.

Stays at Brideshead for Christmas in 1923. Leaves with Julia for another party. Marries Charles Ryder in 1930. People say that she 'made him'. They have two children, John (b. 1931) and Caroline (b. 1935).

Has an affair in 1934, before Charles' departure. Meets Charles in New York on his return from South America. Makes Bertha van Halt godmother of Caroline.

Has Emden convert the barn into a studio for Charles. Promises Lady Anchorage that Charles will paint Anchorage House before it is demolished.

Organizes a cocktail party on board the ship to England. Tries to introduce Charles to film producers. Becomes badly seasick and retires to bed leaving Charles and Julia together. Recovers and is pleased that they are friends. Does not realize that they have begun an affair.

Arranges Charles' private view for a Friday. Becomes quickly aware of his infidelity and accepts it.

After her divorce settles down at the Old Rectory with Robin, who has been mad about her since 1937.
BR 120, 218–224, 227, 245–256, 263, 281

MULLIGAN, JOE
American journalist entertained at the Savoy by Ian Kilbannock in 1941. Friend of Scab Dunz and Bum Schlum. Boston Irish by birth, he does not like the English.
OG 212, 216

MUNICH, BAVARIA
Tony Last visits Munich in 1921 and buys a fur coat which he gives to a girl who speaks no English.
• Where Ambrose Silk has his unhappy love affair with Kurt (q.v.).
• A publisher from Munich is among Mr Ryder's guests for Miss Orme Herrick's concert.
• In 1923 Anthony Blanche takes a flat in Munich, where he has found himself a policeman.
HD 156; PF 34; BR 69, 102

MUNICH AGREEMENT
Agreement signed on 30 September 1938 by Britain, France and Italy and Germany, agreeing not to go to war over Czechoslovakia, and by which the Sudetenland was handed over to Germany.
• John Verney 'pungently' denounces it.
GP 162

MURALS
See ARTHUR; LENNOX, David; RYDER, Charles.

MURDER
The religious maniac at Blackstone Gaol kills Mr Prendergast by sawing off his head.

• The Sakuyu once shaved off the hair from an Italian woman's head and covered it with butter so that white ants ate through into her skull.
• A girl is found strangled with a piece of barbed wire in Wandsworth.
• The Free Spaniards in North Africa murder an Egyptian cabdriver.
• Scarfield (q.v.) thinks that all murderers are mad. Gilbert Pinfold agrees with him and adds that they are always smiling.
• Elizabeth Verney drugs her husband's coffee and throws him down a cliff, as in a film they have seen together.
• Bella Fleace's brother is obsessed with assassination, and paints pictures of every such known occurrence until he is himself murdered with a shotgun in his own drive, during the Troubles.
• Mr Loveday strangles two young lady cyclists.
DF 182; BM 210, 211; BR 267; MA 119; GP 64, 169; WS 14, 79

MURDOCH
A little dark man who sits alone in the saloon of the *SS Caliban*, on which he often travels. He has the accent of the north of England. Tells Pinfold that 'wog trains' are 'filthy dirty and slow'. Gives Pinfold a lift to Cairo.
GP 124, 140–143

MURIEL, LADY
One of the passengers on the *SS Glory of Greece* with whom the young lady correspondent's father has 'a walk out'.
WS 17

MUSEUMS
Seth plans a museum in Azania.
• When the revolution comes Roger Simmonds wants to be director of the 'Museum of Bourgeois Art'.
BM 149; WS 144

MUSIC
Paul Pennyfeather's guardian's daughter plays Gilbert and Sullivan on her gramophone.
• Doctor Fagan insists on music at the Llanabba sports day. The silver band plays 'Men of Harlech' non-stop.
• Paul Pennyfeather visits a prison with Stubbs and sings part-songs with the inmates.
• Adam Fenwick-Symes considers writing in his Mr Chatterbox column that 'Colonel Blount has the curious eccentricity of being unable to shoot his best except to the accompaniment of violin and 'cello'.
• The Harknesses (q.v.) have chamber music every week in the summer under their cherry tree.
• Music is relayed through loudspeakers in the town of Bari in 1944.
• It is also broadcast on the wireless in the RAF hospital to which Guy Crouchback is confined in 1943.
• There is relayed music in the corridors of the hospitals of the New Britain.
DF 15, 49, 82, 86, 211; VB 141; PF 95; US 116; GP 180, 212
(*See also* SONGS, HYMNS, individual composers, TUNES)

MUSIC WHILE YOU WORK
Morale-boosting radio programme of popular music broadcast during WWII.
• Mrs Bristow's morning's housework is crowned with a radio broadcast of 'Music While You Work'.
US 90

MUSPRATT, ADMIRAL
Late husband of Beryl Muspratt (q.v.). Notable for his collection of matchboxes which he left to Falmouth Town library.
BR 270

MUSPRATT, BERYL
Widow of Admiral Muspratt by whom she has two sons, who are sent to Ampleforth. Knows Lord Brideshead for some years before the death of her husband in 1937. Marries Lord Brideshead (q.v.) in 1938. Attends a luncheon party at Lady Rosscommon's. Attends an audience at the Vatican. Dines with Lord Marchmain in Rome.

Stays a few nights at Brideshead after her honeymoon. During the war moves to

Brideshead before being turned out by the army. Returns to Brideshead's house in Barton Street, which is blown up. Moves to another house outside London, which is also requisitioned by the army, and finally to a seaside hotel.
BR 270, 272, 275, 283–284, 301, 305, 328, 329

MUSSOLINI, BENITO *(1883–1945)*
Italian dictator. Founder of Italian Fascism (1919). Established himself by force in 1922, going against the wishes of the League of Nations. Set up the Vatican State by the Lateran Treaty in 1929. Allied with Germany. Annexed Abyssinia in 1936 and Albania in 1939. Defeated in WWII and shot by the Italians.
• In 1939, as Guy Crouchback leaves Italy, he sees 'the lowering, stencilled face of Mussolini' stare at him from every wall on posters which carry the legend 'The Leader is always right'.
• Gilbert Pinfold tells Glover that he once 'had hopes' of Mussolini.
MA 16; GP 109

MUTHAIGA CLUB
See KENYA

MUTINY
Ivor Claire tells Guy Crouchback that 'all successful mutinies have always been led by NCOs'.
OG 112

MYERS, MISS
Paid companion of Lady Amelia who fetches her library books which she then reads aloud.
WS 23–25

MYSTICAL BODY
Catholic term expressing the church as a union of all the faithful, with Christ as their head, as a living, corporate organism. In this way the Holy Eucharist, the body of Christ, is the sacrament of the Mystical Body.
• Mr Crouchback reminds Guy after their conversation about the surrender of Italy, that the Mystical Body 'doesn't strike attitudes and stand on its dignity. It accepts suffering and injustice. It is ready to forgive at the first sign of compunction'.
US 16

McADDER, COLONEL
Predecessor of Sir Wilfred Lucas-Dockery at Blackstone. Gives his successor some good advice: 'Don't bother about the lower warders or the prisoners. Give hell to the man immediately below you, and you can rely on him to pass it on with interest. If you make a prison bad enough people'll take jolly good care to keep out of it'.
DF 167

MacDOUGAL
Barman at Bratt's Club. Reminds John Beaver that he owes ten shillings. Is well-apprised of top security information in 1939.
HD 12; PF 118

MacDOUGAL, MR
Australian. Father of Bessie MacDougal (q.v.). He is tall and lean and wears pince-nez. He owns large expanses of territory in Australia, has an interest in statistics and earns fifty two thousand pounds a year. Traces his family roots to Scotland. In 1933 visits England with his daughter. Friend of the Chasms. Gives Tom Kent-Cumberland a position managing one of his farms in Australia.
WS 101, 103, 105

MacDOUGAL, BESSIE
Fiancée of Tom Kent-Cumberland. She is 'bland and creamy'. Visits England with Tom and her father in 1933. Admires everything English for its antiquity. In Australia finds Tom dignified and cultured, but in England finds that everyone is like that. Transfers her affections to Gervase. Marries Gervase and lives at Tomb. Has two children.
WS 102, 103, 105

MACKENZIE, SIR COMPTON ***(1883–1972)***
British writer. Director of the Aegean Intelligence Service 1917. See his *Sinister Street* (1914), and *Whisky Galore* (1947).
• In 1939 Barbara Sothill sees Basil Seal as Compton MacKenzie: 'spider in a web of Balkan intrigue'.
PF 17

MACKENZIE, MR
A very respectable Englishman and friend of Dr Antonic's father whose factory at Budweis he often visited. In 1946 Dr Antonic asks Scott-King if he can find him, to help him and his family out of trouble.
WS 240

MACKENZIE, DOCTOR
Local doctor at the village at which John and Elizabeth Verney stay in 1946. Known as 'Old Mack', he reads all the latest medical books and is up to date. He is a bachelor with grey hair, who smokes heavily. Is consulted by Elizabeth Verney about John's 'sleep-walking', to provide an alibi for his murder, and then by John himself for precisely the same reason.
WS 173–174

MACKINGTOSH
(Mackintosh, pronounced with a strong Milwaukee accent). One of Bonnie Prince Charlie's closest supporters in the film of the 1745 rising seen by Guy Crouchback before the war.
MA 161

McKINNEY, CAPTAIN
Acting camp-commandant at Kut-al Imara in 1940.
MA 88

MACPHERSON, AIMEE SEMPHILL
American evangelist.
• Aimee Thanatogenos is named after her.
LO 73
(*See also* APE, MRS MELROSE)

MACRAE, SIR JAMES
English film magnate. Lives in Hampstead in a 'low Georgian' house. His night secretary is Miss Bentham. Miss Harper is his day secretary. His night butler is Sanders. His chauffeur is Benson. In 1936 commissions Simon Lent to write the screenplay for his production of *Hamlet*, which he wants to update. Organizes meetings throughout the country, to which he never turns up. When finally cornered in a hotel in the New Forest he rejects Simon's script, falsely denying that it was his suggestion that the play should include Macbeth, Julius Caesar and King Arthur. Decides that what the public wants is 'Shakespeare, the whole of Shakespeare and nothing but Shakespeare'. Produces a version of St John's Gospel, shot in Algeria.
WS 65–76

McTAVISH
Nom-de-guerre of Trimmer (q.v.).

N

NACKTKULTUR
Seth (q.v.) is perplexed about Nacktkultur in Azania in 1932, having spent three days attempting to enforce an edict prescribing trousers as compulsory for the upper class, and then reading that it is more modern not to wear any.
BM 154

NAILSWORTH
Member of Bellamy's who, according to the eccentric member who sits in the corner of the stairs, has a wife and a mother who are both whores; and probably a whore for a daughter.
GP 105

NANNIES
Ambrose Silk's nanny describes Heaven as full of angels playing harps.
• Gilbert Pinfold's nanny, like almost all nannies, is Calvinist.
PF 60; GP 38
(*See also* Nanny PRICE, Nanny BLOGGS and Nanny HAWKINS)

NAPLES, ITALY
Where Cedric and Angela Lyne spend their honeymoon, and where they buy a classical temple, later incorporated into the grounds of their house.
• Anthony Blanche reminds Charles Ryder of a Neapolitan urchin.
• Where, in 1936, Charles Ryder hangs about before crossing to Capri to rendezvous with Julia Mottram.
• From where one of Sebastian Flyte's ancestors brought the fountain at Brideshead, in the late 1770s.
• Where, in 1889, Gervase and Hermione Crouchback join the yacht on their honeymoon before sailing up the coast of Italy.
• One of the stopping-off points of the *SS Glory of Greece* where the passengers see some Baroque churches and 'that bit that got blown up in an earthquake and a poor dog killed they have a plaster cast of him goodness how sad. Papa and Bertie saw some pictures we weren't allowed to see'.
PF 169; BR 47, 265, 317; MA 9; WS 17

NAPOLEON I, NAPOLEON BONAPARTE *(1769–1821)*
Soldier, statesman and Emperor of the French. Born in Corsica. Rose to power during the French Revolution. General 1793. Married Josephine 1796. First consul 1799. Emperor 1804. Defeated the Russians and Austrians at Austerlitz 1805, and the Prussians at Jena 1806. Conquered Germany, Austria and half of Prussia. Invaded Spain 1807. In 1810, desperate for an heir, divorced Josephine and married again. Invaded Russia 1812. Forced to retreat with the loss of most of his army. Defeated at Leipzig 1813 and abdicated. Exiled to Elba. Escaped March 1815. Defeated at Waterloo June 1815. Exiled to St Helena, where he died.
• Otto Silenus thinks that Lady Vanburgh resembles Napoleon.
• Lord Copper reflects that none of the great men of the past have ever enjoyed the devotion they deserved. Napoleon and Josephine are just one such example.
• One of Adam Symes' eccentrics is an earl who wears Napoleonic dress.
• On Crete in 1941 Guy Crouchback, having heard that the Commanding General of the British forces (General Freyberg) is leaving his men, reflects that Napoleon did not stay with his army after Moscow.
• One of Napoleon's marshals made

Santa Maria (q.v.) his base and built the classical garden.
DF 125; Sc 218; OG 220; VB 112

NAPOLEON III, CHARLES LOUIS NAPOLEON BONAPARTE *(1808–1873)*

Nephew of Napoleon I (q.v.). Emperor of the French (1852–1870). Declared war against Prussia in July 1970. Defeated in September. Exiled to England.

• Margot Metroland's great bed in her villa on Corfu, carved with pineapples, once belonged to Napoleon III.
DF 150

NARCISSUS

The beautiful youth of Greek legend whose cruelty to nymphs was avenged by the gods by his being condemned to fall in love with the reflection of himself in a pool. Having discovered his inability to realize this love, he pined to death.

• As Basil Seal kissed his sister Barbara at breakfast 'Narcissus greeted Narcissus from the watery depths'.

• Anthony Blanche describes Sebastian Flyte at Eton as having been 'Narcisus with one pustule'.
PF 87; BR 52

NASH, JOHN *(1752–1835)*

English architect. Engaged by the Prince Regent, later George IV, to plan Regent's Park and its surroundings (1811 onwards). Redesigned Buckingham Palace and built Brighton Pavilion (1815).

• In 1937, as Julia Stitch and John Boot drive to Bethnal Green from St James's, a Nash façade in Piccadilly is being demolished and 'coarse particles of Regency stucco' carried away by the wind.
Sc 9

NATIONAL ACADEMY OF CINEMATOGRAPHIC ART

Film company in the Edgware Road, of which Mr Isaacs (q.v.) is the principal.
VB 148

NATIONAL AND PROVINCIAL UNION BANK OF ENGLAND LIMITED

Where, according to the bogus major, Adam Fenwick-Symes' thirty-five thousand pounds are invested. 'A perfectly sound and upright company . . . One of those fine old companies you know . . . I'd trust that bank with my wife and kiddies.'
VB 179

NATIONAL ART COLLECTIONS FUND

At a luncheon at Margot Metroland's house in 1936, given in honour of Charles Ryder, representatives of the NACF are present, who promise to reserve certain of his pictures for possible acquisition.
BR 255

NATIONAL ART TREASURES

At the outbreak of war in 1939, Arthur Box-Bender arranges to have Kemble accepted as a repository for National Art Treasures, to ensure that it will not be taken over by the military or evacuees.

Unfortunately for his wife, who had been expecting Boucher, Boule and Sèvres, they receive Hittite tablets from the British Museum at which they may not even 'peep'.
MA 20, 27

NATIONAL TRUST

Association, founded in 1895.

• Malfrey (q.v.) is given over to the National Trust after Freddy Sothill is killed in the war. Barbara Seal thinks it 'hell'.
WS 272

NATO

North Atlantic Treaty Organization.

• The 'Gibraltar crisis' of Gilbert Pinfold's hallucinations means the end of NATO. One of the Generals bids it 'good riddance'.
GP 38

NATURE

Otto Silenus sees man as alien from both Nature and the machine.

• Ambrose Silk, as he muses on his life, recalls the quotation from Walter Savage Landor's 'I Strove with None': 'Nature I loved, and next to Nature, Art.' He concludes that nature 'in the raw is seldom mild; red in tooth and claw', and relates this to his experiences with matelots in Toulon.
DF 121; PF 43

NATURAL SCIENCES
The don who lives above Charles Ryder's rooms at Oxford is 'a mouse of a man connected with the Natural Sciences'.
BR 24

NAZIS
Nazi diplomacy postulates, in order to gain popularity, a world of peace and honour.
• Ambrose Silk, in his position at the Ministry of Information, is aware that his task is to show aesthetes that Nazism is agnostic 'with a strong tinge of religious superstition'.
• Hans (q.v.) accepts 'all the nonsense' of the Nazi leaders.
• Guy Crouchback knows the German Nazis to be 'mad and bad. Their participation dishonoured the cause of Spain'.
• In 1944 Madame Kanyi (q.v.) tells Guy that it is too simple to say that it was only the Nazis who wanted war in 1939.
PF 49, 69–70, 110, 187; MA 12; US 232

NEAR EAST
Sebastian Flyte and Mr Samgrass make a tour of the Near East in 1923. It is a hotch-potch of 'Druses, patriarchs, icons, bed-bugs, Romanesque remains, curious dishes of goat and sheeps' eyes, French and Turkish officials – all the catalogue of Near Eastern travel'.
BR 150

NECROPOLIS
Sonia and Alastair Trumpington move to Brookwood, near the Necropolis. 'The most enjoyable place. Three public houses, my dear, insidëthe cemetery, right among the graves ... the Corps of Commissionaires have a special burial place'.
PF 72

NED
Eldest brother of Lady Marchmain (q.v.). Educated Hertford and Oxford. Served Grenadier Guards 1914 onwards. Leaves a quantity of papers, from which Mr Samgrass makes a privately printed book. He was the last of her brothers to be killed during the Great War, on the Western Front.

NEEDLEWORK
In 1963 Sonia Trumpington spends most of her day at her needlework.
WS 277

NEGROES
Margot Metroland's lover in 1922 is a Negro, Chokey (q.v.).
• Colonel Sidebottom saw the Fuzzy-Wuzzy in the Sudan, 'devilish good enemy and devilish bad friend'.
• Chokey is keen to point out that 'all you white folks despise the poor coloured man ... You folks all think the coloured man hasn't got a soul. Anything's good enough for the poor coloured man. Beat him; put him in chains; load him with burdens ... But all the time that poor coloured man has a soul the same as you have'.
• According to Sam Clutterbuck 'niggers ... have uncontrollable passions'.
• Adam Fenwick-Symes watches a coloured singer at the Café de la Paix in 1927.
• Sir Samson Courteney does not indulge in the ostentatious habit of referring to members of the royal household of Azania by name, but simply remembers them as 'the old black fellow who drank so much Kummel', or something of the sort.
• A black archdeacon is among Tony Last's fellow passengers on the journey to South America. On his last day his wife takes round a collection box for an organ which needs repairs.
• William Boot sees a black man at Speaker's Corner telling his audience that

the Ishmaelite patriots are in the right.
• The fascist consul of Ishmaelia in London tells William that the tropical sun has given his countrymen 'a healthy, in some cases almost a swarthy, tan' and that they are pure aryans.
• The Communist consul has features that to William are 'not much different from those of any other Negro' . . . he tells William that Marx was a Negro, that it was a Negro who invented the circulation of the blood, discovered America and won the Great War.
• Bella Fleace's mother suffers from the delusion that she is a negro.
• Charles Ryder, Anthony Blanche and Boy Mulcaster listen to Florence Mills sing at a party in Regent's Park in 1926.
DF 75, 78, 79, 80–81, 84; VB 119; BM 52–53; HD 165; Sc 48–51, 78; BR 197; WS 79

NELSON, HORATIO, VISCOUNT *(1758–1805)*

British sailor. Blinded in one eye at Calvi 1794. Won the battle of Cape St Vincent 1797. Promoted Rear Admiral. Lost his right arm at Santa Cruz 1797. Won the battle of Aboukir Bay 1798. Began an affair with Emma Hamilton. Promoted Vice-Admiral 1801. Won the battle of Copenhagen 1801. Won Trafalgar 1805 and was mortally wounded.
• To Cedric Lyne the Regency is the age of Nelson.
• To Rex Mottram's friends England in 1938 is the land of Clive and Nelson.
• Margaret, seeing Gilbert Pinfold standing on the deck of the Caliban, thinks of Nelson.
PF 171; BR 105; GF 99

NELSON TOUCH, THE

Expression deriving from Nelson's renowned act in 1799 of putting a telescope to his blind eye and, with the phrase 'I see no ships', refusing to obey orders to take his fleet to Minorca.
• In 1940, the major at Penkirk chooses to ignore the orders he receives ordering him to put X Battalion of the Halberdiers on alert against German parachutists. 'That, I think is called the Nelson touch'.
MA 191

NEMESIS

Avenging deity of Greek mythology representing the anger of the gods meted out to the proud and insolent.
• In 1943 Ludovic believes that the things that he has done in the summer of 1941 will, in the belief of the ancients, provoke his doom, 'the arcane operation of nemesis'.
US 87

NEUTRALIA

Southern European state on the Adriatic. In the 1640s part of the Habsburg Empire. Between 1650 and 1946 suffers: 'Dynastic wars, foreign invasion, disputed successions, revolting colonies, endemic syphilis, impoverished soil, masonic intrigues, revolutions, restorations, cabals, juntas, pronunciamentos, liberations, constitutions, coups d'etat, dictatorships, assassinations, agrarian reforms, popular elections, foreign intervention, repudiation of loans, societies'. The Republic of Neutralia in 1946 is typically modern, with a single party government supported by a corrupt administration. Neutral in WWII. Before the war the Marshal was elected by a bloody revolution. Scott-King visits the Bellorius conference here in 1946 (q.v.).
WS 196, 197, 221

NEW BRITAIN

In the New Britain of Miles Plastic (q.v.) the country is ruled by the Minister of Welfare and the Minister of Rest and Culture. The capital is Satellite City (q.v.) and the men from the state-run orphanages provide the corps of the armed forces.

Everyone carries a Certificate of Human Personality. There is no taxation for industrial workers. In the courts, arson, wilful damage, prejudicial conduct, treason and manslaughter are all grouped under the title of Antisocial Activity. It is one of the basic principles of New Law that no man may be held responsible for the consequences of his own acts. 'There are no criminals. There are only the victims of inadequate social services'. Euthanasia is compulsory for the aged and terminally ill. Women can be sterilized with Klugmann's operation.

Courtship is 'free and easy'. Sex is on the school curriculum from an early age. The word Love is not used except by politicians. The state chooses the wine of the month. Christmas is 'Santa Claus-Tide'. The television rules supreme.
GP 188–221

NEW FOREST
Where, in a hotel, Sir James Macrae holds a conference about his production of *Hamlet.*
WS 75

NEWFOUNDLAND
Lord Moping asks Mr Loveday to look up the figures about the Newfoundland fisheries.
WS 9

NEWHILL
House in Ireland of one of Bella Fleace's neighbours. Leased to sportsmen from England.
WS 78

NEWPORT, RHODE ISLAND
Where Virginia Crouchback sometimes, before the war, used to go to a doctor to get him to sign prescriptions for sleeping pills.
US 56

NEWPORT, SYLVIA
Friend of Mrs Beaver (q.v.) who also knows the owners of the house which burned down.
HD 7

NEWSPAPERS
In the words of Corker (q.v.) 'News is what a chap who doesn't care much about anything wants to read. And its only news until he's read it. After that its dead'.

• Tony Last's conduct with Winnie at Brighton simply confirms in the minds of the onlookers the ideas of human nature which they have grasped from the weekly newspapers.

• William Boot believes that people who write to newspapers are 'proverbially unbalanced'.

• The tenor in the concert party which entertains the Halberdiers in 1940 has to admit that there is nothing in the newspapers but lies: 'You can't believe a word they say. But it's all good. Very good indeed. It helps to keep one's spirits up . . . Something cheerful in the morning. That's what we need in these times'.

• Lord Copper's two rules for a special correspondent are 'Travel Light and Be Prepared'.

• The events in Azania do not stimulate the interest of the British public: 'Anything in the paper this morning?' 'No dear, nothing of interest'.

• John Plant compares the Renaissance poets writing of love, trying to out-do each other, to the publishers' lists in the Sunday newspapers.

• In 1958 the newspapers associate long hair with the King's Road, Chelsea.

• Engineer Garcia (q.v.) tells Scott-King that the British newspapers tell lies about Neutralia. Scott-King tells him that they tell lies about everyone.

• The local paper of Los Angeles includes the column of the Guru Brahmin (q.v.), formerly 'Aunt Lydia's Post Bag', much consulted by Aimee Thanatogenos (q.v.).

• *AZANIAN COURIER:* The editor flees from Matodi in the Emperor's motor-boat at the start of the crisis.

• *CONTINENTAL DAILY MAIL:* While in Paris, Charles Ryder notices the announcement of the engagement of Rex Mottram to Julia Flyte.

• *COURIER:* Local newspaper at Malfrey (q.v.) in which the Harknesses advertise for a lodger.

• *COURIER D'AZANIE:* French newspaper of Azania of which M. Bertrand (q.v.) is Editor. Consists of one single, folded quarto sheet printed weekly and occupies one day a week of M. Bertrand's time.

• *DAILY BEAST:* Based at 700–853 Fleet Street, in Copper House, the Megalopolitan building. Owned by Lord Copper (q.v.) and the Megalopolitan

Newspaper Corporation, which also includes Home Knitting, Clean Fun and a number of comic weeklies. There are sixteen peers on the staff. Basil Seal writes the Lush Places column. The Poet Laureate (John Masefield) writes an ode to the seasonal fluctuation of the paper's net sales. Foreign Editor is Mr Salter (q.v.). In 1936 Mr Samgrass is 'one of Lord Copper's middle-aged young men on the *Daily Beast*'. In 1941 Lord Copper prints a number of articles directed against the regular army.

• *DAILY BRUTE:* Rival newspaper to the *Daily Beast*, owned by Lord Zinc. Sir Jocelyn Hitchcock transfers to the *Brute* after his dispute with Lord Copper. Beats the *Beast* in every edition in its coverage of the 'Zoo Mercy Slaying'.

• *DAILY EXCESS:* Owned by Lord Monomark (q.v.). Simon Balcairn writes the Mr Chatterbox column until his suicide, after which he is succeeded by Adam Fenwick-Symes, who in his turn gives way to Miles Malpractice. All q.v.

• *DAILY EXPRESS:* In 1943 their gossip writer suggests that the Sword of Stalingrad (q.v.) should be sent round Britain. His suggestion is taken up.

• *DAILY MIRROR:* The flying officer at No 4 training centre in 1943 reads the *Daily Mirror*. Mr Bentley finds a copy of the *Daily Mirror* in his railway carriage in which he reads an article by Godfrey Wynn about his cottage (q.v.).

• *DAILY TWOPENCE:* Rival newspaper to the *Daily Beast*. Sends Pappenhacker to Ishmaelia.

• *EVENING MAIL:* Carries a report on the death of Flossie at Lottie Crump's.

• *FLINT AND DENBEIGH HERALD:* Dr Fagan gets them to send a photographer to the Llanabba sports day.

• *GAZETTE:* Local paper of Much Malcock. Read by Mr Metcalfe (q.v.).

• *HAVAS:* Their correspondent in Ishmaelia raises an objection at the meeting of the Foreign Press Association.

• *IRISH TIMES:* Read by Bella Fleace.

• *LONDON HERCULES:* Jack Spire writes a column here on the Save King's Thursday Fund.

• *MORNING ADVERTISER:* In which Brideshead suggests placing a notice announcing the cancellation of Rex and Julia's engagement.

• *MORNING DESPATCH:* Lord Vanburgh (q.v.) writes the gossip column. Sponsors the motor race attended by the Bright Young People, and pays for the trophy.

• *NEWS OF THE WORLD:* Read by Sebastian Flyte after attending Mass at Brideshead.

• *NEW YORK GUARDIAN:* Silas Shock is one of their journalists.

• *PARIS SOIR:* Their correspondent in Ishmaelia has an objection to make at the meeting of the Foreign Press Association.

• *RUM, MUCK AND EIGG TIMES:* Local newspaper of the Isle of Mugg (q.v.), read by X Commando.

• *STAR:* In the opinion of Rex Mottram, the only paper which might be difficult to 'square' over reporting Sebastian's arrest.

• *SUNDAY MAIL:* Gives Alastair Trumpington £50 to put his name to an article describing the experience of being best man at the wedding of Paul Pennyfeather and Margot Beste-Chetwynde.

• *SUNDAY TIMES:* In 1944 prints a two-column review of Dennis Barlow's poems.

• *THE TIMES:* Basil Seal reads the news on the Imperial and Foreign page of *The Times* at his club and catches up with the latest on Azania. The British legation on Azania receives, by diplomatic bag, fifty-nine copies at once. Lord Brideshead reads it every day. Brideshead suggests putting an announcement in *The Times* cancelling Rex and Julia's engagement. In which, in 1926, Sir Adrian Porson publishes a poem as an obituary to Lady Marchmain. Julia Flyte, becoming hysterical about her religion, suggests that Charles write to *The Times* about it.

On 2nd November 1940 *The Times* carries an advertisement in the personal column from Guy Crouchback, asking 'Chatty Corner' to communicate with Box 108, 'when he will learn something to his advantage'.

In 1943 *The Times* prints a poem about

the Sword of Stalingrad (q.v.).

Gilbert Pinfold's most frequently recurring dream is that he is doing *The Times* crossword puzzle.

Mr Metcalfe (q.v.) always makes himself read the local paper before allowing himself to open *The Times*.

Mr Hargood-Hood (q.v.) does *The Times* crossword.

Mr Plant, during the anti-semitic thirties, declares his support for the Jewish cause in many unpublished letters to *The Times*.

• *TIMES LITERARY SUPPLEMENT:* Ludovic used a typist in Scotland who he found in the *TLS*.

DF 49, 118, 155; VB 76, 86, 105, 106, 108, 113; BM 7, 67, 103–104, 124; HD 144; Sc 11, 13–16, 19–20, 21, 23, 24, 25, 31–32, 34, 41, 66, 80, 84, 117, 221; PF 48, 92, 113, 117; BR 84, 116, 119, 162, 171, 177, 190, 212, 253, 310; MA 57; OG 39, 48, 154, 212, 246; US 22, 40, 101, 187; LO 22, 80; GP 16; WS 48, 56, 81, 113, 150, 214

NEW WRITING

Periodical edited by John Lehmann from 1936 to 1940. Included contributions from Spender, Auden, Isherwood, Edward Upward and V.S. Pritchett. Was notably unorthodox.

• Parsnip and Pimpernell once contributed.

GP 217

NEW YORK

Home of the yogi who teaches Mrs Hoop to meditate.

• Setting for the film on journalists once seen by William Boot.

• Source of the gadgets beloved by Mrs Stitch.

• Where Charles Ryder has an agent to whom he dispatches his drawings of South America as they are completed.

• To where Charles returns in 1936, en route from South America to England. He and Celia spend one sticky night there at the Savoy-Carlton.

• One of the things for which Guy Crouchback is asked by the Jews at Begoy is an aeroplane to New York.

• At his hotel in Colombo Gilbert Pinfold is approached by a friend of his from New York, a collector from one of the art galleries.

• In 1947 Basil Seal and Angela go to New York where it was still possible to procure luxury items then scarce in Britain.

VB 13; Sc 24, 221; BR 217, 219; US 180; GP 146; WS 256, 266

NEW ZEALAND

The member of the Sudan Police who Charles Ryder meets in Fez regards the town as a New Zealander might see Rome.

• On Crete in 1941 Major Hound meets a sports car in which are a New Zealand officer and a New Zealand Brigadier, both haggard and covered in dust and blood.

• Ralph Bland talks of buying a sheep farm in New Zealand and Billy Cornphillip lends him the money, which he immediately loses in the City.

BR 203; OG 194; WS 27

NGUMO, EARL OF

Member of the Azanian nobility. From a family of forty-eight (most of whom he assassinated to gain the title). Has sixty sons and numerous daughters. He has under his control some five hundred square miles of mountain land and tries to mobilise his tribesmen during the civil war.

BM 114, 143

NICARAGUANS

A Nicaraguan calling himself either Ponsonby or Fitzclarence robs Dr Messinger of £200 and thirty machine guns.

HD 158

NICE, FRANCE

Where Rex Mottram takes Julia Flyte for drives while courting her at Cap Ferrat in the summer of 1923.

• Where the Grand Duchess Elena of Russia, Colonel in Chief of the Halberdiers, lives in a bed-sitting room.

BR 178; MA 76

NICHODEMUS, SAINT, OF THYATIRA

Martyred by having a goatskin nailed to his head. Patron saint of bald heads.

• During the Easter vacation 1923, Sebastian Flyte writes a letter to Charles Ryder on the feast of St Nichodemus, telling him the gruesome history.

BR 44

NICHOLS, MR

Cabbie at Oxford in 1923 who returns Aloysius to Sebastian Flyte.

BR 84

NICHOLS, MARY

Friend of Basil Seal who is also an acquaintance of the Girl at Grantley Green (q.v.) who thought her wonderful when she was sixteen. Basil met her on a ship from Copenhagen.

PF 124

NICKNAMES

The two detectives accompanying Mr Outrage on his painting visit call him 'The Right Honourable Rape'.

• The Pinfolds are addicted to giving people nicknames.

• Reginald Graves Upton is given a number of nicknames by them, on account of his association with the Box.

• Someone in X Commando dubs Ritchie-Hook 'the Widow Twankey', and it sticks.

• Basil Seal is known after the war by his daughter as 'Pobble', on account of having blown away the toes of one of his feet while on manoeuvres.

VB 11; GP 11–12; WS 255; OG 111

NIDGET

Defined in Ludovic's copy of the dictionary as 'an idiot. A triangular horseshoe used in Kent and Sussex'. It is not, he decides, applicable to his reports on the men in his command.

US 85

NIGHTCLUBS

ST CHRISTOPHER'S SOCIAL CLUB, LEICESTER SQUARE: The Bright Young People go here in 1927. It is a little door at the side of a shop and costs £10 to enter. Adam Fenwick-Symes is insulted here by Gilmour, who is a friend of Ginger.

• *THE SUIVI, LONDON:* Angela Lyne goes to dance here in the winter of 1939.

• *THE PERROQUET, DEBRA DOWA:* Managed by a Georgian prince.

• *THE WARREN, LONDON:* Opened in London in 1933. John Beaver goes there.

• At a nightclub in May 1926 Boy Mulcaster and Charles Ryder are filled with drunken patriotism and decide to join Bill Meadows' show.

• In the 1920s Charles Ryder frequents BRICKTOP'S and the BAL NEGRE in Paris.

• *THE BLUE GROTTO:* Homosexual club frequented by Anthony Blanche in 1936. He takes Charles there and becomes objectionable.

• As a young man Gilbert Pinfold seeks out nightclubs where there is a bar out of earshot of the band.

VB 124; HD 27, 70; BM 51; PF 120; BR 109–112, 195, 198, 257; GP 46

(*See also* OLD HUNDREDTH)

NIHILIST

A Jewish nihilist from Berlin makes an unsuccessful assassination attempt on Amurath.

BM 11

NINETEEN TWENTY-TWO COMMITTEE

Rex Mottram's friends in 1938 think that the 1922 Committee are preventing Hitler from 'scuppering himself'.

BR 280

NOAH, MRS

Wife of the Biblical patriarch.

• The lodge keeper's wife at King's Thursday is as 'white-aproned as Mrs Noah'.

DF 123

NOLLEKENS, JOSEPH *(1737–1823)*

English sculptor. Produced likenesses of many of his illustrious contemporaries. See his bust of Johnson (Westminster Abbey).

• Mr Bentley has managed to procure two marble busts by Nollekens from his offices in Bedford Square with which to decorate his office at the Ministry of Information. Ambrose Silk thinks that Nollekens inspired the greatest biography in the English language; i.e. J.T. Smith *Nollekens and his Times* (1828).
PF 62–63

NORFOLK
Ian Kilbannock, creeping up the coast of occupied France with Trimmer on Operation Popgun, quotes from Noel Coward's *Private Lives* to comment on the surrounding countryside: 'Very Flat Norfolk'.
• Next destination for Mr Hargood-Hood and his brother after Much Malcock.
• Location of Tomb (q.v.).
OG 145; WS 62, 87

'NORMALITY'
In 1944 almost all the women in England believe that peace will bring a return to 'normality'. By this they mean their husbands being at home, their basic comforts being restored, 'a full larder and cellar; a lady's maid . . . a butler, a footman . . . a reliable, mediocre cook . . . self-effacing housemaids . . . one man in the stable, two in the garden'.
US 146–147

NORMANDY, FRANCE
After the D Day invasions of June 1944 Ian Kilbannock negotiates a position as a war correspondent in Normandy.
• The *SS Caliban* served in the Normandy landings.
• At the time of the Normandy landings Scott-King finishes his work on Bellorius.
US 185; WS 197; GP 41

NORTH GRAPPLING, GLOUCESTERSHIRE
Village ten miles from Malfrey (q.v.). It is off the main road and a stream follows its single street and has two stone bridges across it. At one end of the street is the church and at the other the Old Mill House. It has been spared from modernization and retains the scent of gillyflowers. Home of the Harknesses (q.v.).
PF 90–91

NORTHCOTE, MRS
The fortune teller discovered by Mrs Beaver and used by Brenda Last, Marjorie, Polly Cockpurse, Daisy, Veronica, Souki de Foucauld-Esterhazy and others. She tells fortunes by reading the soles of the feet.
HD 117

NORTON
Alias used at the Wimpole club by Arthur Atwater (q.v.).
WS 185

NORWAY
Guy Crouchback hears the news on the wireless that all is going well in Norway on 21 April 1940, and that General Paget is at Lillehammer.
• The Norwegian fellow passenger of Gilbert Pinfold on the *SS Caliban* tells him that in her country 'in the forests in the long winter often the men become drunken and fight and sometimes they kill one another'.
MA 170; GP 64

NOTABLE INVALIDS
Series started by Adam Fenwick-Symes in the *Daily Excess*. It is a tremendous success and includes his famous list of the most popular deaf peeresses, deaf peers and statesmen, one-legged blind and bald society figures.
VB 111

NOUGHT, JOHN
Agent of the Credential Assurance Company, present at the dinner at the Savoy Grill given by Silas Shock on the evening of Edward VIII's abdication (11 December 1936).
Sc 80

NOUVEAUX RICHES
Among self-made men there is a 'mystery' about how they made their first ten thousand.
BR 178

NOVELS

• According to Adam Fenwick-Symes, Ginger Littlejohn's novel will soon be finished.
• Reading the will only happens in Victorian novels, not at Broome.
• *The Death Wish* (q.v.) is 'pure novelette'.
• Lady Amelia has been brought up to believe that it is improper to read a novel in the morning, but she notices that people who read novels have better health.
• Lady Peabury has been brought up to believe that it is one of the gravest possible sins to read a novel before luncheon.
• John Plant believes that 'the delicate parts of a story suffer when it is chopped up into weekly or monthly parts and never completely heal'.
VB 120; US 62, 202; WS 23, 24, 50, 106
(*See also* MRS PARKER)

NOVELISTS

Between novels John Boot (q.v.) 'keeps his name sweet' with intellectuals by writing books on history and travel.
• A group of progressive novelists have joined the Fire Brigade in 1941 and happily play their hoses into the burning morning room of Turtles Club.
• Ludovic is following in the footsteps of a number of notable authors in starting with poetry before having written his magnum opus *The Death Wish* (q.v.).
• Gilbert Pinfold thinks that any novelist is condemned 'to produce a succession of novelties, new names for characters, new incidents for his plots, new scenery'.
• Gilbert Pinfold's voices tell him that novelists survive on publicity and headlines such as 'Novelist whipped on liner'.
• Simon Lent is described in the press as a 'popular', 'brilliant', 'meteorically successful', and 'enviable' young novelist.
• John Plant, reading the work of a competitor, will reflect that 'she has a husband to support and two sons at school. She must not expect to do two jobs well, to be a good mother and a good novelist'.
• Only once, after the death of his father, does John Plant need to ask for a postponement from his publishers.
• Roger Simmonds is a very good novelist in his own way, and every bit as good as John Plant.
• Scott-King, not being a reader of popular fiction, is not familiar with the phrase 'It all happened so quickly that it was not until afterwards . . .'
Sc 5; OG 9; US 203; GP 10, 13, 71; WS 64, 106–107, 129, 148, 241

NUDGE

Butler to Basil and Angela Seal in 1963.
WS 260

NUIT DE NOEL

See PERFUME

NUNS

Nanny Hawkins thinks it a ridiculous idea to try to make a nun out of Julia Flyte.
• Father Phipps notes that nuns cut their hair (although not in quite the same way as Julia Flyte and her friends).
• Seven men dressed as Ursuline nuns share Scott-King's passage out of Neutralia.
BR 38; WS 243

O

OAKSHOTT, BUCKINGHAMSHIRE
House near Doubting Hall, where Ginger Littlejohn's parents used to live.
VB 203

OATES
Civilian efficiency expert at HOOHQ in 1943. To Guy Crouchback his presence seems bizarre. He is 'a plump, taciturn little man' and is profoundly peaceful.
US 30

OBERAMMERGAU, GERMANY
German town, reknowned for its passion play.
• Mrs Ape, having confirmed the content of Simon Balcairn's libellous story, leaves the country with her 'Angels' in response to a call to 'ginger up the religious life of Oberammergau'.
VB 109

OEDIPUS
Mythical King of Thebes who fell in love with his mother. See tragedy by Sophocles.
• Basil Seal thinks, if Seth ever discovers psychoanalysis, Debra Dowa will have an Avenue Oedipus.
BM 142

OGADEN DESERT
Desert in the east of Ethiopia.
• Basil Seal once knew a hermit in the Ogaden Desert.
PF 176

O'HARA
Bella Fleace's mother was an O'Hara of Newhill, who suffered under the delusion that she was a negress.
WS 79

OLAFSEN, ERIK
'A gigantic, bemused Swede'; resident correspondent for a syndicate of Scandinavian papers, he is also Swedish Vice-Consul to Ishmaelia, head surgeon at the Swedish Mission Hospital, and owner of the chemist's shop which forms the centre of European life in Jacksonburg.
Sc 80–81, 88, 104, 173, 176

OLD BILL
Cartoon character created by Bruce Bairnsfather in the Great War, famous for the cartoon 'If you knows of a better 'ole, go to it'.
• Angela Lyne's maid sees Basil Seal as 'Old Bill' in 1939.
PF 29

OLD GANG, THE
In 1938 Rex Mottram's friends are keen for a show-down with the Old Gang.
BR 262.

OLD HUNDREDTH, SINK STREET
Nightclub at 100 Sink Street, just off Leicester Square, run by Ma Mayfield Its hours of opening are nine in the evening until four in the morning.
• None of the staff receive wages, but make what they can by going through peoples' overcoat pockets and short-changing the drunken customers. Young ladies are admitted free of charge, on the understanding that they encourage the patrons to spend money. Lots of girls 'work' there.
• It has never been shut. The police have often tried to close it down and Mrs Mayfield has been in prison. There have been questions in the House about it.

Boy Mulcaster goes there in September 1923 and meets Effie.

Charles Ryder, Sebastian Flyte and Boy

Mulcaster slip away to the Old Hundredth from Julia Flyte's party at the Ritz in 1923. Boy Mulcaster tells the others that he has a 'regular' there, Effie, but she does not recognise them. Boy finds Effie and Charles and Sebastian are joined by two girls, one of whom looks like a Death's Head (who takes up with Charles), the other like a Sickly Child. They take Charles and Sebastian for 'fairies' but are persuaded otherwise. The six of them leave for a party at the Death's Head's place and the three young men are arrested for being drunk and incapable.

• Jock Grant-Menzies and Tony Last attend Tony's bachelor party here in 1926. Also present is Reggie St Cloud (Brenda's brother), who breaks the fruit gum machine. They all become 'tight'. Jock and Tony are there again in 1933, having become drunk at Bratt's. They meet Milly and Babs and call Brenda at her flat.

BR 110–112; HD 70–74

OLD MEN

Old men frequently feel the compulsion to 'touch every third lamp-post on their walks', and are disturbed beyond all reason should they pass one by.

WS 161

OLD POBBLE

See SEAL, BASIL

OLDENSHAW, COLOUR-SERGEANT

Training sergeant on Guy Crouchback's return to the Halberdier barracks in 1941.

OG 249

O'MALLEY

Fellow pupil of Charles Ryder at Lancing in 1919. He is ungainly and an 'upstart' who is only able to distinguish himself by his tenacity on cross-country runs.

WS 293

OMANI ARABS

Victorious beseigers of the Portuguese garrison at Matodi in 1632 and for two centuries afterwards the masters of the Azanian coast.

BM 8

OMAR KHAYAM

The Rubaiyat of Omar Khayyam (1859) translated from the Persian by Edward Fitzgerald. (*See* BOOKS)

• Frankie (q.v.) suggests that *Omar Khayam* might have been written by Scott Fitzgerald.

US 200

OMEGA WORKSHOPS

Artistic institution, founded in 1913 by Roger Fry, to produce furniture, textiles and decorative objects with a very distinctive modernist style. Closed in 1919.

• Charles Ryder buys a decorated screen from the Omega Workshops when they sell up. It is part of the decoration of his rooms at Oxford in 1922, but is discarded after he succumbs to the tastes of Sebastian Flyte. Charles eventually sells it to Collins (q.v.) for £10 to cover his end of term expenses.

BR 29, 35, 60

OMNIUM, DUKE OF

One of those people whom Mr Crouchback regards as on the other side from the Crouchbacks, and whose wealth is derived from the spoilation of the monasteries.

MA 34

ONE YEAR PLAN

Basil Seal's plan for the modernization of Azania in 1931.

BM 155

OPALTHORPE, ANNE

Owner of the London house opposite that of Edward Throbbing, who tells Lady Throbbing of the goings-on at her son's house during his absence.

VB 98

OPERA

Julia Stitch is taken to the opera by an aged admirer in 1937.

• At Bari in 1944, Lieutenant Padfield is in charge of organising the opera.

Sc 73; US 158

OPERATION BADGER

Aborted military operation in 1941. Prev-

iously known as Operation Quicksand.
OG 100

OPERATION BOTTLENECK
Cancelled military operation on an island in 1941.
OG 100

OPERATION HOOPLA
Military operation in 1943 whose objective is to attack submarine pens in Brittany with twelve men in a fishing boat. It is at first aborted, and its reappearance at 'Beaches' is met with ironic applause.
US 27–28

OPERATION MOUSETRAP
Aborted military operation in 1941.
OG 100

OPERATION POPGUN
Least ambitious military operation in 1941 which plans to investigate whether a tiny uninhabited island near Jersey is being used by the enemy to investigate the RDF. Ian Kilbannock and Trimmer are sent on it in an effort to make Trimmer into a hero.
OG 118, 137, 141–149

OPERATION QUICKSAND
Military operation in 1941, aborted and renamed Badger.
OG 100

OPERATION STOCK EXCHANGE
Idea of Angel's (q.v.) designed to intimidate Gilbert Pinfold by having the passengers of the *SS Caliban* recount tales of a huge financial slump, within Pinfold's hearing. Does not work. Pinfold has no fortune.
GP 132

OPERATION STORM
Idea of Angel's (q.v.) intended to intimidate Gilbert Pinfold. Does not work as Pinfold is too good a sailor.
GP 132

OPPENHEIM, EDWARD PHILLIPS *(1866–1946)*
English novelist. Author of early examples of the espionage novel. See his *Kingdom of the Blind* (1917) and *The Envoy Extraordinary* (1937).
• Peter Pastmaster tells Paul Pennyfeather that Sir Humphrey Maltravers (later Lord Metroland), has been to see his mother Margot, 'in the most impossible Oppenheim sort of way', to tell her that if she marries him he will secure Paul's release.
DF 160–161

ORDERS
Guy Crouchback, aware that men running amok are sometimes brought to their senses by a response to a command, barks out a parade ground order 'That half-file in front . . . about turn. Quick march', when on the beach near Dakar during the raid on French West Africa in 1940.
MA 226

ORIENT
Dreamed of by Mr Outrage (q.v.).
VB 15

ORME-HERRICK, SIR CUTHBERT AND LADY
Friends of Mr Ryder (q.v.) who gives a dinner party during Charles's summer vacation 1923 to which he invites them and their daughter, who plays the cello.
BR 69

ORME-HERRICK, MISS GLORIA
Daughter of Sir Cuthbert and Lady Orme-Herrick. She plays the cello, has a small moustache and large feet and is engaged to a bald young man from the British Museum.
BR 69–70

ORPHANAGES
The orphanages of the New Britain, such as that attended by Miles Plastic, provide the core of the armed forces.
GP 183

O.S.C.U.
In 1922 Stiggins reads a paper to them on 'Sex Repression and Religious Experience'.
DF 45

OTTAWA
Where, in 1927, Edward Throbbing stays at Government House.
VB 51

OUIDA (LOUISE RAME)
(1839–1908)
English novelist. Author of *Under Two Flags* (1868) and other romantic fiction.
• Mr Joyboy, at ease in his profession, peels off his rubber gloves after a taxing day's embalming, 'like a hero of Ouida'.
LO 79

OUTRAGE, THE RIGHT HONOURABLE WALTER, OM, MP
'Last week's Prime Minister' in 1927. Fellow passenger of Adam Fenwick-Symes on the cross-channel ferry on his return from a trip to Paris. Addicted to chloral, of which he takes twice the maximum dose before breakfast on the day of his crossing, later finishing the bottle on the train. Becomes conscious near Maidstone. Has affair with Baroness Yoshiwara.
VB 12, 15, 22, 23, 42, 48–49, 101, 127–128, 130–131

OVERDRAFTS
In 1926 the Flytes are a hundred thousand pounds overdrawn.
• John Plant has an overdraft until his father dies and leaves him a small legacy.
BR 169; WS 141
(*See also* LENT, SIMON)

OXFORD
Oxford in 1922 is 'a city of aquatint. In her spacious and quiet streets men walked and spoke as they had done in Newman's day; her autumnal mists, her grey springtime, and the rare glory of her summer days . . . when the chestnut was in flower and the bells rang out high and clear over her gables and cupolas, exhaled the soft airs of centuries of youth'.
• John Beaver is at Oxford from 1926–1929. 'Bertie' is at Oxford. John Plant first meets Roger Simmonds at Oxford where they edit an undergraduate weekly.
• Ambrose Silk is there in the mid '20s, 'when the last of the ex-servicemen had gone down and the first of the puritanical, politically minded had either not come up or . . . had not made himself noticed'. He dines at the Spread Eagle at Thame. Barbara Seal is here in 1962.
• *ALL SOULS COLLEGE, HIGH STREET:* In his youth Mr Ryder sat for All Souls and failed. J. Cattermole is a fellow of All Souls.
• *ASHMOLEAN MUSEUM, BEAUMONT STREET:* Founded 1683. Among whose casts from the antique Charles Ryder studies form while at the Ruskin School of Art.
• *BALLIOL COLLEGE, BROAD STREET:* Founded 1264. Attended by Tony Last (1921–1924), Guy Crouchback and J. Cattermole (1921–1924). Guy Crouchback was a friend of Sligger Urquhart (q.v.). Attended by Seth 1926–1929. Attended by Basil Seal who throws lavish luncheon parties which last until dusk, and dinner parties which become riots. A few men from Balliol take their Sunday breakfast in their slippers at the same tea shop in the Broad frequented by Charles Ryder. From the gates of Balliol four Indians walk with a picnic down to the river, carrying copies of Bernard Shaw. When Gilbert Pinfold was at Oxford he used to sing songs outside the Dean of Balliol's rooms.
• *BECKLEY:* Where Paul Pennyfeather and Stubbs go for walks in October 1923.
• *BLACKFRIARS:* To which church, on the last Sunday of the summer term 1923, Charles Ryder sees the congregation hurrying.
• *BLACKWELL'S BOOKSHOP, 50 BROAD STREET:* Paul Pennyfeather finds Dr Fagan's book *Mother Wales* here in 1923. In the spring term of 1924 Charles Ryder meets Mr Samgrass here, beside the German book table.
• *BOAR'S HILL:* Where, at Lady Keble's, some of the senior members of Scone College choose to dine on the evening of the Bollinger Club dinner in 1922. Jasper advises Charles Ryder to stay clear of Boar's Hill. Where Sebastian

Flyte supposes normal undergraduates go to have tea.

• *BODLEIAN LIBRARY:* In 1923 Stubbs argues with Mr Sniggs about plans to rebuild it.

• *BOLLINGER CLUB:* Dining club (q.v.).

• *BOTANICAL GARDENS, ROSE LANE:* Where Sebastian Flyte often comes 'to see the ivy', and where he takes Charles Ryder after his luncheon party in March 1923.

• *BOTLEY ROAD:* Route taken out of Oxford by Charles and Sebastian on their way to Brideshead in 1923.

• *BROAD STREET:* On the last Sunday of the summer term 1923 Charles Ryder walks from Hertford College down the Broad to breakfast at a tea shop opposite Balliol.

• *BULLINGDON:* Dining club. Gervase Kent-Cumberland is a member.

• *CADENA CAFE:* Where Sebastian Flyte supposes normal undergraduates drink coffee in the morning.

• *CARFAX:* Crossed by Charles and Sebastian on their way out of Oxford to Brideshead in June 1923. Where, on the last Sunday of the summer term 1923, Charles Ryder bumps into the Mayor of Oxford and the Corporation with the wand-bearers on their way to the City Church. To where Charles Ryder takes the bus after having escorted Lady Marchmain to her convent in the spring of 1924.

• *CARLTON CLUB:* Jasper advises Charles Ryder to join.

• *CANNING CLUB:* Charles Ryder's cousin Jasper is secretary in 1923. He tells Charles to make his reputation here before standing for the Union.

• *CHATHAM CLUB:* Jasper advises Charles Ryder to make his reputation here before standing for the Union.

• *CHERWELL EDGE:* Anthony Blanche is 'a byword of iniquity from Cherwell Edge to Somerville'.

• *CHRIST CHURCH COLLEGE:* Founded 1525. John Plant's Great Grandfather was Canon of Christ Church. Lord Marchmain was a student here (1883–1886) Where Sebastian Flyte's rooms are, high in Meadow Buildings. He holds a lunch party here in March 1923 at which Charles Ryder meets Anthony Blanche, who recites *The Wasteland* through a megaphone from Sebastian's balcony. In Peckwater Quad Anthony Blanche has his rooms, where he sits in his pyjamas reading *Antic Hay* and watching the light fade.

In the spring term of 1924 Sebastian is found hopelessly drunk in Tom Quad at one o'clock in the morning by the Junior Dean. Gervase Kent-Cumberland is here between 1921 and 1924. His brother Tom gets drunk and is sick in a corner of Peckwater Quad in 1921.

• *CORNMARKET:* Where, on the last Sunday of the summer term, 1923, Charles Ryder notices a group of tourists discussing a road map with their chauffeur.

• *DOLBEAR AND GOODALL:* Chemists in whose hands Sebastian Flyte puts himself on the morning after he is sick into Charles Ryder's rooms.

• *DRUID'S HEAD:* Pub near the theatre, frequented by Charles and Sebastian in Michaelmas term 1923.

• *GARDENERS' ARMS:* One of the pubs frequented by Charles and Sebastian during the Michaelmas term 1923.

• *GEORGE HOTEL:* Where Sebastian Flyte dines wearing false whiskers. Where, in a loud voice, Anthony Blanche challenges convention. Where Anthony Blanche takes Charles Ryder for Alexandra cocktails before their dinner at Thame.

• *GERMERS:* Barber's shop where Charles Ryder first catches sight of Sebastian Flyte.

• *GOLDEN CROSS:* Where 'through the venerable arch of Golden Cross', Charles Ryder greets a group of undergraduates from Hertford who had just had their breakfast there.

• *GRID CLUB:* Jasper advises Charles Ryder to join it at the beginning of his second year.

• *HERTFORD COLLEGE, CATTE STREET:* Founded 1874

Lady Marchmain's brothers Simon and Ned attend here before the Great War. Ned has rooms on the garden front. Their names are carved in gold on the war memorial. Lady Marchmain wanted Sebastian to go there as well. An 'ugly, subdued little college' attended in 1923 by Stubbs. Paul Pennyfeather visits him for tea. Jasper Ryder is here in 1923, president of the JCR. Charles Ryder is here 1922–1924. In early March 1923 Sebastian Flyte is sick through the window of Charles Ryder's rooms on the quad. Collins is here (1922–1925). Waugh's own college when at Oxford.

• *HIGH STREET:* Where Gervase Kent-Cumberland has fashionable lodgings in 1921. Where from his bicycle, in 1923, Paul Pennyfeather sees Philbrick in an open Rolls Royce. On Charles and Sebastian's route out of Oxford to Brideshead in June 1923. Here they almost collide with an old clergyman who is cycling on the wrong side of the road.

• *HOLYWELL:* In the spring term of 1924 Lady Marchmain and Charles walk through Oxford in conversation, by way of Holywell.

• *HOLYWELL PRESS:* Lord Metroland, when Humphrey Maltravers at Scone in the 1900s, proofreads for the Holywell Press.

• *IFFLEY ROAD:* In the 1920s where the lodging houses are to be found of 'proletarian scholars who scramble fiercely for facts'. Where Collins shares digs with Tynegate in the summer term 1924.

• *KEBLE COLLEGE, PARKS ROAD:* Founded 1870. Where Sebastian Flyte supposes normal undergraduates go to hear lectures.

• *MASONIC DANCE HALL:* Where some undergraduates go to dance in 1923.

• *MERTON COLLEGE, MERTON STREET:* Founded 1264. Under whose walls Charles and Sebastian walk on their way to the Botanical Gardens.

• *MERTON STREET:* Where, in the spring term of 1924, Charles Ryder finds lodgings for himself and Sebastian in 'a secluded, expensive little house near the tennis court'.

• *MESOPOTAMIA:* Paul Pennyfeather and Stubbs go for walks here in October 1923. One of the places where Lady Marchmain and Charles Ryder walk in conversation in the spring term of 1924.

• *NAG'S HEAD, HYTHE BRIDGE STREET:* Pub frequented by Charles and Sebastian during Michaelmas term 1923.

• *NEW COLLEGE, NEW COLLEGE LANE:* Founded 1379. The sums spent on the education of Miles Plastic in the New Britain would have at one time sent 'whole quiversful of boys to New College'.

• *NEWMAN:* Room in the parish buildings of St Marys. Unlike the other Catholics, Sebastian Flyte does not go to the Newman.

• *NORTH OXFORD:* Where some of the senior members of Scone College choose to dine on the evening of the Bollinger Club dinner in 1922. Where, by way of the ferry, Lady Marchmain and Charles Ryder walk in conversation in the spring term of 1924.

• *OLD MARSTON:* In October 1923 Paul Pennyfeather and Stubbs go for walks to Old Marston.

• *OLD PALACE:* Where Sebastian Flyte attends Mass on the last Sunday of the summer term 1923.

• *PECKWATER: See* CHRISTCHURCH.

• *PUSEY HOUSE, ST GILES:* Chaplaincy with a high tradition. To where, on the last Sunday of the summer term 1923, Charles Ryder sees the churchgoers hurrying.

• *RAILWAY STATION, BOTLEY ROAD:* Passed by Charles and Sebastian on their way out of Oxford to Brideshead in June 1923.

• *RUSKIN SCHOOL OF ART, WALTON STREET:* Charles Ryder joins the Ruskin at the start of his second year (1923–24).

• *ST ALDATES:* Where on the last Sunday of the summer term 1923, Charles Ryder passes a crocodile of choir boys on their way through Tom Gate of Christchurch and into the Cathedral.

• *SAINT ALOYSIUS', 25 WOODSTOCK ROAD:* Catholic church. On the last Sunday of the summer term 1923, Charles Ryder watches the congregation on their way here.

• *SAINT BARNABAS, WALTON*

STREET: Charles Ryder notices church-goers hurrying here on the last Sunday of summer term 1923.

• *SAINT CLEMENT'S:* Among whose 'Hogarthian little inns' Charles Ryder and Sebastian Flyte pass the evenings of their second year at Oxford.

• *SAINT COLUMBA'S, ALFRED STREET:* Scottish church. Charles Ryder notices the congregation on their way here on the last Sunday of summer term 1923.

• *SAINT EBB'S:* It is in the inns of St Ebb's that Charles Ryder and Sebastian Flyte spend their evenings in Michaelmas term 1923.

• *SAINT MARY'S, MAGDALEN STREET:* As Charles Ryder and Sebastian Flyte drive off to Brideshead in June 1923 the bells of St Mary's strike nine. On the last Sunday of summer term 1923 Charles Ryder watches the church-goers on their way here.

• *SAINT PETER WITHOUT THE WALLS:* 'One of England's oldest and most venerable places of worship.' Transplanted from Oxford to Whispering Glades by Dr Kenworthy in 1935 and 'rebuilt' in glass and steel.

• *SCONE COLLEGE:* Attended by Paul Pennyfeather, Partridge, Sanders, Lord Rending, Lord Reading, Austen and Sir Alastair Digby-Vane-Trumpington in 1922. The porter is Blackall. The Junior Dean is Mr Sniggs and the Domestic Bursar Mr Postlethwaite. The Bollinger Club meets in Trumpington's rooms in 1922. Paul Pennyfeather is debagged by the Bollinger and runs the length of the quad without his trousers. He is sent down. Paul returns to Scone under an alias in 1923. An Annamese student tries to buy one of the Senior Tutor's daughters. Attended in 1926 by Peter Pastmaster.

• *SKINDLES:* Where Philbrick is staying in 1923.

• *SOMERVILLE COLLEGE, WALTON STREET:* Anthony Blanche is 'a byword of iniquity from Cherwell Edge to Somerville'.

• *TOM QUAD: See* CHRISTCHURCH.

• *TRINITY COLLEGE, BROAD STREET:* A few slipper-clad men from Trinity take their Sunday breakfast at the same Broad Street tea shop as Charles Ryder.

• *TURF TAVERN, 'HELL PASSAGE', HOLYWELL STREET:* Pub frequented by Charles and Sebastian in Michaelmas term 1923. They are well known here.

• *THE UNION:* Where, during Eights Week 1923, women are met with 'a wholly distressing Gilbert and and Sullivan badinage'. Where J. Cattermole of Balliol speaks (1921–1924).

• *WALTON STREET:* Where Stubbs has digs in 1926.

• *WELLINGTON SQUARE:* Where, in the 1920s, one might find the lodgings of 'proletarian scholars who scrambled fiercely for facts'.

DF 9, 211, 212; HD 8; BM 7, 6, 112–113; BR 23–25, 28–35, 45, 49, 51, 58, 59, 101, 103, 105, 135, 136, 137, 138, 139, 140–141, 163, 248; US 162, 165; LO 63; GP 69, 183; WS 16, 93, 132

OXFORD UNIVERSITY PRESS

• Scott-King sends his work on Bellorius to the OUP, who are not interested in publishing it.

WS 197

P

P AND O
Peninsular and Orient shipping line.
• On his return from Fez in 1926, Charles Ryder travels by P and O from Tangier.
BR 208

PABLO, JUANITA DEL
Star of Megalopolitan Studios, created in 1936 by Sir Francis Hinsley (q.v.).
LO 24–25

PADFIELD, LIEUTENANT *(b. 1918)*
American Lieutenant, known as 'The Loot', who in 1943 becomes the toast of London society. Attends dinner at the House of Commons, where he meets Guy Crouchback. He attends every society party in 1943 and visits castles in Scotland, politicians, actresses and universities. Visits Broome to watch Sally Sackville-Strutt's daughter play hockey. Becomes a member of Bellamy's. Dines with Ralph Brompton (q.v.). Attends Mr Crouchback's funeral. Meets Virginia in Claridges and tells her that the Crouchback fortune is still intact. Ian Kilbannock suggests that Virginia marry him. Visits Guy in the RAF hospital, bringing with him a copy of *Survival*, a Staffordshire figure of Gladstone and a bunch of chrysanthemums.

Turns up in Bari in 1944, accompanied by Sir Almeric Griffiths (q.v.). Accompanies Guy on the plane flight to see the manoeuvres. Survives the crash. Almeric Griffiths is killed. After the war becomes Ludovic's 'factotum' and finds the Castello Crouchback for him.
US 24, 25, 49, 55, 78–79, 88, 122, 210–211, 222

PAGET, GENERAL
British General.
• On 21 April 1940 Guy Crouchback feels relieved to hear on the wireless that General Paget is at Lillehammer, and all is well in Norway.
MA 170

PALEOLOGUE
Assistant of Wenlock Jakes (q.v.) in Ishmaelia. He finds Jakes difficult to work for. He is a family man he has two wives and 'countless queer-coloured children on whom he lavished his love'.
Sc 82, 86, 90

PALESTINE
Where, in No 64 Jewish Illicit Immigrants' Camp, Scott-King awakens after his escape from Neutralia through the underground. Lockwood is an officer here.
WS 246

PALMERSTON, HENRY, JOHN TEMPLE, 3rd VISCOUNT *(1784–1865)*
British statesman. Foreign Secretary 1830. Prime Minister 1855–1865. Driving force behind victory in the Crimean War. Reknowned for 'gunboat diplomacy'.
• Mr Baldwin (q.v.) sighs for 'the days of Pam and Dizzy'.
• Rex Mottram's friends in 1938 refer to 'my country of Palmerston'.
Sc 172; BR 263

PAMIRS
Mountain range in Tadzhik (USSR).
• Location of Mount Cruttwell, christened by the general of the same name (q.v.).
Sc 43

PANORAMA OF LIFE
See BOOKS

PANOSES, THE DE
Friends of Lord Malton (q.v.) who accompany him on his yacht to Venice in September 1922, but who, because of Lord Marchmain's presence on the yacht, are not invited to the Principesa Fogliere's ball.
BR 55

PANOTROPE
Early form of gramophone player.
• Margot Metroland owns one in 1922.
DF 128

PANRAST, MRS ELEANOR
Mother of Lord Balcairn (q.v.). Attends Archie Schwert's party in 1927. Attends Margot Metroland's party, where her presence scandalizes Lady Throbbing and Mrs Blackwater.
VB 51, 98

PANTELERIA
Island between Sicily and Tunisia.
• Rex Mottram's friends are keen, in 1938, to know why the British did not land on Panteleria.
BR 262

PAOLO AND FRANCESCA
The famous lovers of Italian history, immortalized by Dante in the *Inferno* as well as by Leigh Hunt, d'Annunzio and Tchaikovsky. Francesca was the daughter of Giovanni da Polenta, Count of Ravenna and was given by him in marriage to Giovanni Malatesta of Rimini.
Having fallen in love with Paolo, her brother-in-law, the two were discovered and put to death in 1289.
• Dennis Barlow observes numbers of 'oblivious Paolos and Francescas' emerging from the Lake Island of Innisfree (q.v.), where they have been 'necking'.
LO 67

PAPAL KNIGHTS
See CROUCHBACK, PEREGRINE

PAPPENHACKER
Communist journalist sent to Ishmaelia to report for the *Daily Twopence* in 1937. Corker calls him 'the cleverest man in Fleet Street'. He sometimes hits waiters and is barred from many restaurants. Travels with his typewriter and a lightweight suitcase. Reads Arabic grammar. Takes a toy train everywhere with him, a relic of his college at Winchester. As a boy he had given each part of the mechanism a Greek name. Chairman of the Foreign Press Association in Ishmaelia. Travels to Laku in a two-seater which he has bought from the British Legation. In 1939, now working for the Hearst Press, is told of the arrival of a Polish submarine in Scapa Flow before an American war correspondent.
Sc 31–32, 45, 81, 82, 119; PF 69

PARACHUTING
Guy Crouchback takes a course in parachute training at No 4 training centre in 1943. His instructor tells him that 'on the whole it's a lot safer than steeple-chasing'. When they jump from the plane, Gilpin will not go. Guy jumps and experiences 'a kind of rapture'. However, the rapture soon ends, and when he lands he twists his bad knee.
• Gilbert Pinfold went on a parachute course during the war which resulted in his breaking a leg on his first drop. However, the experience he found 'the most serene and exalted' of his life.
US 97, 102; GP 142

PARAKEET, LORD
Friend of Alastair Trumpington in 1922. Attends his twenty-first birthday party in London. Drives with Alastair to King's Thursday immediately afterwards, quite drunk. Alastair falls out of his car.
Loses £30 to Sir Humphrey Maltravers at cards.
DF 129, 132

PARIS, FRANCE
Paul Pennyfeather charters a special aeroplane here to fly to Marseilles in 1922.
• Margot Metroland carries with her 'the delectable savour of the Champs-Elysées in early June'.
• Adam Fenwick-Symes returns to Eng-

land from Paris where he has been writing his autobiography.
• Walter Outrage returns from a trip to Paris in 1927 on the same ferry as Adam Fenwick-Symes.
• Where 'disgusting dances' are held in the late 1920s.
• Johnny Hoop goes to Paris in the spring of 1928 to study at the studio of a famous painter.
• To Philbrick the whole of Paris reeks of Gracie's English cooking.
• Seth (q.v.) has attended the Paris exhibition. He buys spotted silk pyjamas in the Place Vendôme and has a model of the Eiffel tower which he brought back to Azania.
• According to Fanny Throbbing you never know if the maid at the Lotti will steal your possessions.
• In 1937 William Boot flies to Paris where he catches the Blue Train to Marseilles.
• Father Rothschild looks like one of the gargoyles of Notre Dame.
• Ambrose Silk is in Paris in the twenties, where he knows Jean Cocteau and Gertrude Stein. It is in Paris at that time that he writes and publishes his first book, a study of Montparnasse Negroes.
• Where Virginia Crouchback attends finishing school.
• Charles Ryder and Sebastian Flyte stop at Paris on their way to Venice in 1922. They drive to the Lotti where they bathe and shave, and then have lunch at Foyot's. They then wander around the shops and sit at a café until it is time for their train to leave from the Gare de Lyon.
• Where the Clutterbuck's governess had a friend who married a black American soldier in the Great War.
• In 1924 Charles leaves Oxford and moves to Paris to study in the studio of a painter. He has rooms on the Ile Saint-Louis with a view of the river and Notre Dame. He attends the art school. None of the students ever visit the Louvre.
• In February 1924 Rex Mottram meets Charles Ryder in Paris. Rex offers to take Charles to dinner and suggests Ciro's, but Charles prefers Paillard's, where they go (q.v.).
• In Paris Charles Ryder and his friends frequent two nightclubs – Bricktops and the Bal Negre in the rue Blomet.
• One of the places where Lord Marchmain thinks that he might see Brideshead and his new wife in 1938.
• Angela Lyne, in 1963, owns a panelled seventeenth century apartment in Paris.
DF 189; VB 123, 190; BM 17, 39, 149–150; Sc 45; BR 92, 147, 157, 165, 195, 297; WS 255

PARKER, ARCHBISHOP MATTHEW ***(1504–1575)***
Protestant Archbishop of Canterbury consecrated under Elizabeth I. It was said in Catholic circles that he was consecrated in an inn called the Nags Head.
• In Mr Prendergast's opinion the source of an 'ordinary doubt'.
DF 33

PARKER, MRS
Novelist, under the name Ruth Mountdragon. She is the author of seventeen novels. She is published by Mr Bentley, to whom she is a source of embarrassment. However, her books are greatly enjoyed by Mr Rampole when in prison.
PF 219

PARKS, MR
One of the younger morticians at Whispering Glades (q.v.).
LO 76

PARSEES
Adherents of a Zoroastrian religion, now chiefly found in western India.
• A 'pallid Parsee' is Mr Pinfold's fellow passenger on the flight to Colombo.
GP 144

PARSNIP
English poet of the interwar years. Author of 'Guernica revisited' which is full of 'wonderfully dramatic old chestnuts', and the 'Christopher' sequence. Friend of Ambrose Silk who tells him that he cannot accompany him into becoming 'wholly proletarian'. Believes that this is the only way to become a 'valuable' writer.

Inseparable friend of Pimpernell, with whom his name is alliteratively linked. The Parsnip-Pimpernell controversy is a point of great discussion among Poppet Green's friends. The point is that although the two are inseparable, Parsnip works best in England, and Pimpernell in America.

• In 1939 moves to America. Writes for *Survival*. Becomes Professor of Dramatic Poetry at the University of Minneapolis.

• Flies to London in 1963 for a party at the Ritz in honour of Ambrose Silk.

• In the New Britain he attends the Department of Euthanasia daily, but is always pushed to the back of the crowd. Twice he succeeds in getting in, but both times he runs off. Finally, however, his nerve does not fail him and he passes into the gas chamber.

PF 35, 39; US 124; WS 253; GP 217

PARSONS

Barman at Bellamy's in 1939 and 1941.

OG 11

PARTIES

Alastair Trumpington's twenty-first party in 1922 is attended by Lord Parakeet. They all become very drunk, and on the way to King's Thursday Trumpington falls out of Parakeet's car.

• Agatha Runcible thinks Mrs Ape's evangelical singing as she is seasick on the cross-channel ferry, 'just like one's first parties . . . being sick with other people singing'.

• Johnny Hoop throws a Savage Party at Edward Throbbing's house. The Bright Young People dress as savages. Photographers are present as are Adam Fenwick-Symes and Nina Blount who get 'sentimental'. Afterwards they go on to Lottie Crump's and then to No 10 Downing Street.

• Only Margot Metroland is able to invite both the Old Guard and the Bright Young People to a party and carry it off.

• Adam Fenwick-Symes, Nina Blount, Ginger and the Bright Young People attend a party on an airship, the first of its kind, in the 'degraded suburb' where it is moored. It is only one of the parties which they attend. Adam is rather bored by the succession of parties; They are held in all sorts of locations from nightclubs to windmills, studios to swimming baths. There are also parties in Scotland and at Oxford.

• Basil Seal's parties are inevitably wild. At Oxford his luncheon parties last well into the evening and his dinner parties become riots.

• He, Peter Pastmaster and Alastair Trumpington, have a five day party after a Conservative ball in 1931.

• Lady Seal gives four or five dinner parties a year, which are strictly formal.

• Margot Metroland's dinner parties are devised on the spur of the moment when she is too tired to go out, and consist of twenty people for dinner, whom she insists 'chuck' their prior engagements.

• Lord Copper's banquets are always a little too grand. The food and drink is 'copious, very bad and very expensive'.

• Charles Ryder, in early March 1922, before he meets Sebastian Flyte, has college intellectuals to his rooms for mulled claret.

• Undergraduate dinner parties at Oxford in the 1920s often end with the guests being sick in the rooms.

• Sebastian Flyte's luncheon party at Christ Church in March 1922 opens a new era in Charles Ryder's life. It is full of old Etonians including Anthony Blanche who recites *The Wasteland* through a megaphone from Sebastian's balcony. They eat plovers' eggs and lobster.

• Mr Ryder, in his youth, used to go on reading parties to the mountains.

• Rex Mottram gives a 'squalid' wedding reception at the Savoy in June 1924, and a party before the wedding to see the presents.

• Charles Ryder meets Anthony Blanche and Boy Mulcaster at a party in a house in Regent's Park in May 1926, given in honour of the Blackbirds. Florence Mills is persuaded to sing.

• In 1936 Rex Mottram starts to give lavish parties at Brideshead at which he and his friends make bets on everything they can think of, while the girls play backgammon and gossip and the room is filled with the smell of cigar smoke, which lingers to the next day.

• In 1936 Margot Metroland gives a luncheon party for Charles Ryder's return to England.

• In 1938 Fanny Rosscommon gives a luncheon party in honour of Brideshead's engagement.

• Before the war Arthur Box-Bender often entertains dinner parties of eight or ten at his house in Lowndes Square. The conversation is humdrum.

• The dinner given by the Halberdiers is a most formal affair. The table is struck by the mess-president with an ivory hammer and they dine amidst the regimental silver depicting palm trees and savages.

• The Kilbannocks hold a party in 1940, at which Air Marshal Beech recites his rhyme about Elinor Glyn.

• Everard Spruce has a party on 29 October 1943 attended by Guy Crouchback, Ian Kilbannock, Lieutenant Padfield and Ludovic. The guests drink a concoction of South African sherry mixed with 'Olde Falstaffe Gin', apart from Ludovic to whom Frankie gives some whisky.

• In June 1951 Tommy Blackhouse organizes a reunion party for X Commando at Bellamy's. It is attended by Bertie, Guy, and eleven others.

• On the same evening Arthur Box-Bender throws a party in a hotel for his daughter's eighteenth birthday.

• Bella Fleace gives a party in 1932 for which she forgets to send out the invitations. She has heard tell of parties starting very late, but cannot understand why her guests should not have arrived on time.

• Celia Ryder throws a cocktail party on board ship when she and Charles return to England in 1936. There is a huge ice swan filled with caviar, a present from the chief purser.

• Mr Plant throws a tea-party on the Sunday before sending-in day at the Royal Academy. He has 'Academy cake', supplied by a grocer in Praed Street and 'Academy sandwiches' and his guests eat off a Worcester tea service.

• Basil Seal and Peter Pastmaster attend a banquet at the Ritz thrown by Geoffrey Bentley to honour the sixtieth birthday of Ambrose Silk. Parsnip and Pimpernell are present, as are many other distinguished men of letters.

• Barbara Seal tells her father that the party to which she is going in 1963 is a new kind of party invented by the Americans, called a 'happening': 'Nothing is arranged beforehand. Things just happen. Tonight they cut off a girl's clothes with nail scissors and then painted her green'.

DF 129; VB 21, 53, 100, 122; BM 71, 76, 90, 113; HD 40, 48; Sc 215; BR 31, 32, 62, 192, 195, 228–236, 246, 254, 283; MA 29, 54, 75; US 43, 50, 237; WS 81, 84, 116, 252, 260

PARTISANS

To the British in Begoy in 1944 the partisans are 'quite a revelation'. They are mostly 'ragged, swaggering girls in battle-dress' who have hand grenades strung around them in belts. They walk through the streets singing patriotic songs.

• In Neutralia in 1946 there are bands of partisans living in the hills. In Bellorius' time, Scott-King reflects, they would have called them brigands. They murder the Chinese and the Swiss delegates.

US 165, 178; WS 225, 232

PARTRIDGE

One of the intellectual undergraduates who form Charles Ryder's friends during his first term at Oxford.

BR 32

PASADENA, CALIFORNIA, USA

City near Los Angeles.

• When there is an outbreak of food poisoning here the ice box at the Happier Hunting Ground is packed out and the furnaces are kept going late into the night.

Home of the literary gentleman who Mr Joyboy meets at the Knife and Fork club dinner, and to whom he shows Dennis Barlow's poems.

LO 50, 103

PASTMASTER, PETER BESTE-CHETWYNDE, LORD *(b. 1906)*
Son of Margot Metroland (q.v.). Pupil at Llanabba School (1922). Taught the organ by Paul Pennyfeather (to get out of gym). Plays 'Pop Goes the Weasel' on the organ. Makes rather good cocktails, aged sixteen. At this age his mother thinks him 'rather lovely in a coltish sort of way'.

Drinks brandy and soda. His favourite books are *The Wind in the Willows* and Havelock Ellis (q.v.). Is pleased that Margot and Paul are to be married. Comes up from Llanabba for the wedding. Is very vain in his first morning coat.

Succeeds his uncle as Earl of Pastmaster (1922). Holidays with his mother in Corfu. Goes up to Scone College Oxford 1924. Friend of Basil Seal and Ambrose Silk at Oxford.

In 1939 joins 'a very secret corps' trained to fight in the arctic. His training involves winter sports in the Alps. Takes Molly Meadowes to the cinema in Jermyn Street in 1940 (in uniform). At this time he is looking for a wife. He and Molly are married in London and there is a reception at Lady Granchester's.

• In later life lives at King's Thursday. Has a daughter who lends his shirts to Charles Allbright. In 1962 attends, with Basil, the banquet held at the Ritz for Ambrose Silk's birthday. By this time he is 'stout, rubicund, richly dressed' and looks over sixty. They visit his mother.
DF 25, 39, 50, 88, 117, 118, 125, 127, 128, 154, 186, 187, 213, 214; VB 99; BM 71; PF 35, 50, 77, 152–158; WS 251, 252, 253, 258

PASTMASTER, ROBERT BESTE-CHETWYNDE, EARL OF *(d. 1922)*
Lord Pastmaster directly before his nephew Peter. A bachelor, he has no sons of his own. The title was created in the 1550s. The family seat is King's Thursday (q.v.) and the motto 'Teneat Beste-Chetwynde'.
DF 116–118, 135, 186

PAT
Girlfriend of Frank de Souza who accompanies him to the theatre and the Café Royal on 30 December 1939.
MA 79–80

PATAGONIAN INDIANS
Subject of one of John Boot's travel books, *Waste of Time*. Most of the people who lunch with Margot Metroland are able to remember the names of three or four of them.
Sc 5

PATMORE, COVENTRY *(1823–1896)*
English poet. Author of 'The Angel in the House' (1863), which had tremendous success with the Victorian public. Converted to Catholicism 1864.
• Gervase Crouchback (m. 1889) reads aloud to his bride on their honeymoon from the works of Patmore.
MA 9

PATON, SIR JOSEPH, NOEL *(1821–1901)*
Scottish painter, famous for his allegorical, historical and fairy subjects. See his 'Oberon and Titania' (National Gallery of Scotland).
• The art gallery at Cape Town has two 'remarkable' Patons, seen by Guy Crouchback on his stop there en route to Crete in 1941. He explains to Ivor Claire that the beauty of Paton is that he knew nothing of art.
OG 108

PAUL
Friend of Ambrose Silk who tries to enter a monastery.
PF 43

PAULING, MR
Official at the Ministry of Information in 1939 dealing with cases like that of the Archimandrite Antonios.
PF 67, 68

PAVLOVA, ANNA *(1885–1931)*
Russian ballerina. Formed her own company 1909.

• Ruby's guests in 1943 ask her to tell them her memories of Pavlova.
US 80

PEABURY, LADY
Owner of Much Malcock House, Much Malcock (q.v.), opposite Mr Metcalfe. Thinks that Mrs Hornbeam (q.v.) does not pull her weight at the WI. Is brought up to believe that it is sinful to read a novel before luncheon. Is acknowledged as the leader in the village.
WS 45, 50–61

PEACE BALLOT
Ballot held in 1935 in which ten and a half million voters out of eleven and a half million declared their faith in the League of Nations and economic sanctions.
• At the time of the Peace Ballot Mrs Hornbeam canvasses every cottage around the village of Much Malcock by bicycle.
WS 46

PEACE-PLEDGE
The Peace-Pledge Union was formed in 1937 in an attempt to gain mass support to prevent war.
• One of the topics discussed by Rex Mottram's vociferous house-guests at Brideshead in 1938.
BR 280

PEACHUM, POLLY
Character from *The Beggars Opera* by John Gay.
• Charles Ryder possesses a porcelain figurine of her in his first term at Oxford.
BR 29

PEACOCK
Master of Charles Ryder's in the Upper Fifth at Lancing in 1919. The boys doubt whether he is 'raggable'.
WS 292

PEACOCKS
There are peacocks in Mrs Stitch's garden in Alexandria.
• The flock of peacocks at Mountjoy are found mysteriously slaughtered in the first few days of summer.
LOG 239; GP 179

PEINFELD
According to Gilbert Pinfold's voices, the name by which he was originally known.
GP 70

PEKING, CHINA
Where Sir Samson Courteney had been third secretary at the outset of his career.
BM 48

PELECCI, GIUSEPPE
Proprietor of the Garibaldi restaurant at Southsand (q.v.) where he has come to avoid military service. Part time Fascist spy. Is bored by politics and frightened by wars. Is arrested on the day Italy declares war (10 June 1940) and sent to Canada. Drowns when his ship is sunk in mid-Atlantic.
MA 107, 119, 149; OG 40

PEMBROKESHIRE, WALES
Homeland of the grandmother of one of the sixth-formers at Llanabba. To Dr Fagan it is hardly the same as the rest of Wales, 'quite a different matter'.
DF 66

PEN CLUB
Representatives of the Pen Club are among those present at the banquet held in honour of Ambrose Silk at the Ritz in 1963.
WS 253

PEN NAMES
See Hucklebury SQUIB, Bartholomew GRASS, Tom BAREBONES-ABRAHAM, and Ruth MOUNTDRAGON.

PENDLE-GARTHWAITE, MR AND MRS
Friends of the Flytes who give Julia an early morning tea set from Goode's as a wedding present.
BR 188

PENELOPE
Mythical beauty of Greek legend. Daughter of Icarus of Sparta. Ulysees won her hand in marriage. During his absence at the Trojan war she was courted by a great

many suitors whom she delayed by cunning, in an attempt to gain time until her husband returned.

• Julia Flyte, in making her choice of husband, is certainly no Penelope, inclined to 'the indolent, cat-and-mouse pastimes of the hearth-rug'.
BR 175

PENKIRK, SCOTLAND
Lowland valley twenty miles from Edinburgh, where the Halberdiers are posted in April 1940. At the head of the valley is a small Victorian castle, where they are billeted.
MA 161

PENINSULAR WAR *(1807–1812)*
Conflict between the French under Napoleon and the Spanish, Portuguese and British under Sir John Moore and Wellington (q.v.).

• The setting for the *Journals of Colonel Jasper Cumberland* (q.v.).
WS 95

PENNYFEATHER, PAUL *(b. 1901)*
Orphan. Both his parents died in India. Lives with his guardian in Onslow Square. Educated at 'a small public school of ecclesiastical temper on the South Downs' (Lancing).

Reads for the Church at Scone College, Oxford (1919–1922). Sent down for running without his trousers the length of the quad; an act perpetrated by the Bollinger Club. Finds a job as a schoolmaster at Llanabba School (q.v.). Teaches Peter Beste-Chetwynde the organ. Is sent £20 by Alastair Trumpington, which he accepts. Organizes the sports day. Falls in love with Margot Beste-Chetwynde.

Visits King's Thursday with Peter. Is persuaded by Margot to stay at King's Thursday. Leaves Llanabba. Takes a job with Margot. Asks Margot to marry him. She accepts and 'makes sure' that it is the right thing to do, in bed with him that evening. Has a personal allowance from Margot of two thousand a year.

Flies to Marseilles to help Margot's girls. Compares Marseilles to a scene from the Terror. Is accosted by a negro sailor. His hat is taken by a prostitute. Is laughed at in the street. Flees to his hotel. Goes to Chez Alice and helps the girls by going to the consulates and police bureaux.

Returns to London: is arrested. Tried at the Old Bailey for 'this most infamous of crimes'. Sent to prison at Blackstone Gaol. Meets Philbrick there. Meets Sir Wilfred Lucas-Dockery. Enjoys solitary confinement and asks to extend his period. Takes part in one of the Lucas-Dockery experiments.

Transferred to Egdon Heath. Meets Grimes there. Begins to receive luxuries – caviare, foie gras, roses, sherry, books. Visited by Margot. Is not pained by the fact that she is marrying Maltravers. Removed to a nursing home for an appendectomy. Signs his will. Arrives at Cliff Place. Is declared to be dead.

Travels to Margot's villa on Corfu on her yacht. Otto Silenus joins him there. Returns to Scone under a different name, one year after leaving it. Reads for the church. Makes friends with Stubbs. Meets Philbrick in the High Street. Meets Peter Pastmaster in 1926, during his last year at Scone.
DF 11–14, 15, 16, 17, 45, 47, 98, 105, 115, 122, 123, 150, 155, 210

PEPPERMINT
See HORSES

PERDITA
Friend of Kerstie Kilbannock who takes Everard Spruce to see Virginia Crouchback.
US 189

PERFUME
Margot Metroland's perfume is 'almost unobtainable'.

• Lottie Crump wears 'Nuit de Noel'.

• Aimee Thanatogenos wears 'Jungle Venom'.

• Lady Amelia wears lavender water.
DF 00; VB 61; LO 88; WS 23

PERUVIANS
The Peruvian delegate at the Bellorius

conference in Neutralia is only a student who happened to be in the country at the time.
WS 226

PETERBOROUGH
Town in which Apthorpe claims to have an aunt – whom he later admits to have been an invention.
MA 96

PETERFIELD, DOCTOR
Friend of Toby Cruttwell (q.v.) who did 'something' to Alf Larrigan which ensured that he would never again have 'no use for girls'.
DF 53

PETITIONS
Paul Pennyfeather petitions Sir Wilfred Lucas Dockery, asking to be allowed to remain in solitary confinement.
• Gilbert Pinfold's voices petition the captain of the *Caliban*, asking him to ban Pinfold from his table.
DF; GP 102

PETS
Jack Bannister has a tame cheetah.
• Frau Dressler has a three-legged dog; her guests have baboons, gorillas and cheetahs.
• For one 'disasterous month' in the 1930s, Sonia Trumpington has a pet kangaroo called Molly.
• Cedric Lyne once had a pet octopus, in a tank carved with dolphins and covered in silver leaf.
• Julia Flyte has a pekinese and a tortoise – with her initials in diamonds embedded in its shell – which she is given by Rex Mottram for Christmas 1923, and which buries itself in the garden. Before his demise the tortoise is teased by the peke.
• Dennis Barlow works at The Happier Hunting Ground, the pet cemetery in Los Angeles. At full blast its ovens are able to dispose of six dogs, a cat and a barbary goat in an hour and twenty minutes. Its proprietor, Mr Shultz, complains that in the 1940s: 'there ain't the demand for fancy stuff . . . Folks pretend to love their pets, talk to them like they was children, along comes a citizen with a new auto, floods of tears, and then it's "Is a headstone really socially essential, Mr Shultz?"'
• Mrs Heinkel has a Sealyham.
• Mrs Joyboy has a parrot called Sambo.
• Gervase Kent-Cumberland has a pony.
Sc 99, 109; PF 44, 164; BR 129, 159, 162; LO 19, 50, 82, 91; WS 89
(*See* DOGS)

PHILBRICK
Mysterious butler to Dr Fagan at Llanabba School (q.v.). Peter Beste-Chetwynde notices something odd about him and does not think that he is a butler.

Tells Brigg that before the Great War he used to have 'bushels of diamonds and emeralds . . . and that he used to eat off gold plate'. The boys think that he is an exiled Russian prince. He himself has three stories about who he is:

1 Tells Paul Pennyfeather that he is 'Sir Solomon Philbrick alias "Solly Philbrick of the Lamb and Flag, Camberwell Green"' and that you only have to say his name anywhere south of Waterloo Bridge to see what fame is. He is not really a knight, son of 'Chick' Philbrick, the boxer from Lambeth who put him into the sporting world as a sponge holder at Lambeth Stadium on Saturday nights. Meets Toby Cruttwell (q.v.), with whom he works for five years as a thief. In 1913 he buys the Lamb and Flag on Camberwell Green.

During the war his wife runs the pub. She dies about 1919 and he becomes restless. One evening he meets Jimmy Drage and has a bet with him that he can successfully kidnap Lord Tangent (q.v.), which explains his presence at Llanabba.

2 Tells Mr Prendergast that he is Sir Solomon Philbrick, the ship owner with a large house in Carlton House Terrace where he used to live with an actress who was not his wife. One evening the actress and he gave a party and they played baccarat. Philbrick won everything from a Portuguese count, who eventually bet an enormous diamond against Philbrick's largest assets.

Philbrick won and returned the emerald to the count, who was insulted and challenged him to a duel in which Philbrick shot the count dead. He was changed by the deed, banished the actress from his house, and confessed to a priest who sent him to be a butler for three years as a penance.
3 To Grimes he tells the following story: His father had been eccentric and made his fortune out of diamond mines. The two children were Philbrick and a daughter called Gracie. Philbrick was his favourite. At the age of eight, Philbrick had a sonnet printed in the local paper and could recite from Shakespeare; Gracie was neglected. Went to Cambridge and afterwards settled in London, where he wrote novels. His father died and left him everything. Moved into a bigger house in Cheyne Walk, where he was haunted by the ghost of his impoverished sister who he then contacted through a medium. She told him that to make reparation for the wrong he has done her he must work as a servant for a year and write a book about it to help the plight of servants.

Detectives arrive at Llanabba with a warrant for his arrest for being a confidence trickster. There are five charges against him in different parts of the country for cashing bad cheques for huge amounts. He has already fled to Holyhead.

Paul sees him at the next table at the Maison Basque restaurant in Mayfair, and tells him he is living at Batts and that if he does not look out, Paul himself will be arrested for his involvement with the Latin American Entertainment Co.

Paul next meets him at Blackstone Gaol where he is an inmate and now calls himself Sir Solomon Lucas-Dockery.

Paul meets him in the High Street at Oxford in 1923, in a chauffeur-driven, open-top Rolls Royce, which pulls out of Oriel Street.
DF 25, 31, 40, 51–58, 64, 77, 78, 84, 90–94, 100, 112, 141, 147, 162, 176, 212

PHILBRICK, CHICK
The father of Philbrick (q.v.), according to one of his stories. Boxer at Lambeth Stadium before the Great War. A 'useful little boxer . . . not first class, on account of his drinking so much and being short in the arm'. Twice 'jugged' for beating up Philbrick's mother.
DF 52

PHILBRICK, GRACIE
The sister of Philbrick (q.v.), according to one of his stories. Neglected by her father as a child, she lived like Cinderella with the servants. Runs off with a man in the motor trade who, when he realizes that her father has not left her any money, leaves her. Goes into service as a cook and dies a year later. Her ghost comes back to haunt Philbrick with the smells of cooking and, after he contacts her through a medium, tells him that he will have to go into service for a year to make up for the wrong he has done her.
DF 92–93

PHILLIPS, MISS
Fellow passenger of the correspondent on board the *SS Glory of Greece*; 'Wears a yachting cap and is a bitch'.
WS 17

PHILOCTETES
Greek hero and friend of Hercules who joined the expedition against Troy. By accident he wounded himself with one of Hercules' poisoned arrows, which were in his possession, and the smell from his wound so offended the warriors that they had him carried to the island of Lemnos where he was left. The Greeks, however, realizing that they needed the arrows to capture Troy, persuaded him to rejoin the army and he was cured by Machaon.
• Guy Crouchback, unable to gain himself a front line command on Crete, feels 'set apart from his fellows by an old festering wound; Philoctetes without his bow'.
OG 210

PHILPOTTS, BISHOP HENRY
(1778–1869)
Bishop of Exeter; Fellow of Magdalen,

1795; Dean of Chester, 1828. A keen Tory and High Churchman.
• One of the characters in *A Brand from the Burning* (q.v.), who tells Adam Fenwick-Symes all about the 'shooting' going on at Doubting Hall.
VB 141–142

PHIPPS, FATHER
Catholic priest at Brideshead in 1923: 'A bland, bun-faced man with an interest in county cricket'. Is sorry not to have seen Tennyson make fifty-eight.
BR 82

PHOTOGRAPHS
Basil Seal and Sonia Trumpington pass an evening looking at old photographs in 1962.
WS 278

PHYSICAL TRAINING
The physical training instructor of the Halberdiers is 'a sleek young man with pomaded hair, a big behind and unnaturally glittering eyes'.
• There is a physical training congress in Neutralia at the same time as the Bellorius Conference. Irma Sveningen attends.
MA 51; WS 224

PICABIA, FRANCIS *(1879–1953)*
French painter and leading light of the Dadaist movement which, with Marcel Duchamp, he introduced to America in 1915. See his 'Parade Amoreuse' (1917).
• According to Charles Ryder, half of the students on his Fine Art course in Paris in 1924 are 'out to make a popular splash like Picabia'.
BR 147

PICASSO, PABLO *(1881–1973)*
Spanish painter; important influence on twentieth-century art, particularly in France. Founder, with Braque, of Cubism (1906). See his 'Demoiselles d'Avignon' (1906), 'Three Dancers' (1925), and 'Guernica' (1937).
• To Guy Crouchback, Picasso's works are akin to the drawings of primitive cavemen.
• Gilbert Pinfold abhors Picasso.
• The walls of institutions in the New Britain are hung with reproductions of paintings by Picasso.
• Mr Plant tells John that it is better for people to admire his fake Lelys than to 'make themselves dizzy by goggling at genuine Picassos'.
OG 56; GP 14, 183, 196; WS 116

PICTURES
'The Aphrodite of Melos', by Poppet Green (with a moustache added by Basil Seal).
• 'The Fountain at Brideshead, in the manner of Piranesi', by Charles Ryder (1923).
• 'Sunflowers', by Van Gogh. Hung in reproduction by Charles Ryder in his rooms at Oxford; taken down after his first term.
• 'Three Medallions on the wall of the office at Brideshead', by Charles Ryder (1923).
• Drawings by Daumier; in Sebastian Flyte's rooms at Oxford.
• A Religious Oleograph; in Sebastian and Kurt's house in Fez.
• Four small oils of Marchmain House, by Charles Ryder (1926).
• 'Julia Flyte'; numerous versions by Charles Ryder.
• 'The Awakened Conscience', by William Holman Hunt (1800); to which Charles Ryder compares Julia Flyte's realization of her sin.
• 'The Halberdiers in Square in the Desert', in the Halberdiers' mess, above the fireplace.
• 'Painting of a Fairy Glad', used on a calendar in 1940 and much admired by Ritchie-Hook.
• 'A Wintry Seascape', by an artist with a huge and unintelligible signature. Hangs above the fireplace in the hall at Kut-al-Imara.
• French Impressionists; Angela Lyne's father has a large collection.
• A French eighteenth-century work in the manner of Boucher; Clara.
• A French seventeenth-century work in the manner of Claude; Clara.
• Reproductions after Picasso and Leger; hung on the walls of institutions in the New Britain.

• 'Abraham Lincoln in his box at the Theatre', by Bella Fleace's brother; hangs at Fleacetown.
• 'Paintings of Famous Assassinations', by Bella Fleace's brother; hang at Fleacetown.
• 'Portrait of Jasper Cumberland'; sits in a case of miniatures in the drawing-room at Tomb.
• Two portraits by Romney and one by Hoppner, sold by Gervase Kent-Cumberland.
• 'A Balloon Ascent in Manchester' in the manner of Frith, Mr Plant's first exhibited work.
• 'The Neglected Cue' (1938); Mr Plant's second last picture. It is of the dressing-room of an actress during a party after her first night. Her old parents, dressed in country garb, stand nervously at the open door, while her protector pours her a glass of champagne. It is bought by Julia Stitch for 500 guineas.
• 'Again?'; Mr Plant's last picture, left unfinished at his death. It represents a one-armed veteran of the Great War musing over a German helmet.
• Arundel Prints; hung in Mr Plant's house.
• An engraving of the Royal Yacht Squadron, with a key; owned by Colonel Blount.
• Copies after Lely; by Mr Plant. Sold by Goodchild and Godley.
• Negresses by Gauguin; collected by Sir Lionel Sterne.
• 'Agag before Samuel' (1935) by Mr Plant; bought for 750 guineas.
• 'Vague Assemblages of Picnic Litter'; shown by the Mansard Gallery in the early twenties.
• An engraving after Batty Langley of 'A composed Hermitage in the Chinese Taste' (1767); it shows a pavilion decorated with oriental forms and balconies. The cornices have the line of a pagoda and the roof has an onion cupola. In the foreground a group of Turkish soldiers are performing the bastinado, alongside a camel and a mandarin with a bird in a cage. Roger Simmonds has a collection of such works.
• Prints by Bartolozzi; hung by the landlord in the Simmonds' house in Victoria Square.
• Soviet Posters; inspires Seth in his propaganda for birth control.

PIE WIE INDIANS
Natives of the Upper Orinoco. Dr Messinger is the only white man to have visited them and come back alive. From them he learns where to look for 'The City'. He becomes a blood-brother with one of them. They call 'The City' by a number of different names, including the same name as that of an aromatic jam they make. Tony and Dr Messinger use them as guides, but are abandoned by them when they ask them to be taken to the Macushi ('Pie Wie no go with macushi').
HD 159

PIGGE
Special correspondent in Ishmaelia. Friend of Corker (q.v.). Eternal pessimist. Despondent at the lack of hard news.
Sc 81, 85–6

PIGS
Cordelia Flyte has a pig called Francis Xavier which gets a special mention at the Brideshead Show.
BR 87

PIGSTANTON
Town near Hetton. Home of the Pigstanton hunt (q.v.).
HD 24

PILBURY, GLOUCESTERSHIRE
Village near Much Malcock in the Cotswolds. One can always see Pilbury steeple from Much Malcock when rain is on the way.
WS 44

PILGRIMAGE OF GRACE
Mr Goodall believes that the Poles, Hungarians, Austrians, Bavarians, and Italians will rise up, and embark on a crusade 'to redeem the times'.
OG 40

PILGRIM'S WAY
Julia Flyte recites an ancient pious rhyme

passed down since the days of pack-horses on the Pilgrims' Way.
BR 278

PIMPERNELL
Inter-war poet who with his inseparable companion, Parsnip, is a subject of great interest to Poppet Green and her circle. It is generally agreed that his work is better suited to America than Britain. Ambrose Silk defines his own attitude in an article in *Ivory Tower* entitled 'The Minstrel Boys'. Moves to America during the war. Is present at the banquet held for Ambrose Silk in 1963. Professor of poetic drama at the University of St Paul. One of the first people to seek voluntary euthanasia in the New Britain.
PF 35; WS 253; CP 217

PINDAR ***(c. 522–440 BC)***
Greek lyric poet from Boeotia. *See* his *Epinikia*.
• Charles Ryder's cousin Jasper has the air of someone who thinks that he may not have quite 'done himself full justice on the subject of Pindar's Orphism'.
BR 41

PINFOLD, GILBERT ***(b. 1903)***
English novelist. Author of a dozen books. He is translated into many languages and sells well in America. Sees his books as objects of craftsmanship. He is not vain about his accomplishment. In his childhood he had been 'affectionate, high-spirited and busy', and in his youth 'dissipated and despairing'. As a boy he was extremely sensitive to ridicule. In his youth he sought out nightclubs where there was a bar away from the music. At Oxford he sang disgusting songs outside the Dean of Balliol's rooms.

At the age of twenty-five he frequented the company of a number of bright, cruel girls, with one of whom he is in love. In manhood he had become 'sturdy and prosperous'. Lives at Lychpole. His wife is some years younger than him. He is devoted to her and has a number of healthy children. In his youth he travelled widely. Has never been 'a strenuous philanderer'. When abroad patronizes brothels as a young man. Generally he is faithful and romantic. In 1929 was in Egypt.

Served as a soldier in WWII. Takes a parachute course and breaks his leg. Has never voted in a parliamentary election. His political views are of a sort of Toryism that is not found in any of the parties.

Has a penchant for nicknames. Sceptical about the Box. Is a Roman Catholic, having been received into the church as a young man. In his religion he prefers the least well-attended Mass. Member of Bellamy's Club. Friend of Roger Stillingfleet, Cedric Thorne and James Lance.

Thinks at the age of fifty that he is becoming a bore. Hates Picasso, jazz, plastics and sunbathing. He faces the world with a thick skin. By his late forties he has become physically lazy and corpulent. Suffers from various illnesses (arthritis, gout, rheumatism and fibrositis). Sleeps badly. Takes chloral and bromide as a sleeping draught. Records an interview for the BBC. Sails on the *SS Caliban* to Ceylon. Is a good sailor. Has only been seasick once, during the war.

He is 'neither beautiful nor athletic'. Clutton Cornforth declares that his novels seldom vary and are either tedious or blasphemous or both. Member of the London Library. Speaks clumsy French.

Tells Glover that he is not a Fascist. Is often the object of adolescent crushes. Has no fortune apart from a few fields, a few pictures and books and his own copyrights. By adding a dose of crème de menthe and a new sleeping draught to his normal chloral and bromide, with gin, wine and brandy he renders himself clumsy and suffers a series of hallucinations (*see* HALLUCINATIONS).

Leaves the *Caliban* at Port Said. Is given a lift by Murdoch to Cairo. Flies to Colombo. Has never been to Ceylon before. Writes to his wife. Believes that he may be possessed. Has three suits made in Colombo. Returns to London. His voices return. Gives up the choral. His voices depart. Sits down to write *The Ordeal of Gilbert Pinfold*.
GP 9, 10, 11, 13, 14, 15, 16, 17, 20, 27,

35, 46, 62, 69, 104, 105, 109, 111, 115, 130, 132, 140, 142, 146, 155

PINFOLD, MRS *(b. 1871)*
Mother of Gilbert Pinfold. Widowed. Lives in a pretty little house in Kew. Is not well off. Gilbert's wife is happier in her company than her own son. Her housekeeper is Mrs Yercombe.
GP 30–31

PIPES
Ludovic wonders whether if he smoked a pipe his habit of simply sitting thinking might seem more normal.
• John Verney smokes a pipe.
US 93; GP 172

PIPING DAYS OF PEACE
Dr Akonanga expects that Virginia Crouchback would call the days before the war 'the piping days of peace'.
US 84

PIRANESI, GIAMBATTISTA *(1720–1778)*
Italian architect and engraver. Famous for his views of Rome and fanciful dungeon scenes.
• Charles Ryder draws the fountain at Brideshead in the manner of Piranesi, in 1923.
BR 79

PITT, WILLIAM *(1759–1806)*
British statesman. Chancellor of the Exchequer 1782; Prime Minister 1784. Led England through the first years of the Napoleonic wars.
• Lady Circumference imagines the ghost of Pitt on the stairs at Anchorage House (q.v.) in 1927.
• Tony Last remembers history lessons at his prep school, and the story of Pitt saying 'roll up the map – you will not need it again for how many years', as Doctor Messinger and he advance, mapless into the Brazilian jungle.
VB 126; HD 177

PLASTIC
Detested by Gilbert Pinfold.
GP 14

PLASTIC, MILES
Orphan. Product of the state orphanages of New Britain. Inmate of Mountjoy, where he has been incarcerated for arson. He has a good figure and belongs to a privileged class in the new society. He is the Modern Man. Serves in the Air Force.

Burns down an Air Force station. Is promoted to sub-official at the Ministry of Welfare. This means that he is responsible for opening the doors of the euthanasia department at ten o'clock every day.

Sweeps the waiting room, makes the tea and empties the waste paper basket. Falls in love with Clara. Makes love to her. Is so upset that Clara has had the Clara Operation that he burns down Mountjoy. Is married to Miss Flower.
GP 179, 182, 183, 186, 196, 203, 204, 215, 221

PLANT, ANDREW
Uncle of John Plant (q.v.), his brother's son, who writes to tell him of his father's death. John meets him on his return to London.
WS 108, 125

PLANT, JOHN *(b. 1904)*
Novelist. Writer of crime fiction. His titles include *Murder at Mountrichard Castle*, *Vengeance at the Vatican*, *Death in the Dukeries*, and *The Frightened Footman*. Sells each book for £900. Lives modestly on his royalties.

At prep school says that his father (q.v.) is a naval officer (when in fact he is an artist).

At Oxford (1922–1925) with Roger Simmonds, with whom he edits an undergraduate magazine. Takes a second in Mods and a first in Greats. Runs into debt at University, living the life of a dandy. Becomes a writer in 1925, at the age of twenty-one. Leaves his father's house in 1933. Finds Fez the best place to write, in a small hotel just outside the walls. Learns of his father's death in 1938. Returns to London having not finished his book.

Inherits £2000 and his father's house in St John's Wood. Moves to his club. Visits his publishers. Has a number of hats (q.v.). Asks Roger Simmonds' advice on buying a house.

Meets Thurston, who turns out to be Arthur Atwater (q.v.), the man who killed his father.

Meets Mr Hardcastle (q.v.). Sells him his father's house for £2500. Has a plan to settle in the country. Is keen on domestic architecture. Falls in love with Lucy Simmonds. Takes the Simmonds to lunch at the Ritz. Meets Lucy's cousin Julia (q.v.) who has a crush on him. She guesses that he is in love with Lucy. Takes rooms in Ebury Street.

Becomes a friend of Lucy, and takes her to see a house which he might buy below the Berkshire Downs. They spend the night with relatives of hers near Abingdon.

Buys a house in the country which, during the war is filled with pregnant women and gradually falls to pieces. He never spends a night there. During the war becomes a soldier and often meets Atwater.

WS 106–10, 120–24, 125, 132, 140, 154, 179, 191

PLANT, MR ***(d. 1938)***

Father of John Plant (q.v.). Artist. His grandfather was a Canon of Christ Church and his father in the Bengal Civil Service.

Lives in St John's Wood. His house is decorated like the house of an unfashionable artist of the 1880s, with Morris tapestry curtains and chair covers, Dutch tiles in the fireplace, Levantine rugs on the floors and on the walls, with their Morris paper, Arundel prints, majolica dishes and photographs of old masters. The furniture is of German oak, rosewood, mahogany, and Spanish walnut.

He has a manservant and a housekeeper, the Jellabies (q.v.) about whom he is untiringly scathing.

He is an aetheist purely to be able to express a belief contrary to other people. This he does in all things, from his late-found defence of the Jews to his equally late belief in a Jesuit conspiracy.

Dresses in what he considers painters' garb of the eighteen nineties – poncho capes, check suits, sombrero hats and stock ties.

Believes himself to be the last survivor of his class. Says that in the 1930s there are only three classes in England 'politicians, tradesmen and slaves'.

There is a caricature of him by Max Beerbohm, uttering his famous phrase 'I am a Dodo'. His mind is 'naturally hierarchic'. Tells his son that 'anyone can buy a don' for a good review.

In his work he makes many complicated studies for each picture and paints from left to right across the canvas. For him English painting is in the tradition of Frith, Millais and Winterhalter.

Sells works to Sir Lionel Sterne and Julia Stitch. Paints fakes for Goodchild and Godley.

Once a year throws Academy parties with a special cake from Praed Street and a Worcester tea service.

Having often expressed the view that all motorists should be permanently locked up, he is killed in 1938 by being knocked-down by a motor-car driven by Arthur Atwater (q.v.). He dies with one painting unfinished.

WS 111, 112, 113, 114, 115–17, 119, 127, 128, 138

(See PICTURES)

PLAYS

- *The Cocktail Party* by T.S. Eliot. Gilbert Pinfold's voice, Angel, reminds him of the second act of *The Cocktail Party*, in which there is a little band of people 'doing good, sworn to secrecy, working behind the scenes everywhere', and tells him that this is just what his voices are about.
- *The Duchess of Malfi* by Thomas Webster. In the storm in the Atlantic Charles Ryder feels like the Duchess of Malfi, bayed at by hounds.
- *Hamlet* by William Shakespeare. Sir James Macrae commissions Simon Lent to re-write *Hamlet* for a modern audience, before equally swiftly abandoning the idea.

The attendant at Whispering Glades tells Dennis Barlow that *Hamlet* is so

beautifully written: 'Know that death is common; all that live must die'.
• *Henry V* by William Shakespeare. At school Nina Blount acted in *Henry V*. Ginger Littlejohn, quoting the speech about 'this happy breed', while looking from the window of an aeroplane, insists that it is a poem.

Ian Kilbannock recites from *Henry V* while on Operation Popgun: 'We shall this day light such a candle by God's grace in England as I trust shall never be put out'.
• *Internal Combustion* by Roger Simmonds. Unfunny play in which all of the characters are parts of a motor-car. He describes it as an old-fashioned ballet. It is produced by the Finsbury International Theatre in July 1938.
• *King Lear* by William Shakespeare. Julia Flyte compares herself, Charles and Celia, left alone in the dining-room of the liner across the Atlantic, to Lear, Kent and Fool in the storm in *King Lear*: 'Only each of us is all three of them'. Celia does not understand. Charles feels like Lear on the heath.

Gilbert Pinfold thinks of King Lear when hearing his voices tying the steward to the chair; '"Bind fast his corky arms" . . . Who said that? Goneril? Regan?' Later 'possessed with atavistic panic', he cries in the words of Lear 'O let me not be mad, not mad, sweet heaven'.
• Sir Francis Hinsley, aware that something is not as it should be, feels 'the mantle of Lear about his shoulders' as he takes a taxi to Megalopolitan Studios for the last time.
• *Macbeth* by William Shakespeare. Brideshead tells Charles that were he to paint a picture the subject he would choose would be *Macbeth*.

Sir James Macrae has the idea of incorporating the story of *Macbeth* into that of *Hamlet*.
• *Private Lives* by Noel Coward. Ian Kilbannock's favourite play, from which he recites lines during Operation Popgun (q.v.).
• *The Choice* by Alfred Sutro. Charles Ryder is taken to see by his Aunt Philippa in September 1919.
• *Tractor Trilogy*. Marxist play produced by the Finsbury International Theatre in 1938.
• Mr Ryder tells Charles that he should go to plays as part of his education.
• John Plant thinks that he and Lucy are like 'characters in the stock intrigue of Renaissance comedy'.
VB 199; BR 65, 235–6, 269, 277; OG 145–6, 149; GP 58, 98, 137; LO 26; WS 70, 74, 131, 132, 133, 151, 172

PLENDER

Soldier servant to Lord Marchmain in the Wiltshire Yeomanry during the Great War and afterwards his valet. Meets Sebastian and Charles from their train in Venice in 1923.

At Brideshead, in 1938, he assumes a position equal in status to that of Wilcox (q.v.).
BR 92, 297

PLESSINGTON, CHARLES

One of the young men whom it seems that Angela Crouchback might marry in 1914. Instead marries Eloise Plessington. From a recusant Catholic landed family. Has sons and a daughter, Domenica (b. 1919).
US 201

PLESSINGTON, DOMENICA
(b. 1919)

Daughter of Charles and Eloise Plessington (q.v.). Tries to become a nun but fails. During the war drives a tractor on the family farm. By 1944 she has become a problem to her family who are trying to marry her off. Shy and feminine before the war, four years of work have made her something of a tom-boy. Becomes fond of Gervase Crouchback (b. 1944) and after the war marries Guy. Has two children, both boys. Manages the home farm at Broome, where they live in the Lesser House.
US 201, 239–40

PLESSINGTON, LADY ELOISE

Contemporary of Angela Crouchback (q.v.). Marries Charles (q.v.) *circa* 1914. Converts to Catholicism. Has sons and a

daughter. Visits Virginia Crouchback after the birth of Gervase. Is made godmother. Looks after the baby after Virginia is killed. Arranges Guy's marriage to her daughter Domenica.
US 138, 189, 195, 201, 239

PLUM, COLONEL

Official at the Ministry of Information in 1940, in charge of ADDIS (q.v.). Tells Basil Seal that they have met before: 'Jibuti 1936, St Jean de Luz 1937, Prague 1938', when he was a journalist.
PF 146–50

PLYMOUTH, DEVON

Home of Mr Loveday's stepsister.
WS 11

POET LAUREATE

(*See* MASEFIELD)

POETRY

- 'Abu Ben Adhem'. Read by the boys in Frank's form at Lancing in 1919.
- 'The Dream', by Wilbur Kenworthy. Inscribed in an open book of marble at the gates of Whispering Glades (q.v.)

> God set her brave eyes wide apart
> and painted them with fire; . . .

Dennis Barlow sends to Aimee Thanatogenos. It brings a tear to her eye.

- 'In Memoriam', by Alfred, Lord Tennyson. At Oxford Ambrose Silk recites through a megaphone to the accompaniment of combs and tissue paper.
- 'I Strove with None', by Walter Savage Landor. Ambrose Silk, thinking about his past life recalls the lines of Walter Savage Landor 'Nature I loved, and next to Nature, Art'.
-
> Like those Nicean barks of yore
> That gently o'er a perfumed sea,
> The weary way-worn wanderer bore

Inscribed by Dennis Barlow on the card which Mr Joyboy will receive on every anniversary of Aimee's death.

- 'Milton on his Blindness', by John Milton. Learned by Wykham-Blake for Mr Graves at Lancing in 1919.
- 'My Love is like a Red, Red Rose', by Robert Burns. Inscribed on the step of the Lovers' Seat in Whispering Glades.

Dennis Barlow, and Whispering Glades confuse it with 'John Anderson My Jo'. Aimee thinks it coarse.

- 'Now Sleeps the Crimson Petal', by Alfred, Lord Tennyson. Claimed as his own by Dennis Barlow. It is just the right thing to send Aimee Thanatogenos into romantic rapture.
- Sir Adrian Porson writes a poetic tribute to Lady Marchmain in *The Times* in May 1926.
- 'The Pobble Who has No Toes', by Edward Lear. Barbara Seal quotes to her father from Lear when he is at a loss for words when Charles Allbright takes his Cliquot Rosé:

> His Aunt Jobiska made him drink
> Lavender water tinged with pink,
> For all the world in general knows
> There's nothing so good for a Pobble's
> toes.

- 'Shall I Compare Thee to a Summer's Day', by William Shakespeare. One of the poems which Dennis Barlow claims as his own. Reminds Aimee Thanatogenos of something she learned at school.
- 'There swimmeth one who swam e'er rivers were begun'. Read by the boys in Frank's class at Lancing in 1919.
- ''Twould ring the Bells of Heaven the Wildest Peal for Years', by Ralph Hodgson. The young Charles Ryder, at Lancing, produces an illuminated version.
- 'Under the Wide and Starry Sky'. Read by Frank's class at Lancing in 1919.
- 'The Wasteland', by T.S. Eliot. Recited by Anthony Blanche through a megaphone from Sebastian Flyte's balcony at Christchurch, to a group of rowers on their way to the river:

> I, Tiresias, have foresuffered all . . .
> Enacted on this same divan or b-bed,
> I who have sat by Thebes below the
> wall
> And walked among the l-l-lowest of
> the dead . . .

- 'What have I done for You, England,

My England?' Read by Frank's form at Lancing in 1919.

• John Masefield writes an ode to the seasonal fluctuation of the net sales of the *Daily Beast* in 1937.

• William Boot thinks that he may risk putting something from the poets in his lush places column:

> Nay not so much as out of bed?
> When all the birds have Matins said

• Mr Baldwin (q.v.) reads pre-Hitler German poetry.

• Grimes once knew a poem about a light burning in a tower window.

• Ginger Littlejohn insists that Henry V's speech about 'this scepter'd isle' is a poem which he learned from a blue poetry book at school.

• At the start of WWII Mr Benfleet does very well with his series of war poets, entitled *Sword Unsheathed*.

• On 29 October 1943 *The Times* publishes a poem to celebrate the Sword of Stalingrad:

> I saw the Sword of Stalingrad,
> Then bow'd down my head from the
> Light of it.
> Spirit to my spirit, the Might of it
> Silently whispered – O Mortal, behold
> I am the life of Stalingrad

• Etty Cornphillip brings out a 'very silly book of sonnets about Venice'.

• Sooner or later all of Mr Benwell's novelists tell him that they have written poetry. 'It does them infinite harm.'

• Bellorius' life work is a 1500-line epic poem on the subject of a visit to a mythical utopia.

• There is a sonnet by Sir Francis Hinsley in *Poems of Today*.

• Dennis Barlow attempts to compose a funerary ode to Sir Francis Hinsley:

> Bury the great Knight
> With the studio's valediction
> Let us bury the great Knight
> Who was once the arbiter of popular
> fiction

He abandons this and attempts a more classical approach:

> They told, me, Francis Hinsley, they
> told me you were hung
> With red protruding eyeballs and black
> protruding tongue

Neither, he decides is appropriate.
DF 108; VB 99, 199, 220; Sc 13, 21, 57; PF 43; BR 34; OG 130; US 22, 53, 54; LO 22, 34, 53, 68, 69, 84, 95, 99, 100, 127; WS 29, 130, 196, 261, 307, 308

POETS

• William and Tony are two of Mr Benfleet's poets in 1927.
See also Sir Adrian Porson; Parsnip and Pimpernell; Dennis Barlow; Ludovic; Cavafy; Sir Francis Hinsley; Sophie Krump *and other individual poets.*
VB 99

POINT-TO-POINTS

Captain Angus Stuart-Kerr is regularly seen at a point-to-point meeting.
VB 113

POISON

Aimee Thanatogenos takes her life with poison.
LO 119
(*See also* Drugs and Murder)

POLES

Among the peoples whom Mr Goodall believes will rise up in the pilgrimage of grace (q.v.).
OG 40

POLICE RAIDS

Basil Seal is no stranger to the police raid, which as a young man had seen him escape over the tiles.

• At the St Christopher's Social Club in 1927 waiters are unable to serve alcohol because the management has just heard that there is about to be a police raid.

• John Plant frequents a brothel in Fez until there is a police raid. 'Two seedy figures in raincoats strode across the room . . . a guard of military police stood at the street door'.
VB 124; PF 194; WS 123

POLITICS
Sir Humphrey Maltravers cannot think why he keeps on at politics: 'It's a dog's life, and there's no money in it, either.'
• Azanian politics is a complex machine. There is a bicameral legislature and proportional representation. The system was only set up in the 1890s and is rendered difficult to implement by the difficulties of communication in the country. There should be an election every five years, but what has emerged by the 1930s is a self-electing dynasty of the Jacksons (which preserves order).
• Gilbert Pinfold has no interest whatsoever in politics and has never voted in an election.
• To the Lieutenant Colonel of the Bombardier Guards all politicians are 'not so much boobies as bogies . . . figures of Renaissance subtlety and intrigue'.
• John Verney has hopes of a political career before the war (q.v.) as do at various times Basil Seal and Brideshead.
• In the New Britain the country is governed by a coalition between the Ministry of Rest and Culture and the Ministry of Welfare.
DF 130; Sc 75; GP 11, 162, 186; PF 52

POLYNESIANS
When left to himself, and not disturbed by his family or his faith, Sebastian Flyte is 'happy and harmless as a Polynesian'.
BR 123

POMPEII, ITALY
Paul Pennyfeather has visited Pompeii 'guidebook in hand'. His experience there alerts him to the nature of the trade being plied in Marseilles' dingy streets.

Paul believes that Grimes must have stood 'like the Pompeiian sentry, while the Citadels of the Plain fell about his ears'.
DF 152, 199

PONT STREET
Term of derogatory amusement to Julia Flyte and her friends in 1922.
• Lucy Simmonds speaks in 'a Pont Street manner' which has an element of 'dumb crambo'.
BR 177; WS 157
(See LONDON)

PONTUS
Mr Samgrass has his photograph taken at Pontus during his trip to the Near East with Sebastian Flyte.
BR 145

POOTER, MR
Hero of *Diary of a Nobody*.
• Gilbert Pinfold, gazing at his entry in the *Caliban*'s passenger list as 'Mr G. Pinfold' thinks of Mr Pooter going to the Mansion House.
GP 35
(*See* BOOKS)

POPE, HIS HOLINESS THE
Father Mowbray asks Rex Mottram 'supposing the Pope looked up and saw a cloud and said "It's going to rain", would that be bound to happen?' Rex supposes that it would be raining 'spiritually'.
BR 185

POPE PIUS X
Has a private audience with Gervase and Hermione Crouchback after their marriage in 1889.
MA 9

POPE PIUS XI, ACHILLE RATTI *(1857–1939)*
Has a private audience with Lord Brideshead and his wife Beryl after their marriage in 1938.
BR

POPEYE
American cartoon character.
• Celia Ryder compares him to Captain Foulenough.
BR 234

POPHAM, PAMELA
Guest of Margot Metroland at King's Thursday in 1922. She is 'square-jawed

and resolute as a big-game huntress'.
• Simon Balcairn spots her at Margot's party in 1927.
• Someone sends the *Daily Excess* a spurious story about Miles Malpractice having spent a night with her at Arundel.
DF 128; VB 85–6, 89

POPO, BISHOP OF
At whose consecration the natives of Azania commit embarrassing human sacrifices.
BM 144

POPOTAKIS, MR
Entrepreneur in Jacksonburg. At one time or another he has tried his hand at running a dance hall, a baccarat room, a miniature golf course and a ping-pong parlour. The last is the most successful. He serves up homemade whisky and homemade champagne at ten dollars a bottle. He keeps his genuine absinthe behind the bar.
Sc 128

PORCH, DAME MILDRED
Representative of the RSPCA in Ishmaelia in 1932. Investigates the Wanda methods of hunting. 'An intolerable old gas-bag.' Has been in South Africa. She is stout; wears a sun hat in an oil-cloth cover, a serviceable frock and thick shoes.

Arrives in Debra Dowa; met by William Bland. Does not drink. Banquet is given in her honour by the Azanians.

Has a narrow escape when, with Miss Tin, she is caught in Debra Dowa in the midst of the fighting. Searches for Evian in Youkoumian's bar. Drinks his Koniak on the roof. Rescued by William. Stays at the Legges. Leaves Azania with the legation.
BM 129, 158, 169, 170, 178, 184, 198

PORNOGRAPHY
'Billy' has pictures of girls stuck above his bunk on the *SS Caliban*.
GP 38
(*See also* CUSTOMS)

PORPOISES
(*See* BOOTS)

PORSON, SIR ADRIAN
Poet. Close friend of Lady Marchmain. Stays with her in Venice in September 1922. According to Anthony Blanche she has 'bled him dry'. 'And he, my dear, was the greatest, the only, poet of our time.' Stays at Brideshead over Christmas 1923. He has 'fine old eyes'. Finds Mr Samgrass 'distasteful'. Meets Charles Ryder, in tears, hastening through Marchmain House in 1926, from Lady Marchmain's deathbed (holding a bandana handkerchief to his face). Writes a poem in *The Times* on the death of Lady Marchmain. He has loved her all his life. Yet, according to Cordelia it has nothing at all to do with her.
BR 55–6, 120–21, 199, 212

PORT OF SPAIN, TRINIDAD
Town in Trinidad.
• Thérèse de Vitre tells Tony Last that the shops in Port of Spain 'aren't any good'.
HD 166

PORT SAID, EGYPT
• Basil Seal sends lewd postcards to Sonia Trumpington from Port Said on his way to Azania in 1932 and disposes of his mother's bracelet to an Indian jeweller here at a fifth of the price. He gets drunk with a Welsh engineer in the bar of the Eastern Exchange and fights with him.
• Gilbert Pinfold's voices tell him that they have sent the tortured crooked seaman on to a good hospital in England instead of 'the filth of a wog hospital' in Port Said.
• Gilbert decides to leave the *Caliban* at Port Said. He has been there often, but had never expected to greet it with the affection with which he does in 1953.
• One of the ports at which the *SS Glory of Greece* puts in.
BM 89; GP 50, 135, 141; WS 19

PORT SUDAN
Port on the Red Sea.
• Gilbert Pinfold imagines his wife reading a report in her morning paper from

Port Sudan reporting a physical assault upon his person by his 'voices'.
GP 75

PORTALLON, PRINCE DE
Friend of Anthony Blanche, to whom he promises to introduce Charles Ryder.
BR 52

PORTSMOUTH, HAMPSHIRE
Trimmer tells his sergeant major in 1943 that he is to report to Portsmouth docks immediately for posting to India.
OG 88

PORTUGUESE
In 1632 the Portuguese garrison at Matodi holds out for eight months against a siege by the Omani Arabs, but is eventually overwhelmed.
• The masonry of Fez was cut in 1539 by Portuguese prisoners.
• Some Portuguese Trotskyites are among Scott-King's fellow travellers on the European underground network in 1946.
• Ambrose Silk spent some years after the war in Portugal.
BM 8; WS 120, 245, 254

POSEIDON
Greek god of the sea.
• In the days of Pericles an Athenian colony had built a shrine to Poseidon at Santa Maria (q.v.).
WS 243

POSILLIPO
Where an old Air Force acquaintance of Guy Crouchback's has a flat in 1944. He stays there on the way to Naples.
US 235

POSKI, MISS
Employee of the Happier Hunting Ground (q.v.). The standard product, American Young Woman, of the type which one can leave in a delicatessen in New York and find again at the cigar stall in San Francisco.
LO 45, 127

POSTLETHWAITE, MR
Domestic Bursar at Scone College in 1922. Dines with Mr Sniggs on the evening of the Bollinger Club dinner, after which he feels sure that the fines will ensure that he can look forward to a week of founder's port.
DF 9, 10

POSTMEN'S HATS
At the Old Hundredth in 1933, Jock Grant-Menzies (q.v.) tells Milly and Babs that he designs postmen's hats.
HD 73

POTTS, ARTHUR *(b. circa 1902)*
Fellow student of Paul Pennyfeather at Scone College in 1922. Does not complete his course, having accepted a position with the League of Nations (q.v.). His middle-class morals are irreproachable. Is shocked by Alastair Trumpington offering Paul money as compensation for having had him sent down.

Lunches with Paul at Queen's Restaurant in Sloane Square. Tells him all about King's Thursday and Otto Silenus. Here they have in the past discussed everything from birth control to Byzantine mosaics. Thinks that Silenus is worth watching and that he has really managed to get away from Corbusier.

Arrives at King's Thursday where Paul is staying. Looks over the house.

Watches Margot's office in Hill Street from the other side of the road.

Is the unshakeable chief witness in Paul's trial.

Gives a lecture to the inmates of Egdon Heath on the League of Nations; it is not a success.
DF 43, 70, 121, 123, 142, 146, 148, 151, 159, 186

PRACTICAL JOKES
Ritchie-Hook's favourite pastime (*see* BOOBY TRAPS).

PRAESIDIUM
Government of Yugoslavia in 1944. 'A scratch lot collected from Vis and Montenegro and Bari. The real power, of course,

will remain with the partisan military leaders. The Praesidium is strictly for foreign consumption'. Thus de Souza puts Guy Crouchback 'in the picture'.
US 203

PRAGUE
Capital city of Czechoslovakia.
• Bum, Scab and Joe cover the fall of Prague to the Nazis (15 March 1939).
• Venue, in 1946, for an International rally of Progressive Youth Leadership, attended by Griggs (q.v.).
• One of the cities in which, as a young man, Dr Antonic (q.v.) studied.
OG 214; WS 201, 218

PRAYER
Mr Prendergast instructs Paul Pennyfeather to 'pray for penitence'.
• In the depths of Ishmaelia, William Boot prays to the great crested grebe: 'maligned fowl . . . am I still to be in exile from the green places of my heart? Was there not even in the remorseless dooms of antiquity a god from the machine?'
Sc 166; BR 84

PREGNANCY
Sometimes, during their first pregnancy, women acquire an 'incurious, self-regarding' expression.
WS 151

PRENDERGAST, MR *(b. 1871)*
In 1912 a rural dean of the Church of England with a living in Worthing, where he lives with his mother. Is given the *Encyclopaedia Britannica* by the dentist's wife. All is well until his 'doubts' begin. Meets the Bundles (q.v.). His doubts involve a basic inability to see why God has created the world.

In 1922 he is a master at Llanabba school (q.v.) where he has been for ten years.

Owns sixteen pipes; wears a wig. Finds it hard to keep order. Does not receive any letters; used to receive five or six a day. Has not bought anything since 1920, when he bought his walking stick in Shanklin instead of having tea, having entered the tobacconists and feeling that he was unable to leave without buying something. Would like one day to return to the Ministry.

Meets Paul Pennyfeather.

Becomes drunk and starts the quarter-mile race at the sports day with Philbrick's revolver, shooting Tangent (q.v.) in the foot. Has a drunken conversation with Colonel Sidebottom, who he calls 'Shy-bottom'. Becomes drunker and gains in self-confidence. Canes twenty-three boys. Has a dreadful hangover.

Resigns in 1922, shortly after Paul, to become a 'Modern Churchman' (q.v.).

Becomes chaplain at Blackstone Gaol. Finds criminals as bad as schoolboys in that he is unable to control them.

Is murdered horribly by the religious maniac:

> Old Prendy went to see a chap
> What said he'd seen a ghost;
> Well, he was dippy, and he'd got
> A mallet and a saw.
>
> Who let the madman have the things?
> The Governor, who d'you think?
> He asked to be a carpenter,
> He sawed off Prendy's head'.

His death passes 'almost unnoticed'.
DF 23, 26, 31–4, 36, 39, 41–2, 71, 89–90, 99–104, 141, 165, 183–4

PRENDERGAST, MRS
Mother of Mr Prendergast (q.v.) who used to housekeep for him in Worthing. Furnishes his house with chintz. Is 'at home' to the ladies of the congregation once a week. Files his letters for him under 'charity appeals', 'personal', 'marriages and funerals', 'baptisms and churchings' and 'anonymous abuse'. Friend of the Bundles (q.v.). Never recovers from the shock of her son's 'doubts'.
DF 32–3, 41

PRENDERGAST, MR (SENIOR)
Father of Mr Prendergast (q.v.). At one time receives so many letters of abuse from the curate's wife that he has to call in the police.
DF 41

PRENTICE, COLONEL
Commander of B Commando on Crete. He has a fleshless face and according to Ivor Claire is 'awfully mad'. Wears the stockings worn by his great-great grandfather at Inkermann. Makes his officers have the same drink ration as the Navy.
OG 109, 110, 113

PRESENTS
Margot Metroland buys a vast number of presents for Paul Pennyfeather before their wedding, in 1922. Messengers arrive at his rooms at the Ritz five or six times a day bearing: a platinum cigarette case, a dressing-gown, a tie-pin and cufflinks.
• Adam Fenwick-Symes gives Nina Blount a bottle of scent and a scent spray from Asprey's for Christmas 1927, and she gives him two ties and a new kind of safety razor. Adam gives Colonel Blount a box of cigars and Nina gives him a book about the cinema. He gives Nina a seed pearl brooch which belonged to her mother and to Adam he gives a calendar with a picture on it of a bulldog smoking a clay pipe and a thought from Longfellow for each day of the year.
• Brenda Last gives John Beaver at Christmas 1933, a ring made of three interlocking circles of gold and platinum.
• For Christmas 1923 Rex Mottram gives Julia Flyte a tortoise with her initials inscribed in diamonds on its shell.
• Among the wedding presents which Rex and Julia receive are: a pair of Chinese vases from Aunt Betty, a jade dragon on an ebony stand, and an early morning tea-set from Goode's, from the Pendle-Garthwaites.
• Peregrine Crouchback gives his hosts the Scrope-Welds, at Christmas 1943, a large and highly coloured Victorian album. He gives Virginia a copy of Pyne's *Horace.*
DF 150; VB 213–4; HD 61; BR 159, 188; US 144, 149

PRETTYMAN-PARTRIDGE, MR AND MRS
Previous owners of the Malt House, Grantley Green (q.v.). One of them dies in summer 1939 and sells the house to 'Bill' (q.v.).
PF 121–2

PRICE, NANNY
Bedridden junior Nanny to Nanny Bloggs (q.v.) to whom she is ten years the younger, at Boot Magna Hall (q.v.). Gives her wages to Chinese Missions. Has little influence at the Hall.
Sc 19

PRIESTLEY, J.B. ***(1894–1984)***
English novelist and playwright. See his *The Good Companions* (1927), *Angel Pavement* (1930) and *Time and the Conways* (1937).
• One of the authors read by Seth who form part of his claim to be a man of the New Age.
• Receives a great deal of personal abuse in *Ivory Tower* (q.v.).
• Major Erskine's reputation for 'braininess' among the Halberdiers is chiefly derived from his reading the novels of J.B. Priestley.
BM 17; PF 186; MA 171

PRIESTS
Mr Prendergast (q.v.) hears that there exists such a thing as a 'Modern Churchman' and immediately decides to become one. This is a creature who draws a clergyman's salary but who need not commit himself to any religious belief.

When he is practising in this capacity at Blackstone, the inmates confess the most terrible sins just to see his reaction.
• A black archdeacon is among Tony Last's fellow passengers on the ship to Brazil.
• The Abbot of the Nestorian church at the monastery of St Mark the Evangelist in Azania is thoroughly corrupt (q.v.).
• Lady Marchmain tells Charles Ryder that all Protestants think that Catholic priests are spies.
• Rex Mottram wants to hire some more cardinals from abroad for his wedding to Julia.
• One of Charles Ryder's fellow passengers on his way back to England in 1936

describes himself as an Episcopalian bishop.

• The Alsatian priest to whom Guy Crouchback confesses in Alexandria is a spy.

• Guy asks the priest at Begoy to say a requiem Mass for Virginia. He is suspected of spying. Guy's giving him rations causes an uproar among the Communists.

• Dennis Barlow is keen to become a 'non-sectarian clergyman'. This is an American invention and to Dennis seems to be a good way of making money. 'Some of the non-sectarians stop at nothing – not even at psychiatry and table-turning.'

• Gilbert Pinfold's voices accuse him of having once claimed to have been the nephew of an Anglican bishop.

• John Plant's great grandfather was a Canon of Christ Church.

DF 141, 165; HD 165; BM 175; BR 82, 139, 184, 233; OG 140; US 126, 205; LO 96; GP 131, 146; WS 111, 305

(*See also* Monsignor BELL, Canon GEOGHAN, Fathers FLANAGAN, MACKAY, MEMBLING, MOWBRAY, ROTHSCHILD, WESTMACOTT, WHELAN and WIMPERIS, Reverend BARTHOLOMEW)

PRIME MINISTER

The Prime Minister in 1937 always sleeps with one of John Boot's novels beside his bed. His name is Mervyn. In the vacation he approves the honours, including Boot's KCB.

Sc 12, 182

(*See also* BROWN and OUTRAGE)

PRINGLE, SERGEANT

PT Sergeant involved in the training of Guy Crouchback's officer intake in 1940. Warns them against the dangers of jarring the spinal column. In Guy's view there is no place for him in the Halberdiers.

MA 51–2

PRINTING

Seth's birth control posters are printed by an antiquated lithographic apparatus.

• Mr Graves attempts to gain Charles Ryder's confidence at Lancing by telling him that he is buying a hand printing press. Charles is indeed passionately interested in printing and owning a private press, but refuses to admit as much. Later, however, he takes an active interest in using the press. He happens upon a box full of printer's blocks: 'ornamental initials, menu headings of decanters and dessert, foxes' heads and running hounds for sporting announcements, ecclesiastical devices and monograms, crowns, Odd Fellows' arms, the wood-cut of a 'prize bull', and a great deal more. What fun, he thinks, one might have with such things. The press itself travels in many cases and when assembled is smaller than might have appeared. It has cast iron supports with brass Corinthian capitals and on the top a brass urn dated 1824.

BM 145; WS 296, 313

PRISON

See EGDON HEATH, BLACKSTONE, LUCAS DOCKERY, GRIMES, PHILBRICK, PRENDERGAST, PENNYFEATHER, MOUNTJOY, PLASTIC

PRIVATE VIEWS

Charles Ryder's private view in 1936, is held on a Friday because of the critics: 'If we give them the weekend to think about it, we shall have them in an urbane Sunday-in-the-country mood. They'll settle down after a good luncheon, tuck up their cuffs, and turn out a nice, leisurely full-length essay, which they'll reprint later in a nice little book.'

BR 252

PROCOPUTA INDIANS

The mad masters of the three-eight rhythm (q.v.).

GP 46

PROPAGANDA

Seyid (q.v.) has several thousand copies printed of a photograph of Seth in his cap and gown from Oxford and circulates them among the palace guard telling them that he has deserted the Church of England and become an English Mohammedan. They defect in their hundreds.

• Seth's own campaign for Birth Control (q.v.) is a terrific failure.
• Miss Campbell (q.v.) gives Guy Crouchback a huge pile of leaflets bearing the slogan: 'Call to Scotland, England's peril is Scotland's Hope. Why Hitler must win'.
BM 41–2, 146; OG 69
(*See also* MINISTRY OF INFORMATION and ADVERTISING)

PROPOSALS OF MARRIAGE
Paul Pennyfeather proposes to Margot Metroland on his knees, beside her chair at King's Thursday in 1923. She accepts: 'I don't see why not'.
• Adam Fenwick-Symes proposes to Nina Blount constantly.
• Rex Mottram proposes to Julia Flyte in the library in Marchmain House in May 1924.
• Celia Ryder 'pops the question' to Charles on the night they eat shrimps with a paper knife.
• Dennis Barlow proposes to Aimee Thanatogenos at four o'clock in the afternoon on the lake shore at Whispering Glades.
DF 136; VB; BR 180, 229; LO 87

PROSTITUTES
The bandmaster of the Llanabba Silver Band asks Lord Circumference whether he would like to 'meet' his sister, and that although it would normally cost a pound, he could let him have special terms.
• Some of Margot Metroland's 'young ladies' tend to be 'a bit mannery if they aren't kept in order'.
• Paul Pennyfeather, accosted by prostitutes in Marseilles, realizes the nature of their trade, having visited Pompeii. One of them takes his hat; 'he caught a glimpse of her bare leg in a lighted doorway'.
• The judge at Paul Pennyfeather's trial refers to prostitution as 'white slave trading', and feels sorry for the victims.
• Charles Ryder cannot, in 1923, recognize 'with any certainty' a prostitute in the streets.
• Charles and Sebastian pick up two prostitutes at the Old Hundredth in 1923, one of whom looks like a sickly child, the other like a death's head.
• Virginia Crouchback tells Guy in 1940, that she would far rather have been 'taken for a tart . . . offered five pounds to do something ridiculous in high heels or drive you round the room in toy harness or any of the things they write about in books' than have him attempt to make love to her in her hotel room.
• In 1943, out of the slums of London there swarm 'multitudes of drab, ill-favoured adolescent girls and their aunts and mothers, never before seen in the squares of Mayfair and Belgravia. They are paid with chewing gum, razor-blades and goods from the PX stores'.
• As a young man, abroad, Gilbert Pinfold patronized brothels.
• Jellaby reports to Mr Plant, the presence of prostitutes in St Eustace's.
• Unlike the other girls of the brothel in the Moulay visited regularly by John Plant in the 1930s, Fatima does not use a professional name such as 'Lola' or 'Fifi', or even 'Whiskey-Soda'.
• 'Ten patient Turkish prostitutes' are among Scott-King's fellow travellers on the underground network in 1946.
DF 78, 144–5, 152, 160; BR 97, 112; MA 133; US 24; GP 115; WS 119, 121, 244
(*See also* CHASTITY, FATIMA, Florence DUCANE, Jane GRIMES, THE LATIN AMERICAN ENTERTAINMENT COMPANY, and MILLY)

PROUST, MARCEL *(1871–1922)*
French novelist. Renowned for his thirteen-volume masterpiece *A la Recherche du Temps perdu* (1913–1922).
• Paul Pennyfeather, in his new-found wealth in 1922, buys a set of Proust.
• Anthony Blanche dines with Proust before coming to Oxford in 1922.
• Mr Samgrass is reading Proust when Charles Ryder arrives at Brideshead at Christmas 1923.
DF 150; BR 47, 120

PROVENCE, FRANCE
In Provence the bitter little strawberries,

which they serve in Dover Street at such a price, are very cheap.
DF 147

PROVERBS
'Sense of Sin is Sense of Waste': one of the thoughts for the day at Blackstone Gaol.
• 'East is East and West is West and never the twain shall meet': all that Mr Outrage can think to say to Baroness Yoshiwara on her departure.
DF 169; VB 128

PROVNA
Sculptor, invented by Adam Fenwick-Symes, as Mr Chatterbox, in 1927. He is the son of a Polish nobleman and lives in a top-floor studio at Grosvenor House. He is indifferent to 'conventional beauty'. His work is for the most part made of cork, vulcanite and steel. It is all in private hands, but the Metropolitan Museum of New York is keen to purchase an example, but is outbid by collectors. This announcement precipitates a stream of early Provnas from Warsaw to Bond Street and thence to California. Mrs Hoop tells her friends that he is working on a bust of her son Johnny. He describes Imogen Quest as 'justifiying the century'.
VB 112, 114

PSYCHOANALYSTS
Basil Seal wonders what on earth might happen should Seth (q.v.) ever discover psychoanalysis.
• The mortuary hostess at Whispering Glades tells Dennis Barlow that one of the things that psychoanalysis has taught us is not to shrink from the unknown but to 'discuss it openly and frankly' to remove 'morbid reflections'.
• The doctor at the health farm recommends that Basil Seal visit a psychoanalyst.
BM 142; LO 44; WS 263

PSYCHOLOGISTS
Father Westmacott gives Gilbert Pinfold's wife the name of a trustworthy 'looney doctor'. 'A Catholic, so he must be all right.' Pinfold, however, refuses to see him.
GP 154

PUBLIC HOUSES
• **Mrs Robert's**. Local pub to Llanabba school. Supplied with beer by Clutterbuck's. 'Not such a bad little place in its way.' Paul Pennyfeather and Grimes drink here.
• **The Lamb and Flag**, Camberwell Green. Owned by Philbrick (q.v.).
• **The Sothill Arms**, Malfrey. Local public house of the Sothills.
• **An Inn** near Swindon. Where Charles Ryder and Sebastian Flyte lunch on eggs and bacon, pickled walnuts and cheese and beer on the way to Brideshead in 1923 'in a sunless parlour where an old clock ticked in the shadows and a cat slept by the empty grate'.
• **The Trout**, Godstowe. Where Charles and Sebastian have a drink on their way back to Oxford from Brideshead in June 1923.
• **The Gardeners' Arms**, Oxford. One of the pubs frequented by Charles and Sebastian in Michaelmas term 1923.
• **The Nag's Head**, Oxford. One of the pubs frequented by Charles and Sebastian in 1923.
• **The Turf**, Oxford. One of the pubs frequented by Charles and Sebastian.
• **The Druid's Head**. One of the pubs frequented by Charles and Sebastian in 1923.
• **The Pub**, Flyte St Mary. Has the capacity to billet twenty soldiers in 1944. Out of bounds to officers.
• **The Brakehurst Arms**, Much Malcock (later **The Metcalfe Arms**). Where Mr Hargood Hood stays, and where he has his meeting with Colonel Hodge.
• **The Cumberland Arms**, Tomb. Where Tom Kent-Cumberland stays on the night of his brother Gervase's twenty-first birthday party.
• The reporters of the *Daily Beast* congregate at a pub on the corner of Fleet Street.
• Women run to fat in the public house business.

• Ralph Bland (q.v.) used to drink far too much in public houses.
DF27,52,54;PF11,34;BR35,41,105,325; MA 89; WS 29, 56, 96; Sc 28

PUBLISHERS

As Mr Rampole never likes paying large advances to young authors, Mr Benfleet advises Adam Fenwick-Symes, having had his manuscript burned by customs officers, to repay the advance 'plus interest of course'. As this is impossible he advises him to rewrite the book for the spring list. The new contract is on the standard first novel terms: 'No royalty on the first two thousand, then a royalty of two and a half per cent, rising to five per cent on the tenth thousand. We retain serial, cinema, dramatic, American, colonial and translation rights, of course. And, of course, an option on your next twelve books on the same terms.'
• Geoffrey Bentley (q.v.) admits that he has never liked books.
VB 32–3; PF 61–2
(*See also* Benfleet, Bentley, Benwell, OUP, Rampole, Spruce, Tiffin)

PUKKAPORE, MAHARAJAH OF

Attends a party of Archie Schwert's in 1927 at which he meets Miss Mouse and is displeased by the fact that Johnnie Hoop is dressed as the Maharani (q.v.). Is later discovered at the party in the airship by Adam, Ginger and Nina, making love to Miss Mouse on a cushion on the terrace.
VB 53, 122

PUKKAPORE, MAHARANI OF

Dressed as whom Johnnie Hoop attends Archie Schwert's savage party in 1927, incurring the displeasure of the genuine Maharajah.
VB 53

PULLITZER'S SOUP

(*See* Food)

PUNISHMENTS

The doctor at Blackstone Gaol certifies Paul Pennyfeather capable of undergoing 'restraint of handcuffs, leg-chains, cross-irons, body-belt, canvas dress, close confinement, No. 1 diet, No. 2 diet, birch-rod, and cat-o'-nine-tails'.
• The Eastern neighbours of the New Britain employ 'chain gangs, solitary confinement, bread and water, cat-o'-nine-tails, the rope and the block'.
DF 163; GP 188

PUTTOCK, DOCTOR

Kerstie Kilbannock's doctor in Sloane Street, who tells Virginia Crouchback in 1943, that she is pregnant.
US 74

PYNE

Kerstie Kilbannock is left a copy of Pyne's *Horace* by Virginia Crouchback in 1944 as a 'little token for Ian'.
US 149

Q

QUEST, MRS ANDREW (IMOGEN)
Invention of Adam Fenwick-Symes as Mr Chatterbox. She is the loveliest and most popular of the young married set. Just above average in height, she has 'Laurencin eyes' and is dark and slim. She fences sabre for half an hour every morning before having breakfast. Provna (q.v.) says that she justifies the century. She dresses impeccably 'with just that suggestion of the haphazard'. She is 'witty and tender hearted; passionate and serene, sensual and temperate; impulsive and discreet'. She mixes with a set which falls between those of Margot Metroland and Lady Circumference. Adam hears her name mentioned in a hat shop in Hanover Square. She is the pinnacle of social climbing. Gives a party at her house in Seamore Place (it is in fact untenanted). When Lord Monomark expresses an interest in her, she and her husband sail for Jamaica.
VB 114–5

QUISLING, VIDKUN ***(1887–1945)***
Norwegian fascist leader and League of Nations official. In 1933 formed the Norwegian National Party. Became Prime Minister under the Germans. Executed 1945.
• During the war his name became a synonym for all traitors.
GP 103

QUOTATIONS
'God gave all men all earth to love'; inscribed on a calendar in Mr Metcalfe's office in Alexandria.
WS 47

R

RABAT, MOROCCO

One of the places to which the British Consul in Fez suggests Sebastian Flyte might move in 1926.
BR 201

RACING

Lady Circumference and Lord Tangent attend Warwick races in 1921. Their picture is in the national press.
• The reception cleaner at Blackstone Gaol often hears racing tips.
• Indian Runner is a twenty-to-one outsider for the November handicap in 1927. The drunken major gives Adam Fenwick-Symes a tip to put his money on it. He takes Adam's thousand pounds, which he has just won, and says he will put it on for him. The horse is owned by Mary Mouse's mother.
• Adam and Nina go to the race and meet Ginger Littlejohn and watch Indian Runner win at thirty-five to one. The crowds are very dense and 'brandish' flasks and sandwiches. Adam sees the drunken major there. A pickpocket is arrested by two policemen.
• Lottie Crump has 'a little flutter' on the November handicap.
• Nanny Bloggs (q.v.) has a penchant for 'bringing off showy doubles' in the flat racing season. Her only reading apart from the Bible is the Turf guide. She promises William Boot that if she should win the Irish Sweepstake she will buy him a flight in an aeroplane. However, she does not win and gives it up as a Popish trick.
• Basil Seal, disguising Ambrose Silk as an Irish priest to effect his escape from England in 1940 advises him to read a racing paper.
• Gervase Kent-Cumberland keeps six racehorses after he is married.
DF 57, 175–6; VB 45–6, 84, 117; Sc 19, 46; PF 195; WS 105

RADIO TRANSMITTERS

In his hallucinations, the table lamp with a little rose-coloured shade which stands on Gilbert Pinfold's breakfast table on the *SS Caliban* suddenly 'pings' into life as a radio transmitter.
GP 78

RAGUZA, SICILY

Town in the south of Sicily where Dr Antonic once lived, and where he often developed hiccups from laughing.
WS 218

RAILWAYS

John Beaver travels to Hetton on the Great Western Railway 'recklessly mixing starch and protein in the Great Western three and sixpenny lunch'.
• The wheels of the train from Dover to London seem to Mr Outrage to say 'Right Honourable gent. Right Honourable gent. Right Honourable gent', over and over again.
• The Grand Chemin De Fer Imperial d'Azanie runs on a narrow gauge rail. Amurath travels from Matodi to Debra Dowa in the sixteenth year of his reign. On the way a Jewish nihilist from Berlin throws a bomb which does not explode. The first few trains on the line killed a number of people who did not understand the power of the train. Amurath draws up a timetable, express trains, goods trains, excursions, boat trains, cheap local returns, and plans for future developments. It is his last great achievement. After his death his plans do not come to fruition. By

the time Seth returns from Oxford there is only one goods train with a shabby saloon upholstered in threadbare velvet.

• William Boot travels up to London to see Mr Salter. He goes from Boot Magna Halt to Paddington, via Westbury. He orders a whisky and is told by the steward that there are no whiskies until after Reading. After Reading he is told that they are serving dinners. He gives a sovereign to the steward by mistake and the steward refuses it.

• At Taunton Mr Salter, on his way to Boot Magna, changes to a train 'such as he did not know existed outside the imagination of his Balkan correspondents; a single tram-like, one class coach'. It stops at every other station and the passengers, instead of 'slinking and shuffling and wriggling themselves into corners and decently screening themselves behind newspapers, as civilized people should when they are travelling by train, had sat down quite close to Mr Salter, rested their hands on their knees, stared at him fixedly and uncritically and suddenly addressed him on the subject of the weather in barely intelligible accents; it had been a horrible journey'.

• Charles Ryder travels third class to Brideshead in 1923 from Paddington. His suitcase is placed by a porter in the third-class carriage and he sits in the dining-car. He drinks gin and vermouth and discovers that the first dinner after Reading is at seven o'clock. The knives and forks have a 'regular jingle'. After he has dined he changes trains for Melstead Carbury.

• On their way to Venice Charles and Sebastian travel in a third-class carriage 'full of the poor visiting their families . . . and sailors returning from leave'. The carriage has wooden seats and a trolley comes round with bottles of Orvieto.

VB 28; HD 25; BM 11; Sc 23, 196; BR 72, 92

RAITH, MR

Bank Manager who visited the British Legation in Azania and has a terrible time at the procession.

BM 199–200

RAMLEH

Town in Egypt beyond which the Stitch's villa in Alexandria lies.

OG 129

RAMPOLE, MR

Director of Rampole and Bentley. A relatively small publishing firm. He is a widower of many years. He is a 'benign old gentleman'. In 1927 once a week he drives up from the country for a board meeting. He has written a book about bee-keeping, published in 1907, and by 1927 long out of print.

• Sam Benfleet creates a myth that he is a harridan who hates young authors.

• One or two times a year introduces new writers whom he knows will fail. By 1939 he lives in a 'small but substantial' house in Hampstead. Has a spinster daughter who lives with him. Leaves home at 8.45. Travels on the Underground from Hampstead. Deplores the 'propagation of books . . . no one ever reads first novels'. Publisher of Adam Fenwick-Symes' work.

• He deplores *Ivory Tower*, but has a certain grudging regard for Ambrose Silk, who he also publishes. Has 'an ingenious way of explaining over advances and overhead charges and stock in hand in such a way that seemed to prove that obvious failures had indeed succeeded'. Eventually concedes to publish *Ivory Tower*.

• Is arrested by the police in 1940 for publishing *Ivory Tower* (q.v.). Imprisoned in Brixton Gaol. Despite his privileges he misses his house and his club. Enjoys the novels of Ruth Mountdragon (q.v.). In prison he is happier than he can ever remember.

VB 31, 32, 33; PF 183, 184, 185, 197, 198, 219–20

RANDAL

'That beast Randal' manages to win first prize in the pig competition at the Brideshead Show in 1923 with 'a mangy animal'.

WS 87

RANDAL CANTAUR

Stubbs (q.v.) 'lighthearted at the fresh weather, and their long walks, and their

tea' signs the visitors' book 'Randal Cantaur'.
DF 211

RANGOON
Destination of the Burmese who are Gilbert Pinfold's fellow passengers on the *SS Caliban.*
GP 35

RAPHAEL (RAFFAELLO SANTI) *(1483–1520)*
Italian painter, pupil of Perugino, influenced by Leonardo and Michelangelo. See his 'School of Athens', 'Leo X', 'Madonna della Sedia'.
• Father Mackay (q.v.) asks Charles Ryder whether Titian was 'more truly artistic' than Raphael.
BR 311

RATTERY, MRS
Jock Grant-Menzies' 'shameless blond' who spends the weekend at Hetton. She is a tall American divorcee, once married to a Major Rattery. Meets Jock at Biarritz 1932. Plays bridge for seven hours a day. Changes her hotel once every three weeks. Takes morphine. Flies to Hetton. Has two sons. Plays animal snap with Tony Last after John's death. Drinks whisky. Tony thinks her very severe.
HD 95–9

RAVENNA, ITALY
Charles Ryder spends 'several economic and instructive weeks' here with Collins, at Easter 1923.
BR 44

RAWKES, SERGEANT-MAJOR
Company sergeant-major of the Halberdiers in 1940. Sergeant-major to Guy Crouchback's D-Company in 1940.
MA 198

READING, BERKSHIRE
The train from Boot Magna Halt to London goes through Reading, after which they serve drinks.
• Where, in the 1920s, Peter Pastmaster goes to a Palais de Danse dressed as a woman.
• Charles Ryder's train to Brideshead passes through Reading in 1923.
SC 23; PF 35; BR 72

REGENCY
Decorative style given its name by the rule of the Prince Regent, later King George IV (1810–1820). It is characterized by a number of enthusiasms for antique styles, each of them earlier than the last. These were Pompeiian, Etruscan, and Egyptian, along with a renewed enthusiasm for the Chinese taste and other Rococo excesses.
• David Lennox's paintings in Angela Lyne's bedroom are Regency in character. Cedric Lyne is depressed that this feebleness is all that decorators are able to make of the Regency: 'the age of Waterloo and highwaymen and duelling and slavery and revivalist preaching and Nelson having his arm off with no unaesthetic but rum and Botany Bay'.
PF 171

REIGATE, SURREY
Where Mr Cholmondeley (q.v.) asks Flossie Fagan to spend a weekend with him in 1922.
DF 84

RELIGION
Stiggins reads a paper to the OSCU on 'Sex Repression and Religious Experience', in 1922.
• Chokey (q.v.) thinks that religion is 'just divine'.
• Religion is a predominating aspect of life at Brideshead.
• Lady Marchmain tells Charles Ryder about the '*Alice in Wonderland* side' of religion.
• Rex Mottram likes a girl 'to have religion'. He admits that he is not devout, but he knows that it is a bad thing to have two religions in one house. 'A man needs a religion.'
• No one more than Lord Marchmain could have made it more obvious, throughout his life, exactly what were his feelings on religion.

• Charles Ryder calls it 'such a lot of witchcraft and hypocrisy'.
• Aimee Thanatogenos' father lost money in religion, by investing in the Four Square Gospel.
• His voices tell Gilbert Pinfold that he does not really believe in his religion. 'He just pretends to because he thinks it aristocratic. It goes with being Lord of the Manor'.
DF 45, 83; BR 121, 123, 170, 185, 309, 310; LO 73; GP 102
(*See also* CATHOLICS, PRIESTS, and individual characters)

REIGN OF TERROR
Period during the French Revolution between 1793 and 1794 during which the Jacobins, under Robespierre, condemned to death some 3,000 people in Paris and perhaps another 14,000 in the rest of France.
• To Paul Pennyfeather the cramped and filthy streets of Marseilles in 1922 seems like a Hollywood stage set from the Reign of Terror.
DF 152

RENAISSANCE
Intellectual movement in European history between the medieval and the modern, of the fifteenth and sixteenth centuries, characterized by a rediscovery of classical art and literature and the growth of scientific knowledge.
• On the first evening of painting his four pictures of the interior of Marchmain House, Charles Ryder feels himself become a Renaissance man.
BR 213

RENDING, LORD
Fellow student of Paul Pennyfeather at Scone college in 1922, and victim of the Bollinger Club (q.v.). He can afford to hunt, but eschews this and collects china and smokes cigars in the college garden after breakfast. The Bollinger smash his china and grind his cigars into his carpet.
DF 10–11

REPPINGTON, MR
District Magistrate at Matodi after the Azanian crisis. Drives a two-seater car which he calls 'the little bus'. He and his wife have a drink with the Brethertons and dine with the Lepperidges. They live in the fifth bungalow along above the town.
BM 234

REPTON, HUMPHREY *(1752–1818)*
Leading British landscape gardener of the generation after Capability Brown. See his *Observations on the practice and Theory of landscape Gardening* (1803).
• The park of Boot Magna Hall was laid out by 'some forgotten, provincial predecessor of Repton'.
Sc 17

REQUIEM
Cordelia Flyte tells Cara that having a requiem does not necessarily ensure that you will go to Heaven.
BR 313

RESTAURANTS
• **ABC Shops**, at one of which Mrs Kent-Cumberland lunches with Gladys Cruttwell in 1938.
• **Amurath Café**, Debra Dowa, Azania. Proprietor Mr Youkoumian (q.v.).
• **Basso's**, Marseilles. Where Paul Pennyfeather dines in 1922. He has bouillabaisse and Meursalt in the covered balcony and watches the lights reflected on the water.
• **The Berkeley**, London. Tamplin's brother takes him here for lunch in 1919. It is rather rowdy and full of 'Sandhurst men'.
• **Braganza Hotel**, London. Has a restaurant purpose-built for banquets in which Lord Copper throws the banquet in honour of Boot in 1937.
• **Cadena Café**, Oxford. Where Sebastian Flyte supposes that 'normal' undergraduates go to drink coffee every morning in 1923.
• **Chez Espinosa (Espinosa's).** Second most expensive restaurant in London. The bill always comes to the same amount,

whatever you eat. Decorated with oilcloth and Lalique glass. People who like that sort of decoration go there all the time and comment on how frightful, it is. The commissionaire is a veteran of the Boer War. The head waiter keeps a list of all the guests, expressly for the gossip-columnists.

In 1927 Adam Fenwick-Symes is taken there by Simon Balcairn, and later takes Nina there for lunch.

In 1933 John Beaver takes Brenda Last there for dinner. She pays.

In 1936 Simon Lent dines there with Sylvia.

• **Café de la Paix.** Adam Fenwick-Symes reports seeing Count Cincinnati here in 1927. Where Adam and Ginger meet Hoop and watch a coloured singer.

• **Café de Paris.** Where Brenda Last sees Jock Grant-Menzies in 1933.

• **Café Lenin.** *See* **Café Wilberforce**

• **Café Royal**, Regent Street, London. Restaurant associated in the 1890s with the aesthetic and Bohemian circle of Wilde and Beardsley.

Charles Ryder dines here with Jean de Brissac de la Motte in May 1926. Roger and Lucy Simmonds dine here in April 1939. Frank de Souza and Pat eat here after the theatre on 30 December 1939. Ambrose Silk always feels at home here. Basil Seal goes here to observe Poppet Green in 1940

• **Café Royal.** Tea shop restaurant in the town near the motor-racing circuit.

• **Café Wilberforce**, Jacksonburg, Ishmaelia. Changes it name to the **Lenin** with the coming to power of the Communists in 1932.

• **Casanova Hotel**, Bloomsbury, London. Adam Fenwick-Symes as Mr Chatterbox, reports that this is the smartest place to dance in London.

• **The Château de Madrid**, The Station Hotel, Glasgow. Where Trimmer and Virginia Crouchback dine in November 1940. The waiter is a bogus Frenchman.

• **Ciro's**, Paris. Nightclub and restaurant favoured by Rex Mottram.

• **Florian's**, Venice. Where Sebastian Flyte, Charles Ryder and Lord Marchmain have coffee after dinner, and are spotted by an English couple.

• **Foyot's**, Paris. Where Charles Ryder and Sebastian Flyte have lunch en route to Venice in 1922.

• **The Garibaldi**, the Seafront, Southsand. Owned by Guiseppe Pelecci (q.v.). Guy Crouchback and Apthorpe dine here frequently in March 1940. It is closed down by the Government on 10 June 1940, after Italy declares war.

• **A Grill Room** in The Strand, London. Where the staff of the *Daily Beast* always entertain when on expenses. Mr Salter cooks his own Magyar food here. William Boot asks for a mixed grill.

• **Gunter's** Berkeley Square, London. Where Charles and Sebastian meet Julia Flyte the morning after their arrest.

• **The Holborn Grill.** According to Jorkins (q.v.) in 1919 they serve the best meal in London at the four and sixpenny table d'hôte.

• **The Honest Injun.** Workmen's café in the town near the motor-racing circuit. Serves fried fish.

• **Hotel Eden**, Santa Dulcina, Italy. Café Restaurant which changes its name to the Albergo de Sol during the Abyssinian crisis.

• **Hotel Metropole**, Cympryddyg, Wales. Where Philbrick dines frequently, always on his own, and always on the best of everything. Also where Paul Pennyfeather, Grimes and Prendergast dine in 1922. The soup is served in small aluminium bowls.

• **The D'Italie**, Soho, London. Where Charles Ryder is taken for dinner by his Aunt Philippa on 23 September 1919. It is 'a little place', not well known, and full of literary people and artists.

• **The Lotti**, Paris. Where Rex Mottram leaves Sebastian after dinner in 1923.

• **The Luna**, Venice. According to Lady Marchmain it is full of English.

• **Overton's**, Victoria, London. Peregrine Crouchback takes Virginia to dinner here in December 1943. It is approached up side stairs and known to the discriminating. They eat oysters and turbot.

• **An Oyster Restaurant** next to a

theatre, London. Where Guy Crouchback dines alone on 30 December 1939.

• **Paillard's**, Paris. Where Rex Mottram takes Charles Ryder for dinner in 1923. It is 'a sombre little place' but the food (q.v.) is excellent.

• **Raineri's**, Rome. Lord Marchmain dines here with Beryl Muspratt and Brideshead in 1938.

• **The Restaurant**, Bari, Italy. In 1944 there is an illicit restaurant in a small ancient town near Bari. It does not take any paper currency but rather petrol and cigarettes.

• **The Restaurant de Verdun**, Marseilles. Where Basil Seal dines on his way to Azania in 1932.

• **A Restaurant** in Albemarle Street, London. Opened in 1933. Brenda Last and her sister Marjorie go here for lunch and meet Mrs Beaver.

• **A Restaurant** in Charlotte Street, London. The tables are too squashed together, the menus are sheets of purple handwriting and the waiters forget the orders.

• **A Restaurant** in Tottenham Court Road, London. Where in 1927 one can buy oysters at three and sixpence a dozen.

• **The Ritz**, Piccadilly, London. Paul Pennyfeather lunches here with Alastair Trumpington and Peter Pastmaster on the day of his wedding in 1922, and is arrested. Julia Flyte lunches here in the 1920s. Roger Simmonds does not like it here. He hates the attention. In 1939 John Plant invites Roger and his wife Lucy to lunch here.

• **The Ritz Grill**, Piccadilly, London. Where Charles Ryder takes Cordelia Flyte for dinner in early June 1926.

• **Romano's**. One of Theodore Boot's old haunts in the 1890s.

• **Ruben's**. Small fish restaurant run by Ruben, which during WWII manages to get hold of the most unobtainable foods: Colchester oysters, Scotch salmon, lobsters, prawns, gull's eggs and caviare. There are also French cheeses delivered by parachutist and submarine, and good wines. It is 'a rare candle in a dark and naughty world'. Guy Crouchback asks Jumbo Trotter to lunch here on 29 October 1943.

• **The Savoy Grill**, The Strand, London. Where Wenlock Jakes dines as the guest of Silas Shock on 11 December 1937.

• **A Tea Shop**, Broad Street, Oxford. Where Charles Ryder regularly has breakfast on Sundays.

DF 99–104, 151; VB 84, 108, 113, 116, 119, 151, 177, 178; HD 40, 45, 46, 83; BM 18, 88; Sc 31, 80, 169, 213, 215; PF 59, 173, 174; BR 58, 92, 95, 96, 101, 117, 165, 194, 211, 284, 305; MA 11, 80, 107; OG 40, 73; US 134, 135, 169; WS 63, 104, 151, 155.

REVOLUTION

In 1926 Charles Ryder expects England to be in a state of revolution: 'the red flag on the post office, the overturned train, the drunken NCO's, the gaol open and gangs of released criminals prowling the streets.'

BR 194

REYKJAVIK, ICELAND

Mr Salter does not know where Reykjavik is, and asks William Boot.

Sc 28

RHINEBECK

Gilbert Pinfold's voices accuse him of never having stayed here.

GP 147

RHODES, CECIL *(1853–1902)*

African statesman. Secured Bechuanaland and Rhodesia for Britain. Mr Baldwin's activities in Ishmaelia recall Rhodes exploits.

Sc 177

RHODES

Island in the Aegean, where Sebastian Flyte and Mr Samgrass start their tour of the Near East, staying with the Military Governor.

BR 152

RHODESIA, AFRICA

Where Arthur Atwater has a pal.

WS 137

RIBBENTROP, JOACHIM VON
(1893–1946)
German politician. Became a Nazi 1932. Ambassador to Britain 1936–39. Executed 1945.
• Freddy Sothill thinks that one cannot blame Ribbentrop for thinking the English decadent if he has been taking Basil Seal as his model. Lady Seal would never have 'that vulgar man Ribbentrop' in her house, even when Emma Granchester was trying to get everyone to be sweet to him.
• Ribbentrop tells one of Rex Mottram's friends in 1938 that the German Army only keeps Hitler in power as long as they can get something for nothing.
• In 1943 Dr Akonanga (c.v.) is giving Ribbentrop 'the most terrible dreams'.
PF 16, 19; US 84

RICH, THE
Among the rich 'a sharp instinct for self-preservation' passes for wisdom.
PF 13

RILEY
Butler to Bella Fleace (q.v.). He has a sympathetic glitter in his eye when she announces her intention to hold a dance. For the party he is dressed in knee breeches and black silk stockings.
WS 82, 85

RIMBAUD, ARTHUR *(1854–1891)*
French poet; associate of Verlaine. See his 'Les Illuminations' (1872).
• At the age of eighteen John Boot (q.v.) writes a life of Rimbaud.
• Anthony Blanche tells Charles Ryder that he has heard Mrs Stuyvesant Oglander and her friends say that he has become a second Rimbaud with his pictures of South America.
Sc 5; BR 259

RIO DE JANIERO, BRAZIL
Where, in 1922, Margot Metroland has a vacancy for one of her girls, which she fills with Jane Grimes (q.v.).
DF 145

RIPON, MISS
Member of the Pigstanton Hunt whose horse rears at the backfiring of Mr Tendril's niece's motor-bicycle and kicks John Last into a ditch, killing him.
HD 102–4

RITCHIE-HOOK, GENERAL BEN
(d. 1944)
'The great Halberdier enfant terrible of the Great War.' Youngest company commander in the history of the corps. Wounded many times. Recommended for the VC. Once came back from a raid on German lines with the head of a German sentry in either hand.

Has one eye; wears a patch over the other. His hair and eye are black. Wears a steel-rimmed monocle. His right hand is maimed with two fingers and half a thumb which he hides in a black glove. His soldier servant is called Dawkins. Between the wars he fights in Ireland, the Matto Grosso, and the Holy Land. Brigadier of the Halberdiers in 1940.

Travels light with pyjamas and hairbrushes. Rides a motor-bike. He is no bully but revels in surprise. The War Office call him 'the one-eyed monster' and are terrified of him.

Has a vendetta with Apthorpe over his 'thunder-box' (q.v.) which he eventually blows up (with Apthorpe inside). Apthorpe considers him a certifiable maniac.

Onboard ship bound for Africa he prowls the decks with 'a weapon like a hedging implement which he had found invaluable in the previous war'. Sneaks ashore with Guy, kills a native and returns with his head. Demands to have the head pickled. Is wounded in the leg. Is evacuated by plane. Reappears on the Isle of Mugg on Julia Stitch's yacht as commander of 'Hookforce' of which X Commando is a part. He is nicknamed 'the Widow Twankey' by X Commando to whom he appears slightly absurd. In Guy Crouchback's eyes he is something of a hero.

Flies to join his command in the Middle East and is lost. Turns up again leading 'a group of wogs' in Abyssinia. Arrives in Cairo in June 1941.

By 1943 he is a major-general.

Survives the plane crash in Yugoslavia. Of the crew's death he can only remark 'the dog it was that died'.

Accompanies Guy, General Spitz and de Souza to watch the manoeuvres. Launches a one-man raid on a block-house. He is hit several times by rifle fire and killed. His body is found by the Germans and provokes wonder and suspicion.

Dawkins informs Guy that his master had died as he would have wanted having told him: 'Dawkins, I wish those bastards would shoot better. I don't want to go home.'

MA 54, 66, 67, 68, 69, 72, 117, 123, 153, 221, 240; OG 98, 111, 241; US 95, 209, 211, 221, 222, 223

ROBERT

Young man to whom the correspondent on the *SS Glory of Greece* becomes engaged, and then breaks it off.

WS 21

ROBERTS, MRS

Landlady of the local pub at Llanabba (q.v.).

DF 27

ROBIN *(b. 1912)*

Lover of Celia Ryder who settles down with her and her children at the Old Rectory after her divorce from Charles who remembers him as 'a half-baked, pimply youth'. He is immature for his age but 'absolutely devoted' to Celia, who is seven years his senior.

BR 281, 284

ROCHFORTS, THE

Ancient family of Ireland whose blood long ago merged with that of the Fleaces.

WS 79

RODERICK

Rubber planter from Malaya who is Apthorpe's equivalent in the batch of Halberdier officers from the training depot in 1940.

MA 93

RODIN, AUGUSTE *(1840–1917)*

French sculptor. Key figure among the impressionists. See his 'Le Baiser' (1898), 'Porte d'Infer' (1880), and 'Le Penseur' (1904).

• The 'Lovers' Nest' at Whispering Glades (q.v.) is 'zoned' about a 'very, very beautiful marble replica of Rodin's famous statue, "The Kiss".'

LO 38

ROLAND, THE HORN OF

The horn, Olivant, of Roland, knight of Charlemagne. When attacked in the pass of Roncesvalles he sounded it to warn the king. It was so loud that it struck terror into the Saracens and even killed the birds.

• 'Fido' Hound (q.v.) is called to life on Crete by a new note 'clear as the horn of Roland'. It is the smell of a bubbling cauldron of food, tended by the deserters.

OG 202

ROMANS

Mr Crouchback tells Guy that in the 1870s and 1880s 'every decent Roman disliked the Piedmontese'.

US 16

ROME, ITALY

Lady Marchmain tells Charles Ryder that in pagan Rome wealth was necessarily cruel.

• The Sudanese police regard Fez as a New Zealander would see Rome, so far apart are their cultures.

• Where Lord Marchmain meets Brideshead and his new wife, Beryl.

• When Gervase and Hermione Crouchback visit Italy on their honeymoon in 1889, there are French troops at the defences of Rome and the Cardinals ride side-saddle on the Pincian Hill. They have an audience with the Pope. Hermione paints the ruins. Gervase is all the Romans expect an Englishman to be.

• Where Guy Crouchback sees Ivor Claire ride, at the Concorso Ippico, before the war.

• Thinking of the Lateran Treaty, what, wonders Guy, in the history of Rome is fifteen years,and was there not once a boy called the King of Rome?

• The lamp in the chapel at Broome was bought by Hermione Crouchback in the Via Babuino.

• To Guy, Moses conjures up an image of the statue of the patriarch striking the rock near the Grand Hotel in Rome, in the Church of St Peter in Chains.

• Where Gilbert Pinfold breaks his journey from Colombo to England. He breakfasts here.

• Having 'left his coin in the fountain of Trevi' Scott-King is 'a Mediterranean man'.

BR 122, 203, 297; MA 9; OG 48; US 15, 72, 226; GP 149; WS 201

ROMMEL, FIELD-MARSHALL, ERWIN VON *(1891–1944)*

German soldier. Served in the Great War. An early Nazi. Commanded the Afrika Korps. Defeated by the Eighth Army. Plotted to kill Hitler. Committed suicide 1944.

• In 1953 the road to Cairo from Port Said presents more warlike an aspect than it did in 1943 when Gilbert Pinfold was there and 'Rommel was at the gates'.

GP 140

RON

One of the sentries at the gate of the Headquarters of the British Mission to the Anti Fascist forces of National Liberation (Adriatic) in 1944.

US 153

RONCESVALLES

Pass in the Pyrenees where according to legend in AD 778, the hero Roland and the rearguard of Charlemagne's army were slain by the Saracens.

(*See* ROLAND)

• The advertisement placed by Guy Crouchback in *The Times*, seeking Chatty Corner sounds, he feels, 'a despairing note, as though from the gorge of Roncesvalles'.

OG 39

ROOTS, CAPTAIN

Staff Captain of X Commando in 1941.

OG 165

ROOTS

(*See* BOOT, WILLIAM)

ROSENBAUM, MRS

Madame of a brothel in Jermyn Street in 1922. Bessy Brown is one of her girls.

DF 145

ROSS

Butler to Lady Amelia (q.v.).

WS 30

ROSSCOMMON, LADY (FANNY)

Lady in waiting. Sister-in-law of Lady Marchmain. Is always telling her that she brought up the children badly. Has a villa at Cap Ferrat where Julia Flyte stays in the summer of 1922, and where she meets Rex Mottram. After Lady Marchmain's death in 1926 wants Cordelia to live with her.

• Give a luncheon party in 1938 in honour of Brideshead's engagement.

BR 118, 176, 182, 211, 283

ROSSETTI, DANTE GABRIEL *(1828–1882)*

English painter and poet. Founder of the Pre-Raphaelite brotherhood. His paintings gradually became more and more ornate and romantic in feelings. See his 'Annunciation' (1850), 'The Blessed Damozel', and 'The Wedding of St. George'.

• Everard Spruce compares Ludovic's writing *The Death Wish* to the humble beginnings of Hall Caine (q.v.), the protégé of Rossetti.

US 203

ROTHSCHILD, FATHER, S.J.

Fellow passenger of Adam Fenwick-Symes on the cross-channel ferry in 1927. In his small, borrowed suitcase he carries six new books in six languages, a false beard and a heavily annotated school atlas. He is able to remember everything about anyone of even small importance. Looking over the rail of the ship he looks not unlike a gargoyle. Met Adam Fenwick-Symes at lunch with the Dean of Balliol in 1922. Knows Colonel Blount. Finds Mrs Ape 'extremely dangerous and disagreeable'. On the crossing he thinks of martyred saints and repeats penitential psalms. During his childhood had been dandled on the knee of Doge, the butler.

• Telephones Mr Outrage at Lottie Crump's and advises him to leave at once.

• 'Conspires' with Mr Outrage and Lord Metroland at a party of Margot's on 11 November 1927. Wonders whether the Bright Young People are not all 'possessed with an almost fatal hunger for permanence'. He wonders whether they are not right. Rides a motor-cycle.

VB 9, 13, 15, 37, 49, 101, 132, 133

ROUAULT, GEORGES ***(1871–1958)***

French painter. His subjects are often clowns, prostitutes or Biblical. The house visited by Angel and his team of BBC interviewers before they reach Lychpole contains a Rouault watercolour. Gilbert Pinfold remarks that he did not know that he painted in watercolour: 'Anyway he's a dreadful painter.'

GP 19

ROYAL ACADEMY, LONDON

Mr Plant looks on the Academy as a club. He enjoys the dinners and often attends the schools, where he states his opinion of art 'in Johnsonian terms'.

WS 113

ROYAL AIR FORCE

Mrs Leonard wishes Jim had joined the RAF. 'You just settle down at an RAF station as though it was business with regular hours and a nice crowd.' 'Their wives live comfortable, and what's more they're the people who are winning the war.'

• Ian Kilbannock admits that 'the RAF does not understand about servants'.

• To de Souza: 'Air Force jokes are deeply depressing'.

The RAF does not read newspapers.

• Trixie (q.v.) has cousins in the RAF.

MA 65, 215; OG 99; US 109, 116; GP 183; WS 147

(*See also* BEECH, BARLOW, KILBANNOCK, AND PLASTIC)

ROYAL GEOGRAPHICAL SOCIETY, LONDON

General Crutwell is a member. His subscription is one of the reasons that he works in a department store.

SC 44

ROYAL NAVY

John Plant tells his fellow pupils at his prep school that his father is an officer in the Royal Navy.

WS 168

(*See also* DARTMOUTH)

ROYAL YACHT SQUADRON

Colonel Blount is a member and has an engraving with a key in the library at Doubting Hall.

DR 67

(*See also* COWES)

RUBEN

London restaurateur able in 1944 to supply his patrons with almost anything. When Kerstie Kilbannock asks him how he can make such good mayonnaise he replies: 'Quite simply, my lady, fresh eggs and olive oil.'

US 23

RUBENS, SIR PETER PAUL (1577–1640)

Flemish painter. Worked in England at the court of Charles I. Renowned for his extravagantly fleshy nudes and use of deep colour. See his 'Rape of the Sabines', 'Birth of Venus' and 'Peace and War'.

• Mr Plant advises art history students to 'trot round Europe studying the Rubenses'.

WS 128

RUBY

London society figure between the 1900s and 1940s. Used to have a house in Belgrave Square. Before the war Virginia Crouchback used to go to her parties. Friend of Lord Curzon, Elinor Glyn, Boni

de Castelane, the Marchesa Casati, Pavlova, J.M. Barrie. For thirty years she had glittering parties at Belgrave Square. By the 1940s her skin is brown and wrinkled. She wonders what it was all in aid of. Most of her possessions are French. Her husband was in Asquith's cabinet.
US 78, 80, 122, 123

RUM (RHUM), ISLE OF, INNER HEBRIDES
From where the isle of Mugg is visible as two cones.
OG 47

RUNCIBLE, THE HONOURABLE AGATHA
One of the Bright Young People. Daughter of Viola Chasm. Crosses on the ferry from France and enjoys having her tummy strapped with sticking plaster. At Dover she is mistaken for a well-known jewellery smuggler and is strip searched 'by two terrific wardresses'. Afterwards she appears in the newspapers saying that it was 'too shaming'.

Dines with Adam Fenwick-Symes, for which she pays. Lottie Crump calls her a tart. Wears a Hawaiian costume to Johnnie Hoop's savage party.

Appears in court several times as a plaintiff in the Simon Balcairn case, as a member of the public, and as a prisoner sentenced to a fine or seven days for contempt of court. She puts all the cuttings into a scrap book.

Goes to the St Christopher's club with Adam, Ginger, Miles and Nina. Goes to the motor races with Miles and Adam and Archie Schwert. Feels ill. Happens to put on an armband saying 'Spare Driver'. Smokes cigarettes in the pits. Takes over from the driver of No 13. She wins the race and goes on driving and crashes into a village pump. She never recovers.

She is taken to a nursing home in Wimpole Street where she becomes delirious. She receives the Bright Young People and has cocktails.

She dies.
VB 11, 24, 26, 34, 44, 53, 58–59, 124, 158, 167, 174–180, 200, 206

RUPERT, PRINCE (1619–1682)
Third son of the Elector Palatine. Served for the Royalist cause from 1642–1645. Redoubtable in his reckless bravery.
• Charles Ryder knows that Hooper did not, as a child, ride in his mind with Prince Rupert.
BR 14

RURITANIA, THE KING OF
Patron of Shepheard's Hotel (q.v.). He is in fact the ex-king, expelled after the Great War. He is a sad man with a beard. He is penniless and his wife, Maria Christina, is in a 'looney bin'. She thinks that everyone is a bomb. His uncle Joseph was blown to bits at the opera. Tells Adam Fenwick-Symes about a major from Prussia who had tried to reorganize the Ruritanian Army and had run off with the regimental silver of the Royal Guard, a pair of candlesticks from the Chapel Royal and the Lord Chamberlain's wife.
VB 38–39, 46

RUSKIN, JOHN (1819–1900)
English author and art critic. Defender of Turner and later the Pre-Raphaelites. See his 'Modern Painters', 'Unto This Last' (1860) and 'The Seven Lamps of Architecture'.
• Charles Ryder, from school to university, makes the leap from Ruskin's puritanism to that of Roger Fry.

Charles reads Julia Flyte Ruskin's description, in *Pre-Raphaelitism*, of which there is a copy in the library at Brideshead, of Hunt's 'The Awakening Conscience'.
• On the first morning at Penkirk, Ritchie-Hook (q.v.) behaves like 'a second Ruskin' and orders his officers to 'dig and carry'.
BR 79, 276; MA 162

RUSSIANS
The Perroquet nightclub in Debra Dowa is managed by a Georgian prince.
• Katchen's father is Russian.
• Mr Baldwin tells Erik Olafsen that Russians are 'bad people'.
• At Bellamy's in 1940 the question is asked 'Why go to war at all? . . . If we are

concerned with justice the Russians are as guilty as the Germans.'

- In 1941 the experts believe that the Russians do not have a chance against the invading Germans.
- Colonel Tickeridge is of the opinion that the Russian sort of government is 'rotten': 'So it had been last time. And the Russians changed it. Probably they would again.'
- Nearly all the British workers are keen to help Russia in 1941: 'It's how they've been educated.'
- To the inhabitants of the New Britain Russia is 'our Great Neighbour in the East'.

BN 51; SC 134, 174; MA 25; OG 239, 240, 246; GP 188

(*See also* COMMUNISM)

RYDER, ALFRED

Cousin of Mr Ryder who gives him the invaluable advice to always wear a tall hat on Sundays during term at Oxford.

BR 27

RYDER, CAROLINE *(b. 1934)*

Daughter of Charles and Celia Ryder. Her godmother is Bertha van Halst.

BR 219

RYDER, CELIA

(*See* MULCASTER)

RYDER, CAPTAIN CHARLES *(b. 1903)*

Son of Mr (Ned) Ryder (q.v.). Educated Lancing and Hertford College, Oxford. His home is not 'God fearing'.

Mother killed nursing with the Red Cross in Serbia in the Great War.

At Lancing he is in the upper fifth in 1919. Keeps a diary. Reads *Fortitude*. Loves Gothic architecture and breviaries. Works on an illuminated version of Hodgson's *Bells of Heaven*. Longs to have a printing press. Helps Graves with his.

At Hertford, Oxford (1922–1924); reads History.

Has rooms on the ground floor in the front quad which are filled on summer evenings with the scent of gilly flowers. His scout is Lunt. During his first two terms his rooms are furnished with a reproduction of a Van Gogh, an Omega screen, a poster by Mcknight Kauffer and a figurine of Polly Peachum. His books are Fry's *Vision and Design*, *A Shropshire Lad*, *Eminent Victorians*, *Georgian Poetry*, *Sinister Street* and *South Wind*.

First sees Sebastian Flyte at Germer's. Sebastian is sick in his rooms one evening, a little before midnight in early March 1923. Sebastian takes him in hand. Visits Brideshead for the first time during Eights Week 1923.

Is astounded by Brideshead. Takes to expensive clothes, cigars, Lalique and drink, particularly champagne. Is often drunk in the afternoon.

With Sebastian he seems to enjoy a happy childhood previously denied him with 'naughtiness high in the catalogue of grave sins'.

Returns to London in the long vacation 1923. Has no money left, and no allowance due until October; is bored; does not get on with his father. Receives a telegram from Sebastian telling him to come at once. Travels to Brideshead. Meets Julia Flyte and feels her sexuality.

Stays at Brideshead; paints panels in the office. Tastes the wine from the cellars. Is drunk every night. Meets Father Phipps – Catholicism is an enigma to him.

Back at Oxford is possessed by an Autumnal mood. Joins the Ruskin school of Art. Spends the entire autumn term 1923 in the company of Sebastian.

Travels to London with Boy and Sebastian for Julia's dance. They leave early, drunk, and go to the Old Hundredth. Picks up a prostitute; is arrested and locked up. Bailed out by Rex Mottram. Fined a pound.

Visits Brideshead over Christmas 1923. Talks to Lady Marchmain. Is not touched by her faith. As he grows closer to the Flytes grows further away from Sebastian.

Back at Oxford in the spring of 1924 he feels unable to help Sebastian, who he realizes is a drunkard.

In the summer term the shadows seem to close round them. Finds lodgings for himself and Sebastian in Merton Street.

Has a long talk with Lady Marchmain who, next day takes Sebastian away. Returns to London at the end of term. Tells his father that he is leaving Oxford to become an artist.

Goes to Paris to study at the art school. Takes rooms on the Ile St Louis.

Stays at Brideshead over Christmas 1924. Tells Cordelia that modern art is 'all bosh'. Talks to Julia about Sebastian. Gives Sebastian two pounds for a drink. Paints a panel in the office. Is chided by Lady Marchmain for giving Sebastian money. Leaves Brideshead and is determined never to return: 'henceforth I live in a world of three dimensions'.

At the beginning of May 1925 reads of Rex and Julia's engagement.

Is commissioned by Brideshead to paint four pictures of Marchmain House.

For ten years after 1926 he is 'borne along a road outwardly full of change and incident, but never during that time, except sometimes in my painting . . . did I come alive as I had been during the time of my friendship with Sebastian'.

Becomes an architectural painter. Publishes three folios: *Ryder's Country Seats*, *Ryder's English Homes*, and *Ryder's Village and Provincial Architecture*. Each sells a thousand copies at five guineas each.

Marries Celia Mulcaster 1930. They live at The Old Rectory. They have two children John (1931) and Caroline (1934). In 1934 Celia has an affair.

In 1934 travels to Mexico and Central America and produces *Ryder's Latin America*.

In 1936 returns to England via New York. Meets Julia Flyte. On board ship they begin an affair.

Between 1936 and 1938 paints many portraits of Julia; visits Naples to be with her.

In 1938 in December is divorced from Celia. Plans to marry Julia. Calls Sebastian the 'fore-runner'. Talks to Cordelia about Sebastian.

At the first signs of war negotiates for a commission in the special reserve.

In June 1940 his divorce is made absolute.

Talks to Lord Marchmain on his deathbed. Julia cannot marry him. By 1942 he feels 'very old'. Goes to bed after the nine o'clock news.

Arrives at Brideshead, where is battalion is billeted in 1942, by which time he is 'homeless, childless, middle-aged, loveless'. He visits Nanny Hawkins and the chapel and says a prayer.

Sometime between 1938 and 1942 he has become converted to Catholicism. It is all he has.

BR 9–22, 24, 26, 29, 32–3, 43, 44, 45, 46, 57–9, 78, 79, 80, 83, 96, 102–17, 120, 123, 130–33, 142, 156, 166, 193–206, 209, 210, 213, 215, 216–18, 223, 227, 235, 254, 255, 256, 259, 261, 264, 268, 273, 277, 282, 296, 302, 310, 315, 324, 330; WS 287, 301, 302, 305–7, 313

RYDER, JASPER ***(b. 1900)***

Cousin of Charles Ryder (q.v.), the son of his father's elder brother. Lives at Boughton. At Oxford 1918–22. Secretary of the Canning, president of the JCR. Smokes a pipe. Advises Charles on how to behave at Oxford, and to change his rooms. Visits Charles again in the summer term 1923 and tells him that his behaviour is letting down the college and that he has made him 'a figure of mockery' at his dining club. Writes to Charles' father, who does nothing. Is missed by Charles during his second year. By 1936 has a wife and children. Charles spends Christmas there in 1936 and 1937.

BR 264

RYDER, JOHN ***(b. 1931)***

Son of Charles and Celia Ryder (q.v.). Calls himself John-John. Gets on well with his uncle, Boy Mulcaster.

BR 219, 222

RYDER, MELCHIOR

Cousin of Charles Ryder who is 'imprudent' in his investments and has to emigrate to Australia. At the age of twenty he is part owner of a musical show. ('One of his few happy ventures.')

BR 63, 65

RYDER, MR (NED) ***(b. 1866)***
Father of Charles Ryder. The Summer before he goes up to Oxford is given advice by his cousin Alfred to always wear a tall hat on Sundays, which he does.

Lives in London, in a house near the Bayswater Road. Member of the Atheneum. Is keen on 'Etruscan notions of Immortality'. Gives Charles an allowance of five hundred and fifty pounds a year. Does not allow Charles into his library. Seems older than his years. Wears a frogged velvet smoking suit when dining at home. Dines at his club on Mrs Abel's evening off.

Snuffles a great deal. Reads a book over dinner, making notes in the margin with a pencil in a gold case. Hardly ever sees Charles.

Is puzzled as to why Charles, at the age of thirty-four, should want to be divorced and remarry. Seems impervious to change.
BR 26, 27, 41, 45, 61–4, 68, 72, 142, 282, 286

RYDER, PHILIPPA
Aunt of Charles Ryder (q.v.). After the death of Mrs Ryder she comes to lives in the Ryder house and makes herself Charles' companion. In September 1919 takes Charles to dinner at the D'Italie in Soho, and to see *The Choice*. Knows many literary figures and artists. Says that it is middle-class to have only three courses at dinner. Gives Mrs Abel ten menus after the death of Charles' mother, from which the household never deviates. After a year she leaves the house, and eventually England.
BR 65, 66; WS 289, 291

S

SACKVILLE-STRUTT, SALLY
Friend of Lieutenant Padfield whose daughter is at Broome School. She is captain of Crouchback House, and wins the hockey in 1943.
US 25

SACRIFICE, HUMAN
Human sacrifices are an embarrassing feature of the consecration of the Bishop of Popo in Azania.
BM 144

ST ALBANS, HERTFORDSHIRE
Where, in 1943, on their way from London to Mugg, Jumbo Trotter and Guy Crouchback turn on the lights of their car and hear the air-raid sirens begin to wail.
OG 46

SAINT-CLOUD, LADY
Mother of Brenda Last, Marjorie and Reggie. Writes to Brenda at the time of John's funeral. Tells her 'love is the only thing stronger than sorrow'. Cables to Reggie to return from Tunisia to sort out Brenda's divorce. Attends the commemoration of Tony's monument in 1934. Believes that it is what he would have wanted.
HD 124, 220

SAINT-CLOUD, LORD REGGIE
(b. 1900)
Brother of Brenda Last. Bachelor. Archaeologist. Sells Brakeleigh. Is entirely different to Brenda. Prematurely stout. 'There was an instability in his gait and in his eyes a furtive look as though he were at any moment liable to ambush.' Spends half of his time abroad on archaeological expeditions. His house is full of artifacts–amphoras, axe heads, bone splinters and a marble head. He has written two books on the subject. When in London he regularly attends the House of Lords. Is a bore about archaeology.

Meets Tony for dinner at Brown's. Tries to persuade Tony to settle on Brenda a payment of two thousand pounds a year, and sell Hetton. He fails and provokes Tony into sailing to Brazil.
HD 19, 145–61

SAINT-CLOUD, MARJORIE
Sister of Brenda Last. Married to Allan.
HD 38, 51, 56

ST OMER'S RECORDS
From which Challoner misread a transcript, thus plunging the history of the Crouchback family into confusion by saying that it was the steward who gave away the hiding place of the Blessed Gervase (q.v.).
OG 21

ST PAUL, MINNESOTA
Where, in 1963, Pimpernell (q.v.) is professor of poetic drama.
WS 253

SAINTS, THE
In whose lives, according to Lady Marchmain, 'animals are always doing the oddest things'.
BR 123

SAKUYU
In Arabic Sakuyu means 'man without mercy'.
• Black native tribe of Azania. They are herdsmen who live with their emaciated cattle in the hills. They wear their hair, 'in

a dense fuzz; their chests and arms were embossed with ornamental scars'.
BM 8, 36, 210

SALAMANCA
(*See* BATTLES)

SALERNO, ITALY
During which battle in 1943 Brigadier Cope (q.v.) is wounded.
US 155

SALFORD, LANCASHIRE
Where Engineer Garcia worked for seven years with Green, Gorridge and Wright.
WS 212

SALISBURY, WILTSHIRE
Nearest town to Twisbury Manor (q.v.).

SALLUST *(86–34 BC)*
Roman historian. See his *Catalina*, *Jugurtha* and *Historiarum Libri Quinque*.
• One of the authors with whom Scott-King (q.v.) crams the lower forms at Granchester.
WS 195

SALONIKA, GREECE
Where Cruttwell's Folly stands as a memorial to General Cruttwell (q.v.), who served here during the Great War.
Sc 44

SALTER, MR
Foreign editor of the *Daily Beast*. Married.

Served 1914 to 1918 in Flanders. Blown up and buried while sheltering in a farm. Has worked at Megalopolitan for fifteen years. 'Normal life, as he saw it, consisted in regular journeys by electric train, monthly cheques, communal amusements and a cosy horizon of slates and chimneys; there was something un-English and not quite right about the country.' Sometimes holidays on the east coast. He thinks that the country is what you can see from the train to Frinton. Lives in Welwyn Garden City. His garden has crazy paving.

He was once carefree at the woman's page and then chose the jokes for one of Lord Copper's comics. (*Clean Fun*). When he wants to tell Lord Copper that he is right says 'Definitely, Lord Copper', and when he is wrong says 'Up to a point, Lord Copper.'

Addresses William Boot on the subject of mangel wurzels, but gets his words muddled and asks him 'How are your boots, Root?'

His most frequent phrase is 'Oh, dear, oh dear'.

Through Bateson, loses William on his return from Ishmailia. Travels to Boot Magna Hall to try and bring William back. Is appalled by the manners of country people; has a horrible journey and refuses a lift in the back of a slag lorry and walks the three miles to the hall over the fields in the darkness. He walks six miles and arrives at eight o'clock having been chased by a herd of cattle and barked at by farm dogs. Lapses into a coma.

Stays in Priscilla's room, with Annabel her dog. Dines with the Boots, is denied wine and port. Tries to win William back but William refuses all offers. Has the idea of using Theodore as 'The Boot'.

Becomes art editor of *Home Knitting.*
Sc 14, 16, 26–34, 194–215

SALZBURG, AUSTRIA
Location of an international music festival.
• In 1939 a Swiss paper reports that storm troopers have attended a requiem mass in Salzburg.
• Angela Lyne refuses to accompany Cedric to Salzburg one summer in the 1930s.
• Julia Flyte accompanies her mother to Salzburg after her initial courtship by Rex Mottram at Cap Ferrat in 1923.
• Arthur Box-Bender travels twice to Salzburg in the 1930s for the festival.
PF 113, 169; BR 178; MA 160

SAM
Fellow pupil of Guy Crouchback at Downside.
• Director of publicity at Megalopolitan Pictures.
MA 23; LO 25

SAMBO
Mrs Joyboy's parrot, buried at The Happier Hunting Ground.
LO 91

SAMGRASS, MR
Fellow of All Souls. Sebastian Flyte calls him 'someone of mummy's'. He is a history don 'a short, plump man, dapper in dress, with sparse hair brushed flat on an over-large head, neat hands, small feet, and the general appearance of being too often bathed'.

Author of several books. He is a genealogist and 'a legitimist'. Loves dispossessed royalty and knows the claims of pretenders to thrones.

Not a Catholic but has friends at the Vatican and knows the 'ins and outs' of the Catholic clergy. But there is something bogus about him. Charles Ryder suspects that he has a dictaphone in his panelled rooms.

After Sebastian's arrest he gives evidence of good character which stops the judge giving him an exemplary sentence, and at Oxford he helps by talking to the college authorities. The three offenders are gated for a term and the affair blows over.

Not an evening passes without Charles and Sebastian being harassed by him. He tries desperately to forge bonds with them.

Visits Brideshead at Christmas 1923. Works on the memoirs of Lady Marchmain's brother (published 1924).

Sebastian composes a ditty about him 'Greenarse, Samgrass – Samgrass, greenarse', sung to the chime of St Mary's church.

Over Christmas 1924 takes Sebastian on a tour of the Near East and loses him.

By 1936 he is 'one of Lord Copper's middle-aged young men on the *Daily Beast*'. Attends Charles' private view.
BR 101, 105, 106, 119, 120, 121, 124, 152–4, 167, 253

SAMOTHRACE, GREECE
Island in the Aegean. One of the places visited by Mr Samgrass and Sebastian in 1924.
BR 145

SAMPSON, SISTER
Second nurse of old Mrs Boot at Boot Magna Hall. Cuts out old coupons and loses them in the bedclothes.
Sc 19, 20

SAMSON, MRS
Cook to Lady Amelia. Makes very good scones.
WS 30

SAN FRANCISCO, CALIFORNIA
Where, in 1944 Trimmer finds himself on his grand morale-raising tour of America which falls flat.
US 186

SAN VITALE
Byzantine church.
• One of those mentioned by Collins (q.v.) in the dedication of his book on the subject to Charles Ryder.
BR 45

SANDERS
Aide to Lord Monomark in 1932.
BM 73

SANDERS, CAPTAIN
Brother officer of Athorpe's whose brother lives in Kasanga. Plays 'pretty rotten golf'. Wins the company game of Housey Housey.
MA 58, 59, 139

SANDHURST, BERKSHIRE
The Royal Military Academy.
• Tony Last and Jock Grant-Menzies, drunk in Bratts, behave as if they were 'up for the night from Sandhurst'.
• Major Hound (q.v.) was at Sandhurst in 1925.
• When Brigadier Cape was at Sandhurst no one talked about the war. 'We learned about it, of course; a school subject like Latin or geography; something to write exam papers about.'
• In 1919 the Berkeley is full of Sandhurst men.
HD 76; OG 19; US 170; WS 291

SANTA DULCINA DELLE ROCCE, ITALY
Coastal town near Genoa. Location of the Castello Crouchback. The houses rise up steeply from the quay and two buildings stand out from the others, the church and the castello. Behind the town the hillside is terraced and planted. Visited by Gervase and Hermione Crouchback in 1889. There is an inn, the Hotel Eden. In the parish church are the bones of Santa Dulcina and the tomb of Sir Roger de Waybrooke.
MA 10–13

SANTA MARIA
Port in Neutralia established by the Athenians in the time of Pericles. It is from here that Scott-King makes his escape.
WS 243

SARUM-SMITH (b. circa 1915)
Fellow officer of Guy Crouchback in 1940. Guy does not particularly like him, but does lend him some money before they are all paid. Is fond of sarcasm and facetious jokes. Calls the depot batch 'matey bastards'. He is a 'townsman'.

Apthorpe thinks him 'just the sort of young idiot' who would catch the claps and suspects him of sabotaging the Thunder Box.

Is made Adjutant of Y Battalion under Apthorpe. Appointed entertainments officer.

Reappears in Crete in 1941, by which time he has matured into a man. Smokes a pipe.

Killed in action sometime between June 1941 and 1943.
MA 48, 49, 50, 89, 113, 145, 190, 206, 245; OG 207; US 95

SASSOON, SIEGFRIED ***(1886–1967)***
English poet and novelist. Renowned for his poetry of the Great War and for two books *Memoirs of a Fox-Hunting Man* and *Memoirs of an Infantry Officer*. Converted to Catholicism in 1957.

• In 1939, Barbara Sothill sees her brother Basil as Siegfried Sassoon 'an infantry subaltern in a mug-clogged trench standing to at dawn, his eyes on his wrist watch, waiting for zero hour'.
PF 17

SATELLITE CITY
One of the large cities of New Britain. It is planned around the Dome of Security (*see* ARCHITECTURE) and this as yet, is all that it consists of.
GP 191

SCARFIELD, MRS
One of Gilbert Pinfold's fellow passengers on the *Caliban* in 1953. She is pretty and 'youngish' and sits at the captain's table. Does not read. Her husband is in the teak trade. Gradually Pinfold begins to see her as sly. Her husband wins a small prize in the ship sweepstake and buys a round of drinks.
GP 42, 43, 44, 53

SCHLUM, BUM
One of the American journalists entertained at the Savoy by Ian Kilbannock in 1941. Naturally anti-fascist.
OG 212

SCHONBAUM, MR ***(b. 1884)***
United States representative in Debra Dowa, Azania. He has come late to diplomacy. Between ten and forty he was involved in 'journalism, electrical engineering, real estate, cotton broking, hotel management, shipping and theatrical promotion'. In 1914 he had returned to America and after 1917, to Mexico. In 1919 becomes an American citizen and goes into politics. After an unsuccessful presidential campaign he is offered Debra Dowa in 1924.
BM 46–7

SCHOOLS
• **Aircastle School.** Correspondence school of journalism. Bateson (q.v.) is a graduate.

• **Amurath Memorial High School, Azania.** Founded by the Empress to look after the orphans of murdered officials. The embroidery and dressmaking class work for several weeks on a banner reading 'Women of tomorrow demand an empty cradle'.

- **Granchester**. Where Scott-King is classics master.
- **Harrow**. Where Grimes says he was.
- **Llanabba School,** North Wales. *See* LLANABBA.
- **Madame de Supplice's,** Paris. Attended by Thérèse de Vitre, and also by Antoinette (q.v.).
- **Marlborough.** Attended by Glover (q.v.). Potts believes that the great problem of education is to train the moral perceptions, not merely to discipline the appetites.
- **Our Lady of Victory,** Matchet. Preparatory school at which Mr Crouchback takes a job as classics master in 1941. Greswold and Challoner are pupils and easily divert him from Livy on to the Blessed Gervase Crouchback.
- **Rugby**. Attended by Mr Graves and Lord Circumference.
- **Staplehurst,** Southsand. Attended by Apthorpe. Mr Goodall was a master there. Demolished before 1940.
- **Stonyhurst.** Attended by Lord Brideshead. Sebastian should have gone there, but his father insisted on Eton.
- **Uppingham**. Attended by David Legge.
- A Jewish schoolteacher is elected to John Verney's constituency in 1946.
- De Souza thinks that all army courses are like prep schools. Grimes believes that the English public school man is ensured against starvation. The sight of Millicent Blade's nose (q.v.) takes the thoughts of any Englishman back to his schooldays 'to the doughy-faced urchins on whom it had squandered its first affection, to memories of changing-room and chapel and battered straw boaters. Three Englishmen in five, it is true, grow snobbish about these things in later life.' Dr Fagan realizes that no one enters the scholastic profession 'unless he has some very good reason which he is anxious to conceal'.

DF 20–190; HD 164; BM 57, 189; SC 187; BR 86' MA 97. 110; OG 21; US 97; GP 108, 164; WS 32, 294

(*See also* DOWNSIDE, ETON, FAGAN, FRAN, GRAVES, GRIMES, LANCING, PENNYFEATHER, PRENDERGAST, SCOTT-KING)

SCHULTZ, MR

Owner of the Happier Hunting Ground (q.v.). Despairs about the modern attitude to pets. Is jealous of Whispering Glades. Will not pay Dennis Barlow for his days off.

LO 50.

SCHWERT, ARCHIE

One of the Bright Young People. He is 'rather sweet, only too terribly common, poor darling'. Throws the 'savage party' at Edward Throbbing's house, in 1927. Lives at the Ritz. Miles Malpractice discovers him. Drives Adam Fenwick-Symes, Agatha Runcible and Miles to the motor races. Orders champagne in a hotel at luncheon.

His humanitarian interests are narrower than those of Miss Runcible. His armband at the track reads 'Owner Representative'. Adam uses his account at Asprey's to buy Nina a Christmas present. During WWII is interned as an undesirable alien. (Ginger arranges it.)

VB 28, 29, 153, 155, 213, 220

SCOPE, MISS

Governess of Aunt Anne at Boot Magna Hall. A watercolour by her of the village church hangs in Priscilla Boot's bedroom.

Sc 19, 35

SCORPIONS

Dr Akonanga (q.v.) is waiting for a consignment of scorpions in 1943, and wonders whether Virginia Crouchback has brought them. They have in fact been sent to Alexandria and given to an officer to take to London. However, they escape and he becomes delirious and ends up in the same RAF hospital as Guy Crouchback.

US 83, 110

SCOTLAND

During the parliamentary vacation of 1937, the principal private secretary of the Prime Minister is in Scotland.

• Anyone with a knowledge of Highland geography could have told the American director of the film about the '45 seen by Guy Crouchback, that the Highlanders marching away from Glenfinnan are going straight into 'the chilly waters of Loch Moidart'.
• Two cowmen are arrested at Penkirk on account of their strong Scottish accents being mistaken by the Halberdiers for German.
• Miss Carmichael (q.v.) is keen to tell Guy Crouchback that every generation the Scots see the best of their men march off to fight battles for the English, and determines to use the German threat to incite a Scottish rebellion.
• In the outer islands of Scotland one finds isolated communities of Catholics like that at Broome.
• According to Guy Crouchback a lot of Scots are Liberals.
• At Bari in 1944 there is a 'euphoric' Scottish officer who sits surrounded by books and who intends to 'inculcate a respect of English culture'.
• De Souza tells Guy Crouchback that to start distinguishing between Jews and Christians in 1944 will get him as far as trying to agitate Auchinlek about Scottish nationalism.
• Some Scots are nursing the passengers on the *SS Caliban* in 1955.
• Sir James Macrae wants to set his production of *Macbeth* in the Highlands in order to be able to include 'some kilts and clan gathering scenes'.
SC 182; MA 161, 191; OG 66; US 60, 123, 168, 204; WS 74; GP 34
(*See also* CAMPBELL, MCTAVISH, PENKIRK, MUGG, KILBANNOCK, GLENOBAN, STUART-KERR, ANSTRUTHER-KERR, GAELIC BOOKS *and individual locations)*

SCOTSBORO TRAILS

During the time of which a cellist invited to play at an anniversary breakfast of the Colonial Dames is tied to a lamp-post, covered in tar and set alight by the Communists.
PF 112

SCOTT, SIR WALTER *(1771–1832)*

Scottish novelist. See his *Ivanhoe*, *Waverley* and *Heart of Midlothian*.
• John Plant remembers reading that Scott's hand had been seen at a lighted window moving evenly across the page as he wrote *Waverley*.
WS 166

SCOTT FITZGERALD, FRANCIS *(1896–1940)*

American novelist. See his *The Great Gatsby* (1925). Frankie (q.v.) thinks that he might be the author of '*Omar Khayyam*'.
US 200

SCOTT-KING *(b. 1904)*

Attends Granchester. At university from 1922 to 1925. After university fails a fellowship and goes straight to teach at Granchester. Classics master of Granchester School from 1925.

By 1946 he is 'slightly bald and slightly corpulent' and is a much-parodied school institution. He has a 'smoky gothic study' above the quad, furnished with pitch pine.

He is fascinated 'by obscurity and failure', a feeling best summed up in the word 'dim'. He is an intellectual 'almost a poet' and no chauvinist. His favourite writer is Shakespeare.

Makes a study of Bellorius (q.v.) and write a book on the subject which he sends, in June 1944, to the OUP. It is not published. Distills the book into an essay 'The Last Latinist' which is published in a learned journal.

Invited in 1946 to the Bellorius conference in Neutralia (q.v.). Thinks it a hoax. Flies to Neutralia. Is met by Arturo Fe who he thinks looks like an ageing film actor.

Visits the university. Attends the banquet. Feels an empathy with Whitemaid. Cries because of Miss Sveningen's party frock. Sleeps badly. Goes to Simona and visits the national memorial. Does not share the others' indignation. They call him a fascist beast. Attends the unveiling of the statue.

Returns to Bellacita and visits the British Consulate. Is stranded in Neutralia, following the disappearance of Dr Antonic. Is terrified of being left there, forgotten. Despite lack of money, remains in the Ritz.

Meets Miss Bombaum who gets him out through the underground. Travels to the suburbs and hands over all of his money. Has to leave his luggage behind. Travels to Santa Maria and from there by ship to Palestine. Meets Lockwood. Returns to England.

Refuses to take a class for economic history. His experience gives him a shrewd idea of a modern world unfit for men to live in.

WS 195–247

SCROPE-WELD, MR AND MRS

Friends of Peregrine Crouchback, distant cousins of his mother, with whom he always spends Christmas. After their deaths their son and his wife take over in this capacity.

They live in 'an agricultural island among the industrial areas of Staffordshire', in a large house. The son has four children and in 1939 serves with the army. Part of the house becomes a children's home. Young Mrs Scrope-Weld has a firm idea in her mind of what normal life is all about. (*See* NORMALITY)

US 142–3, 146–7

SCULPTURE

(*See* PROVNA)

SCUNTHORPE, LINCOLNSHIRE

One of the towns visited by Trimmer (q.v.) with Virginia Crouchback on his morale–raising tour of Britain in 1941.

OG 248

SEA OF GALILEE

Inland sea in the Holy Land. The young lady correspondent sends a postcard of the Sea of Galilee, 'all very Eastern with camels' to England.

WS 18

SEA LIONS

Jock Grant-Menzies tells Milly and Babs that Tony Last trains sea lions.

HD 73

SEAL, BARBARA ***(b. 1945)***

Daughter of Basil and Angela Seal. Attends a 'Happening' in 1962. Calls Basil 'Pobble'. Has an affair with Charles Allbright (q.v.) at the age of seventeen. Sent to her aunt Barbara at Malfrey while Basil and Angela are at the health farm. Escapes and returns to London and Charles. Is found by her father sitting in pyjamas and a fur coat of her mother's in their house in Hill Street. Is in love with Charles. Basil tells her that Charles is her half-brother and she runs off into the night, back to her mother at Claridges.

WS 259–260, 266, 272

SEAL, BASIL ***(b. 1903)***

Son of Sir Christopher and Lady Seal. Black sheep of the family. Resembles his sister. The girls of London society think he is 'a corker'. He has dark hair which falls over his forehead, 'contemptuous' blue eyes, a 'proud, rather childish mouth' and a scar on one cheek. He is 'fartouche'.

At Balliol, Oxford (1921–1924) where he has a reputation for brilliance among his friends, and for debauchery among evangelical undergraduates. Plays poker for high stakes. His lunch parties last till dusk and his dinner parties become riots. 'Lovely young women' drive down from London to see him.

Friend of Ambrose Silk with whom he was at Oxford. Naturally shabby. Member of Bratt's and Bellamy's. In later life joins the Travellers'.

Disinherited by his father on his deathbed in 1924.

Angela Lyne is in love with him and can talk of nothing else. Is only attracted to very silly girls (apart from Angela).

Reads *The Times*. As a young man he has promise and is taken up by Lord Monomark who invites him for a cruise on his yacht which he says he will join, but does not, thus ending the relationship. 'Countless incidents of this kind had contributed to Basil's present depreciated popularity.'

In 1930 spends all of the money left to him by his Aunt on an idiotic expedition to Afghanistan.

His mother gives him a reasonable allowance and always pays off his debts.

Has a long-standing affair with Angela Lyne.

In 1931 is adopted as a candidate in the West Country, for which Angela Lyne is paying his expenses. But he does not get in, having gone on a racket for four days after the Conservative ball, with Peter Pastmaster and Alastair Trumpington. They begin at Lottie Crump's. Leaves a lot of bad cheques. Has a motor accident. Sonia Trumpington throws something at the mayor. One of them is arrested. Thus he has to stand down and he wakes up on a sofa in someone's flat in King's Road Chelsea.

Takes a keen interest in Azanian politics.

Friend of Margot Metroland. Attends a cocktail party at her house in Hill Street in 1931 to which he has not been invited. Drinks Pernod and water, and whisky.

Leaves for Azania, having stolen his mother's emerald bracelet.

At Port Said he sends dirty postcards to Sonia and sells his mother's bracelet for a fifth of its value.

Smokes cheroots. Visits a brothel in Jibuti with a Dutch South African. Talks about world monetary systems. Arrives at Matodi. Steals his cabin companion's topee, slippers, and shaving soap.

Travels to Debra Dowa and attends the victory ball at the Perroquet. Appointed Minister of Modernization, High Commissioner and Comptroller General. Mr Youkoumian is his financial secretary. He takes on too much. Everyone else in the government gives him their work.

Lives in a large room over Youkoumian's shop. He has a veranda which faces a junk yard with an outside staircase. Uses a tin hip bath.

Has an affair with Prudence Courteney. Is interrupted in his love-making by Youkoumian.

Tells Prudence that 'he would like to eat her'. Tells tales of Sakuyu savagery at the legation dinner. Organizes defence of the legation. Wears white Sakuyu robes.

Stays on alone in Azania when the rest of the British flee.

Discovers Seth is dead. Takes Seth's body to Moshu; feasts with Joab and the chiefs. Tells Joab to kill Boaz. Eats Prudence in a stew.

Returns to England. Visits the Trumpingtons. Thinks of staying in London or Berlin.

Has always been 'mixed up in fighting'. He 'never condescends to the art of the toilet'.

Set up in The Temple in chambers with an allowance of £1000 a year. Abandons it.

Leader writer of the *Daily Beast*. Sells champagne on commission. Composes dialogue for the cinema. Gives a talk to the BBC. Press agent for a female contortionist.

Takes tourists around the Italian lakes, leaving them all penniless at Lake Garda: 'for all Basil knew they were still there'.

Friend of John Plant, whom he tells how one might go about finding an heiress to marry. Says 'you must go to the provinces ... the very rich have a natural affinity for one another'.

Stands three times for Parliament, on two of which he falls out with the committee before the election.

He finds it bitter to be still living at home at the age of thirty-five, dependent on his mother for money.

Tells John Plant that Lucy Simmonds has been left an orphan at any early age and that all she has is £58,000 in trustee stock.

Breakfasts with Poppet Green whom he meets through Ambrose Silk in 1939. Tells her that London will not have any air raids. Thinks a surreal artist would find air raids useful material. Paints a ginger moustache on her painting of the head of Aphrodite. Poppet Green sees him as 'a kind of dilapidated Bulldog Drummond'.

Is always able to find the Trumpingtons' latest house. Visits them in Chester Street in 1939.

Lunches with Sir Joseph Mainwaring and the Lieutenant Colonel of the Bombardier Guards. Tells the colonel that they ought to do something about Liberia. The colonel does not take to him. Visits the colonel at his office, having been smartly dressed by Angela. Tells him that he wants to join the Bombardiers because they are not as stuffy as the Grenadiers and do not have any bogus regional connections like the Scots, Irish and Welsh, and that he does not want to lead men into action but requires a staff job. The colonel throws him out.
Volunteers for counter-espionage. Is given a uniform and a post on the General Service list catching Communists.

Visits Mr Bentley and Ambrose. Returns to Colonel Plum and tells him that they are dangerous. Falls briefly in love with Susie (q.v.) and seduces her. Steals Father Flanagan's passport from the Ministry of Information and gives it to Ambrose Silk who he smuggles out to Ireland. Subsequently moves into Ambrose's flat. Asks Angela to marry him. She agrees.

Is made liaison officer of the top secret new force in which Peter Pastmaster and Alastair Trumpington are serving in summer 1940. Early on in the war he blows off the toes of one foot while demonstrating a bomb of his own for destroying railway bridges to his commando section.

Drains the cellars of the dead Freddie Sothill and Cedric Lyne. Becomes a creature of habit and develops the 'set opinions' of the rich. In 1962 attends, with Peter Pastmaster the banquet in honour of Ambrose Silk at the Ritz. By this time he is 'stout' and 'rubicund'. Has a daughter by Angela, Barbara (q.v.) who calls him 'old pobble', on account of his lameness. (He walks with a stick.) After his accident he is listed as a 'farmer'.

Lives in Hill Street in Mayfair in Angela's house which is 'almost the sole survivor of the private houses of his youth'.

Tells his daughter her fiancé, Charles Allbright, might be his son to stop her marrying him.
BM ff; PF ff; WS 251, 252–7, 260, 263–81

SEAL, SIR CHRISTOPHER *(d. 1924)*
Wife of Lady Cynthia and father of Basil (q.v.). He is never seen without his silk hat and orchid in his buttonhole. Conservative chief whip for twenty-five years. Too old to fight in the Great War. Says that they will all have to pay for the peerage handout after the Armistice. On his deathbed he disinherits Basil.
BM 69; PF 18, 23, 47

SEAL, LADY CYNTHIA
Long-suffering mother of Basil Seal. When her husband is chief whip she entertains on a lavish scale. As a widow she has five or six dinner parties a year. They are extremely formal. Lives in Lowndes Square. Has ammonia in her bath. Wears lavender water behind her ears.

Her butler is Anderson. Has never liked Neville Chamberlain, or his brother, but decides that she will ask him to luncheon. In 1939 she is keen to offer Basil to the country. Hates Ribbentrop. Friend of Emma Granchester, and Sir Joseph Mainwaring who she persists in asking to find a job for Basil. Her major fault is lack of imagination.
BM 75–6; PF 17–19, 21, 55

SEAL, EDWARD
During the Great War he was stuck in Dar es Salaam.
PF 18

SEAL, TONY
Elder brother of Basil Seal. Just too young to serve in the Great War. Disliked by Freddie Sothill, who finds him 'supercilious and effeminate'. Brilliant diplomat; has weak eyes.

In the 1960s, after a 'tediously successful diplomatic career spent in gold-lace or starched linen', becomes lax in his dress and looks 'like a scarecrow'.
PF 14, 18, 20; WS 256

SECOND COMING

The religious maniac at Blackstone Gaol looks daily for the second coming: 'It's all in the Bible . . . It was a vision brought me here, an angel clothed in flame . . . crying "Kill and spare not. The Kingdom is at hand".'
DF 177

SENEGALESE

Senegalese infantrymen wash their clothes in the ravine below John Plant's window at Fez.
WS 108

SERBIA

Where Charles Ryder's mother serves with the Red Cross in the Great War, and where she is killed.
BR 41

SERMONS

The vicar who marries Grimes and Flossie gives a long sermon on 'Home and Conjugal Love'.
DF 106
(*See* TENDRIL)

SERVANTS

- The Beste-Chetwyndes find that servants are 'less responsive than their masters to the charms of Tudor simplicity; . . . housemaids tend to melt away under the recurring strain of trotting in the bleak hour before breakfast up and down the narrow servants' staircase'.
- At Lottie Crump's there are always innumerable housemaids with cans of hot water and clean towels.
- Lady Circumference's butler is a source of gossip for Mr Chatterbox.
- Edward Trobbing's butler is driven to drink and insanity by the Bright Young People.
- Colonel Blount says that after they have been with you for a while servants seem to think that they can do what they like.
- Lady Graybridge's butler and his boarders eat all of her fruit in the north wing which he has let out.
- Ten servants wait upon the Boot household at Boot Magna Hall in a 'desultory fashion', being able to spare little time from their traditional five meals a day.
- A page 'with a face of ageless evil' is employed by the hotel in London where William Boot stays in 1937.
- Barbara Sothill's housemaids walk out when the Connollys move in.
- The only servants left at Kemble in 1940 are the gardener's wife and a girl from the village.
- There are Goanese stewards on the ship taken by the Halberdiers to Dakar in 1940.
- Colonel Campbell's butler is large and bearded. His father is the piper.
- A butler, a footman, a cook, a kitchen maid and housemaids are a part of normal pre-war life for Mrs Scrope-Weld.
- Mrs Joyboy's family has a coloured girl as a housemaid on 'fifteen bucks a week and glad of it'.
- The servants on the *Caliban* are from Travancore.
- In Ceylon Gilbert Pinfold is served by old servants of the Raj.
- John and Elizabeth Verney have no servants in 1945: 'the old had fled, the young had been conscribed for service'.
- Mrs Metcalfe thinks that servants seem to take up so much time in England and longs for her Berber servants in Alexandria.
- Mr Hargood-Hood employs three gardeners.

DF 117; VB 37, 88, 110, 204; Sc 18, 19, 37; MA 29, 218; US 147; LO 91; GP 42, 147, 163; WS 46, 47, 61

SETH *(1906–1931)*

Emperor of Azania. Educated Oxford (Balliol, 1921–1924). Likes to think of himself as 'the Modern age'. He is 'Emperor of Azania, Chief of the Chiefs of Sakuyu, Lord of Wanda and Tyrant of the Seas, Bachelor of the Arts of Oxford University.' His Indian secretary is Ali. Wages war against Seyid. He wins. Despite his acquired civilization he still has deep ancestral fears of the jungle and

darkness. Employs Basil Seal as Minister of Modernization. Killed by Boaz.
BM 7, 22, 26, 228

SETTRINGHAM, LORD AND LADY
Couple who dine at the Ritz in 1939 and are mistaken by Roger Simmonds for being mid-west Americans.
WS 155

SEVERN, RIVER
River passed on the way from London to Kemble. It 'shines gold and brown in the evening sun'.
MA 27

SÈVRES
Type of porcelain, taking its name from the French town where production began under Louis XV in 1756.
• Lady Seal owns a Sèvres service which is packed in crates in her basement during the war.
• Sebastian Flyte has two outsize Sèvres vases in his rooms in Christ Church in 1923.
• Angela Box-Bender had hoped for Sèvres porcelain rather than Hittite tablets at Kemble in 1939.
PF 17; BR 33; MA 27

SEX
Margot Beste-Chetwynde climbs into bed with Paul Pennyfeather at King's Thursday, after he has proposed to her: 'It's best to make sure, isn't it, darling . . . '
• Adam Fenwick-Symes takes Nina Blount to Arundel for the night. 'It's great fun', he tells her. Afterwards she says that she does not think it divine at all and that it has given her a pain. She is of the opinion that there is not much to sleeping together. 'For physical pleasure I'd sooner go to my dentist any day.' Adam tells Nina that unless she stops going on he will ravish her there and then on her own hearth-rug: 'Then Nina went on. But by the time that Adam went to dress she had climbed down enough to admit that perhaps love was a thing one could grow fond of after a time, like smoking a pipe.'
• William Bland and Prudence Courteney are very keen on sex. Prudence has 'a whole lot of new ideas' for them to try. In her book, the *Panorama of Life,* she writes; 'Sex is the crying out of the spirit of humanity for Completion.' In summer, 'the arid season when Nature seems all dead under the hot soil, there is nothing to think about except sex'.

Later she and Basil Seal are interrupted in their love-making by Mr Youkoumian.
• Dr Borethus in Zurich takes sex cases.
• Celia Ryder makes love in 'neat hygienic ways'.
• In Charles Ryder's dreams Julia Flyte takes on 'a hundred fantastic and terrible obscene forms'. When they make love it is: 'as though a deed of conveyance of her narrow loins had been drawn and sealed. I was making my first entry as a freeholder of a property I would enjoy and develop at leisure.'
• Everything is not right with Gervase and Hermione Crouchback on their honeymoon: 'there was a sad gap between them, made by modesty and tenderness and innocence'. It is only when they moor at Santa Dulcina that: 'all at last came right between them and their love was joyfully completed'.
• Apthorpe is above sex: 'You have to be in the bush, or it gets a grip on you.'
• Virginia Crouchback resents being seduced by Guy in 1940, and tells him that she would prefer to : 'do something ridiculous in high heels or drive you around the room in toy harness'.
• Peregrine Crouchback has only twice been to bed with a woman, the same one, once at the age of twenty and once at forty-five: 'I didn't particularly enjoy it.'
• After they are re-married at the registry office in 1944, Virginia joins Guy Crouchback in bed and: 'with gentle, almost tender, agility adapted her endearments to his crippled condition. She was, as always, lavish with what lay in her gift.'
• The General tells Margaret that: 'many a young couple spend a wretched fortnight together through not knowing how to set about what has to be done'. Margaret is prepared for Gilbert Pinfold

by: 'a whole choir of bridesmaids who chanted an epithalamium as they disrobed her and tied her hair'. At the same time 'amorous expectations' begin to stir in Gilbert. His cabin is not designed for sex. Nevertheless he is 'strongly armed for the encounter'.

• For Miles Plastic, 'sex' had been part of his educational curriculum from the very early stages: 'first in diagrams, then in demonstrations, then in application'. After making love to Clara, Miles: 'all male, post coitum tristis, was struck by a chill sense of loss. No demonstration or exercise had prepared him for the strange new experience of the sudden loneliness that follows requited love.'

• Basil Seal asks his daughter outright whether she has slept with Charles Allbright:

'Oh, no sleep?'

'You know what I mean. Have you had sexual intercourse with him?'

'Well, perhaps; not in bed; on the floor and wide awake; you might call it intercourse, I suppose.'

DF 137; VB 81, 90–91; BM 55, 61–2; BR 160, 219, 238, 248, MA 9–10, 59, 133; US 136, 196; GP 114, 116, 203, 204; WS 274

SEYID, PRINCE

Father of Seth (q.v.). Rebel leader of the war against Seth after the death of the Empress of Azania in 1931. Circulates a photograph among the Imperial Army of Seth dressed in his Oxford robes and tells them that he has abandoned the Church of England and become a Mohammedan. Defeated by General Connolly at Ukaka and surrenders to the Wanda, who eat him.

BM 43

SHAKESPEARE, WILLIAM
(1564–1616)

Pre-eminent English playwright.

• 'Chokey' has read *Hamlet*, *Macbeth* and *King Lear*.

• Ginger Littlejohn quotes from *Henry V*.

• Lord Copper remembers that Shakespeare, one of the great men, had to pay the price of loneliness and had not enjoyed the devotion he deserved from 'someone'.

• Ian Kilbannock quotes from *Henry V*.

• Dennis Barlow recites 'Shall I Compare Thee to a Summer's Day'.

• Sir James Macrae, having previously told Simon Lent that the modern public want Shakespeare's 'beauty and thought and character translated into the language of everyday life', later tells him that 'what the public wants is Shakespeare, the whole of Shakespeare and nothing but Shakespeare'.

• Scott-King supposes that his favourite writer is Shakespeare.

DF 80; VB 199; SC 218; LO 84; OG 149; WS 70, 74, 75, 220

SHAMELESS BLOND
(*See* RATTERY)

SHANGHAI, CHINA

From where Sir Jocelyn Hitchcock reports for the *Daily Beast*. He charges three hundred pounds for camels.

• One of the places where Miss Bombaum pops up during the time of unpleasantness in the 1930s.

Sc 33; WS 203

SHANKS

One of Guy Crouchback's company of the Halberdiers. Requests leave to travel to Blackpool to enter the slow valse competition, which he has previously won at Salford. Permission is denied. In May 1941 is wounded by a mortar bomb on Crete.

MA 205; OG 208

SHAW, MRS

Cleaner to Simon Lent to whom he pays four shillings and sixpence a day to make his bed and orange juice.

WS 64

SHAW, GEORGE BERNARD
(1856–1950)

Irish playwright, novelist, essayist and political activist. Socialist. Served in local government. See his *Arms and the Man*, *Man and Superman*, *Major Barbara* and *Pygmalion*.

• One of the modern writers read by Seth who form his claim to being a man of the New Age.
• The group of Indians on their way to the river in Oxford in 1923, carry in their basket a copy of Shaw's *Plays Unpleasant*.
BM 17; BR 59

SHELLEY, PERCY BYSSHE
(1792–1822)

English poet. See his 'Prometheus Unbound', 'Queen Mab', 'Adonais' and 'To a Skylark'.
• On his discharge from the RAF in 1946, Dennis Barlow goes to Hollywood to write the life of Shelley for Megalopolitan Films.

According to the notice outside, it was in the church of St Peter Without the Walls (q.v.) that Shelley planned 'his great career in poetry'.
LO 22, 63

SHERIDAN, RICHARD BRINSLEY
(1751–1816)

Irish-born playwright. See his *The Rivals* (1775), and *School for Scandal* (1777).
• One of the writers who comes to Ambrose Silk's mind on his arrival in Ireland in 1940.
PF 218

SHIPS

The Bright Young People have a bad channel crossing in 1927: 'Sometimes the ship pitched and sometimes she rolled and sometimes she stood quite still and shivered all over, poised above an abyss of dark water; then she would go swooping down like a scenic railway train . . . and sometimes she would drop dead like a lift. It was this last movement that caused the most havoc among the passengers.'

The captain and the Chief Officer meanwhile are happily doing a crossword puzzle on the bridge.
• The ship on which Tony Last travels to Brazil in 1934 is planned for the tropics rather than the Atlantic. They pass the *Yarmouth Castle*.
• The Messageries vessel on which Basil Seal travels to Azania in 1931 is 'an ugly old ship snatched from Germany after the war as part of reparations'.
• To one of the *Beast's* readers Azania sounds like the name of a Cunarder.
• Dame Mildred Porch sails from Durban to Azania on the French ship *SS Le President Carnot*, which is 'very dirty and unseamanlike'.
• William Boot sails to Ishmaelia in late June 1937 on the *Francmaçon*: 'She had been built at an earlier epoch in the history of steam navigation and furnished in the style of the day, for service among the high waves and icy winds of the North Atlantic. There is thus nowhere on her decks for deckchairs and her cabins only have tiny portholes for ventilation. She is furnished with red velvet and mahogany. Half of the boat deck is the captain's quarters in which he has a brass bedstead, and where his wife irons on the verandah, accompanied by their small hairless dog.'
• In 1940 Cedric Lyne's battalion travels to France on the *Duchess of Cumberland*. It is full of Highlanders who should be on the *Duchess of Clarence*. In the summer of 1939 the ship, whose stewards still remain on the journey to France, was in the Mediterranean filled with 'a hundred cultured spinsters'.
• Charles Ryder returns from Tangier to England by a P and O ship in June 1926.
• The ship on which Charles and Celia return to England in 1936 has huge halls like enormous railway coaches, with bronze gates decorated with Abyssinian animals and carpets the colour of blotting paper: 'the painted panels of the walls were like blotting paper, too . . . and between the walls were yards and yards of biscuit-coloured wood . . . that had been bent round corners, invisibly joined strip by strip, steamed and squeezed and polished'. There are tables 'designed perhaps by a sanitary engineer, square blocks of stuffing with square holes for sitting in'. Light comes from 'scores of hollows' which cast no shadows. They occupy a suite of rooms, which is only the hall in miniature.

• Julia Flyte thinks that being on a boat 'makes everyone behave like a film star'.
• De Souza calls the boat on which the Halberdiers sail to Dakar in 1940 'the refugee ship'. It is accompanied by a battleship, the *Barham*, and a small vessel the *Belgravia* which reputedly carries champagne and bathsalts for the garrison of Dakar. The cruiser *Fiji* is torpedoed. The convoy expects opposition from the French battleship *Richelieu*.
• Before the war Trimmer (q.v.) was a hairdresser on the *Aquitania*.
• Julia Stitch's yacht is called the *Cleopatra*. In it she travels to Santa Dulcina in the thirties. During the war it serves to take the commanding officers of X Commando to and from Mugg. The bachelors' cabins are not luxurious.
• In May 1941, *HMS Plangent* lands Hookforce on Crete and evacuates 400 wounded.
• Guy Crouchback travels back to England from Alexandria in 1941, aboard the old 'hulk' *Canary Castle*.
• The *SS Caliban*, on which Gilbert Pinfold sails to Ceylon in 1953 is a one class ship and not large enough to command a special train. Her master is Captain Steerforth. There are no private bathrooms and meals are not served in cabins. Her rooms are panelled in fumed oak. The crew and stewards are Lascars, the window of Pinfold's room is of opaque glass with muslin curtains and a sliding shutter. There are electric cables in a white beam in the ceiling. There are two narrow bunks, not designed for making love. During the war she had been manned by the Royal Navy, serving in the landings in North Africa and Normandy.
• During the war Pinfold travels on troopships with amplifiers on every deck issuing alarms, orders and popular music.
• The *SS Glory of Greece* takes a young lady correspondent to Algiers. The purser tells her that on the cruise to Egypt people always get engaged and have quarrels.
VB 14; HD 160; BM 66, 89, 156; Sc 58, 60; PF 178, 182; BR 208. 225. 228. 239. 240; MA 220, 221; OG 75, 97, 98, 168, 242; GP 27, 29, 34, 41, 116; WS 16, 21

SHOCK, SILAS
Journalist of the *New York Guardian* who entertains a party at the Savoy Grill on 11 December 1936 which includes Wenlock Jakes, Mrs Tiffin, Prudence Blank, John Titmuss and John Nought.
Sc 80

SHOOTING
Adam Fenwick-Symes considers writing about Colonel Blount in his Mr Chatterbox column as the man who is 'unable to shoot his best except to the accompaniment of violin and 'cello'. He then falls victim to a misunderstanding over the nature of the shooting taking place at Doubting Hall during the sojourn there of The Wonderfilm Company:

'I came to see Colonel Blount.'

'Well, you can't, son. They're just shooting him now.'

'Good heavens. What for?'

'Oh, nothing important. He's just one of the Wesleyans, you know – we're trying to polish off the whole crowd this afternoon . . .'.

• Tony Last and his brother-in-law Allan shoot rabbits with rifles in the twilight at Hetton.
• Algernon Stitch shoots partridges in 1937.
• Freddy Sothill intends to get leave from his battalion in 1939 to shoot his pheasants, and at the end of the season has some of his regiment over to shoot the cocks. The bags are small and mostly hens.
• Angela Lyne's father has a celebrated shoot in Norfolk. Cedric finds the birds too tame.
• Guy Crouchback once shot a lion on his farm in Kenya. He is teased about it incessantly by the non-commissioned officers in charge of training the Halberdiers.
VB 141; HD 94; Sc 184; PF 16, 75, 169; MA 68, 95

SHOPS
• **Amurath Universal Stores**, Azania. Run by Mr Youkoumian.
• **Asprey's**, Bond Street, London.

Where Adam Fenwick-Symes buys Nina Blount a scent bottle for Christmas.

• **Bassett-Lowke's**. Where Cedric Lyne buys his son Nigel a model of a Blenheim bomber in 1940.

• **Benakis**, Jackonburg, Ishmaelia. Where one can buy tinned caviar.

• **Cartier's**, Bond Street, London. Where Julia Flyte expects Rex Mottram to buy her an engagement ring.

• **Flannigan's Store**, Ballingar.

• **Goode's**, South Audley Street. Where the Pendle-Garthwaites buy a tea service as a wedding present for Julia Flyte.

• **Liberty's**, Regent Street, London. Margot Metroland thinks that even the Liberty building is better looking than the original King's Thursday.

• **Mulligan's Store**, Ballingar.

• **Riley's Store**, Ballingar.

• **Swaine, Adeney and Brigg**, of Piccadilly. Gentlemens' outfitters and umbrella-makers. Responsible for Briggs' nickname.

DF 118; VB 213; BM 18; PF 172; DP 26; BR 183, 188; WS 77; Sc 142

SHUMBLE

Special correspondent in Ishmaelia in 1937. Plays cards. Looks through the keyhole at Hitchcock. Gets the scoop on the arrival of the 'red agent'.

Sc 80, 97

SHUTTER, MRS

Rival interior decorator to Mrs Beaver who calls her 'that ghoul'.

HD 7

SIDDONS, SARAH ***(1755–1831)***

English actress.

• In 1940 Geoffrey Bentley has a portrait of Mrs Siddons in his office at the Ministry of Information.

PF 65

SIDI BISHR

Where Hookforce are encamped before their move to Crete in May 1941.

OG 121

SIERRA LEONE

The Ishmailian fascist consul in London was brought up in Sierra Leone.

Sc 52

SILENUS, PROFESSOR OTTO FRIEDRICH ***(b. 1897)***

Modernist architect. Born in Hamburg of rich parents. Educated Moscow and the Bauhaus (q.v.). Lives in a bed-sitting room in Bloomsbury.

In 1922 commissioned to build King's Thursday (q.v.). He is a 'find' of Margot's.

Arthur Potts thinks that he is someone to watch, as he has managed to get away from Corbusier. He is not yet very famous, but everyone can see that he is a genius.

Tells a journalist that he sees the problem of architecture as 'the eliminations of the human element from the consideration of form. The only perfect building must be the factory, because that is built to house machines.' Thinks it is impossible for domestic architecture to be beautiful.

Once a house is finished he hates it and says that only the drains are satisfactory.

Absent-minded. Wants to marry Margot – or he would if she were more perfect. Goes to bed at quarter to ten, not having slept at all for over a year.

Meets Paul Pennyfeather again a year later on Corfu and invites himself to Margot's villa. Visits Greece. Thinks classical Greek buildings 'unspeakably ugly, but there were some nice goats'.

DF 119, 120, 121, 122, 124, 126–7, 206–9

SILK, AMBROSE, OM ***(b. 1902)***

English Jewish homosexual aesthete and writer. He has sleek black hair and a 'pale semitic face'. Goes to the same barber as Alastair Trumpington and Peter Pastmaster. Wears a dark suit a little too close-fitting at the waist and wrist, a plain cream-coloured silk shirt and a dark, spotted bow-tie. Also has Charvet ties and crêpe de chine pyjamas.

His favourite phrase is 'My Dear'.

Educated at Eton, where he collects Lovat Frazer rhyme sheets. At Oxford with Basil Seal.

At Oxford he rides in Christ Church Grind, tells Alastair Trumpington about his love for a rowing blue, and recites 'In Memoriam' through a megaphone.

Since Oxford he has 'maintained a shadowy, mutually derisive acquaintance' with Basil.

In Paris he write and publishes his first book, a study of Montparnasse negroes, which is banned in England. Turns away from the aestheticism of Neapolitan grottoes and Cochran stage-sets towards a more austere life.

Represents himself as a martyr to art and says that he belongs firmly to 'the age of the ivory tower'. Poppet Green sees him as a survivor of the *Yellow Book*.

He walks with a swagger and cuts an incongruous dash. He has picked up a little from Poppet and her set. Has a reverence for the Prince Regent. If at a dead end in a conversation uses 'Russia' to get out of it.

Joins the Ministry of Information as atheist representative in the religious department. He is responsible for showing British atheists that Nazism has a religious base.

Proposes the foundation of a new magazine and becomes editor of *Ivory Tower* for which he writes all the articles himself under the pseudonyms Hucklebury Squib, Bartholomew Grass and Tom Barebones-Abraham.

Writes *Monument to a Spartan*.

Basil Seal persuades him that *Ivory Tower* will get him arrested and arranges to smuggle him to Ireland as an Irish priest. Settles in Ireland, in the country, before moving to the west coast where he takes rooms in a fishing town.

Determines to move on: moves to Tangier, Tel Aviv, Ischia, and then to Portugal before returning to London.

In 1962, at the age of sixty he is invested with the Order of Merit and a banquet is given in his honour at the Ritz. Parsnip makes a speech which might be sarcastic in which he says Ambrose has maintained the 'silence of genius' for twenty-five years.

PF 30, 34–5, 36, 40, 43, 58–73, 109, 113, 174–7, 185, 188, 194–7, 203–4, 218–9; WS 251, 253–4

SIMMONDS, LUCY ***(b. 1914)***

Wife of Roger Simmonds (q.v.). Has £58,000 in trustee stock. Meets Roger at a ball thrown by one of his relatives in Pont Street, having been sent to dances by her aunt for six years.

Sheds her Pont Street ways before marrying Roger in November 1938. Lives in Victoria Square.

When John Plant first meets her she is pregnant. He falls in love with her.

Writes like a man. Has few friends, namely Peter Baverstock and Muriel Meiklejohn (q.v.). Tells confidences to Muriel.

She loves sunlight and is taken into Marxism by Roger.

Becomes impatient for the birth of her baby. Is taken to the zoo every noon by John. Gives birth on 25 August 1939. During the war moves back to her aunt's.

WS 145, 146, 147, 153, 166, 172–91

SIMMONDS, ROGER ***(b. 1904)***

Marxist playwright, humourist and novelist. Friend of John Plant with whom he was at Oxford (1922–1925), where, during their second year they together edited an undergraduate weekly. In the late twenties makes his reputation as a writer of funny novels, which get him jobs at newspapers and film companies. People find his writing 'delicious'.

Lives in Victoria Square. In 1938 he marries Lucy, joins the Socialist party and becomes conventional. Does not wear a hat after he is married.

Writes *Internal Combustion* (q.v.).

Has a good collection of the printed works of Batty Langley and William Halfpenny. When the revolution comes wants to be director of the museum of Bourgeois Art.

Lunches with John at the Ritz, which he detests. Mistakes Lord and Lady

Settringham for a couple of mid-West Americans.

During the war rises to a position in the department of Political Warfare.
WS 107, 130, 132, 144, 147, 148, 155, 170, 191

SIMON
Young man who fell out of an aeroplane and is commited to the same nursing home as Agatha Runcible in 1927.
• The Nephew of Lady Amelia who tells Etty Cornphillip's son that his real father is Ralph Bland.
VB 187; WS 30

SIMONA
Mediterranean coastal town of Neutralia visited by Scott-King in 1946. Around it grow groves of walnut and cork-oak and orchards of lemon and almond trees. It has a medieval university, a baroque cathedral, twenty churches, a rococo square, two or three 'tiny shabby palaces', a market and one shopping street.
WS 225

SIMPSON, MRS WALLIS, DUCHESS OF WINDSOR *(1896–1986)*
American socialite. Born Bessie Wallis Warfield. Married 1916 E.W. Spencer, and 1928 Ernest Simpson. London society hostess in the 1920s. In 1936 her affair with Edward VIII sparked a constitutional crisis and provoked his abdication.
• The talk at Margot Metroland's luncheon party for Charles Ryder in 1936 is entirely of Mrs Simpson.
BR 255

SIN
The naughtinesses enjoyed by Charles Ryder and Sebastian Flyte at Oxford in 1923 are 'high in the catalogue of grave sins'.

It takes a harsh word from her brother Brideshead to make Julia Flyte realize the reality of her sin. She sees it as an idiot child which she has always to look after, preventing her from going out and enjoying herself. She sees her mother carrying it with her to church and dying with its burden and becomes hysterical.
BR 46, 273–4

SINAI, EGYPT
Ambrose Silk compares the English people of the 1890s to 'the Voice of Sinai smiling through the clouds'.
PF 175

SKIMP, JUDGE
Resident at Lottie Crump's, who she calls 'Judge thingummy'. It is in his suite that one of her young ladies, Flossie, tries to swing from the chandelier and falls to her death.
VB 42, 55

SLAVING
Paul Pennyfeather is convicted for white slaving. 'Well I'm afraid you wont have much opportunity for that here,' Sir Wilfred Lucas-Dockery tells him.
DF 167

SLIMBRIDGE, CAPTAIN
Signaller officer on Crete with Hookforce.
OG 165

SLOGANS
NO BATHING IN BRAZIL: cry taken up by Tony Last's hallucinations in Brazil.
• WOMEN OF TOMORROW DEMAND AN EMPTY CRADLE: slogan on the banner carried by the Amurath Memorial High School girls at Seth's pageant in Azania.
• THROUGH STERILITY TO CULTURE: slogan on the banner carried by the Azanian beauties at Seth's pageant.
HD 202; BM 189, 190

SLOVAKS
Rex Mottram's friends think in 1938 that the Slovaks are bound to rise against Hitler.
BR 28

SITWELL, SIR OSBERT *(1892–1969)*
English writer – see his autobiography in three volumes *Left hand, Right hand.*
• Gilbert Pinfold's voices accuse him of not knowing Osbert Sitwell.
GP 147

SLUMP, THE
In the year of the great slump Ambrose Silk is afflicted by ascetic promptings and moves into his attic in Bloomsbury.
• Gilbert Pinfold's voices tell him that there has been a financial slump and that he has lost all his money.
PF 194; GP 132

SLUMP, MR
Deals with the letters to the Guru Brahmin which need private answers. He has worked at the paper since the days of Aunt Lydia's *Postbag*. He still writes in her style. Smokes incessantly and has a terrible cough which only whisky will revive. He gradually falls into slovenly habits. The managing editor notices and says that unless he pulls himself together he will be fired. He is fired. Aimee Thanatogenos finds him in Mooney's saloon. He tells her to 'go and take a high jump'. She does.
LO 93, 106, 114, 115

SMART WOMAN, THE
Present at Everard Spruce's party in 1943. She is an air-raid warden and has soot on her face. The 'smart' denotes rank rather than chic. She is the woman at whose wedding Ludovic had been in the guard of honour. Her name is Lady Perdita. Calls Ludovic a snob because he will not drink Frankie's cocktail.
US 41–2

SMELLS
The chapel at Broome smells of beeswax and chrysanthemums and incense.
• The smell of his tobacco jar reminds Miss Vavasour of Mr Crouchback.
• Mr Plant's house smells of cigar smoke and cantaloup: 'a masculine smell'.
US 63, 73; WS 127

SMERDYAKEV
The Russian agitator from Moscow who arrives at Jacksonburg in 1937 disguised as a ticket collector, to help Dr Benito.
Sc 100

SMETHWICK, MISS CONSTANTINA
Friend of Mr Ryder who he invites to dinner in the same party as the Orme-Herricks in 1923.
BR 70

SMILEY, SERGEANT
Physical training instructor of Guy Crouchback's platoon at Sidi Bishr in 1941.
OG 120

SMITH, F.E., LORD BIRKENHEAD *(1872–1930)*
English Conservative statesman and lawyer. Secretary of State for India from 1924 to 1928.
• Rex Mottram is friendly with 'F.E.' in 1924.
BR 177

SMITH, LOGAN PEARSALL *(1865–1946)*
American writer and essayist. See his *All Trivia* (1933).
• Everard Spruce tells Frankie that Ludovic's *Pensées* reads as if Logan Pearsall Smith had written Kafka. He is a friend of Spruce but does not attend his party in 1943, as he does not go out.
US 42

SMUDGE, HORACE
Second secretary in the British Consulate at Bellacita. Is unable to help Scott-King get home in 1946.
WS 236

SMYRNA, TURKEY
Port to which Basil Seal imagines himself being posted as a secret agent in 1939.
PF 51

SNIEFEL
American photographer. He is a 'very young, very lively manikin'. Accompanies General Spitz to the Balkans. Survives the crash in Yugoslavia, perched in a chestnut tree. Accompanies Ritchie-Hook on his assault on the blockhouse, 'like a terrier, like the pet dwarf privileged to tumble

about the heels of a prince of the renaissance' and manages to escape. His scoop fills half a dozen pages of an illustrated weekly paper.
US 209, 214, 215, 221, 223

SNIGGS
Junior Dean of Scone college in 1922. Sits with Mr Postlethwaite in his rooms on the night of the Bollinger dinner, hoping for a week of founder's port.

Is seen by Paul Pennyfeather in 1923 being supercilious to the chaplain.
DF 9–10, 210

SNUFF
The Halberdiers have a huge, silver mounted horn of snuff which circulates with spoon, hammer and brush after regimental dinners.
MA 77

SOAMES
Guy Crouchback's platoon sergeant in the Halberdiers in 1940. They do not get on. He sees Guy 'as a nannie might some child, not of "the family" but of inferior and suspicious origin, suddenly, by a whim of the mistress of the house, dumped, as a guest of infinite duration, in her nursery'. Signs on for long service in 1937. Corporal for three months. Wears a moustache in a gangster's cut. Reminds Guy of Trimmer. Guy recommends him for a commission.
MA 172

SOANE, SIR JOHN *(1753–1837)*
English architect. Designed the Bank of England. Made use of interesting decorative features in a severe neo-classical style.
• The library at Brideshead is Soanesque.
BR 78

SOAPY
Inmate at Mountjoy prison. In his opinion the string quartet play Mozart as if it were Haydn, and there is no feeling in their Debussy pizzicato.
GP 181

SOCIALISTS
A Socialist from the coal mines is among Rex Mottram's friends staying at Brideshead in 1938.
• Socialism has a double attraction for Lucy Simmonds. It is part of her break with Aldershot.
BR 26; WS 169

SOCIETY FOR THE PRESERVATION OF ANCIENT BUILDINGS
Paul Pennyfeather tells Arthur Potts that Grimes is from the SPAB.
DF 142

SOCRATES *(BC 469–399)*
Athenian philosopher. According to the Delphic Oracle the wisest man in the world. Friend of Xenophon and Plato. Exposed Sophistry. Held the principle that virtue was knowledge, a knowledge divined from dialectic.
• Ambrose Silk, in his pantheon of courageous writers, pictures Socrates marching to sea with Xenophon.
PF 40

SODOM AND GOMORRAH
The two old Testament cities in the vale of Siddim which were destroyed by Jehovah with fire and brimstone as recompense for their debauchery, despite the pleas of Abraham.
• Anthony Blanche thinks that society treats Lord Marchmain as if he had 'roasted, stuffed and eaten his children, and gone frolicking about wreathed in all the flowers of Sodom and Gomorrah'.
BR 55

S.O.E.
The highly secret British Special Operations Executive of WWII , responsible for co-ordinating resistance activity in occupied Europe.
• There is something about Fosker (q.v.) thinks Gilbert Pinfold, which reminds him of the sort of subalterns he had met during the war who, disliked by their regiment, had been posted to SOE.
GP 67

SOLAR POWER
The great sheets of glass of the Dome of Security, designed to trap the sun are now rendered useless having been covered with coats of tar as camouflage during one of the frequent weeks of international panic.
GP 194

SOLOMON
The king of the Old Testament, renowned for his wisdom, and the 'judgement of Solomon'.
• Sir Wilfred Lucas-Dockery (q.v.) always feels like Solomon when at ten o'clock every morning except Sunday, he sits in judgement on cases of misconduct among the prisoners.
DF 179

SOMALILAND, AFRICA
Abandoned 'precipitously' by the British in 1940.
• De Souza, on seeing the Halberdiers' tropical kit arrive shortly after the withdrawal presumes that they are to be sent to re-take Somaliland.
MA 214

SONERSCHEINS
Dealers in antiquities, from whom in 1923, Ryder purchases a fifth-century terracotta bull.
BR 62

SONGS
• 'Auld Lang Syne'. Sung by the passengers at the end of their cruise on the *SS Glory of Greece*.
• 'Father wouldn't buy Me a Bow-Wow'. Sung by Ludovic in his madness, to Fido.
• 'Gilbert the Filbert'. Broadcast on the wireless by Gilbert Pinfold's voices.
• 'God Save the King'. The boys at Llanabba refuse to sing it because of the pudding they have had at luncheon.
• 'Home they brought the Warrior Dead'. Sung by one of the Etonians at Sebastian Flyte's luncheon party at Christ Church in 1923.
• 'Night and Day'. Sung by Trimmer, incessantly, in 1941. Virginia Crouchback cannot get it out of her head and seems, when pregnant to hear a voice within her saying 'you, you, you'.
• 'Nobody Knows How Bored We Are and Nobody Seems to Care', 'Take Me Back to Dear Old Blighty', 'We're Here Because We're Here'. Songs of the Great War remembered by de Souza, which he thinks would not have been approved of by the Ministry of Information in 1940, because of their lack of 'morale-building qualities'.
• 'Pull for the Shore, Sailor, Pull for the Shore'. Gilbert Pinfold's nanny sings this.
• 'Roll Out the Barrel'. Guy Crouchback tells Bakik that this might be an anti-fascist song. Sung by Halberdiers when on the march in 1940.
• 'Show Me the Way to Go Home'. In 1944 Guy Crouchback tells Bakik that this is an English anti-fascist song.
• 'Song of Solomon'. The song of songs of the Old Testament. John Plant wonders how the 'Song of Solomon' can compare with the true voice of love.
• 'The Eton Boating Song'. Sung by Ginger Littlejohn when drunk with an American at the Café de la Paix.
• 'The Man on the Flying Trapeze'. Sung by Basil Seal when drunk at the health farm in 1962.
• 'The Quartermaster's Stores'. Sung by the Halberdiers on the march in 1940.
• 'The Wearing of the Green'. Sung by Juanita De Pablo at the funeral of Sir Francis Hinsley.
• 'This Time Tomorrow I shall be far from this Academy'. Sung in the dormitories at Kut al Imara by the Halberdiers in 1940.
• 'Three Little Maids from School' (from *The Mikado*). Played by the Lepperidges in Azania.
• 'Tit Willow' (from *The Mikado*). Played on a record by the Lepperidges in Azania.
• 'We'll Hang out the Washing on the Siegfried Line'. Sung by the conscripts of the Halberdiers in 1940 when on the march.
• 'When Father Papered the Parlour'. On a record played by the little gramophone which Reggie St Cloud gives John Last for Christmas 1933.

• 'When first I saw Mabel'. Broadcast on the wireless by Gilbert Pinfold's voices.
• Songs about Bells. Prendergast knows several.
• Mrs Ape tells her angels 'If you feel queer, sing. There's nothing like it'.
• A Song about Sex Appeal. Played on the gramophone by Prudence Courteney and William Bland. Includes a good line about 'start off with cocktails and end up with Eno's'.
• A Neapolitan Song. Sung by Josephine Stitch.
• A Song about a Little Broken Doll from the 1910s. Virginia Crouchback to Guy in 1943.
• American songs are all above love, which is not anti-fascist.
• There is community singing in the New Britain.
• Paul Pennyfeather and Stubbs sing part-songs to the inmates of Oxford Prison.

SOTHILL, BARBARA
Daughter of Lady Cynthia and Sir Christopher Seal, and sister of Basil (q.v.) to whom she bears a close resemblance. She has curly dark hair and clear blue eyes.

For the first twenty years of her life she hero-worships Basil. She has a breathless charm and is 'fartouche'.

Marries Freddy Sothill 1931. Lives at Malfrey. After the birth of her children she is less wild.

In winter 1939, after Freddy goes off with his regiment, she moves into the octagonal parlour and shuts off the rest of the house. Before the war breakfasts in bed from a wicker tray.

In 1939 takes in refugees from Birmingham including the Connollys. Has no idea about Basil's deal with the Connollys.

Her husband is killed during the war.

Telephones Basil at the health farm in 1962. Looks after her niece, Barbara.
PF 9, 14, 15, 74, 87; Bm 74; WS 254, 267

SOTHILL, FREDDY (1903 c. 1942)
Contemporary of Basil Seal. Owner of Malfrey (q.v.). In 1929 joins the Gloucestershire Yeomanry. Marries Barbara Seal 1931.

He is 'large, masculine, prematurely bald and superficially cheerful'. In reality he is misanthropic. Takes in most people excepting his wife and her family. When he tells a joke he uses a special facial expression. Has a happy marriage and enjoys, when in private, making his wife swear and kick him playfully.

At Yeomanry camp 1937. Called up in 1939, by which time he has put on so much weight that his trousers are uncomfortable.

Dislikes Tony Seal who, despite his obvious diplomatic brilliance he finds 'supercilious and effeminate'.

Returns to Malfrey with his regiment in spring 1940 and billets them in the house. Takes the officers on a shoot.

Killed in action in WWII. After his death his ample cellar is drained by Basil.
PF 10, 13, 14, 46, 136; WS 254, 255

SOUM, SMILES
Leader of the Fascists in Ishmaelia. He is one quarter Jackson, being the grandson of President Samuel Smiles Jackson, in the female line. In the family hierarchy he is only Assistant Director of Public Morals. He is dissatisfied with this post and he leaves Jacksonburg and issues a manifest of the White Shirt movement. His thesis is that the Jacksons have usurped the power of the Ishmaelites, who are in fact a white race and are behind an international negro Bolshevist movement. In short that they are responsible for every ill facing the country. The Jacksons are unaffected.
Sc 77–8

SOUP, IN THE
Talking about Prendergast's Doubts, Grimes admits to Paul Pennyfeather that 'when a chap's been in the soup as often as I have, it gives you a feeling that everything's for the best'. When he turns up at King's Thursday he is 'in the soup' again. And at Egdon Heath he is, of course, 'in the soup' as usual.
DF 34, 95, 189

SOUTH DOWNS, SUSSEX
Location of Lancing School (*see* CHARLES RYDER) and the school of Paul Pennyfeather.

SOUTH POLE
Destination, in 1937 of an all-woman expedition which Lord Copper does not want the *Beast* to cover.
Sc 181

SOUTH TWINING, WILTSHIRE
Village near Brideshead, where Sebastian Flyte gets drunk in a hotel on the day of the hunt in 1924.
BR 161

SOUTHERN CROSS
Constellation of stars seen by Ivor Claire and Guy Crouchback from the deck of their ship on the way to North Africa.
OG 109

SOUTHSAND
Location of Kut al Imara, Staplehurst, the Ristorant Garibaldi, the Grand Hotel, and the Southsand and Mudshore Yacht Squadron. It has a dance hall, a cinema and several hotels.
MA 85, 94, 97

SOUTHSAND AND MUDSHORE YACHT SQUADRON, SOUTHSAND
Sailing club which occupies a villa on the seafront. There are a flag and burgee at a pole on the lawn and two brass cannon at the door. It has large plate-glass windows. Mr Goodall is a member, and Sir Lionel Gore the Commodore. Guy Crouchback and Apthorpe become members in 1940, at the temporary member's rate of ten bob a month.
• Around the fire are a collection of charts, burgees, binnacles and model ships.
MA 107–11

SOUVENIRS
Seth brings back a model of the Eiffel Tower from Paris.
• Corker buys a bakelite elephant, some Japanese shawls, Benares trays, cigarette boxes, an amber necklace and a model of Tutankhamen's tomb.
• The correspondent of the *Glory of Greece's* mother buys a shawl in Taormina.
BM; Sc 70–71; WS 17
(*See also* COCONUT)

SPAHIS
French colonial cavalry of North Africa.
• In the evenings Spahi officers play bagatelle at the hotel in Fez frequented by John Plant in the 1930s.
WS 108

SPAIN
In the summer of 1934 Lord Monomark takes his yacht and a party including Marjorie St Cloud and Allan, down the coast of Spain, attending bull-fights.
• Where Basil Seal lives at the time of the Civil War.
• Fifty Free Spaniards are placed under the command of X Commando in North Africa in 1941. They are quite anarchic and have women in the camp at all times. They slit the throat of an Egyptian cab-driver. They are always boasting about having blown up convents during the Civil War.
HD 200; PF 16; OG 119; GP 87
(*See also* PENINSULAR WAR *and* MADRID)

SPANISH CIVIL WAR *(1936–1939)*
Bloody conflict between the Nationalists, under Franco, and the Socialists. The struggle against a dictatorship inspired many anti-fascists to come to the aid of the Socialists, including a number of intellectuals and writers (Hemingway, Orwell, Spender, Auden). However, brute force, in the shape of military aid from Germany and Italy prevailed and the Nationalists were victorious.
• Ambrose Silk, having picked up a little from Poppet Green's set in 1939, is able to say that the war in Spain is 'contemporary' because it was a 'class war'.
• A Bishop travelling back to England on the same ship as the Ryders in 1936 is on his way to Spain to attempt to reconcile the Anarchists and the Communists.
• Basil Seal is in Spain, at the front, at

the time of the Civil War, although just why is unclear.

• Cordelia Flyte drives an ambulance in Spain and stays on to help refugees after most of her colleagues have left, returning in late 1938 to Brideshead.

• Ian Kilbannock tells Guy Crouchback in 1941 that he has been 'pretty red' since the Civil War.

• The Free Spaniards in North Africa in 1941 blew up a great many convents in the Civil War.

• In 1938 Roger Simmonds works with a committee of relief for Spanish refugees.

PF 40; BR 234, 285; OG 100, 152; WS 150, 278

(*See* FIFTH COLUMN)

SPARROW, MRS

Cook to Lady Brown in 1927, who, puzzled at the scarcity of eggs after the Bright Young People have had their party at No. 10, thinks that there must have been burglars.

• Villager at Kemble, who in 1940 falls out of the apple loft and cannot be taken to the hospital for her two broken legs as it is being kept free for air-raid casualties.

VB 58; MA 30

SPARTA

City state of Ancient Greece famed for its hardiness and asceticism.

• Angela Lyne is puzzled to know what, if they combed their hair before Thermopylae, and if Alcibiades cut off his hair, did the Spartans really think about hair.

• She also feels that, 'like the Spartan boy and the fox', Basil Seal has been 'eating her' for the past seven years.

PF 28

SPEECHES

In 1932 Viscount Boaz welcomes to Azania Dame Mildred Porch and Miss Tin 'two ladies renowned throughout the famous country of Europe for their great cruelty to animals' and gives a detailed account of what he had once done with a woodman's axe to a wild boar.

• Lord Copper's speech at the Boot banquet in 1937 lasts for thirty-eight minutes.

• In 1962 Parsnip makes a speech at the banquet in honour of Ambrose Silk which Basil Seal considers might be sarcastic.

BM 171; Sc 220; WS 254

SPECIAL SERVICES FORCES

Department of HOOHQ to which Guy Crouchback is attached in 1943.

US 27

SPEED KINGS

The racing drivers at the motor races in 1927. They are 'unimposing men mostly with small moustaches and apprehensive eyes'.

VB 158

SPENDER, SIR STEPHEN *(1909–1989)*

English poet. His early left-wing views eventually changed to a form of Liberalism. See his *Poems from Spain* (1930) and *Runes and Visions* (1941).

• Dr Beamish, stood, as a young man, alongside Spender at 'great concourses of youth'.

GP 195

SPEZIA

One of Rex Mottram's friends in 1938 wants to know why on earth the British did not simply blow Spezia to blazes, and send the Italian fleet to the bottom.

BR 262

SPHAKIA, CRETE

Where the final evacuation of British troops from Crete took place on 31 May 1941. On this day Guy Crouchback is sitting in a cave which overhangs the beach at Sphakia watching the Second Halberdiers in column of companies in the ravine below him. He meets Ivor Claire, sleeps there overnight, and prepares to surrender.

OG 219–21

SPHINX, THE
Seen by the correspondent on the *SS Glory of Greece* in 1932: 'Goodness how sad'.
WS 20

SPIERPOINT
Charles Ryder's house at Lancing.
WS 291

SPIES
In 1937 Algernon Stitch (q.v.) is sacking ten spies a day.
• Seth is spied upon but does not see the spy, only hears the scamper of his retreating feet.
• Gilbert Pinfold's voices tell each other that he is a spy in the employ of HMG.
• Basil Seal imagines, in 1939, that he might be sent to Smyrna on a secret mission on behalf of the government. When he does come to spy for the Ministry of War, the reality, and the outcome are rather different.
• According to Dr Antonic, there are spies everywhere in Neutralia in 1946.
• Spies permeate the amateur underground organizations that spring up in Europe just after the war.
BM 31; GP 91, 95; WS 218, 242; Sc 11

SPIRE, JACK
Conservationist. In 1922 saves St Sepulchre's Egg Street and can thus do nothing about King's Thursday. Paul Pennyfeather thinks that the back streets of Marseilles are so 'picturesque' that they would, in England, have immediately been saved by Mr Spire.
DF 118–19, 152

SPITSBERGEN, NORWAY
Island in the Arctic Circle. Location of a glacier named after General Cruttwell.
Sc 43

SPITZ, GENERAL
American general who is at the head of the observation party in Begoy in 1944. He has 'a round, stern face' and is hung with weapons and haversacks. He is attended by an aide and by Sneiffel (q.v.). Survives the plane crash.
US 209

SPLIT, YUGOSLAVIA
An old lawyer from Split is the Minister of the Interior of the Yugoslav partisan general staff in 1944.
• Guy and his men travel in 1944 from Begoy to Split, where in February 1945 they leave for Brindisi.
US 173, 232

SPONGE, SOAPY
Central character in *Mr Sponge's Sporting Tour* by R.S. Surtees (q.v.).
• Basil Seal approaches the twenty closed doors of the Ministry of War with the same purposeful manner as that with which Soapy Sponge approached Jawleyford Court.
PF 145

SPORTS DAYS
The Llanabba School sports day is a great event. Dr Fagan calls for fireworks and music. They employ the Llanabba Silver band. Everyone dresses up. During Dr Fagan's sixteen years at Llanabba there have been six sports days, all 'utterly disasterous'. At one Lady Bunyan was taken ill. At another there is the matter of the press photographers and the obstacle race; at another, one of the parent's dogs bites two of the boys and one of the masters, who swears terribly and is sacked. There is a marquee. The hurdles are spiked iron railings. The events are weight, hammer, javelin, long-jump, high jump, hurdles, egg and spoon, and greasy pole, which have all been competed for already. The races are started with Philbrick's service revolver. Lord and Lady Circumference attend. The first race is the quarter mile. Lord Tangent is shot in the foot by Mr Prendergast, with Philbrick's revolver, and filled up with cake. Mr Prendergast becomes drunk. Colonel Sidebottom turns up along with the Clutterbucks and Margot Metroland with 'Chokey'. There is some question as to

whether Clutterbuck should have won the race.
DF 59–83

SPOT
Fox terrier belonging to the matron of the nursing home in Wigmore Street to which Agatha Runcible is taken after her crash.
VB 185

SPRATT
A 'tick' in Boucher's house at Lancing in 1919 who is made Platoon Commander of the cadet force.
WS 302

SPRING
'When the earth proclaims its fertility, in running brooks, bursting seed, mating of birds and frisking of lambs, then the thoughts of man turn to athletics and horticulture, watercolour painting and amateur theatricals' writes Prudence Courteney (q.v.).
BM 138

SPROGGIN, COLONEL
Colonel of Freddy Sothill's regiment, the Gloucestershire Yeomanry, who moves into Malfrey in the spring of 1940.
PF 141

SPRUCE, EVERARD *(b. circa 1909)*
English literary critic of the 1940s. Publisher of *Survival* (q.v.). Publishes Ludovic's *Pensées* which he thinks are like Logan Pearsall Smith writing Kafka.

Believes that the human race is bound to dissolve in chaos. In 1929 he is not particularly esteemed. Most of his friends flee to America during the war or joined the fire brigade. Largely because of this he finds himself elevated and launches Survival given over to the survival of values.

Lives in a fine house in Cheyne Walk and is cared for by four secretaries. In his youth he had attempted to appear proletarian, but by the time of his middle thirties he presents the negligent elegance of a don. He wears the Charvet shirts and pyjamas of a dead friend from the fire brigade killed by a falling chimney. His suits are thus far too large for him. He wears a huge fur-lined overcoat, and when at home does not wear a jacket, whatever the weather. Is taken to see Virginia Crouchback and her child; takes her smoked salmon from Ruben's. Has always studied the gossip columns, as a man of the left studying his enemy. Calls Virginia Crouchback 'the last of twenty years' succession of heroines'.
US 35, 39, 40, 49, 123, 189, 195, 199, 200

SPRUCE'S VEILED LADIES
See CONEY and FRANKIE

SPY
Cartoonist for *Vanity Fair* in the Edwardian era. Caricatures by him decorate Shepheard's Hotel.
VB 38

SQUIBB, HUCKLEBURY
Pseudonym used by Ambrose Silk as a byline in *Ivory Tower*. Mr Bentley tells the police that he is 'a very tall young man; easily recognizable for he had lost the lobe of his left ear in extraordinary circumstances when sailing before the mast; he had a front tooth missing and wore gold earrings'.
PF 99

STAFFORDSHIRE
Home of Mrs Scrope-Weld.
• Where Mr Hornbeam's father is a commercial potter.
US 146; WS 46

STAFFORDSHIRE FIGURES
Lieutenant Padfield buys a Staffordshire figure of Gladstone for the Glenobans. Guy Crouchback thinks that one of a Highlander might be more appropriate.
US 122

STALIN, JOSEPH *(1789–1953)*
Russian leader and notorious dictator. In 1943 the British public have a popular enthusiasm for 'Uncle Joe' Stalin.
US 23

STANLEY, DEAN ARTHUR PENRHYN *(1815–1880)*
English prelate and author who travelled to the east, and to the Holy Land, in 1851 with the Prince of Wales.
• Paul Pennyfeather has a copy of his *Eastern Church*, at Scone in 1923.
DF 212

STATUES
An equestrian statue stands before the façade of Doubting Hall, pointing down the avenue.
• A statue of Lord Copper in coronation robes (Chryselephantine effigy), stands in the hall of Copper House, Fleet Street.
• The statue of Bellorius in Neutralia is 'appalling'. It was originally a portrait of a businessman and bears no possible relation to Bellorius or any Renaissance prince.
• Whispering Glades is decorated with bronze and Carrera statuary 'allegorical, infantile or erotic'.
VB 67; Sc 25; WS 233; LO 65

STAYLE, BETTY (ELIZABETH ERMINTRUDE ALEXANDRA) *(1920–1956)*
Younger daughter of the Duchess of Stayle. Likes the work of Hemingway. Attends a party at King's Thursday 1937. Has an affair with Basil Seal. Is considered for marriage in 1939 by Peter Pastmaster. The Duke of Connaught stands as sponsor for her. Marries 1940 Clarence Allbright who is killed in WWII. Has one son, Charles. Contracts cancer.
PF 152; WS 278–80

STAYLE, DUCHESS OF
Has two daughters Ursula and Betty (b. 1920). In 1931 she and her husband dine with Lady Seal. Her husband thinks Basil Seal 'a clever young fellow'. In 1937 gives a ball. John Boot attends and finds Julia Stitch there in the duke's dressing-room eating *foie gras* with a shoehorn. By 1962 the duke is dead.
VB 128; BM 77' SC 72; PF 152; WS 278, 279, 280

STAYLE, URSULA
Eldest daughter of the Duchess of Stayle. She is a few inches taller than Edward Throbbing and wears a frock decorated with lace 'in improbable places'. Her hair is colourless, worn long and bound across her forehead in a broad fillet. It is understood that she will marry Edward. Does not wear make-up. She is involved with organizing a girls' club in Canning Town.
VB 128

STEAM ENGINES
The Empress of Azania is keen to choose a steam roller. The Metropolitan Archbishop is keen on the Pennsylvania Monarch, while the Prince Consort is in favour of the smaller Kentucky Midget.
BM 50

STEBBING, MAJOR
Adjutant of the OTC at Lancing in 1919. Has no academic gown.
WS 304

STEERFORTH, CAPTAIN
Master of the *SS Caliban* in 1953. He is middle aged and middle class. He had once seen a murderer, a stoker, who had killed another with a shovel.
WS 34, 64

STEIN, GERTRUDE *(1874–1946)*
American writer. Lived in Paris. Formed a collection of Modern paintings and befriended many major writers. See her *Autobiography of Alice B. Toklas* (1933).
• When in Paris in the 1920s Ambrose Silk frequents her company.
PF 43

STERNE, SIR LIONEL
Patron of the arts. Collects pictures by Mr Plant. Lives in Kensington Palace Gardens. To Mr Plant he is 'a fine meaty fellow with a great gold watch-chain across his belly'. He is in fact a 'youthful and elegant millionaire' who has, since 1928 been a leader of aesthetic fashion.
WS 115

STEYLE, MARJORIE
Friend of Mr Plant. Her eldest son sells haberdashery for four pounds a week.
WS 111

STEYNING
Near where Sir Samson Curtis–Dunne has his country house.
WS 312

STIGGINS
Undergraduate at Oxford in 1922. Friend of Paul Pennyfeather and Potts. Reads a paper to the OSCU on 'Sex Repression and religious experience'.
DF 45

STILLINGFLEET, ROGER
One-time friend of Gilbert Pinfold. Writer. Pinfold likes his work. In the fifties he becomes odd and no longer goes to Bellamy's where he is a member, unless to entertain a visiting American. Jazz to him is 'a necessary narcotic'. Is spoken of by Pinfold's voices.
WS 46, 63

STITCH, ALGERNON
Married to Julia (q.v.).

English Minister of Imperial Defence in 1931. He has 'a long, thin nose and long, thin moustaches'. He is loved by all (even Labour politicians). In 1931 he is sacking ten spies a day. Wears a bowler hat and carries a crimson dispatch case with the Royal Arms. In 1941 he is in Alexandria 'keeping his eye on the King'.
SC 6; OG 125

STITCH, JOSEPHINE *(b. 1924)*
Child of Julia and Algernon Stitch. In 1937, at the age of eight she is a prodigy. Construes Virgil every day. Thinks Arthur's ceiling 'very banal'. Thinks *Waste of Time*, which she has read 'very banal'. Banal is a word which she can apply to everything, including her gymnasium at which she is the best of her class. Is able to imitate the Prime Minister, sing a Neapolitan song and stand on her head.
Sc 7–9

STITCH, JULIA
She is 'lovely'. All of her friends always bring their problems to her. Lives with her husband Algernon in a Hawksmoor house in a cul de sac in St James's.

Her grandparents spent their lives 'in the service of Queen Victoria and in that court had formed standards of living which projected themselves over another generation and determined Mrs Stitch's precocious but impressionable childhood'.

She has grown up believing that comfort is common. Although she enjoys good living, surprise and change, her male guests always have a rough time of it.

She is still in bed at eleven o'clock in the morning. Wears a clay face pack. Her secretary is Miss Holloway. Designs costumes for a charity ballet. Her maid is Brittling. One child, Josephine (born 1924). Discovers a carpet shop in Bethnal Green. Has a 'Model Madhouse'. Reads *Waste of Time* by John Boot aloud at Brakewell. Does *The Times* crossword at the same time as many other things. Drives the latest baby car in a brilliant black.

Drives along the kerb in St James's Street. A policeman taker her number. Takes John Boot to Bethnal Green. Drives on the kerb driving a young man on to Brooks' steps for safety.

Drives her car in pursuit of a man to whom she had been wanting to speak for weeks, down the steps of a gentlemen's lavatory in Sloane Street. The newspapers report the incident: 'Society Beauty in Public convenience', 'Mrs. Stitch again'. William Boot thinks her 'The most beautiful woman he had ever seen'.

John Boot finds her at a party of the Duchess of Stayle's in 1931, eating *foie gras* with a shoehorn surrounded by three elderly admirers, in the duke's dressing-room.

In 1940 her yacht is requisitioned to transport the officers of Hookforce to Mugg. Ivor Claire thinks that she might be able to keep order among the sergeants.

In 1941 she is in Alexandria with her husband. Half of X Commando spend their evenings with her.

Visits Guy Crouchback in hospital. Takes him away with her in a little open car and drives madly down the rue Sultan turning left at the Nebi Daniel. Stands up in the car and points out Alexander's tomb. The Egyptian police become enraged with her. Finds Egypt disappointing, 'can't get to like the people'.

Her villa is beyond Ramleh and Sidi Bishr. It has the atmosphere of the Alpes Maritimes.

She seems to be the protectress of X Commando.

Keeps cats. Looks after Guy. He is at her villa on 22 June 1941, when Hitler invades Russia.

Guy gives her the identity tag which he had taken from the dead soldier on Crete to give to Algie. She drops it in a waste-paper basket: 'her eyes were one immense sea, full of flying galleys'.

SC 5–14, 40, 48, 72; OG 97, 98, 103, 125, 129, 157, 232, 237, 239, 241, 243, 244; WS 117

STOCKHOLM, SWEDEN

Where in the 1920s Sir Samson Courteney's diplomatic career is finally doomed. Here, as Chargé d'Affaires, he had invited Scott-King to luncheon in mistake for someone else.

WS 235

STOPES, MARIE *(1880–1958)*

English pioneer of birth control.

• Seth renames the site of the Anglican cathedral in Debra Dowa the Place Marie Stopes.

BM 142

STORM, IRIS

Fictional character 'That shameless, shameful lady, dressed pour le sport . . . "I am a house of men" she said.' Everard Spruce reads the book at school, 'where it was forbidden'. Frankie has not heard of her.

US 200

STRAPPER, GENERAL

Incensed general who arrives at the offices of the *Daily Excess* in 1927 determined to see Simon Balcairn about a lie about his daughter in the paper which says that she has been seen in a nightclub: 'to anyone better acquainted with Miss Strapper's habits the photograph was particularly reticent'. Corners Mrs Brace who refers him to Simon.

VB 88

STRAPPER, COLONEL

Name on the passenger list of the boat to Brazil which Thérèse de Vitre associated with Tony Last.

HD 162

STRATFORD-ON-AVON, WARWICKSHIRE

Where, in 1953 Cedric Thorne is acting, and where he hangs himself in his dressing-room.

GP 20

STRICKLAND-VENABLES, SIR WALTER and LADY

Joint-master of the Marchmain Hunt with Lord Brideshead.

Mr Samgrass finds him 'a figure of fun'. In 1924 they take their grooms out of top hats. Their daughter Jean falls in the mud during the hunt.

BR 120, 154, 160

STRIKES

A strike in Glasgow in 1941 is brought to a halt by 'Aid to Russia week'.

OG 246

(*See also* GENERAL STRIKE)

STRONGBOW (RICHARD DE CLARE) *(1130–1176)*

Gave military aid to Dermot, King of Leinster in Ireland in 1170 and married his daughter.

There have been Fleaces and Fleysers in Bellinger since his time.

WS 79

STROUD, GLOUCESTERSHIRE

To reach Kemble one can take the bus from Stroud. In 1939 Caroline Maiden is stopped here by a policeman because she is not carrying her gas-mask.

MA 26, 30

STUART DYNASTY, THE

Scottish family which produced the Kings of Scotland and Great Britain from 1177 to 1714, at which date their power was given to the Hanoverians.

• Mr Crouchback has 'acknowledged no monarch since James II'.

MA 34

STUART-KERR, CAPTAIN ANGUS

One of Adam Fenwick-Symes' creations during his time as Mr Chatterbox. He is a big-game hunter and an expert dancer.

• The character is taken up, to Adam's disgust, by a gossip columnist in a two-penny illustrated weekly, who sees him at a point-to-point and says that he is known to be the 'hardest rider in the Hebrides'. Adam responds by writing that this must be a confusion with Alastair Kerr-Stuart of Inverauchty, a distance cousin. Angus, says Adam, never rides; 'for a very interesting reason. There is an old Gaelic rhyme repeated among his clansmen which says in rough translation "the laird rides well on two legs". Tradition has it that when the head of the house mounts a horse the clan will be dispersed.'

VB 113–14

STUBBS

Fellow student at Oxford with Paul Pennyfeather in 1923. He is 'a grave young man with a quiet voice and with carefully formed opinions'. Reads theology at Hertford College. Argues with Sniggs about plans to rebuild the Bodleian. Entertains Paul to tea with the College secretary of the League of Nations Union and the chaplain of Oxford prison. Walks with Paul around Oxford. Together they sing part songs to the inmates of the prison. Has read Dr Fagan's book. Paul tells him that Philbrick is Arnold Bennett. During his third year has digs in Walton Street. Smokes a pipe.

DF 210–13

STUYVESANT-OGLANDER, MRS

Guest of Celia Ryder at her cocktail party on the Atlantic in 1936. Anthony Blanche lunches with her on her return to England. She is a friend of his mother's: 'Such a frump!' They talk of Charles Ryder. She is one of the 'old trouts' whose hair is cut by Trimmer on ocean liners in the late 1930s.

BR 231, 259; OG 217

SUDA BAY, CRETE

Into which Hookforce sail to disembark in May 1941

OG 165

SUDAN, THE

Where, in Khartoum, Katchen's husband was once in trouble.

• Charles Ryder is conducted through the streets of Fez by an officer of the Sudan Police.

SC 159; BR 202

SUICIDE

Grimes apparently takes his life at Llanabba, but few people believe in it, as he does not leave his leg behind when he walks out to sea. A note is found in the pocket of his trousers which reads: 'Those that live by the flesh shall perish by the flesh.'

• Suicide is not allowed in Blackstone goal and thus wire-netting is stretched between the landings.

• Simon Balcairn kills himself by putting his head in the gas oven, being sure not to lay it on a copy of Lord Vanbrugh's column from the *Morning Despatch*.

• David, one of Ambrose Silk's boy-friends throws himself under a train.

• One of Cordelia Flyte's governesses throws herself from a bridge into one of the ornamental lakes at Brideshead.

• Cedric Thorne hangs himself in his dressing-room at Stratford.

• Gilbert Pinfold's voices accuse him of having been responsible for the suicide of a staff-officer in the Middle-East in WWII.

• Dr Beamish's parents hang themselves with their own clothes-line rather than wait for euthanasia.

• Sir Francis Hinsley, fired by Megalopolitan, hangs himself with his braces.

• Leo throws himself off the roof of the Garden of Allah Hotel.

• Aimee Thanatogenos poisons herself.
• Lord Moping threatens suicide for some years at the time of his wife's garden party, and one year is found, not quite dead, hanging by his braces in the orangery.
• There is a suicide at St Eustace's. An occurrence which pleases Mr Plant.
DR 139, 164; VB 106; PF 43; BR; GP 20, 131, 197; LO 33, 116; WS 119

SUNBATHING
In 1923 Charles Ryder and Sebastian Flyte are sunbathing on the roof of Brideshead when happened upon by Cordelia.
• Gilbert Pinfold abhors sunbathing.
BR; GP 14

SUNNINGDALE, BERKSHIRE
Town near Windsor where Rex Mottram spends a weekend with a stockbroker friend in 1924 and continues his affair with Brenda Champion.
BR 181

SUPERSTITION
• Jenny Abdul-Akbar believes that a terrible curse hangs over her.
• The Macushi are afraid of the evil spirits of the Pie Wie.
• M. Ballon keeps a small curved nut under his bolster to bring him good luck.
• The words 'His contract wasn't renewed' are 'words of ill omen' to Englishmen in Hollywood.
HD 115, 163; BM 61; LO 30
(*See also* RELIGION, and OLD MEN

SUPPLICE, MADAME DE
Principal of the school in Paris attended by Thérèse de Vitre and Antoinette (q.v.).
HD 163–4

SURREALISTS
Exponents of an artistic movement born in 1922 from a fusion of Constructivism, Dada and Cubism. The chief driving force was André Breton and the artists Ernst, Klee, Picabia, de Chirico, Man Ray, Magritte, Dali and Delvaux. See the Surrealist Manifesto of 1924. Its basic tenet was the juxtaposition of apparently unrelated objects and figures to create a disturbing image.
• Poppet Green falls into the term 'surrealist'. Basil Seal tells her that he would have thought that an air raid would have been just the place for a surrealist: 'limbs and things lying about in odd places, you know'. Her picture of Aphrodite (q.v.) is just one example of her work. Other 'evidence of her silliness abounded in the canvases . . . which crowded the studio . . . bodiless heads, green horses and violet grass, seaweed, shells and fungi, neatly executed, conventionally arranged in the manner of Dali'.
PF 30–31

SUSIE
Female lance-corporal at the Ministry of Information. Secretary to Colonel Plum. She has a face 'of transparent, ethereal silliness'. Basil Seal falls in love with her and follows her along the passages to Colonel Plum. She is a popular girl with all ranks. Colonel Plum addresses her as 'Susie, you slut'.

Calls Basil 'handsome' and the Colonel 'Plummy'. Basil asks her to come with him to investigate nightclubs. She tells him that although she goes to nightclubs, he does not.

Basil calls her to see the Director of Internal Security, who arranges to have her transferred to his own office. Basil, having arranged this promotion for her asks her to his (Ambrose's) flat which he wants to decorate. She accepts. Basil sets her to work taking off the 'A's from Ambrose's underclothes and stitching on 'B's.
• Communist sergeant with golden curls who in 1943 works in 'the studio' at the Royal Victorian Institute in London.
PF 189, 192, 201, 202, 204; US 28

SVENINGEN, IRMA
Young Scandinavian delegate to the Bellorius Conference in Neutralia. Meets Pinfold (q.v.) and Whitemaid (q.v.), who has an affair with her. Wears shorts.

Pinfold cries at the sight of her evening gown.
WS 224, 236

SWANS
Paul Pennyfeather and Margot Metroland have 'a rather fearful encounter with a swan' beside the lake at King's Thursday.
DF 134

SWEAT, MR
Next-door neighbour of Miles Plastic at Mountjoy prison. A veteran criminal of another age of Wormwood Scrubs. Tells Miles that there is no understanding of crime in the New Britain. With Soapy, kills the peacocks as a security measure against being released.
GP 180–82

SWEDEN
Where Sir Samson Courteney's career is finally doomed.
• Corker does not feel that Swedes are really foreign: 'More like you and me, if you see what I mean'.
BM 48; SC 105
(*See also* OLAFSEN)

SWITZERLAND
A Swiss firm pushes Margot Metroland's Latin American Entertainment corporation out of business in 1924.
• A Swiss used to come and stay at Broome in Mr Crouchback's day. Mr Crouchback thinks that he may be able to help the imprisoned Tony Box-Bender in 1940.
• Where Virginia Crouchback's stepmother lives.
• Swiss scientists have made a special record designed to enable neurotic factory workers to sleep. It is of factory noises, and is played to Gilbert Pinfold by his voices.
• The Swiss delegate at the Bellorius conference in Neutralia is murdered by partisans.
DF 195; OG 28; US 45; GP 134; WS 232–6
(*See also* GENEVA AND ZURICH)

SWORD OF STALINGRAD
On 29 October 1943 crowds queue up outside Westminster Abbey to view the Sword of Stalingrad. It is upright between two candles at a table used as an altar next to the shrine of Edward the Confessor. Lieutenant Padfield notices that, if worn on a baldric, the escutcheon will be upside down. Guy Crouchback supposes that Stalin will not wear it on a baldric. It has been made on the command of the King as a gift to 'the steel-hearted people of Stalingrad'. It is forged by 'an octogenarian, who had made ceremonial swords for five sovereigns'. It is embellished with silver, gold, rock-crystal and enamel. It was previously exhibited at Goldsmiths' Hall and the Victoria and Albert Museum. Poems to it are published in *The Times*, and *Time and Tide*. According to Ian Kilbannock it was Trimmer who first gave the King the idea of the sword by being given a Commando dagger to brandish in the newspapers.
US 21, 22, 26, 44

SYD
One of the deserters on Crete who pulls the stew away from Major Hound.
OG 202

SYLVIA
Girlfriend of Simon Lent, with whom he is 'half in love'.
WS 63

SYLVIA
Heroine in *The Frightened Footman* by John Plant (q.v.).
WS 159

SYMONDS
Prefect at Lancing in 1919.
WS 303

SYRIA
Where Sebastian Flyte and Anthony Blanche meet Mr Samgrass, by appointment, after Sebastian's independent venture on their near-eastern trip in 1924.
• Syrian anarchists are among Scott-King's fellow travellers.
BR 153; WS 244

T

TAILORS
Gilbert Pinfold has three suits made by a tailor in Colombo.
• Simon Lent owes his tailor £56. It is long overdue.
• Anthony Blanche always has his suits made at Lesley and Roberts.
GP 140; WS 63; BR 196

TALLEYRAND, CHARLES MAURICE DE ***(1754–1838)***
French statesman. Bishop of Autun under Louis XVI (1788). Helped to consolidate Napoleon's power. Consorted with the Bourbons and under Louis XVIII became Minister of Foreign Affairs.
• Scott-King is more blasé than even Talleyrand.
WS 199

TAMPEN, COUNT
Liberal minister of Ruritania who stole the ex-King's fountain pen.
VB 41

TAMPLIN
Fellow pupil of Charles Ryder at Lancing in 1919.
WS 289

TANGA, TANGANYIKA
One of the destinations of the Arab dhows sailing from Matodi from the seventeenth to the nineteenth centuries.
BM 9

TANGANYIKA, AFRICA
From where Frau Dressler drifts to Ishmaelia after the Great War.
Sc 110

TANGENT, LORD ***(1910–1922)***
Son of Lord and Lady Circumference (q.v.). Pupil at Llanabba School, where he arrives at the same time as Paul Pennyfeather. He is 'erratic' but he has 'tone'. All of the boys in Paul's class tell him that their name is Tangent. He is no athlete, but is nevertheless put in the quarter mile at the sports day. Mr Prendergast shoots him in the foot with Grimes' revolver. 'Am I going to die?' he asks Dingy as she stuffs him full of cake. Two days later his foot swells up and turns black. Seven days later his foot is amputated in a local nursing home. He dies just before Paul and Margot's wedding.
DF 19, 37, 70, 71, 94, 105, 149

TANGIER, MOROCCO
To where Anthony Blanche and Sebastian travel from Marseilles in 1924, and where Sebastian meets Kurt, who says that it is 'a stinking place'.
• One of the places where Ambrose Silk has lived.
BR 196, 205; WS 253

TAORMINA
One of the stopping-off places of the *SS Glory of Greece* in 1932.
WS 17

TATTON, PRIVATE
Soldier in Alastair Trumpington's company in 1939 who loses 'by neglect one respirator, anti gas, value 18s. 6d.'
PF 103

TAUNTON, SOMERSET
Where William Boot sees a film about newspaper life in New York.
Sc 24

TEHERAN, PERSIA
Where, from 28 to 30 November 1943, Churchill, Stalin, Roosevelt and Chiang

Kai-Shek met to discuss the D Day offensive of summer 1944.
US 128

TEL AVIV, ISRAEL

One of the dreams of the Jews at Begoy in 1944 is a passage to Tel Aviv.
• One of the places stayed in by Ambrose Silk after the war.
US 180; WS 253

TELEGRAMS

ENGAGED TO MARRY ADAM SYMES EXPECT HIM LUNCHEON: Nina Blount to her father.
DRUNK MAJOR IN REFRESHMENT TENT NOT BOGUS THIRTY-FIVE THOUSAND MARRIED TOMORROW EVERYTHING PERFECT AGATHA LOST LOVE ADAM: Adam Fenwick-Symes to Nina Blount.
• ARRIVING 2.18 SO LOOKING FORWARD VISIT BEAVER: John Beaver to the Lasts.
• REQUEST YOUR IMMEDIATE PRESENCE HERE URGENT LORD COPPERS PERSONAL DESIRE SALTER BEAST: Salter to William Boot.
OPPOSITION SPLASHING FRONTWARD SPEEDIEST STOP ADEN REPORTED PREPARED WARWISE FLASH FACTS BEAST: Salter to William Boot.
CO-OPERATION BEAST AVOID DUPLICATION BOOT UNNATURAL: Corker's bosses to Corker in Ishmaelia.
ADEN UNWARWISE. Boot to the *Beast*.
NO NEWS AT PRESENT THANKS WARNING ABOUT CABLING PRICES BUT I'VE PLENTY MONEY LEFT AND ANYWAY WHEN I OFFERED TO PAY WIRELESS MAN SAID IT WAS ALL RIGHT PAID OTHER END RAINING HARD HOPE ALL WELL ENGLAND WILL CABLE AGAIN IF ANY NEWS: Boot to the *Beast*.
NOTHING MUCH HAS HAPPENED EXCEPT TO THE PRESIDENT WHO HAS BEEN IMPRISONED IN HIS OWN PALACE BY REVOLUTIONARY JUNTA HEADED BY SUPERIOR BLACK CALLED BENITO AND RUSSIAN JEW WHO BANNISTER SAYS IS UP TO NO GOOD THEY SAY HE IS DRUNK WHEN HIS CHILDREN TRY TO SEE HIM BUT GOVERNESS SAYS MOST UNUSUAL LOVELY SPRING WEATHER BUBONIC PLAGUE RAGING SACK RECEIVED SAFELY THOUGHT I MIGHT AS WELL SEND THIS ALL THE SAME: Boot to the *Beast*.
CONGRATULATIONS STORY CONTRACT UNTERMINATED UPFOLLOW FULLEST SPEEDILIEST: Salter to Boot.
• GRAVELY INJURED COME AT ONCE: Sebastian Flyte to Charles Ryder.
• ENTIRELY CURED ALL LOVE: Gilbert Pinfold to his wife.
IMPLORE YOUR RETURN IMMEDIATELY: Mrs Pinfold to her husband.
VB 70, 175; HD 25; Sc 22, 68, 69, 72, 121, 146; BR 72; GP 123, 147

TELEPHONE

Adam Fenwick-Symes and Nina Blount spend a great deal of time discussing on the telephone whether or not they will get married.
• Mr Samgrass is the first don to have a private telephone installed in his rooms.
• In London, just after the war, telephones used to behave erratically: 'the line would go dead; then crackle; then, when the tangled wire was given a twist and a jerk, normal conversation was rejoined'.
VB ff; BR 124; GP 52

TELEVISION

In the New Britain everyone has a television set, including the hall porter at the hospital, who, on Christmas Day is engrossed in watching an obscure old folk play about an ox and an ass and a young mother.
• In 1962 television is Margot Metroland's chief pleasure in life. Basil Seal and her son Peter find her sitting in darkness 'save for the ghastly light of a television set'.
GP 210; WS 258, 259

TELLING 'MEAT'

One of the basic skills taught to Halberdier officers in 1940 is how to 'tell' cat from rabbit by the number of ribs.
MA 49

TENDRIL, THE REVEREND

Local elderly parson at Hetton, whose sermons, following his time as a military padre on the Afghan frontier are always of

a patriotic nature (q.v.). His voice is 'noble and sonorous'. In 1926 he was in Bournemouth. Married to Mrs Ada Tendril.
HD 32–3

TENNYSON, LORD ALFRED
(1809–1892)
English poet. See his 'In Memoriam' (1850), 'Maud' (1855), 'Locksley Hall' (1886) and 'Idylls of the King' (1859–85).
• Ambrose Silk recites 'In Memoriam' through a megaphone to the accompaniment of comb and paper when at Oxford.
• Gervase Crouchback reads aloud from the poems of Tennyson to his bride Hermione when on their honeymoon in Italy.
• Miles Plastic's last night at Mountjoy is 'rich, old-fashioned, Tennysonian'.
• In the 1930s eighteenth-century Whiggery is to John Plant and his contemporaries what the Arthurian knights were to his equivalent in the times of Tennyson.
PF; MA 9; GP 179; WS 144

TENNYSON
English test cricketer in 1923 who Father Phipps wishes he had seen make fifty-eight runs, and who played well against the South Africans.
BR 82

TERRITORIAL ARMY
John Verney secures a commission in the Territorial Army in 1938 after the Munich agreement.
GP 162

TETBURY
Nearest town to Lower Chipping Manor (q.v.).
OG 26

TEXAS, USA
Place of origin of a 'jaunty young embalmer' once employed for a week at Whispering Glades, who referred to the deceased as 'meat'.
LO 54

THACKERAY, WILLIAM MAKEPEACE *1811–1863)*
English novelist. See his *Barry Lyndon*, *Henry Esmond*, and *Vanity Fair*.
• Roger Simmonds thinks Sister Kemp's nursing snobbery is 'like something out of Thackeray'.
WS 176

THANATOGENOS, AIMEE
(1923–1946)
Junior cosmetician at Whispering Glades, where she works with the serenity of a nun. She has dark, straight hair, wide brows, pale transparent skin, and sensual lips. Her face is full and oval and her profile classical. Her eyes are green 'with a rich glint of lunacy'. Wears large, elliptycal violet sun-glasses. She 'speaks the tongue of Los Angeles'.

Her father lost all of his money in the Four Square Gospel. She herself is named after Aimee Semphill Macpherson. Her mother was an alcoholic.

Educated at the local high school and university. However, her spirit is lost in ancient Greece. At college she studied Psychology and Chinese, majoring in Beauticraft. Her thesis is on 'Hairstyling in the Orient'. She graduated in 1943.

Her first job was at the beauty parlour at the Beverly-Waldorf Hotel. She gives Mrs Komstock's corpse a blue rinse and becomes a novice cosmetician (in 1944).

She thinks of herself as an artist. Looks up to Mr Joyboy: he is 'kinda holy'. Death and Art fill her thoughts. She has no religion.

Is chosen to be trained as an embalmer. Meets Dennis Barlow. Writes incessantly to the Guru Brahmin (q.v.) about her love for Mr Joyboy, and latterly her love for Dennis. Is proposed to by Dennis. She refuses and dines with Mr Joyboy and his mother.

Decides to marry Dennis, and becomes engaged to him. Decides that having learned of Dennis's deceit, she cannot marry him.

Seeks out Mr Slump at Mooney's Bar, who tells her to 'go take a jump'. Commits suicide by taking poison. As she dies

thinks of Ancient Greece. Cremated at Whispering Glades.
LO 46, 54, 72–8, 81–2, 86–92, 105, 119

THEATRE
Guy Crouchback attends an 'intimate revue' in London on the evening of 20 December 1939, where he meets de Souza and Pat.
• Roger Simmonds believes that the trouble with ideological dramas is 'that they're too mechanical'.
• The fact that the Finsbury International Theatre starts at seven o'clock is designed to suit the workers.
• Charles Ryder is taken in 1919 to see *The Choice* at Wyndham's Theatre.
MA 79; WS 133, 151, 289
(*See also* PLAYS)

THEATRICAL DESIGN
Otto Silenus' first commission is a set design for a play.

One of the books sent to Paul Pennyfeather at Egdon Heath is on Theatrical Design.
DF 119; 190
(*See also* CRAIG)

THEOLOGY
Subject studied by Stubbs and Paul Pennyfeather at Scone College in 1923.
• Ludovic can see that Guy Crouchback has some knowledge of Theology, and asks his advice as to the moral implications of swimming out to sea from Crete.
DF 11; OE 224

THORNE, CEDRIC *(d. 1953)*
Shakespearean actor. Friend of Angel of the BBC who hangs himself in his dressing-room at Stratford.
GP 20

THORNTON
Thornton's flower prints adorn the walls of Mr Harkness's house at North Grappling.
PF 91

THROBBING, LORD EDWARD
Eldest son of Lord and Lady Throbbing, and brother of Miles Malpractice (q.v.). Has a house in Hertford Street which is taken over by Miles when he goes to Canada in 1927. The Bright Young People think him 'frightfully dim and political'. On his return, with two secretaries, he throws Miles out. Discovers 'curious and compromising things' all over his house. His butler has become an alcoholic and has to be removed. It is generally understood that he will marry Lady Ursula Stayle. Attends a party at Anchorage House, where he proposes to Ursula, who refuses. Her mother, however is determined that they will marry.
VB 11–12

THUNDER-BOX
Properly 'Connelly's Chemical Closet'. Portable field water-closet belonging to Apthorpe (q.v.). It is a 'rare and mysterious' object about which he is tremendously possessive. It is a brass-bound cube of oak which when opened displays a heavy, cast-brass mechanism and patterned earthenware bowl. Apthorpe obtained it from a High Court Judge in Karonga, the year that they put in the drains there, for five pounds. Talk of it complicates the Box-Bender secrets smuggled out by Mr Pelecci, and intercepted by Grace-Groundling-Marchpole. He attempts to keep it secret from all but Guy Crouchback. However, it soon becomes clear that someone else is using it. Apthorpe thinks that it might be Sarum-Smith, but it turns out to be Ritchie-Hook, who blows it up, with Apthorpe in possession. 'Thunder-Box', thinks Guy is the *mot juste.*
MA 98, 144, 154–5, 157

THURSTON
Alias adopted by Arthur Atwater (q.v.).
WS 134

TICKERIDGE, BRIGADIER
Brigadier in the Halberdiers. Guy Crouchback first meets him when he is a major in 1939, at Matchet, where he comes down for Sunday to see his wife. He has huge handlebar moustaches and tufts of ginger hair on his cheekbones, just below his

eyes. Drinks pink gin. Is full of quaint expressions: 'Pardon my glove', 'Here's how', 'light shopping', calls his wife 'the madam'.
- Arranges for Guy's commission in the Halberdiers.
- At the mess dinner he gives a performance of 'the One-armed Flautist'.
- Promoted Colonel 1940. Explodes at Apthorpe over the question of saluting.
- Guy meets up with him on Crete in May 1941. To Guy he is the perfect soldier, who always knows how to get out of a spot.
- Julia Stitch finds him at the camp in Mariout and invites him, at Guy's request, to dinner at her villa in Alexandria in June 1941. Cannot understand French. Takes Guy back into the Halberdiers.
- Promoted Brigadier between 1941 and 1943.

MA 37, 38, 39, 77, 180; OG 179, 240; US 95

TICKERIDGE, MRS 'VI'
Wife of Brigadier Tickeridge. She is 'mousy'. Her husband calls her 'the madam'. Stays at the Marine Hotel, Matchet during 1940 and 1941. Every evening she dines with Mr Crouchback in the Residents' Lounge. They always converse on Felix's exercise. Does not think that she has ever read *Trumper's Eucris*. Discusses the contents of his American parcel with Mr Crouchback. She knows Colonel Trotter. Meets him in the Marine Hotel.
MA 38; OG 27, 33

TICKERIDGE, JENNIFER *(b. 1933)*
Daughter of Brigadier and Mrs Tickeridge. Stays with her mother at Matchet in 1939. 'A beautifully behaved child.'
MA 38, 39

TIFFIN, MRS
Wife of the famous publisher, who on 11 December 1936, attends a dinner party at the Savoy Grill thrown by Silas Shock.
Sc 80

TILSIT, USSR
Location of the historic meeting between Napoleon and Tsar Alexander in 1807 when France and Russia signed the treaty of the same name.
- One of the topics of conversation at luncheon at Julia Stitch's villa in Alexandria in June 1943, just after the German invasion of Russia.

OG 240

TIM
Brother of Virginia Crouchback (q.v.), five years her junior. Killed in 1940.
US 45

TIMING
Faultless timing was always Hitler's strongpoint, according to Basil Seal.
OG 240

TIN, MISS
Companion of Dame Mildred Porch (q.v.) on her visit to Azania in 1931. In build she is spare. In character and clothing she is like a smaller version of Dame Mildred. Arrives in Debra Dowa. Met by William Bland. Attends banquet in her honour. Caught in Debra Dowa in the midst of the coup. Has a narrow escape. Drinks Koniac on the roof of Youkoumian's. Rescued by William. Stays at the Legges' house. Leaves Azania with the legation.
BM 158, 169, 170, 184–98

TINTORETTO, JACOPO *(1518–95)*
Venetian painter. Studied under Titian. He forms a link between Renaissance and Baroque art. See his 'Origin of the Milky Way', 'Last Supper', and 'Crucifixion' of 1565.
- The piano nobile of Lord Marchmain's palazzo in Venice is decorated with frescoes by a follower of Tintoretto.

BR 93

TIPPING, MRS
London society hostess of the 1930s. Invites John Beaver, at the last minute, to make up the numbers at a luncheon party in 1933, after having first tried to get hold of Jock Grant-Menzies.
HD 10

TIPPERARY, IRELAND
Origin of the brooch made from bog-oak given by his American girl to John Boot when she says goodbye in 1937.
Sc 73

TIPS
John Beaver, not intending to return to Hetton, decides only to tip the footman five shillings and the butler nothing. In fact he leaves them both ten shillings.
• Later, in London, as she insists on paying for the bill, Brenda Last pretends not to know how much to leave as a tip at Espinosa's and asks Beaver.
HD 29, 37, 47

TITCHOCK, MR
One of the guests at the Royal George Hotel. The landlady tells the Bright Young People that to accommodate them she can put him on the floor. He is duly woken up, given some gin, and moved.
VB 156

TITIAN, *(d. 1576)*
Venetian painter. Student of the Bellini and assistant to Giorgione. Influenced Tintoretto, Rubens, Velasquez and others. See his 'Venus of Urbino', 'Three Ages of Man', 'Bacchus and Ariadne' and 'Diana and Actaeon'.
• Father Mackay asks Charles Ryder whether he considers Titian or Raphael the more truly artistic painter.
BR 311

TITLED ECCENTRICS
Popular feature of the Mr Chatterbox column under the aegis of Adam Fenwick-Symes (q.v.). Includes: 'The Earl of —, who lives in strict retirement, has the unusual foible of wearing costume of the Napoleonic period. Lord —, whose public appearances are regrettably rare nowadays, is a close student of comparative religions . . . Lady —' whose imitations of animal sounds are so lifelike that she can seldom be persuaded to converse in any other way . . .'.
VB 112

TITMUSS, JOHN
Journalist on the *News Chronicle* whose desk 'holds more secrets of state than any ambassador's'. He is one of the guests at the dinner at the Savoy Grill thrown by Silas Shock on 11 December 1936.
Sc 80

TITO, MARSHAL *(1892–1980)*
Yugoslav political leader. Served in the Great War with the Austro-Hungarians. Adopted Communism 1917. Organized the Yugoslav Partisans in 1941. Effectively disrupted the operations of the German Army. Managed to discredit Mihajlovic in the eyes of the Allies. On victory in 1945 engineered his way into power as President; a position which he retained for many years.
• Sir Ralph Brompton tells Guy Crouchback in 1943 that Tito is the Allies' real friend, not Mihajlovic.
• De Souza tells Guy that Tito is 'a highly trained politician', and will 'make rings around' Churchill when they meet in 1944.
US 29, 204

TOBRUK, LIBYA
Scene, between 10 April and 28 November 1941, of an heroic defence by the British and Australians, resulting in a serious supply problem for the Germans under Rommel.
• Where the lame hussar who brings round the whisky at the hospital in Alexandria in May 1941 'caught a packet'.
OG 227

TODD, JAMES
Inhabitant of the Amazonas where he has lived since 1928. Had a Barbadian father who came to Guiana as a missionary, married a white woman, left her to look for gold and took Todd's mother, an Indian. Todd has had most of the Indian women in his camp, and most of the Indians there are his children. Is illiterate. He is known only to the Pie Wies. Lives in a house in a small savannah bounded by a forest. Owns a dozen puny cattle, a cassava plantation, banana and mango trees, a dog and a

single-barrelled breech-loading shotgun. Makes his own cartridges. Has a beard.

Until 1929 Barnabas Washington used to read Dickens to him. Finds Tony Last delirious in the jungle. Nurses him and when he is well makes him read Dickens to him. They begin with *Bleak House*. Cries at sad episodes in the book. He always weeps at *Little Dorrit*.

Gives Tony's watch to a search party with the implication that he has perished. Compels Tony to remain with him and read Dickens, forever.
HD 204, 207–217

TODHUNTER, MR
Billeting officer for Grantley Green and the area. Has a game leg gained in a motor race. Has ginger hair, a ginger moustache, a 'red nob' and 'malevolent pinkish eyes'. Looks 'like a drawing by Leach for a book by Surtees'.

In 1939 Basil Seal takes the Connollys to him and finds that he realizes what he is up to. Basil sells them to him for 'five pounds a leg'.
PF 137–141

TOKATLION
Hotel in Constantinople where Sebastian Flyte meets Anthony Blanche in 1914.
BR 153

TOLPUDDLE MARTYRS
Six agricultural workers from Tolpuddle in Dorset who, having formed an illegal trade union in 1834, were sentenced to transportation to Australia on a trumped-up charge, and were pardoned in 1836.
• Griggs, civics master at Granchester extolls the Tolpuddle Martyrs.
WS 200

TOLSTOY, COUNT LEO
(1828–1920)
Russian writer and philosopher. See his *War and Peace* (1869) and *Anna Karenina* (1876).
• One of the topics of conversation at Julia Stitch's luncheon party in Alexandria on the day that Germans invade Russia in 1941 (22 June).
OG 240

TOMB, NORFOLK
Home of the Kent-Cumberlands (q.v.). Built in the eighteenth century, after which date the original gabled manor became the Dower House, let in 1935 on a long lease to a manufacturer of sporting goods. Has a mill, quarries and a farm.

In the Victorian baronial turret there is a lancet window which lets light into the bedroom with its 'hard, irregular bed'. Has Palladian entrance gates. The billiard-room has Victorian panelling. There is a library with 'a dusty collection of books amassed by succeeding generations'. Tom catalogues them into a fumed-oak cabinet.

After the death of Mr Kent-Cumberland in 1915 his widow closes a wing. In 1934 Gervase installs central heating.
WS 82–104

TOMB BEACON
Hill near Tomb on which celebratory bonfires are lit.
WS 87

TORQUAY, DEVON
Where, in 1938, Mrs Muspratt takes a furnished villa on the return of Lord Marchmain to Brideshead.
BR 297

TOULON, FRANCE
Where Ambrose Silk found matelots 'smelling of wine and garlic, with tough brown necks'.
PF 43

TOULOUSE-LAUTREC, HENRI DE
(1864–1901)
French painter. Influenced by Degas. From an aristocratic family, he was disabled at the age of fourteen by breaking his legs which ceased to grow. Died of venereal disease. See his 'Jane Avril' (1892) and 'Moulin Rouge' (1894).
• Charles Ryder is surprised to find that 'Cara' is not 'a voluptuous Toulouse-Lautrec odalisque'.
• Guy Crouchback tells Virginia that being over-bred and under-sexed do not

always go hand-in-hand: 'Think of Toulouse-Lautrec'.
BR 97; US 146

TOURISTS
In Venice in 1923, Charles Ryder and Sebastian Flyte are not ashamed to become tourists.
BR 97

TOURS, FRANCE
Where, at the age of eighteen, in 1920, Tony Last spent the summer with two other English boys, before going up to Oxford. He visits the châteaux on a bicycle. He sets free a pigeon at a tombola stall.
HD 156

TOYS
An inflatable indiarubber sea serpent: Prudence and William, and Sir Samson Courteney in the bath.
• Clockwork mice, the size of rats, painted with green and white spots, with large glass eyes, stiff whiskers and tails ringed in green and white, which run on hidden wheels and have bells inside them: taken by Dr Messinger to barter with the Pie Wies who are so terrified of them that they run away.
• A toy train: Mr Pappenhacker.
• A red toy car: Gervase Kent-Cumberland, intended for his brother Tom.
BM 62; HD 189; Sc 81; WS

TRAINS
The wheels of the train on which Mr Outrage travels from Dover to London seem to say 'Right Honourable gent, Right Honourable gent, Right Honourable gent', over and over.
• Adam Symes travels on the train to Doubting Hall (Marylebone to Aylesbury). He overhears two women in conversation.
• Brenda Last always has chocolate and buns on her train to Hetton from London (the Great Western from Paddington).
• John Beaver comes down to Hetton on the 3.18.
• After she hears of her son's death, Brenda returns by the seven o'clock train which is full of women coming back from their weekly Wednesday shopping trips to London.
• On his journey by train to London, William Boot has difficulty ordering a whisky, which is only served after Reading, and loses a sovereign in a bet.
• Mr Salter travels from Liverpool Street to Frinton on holiday. He considers what he can see from the train to be 'the country'. Mr Salter travels to Boot Magna Halt by train from Paddington (change at Taunton). He spends an hour on the train from Taunton. It is to him an unimaginable journey in a single tram-like coach, full of country people who 'instead of slinking and shuffling and wriggling themselves into corners and decently screening themselves behind newspapers, as civilized people should when they travel by train' sit too close to him and fix him with stares.
• Charles Ryder travels to Brideshead from Paddington (to Melsted Carbury).
• He and Sebastian travel to Venice by train, from Charing Cross to Dover and then third class from Paris. There are wooden seats and the carriage is full of the poor visiting their families, with small bundles 'and an air of patient submission to authority', and sailors returning from leave. They change trains at Milan.
• Charles and Julia dine on the train to Brideshead in 1936.
• Guy Crouchback remarks to his father that the English trains in 1939 are not luxurious. He travels by train from Charing Cross to the Halberdiers' barracks in 1940. When travelling on the Tube railway in 1943 notices the refugees at Green Park station making up their beds.
• Mr Murdoch tells Gilbert Pinfold that 'wog trains' are 'filthy dirty and slow'.
• John Verney makes crowded tube journeys in 1946.
• Simon Lent travels by tube to Hampstead in 1935.
• John and Elizabeth Verney travel to Good Hope Fort, Cornwall, by a 'train journey of normal discomfort'.
VB 28; HD 120; Sc 23, 26, 196–7; BR 92, 260; MA 37; OG 16; US 46; GP 140, 167, 170; WS 69
(*See also* AZANIA)

TRANSEPT, LADY MARMADUKE
Heroine of *The Death Wish*, second wife of Lord Marmaduke.
US 188
(*See* Books)

TRANSJORDAN
Where Basil Seal had once visited a prison where the punishment was to be shut into a cell with a madman who would outstare the delinquent until, when he eventually shut his eyes the madman would attack him 'tooth and nail'. He is reminded of this by Mr Harkness's demeanour after his experience of the Connollys (q.v.).
PF 98

TRAVANCORE
Place of origin of the servants on board the *SS Caliban* (q.v.). It is a complex culture full of 'ancient rites'.
GP 42, 65

TREBISOND
One of the sites visited by Mr Samgrass and Sebastian Flyte on their trip to the Near East in 1924.
BR 145

TRENCHARD, SERGEANT
Female sergeant at HOOHQ at Marchmain House in 1940, who makes out Guy Crouchback's travel warrant for Mugg. Is frightened of General Whale.
OG 45

TRENT, SOMERSET
One of the places where, in a hothouse, Anthony Blanche presumes that Charles Ryder must have concocted his paintings of South America.
BR 257

TRIESTE, ITALY
Where Lord Malton sends Lord Marchmain and his valet after discovering that Lady Marchmain is in Venice in 1922.
BR 55

TRILBY (*See* Books)

TRILBY, LADY AGNES (ANNE)
Great-Aunt of William Boot. A widow. Owns the only motor-car at Boot Magna Hall, with a horn which she can operate from the back seat. Goes to church once a week.
Sc 18, 204

TRIMMER
Before the war, under the name of Gustave, a hairdresser on transatlantic liners. In this capacity meets Virginia Crouchback.

One of the batch of twenty probationary officers of the Halberdiers in 1940. He is not one of the youngest. His eyes are long-lashed and close set and have a 'knowing' look. He has golden hair, a lock of which falls over his forehead when bare-headed. Speaks with 'a slightly refined Cockney accent' and when the wireless plays jazz he dances about 'with raised hands in little shuffling dance steps'. Guy dislikes him. His only friend is Sarum-Smith (q.v.). He is 'marked for ignominy' thinks Guy. He dresses sloppily: 'instead of buttoning his greatcoat across the chest and clipping it tight at his throat, he had left it open. Moreover he had made a mess of his equipment. He had let one side down at the back,the other at the front with monstrous effect'.

Leaves the Halberdiers and the Army; his firm has been bombed out.

Not wanting to be called-up, goes to Glasgow and joins up under an assumed name and is commissioned.

Turns up on Mugg transformed in bonnet, kilt and sporran under the name of Ali McTavish where he has made friends with Ivor Claire. Tells Guy that his mother is a McTavish.

In November 1940. Although a lieutenant he changes his pips for major's crowns on the train. Takes up with Virginia.

Returns to Mugg. He is worried that 'papers are slowly passing from tray to tray which might at any moment bring his doom' by revealing his true rank and identity. Sends his men off on leave and tells them not to return but to go to join their battalion in India.

Bribes his sergeant-major not to give him away.

Joins the 'specialists' and is given command of the Sappers and the demolition squad. Is sent on Operation Popgun with Ian Kilbannock (q.v.) Finds himself a hero after demolishing a section of railway near Cherbourg.

Christened 'the demon barber' by the press. Ian tells Virginia that she must go out with him for reasons of national defence. She is nauseated by him. Goes on a morale-boosting tour of Britain, Scunthorpe, Hull, Huddersfield and Halifax, with Virginia. His name is changed to Trimmer 'there were too many Scots heroes'.

Delivers, in 1943, a series of Sunday-evening postcripts as 'the voice of Trimmer'. It does not catch on. Stars in a film of his exploits of which a preview is shown to the King.

Goes to America on a morale-boosting tour in 1943. Ends up in San Francisco having 'flopped' all over the USA. The Americans see him as a typical British officer.

Virginia has his baby in 1944. After the war he has disappeared and cannot be found for the reunion party in 1951.

People say that he jumped ship in South Africa, bound for Burma where he had been sent by Ian.

MA 46, 48, 104; OG 52–55, 72–78 80, 82, 87, 90, 118, 150, 155, 212, 215, 248,; US 10, 11, 44, 55, 89, 186,

TRINIDAD

Home of Thérèse de Vitre. There are not many colonels there. The sea is opaque and colourless.

HD 162–3, 166–7

TROLLOPE, ANTHONY *(1815–1882)*

English novelist. See his *The Warden*, *Barchester Towers* and *Can You Forgive Her?*

• Peregrine Crouchback reads aloud to Virginia from *Can you Forgive Her?* during her pregnancy in 1944.

US 159

TROMMET, MRS DE

American society figure in London in 1933. Client of Mrs Beaver, whose bill for *toile-de-jouy* chair covers she has not paid. Throws a party which John Beaver attends.

HD 8

TROTSKYISM

Brand of Communism inspired by Leon Trotsky, opposed to Stalinist opportunism.

• The red-headed girlfriend of Poppet Green is suspected of Trotskyism.

PF 39

TROTTER, MR

History teacher of Tony Last at school.

HD 177

TROTTER, COLONEL JUMBO

An elderly colonel of the Halberdiers encountered by Guy Crouchback playing billiards in the mess in 1940. Served in Flanders in the Great War. His constant refrain is 'care for a hundred up? . . . not much in the paper today'.

Guy cannot remember what the regulars used to call him 'Ox? Tiny? Hippo?' Had retired from the Army with the rank of colonel in 1936. An hour after the declaration of war he had returned to barracks 'and there he had sat ever since. No one had summoned him and no one cared to question his presence. His age and rank rendered him valueless for barrack duties. He dozed over the newspapers, lumbered round the billiard-table, beamed on his juniors; scrimmaged on guest nights, and regularly attended Church parade . . . Mostly he slept.' His soldier-servant is Halberdier Burns.

• Is unable to make sense of *Don't Mr Disraeli*. Becomes attached to X Commando.

• In 1944 rescues Guy from the RAF hospital in Essex.

OG 20, 31–37, 41–45, 81; US 10, 119

TROPHIES
The *Morning Despatch* provides the trophy for the motor races: 'a silver-gilt figure of odious design, symbolizing Fame embracing Speed'.
VB 163
(*See also* DOCTOR FAGAN)

TROUBLES, THE
The Irish conflict of the 1920s during which Bella Fleace's brother is shot in his own drive at Fleacetown.
WS 79

TROUTBECK
Butler to the Boots. He is an 'aged boy'.
Sc 21

TROY
Legendary city besieged by the Greeks after the abduction of Helen by Paris.
• Charles Ryder compares the stone balustrade on the terrace of Brideshead Castle to the walls of Troy.
• Gilbert Pinfold thinks of the ice-floes of the Black Sea racing past Troy.
BR 280; GP 89

TROY, HECTOR
Third husband of Virginia Crouchback (q.v.). Lives in America. In 1943 divorces Virginia.
MA 83; OG 75; US 46

TROY, VIRGINIA ***(1910–1944)***
At an early age she is seduced by a friend of her father's 'who had looked her up, looked her over, taken her out, taken her in'. Attends finishing school in Paris. Has one brother, Tim, killed in 1940, and a stepmother in Switzerland.

Marries Guy Crouchback. Lives at the Castello Crouchback and in Kenya. In Kenya she says that she needs a year at home in England – returns. Writes to Guy and eventually tells him that she has fallen in love with a friend of theirs called Tommy Blackhouse and wants a divorce.

Marries Tommy. Experiences 'London hotels, fast cars, regimental point-to-points'.

After Tommy she goes out with Augustus (Gussie), and then marries 'Bert' Troy. 'She's a grand girl' everyone at Bellamy's thinks. Her clothes are from a grand couturier, a new wardrobe in 1938.

In the 1930s she often has her hair done and is given a massage by Trimmer, alias Gustave.

In 1940 she returns from America and stays at Claridges and has a brief fling with Tommy Blackhouse. Lunches with Guy. Feels sorry for him. Dislikes his moustache and monocle.

Dines with Guy in her room at Claridges on St Valentine's day 1940. Guy attempts to seduce her; she says that he was not an expert lover on their honeymoon. Is appalled that he should try to seduce her. Leaves Claridges during the blitz and moves out of London.

Turns up at the Station Hotel, Glasgow in November 1940, to see off a sailor boyfriend, where she meets Trimmer. Has an affair with Trimmer who falls hopelessly in love with her.

She is the antithesis of Kerstie Kilbannock (q.v.). Works with Kerstie at No. 6 transit camp, London District. Trimmer finds her again. Stays with the Kilbannocks.

By October 1943 she is no longer living with the Kilbannocks. Divorced by Hector Troy. Sells her own jewels for which she has already claimed the insurance. Sells her furs to Kerstie. Is penniless. Moves back in with the Kilbannocks, but cannot pay the rent.

Asks Kerstie to find her a doctor. Visits doctor Puttock and discovers that she is carrying Trimmers's baby. She is 'remarkable for the composure' with which she accepts 'the vicissitudes of domesticity'. From the day of her marriage to Guy to that of her most recent divorce she has managed a '*douceur de vivre* that is alien to her epoch; seeking nothing, accepting what came and enjoying it without compunction'. It is only after her meeting with Trimmer in Glasgow that 'shadows begin to fall'. Tells Kerstie about her problem. Kerstie gives her the address of a doctor in Brook Street who might perform an abortion for her. Goes to see him and finds his surgery blown up.

Visits Dr Akonaga (q.v.) recommended to Kerstie by Mrs Bristow. From deep within her womb she seems to hear Trimmer's baby crooning 'You, you, you'. Dr Akonanga cannot help her.

In early December 1943 she visits Guy at Peregrine's flat in Carlisle Place. To Peregrine she is a scarlet woman.

Starts to visit Guy every day, calls Peregrine an 'old pet'. Her motto is 'there's fun ahead, always'.

Peregrine takes her to dine at Overton's. Talks to him candidly about sex. Her spontaneous laughter (seldom heard during the war) is one of her main charms.

Tells Peregrine that she is thinking of converting to Catholicism.

Thinks of going back to Guy. Spends Christmas 1943 with Guy at Peregrine's flat. She has confidence that the war is only a temporary upset to the normal routine of her life. Tells Guy that she is pregnant. Remarries Guy at a registrar's office. Makes love to Guy 'as always, lavish with what lay in her gift'. Lives with Guy at Carlisle Place over January 1944. Converts to Catholicism. Befriends Eloise Plessington. Gives birth to a son on 4 June 1944. Cannot bear to see her child. Killed by a flying bomb in Carlisle Place, with Peregrine and Mrs Corner on 15 August 1944.

Everard Spruce calls her one of the last great heroines and compares her to Mrs Viveash.

MA 18, 22, 82–4, 81, 123, 129–133; OG 14, 74, 77, 133, 218; US 9, 44–6, 51, 58, 84, 90, 146, 185, 195, 196

TRUSLOVE

Character in a boyhood story much beloved by Guy Crouchback. He is an officer: 'I've chosen your squadron Truslove . . . If anyone can do it, you can'.

MA 165, 166, 217

(*See* Congreve)

TSARKO SELOE

Palace of the Tzars of Russia in whose grounds Catherine the Great had once seen a flower which she wanted to preserve, thus creating the necessity of having a guard on that spot every since.

OG 49

TUNBRIDGE WELLS

Where Apthorpe (q.v.) has an aunt.

MA 97

TUNES

'The Roast beef of old England', the band at the Halberdiers' mess night: 'The Hindu love song', Whispering Glades: 'The Blue Danube', Bella Fleace's party.

MA 75; OG 20; LO 35; WS 85

TUNISIA

Where in 1933 Reggie St Cloud desecrates tombs.

• Where Sebastian Flyte stays with the monks in 1938.

HD 145; BR 287

TURKEY

One of the places visited by Mr Samgrass and Sebastian Flyte on their tour of the Near East.

BR 144

TURNER, JOSEPH MALLORD WILLIAM *(1775–1851)*

English painter. Renowned for his use of oil and watercolour in the northern European romantic tradition. See his 'Ulysses deriding Polyphemus' (1829), 'The Fighting Temeraire' (1839), and 'Rain, Steam and Speed' (1844).

• Guy Crouchback compares the blitz sky over London to a painting by Turner.

OG 9

TUTENKHAMEN *(d. circa 340 BC)*

Egyptian Pharaoh (18th dynasty).

• Corker (q.v.) buys a replica of Tutankhamen's tomb on his journey to Ishmaelia in 1937.

• His tomb is visited by the passengers of the *SS Glory of Greece* in 1931. Bertie says it is vulgar.

Sc 71; WS 20

TYLER, BERT
He has had a driving licence for twenty years in 1937 and is the only man at Boot Magna with whom the slag-lorry driver is permitted to drive, not having a licence of his own. Has a mare who is sick.
Sc 198–9

TYNGATE
Secretary of the College Essay Society at Hertford in 1924. Friend of Collins, with whom he shares digs.
BR 140

U

UKAKA
(*See* BATTLES)

ULEY
Town near Malfrey where Angela Lyne picks up some evacuees in 1940.
MA 32

UNDERTAKERS
According to John Plant's uncle there is a great deal of sharp practice among undertakers 'they trade upon the popular conception of delicacy. In fact they are the only profession who literally rob the widow and the orphan'.
WS 125
(*See* JOYBOY, THANATOGENOS, BARLOW, SCHULTZ)

UNIVERSAL NEWS
Biggest news agency in England. Corker is a reporter for them.
Sc 64

UNIVERSITY
The staff of the *Twopence* are 'university men'.
Sc 32
(*See* OXFORD, SIMONA, BELLACITA)

UNKNOWN SOLDIER
One of the guises of Basil Seal in 1939.
PF 29

UNRRA
In 1944 they mysteriously import Almeric Griffiths into Yugoslavia.
US 169

UPPER EASTNEY, WILTSHIRE
Village near Brideshead to where the Marchmain Hunt runs.
BR 160

UPPER MEWLING
Village near Lychpole.
GP 11

UPPSALA, SWEDEN
Whitemaid visits in summer 1945 and eats caviar. He is made a doctor of the university.
WS 203, 211

URIAH THE HITTITE
Treacherous character of the Old Testament.
• One of the stories which Ludovic remembers from his childhood is that of Uriah the Hittite with whom he is tempted to compare Guy Crouchback.
US 120

URQUHART, FRANCIS FORTESCUE (SLIGGER)
Dean of Balliol, Oxford from 1916. Infamous Oxford figure. At Oxford in 1922 Waugh used to stand underneath his windows and shout 'the Dean of Balliol sleeps with men'. Described by Peter Quennell as 'curly-headed, wrinkled and rosy-cheeked'.
• Adam Symes and Father Rothschild have luncheon with him in 1922.
• Guy Crouchback was 'a friend of Sligger's'.
• According to his voices Gilbert Pinfold was sent down from Oxford for making a row outside the Dean's rooms, and accusing him of 'the most disgusting practices'.
VB 13; US 162; GP 69

USHANT, FRANCE
Island where, in the 1790s, Captain Montagu had gazed at the French revolutionary fleet.
US 21

USTACHI
Croatian quislings (q.v.) fighting on the side of the Germans in Yugoslavia in 1944. They burn down a mosque in a Mohammedan village, and after the king flees, start to massacre the Jews.
US 163, 172, 176

UTRILLO, MAURICE ***(1883–1955)***
French painter. Renowned for his views of Montmartre.

• Angela Lyne's make-up in 1940 is 'rather garish, like a later Utrillo'.
PF 159

UTTERIDGE, LORD
Lives in Utteridge House, Belgrave Square, which is protected with electric burglar alarms. His son is kidnapped by Jimmy Drage (q.v.) and he refuses to pay the ransom.
DF 55–56

V

VALKYRIE
The handmaids of the Norse god Odin. They are portrayed as mounted on swift steeds, with swords, and traditionally charge into the thick of battle and pick out those who will die. These heroes they then conduct to Valhalla where they wait on them with mead and ale.
• Miss Sveningen looks like a Valkyrie, when dressed in her shorts.
WS 216

VALPARAISO, CHILE
Where Basil Seal once knew 'a chink'.
PF 176

VAMPIRES
The judge at Paul Pennyfeather's trial refers to him as a 'human vampire'.
• Dr Messinger is bitten on the toe by a vampire bat in Brazil.
DF 160; HD 171

VAN GOGH, VINCENT *(1853–1890)*
Dutch Post-Impressionist painter. Friend of Toulouse-Lautrec and Gauguin whom he threatened with an open razor and afterwards in a fit of remorse, cut off his own ear. He spent some time in an asylum and shot himself at the scene of his last painting 'Cornfield with Flights of birds'. See his 'Sunflowers (1888). 'The Bridge' (1888) and various interiors of the same period.
• During his first term at Oxford Charles Ryder hangs a reproduction of Van Gogh's 'Sunflowers' on the walls of his room, over the fire.
BR 29

VANBRUGH, SIR JOHN *(1664–1726)*
English architect, playwright and adventurer. He is chiefly memorable for Castle Howard (1699–1726) and Blenheim Palace (1705) both built in the grand Baroque style at which he excelled.
• He was the architect of the St Cloud's seat, Brakeleigh.
HD 36

VANBURGH, LADY
Friend of Margot Metroland. Otto Silenus thinks that she is like Napoleon. Dislikes the rebuilt King's Thursday, but supposes that the drains are all right. Lives in Lowndes Square.
• She is one of the stuffy people who boycotts Julia Flyte's wedding in 1924.
DR 125, 149; BR 192

VANBURGH, FIFTH MARQUIS OF *(Earl Vanburgh de Brendon, Baron Brendon, Lord of the Five Isles and hereditary Grand Falconer to the Kingdom of Connaught)*
Gossip columnist on the *Morning Despatch*. Rival to Simon Balcairn. Hates the savage party. Steals Simon's stories. During WWII gets 'a divine new job making up all the war news'. Invents a story about how Adam Symes saves hundreds of peoples lives and creates a public demand to give Adam the VC.
VB 89, 220

VANDERBILTS, THE
American landed family descended from Cornelius Vanderbilt (*1794–1877*).
• Trimmer cuts the hair of the Vanderbilt ladies on the *Aquitania* in the 1930s.
OG 217

VATICAN, THE
The palace of the Pope in Rome, on Vatican Hill.
• Mr Samgrass has friends there.
• Cordelia Flyte tells Rex Mottram that

there are holy monkeys there, to confuse him during his conversion.
BR 106, 187

VAVASOUR, MISS
Fellow guest of Mr Crouchback's at the Marine Hotel, Matchet (q.v.). Likes the doggy smell of Felix. Tells Mr Crouchback that the Cuthberts intend to turn him out. She is fearless and 'would willingly have thrown herself on any German paratrooper and made short work of him with poker or bread-knife'. Like all the British public she is captivated by the heroic exploits of Captain McTavish (Trimmer) and puts a cut-out photograph of him from the newspaper into a small photograph frame. Attends Mr Crouchback's funeral and ask Guy if she might have his tobacco jar as a keepsake.
OG 22–24, 35, 152; US 72–73

VENEZUELA
Location of Cruttwell Falls.
Sc 43

VENICE, ITALY
Where the second secretary to the Prime Minister takes his holiday (on the Lido) in 1937.
• Angela Lyne normally goes there at the end of the summer, but does not do so in 1939.
• Lord Marchmain lives in exile with Cara in Venice.
• Anthony Blanche tells Charles Ryder that Venice is the only town in Italy 'where no one has ever gone to church'.
• Lady Marchmain visits Venice with Sir Adrian Porson in September 1921, and stays at the Palazzo Fogliere. Anthony Blanche is there at the same time and knows all the gondoliers. Lord Malton's yacht puts in with Lord Marchmain on board, who is sent off to Trieste to avoid embarrassment.
• Charles Ryder travels to Venice with Sebastian Flyte to see Lord Marchmain in summer 1923. They are met by Plender in a gondola. Their luggage follows by vaporetto.
• Lord Marchmain's palazzo has a narrow Palladian façade, moss-covered steps and a dark, rusticated, arched entrance. The *piano nobile* is decorated with frescoes in the manner of Tintoretto.
• Charles and Sebastian sleep on the floor above, up a 'precipitous' marble staircase. The beds have mosquito nets. In each room there is 'a bulbous press . . . a misty, gilt-framed mirror and no other furniture. The floor was of bare marble slabs.' Their bathroom has an exploding geyser. Downstairs the saloon has a balcony. Everything in the house is made of marble, velvet or dark, gilt gesso.

They go to Florian's for coffee after dinner, and watch the crowds crossing under the campanile. They attend the Corombona ball at the Pallazo Corombona. Cara takes them around the city, guidebook in hand. They spend a fortnight there, and go fishing for scampi in the shallows at Chioggia. They drink and eat hot cheese sandwiches at Harry's Bar. Sebastian looks up at the Colleoni statue and reflects on war.
• A popular restaurant is the Luna, which is full of English.
• Charles Ryder later reflects that the pigeons of St Mark's get everywhere.
• The ice sculpture presented to Celia Ryder would, in sixteenth-century Venice, have been 'a somewhat different shape'.
• Virginia Crouchback once fell down the stairs at the Palazzo Corombona and was 'patched-up' by a 'rather ghastly' English doctor.
• Etty Cornphillip writes a book of sonnets about Florence and Venice. Ralph Bland takes her off there. She develops a septic throat and Ralph runs off with an American.
• Angela Lyne owns a little palace in Venice 'which she had once bought for Cedric Lyne but never visited in his lifetime', and which is frequented in the 1950s by Angela, Basil Seal, and their daughter Barbara.
Sc 182; PF 24; BR 55, 71, 93–98, 215, 230; US 56; WS 29–30; WS 256

VERMONT, USA
Where the Joyboys used to live before moving to Los Angeles.
LO 91

VERNEY, ELIZABETH ***(b. 1912)***
Cousin and wife of John Verney. She is calm and handsome, and is an only child with some money of her own. Has a reputation for 'deep' cleverness. Attends balls in Pont Street in the 1930s, where she languishes. Married 1938. She is a linguist and during the war works in a clandestine branch of the Foreign Office. In 1945 she is living in Hampstead with her parents. Tells John that he is lucky to have a home. John begins to hate her as a part of the new age, a symbol of 'the century of the common man'. Snores. Takes sleeping pills. Goes to the cinema with John and sees a film about a husband being murdered by his wife by being thrown over a cliff. Finds them Good Hope Fort to go to on holiday, in April 1946. Tells Dr Mackenzie an invented story about John's sleep-walking. She drugs him and leaves him asleep beside the open window above the cliffs.
GP 161–176

VERNEY, JOHN ***(1908–1946)***
Cousin and husband of Elizabeth Verney (q.v.). He is normally good-tempered and phlegmatic. Before the war he has a little money and hopes for a career in politics. As a bachelor he runs in two hopeless by-elections as Liberal candidate. Is given a constituency in outer London. Has a flat in Belgravia. Studies on the Continent.

Marries 1938. Denounces the Munich Agreement and gets a commission in the Territorial Army.

During the war he is a captain. Hates the 'annoyance of the army'. Wounded in the knee. Spends three months in a hospital outside Rome. Discharged from the army in early 1945 with one leg two inches shorter than the other. His leg gives him constant pain. His flat has been requisitioned and furniture destroyed by bombs. Lives with Elizabeth and her parents in Hampstead. Is awarded a medal.

Loses the election against a Battle of Britain pilot put up by Tories and a 'rancorous Jewish schoolteacher', who wins. Stays in Hampstead and does the housework. Hates Elizabeth because she stands for the age of the common man. Wishes that she were dead.

Dines once a week at his club. Travels by tube.

Notices his wife's sleeping pills. Goes with her to see a film in which a wife murders her husband by drugging his coffee and throwing him off a cliff. Goes with Elizabeth to holiday at Good Hope Fort. Notices its similarity to the house in the film and starts to plan her murder. Tells the men at the golf club and Dr Mackenzie about her sleep-walking. Discovers to his horror, that Elizabeth has told Dr Mackenzie that *he* sleep-walks. Feels drugged after dinner. Falls asleep in a chair near the broken balustrade above the cliffs . . .
GP 161–176

VIENNA, AUSTRIA
Basil Seal is there in 1929.
- Home of Griffenbach (q.v.).
- Where Anthony Blanche is cured of his Oedipus complex.
- Bum, Scab and Joe (q.v.) cover the fall of Vienna in March 1938.
- Lucy Simmonds and Muriel Meikeljohn attend singing classes in Vienna in the 1930s.
- Dr Antonio studied as a young man in Vienna.

BM 73; BR 47; OG 214; WS 167, 218

VIKINGS
Dr Messinger tells Tony Last that they will arrive under the walls of 'The City' 'like the Vikings at Byzantium'.
HD 164

VINCENNES, ARMAND, DUC DE
Challenges Anthony Blanche, aged seventeen, to a duel over the affair which he has had with the Duchess Stefanie. Is taken in by Anthony's telephone impersonation of Stefanie.
BR 50

VINCENNES, PHILIPPE, DUC DE
Son of the old duke, who would never dream of challenging Anthony Blanche to a duel.
BR 50

VINCENNES, POPPY, DUCHESS OF
Old Duchess, with whom, of course, Anthony Blanche did not have his affair.
BR 50

VINCENNES, STEFANIE, DUCHESS OF
Charming young duchess with whom Anthony Blanche had an affair of the heart, 'and very much more than the heart' in 1921. He used her words and lit his cigarette in the way that she did, and even wore the same coloured nail varnish on his tow-nails. However, she was 'positively cretinous'.
BR 50, 52

VIRGIL ***(70–19 BC)***
Greatest of the Latin poets. See his 'Eclogues' (37 BC), 'Georgics' (30 BC), 'Aeneid' (19 BC). His writing was a profound influence on literature in the Middle Ages, the Renaissance and after.
- In 1937 Josephine Stitch has to construe a passage of Virgil every day.
- Ambrose Silk thinks in 1939 of Virgil 'sanctifying Roman military rule'.

Sc 7; PF 40

VIRGIN MARY
Cordelia Flyte tells the Reverend Mother at her convent school that she does not believe that 'our Blessed Lady cares two hoots whether I put my gym shoes on the left or the right of my dancing shoes'. Lady Marchmain tells her simply: 'Our Lady cares about obedience'.
BR 88

VIS, YUGOSLAVIA
Where, in 1944, Tito (q.v.) sets up his headquarters under the protection of the Allies.
US 179

VITRE, THÉRÈSE DE ***(b. 1915)***
Fellow traveller of Tony Last on the boat to Brazil in 1933. She spends the Atlantic crossing wrapped in furs and rugs. Her face is colourless with wide dark eyes. Thinks that Tony might be Colonel Strapper.

Lives in Trinidad to where she is returning after two years at Madame de Supplice's finishing school in Paris. Her face has a soft pointed chin, grave eyes and a high forehead. She returns to be married. She must marry a Catholic from one of the islands and is an only child.

They dance after dinner to an amplified gramophone, and she drinks lemon squash through two straws. When they reach warmer weather Tony plays quoits with her and buys her a woollen rabbit. At the first of the islands they go ashore and bathe. They return to the ship and dine, and later, leaning on the ship's rails, Tony kisses her. At Barbados they bathe again and drive about the island visiting churches. They dine on flying fish. She does not like Dr Messinger. She is upset to hear that Tony is married. At Trinidad she leaves the boat with her father, 'a wiry, bronzed man with a long grey moustache'.
HD 162–167

VIVEASH, MRS
Character in *Antic Hay* (q.v.). Everard Spruce compares her to Virginia Crouchback.
US 200

VOGEL, MR
Fellow embalmer, with Mr Joyboy at Whispering Glades.
LO 58

VOLES
Subject of William Boot's 'Lush Places' column of the *Daily Beast* in the issue after the mix-up over the badgers and the great-crested grebe (q.v.). Their antics are described in the immortal piece of prose: 'Feather-footed through the plashy fens passes the questing vole.'
Sc 21

W

WAGSTAFF
Secretary to Lord Copper (q.v.).
Sc 217

WAITERS
(*See* Ritz, Espinosa's, Château de Madrid and Corker)

WAITRESSES
When Brenda, Zita, Virginia Crouchback and Kerstie Kilbannock work as waitresses during the war they giggle and gossip about their customers, just as real waitresses do.
OG 134

WAL WAL
One of the centres of 'unpleasantness' where Miss Bombaum had popped up in the 1930s.
WS 203

WALES
Dr Fagan tells Paul Pennyfeather all about the Welsh: 'They are not Celts but "pure Iberian stock . . . From the earliest times the Welsh have been looked upon as an unclean people . . . Their sons and daughters rarely mate with human-kind except their own blood relations".' In his opinion it is possible to trace almost every disaster in English history to the Welsh: 'Think of Edward of Caernarvon . . . then the Tudors and the dissolution of the Church; then Lloyd George; the temperance movement; nonconformity.' They are he says: 'the only nation in the world that has produced no graphic or plastic art, no architecture, no drama. They just sing . . . They are deceitful because they cannot discern truth from falsehood, depraved because they cannot discern the consequences of their indulgence.'
• Home of the major who challenges William Boot on the fact that a great-crested grebe has never attacked a rabbit.
• In 1944 Guy Crouchback is offered an administrative post here at a school of 'photography interpretation'.
DE 65–66; Sc 20; US 18

WALES, PRINCE OF
(*See* Edward VIII)
BR 170–171

WALKER
American Secretary in Azania. Visits Sir Samson Courteney with news of the battle of Ukaka (q.v.).
BM 63–64

WALLACE COLLECTION
Collection of fine painting and decorative art bequeathed to the nation in 1897, by the widow of Sir Richard Wallace (1818–1890), who had inherited the core from his father the Marquis of Hertford. The collection, housed in Hertford House in London, is mainly French in taste and includes many fine examples of work by Boucher, Fragonard and Meissonier, Sèvres porcelain and Boule furniture.
• In 1939 Angela Box-Bender rather hopes that the art treasures to be stored at Lower Chipping Manor will come from the Wallace Collection.
MA 27

WALPOLE, SIR HUGH SEYMOUR *(1884–1942)*
English novelist. A prolific writer of many popular books. See his *Fortitude* (1913), *The Secret City* (1919) and *The Cathedral* (1922).
• When thinking of Ludovic's early writings Everard Spruce remembers that the young Hugh Walpole emulated Henry James.
• At Lancing in 1919 Charles Ryder is

reading *Fortitude* which he considers 'strong meat but rather unnecessary in places'.
US 230; WS 297, 301

WALSH, CAPTAIN
One of the inhabitants of the British Legation in Azania in 1931.
BM 54

WANDA, THE
Tribe of Galla immigrants from the mainland of Africa, who many centuries before 1631 had settled in the north of Azania and farmed it in an irregular fashion.
BM 7, 8

WAR
It is apparently very patriotic to have babies in wartime. Nina Blount wonders why.
• The scene around Adam Symes in WWII (imagined) is of 'unrelieved desolation; a great expanse of mud in which every visible object was burnt or broken. Sounds of firing thundered from beyond the horizon, and somewhere above the great clouds there were aeroplanes. He had had no sleep for thirty-six hours.'
• Barbara Sothill tells her housemaid that 'we can't expect things to be easy in war-time. We must expect to make sacrifices.'
• Margot Metroland tells Sonia Trumpington that the war is 'absolute heaven'.
• Sebastian Flyte remarks shortsightedly to Charles Ryder, while looking at the Colleoni statue in Venice that it is sad that neither of them can ever possibly become involved in a war.
• At the War Office in 1939 no one speaks the word 'war'. It is taboo. Charles Ryder sees it as 'something coming out of the waters, a monster with a sightless face and thrashing tail thrown up from the depths'.
• To Guy Crouchback there are two moral requisites necessary for a lawful war: 'a just cause and the chance of victory'.
• In the next war, Ivor Claire supposes, in 1941, it will be honourable for officers to leave their men behind.
• When Major Hound was at Sandhurst no one talked about 'war' . . . 'it was a school subject like Latin or geography'.
• The Yugoslav commissar tells Guy that war 'is not a time for trade'.
• Wars simply do not interest Aimee Thanatogenos (q.v.). (In 1947 everyone is like that.)
VB 221; PF 11, 38; BR 315; MA 174; OG 221; US 170, 230; LO 73

WAR OFFICE, THE
Basil Seal visits the War Office in the spring of 1940 to try and find himself a job as a spy.
• In late 1938 Charles Ryder is called to the War Office, interviewed and put on an emergency list in the event of war.
PF 144; BR 315
(*See also* SUSIE and PLUM)

WAR AGRICULTURAL COMMITTEE
In 1945 the WAC are involved in giving his field back to Gilbert Pinfold.
GP 18

WARWICK, GILBERT
English novelist of the 1930s. Anthea (q.v.) has a crush on him until he writes her the same letter twice.
WS 159

WARWICKSHIRE
Where, among its leafy lanes, Tom Kent-Cumberland courts Gladys Cruttwell.
WS 98

WASHINGTON DC, USA
Where Sir Samson Courteney is posted between Peking and Copenhagen (here he takes up long-distance cycling).
• Where one of Mrs Komstock's sons lives (q.v.).
BM 48; LO 74

WASHINGTON, BARNABAS *(d. 1928)*
Black man from Georgetown who was trapped by Mr Todd into reading him

Dickens in much the same way as Tony Last. He is buried beside Todd's camp.
HD 213

WATCHES
Paul Pennyfeather has a platinum watch.
• Otto Silenus has a platinum disc from Cartier given to him by Margot Metroland.
• Tony Last is undone by his watch, which Mr Todd gives to the search party as proof of his death.
• Julia Stitch is given a watch by the King of Egypt in 1941: 'a weighty, elaborate, hideous mechanism of the Second Empire, jewelled and enamelled and embellished with cupids which clumsily gavotted as the hour struck'.
DF 127, 162; HD 216; OG 232

WATTS, SISTER
First nurse of old Mrs Boot (q.v.) and inhabitant of Boot Magna Hall.
Sc 19

WATTS, GEORGE FREDERICK *(1817–1904)*
English painter and sculptor. Specialized in portraits and romantic genre, often with historical or literary subject matter. See his 'Caractacus', 'Ariadne' and 'The Sower of the Systems'.
• In 1933 Brenda Last and her sister Marjorie take Djinn for a walk in Kensington Gardens and visit Watt's statue 'Physical Energy'. Djinn stares at the asphalt.
HD 39

WAURAPANG RIVER
River in Brazil, down which Dr Messinger and Tony Last travel in 1934.
HD 175

WAYBROOKE, ROGER DE *(d. 1148)*
English crusader knight. His tomb is in the church at Santa Dulcina. His arms are five falcons. Left England for the Second Crusade in 1147. Sailed from Genoa. Shipwrecked on the coast at Santa Dulcina. Enlisted under the local count who promised him a passage to the Holy Land. He was, however, killed besieging a local castle before the expedition set sail. The people of Santa Dulcina touch his sword for luck and know him as 'Il Santo Inglese'.

Guy Crouchback asks him to pray for him and for England.
MA 13

WEAPONS
Liquid fire-projector: The Drunk Major, when a general in WWII.
• Huxdane-Halley bomb for the dissemination of leprosy germs: Adam Symes in WWII.
• The tank. Made by Mr Marx. Totally unsuitable for fighting in Azania. The two operators nearly go mad with heat. In the end it is used as a punishment cell.
• Arsenical smoke: Basil Seal's imaginary weapon in WWII with which he confuses an air-raid warden.
• Commando daggers: purely for decorative use by the Commandos. A Glasgow policeman is given 'a nasty poke'. General Whale's idea.
VB 221; BM 30, 40, 41; PF 30; US 44

WEATHER
The politicians of the New Britain promise at the election manifesto, to change the climate.
GP 179

WEDDINGS
The wedding of Paul Pennyfeather and Margot Metroland 'bridesmaids, Mendelssohn and Mumm' is postponed indefinitely.
• Peter Pastmaster and Mary Meadows are married under an arch of cavalry sabres. She wears a veil of old lace. At the reception at her mother's house they stand at one end of the drawing-room and shake hands.
• Rex Mottram attends a royal wedding in Madrid.
• Rex Mottram and Julia Flyte are married at the Savoy Chapel. It is a 'squalid' wedding. The reception is held at the Savoy. All of the stuffy families stay away. They do, however, have 'bridesmaids and orange blossom and the Wedding March'.

• Guy and Virginia Crouchback are married for the first time at Brompton Oratory, and for the second at a registry office.
• In 1932 Ludovic forms part of the guard of honour at a wedding at St Margaret's, Westminster, and afterwards meets Sir Ralph Brompton at the reception.
DF; PF 162; BR 171, 184, 191; US 32

WEEKEND PARTIES
At the weekend party at King's Thursday in 1922, Paul Pennyfeather never learns everyone's name: 'nor was he ever sure how many of them there were. He supposed about eight or nine, but as they all wore so many different clothes of identically the same kind, and spoke in the same voice, and appeared so irregularly at meals, there may have been several more or less'.
DF 128

WEICH, VON
German general, commanding in Yugoslavia in 1944.
US 163

WELD, CANON
Catholic priest who receives Virginia Crouchback into the faith at Westminster Cathedral in 1944.
US 159

WELLINGTON, ARTHUR WELLESLEY, FIRST DUKE OF ***(1769–1852)***
British general. The hero of the Peninsular War and the battle of Waterloo. Educated at Eton. Served in the 33rd Foot. Irish Secretary 1807; General 1808; Field Marshal 1814; Prime Minister 1827.
• To Ambrose Silk Ireland is the country of, among others, Wellington.
• De Souza compares the funeral of Apthorpe with that of the Duke of Wellington at St Paul's.
• Mentioned in the journal of Jasper Cumberland.
PF 218; MA 245; WS 95

WELWYN GARDEN CITY, HERTFORDSHIRE
Home of Mr Salter (q.v.).
Sc 26

WESLEY, JOHN ***(1703–1701)***
English evangelist. Founder of Methodism. Son of the rector of Epworth.
• A sect of his movement was formed under the Countess of Huntingdon (q.v.).
VB 141–9
(*See* A BRAND FROM THE BURNING)

WESTMACOTT, FATHER
Local priest to Lychpole. He knows all about 'existentialism and psychology and ghosts and diabolic possession'.
GP 146

WEYBRIDGE, CAPTAIN
Fictitious character who invites his guests to 'a Bottle Party at 100 Sink Street' (the Old Hundredth).
HD 70

WHALE, GENERAL
General at HOOHQ in 1941. Director of Land Forces in Hazardous Offensive Operations. Known to his old friends as 'Sprat'. On Holy Saturday 1941 attends a CIGS meeting at the War Office. His particular concern is the future of Special Services Forces in UK. At the meeting are DSD, AG, QMG, DPS, etc. The consequence of the meeting is Operation Popgun.

Is sceptical about Doctor Akonanga's expenses but thinks that he is doing a good job playing on Hitler's superstitions. Loses his sobriquet of 'Sprat' and becomes known as 'Brides in the bath'. Goes to the sick-bay in HOOHQ for 'sun rays' every afternoon in 1943. In 1944 moves to the air-raid shelter and spends all his time underground. His nerve has gone. Feels 'like a beautiful and ineffectual angel beating in the void his luminous wings in vain. "What am I doing here?" he asked. "Why am I taking cover when all I want to do is die?"'
OG 45, 115; US 26, 28, 56, 191

'WHAT WE ARE FIGHTING FOR'
Series of pamphlets produced by Geoffrey Bentley in 1939. Includes contributions from a retired admiral, a C of E curate, an unemployed docker, a negro solicitor from the Gold Coast, and a nose and throat specialist from Harley Street.
PF 64

WHEATLEY
'Buxom' fellow pupil of Charles Ryder at Lancing in 1919.
WS 290

WHELAN, FATHER
Priest at the church at the Halberdiers' barracks in 1940. A recent graduate of Maynooth. Offers Guy Crouchback a whisky after church.
MA 61, 62

WHELPER
Special correspondent in Ishmaelia in 1937. Friend of Shumble and Pigge (q.v.).
Sc 81

WHIGS
Parliamentary supremacists in the governments of the eighteenth century. Supporters of the Hanoverian succession. Monopolized power from the Glorious Revolution of 1688 to the reign of George III. By 1863 their name had been replaced by 'Liberal'.
• In 1939 Peter Pastmaster's prospective brides, Molly Meadows, Sally Flintshire and Betty Stayle are all from families which are survivors of the Whig oligarchy.
• For John Plant's generation, the 'nobilities of Whig society' are what King Arthur's knights were for that of Tennyson.
PF 152; WS 144

WHISKY SODA
Fellow prostitute of Fatima's at the brothel in the Moulay Abdullah, Fez.
WS 121

WHISPERING GLADES, LOS ANGELES
Necropolis. Place of employment of Mr Joyboy and Aimee Thanatogenos. Founded by Wilbur Kenworthy. Has gold entrance gates. After passing through these before you is a semicircle of yew trees and an island of grass on which is a huge wall of sculpted marble in the form of an open book and on which is inscribed:

> The Dream
> Behold I dreamed a dream and
> I saw a New Earth sacred to HAPPINESS
> And behold I awoke and in the
> Light and Promise of my DREAM
> I made WHISPERING GLADES
> ENTER STRANGER and BE HAPPY

The house is in the style which in England would be that of the country house of an Edwardian financier – black and white, timbered and gabled, with twisting brick chimneys and wrought-iron wind vanes. The 'Hindu Love Song' is piped throughout. It is in fact made of Grade A steel and concrete. The gardens are approached through a florist's shop. The Park is 'zoned' into different areas with their own works of art.The cheapest sites are fifty dollars in the Pilgrim's Rest (behind the Crematory fuel dump). The most expensive are on the Lake Isle of Innisfree. These cost $1000. The Lovers' Nest, based about a marble replica of Rodin's 'The Kiss' costs $750 a double plot. There are also a Poets' Corner with a statue of Homer, two non-sectarian churches and Shadowlands, for film people. The University church is the most convenient for Poets' corner. The park is restricted to Caucasians.
LO 33–9
(*See also* CHURCHES, BARLOW, Dennis)

WHISTLER, JAMES ABBOT McNEILL *(1834–1903)*
American artist. Doyen of the Aesthetic movement (q.v.). See his 'Arrangement in Grey and Black' and various 'nocturnes'.
• Mr Plant is brought up in 'the hey-day of Whistlerian decorative painting'.
WS 114

WHITE LADY OF DUNSINANE
Alternative title for Sir James Macrae's film version of *Hamlet*.
WS 74

WHITE MAN'S GRAVE
European cemetery at Freetown, Sierra Leone. Apthorpe is buried here.
MA 245

WHITEFIELD, GEORGE
(1714–1770)
English evangelist. One of the founders of Methodism and follower of Wesley whom he accompanied to America. Split from Wesley because of his Calvinist views. Chaplain to the Countess of Huntingdon. In *A Brand from The Burning* (q.v.) his character fights a duel with Wesley.
VB 145

WHITEMAID, DOCTOR
Fellow delegate of Scott-King at the Bellorius conference in Neutralia. Holidays in Uppsala in summer 1945 and is given a doctorate. He is 'dim', like Scott-King and of the same age. He is an expert in Roman law. Falls for Irma Sveningen (q.v.). Has an affair with her. Abandons the conference. Tries to cash a cheque with the British Consul. No one knows what became of him. It is presumed that he did not get home.
WS 203, 224, 236

WHITNEYS, THE
American landed family, descended from Eli Whitney (*1765–1825*).
• In the 1930s Trimmer cuts the hair of the Whitney women on board the *Aquitania*.
OG 217

WILCOX
Butler to the Flytes at Brideshead. Brideshead thinks him grudging. He holds the keys to the cellar and the drinks cabinet. On Lord Marchmain's arrival back at Brideshead in 1938 he shares his duties with Plender. Does not like Rex Mottram's friends.
BY 88, 164, 298, 329

WILCOX AND BREDWORTH
Chemist. According to Gilbert Pinfold's voices 'one of the most respected firms in the country'.
GP 131

WILDE, OSCAR *(1854–1900)*
Irish poet and playwright. Leading figure of the Aesthetic movement. Served two years hard labour for homosexual practices. See his *Lady Windermere's Fan* (1893). *The Importance of Being Earnest* (1899), and *Salome* (1893).
• In Ambrose Silk's mind he was 'driven into the shadows, tipsy and garrulous, but, to the end, a figure of tragedy, looming big in his own twilight'. The Café Royal attracts Ambrose because of its associations with Oscar and Aubrey. Ireland is to Ambrose the country of Wilde.
PF 42, 174, 218

WILMARK, MARY SELENA
Prudence Blank is the Mary Selena Wilmark of Britain.
Sc 80

WILMOTS, THE
Neighbours of Guy Crouchback at Santa Dulcina. They live at the Castello Musgrave. They are 'gross vulgarians' who use Santa Dulcina as a pleasure resort, giving rowdy parties, 'wear indecent clothes' and speak of 'wops'. They have 'four boisterous and ill-favoured daughters' and had lost a son bathing from the rocks.
MA 12, 15

WILTSHIRE
Home of the Cornphillips (q.v.).
WS 25
(*See also* BRIDESHEAD)

WIMPERIS, FATHER
Priest at a northern suburb of London seen by Charles Ryder and his Aunt Philippa in September 1919. She thinks him 'irresistibly common'.At the end of his sermon he scatters salt before him and says 'My people, you are the salt of the earth.'
WS 305

WINCHESTER COLLEGE, HAMPSHIRE
Public school. Pappenhacker is an old boy.
Sc 81

WINN, GODFREY
Writes an article about his cottage and his flowers and his moods in the *Daily Mirror* in spring 1940. Geoffrey Bentley cannot see any difference between him and Yan Ts'e-tsung (q.v.).
PF 177

WINNIE
Illegitimate daughter of Milly (q.v.) who accompanies her and Tony Last on their trip to Brighton in 1933. She is plain and wears gold-rimmed spectacles. Two of her front teeth are missing. Forever demands an ice cream and to be taken paddling. She is 'The Awful Child of popular fiction'.
HD 133–4

WINTERHALTER, FRANZ XAVIER *(1805–1873)*
German painter. Painted many portraits of Queen Victoria and Prince Albert.
• John Plant thinks of his father's painting as 'Winterhalter suffused with the spirit of Dickens'.
WS 128

WIPERS
(*See* YPRES)

WIRELESS
Seth digests a catalogue of wireless apparatus and decides on a Tudor model in fumed oak.
• One of Nanny Hawkins' few pleasure in 1938, is a wireless set.
• Mr Crouchback speaks of the wireless in derogatory tones.
• According to Gilbert Pinfold's voices, a new device is developed in 1953 for creating wireless silence.
• Mr Jellaby had a thriving trade in Portsmouth in second-hand wireless apparatus.
BM 21; BR 286; OG 28; US 116; GP 12, 90; WS 126

WISEMAN CLUB, THE
Angela Box-Bender confounds the matchmakers of the Wiseman Club by marrying Arthur Box-bender.
US 201

WITCH DOCTORS
(*See* AKONANGA)

WODEHOUSE-BONNER, BERTIE
Friend of Theodore Boot's in the 1890s and also of a fellow guest at the Boot banquet in 1937.
Sc 218

WOOLF, VIRGINIA *(1882–1941)*
English novelist. She developed a distinctive, impressionistic style based on the stream-of-consciousness technique. See her *To the Lighthouse*, *Orlando* and *A Room of One's Own*.
• Margot Metroland sends Paul Pennyfeather the latest novel by Virginia Woolf at Egdon Heath in 1922.
DF 190

WOLVERHAMPTON, STAFFORDSHIRE
Where, in 1934, Tom Kent-Cumberland is employed in the motor business. He takes lodgings in a fruit shop on the outskirts of town.
WS 96

WOMEN
To Grimes they are 'an enigma'.
DF 30

WONDERFILM COMPANY OF GREAT BRITAIN
(*See* ISAACS)

WOOD, KINGSLEY
Dominant member of the new Cabinet recalled in the memoirs of Wenlock Jakes (q.v.).
Sc 87

WORCESTER, WORCESTERSHIRE
Final home of Canon Chatterbox (q.v.).
VB 150

WORD ASSOCIATION
If someone had said 'farm' to Mr Salter he would have replied 'bang', having once been blown up and buried when in a farm in Flanders during the Great War. A psychoanalyst might do so.
Sc 26

WORKERS
In 1941 the workers are keen to give aid to Russia. 'It's how they've been educated'.
• The Finsbury International Theatre starts its performance at seven o'clock because it is more convenient for the workers.
OG 246; US 151

WORLD WAR I
Also known as The Great War. For Lunt (q.v.) 'as for thousands of others, things could never be the same as they had been in 1914'.
• Charles Ryder's mother is killed as are Lady Marchmain's brother Ned, and her other two brothers.
• In the war Rex Mottram serves with the Canadians and wins a good MC.
• Foreigners, returning home from Mayfair in the 1920s, write of 'a glimpse of a world they had believed lost for ever among the mud and the wire'.
• The mud of Flanders and the flies of Mesopotamia are part of Charles Ryder's experience, received second-hand through the papers and films.
• Lord Marchmain served in the war in the Wiltshire Yeomanry, who are dismounted and sent into the line.
• In 1914 many retired colonels had dyed their hair in order to enlist in the ranks.
• Gervase Crouchback is killed on his first day in France, by a sniper. He was in the Irish Guards.
• Angela Box-bender was one of the girls who danced with the men who were being killed. She remembers the first lot who went out 'there wasn't one of them left at the end . . . there weren't any nice wounds'. She worked in a hospital.
• The Kent-Cumberlands' father is killed early in 1915. Tom makes a collection of war souvenirs, including a captured German helmet, shell-splinters and *The Times* for 4 August 1914.
BR 24, 41, 105, 108, 173, 194, 317; MA 19, 32, 166

WORLD WAR II
To Guy Crouchback it is 'the Modern Age in arms'. He had realized that after Prague fell war was inevitable. 'Whatever the outcome there was a place for him in that battle.'
• Arthur Box-Bender thinks that it will not be a soldiers' war. It will he thinks, be a war of economics.
• The songs of the Great War would be inappropriate for WWII, not being sufficiently morale-boosting to please the Ministry of Information.
• With the coming of the war the scattered pieces of jigsaw of Guy's past are fitted back into place.
• It seems to Madame Kanyi in 1944 that everyone wanted war in 1939: 'there was a will to war, a death wish everywhere. Even good men thought their private honour would be satisfied by war.'
• The weeks which precede the outbreak of World War II hold 'days of surmise and apprehension, which can, without irony, be called the last days of peace'.
• On the Prime Minister's speech Barbara Sothill feels 'personally challenged and threatened, as though, already, the mild autumnal sky were dark with the circling enemy and their shadows were trespassing on the sunlit lawns'.
• World War II brings an end the epoch of John Plant: 'Intellectually we had foreseen the event, and had calmly discussed it . . .'. He compares his friends to 'Beavers, bred in captivity, inhabiting a concrete pool' who will attempt to damn an ancestral stream. During the war his house is requisitioned.
PF 9; MA 12, 20, 201; OG 71; US 23; WS 191
(*See also* NAZIS; HITLER; FASCISTS; CONCENTRATION CAMPS; CROUCHBACK (Guy, Virginia and Peregrine); BRITISH ARMY; Alastair TRUMPINGTON; Basil

SEAL; APTHORPE; RITCHIE-HOOK; PADFIELD; WHALE; CLARE TICKERIDGE)

WORTHING, SUSSEX
Where Mr Prendergast (q.v.) had his first living.
DR 202

WRACKAM
Country house of the Luxmores (q.v.). General Militiades and the King of Greece stay there before the war. They eat Irish stew and shoot pheasant in high bare coverts. The house has a pillared entrance portico.
OG 186

WRITERS
(*See* FENWICK-SYMES; Basil SEAL; John BOOT; Ambrose SILK; PARSNIP; PIMPERNEL; LUDOVIC; BARLOW; HINSLEY; PINFOLD; LANCE; STILLINGFLEET; PLANT; Roger SIMMONDS; LENT NOVELISTS and BOOKS)

WRITING
After Adam Symes has written twelve books he will have fifty pounds advance on his thirteenth, and no more. It will take him a year to write them, and would take most people twenty.
• John Plant's idea, in becoming a writer is 'to produce something saleable in large quantities to the public, which had absolutely nothing of myself in it', unlike Roger Simmonds.
VB 74; WS 107

WROTMAN OF SPEKE
One of the distant ancestors of the Crouchbacks, who are extinct in the male line. So Mr Goodall informs Guy, who tells him that he has cousins of that name. They, of course are not Wrotmans of Speke, but of Garesby.
MA 110

WYCKHAM-BLAKE
A fellow pupil of Charles Ryder's at Lancing in 1919.
WS 287

X

XANTHUS
Ancient name for the river Scamander. So it is known by Homer. It is so called after the Greek hero of the same name who defeated the Trojans on its banks.
• Charles Ryder is sure that Homer, unlike himself, had not as a child, 'sat among the camp-fires at Xanthus' side'.
BR 14

XENOPHON *(435–354 BC)*
Greek writer and military commander. Led the Ten Thousand on their epic march from Armenia to Trebizond and Byzantium in 399 BC. See his *Hellenics*, *Memorials of Socrates* and *Symposion*.
• He is called to mind by Ambrose Silk as he considers those writers who have fought for their country.
• Scott-King teaches Xenophon to some of the lower boys at Granchester.
PF 40; WS 195

Y

YOUKOUMIAN, MR KRIKOR
Armenian entrepreneur in Azania in 1931. Owner of the Amurath Café and Universal Stores. Has a brother in Malindi. Sells his wife's seat to Basil Seal on the train. Is out to make money in any way that he can. Becomes Basil's secretary in the Ministry of Modernization (q.v.). His favourite expression is 'You come to me. I fix everything'. After the crisis blows over buys the rails and engines from the Grand Azanian railway and tries to sell them in Eritrea.
BM 18–19, 20, 98, 233, 237

YOUNG MAGICIAN'S COMPENDIUM
Child's conjuring set: 'that neat cabinet where the ebony wand had its place beside the delusive billiard balls, the penny that folded double, and the feather flowers that could be drawn into a hollow candle'. Charles Ryder compares it to the youth which he left behind him when he left Brideshead in January 1925.
BR 165

YOUNGER SONS
In 1924 they are 'indelicate things, necessary, but not much spoken of'. It is their duty to remain in the shadows until some disaster promotes them, and they must thus remain bachelors as long as possible.
BR 175

YPRES
The 'Wipers' of the Great War, close to where Peppermint, the mule, drank all of the rum ration of Ben Hacket's company in 1917.
HD 31

YUAN TS'E-TSUNG
Geoffrey Bentley cannot tell the difference between Godfrey Winn and Yuan Ts'e-tsung.
PF 177

YERCOMBE, MRS
Housekeeper to Gilbert Pinfold's mother at Kew.
GP 31

YORKSHIRE
Location of Angela's house. Tony Last thinks that there can be very little pleasure to be had from going all the way to Yorkshire in the middle of winter.
HD 17

YOSHIWARA, BARONESS
Japanese noblewoman who, in London in 1927, has an affair with Mr Outrage (q.v.). She wears Paquin frocks and finds it hard to know what to do to please her lover. Her husband is a diplomat at the embassy in London, and when he is moved to Washington her affair with Outrage comes to an abrupt end. She tells him 'twenty damns to your great pig-face'.
VB 48, 127–128

Z

ZAGREB, YUGOSLAVIA
One of Major Cattermole's stretcher-bearers during the sixth offensive in 1943 was a boy from Zagreb University.
• A lawyer from Zagreb is one of the leaders of the Jews at Begoy in 1944.
• One of the places where Dr Antonic studied before the war.
US 163, 175; WS 218

ZEPHYR
In classical mythology a gentle wind, most especially the west wind, son of Aurora and Astraeus.
• Major Hound (q.v.) is transported to his hiding place on Crete as though 'by a benevolent Zephyr of classical myth'.
OG 199

ZEPPELINS
German airships of the Great War.
• Tom Kent-Cumberland is thrilled by the sight of a zeppelin, hit by gunfire in sight of his school, sinking to the earth 'in a globe of pink flame' while a young master, unfit for the forces, shouts out 'there go the baby killers'.
WS 91

ZINGERMAUN
Inhabitant of Agadir. Friend of Dr Messinger. Used to sell ammunition to the Atlas Caids before they were pacified. Leaves to run a restaurant in Mogador.
HD 158

ZIONISTS
Followers of the Jewish movement to establish a state in Palestine. Founded in Vienna in 1895. Recognized by the British in 1917. Established Israel 1948.
• In Yugoslavia in 1944 the Zionists are only interested in helping young Jews.
• The Zionist underground organization has, by 1946, been put out of business by the network with which Scott-King escapes from Neutralia.
US 234; WS 242

ZITA
Friend of Kerstie Kilbannock who in 1941 stays with her as a paying guest at Eton Terrace, and works with her at the canteen.
OG 133

ZOMBIES
Dead bodies brought to life in an automaton form by Voodoo magic.
• De Souza wonders whether Ludovic is a zombie.
US 109

ZULU CAMPAIGNS *(1879)*
War against the South African natives of the Bantu nation, after the annexation of the South African Republic by the British.
• Veterans of the Zulu campaign guard the doors of the War Office in 1940.
PF 144

ZURBARAN, FRANCISCO *(1598–1664)*
Spanish painter of religious works. See his 'Crucified Christ' (1627, Chicago), 'Assumption' (Edinburgh) and 'Saint Francis in Meditation' (1639, London).
• Guy Crouchback compares Major Cattermole's face with that of 'a Zurbaran ascetic'.
US 162

ZURICH, SWITZERLAND
Where Doctor Borethus has his practice. Rex Mottram is taking Sebastian Flyte there in 1925 when he runs away from him in Paris.
BR 159–60

THE WRITINGS OF EVELYN WAUGH

FICTION

'The Curse of the Horse Race' (1910, unpublished)
'Anthony, Who Sought Things That Were Lost' (The Oxford Broom, June 1923)
'The Temple at Thatch' (1924–1925, unpublished)
'The Balance' (Georgian Stories, 1926)
Decline and Fall (1928)
Vile Bodies (1930)
Black Mischief (1932)
Incident in Azania (1932, not available)
'Cruise' (1932)
'Bella Fleace Gave a Party' (1932)
Out of Depth (1933, not available)
A Handful of Dust (1934)
'Mr Loveday's Little Outing' (1934)
'On Guard' (1934)
'Winner Takes All' (1935)
'Period Piece' (1936)
'Excursion in Reality' (1936)
Love in the Slump (1936, not available)
Scoop (1938)
'An Englishman's Home' (1939)
'Work Suspended' (1942)
Put Out More Flags (1942)
Brideshead Revisited (1945)
'Charles Ryder's Schooldays' (1945)
'Scott-King's Modern Europe' (1946)
The Loved One (1948)
Helena (1950)
Man at Arms (1952)
Love Among the Ruins (1953)
Officers and Gentlemen (1955)
The Ordeal of Gilbert Pinfold (1957)
Unconditional Surrender (1961)
Tactical Exercise (1962)
'Basil Seal Rides Again' (1963)

TRAVEL

Labels (1930)

Remote People (1931)
Ninety-Two Days (1934)
Waugh in Abyssinia (1936)
Robbery Under Law (1939)
When the Going was Good :1946)
The Holy Places (1952)
A Tourist in Africa (1960)

BIOGRAPHY

Rossetti (1930)
Edmund Campion (1935)
Ronald Knox (1959)

AUTOBIOGRAPHY

A Little Learning (1964)

DIARIES, LETTERS AND JOURNALISM

Diaries (1976, edited by Michael Davie)
Letters (1980, edited by Mark Amory)
Essays, Reviews and Articles (1983, edited by Donat Gallagher)

MISCELLANEOUS

PRB: An Essay on the Pre-Raphaelite Brotherhood (1926, printed privately, reprinted in a limited edition in 1982)
Wine in Peace and War (1947)